The Social Mind

The Social Mind charts the intellectual history of the
idea of socially constructed mind through the exami-
nation of four key theorists – Lev Vygotsky, George
Herbert Mead, James Mark Baldwin, and Pierre Janet.
All four are widely recognized as seminal, early thinkers, yet there is a paucity of contemporary scholarship
on the work of Janet and Baldwin, and there is nothing before this book that connects the work of all four.
An analysis of the theories of these scholars and the
social climate in which they worked will be invaluable
to contemporary social scientists.

In their analysis of the social construction of mind,
Jaan Valsiner and René van der Veer elaborate on their
notion of intellectual interdependency in the development of scientific ideas and the role of such interdependency in the history of the social sciences. They
take a new look at how progress in science is a socially
constructed entity. Their well-constructed, ambitious
volume makes an important and timely contribution to
the theory and history of psychology.

Jaan Valsiner is Professor of Psychology at Clark University.

René van der Veer is Professor of Education at Rijksuniversiteit Leiden.

The Social Mind

Construction of the Idea

JAAN VALSINER
Clark University

RENÉ VAN DER VEER
Rijksuniversiteit Leiden

PUBLISHED BY THE PRESS SYNDICATE OF THE UNIVERSITY OF CAMBRIDGE
The Pitt Building, Trumpington Street, Cambridge, United Kingdom

CAMBRIDGE UNIVERSITY PRESS
The Edinburgh Building, Cambridge CB2 2RU, UK   http://www.cup.cam.ac.uk
40 West 20th Street, New York, NY 10011-4211, USA   http://www.cup.org
10 Stamford Road, Oakleigh, Melbourne 3166, Australia
Ruiz de Alarcón 13, 28014 Madrid, Spain

First published 2000

Printed in the United States of America

Typeface Palatino 10/13 pt.   *System* DeskTopPro$_{/UX}$ [BV]

A catalog record for this book is available from the British Library.

Library of Congress Cataloging in Publication Data
Valsiner, Jaan.
    The social mind : construction of the idea / Jaan Valsiner and
René van der Veer.
        p.   cm.
    Includes bibliographical references and index.
    ISBN 0-521-58036-6 (hb). – ISBN 0-521-58973-8 (pbk.)
    1. Intellect – Social aspects.   2. Intellect – Social aspects –
History.   3. Discoveries in science – Social aspects.
4. Inventions – Social aspects.   I. Veer, René van der, 1952–   .
II. Title.
    BF431.V25   2000
    302—dc21   99-28458
                                                                   CIP

ISBN 0 521 58036 6 hardback
ISBN 0 521 58973 8 paperback

Contents

Preface

This book is a result of long-time joint work of its authors. Its idea emerged when the European came to visit his American counterpart, who then lived in Chapel Hill, North Carolina, in 1985. In the process of discovering that in America everything (ranging from milk cartons to Thanksgiving turkeys, and to frequent statements as to how fine everybody is), is bigger than in Europe, the two men decided it would be good to write a book together. The idea to write a general book about the history of the idea that persons are social emerged from their discussions during that visit. Of course they could not think clearly that such a book would be another example of big things. Now, years later (and after jointly writing another major book)[1], the two authors are resigned to their destiny of jointly accomplishing voluminous works.

Indeed, the present book was for years left "on hold" as the authors were busily trying to understand the work of Lev Vygotsky in its complexity, and in its cultural-historical context. That experience alerted them against easy acceptance of various myths that were circulating among the fascinated followers of that interesting scholar. The authors contributed to creation of countermyths about Vygotsky, in the form of pointing to his intellectual interdependency with his contemporaries. From wherever the authors happened to be – Haarlem, Leiden, Berlin, Chapel Hill, Melbourne, Brasilia, Worcester, and elsewhere – emerged their focus on understanding intellectual interdependency in scientific creativity as a whole.

Our inquiry into this topic is somewhere between psychology and

---

[1] Van der Veer, R., & Valsiner, J. (1991). *Understanding Vygotsky: A Quest for Synthesis.* Oxford: Basil Blackwell.

the sociology of science. Similarly to our way of "unpacking" Vygotsky in our previous work, here we attempt to examine the work of Pierre Janet, James Mark Baldwin, and George Herbert Mead. We also zoom in on the curious history of the arrest of methodological innovation that the history of the sociogenetic ideas entails. This topic is important to us. It is sad to see potentially productive ideas of sociogenesis become trivialized by temporary fashions in the thinking of social scientists. As we document in this book, there have been a number of such fashions over the last century, taking somewhat different forms in different countries, and migrating between continents. Fashions remain fashions, they come and go. However, we hope that elaborate understanding of the history of the sociogenetic ideas would help these to stay, and become productive in our knowledge construction.

We want to acknowledge the support of various institutions, as well as help given by a number of colleagues who did not despair of our several drafts, but gave us constructive feedback. The N.W.O. travel grant brought René van der Veer to America, and Jaan Valsiner to the Netherlands. Further support by the Dutch Ministry of Education through the Institute for the Study of Education and Human Development (ISED) sponsored the follow-up visit in 1995. Jaan Valsiner is also indebted to the Alexander von Humboldt Stiftung of Germany whose *Forschungspreis für Geisteswissenschaften* (1995) allowed him to spend an academically productive year at Technische Universität Berlin in 1995–6. The Fulbright Visiting Professorship at the Universidade de Brasilia allowed him to continue the work on the book during his escapes to the southern hemisphere.

Numerous colleagues deserve our gratitude for helping us to clarify our understanding of the complex issues. For Jaan Valsiner, years of collaboration with Robert B. Cairns and Gilbert Gottlieb in North Carolina, and Jeanette Lawrence and Agnes Dodds in Australia, have been important for the incubation of many of the ideas. Ingrid E. Josephs from Otto-von-Guericke Universität in Magdeburg, Germany, has provided constructive input on many of the chapters. Likewise, Leonard Cirillo, Roger Bibace (Clark University), Angela Branco (University of Brasilia), Kurt Kreppner (Max-Planck-Instutut für Bildungsforschung, Germany), Ivana Markova (University of Stirling, Scotland), and Gert Biesta (University of Utrecht, The Netherlands) have been very helpful in commenting on different parts of the text.

Having finished the big book, we look forward to further inquiry into the history of ideas, and hope that our effort will be of help to those readers who like diving into the complexity of the history of ideas. It is for such sophisticated readers – who do not expect to be given "the final truth" in a persuasive effort, but rather who become our co-constructors of ideas while reading this book – that our efforts have been made. Therefore, we express our gratitude, in advance, to the avid readers of this complex book.

Jaan Valsiner
Worcester, Massachusetts

René van der Veer
Leiden, The Netherlands

Introduction

How Can the Mind Be Social, and Why Do We Need to Mention It?

Language may be compared with the spear of Amfortas in the legend of the Holy Grail. The wounds that language inflicts upon human thought can not be healed except by language itself. Language is the distinctive mark of man and even in its development, in its growing perfection it remains human perhaps too human. It is anthropocentric by its very essence and nature. But at the same time it possesses an inherent power by which, in its ultimate result, it seems to transcend itself. From those forms of speech that are meant as means of communication and that are necessary for every social life and intercourse it develops into new forms; it sets itself different and higher tasks. And by this it becomes able to clear itself of those fallacies and illusions to which the common usage of language is necessarily subject. Man can proceed from ordinary language to scientific language, to the language of logic, of mathematics, of physics. But he never can avoid or reject the power of symbolism and symbolic thought. (Cassirer, 1942, p. 327)

This book is about human rigid creativity. At first glance, such a formulation seems to be a contradiction in terms. Isn't it the case that creativity is the opposite of rigidity? Yet, the history of humans' understanding of themselves indicates that these two sides of reflection go together: New ideas about what we are like are invented, and then rigidly applied to ourselves. It is as if any invention of a term or concept is both liberating and enslaving at the same time (as was already stated by Von Humboldt; see Chapter 8). By its invention, a concept allows for a new way of organizing understanding. However,

1

its immediate implications also make the position that the concept entails rigid. This happens in everyday life, and it also happens in science.

More specifically, we are interested here in the ways in which new ideas in the social sciences have been made rigid through social means. The basic sociogenetic credo, that human personal-psychological functioning is a social process, has been invented, and has become a popular slogan in the social sciences. Yet slogans do not make science: They may help to get a head start, but then their role will be lessened for knowledge construction. In numerous biological and physical sciences, the invention of loose metaphors has been liberating for the knowledge construction process. But this can't be said about the social sciences, and psychology, in particular. There may be social reasons in these disciplines for wariness of loose metaphors. Yet by avoiding the play with such metaphors, psychology has turned into a stern, uninventive discipline, in which the the right ways of acquiring knowledge suppresses the potential for major intellectual breakthroughs. By such singing to the Kuhnian tune of normal science forever, psychology may eventually commit intellectual suicide as a discipline. We will examine the social processes of construction of ideas in psychology based on the example of sociogenetic concepts.

The Nature of Sociogenesis

In this book, we are interested in charting out what implications the meaning complex *the human mind/psyche is social* has for basic knowledge construction in the social sciences. More specifically, we take a cultural-historical look at the uses of that meaning complex during the formative years of psychology, roughly delineating our coverage of the period from the 1880s to the 1930s. Of course, our historical analysis is aimed at rejuvenating contemporary knowledge construction at the turn of our own century. As in our previous work (e.g., Van der Veer & Valsiner, 1991), we have tried to pave the way to that goal through detailed analyses of the history of ideas and their sociocultural contexts. We look at different versions of the sociogenetic tradition in the social sciences.

This tradition has been built around two basic postulates (see Valsiner, 1989, p. 43). The ontological postulate is a claim that all human psychological processes are social in their nature. The developmental postulate emphasizes the idea that human personality emerges through social experience. Hence the notion of sociogenesis, the social genesis (i.e., development, emergence) of the person.

The sociogenetic tradition in psychology and other social sciences has made episodic appearance on the scene of the drama of science. At times (like our 1990s, or likewise a hundred years ago, in the 1890s) it was actively discussed. At other times, it was hushed up in favor of the dominance of the biologically deterministic perspectives. But it has returned. The waves of emphasis on social (in contrast to biological) deterministic beliefs has its societal repercussions. Not surprisingly, the sociogenetic perspective has flourished in contexts in which the given society has been in a phase of social upheaval, with hope for its basic change into a new (and better!) state. Sociogenetic ideas in the social sciences have thus been rather silent corevolutionaries (or co-mutineers, depending upon the position of the evaluator) to other efforts to change society. In contrast, at the historical phases of relative stability and fixation of social system, the biological determinism with its implications (e.g., differences between persons are predetermined by nature). Hence the complex of ideas of sociogenesis has closeness to the social processes within society that makes it into a good target for our analysis of intellectual interdependency (see Chapter 1).

Not only are the processes of constructing ideas about the psychology of human beings interdependent between different scientists, but they may be parts of the nebulous social contexts (of the given society at the particular historical period, such as Soviet Russia and Germany in the 1920s, the United States in the 1890s, Spain in the 1980s) that create the background guidance for the particular theoretical inventions by the scientists. Social discourse between scientists about a particular subject matter is embedded in the social context within which these scientists live. They may find that the result of their work transcends the confines of their time and their own background. Again, the process of arriving at these results is socially embedded.

Human Psyche as Social

In the last three decades of the twentieth century, it has again become acceptable (even fashionable, see Chapter 9) to consider human psychological functions as social in their nature. Often this position is simply declared by brief, but frequently glorifying, references to thinkers from the past who held such a position. Oftentimes, the names of

Lev Vygotsky, George Herbert Mead, and others are used to emphasize the social nature of human psychological functions. Declarations
of faith are, of course, often made in conjunction with evoking an
authority figure: "as X (e.g., Vygotsky, Mead, Tom Sawyer, Marx)
showed, the mind is A (e.g., social), and not B (e.g., biologically determined)."

However, it is often an open question as to what functions such
declarations can have in science. From a position of in-depth analysis,
such statements seem merely to be stating the obvious (compared with
statements like the rain is wet or the rich are affluent). And yet, such
general claims about the sociality of the human psyche are made with
remarkable vigor and repetitiveness; thus their function cannot be
merely descriptive. Rather, repeated claims about the social nature of
the mind are part of some ongoing social discourse in science. These
claims are about a fight for positioning the researcher in relation to
the object of investigation. Furthermore, it is not only the researchers'
positioning of themselves (for which some kind of repeated prayer,
uttering to oneself "the mind is social," might suffice), but efforts to
position other researchers into their viewpoint, that seem to underlie
the repetition of this simple idea. Efforts are being made to persuade
others to accept the productivity of looking at the human psyche as if
it were social. Thus, many of the contemporary sociocultural, cultural,
and sociogenetic orientations in psychology carry with them a missionary spirit: to persuade the world that their viewpoint is the
"right" one.

Of course, there is always some persuasive (rhetorical) role embedded in scientific discourse. Galileo's well-known claim that the earth
moves around the sun had more rhetorical than knowledge-creating
functions. Yet it is in the twentieth-century social sciences, with their
widened realms of discursive relations, that the rhetorical functions of
general scientific assertions begin to acquire centrality, and at times
dominate. The latter is particularly evident in cases in which some
social institution attempts to take over some area of science. This has
happened in various ways in the history of sciences. For example, the
Soviet system in the 1930s and 1940s attempted to take over the social
sciences (Valsiner, 1988) and genetics (Dobzhansky, 1955). The result
was that for some decades, the knowledge-constructive activities of
scientists were replaced by active rhetoric assertions about the "righteousness of the Soviet science" in contrast to its international counterpart. But such a socioinstitutional takeover need not occur solely from
the side of political systems. It can be observed in the institutionalizing

of a particular knowledge-construction device (e.g., statistics as one of many forms of inductive knowledge constructions) and getting it to take over the social sciences as if it were the "scientific method." The latter, of course, is a rhetorically constructed role, which is set to operate as a starting position of no doubt (e.g., the internal heterogeneity of statistics is hidden in order to create the monolithic methodological imperative; see Gigerenzer et. al., 1989).

Obviously, there are many varieties of institutional takeovers of disciplines. Our examples here tap only into some of these. Yet the general principle remains: By combining power and persuasive or declarative rhetorics, a social institution can work toward appropriating a particular science to its needs (of control, elimination, transformation, application, or enhancement). The relationships between a science and a society are multifaceted, and far from the mutually benevolent recognition of each other's value.

The rhetorical role of general (axiomatic) positioning claims becomes maximized under conditions of a need for negotiating a science's role in the social matrix of different sciences in a society. At times, a particular discipline can become a playground for power games played by the rules of social bureaucracies or religious orthodoxies. But the terminology used in these games need not differ from that of knowledge-constructing science. For example, there is a delicate difference in implications between two interpretations:

(A) *The mind is social*, and therefore we proceed to study it in ways X, Y, Z;

in contrast with

(B) *The mind is social*, and therefore it is not true that it is *not social*, or that it is of any other nature.

The first interpretation opens the door for new inquiries into the specifics, while the second leads to intergroup warfare between the proponents of one or another position. In the first case, the new generic meaning ("social") opens to us a realm of new possibilities to look at the phenomena. The second interpretation closes opportunities for new ways of looking at the mind, as it eliminates our possible doubt as to the position.

Reductionism and Consensus versus Construction

Without doubt, our interest is in the first interpretation. Our cultural-historical analyses in this book are undertaken with a goal of finding out how different sociogenetic thinkers of the past tried to move from the general statement of the mind's social nature to actually investigating it as such. They did it in their own unique ways, some being caught in the pleasures of rhetorical declarations, others in the difficulties of descriptions of the individual and the social at the same time. Yet the major themes around which the construction of sociogenetic ideas revolved remain interestingly constant. First, there is the axiomatic preference for fusion (of person and the social environment) or inclusive separation (i.e., the person is viewed as distinguished from the environment, yet interdependent with it) bases for sociogenetic models. Theoretical constructions following the former may idealize the communion of the person and the social context. They are likely to deny the individuality of the person within the social context, and are often based on implicit sociomoral stance about the person necessarily setting the priorities of the social world ahead of one's own. In fact, the existence of the latter may be denied, or if not denied, considered to be a social aberration (e.g., some persons might not show sufficient membership in the society). These perspectives do not need concepts like internalization and externalization, and find notions of participation and appropriation sufficient for their conceptual needs.

In contrast, sociogenetic theorizing based on the inclusive separation basis emphasizes the personal individuality as the demonstration of the social nature of the person (see Chapter 4). Theoretical constructions from this basis are likely to emphasize the notions of internalization and externalization, and to doubt the imperative that persons should merge themselves within social units through giving up their personal uniqueness.

Thus the crucial question is: How to construe persons as being social without abandoning their obvious personal autonomy, separateness from any social unit (group, crowd, community), while being members of such units. The conceptual imperative of the common-sense "either-or" thinking holds scientific terminologies in its iron grip. Sociocultural thinkers often counter the tendencies of explaining psychological phenomena by their underlying biophysiological substrate (reductionism "downward") by reducing the complexity of personal psyches to social-explanatory constructs (texts, discourse, narratives, culture; i.e., reductionism "upward"). Both versions of reductionism are similar in their construction features. An alternative theoretical route is to make sense of the ways in which the person and social units actually relate. In contemporary sociocultural theorizing, disputes about internalization/externalization, appropriation, mastery, guided participation, etc. abound. All these indicate efforts to overcome the limits of the either-or thought model that is firmly entrenched in human everyday language. This problem was paralleled in the social sciences of the beginning of the twentieth century. As Vincent critically elaborated,

A mere enumeration of terms and phrases brings up a panorama of theories: 'social growth', 'social evolution', 'the general mind', 'co-operation', 'coercion', 'social control', 'contact', 'contract', 'consciousness of kind', 'the dialectic of personal growth', 'the social self', 'the looking-glass self', 'the social nature of conscience', 'the dialectic of social growth', 'imitation, opposition, invention', 'the individual an abstraction', 'social consciousness', 'the social mind', 'the persistence of social groups', 'the role of unconsciousness', 'the cake of custom', 'the folkways' and 'the mores', 'instinct and habit', 'psychic planes.' 'mob-mind', 'like-mindedness', 'conflict and rivalry', 'group struggle', 'social selection', 'survival value', 'crisis', 'adaptation', 'the elite as the social brain', 'making up the group mind', 'the social process'. To one who knows the field these ideas are familiar, many of them commonplace. At first they may seem fragmentary and detached; but they quickly arrange themselves into something like order and unity. (Vincent, 1910, p. 469)

Efforts to make sense of the personal as social have been around a long time, and have generated a multivoiced discourse for the social sciences. Perhaps such overdetermination by meaning (to use Boesch's, 1991, terminology here) has been an obstacle for solving the problem. Very easily, many partly overlapping concepts are disputed within a scientific community as to which of these terms explain the phenomena better than others. The focus here is on the evaluation of the attributional value (or symbolic adequacy) of one or another complex meaning as explainer. Some of such meaning complexes are ruled out as valid scientific explanations from the outset (e.g., "ancestors' spirits"), yet others (of a not necessarily less mythical nature, like "libido") are considered possible (if not preferable). Still others may be prioritized in the discourse of scientists at a given historical time (hence the needs by proponents of the sociocultural perspective for the rhetorical repetition that *the mind is social*, in contrast to their opponents equally rhetorical claim that the mind is innate/personal). What is being discursively constructed, and reconstructed, is the consensual acceptability of one or another symbolic means of explanation. Whichever consensual solution is reached will not automatically lead to new knowledge construction. The latter cannot happen on the basis of consensus about general causal entities, but requires the building of a systemic explanatory system "downward" from the general axiomatic position, toward the empirical phenomena. Thus, discursive construction of a shared position in a science can be a starting point for a productive research program. Yet whether such productivity follows from discursive negotiation of the position, or not, does no longer depend upon that position per se, but on how it is used for making sense of the reality. Thus, the winners of the rhetorical battlefields of science may lose the whole war, which is fought not against opponents, but against the ever-elusive nature of the reality of the objects of our investigations.

History of Construction Efforts: Toward a Theory of Intellectual Interdependency

In this book, we attempt to continue the line of developmental analysis of ideas that was earlier applied to the case of Lev Vygotsky (Van der Veer & Valsiner, 1991). We try to trace the construction and elaboration of the idea that the human psychological system is social in the work of four main authors of the sociogenetic kind: Pierre Janet, James Mark Baldwin, George Herbert Mead, and Lev Vygotsky. In order to demonstrate how their particular ways of conceiving the texture of the sociality of the mind emerged in their life contexts, we analyze relevant other directions of thought that constituted the background for their work. The historical period we cover – roughly designated as that of five decades, from the 1880s to the 1930s – is meant to capture the period of the emergence of various elaborations of the social concept of the human psyche. However, aside from analyzing the concrete development and transformation of ideas, we address a more general issue that faces anybody who tries to make sense of development of ideas: the intellectual interdependency of the author of ideas and others whose activities are relevant for these ideas. Furthermore, the ill-defined (and perhaps in principle undefinable) notion of the intellectual atmosphere, or Zeitgeist, of a historical epoch may direct different authors toward identical or similar new discoveries. In its focus, the present approach is a sociogenetic look at the notion of the sociogenesis of the psyche in the social sciences. In this, self-inclusiveness is both the pleasure and pain of our analytic efforts. We concentrate on the complex ideas that have been used by proponents of sociogenetic ideas, as these reflect the realities of human personality. At the same time, we situate the thinking of these promoters in their sociohistorical contexts. Intellectual interdependency – as we have labeled the mutual constitution of ideas between scientists and societies – is thus a meta-level sociogenetic process itself. Only here what emerges in social discourse and actions a view on the persons becoming personal through social experience. Notice the absence in the English language of an appropriate generic term that could capture the whole of the psychological functions, or psychological processes. We here revert to the use of *mind* as a convenient analogue for psyche, yet the mind carries a rationalist connotation that is not assumed by us.

CHAPTER ONE

The Development of Ideas in Science: Intellectual Interdependency and Its Social Framework

In this chapter we outline a general scheme of *intellectual interdependency*. Our coverage of the issue is based on the assumption that new understanding of phenomena in science is actively constructed by intentional persons, who are involved in a field of mutually communicable meanings, or ideas. Within this field, persons act in a goal-oriented manner: communication is directed toward personally desirable possible future state of affairs. Each of the persons is unique, and constructs knowledge from the basis of personal uniqueness, yet in ways that are related both to the interpersonally communicable ideas, and to the nature of the object world of the given science. These persons are also members of different social institutions, and assume social roles that are set up by these institutions. Thus, we try to make sense of a threefold relation: – *social institutions, scientists, nature* – of the object of the given science. Our focus in the latter case is the issue of humans (scientists) making sense of fellow humans. This is the crucial epistemological problem for the social sciences, where the distance between the subject and object of investigation is essentially absent. A social scientist who looks at another person (or social phenomenon, like social class, gender, etc.) inevitably can't escape the obvious fact that the roles of the researcher and the research participant are always close to being reversible. It often happens that the research subject investigates the thinking of the researcher, while not providing much evidence about one's own. Thus, the researcher is constantly under the uncertainty about his or her control over the research encounter. Furthermore, the closeness of the researcher and the research participant makes it easy to project into the other one's implicit assumptions about perspectives that can be taken (or ought to be taken, from the researcher's viewpoint) upon an object of investigation. The closeness of social sciences' research to societal sociopolitical or sociomoral local imperatives creates a framework for intellectual interdependency where particular decisions by scientists become implicitly guided in directions which emerge from the researcher being "too close for comfort" to the research participants. The issue of intellectual interdependency is undoubtedly complicated by that closeness.

Intellectual Interdependency as Constructive Communication

Intellectual interdependency entails *a process of construction of ideas* by persons, while *that construction of ideas is aimed in a selected direction* in the communicative process with other persons. The other persons are involved in a similar communicative construction of ideas, communicated with some orientation toward goal states. Intellectual interdependency is thus a state of affairs in the process of purposive communication efforts by persons and institutions, in which the constructed ideas are transformed into new forms. Such creation of novelty is possible due to persons' constructive internalization and externalization processes. Communication takes place between participants who are necessarily assuming different positions, and create their potentially different goal orientations. The state of intersubjectivity that emerges in communication can be transitory and often is purposefully illusory, since it is a constructed artifactual basis for maintaining the communication flow.

The communicative process entails construction and use of signs – in this sense, it is a semiotic process. A particular insight (X) of person A becomes externalized by him or her in the form of a semiotically encoded message (X'), and thus made publicly available to other persons. Among these other persons, X' may be ignored by many, neutralized or downplayed by some, and taken seriously by a few others. Among the latter, X' may become transformed in the internalization process and become different (e.g., person B turning X' into Y), followed by constructive externalization of Y into a novel publicly available form (Y'), which in its turn is a message for A and other persons.

This process continues ad infinitum, constantly producing novelty. The interdependency notion emphasizes the developmental continuity between persons (A and B) and their ideas (X and Y), which are linked through externalized communicative messages (X' and Y'). Intellectual interdependency is the process of construction of new ideas through the transformation of old ones in a communicative process. As such, intellectual interdependency is a universal human phenomenon.

Our elaboration of intellectual interdependency is based on the notion of *bidirectional culture transfer* (Valsiner, 1989, 1994c); a view on human communication that is built on the notion of active construction (and reconstruction) of cultural messages by individual persons. This axiomatic notion is based on Karl Bühler's Organon model of communication (Bühler, 1934/1990), and involves a focus on the novelty constructed in the domain of abstractive generalization. Much of scientific discourse – as well as of sociological discourse about what is "appropriate" in "scientific discourse" – is devoted to questions of acceptability, or unacceptability, of generalization, and to the issue of the value of abstract concepts in the reasoning of scientists.

In the history of the social sciences, opposite tendencies of either eliminating abstraction and generalization from scientific discourse (e.g., focus on "knowledge" being "local" or "context specific") have alternated with tendencies to create high-level (often mathematical) abstractions that have lost all direct connections with the common-language meaning systems. Our communicational perspective on intellectual interdependency focuses on the inevitable uncertainty about the abstractness of any scientific communicative message. The same concept – X – as abstracted from its common-language "parent" (x), enters into a tension between the remaining set of connotations of the common language on the one hand, and the ideal infinite abstractedness (with potential for generalization), on the other. Thus, the everyday notion of "attachment" (a mother's feeling toward her child, or vice versa) continues to disallow extreme abstraction of the scientific concept attachment (used by psychologists who study that topic). On the other extreme, the notion of attachment could be defined purely abstractly (e.g., attachment of function F to that of W), without tension between the common language.

The present perspective does not overlook the role of collectively available means of communication – sign systems. Rather, it indicates how such "shared" systems are put to constructive practice by people. One person may construct a cultural message, directed at another, in his or her personal, idiosyncratic way, yet utilizing common cultural tools (e.g., commonly understood words of a language) for such encoding. The other person, while receiving that message, does not accept it as a "given," but instead actively reconstructs it in accordance with his or her own personal position. That reconstruction entails analysis of the message and its synthesis into a new (personal–cultural) understanding, which may be very different from the one intended by the creator of the message.

From here it follows that intellectual interdependency in the history of scientific ideas is not a tale about how equivalent (or similar) ideas are accepted and proliferated by communities of scientists, social institutions, and laypersons. Instead, it is a glimpse into the dialogical process of knowledge construction, in which scientists are involved in dialogues within themselves (Hermans, 1995), and with others. These dialogues do not entail the simple acceptance of ideas, but rather tension-filled processes of relating of different "voices" (Wertsch, 1997) or positions (Rommetveit, 1992). The definitive issue involved is the construction of new understanding on the basis of what was previously achieved by the given discipline. This process involves the proliferation of similar versions of understanding both as a result of the construction of novel ones, and as a basis for (still more) novel understanding. Furthermore, such construction of novelty is part and parcel of the goal orientation of scientists: "The goals of scientific practice are imaginatively transformed versions of its present. The future states of scientific culture at which practice aims are constructed from existing culture in a process of *modeling* (metaphor, analogy) . . . the existing culture predisciplines the extended temporality of human intentionality" (Pickering, 1995, p. 19).

The notion of science as the constant construction of new – yet predisciplined – understanding of phenomena is crucial here. This future orientation has its side effect of dismissing the history of the discipline as part of the construction of the new. Scientists are constant producers of novelty, even when they repeat (and often fight for) meaningful constructions that have been worked out by others. The latter can occur in a generalized form of an interpersonally accepted matrix of meanings within which to look for solutions (outlawing other matrices in which solutions are not to be sought). At a particular historical period of a science, different scientists may arrive at similar solutions to a basic problem. These phenomena – the feeling that "this solution was just in the air" (in some science, during some historical period) – are a case of intellectual interdependency where the scientific (or wider) community was oriented in a specific direction in its efforts to arrive at novel understanding. Often such phenomena can be directed by wider social processes in the given society (e.g., the construction of various kinds of "activity theories" in Soviet psychology under the ideological orientation towards the Marxist notion of practice; Valsiner, 1988).

Assumed Intersubjectivity and Intellectual Interdependency

Intellectual interdependency is possible on the basis of socially shared intersubjectivity (see Rommetveit, 1992) of scientists within their community, as well as on the basis of the establishment of domains of intersubjectivity between the scientific communities and laypersons' or bureaucracies' discourses. The central focus is on the construction of the understanding of some (target) phenomenon by individual scientists within a loosely defined social group (the "scientific community"), within social contexts of such intersubjectivity. The constructor of the new knowledge is necessarily a human being, a creative person, who may indeed be very much intertwined with his or her intersubjective world. In other terms, the role of a particular scientist in providing novel solutions is enhanced (rather than dismissed) by the social embeddedness of that scientist. One scientist may take a notion of others (X', see above) and proliferate it as if it were given (X' = X'). Another may take the same notion X' and turn it into its opposite (Y'). A third may spend his or her career proving that X' is "wrong" and finding many reasons why this is so. For example, consider our contemporary habit of deconstructing different views in psychology. A deconstructionist fails to provide new understanding, but can succeed in reorienting the field toward the rejection of the old one. The scientists in a given field may become active in tearing down the previous ways of creating knowledge, but fail to create new ones. All this (and greater) variety of relating to the previous notion (X') is included in the notion of intellectual interdependency. Followers and critics, skeptics and propagandists, deconstructors and reconstructors, are all in relations of intellectual interdependency with their target understandings in a particular science. Within this corpus of knowledge, all of these different positions can be claimed to operate within the system of assumed intersubjectivity. In order to deconstruct a particular scientific tradition, it needs to be assumed that the deconstructor understands at least the basics of the object of such effort, sharing this with the proponents of the deconstructed tradition. As has been shown (Markova, 1994; Rommetveit, 1992) the assumption of intersubjectivity is a necessary, productive (but counterfactual) construction that enables the communication process to proceed. At times, such intersubjectivity is achieved by the use of general concepts of an open-ended nature (e.g., the "self" vs. "non-self" contrast in immunology, borrowed from William James's psychology; Löwy, 1992). Intellectual interdependency between scientists is based on the assumption of a shared "common ground," even if in reality the ground is not common at all. Instead, it is a heterogeneous field of varied personal positions, guided by the social institutionalization of sciences.

Realms of Intellectual Interdependency in Science

All sciences are both knowledge constructive and social-institutional systems. It is because of the latter that different realms of intellectual interdependency need to be elaborated. Thus, interdependency may be found between scientists interindividually (e.g., Dr. Smith thinks that Dr. Jones understands his or her argument), between scientists of a given discipline and these of another discipline (i.e., "interdisciplinary" relations; e.g., Dr. Smith thinks that physicists understand her ideas better than fellow psychologists), and between scientists as such (a social-institutional structure) and other social institutions within societies (e.g., Dr. Jones applies for government funding, persuading the appropriate bureaucracy that his project deserves it). This parallel multiple intellectual interdependency situates our analysis in this book in the realm of relations between the process of construction of ideas on the one hand, and the sociopolitical guidance of that construction, on the other.

Psychology may be a discipline in which the tension between those two sides – those of the scientist and his/her social context – are experienced in an extreme fashion. On the one hand, psychology as science strives toward constructing basic knowledge on the basis of ever-specific particulars of an empirical kind. At the same time, psychology is built on numerous sociomoral value presuppositions (Cirillo & Wapner, 1983) that make some research questions and ways of knowing adequate for the discipline, while ruling out possible alternatives. Thus, research on why children drop out from U.S. schools is built on the assumption that such drop-out is a sociomoral problem for the given society (at the given historical time). The opposite idea – that the schools are of such quality that the best adaptation for enterprising children would be to drop school – is not only weird, but morally wrong. However, the question of how adolescents may "drop out" from their neighborhood drug-using gangs would be a morally legitimate research issue. When a similar issue is played out on stockholders' "dropping out" from backing a particular company (by selling its stock, in mere anticipation of its failure), that can be hailed as a positively valued business decision.

The moral evaluation is the reverse: the free-market ideology is valued in the one decision and denounced in the other. Psychological problems are formulated in a socially predisciplined way, which – as it is implicit in the background of the research questions – creates a tension for psychology as science. Psychology – for all of the time of its independent existence – has been torn to pieces (almost literally; divided into various sub-areas) between "natural science" and "sociomoral ideology." Because its object of investigation is both a biological species and a cultural self-organizer, it cannot escape this tension by rejecting either of the two poles that create the tension. The alternative, a synthesis of the two at a superordinate level, has become difficult to construct in the context of the proliferating fragmentation of knowledge (supported by the ideology of empiricism), and the irreconcilability of different underlying sociomoral sentiments.

Science and Common Sense: The Role of Empiricism

In the case of the social sciences, particularly psychology, the issue of intellectual interdependency is crucial for the science if it tries to transcend the limits of common sense (and language; Valsiner, 1985, 1994b) and move beyond being a game of pseudoempiricism (Smedslund, 1995). According to Smedslund, most of the results of the empirical investigations in psychology are actually expressions of "given truths" already encoded into our thought through language.

Smedslund argues that the world is known to us through the acceptance of the logic of the psyche: *psychologic* (Smedslund, 1997). This logic is encoded in the language used. Thus, meanings of particular words (e.g., bachelor) set up implications that are necessarily true (e.g., a bachelor is a man who is not married), and do not require empirical evidence for us to begin to know that these implications are true. For instance, in order to find out if bachelors are unmarried men, we do not need to question an increasingly large number of unmarried men about whether they are bachelors. Empirical efforts of the latter kind are examples of pseudoempiricism in Smedslund's critical account. Claiming that it is necessary to prove empirically what we know to be true by the meaning system of our language is pseudoempirical. For example, the empirical demonstration that men are showing higher levels of masculinity than women (and vice versa for femininity) is pseudoempirical. In their practice of "doing science," psychologists are involved in an extensive self-fulfilling prophecy – empirically demonstrating the obvious – rather than constructing new knowledge. Pseudoempiricism dominates psychology, despite its obvious irrelevance.

How can such a state of affairs dominate a particular discipline? Wouldn't such a pseudoempiricistic production of information about what we know already lead to the extinction of the given area of science? Perhaps, pseudoempiricism can be utilized in psychology because of the different social functions that psychological research evidence carries, due to the discipline being caught in-between the natural sciences and sociomoral ideologies. Part of the ideological function of psychological empirical evidence is to provide the "scientific halo" for obvious common-sense truths. This is valued by social institutions, which can utilize such pseudoempirical evidence for the social legitimization of their political actions, now based on "scientific evidence."

If our description is adequate, then – at the level of the work of individual scientists – we can see discrepancies between the parallel communication channels of intellectual interdependency. A scientist can agree that a given project – involving a large number of subjects – is pseudoempirical. Yet he or she may do the study anyway, citing the need to communicate to his or her peers that the work done is "trustworthy," rather than "mere speculation." The peer-peer institutionalized communication channel (which regulates the boundaries of the notion of science in psychology) here overrides the interdependency of ideas between individual scientists. In terms of the social psychology of construction of norms (Sherif, 1936), this situation is to be expected. Social scientists build their norms of what amounts to "science" in their everyday research practices similarly to persons (in autokinetic experiments of Sherif) decided about the movement of light dots – by reaching consensus about inevitably personal positions. A consensus can reflect shared understanding about a clearly specifiable object – in which case consensual validation improves our individual understandings by social referencing. But equally possible, in the case of objects which are not immediately perceivable, is a scenario according to which consensus leads to construction of shared (and, hence, socially fortified) illusions. Thus, pseudoempirical studies in psychology can be viewed as "breakthroughs," the reviewers of the research results may praise the large work done, and hail the conclusions, yet fail to see that the conclusions are unconnected with the research results. The logical imperative of the interpretation becomes masked *as if* the interpretation emerged from the data, whereas in reality the data give an analogous picture precisely because the imperatives for the researchers' interpretation were the same as the ones for the many subjects tested. Furthermore, a governmental agency may institute a policy of providing research funds for projects with large numbers of participants. Again, a pseudoempirical trajectory for research is set into function. Intellectual interdependency between thinkers is canalized by local social norms of institutions as to what is admissible as scientific knowledge.[1] The definition of the boundaries of a discipline is a social-institutional enterprise, carried out by persons in their appropriated social roles.

In terms of intellectual interdependency, pseudoempiricism is but one indication that the system of thought called "science" (or *Wissenschaft*; compare with the weird-sounding verb of "knowledg*ing*" = constructing knowledge) is an intricate web of meaning-making activities, which involve understanding and ignorance side by side. The scientific meaning construction is filled with the use and invention of hierarchies of semiotic devices, as well as symbolic practices. The latter are at times publicly displayed, at others carefully hidden from the public view. During some historic periods political leaders (or parties) may interfere directly in the affairs of science, at other times such intervention may be hidden behind slogans of "taxpayers' right to know," and sometimes the sociopolitical system leaves scientists to their own devices. The intellectual interdependency of ideas in science is embedded in the web of social-personal interdependencies of the makers, carriers, and users of these ideas.

---

[1] As is often the case, such local norms may be upheld by a religious fervent of righteousness. Advisors may crush the "wrong ideas" in their doctoral students, or senior figures in a particular field may try to force younger colleagues to "return to the right path" (e.g., see Mahoney, 1989, p. 140). Fortunately, such social regulation of ideas in science is doomed to fail, as scientists, historically ranging from Galileo to Soviet geneticists, have repeatedly demonstrated.

Elaboration of the Roots of Intellectual Interdependency

It can be said that the issue of intellectual interdependency in science has haunted us in many ways, while we were working on the history of ideas in psychology. The intellectual interdependency was there in the case of Soviet developmental psychology at large (Valsiner, 1988), as well as in the case of Lev Vygotsky (Van der Veer, 1984; Van der Veer & Valsiner, 1991). Whenever we tried to make sense of ideas in what was charted out to be "Soviet psychology" or "the genius of Vygotsky," we would find an intricate web of intellectual interdependency with others. Hence, the need to make sense of that notion in general.

Back in 1988, we started by noting similarities between sociogenetic epistemology in general and the development of scientific ideas:

There is an interesting parallel between the sociogenesis of children's thinking and the issue of intellectual influence in scientific discourse. Children are no passive copiers of adult behaviors or passive recipients of ready-made cultural tools. They try to make sense of their environment, test hypotheses, integrate the results of these tests into their 'body of knowledge,' and actively master cultural tools (sometimes putting them to new use). The same is true, in a much more deliberate and systematic fashion, for mature scientists. It is obvious that the theoretical thinking of a good scientist cannot be reduced to the sum of influences undergone by that person. First, that would amount to denying the active role of individual scientists transforming ideas in various subtle ways . . . Second, scientists actively select their sources of influence. At the basis of this selection process are both theoretical considerations and results of empirical investigation . . . Investigators should be seen as active co-constructors of gradually developing ideas. (Van der Veer & Valsiner, 1988, pp. 61–2)

The appeal of the comparison of scientists with children depends upon the particular valuation of children in the personal culture of the evaluator. If that is of the kind in which children are viewed as inexperienced persons who need to learn the know-how of the world, then our comparison may read as an insult. If, in contrast, the evaluator considers positively the inquisitiveness, experimenting energy, and openness to new ideas that can be seen to characterize children, our comparison may be taken as a compliment. We have emphasized the latter interpretation: looking at scientists as children is a compliment to the youthful energies of scientists, who, even in old age, remain inquisitive about the world. The loss of childlike playful inquiry would amount to the end of knowledge construction. It is there where the *process of doing science* becomes transformed into social discourse *about* science, with all the ritualistic parapharnelia (ranging from Nobel prizes to decisions about what "appropriate" doctoral dissertation is like in the given discipline) being tools for the latter.

The tension-filled complexity that is the basis for our intellectual interdependency notion is not overlooked by other analysts of the processes of science. Pickering's (1995, pp. 22–3) "mangle of practice" emphasizes the dialectical relation of resistance and accommodation to new ways of acting (and thinking) in science. Pickering's theoretical construction allows him to concentrate on the real-life practices of scientists. In contrast, our effort here is to reconstruct the realms of developing scientific thought (rather than practices).

Multiple Participants and Multiple Goals

It became clear to us that intellectual interdependency entails multiple participants: not just scientists but also their grandmothers, their doctoral students, research assistants, or other laypersons, social institutions (universities, research institutes, popular media, governmental and private agencies), and scientific institutional categories called "disciplines." All of these participants in the process of intellectual interdependency act in a goal-oriented manner. Scientists want to solve selected problems in their knowledge domains (as well as secure their employment). Scientific institutions attempt to guide disciplines and scientists in directions of their interest. Different disciplines try to maintain (and others gain) their symbolic power positions (e.g., psychology pretending to be a "hard" or "natural" science, rather than a "soul science" or *Geisteswissenschaft*).

Such multiple participation can be documented through the study of communicative messages that exist in the knowledge construction process. Different kinds of narrative forms are used for different goals (Valsiner, 1994a). Frequent rhetorical efforts to specify "where the science is heading" or "where should it develop" indicate the self-interested, goal-oriented discourse about science. Social institutions make public claims (and encode those into their actual funding practices), making claims about where sciences should go in the present and in the near future. This amounts to the goal-oriented social guidance of different sciences, where the reasons for the promotion of one or another direction of a science are built on extra-scientific (economic, sociopolitical, etc.) grounds.

The academic world of the end of the twentieth century may be witnessing its own eradication (or at least the elimination of the historically developed relative autonomy from the sociopolitical world), all under the rhetoric niceties of "making science accountable" to governmental bureaucracies, and/or making it "applied" so that modern multinational corporations could appropriate it. The construction of basic knowledge by social institutions of science per se can become under siege from two sides. Efforts to control the directions by governmental institutions (of any country) and selective "buy out" of some directions of science by the contemporary global economic power (multinational corporations) may result in the loss of the relative autonomy of sciences from other institutions of societies that have been the benchmark of sciences since the Middle Ages. Becoming "socially *accountable*" for sciences means simultaneously becoming socially *controlable* by other social institutions, and, consequently, becoming politically driven.

As we here show, intellectual interdependency in science is not just a purely personal and intellectual phenomenon. It is simultaneously based on social power relations between the given science and the sociopolitical texture in which they are embedded. Nuclear physicists were heroes at the time of social utopias about new energy resources (followed by the nuclear bomb), and have lost that "halo" at a time when even mere transport of nuclear waste by rail or ship evokes explosive social protests. And psychologists, who after they had created their theoretical ideas, became tainted by either "immoral" (e.g., Watson, or Baldwin, in Chapter 4) or "wrong" political affiliations (e.g., Krueger, see Chapter 7) can be easily forgotten within their disciplines. Others, whose political affiliations have not been marked by moral condemnation (e.g., the history of A. N. Leontiev's activity theory in Soviet psychology, or Francis Galton's and Karl Pearson's contributions to statistics – separate from their hopes for eugenic purification of society) fare well in retrospective and politically corrected accounts of the history of the discipline. The sociopolitical side of human life is necessarily in the background of our construction of historical narratives and counter-narratives (Ahonen, 1997; Luczynski, 1997). The same sociohistorical event becomes narratively constructed in accordance with the direction of desirability that a particular social

institution ascribes to it. The person who encounters such narrative constructions can cordinate different stories (e.g., narrative
and counter-narrative), if such dialogicality is in place. Yet one of the
goals of narrative constructors of a story can be the eradication of
the possibility for such dialogicality – the privileged (by a social institution) an account may be created in ways that disallow the construction of its opposing narrative. In some cases of historical narratives
the latter has succeeded (in the U.S. – see Wertsch, 1997), in others
failed.

Narrative construction of historical accounts in science has similar
nature of it. Hero myths are created about scientists, while others
become "counter-heroes." For example, the simplification and stigmatization of the developmental ideas of Jean-Baptiste Lamarck began
already in his lifetime, and has continued to our days (Burkhardt,
1984). Images of the ever-increasing length of the neck of the giraffe
are easily evoked when Lamarck is mentioned, and bold developmental thinkers at times have to prove to their scientific colleagues that
they "are not lamarckians." The socially constructed counter-myth
about Lamarck's ideas as "not adequately scientific" has eliminated
the interest in these ideas. Yet the myth around Darwin is a positively
valued story of a grand breakthrough in evolutionary biology. Similar
myths have been constructed around the life and work of Lev Vygotsky (e.g., that he studied mother–child interactions) as we have
pointed out elsewhere (Van der Veer & Valsiner, 1991). To summarize,
discourse about science is not merely talking about science in its actual
reality (of the process of knowledge creation) as it is: It involves
talking about science from the position of whoever does the talking.
The need to do such talking is often sociopolitical and does not contribute to science itself. This discourse is meta-scientific (discourse
about science's discourse), and since the positioning of the participants
in that talking is variable, we can describe it as multivoiced or polyphonic.

Discursive Battlefields: Why So Much Fuss about Wording?

The polyphonic nature of any scientific and meta-scientific discourses makes them necessarily heterogeneous, and value-laden. In
contrast with the iron-clad image of the "rationality" of scientists – a
message that is proliferated between sciences and the rest of society –
scientists are human in being passionately devoted to their pet ideas.

Inside disciplines as wholes, the issue of semiotic codes for constructing knowledge is often non-neutral (see Thompson, 1993; on moral
rhetoric embedded in economists' discourse about causality). While
the issues of particular explanations (or descriptions) are being disputed in scientific discourse, in the background may lure implicit
moral preferences about the subject matter being explained.

The whole vocabulary of the given direction in a discipline can
become a discursive battlefield for the development of the given discipline. Psychology's conventionalization of ways of talking (e.g.,
frowning at the use of the plural "thoughts," while accepting its
synonym "cognitions"; or contrast between "observers" with "subjects" and with "research participants") flavors the way of making
sense of the issues from an ideological perspective. Issues about building a universal scientific terminology for psychology have been high
on the agenda of intradisciplinary dialogues. For example, at the 6th
International Congress of Psychology in Geneva, Claparède (1910)
called for the definitive setting up of a nomenclature of psychological
terminology. Recommendations by a special terminology commission
called for an austere simplicity of terminological equivalents between
languages (Baldwin, 1910). Efforts to emulate chemistry in the construction of a symbolic system were revealed in a proposal for a new
sign system (Courtier, 1910). Construction of unified terminology led
to heated discussions about the potential of Esperanto as a language
that could unify psychology (de Saussure, 1910).

The major dispute of psychology in the course of the twentieth
century has been the opposition between uses of terminologies with
mental and non-mental implications (cf. Vygotsky, 1926b/1997). Starting from the North American context (see Chapter 5) and proliferating
worldwide, the notion of behavior has been a consensually accepted
and vigorously defended (and attacked) concept. As Carl Graumann
has observed,

The ease with which the superfluous word 'behavior' could, and still can,
be added to any other word designating animal and human activities
(from crowding to milling, from dating to mating, from littering to
energy-saving behavior) is at least indicative of the belief in the ubiquitous
potency of psychology alias behavioral science. . . . Behavior . . . originally
was, and in the educational field still is, a moral concept. In its originally
reflexive form it meant to conduct oneself in a proper manner, that is,
according to moral standards. Only by virtue of this meaning does the
imperative "Behave!" make any sense (Graumann, 1996, p. 88).

Building psychology on the root term of behavior eliminated reflexivity from further consideration (animals behave, rather than think), and the complex nature of the phenomena was lost (as behavior, in the generic sense, was turned into analyzable discrete units of the observed phenomena: "behaviors"). The role of the behaviorist consensus in the American psychology of this century was based on the moral imperatives of pragmatist philosophies of different kinds, meant to take the place of religious belief systems (e.g., James, 1907, p. 301)

Social canalization of psychologists' thinking moved further in the 1930s, with the introduction of discourse about "variables." The previous "stimulus" now became "independent variable," while "response" was translated into "dependent variable." This

gave the language of dependent and independent variables a greater apparent degree of theoretical neutrality than the language of stimuli and responses. . . . Different interpretations of what variables represented were permissible, as long as all psychologists agreed that the units of their investigative practice were "variables." Second, the language of variables could accommodate the practice of psychologists who were engaged in establishing correlations between measures – for example, personality traits – that had not been experimentally manipulated and hence were not expressible in the language of stimulus and response (Danziger, 1996, p. 23).

Thus, psychology's discursive battlefield first barred psychologists' thinking from the possibility to explain phenomena in mentalistic terminology, and consequently guided it into a pseudo-physicalistic discourse about "variables." The latter is still accepted, despite the blatant mismatch between the implications of the meaning of "variable" (= something to be varied) and the indexical nature of psychologists' use of the term. As a result, psychology could create an image of "natural scientificalness" for itself (and for outsiders), while remaining internally a sociomoral discipline (Maiers, 1988). Further differentiation of the discursive battlefields in the discipline brought back the mentalistic explanatory terminology (through the "cognitive revolution"), yet in a form that maintained distance from the commonsense mentalistic expression (e.g., "cognitions" versus "ideas," "affects" versus "feelings"), and in ways that maintained the terminology of "variables" (e.g., "cognitive variables").

The social fights about the prescriptions for, and meanings of, explanatory terms used in contemporary psychology have a basic theme: It is the fight between maintaining the "common-language-nearness" of the terminology, or abstracting from it. This theme is known in the history of other sciences as well. Notions like "force," "horse power," "purity" (of chemicals), the permanence of the substance in lieu of a change in its form (Crosland, 1995), chemical "reaction" (Holmes, 1995) in the history of the physics and chemistry of the seventeenth and eighteenth centuries indicate a constant fight for overcoming animistic or moralistic (i.e., common-sense) reasoning and the organismic view on non-organismic substances (Bensaude-Vincent & Stengers, 1996; Klein, 1995). At the time, the chemical science struggled to overcome the common-sensical and perceptually immediate nature of the relation of alchemy to the chemical substances. Psychology has been struggling with similar issues throughout the twentieth century. Once these disciplines succeed, general science is born out of sociocultural knowledge complexes. The latter are certainly a domain for the struggle for dominance between scientific and political institutions.

Cultural Systems of Knowledge in Construction

Sciences (and scientists) operate in their particular social contexts, and their intellectual interdependency is constrained by these contexts. A scientist's thinking is always integrative of the habits of the common language, rules of the given science, and voices of his or her colleagues. History of science has not been profoundly cultural-psychological in the past, even if it needs to be. As Renn has remarked,

The texts of the individual authors which are usually in the center of attention of historians of science only reflect very specific aspects of the socially available knowledge. And even these texts cannot be properly understood without taking into account their specific role in the larger cultural system of knowledge. In a given culture, knowledge about bodies in motion, for instance, is built up and transmitted by ordinary experiences with unspecific objects accompanied by every-day language, but also by specific, socially-determined experiences with the material artifacts of that culture, such as machines, experiences which are reflected in technical language, and finally also by appropriating and exploring the theoretical constructs represented by the writings usually studied in the history of science. Since the knowledge of an individual scholar partakes in some or all of these currents of the socially available knowledge in a given culture, the individual knowledge itself is, as a rule, composed of various cognitive layers, each with its own specific structures (Renn, 1996, p. 7).

It is in the analysis of these "cognitive layers" and their counterparts in the social world of the scientist that the focus on intellectual interdependency entails. The cognitive structure of the intellectual interdependency is guided first and foremost by the cultural meanings of "science" (in contrast with other human enterprises) themselves. Not surprisingly, religious changes within societies can be traced to leave their substantive marks on the ways in which science becomes conceptualized (Merton, 1936). It may be possible to trace the divide between Anglo-American empiricist focus in science, and Continental-European primacy on theoretical discourse, to the differential histories of religions in the different cultural areas. While looking at the background role of Puritanism in the framing of science, Merton noted

It may well be that the Puritan ethos did not directly influence the method of science and that this was simply a parallel development in the internal history of science, but it is evident that through the psychological compulsion toward certain modes of thought and conduct this value-complex made an empirically-founded science commendable rather than, as in the medieval period, reprehensible or at best acceptable on sufferance (Merton, 1936, p. 8).

The "faith in *empirical* science," in whatever form it occurs, is primarily a faith and only secondarily empirical. It specifies the direction of inquiry, the desired realm within which scientists should act. The role of the Puritan/Protestant ideology in directing sciences toward the concrete can be seen via its opposition to medieval scholasticism. Likewise, the advent of behaviorism in the United States in the beginning of the twentieth century was an ideological movement away from the context of Protestant theological speculations. In a way, behaviorism turned the pietist focus upon pietism itself.

Who Is Doing the Talking?

Talking about intellectual interdependency of science involves taking a stance – a perspective – upon that science. However, this immediately distances any statement about a science from that science itself. Any statement *about* science – moralistic, futuristic, critical, or glorifying – is a statement of some ideal position relative to science. Hence it belongs to the realm of the social organization *of* science, not *into* science as such. Thus, what is attempted in this book is a meta-level analysis of the social canalization of ideas of the person as a social agent in the social sciences. In that sense, our effort might qualify as an example of a sociogenetic epistemology of science, carried out on the materials of the social sciences. As such, our effort does not belong to psychology (or other social sciences) per se. These are meta-scientific statements, i.e., they belong to the realm of the social organization of science. When this level of discourse is made into the target of investigation, we can talk about a discipline of the *developmental sociogenesis* of scientific ideas. Discourse about science is of value in its own right – only that value is in its being an object for investigation, not reflection of the state of affairs in a given science.

Who is likely to create discourse about science? The knowledge created within a given discipline is by its nature non-neutral as to the goal orientations of different institutions in a society. First, and historically foremost, sciences produced know-how that would lead to material gains in producing and distributing goods. The organization of society on its sociomoral side was sufficiently removed from the potential products of science and, hence, science could be perceived as a social institution in and by itself. This may be sufficiently well described by the representations of "paradigm" and "paradigm change" (Kuhn, 1970).

In the recent two decades, the study of the social organization of science has received increasing attention from sociologists and historians (Latour, 1987; Pickering, 1992, 1995; Renn, 1996; Shapin, 1995; Woolgar, 1988). Investigation of intellectual interdependency borders on these research foci, yet it differs from these in a substantial way. We are interested in the development of concepts in their social contexts, in the process of communication between scientists and societies. The focus of our investigation remains on the individual scientist and his or her creative efforts (and their successes and failures). The social embeddedness of these efforts is given careful consideration as the supportive basis for successes or failures, yet it is the personal creativity in a discipline that is the ultimate location of novelty construction. That creativity, however, is always embedded in the texture of the social guidance efforts of a science.

It may have been up to the scientists to interact about the substance of science, without having to take the social politics into account. Yet in conjunction with changes in the types of societies (moves toward "democratic" organization of society) and sciences' moves into the realms close to sociomoral arenas of institutional activities, this autonomy of the institution becomes lost. Sciences discover the need for *popularizing persuasion*, i.e., showing off certain kinds of their "successes" to the laypublic or powerful interest groups, gaining support via such communication. This necessity becomes important only if the lay populace acquires social mechanisms of control over the given discipline, either as a "client" to its applications, or as a potential power source over its support by governments. Thus, the pressure to persuade the laypublic about the effectiveness of psychotherapy is substantial, while that about the precision of psychophysical experiments is not. Yet the latter may need explaining to a grant review panel.

Contemporary research grant obtaining in U.S. federal funding agencies is a good example: even when peer review entails institution-mediated communication with (anonymous) peers, the final decision about funding is based on institutional decisions on the basis of "priority ratings." Organizing the institution of a science by way of a "peer community" (which discusses the contents), while retaining the control over the actual provision of support, is a natural tactic for any institution (the "professional power" is obtained by purchasing the services of selected "experts" for the institutions in consultant roles).

This example leads us to the question of the structural organization of "the scientific community" and to the role of social institutions in setting it up. The scientific community is not a group of equal persons who are operating a club that functions on the basis of democratic governance. Different forms of the organization of institutions in the given society at the given historical epoch inevitably leave traces in (or give full form to) the way the given science is institutionally organized (e.g., through conventionalization of discourse; Bazerman, 1987). At the same time, it is the scientists themselves who actively assume the expected institutional roles and use them for the advancement of the social status of their particular knowledge.

At different historical periods the linkage between extra-scientific institutions and sciences is more explicit than at others. Thus, the "great break" in Soviet philosophy (Valsiner, 1988, pp. 90–5) that carried over to psychology. It led to the demise of paedology as the interdisciplinary investigation of children, and with it of the cultural-historical school of thought. This ideological transition was institutionally organized by coordination of the "vertical" (scientific institutions–political powers) and "horizontal" (competitive actions in scientists' peer-groups, and inter-"schools" warfare) communicational processes. It was not "Stalin's tyranny" superimposed upon social sciences from above, but rather a social opportunity, provided "from the above," that led competing peer groups to denounce one another in competition to "win" a better position for themselves. It was the "next-door neighbor" (or a competing scientific group) who was the initiator and henchman of the "Stalinist purges" in everyday life and in "Soviet psychology" in the 1930s. Similar ritualistic coordination of the two channels of communication occurred in the Soviet Union during 1947–1951, through different waves of reorganization in philosophy, biology, and linguistics (Kojevnikov, 1996).

All these changes were organized by public institutional rituals of "discussion," during which "criticism" and "self-criticism" was publicly practiced by participating scientists and public officials. The effort to guide the scientific knowledge construction practices toward fit with the ideology in the Soviet Union were in principle not different from the institutionalization of psychology in Nazi Germany, and from the advent of behaviorism in North America (see Chapter 5).

Professionalization of a "Quasi-object"

Intellectual interdependency acquires new nuances in a world filled with rituals of professionalization, advertising of credentials, and competition for rewards. Usually it takes some time for a discipline to construct its own institutionalized system (e.g., for American sociology this is said to have taken four decades; Kuklick, 1980, p. 209; see also Chapter 5). As a result, the practical activities of scientists become institutionally determined:

At the highest, most general, level of the organization of the society, it sets up conditions that determine who among the population becomes involved in one or another area of science. For example, in all societies, becoming a scientist in a particular field involves a lengthy process of education with a selection of the appropriate candidates built into it (in the form of examinations, theses, degrees, honorary insignia, etc.). Furthermore, the content matter and language of exchange of information within a thus 'socially legitimized' science is constrained both by the society and the scientific community itself which may make its 'boundary maintenance' an important task. Undoubtedly, the form of conventions of scientific discourse and boundaries maintained between disciplines are constantly in the process of dynamic change (Valsiner, 1988, p. 11).

When seen from this light, contemporary institutional insistence upon "interdisciplinarity," "multidisciplinarity," and "research productivity" constitutes a marker of enforcing change in the ways science functions. This is the social-institutional discourse about science, which – after providing convenient "modernist" and "postmodernist" labels for mixing scientific and meta-scientific discourses – ends up in fragmented talk about *quasi-objects* (see Latour, 1993). Quasi-objects are objects "in between" the realms of nature and society, belonging to both, yet not distinguishing either. The notion of such objects is an effort to fight "dualisms," which is a social representation that organizes much of social sciences' discourse.

If we were to use Latour's terminology, the whole of psychology could be viewed as a quasi-object. That role is inherently contradictory, and instead of Latour's preferred notion of fusing the realms of nature and society, our coverage here emphasizes the inclusive separation of the two sides, natural and social, of the quasi-object. Latour's efforts to overcome dualistic views on the world have failed, as the application of quasi-object status to one's object of investigation effectively replaces making sense of the systemic functioning of the object by the assignment of an appealing (but imprecise) label to it. By declaring psychology to be a "quasi-object" we have only attached a Latourian label to it, while the fermenting processes that go on behind the label, and that make so many psychologists intoxicated by the "crisis" in their science, continue.

Secular Sanctity of Science

Science as an example of human activity has become intensively investigated by the sociology of scientific knowledge, where largely empirically based ethnographic descriptions, oriented toward describing what happens when scientists are involved in their work, prevail (Gilbert & Mulkay, 1984; Latour, 1987; Latour & Woolgar, 1979; Pickering, 1992). These studies have demonstrated how scientific activities are versions of human activities, and cannot be ascribed a completely separate status.

Scientific institutions make use of forms of socially representing themselves in ways that are borrowed from religious contexts. The notion of the "purity" of the character of scientists is comparable to that of saints. Furthermore, different systems of ideas can proliferate among scientists similarly to religious revitalization movements. Thus, the energeticist credo of Wilhelm Ostwald (see Hakfoort, 1992), or notions of "Marxist science" (Kojevnikov, 1995), utilized similar ritualistic techniques for their social proliferation. The emergence of sect-like groups in science is widespread. In psychoanalytic circles each of these is likely to become a small veritable sect that verifies the trustworthiness of people joining, and stigmatizes the "out-group."

In a similar vein, infighting between rival groups in science can take upon itself a character of a holy war (*jihad*), and sometimes numerous crusades are launched to liberate the given science from the reign of some tyrannical idea. The latter is usually linked with some out-group community of scholars. As such, fights are wars, with all of the psychological characteristics of the latter. John B. Watson's "behaviorist manifesto" (Watson, 1913) reads like a persecutor's speech at a trial of war criminals, in which the culprits (introspectionists) are clearly declared guilty. In contemporary psychology, we can witness fights with "positivism" and "dualism," often glossing over the full richness of the thought of particular scientists who are perceived as belonging to the camp of the opponents (e.g., see the analysis of Ernst Mach; in Feyerabend, 1984). Fights against dualism may color the knowledge-construction efforts (see Chapter 9), and result in infighting that is sectarian and not constructive.

Science as Situated Activity: Symbolic Organization of Its Territories

Science is territorial, i.e., its social institutions designate some areas of its activities to be "off limits" for different "outsiders," both in terms of physical territory (of laboratory rooms, offices, meeting rooms) and in the sense of the realm of ideas (use of special jargons). The access to the "inside" of these territorial havens is organized by way of symbolic markers: laboratory uniforms and labels on doors, degrees-indicating letters used to sign one's name, etc. Elaborate "initiation rites" are institutionally constructed for the "novices" to become "experts" (curricula, fieldwork requirements, expectations for doing one's own or the advisor's empirical work). Distinctions between "applied" and "basic" science can be encoded into the material culture of the marking of the territories (e.g., Löwy, 1996 for a description of contrasts between "research" and "application" contexts in French cancer research).

Inside the territoriality of the situated activity contexts of science is the *differential valuation* of territories. The active person – the scientist – is likely to be involved in the construction of ideas anywhere he or she might be: Basic breakthroughs in science may occur in a bathtub, on a toilet seat, in the middle of a concert, or during the usual empty talk at a cocktail party. Yet none of these contexts would be considered institutionally "proper" places for "doing science." Instead, special rooms (and buildings) called "laboratories," "centers," or "institutes" are erected for such purposes. Valuation emerges on the basis of such creation of symbolic places. "Laboratory research" can be valued more highly than "field research" (even if in the laboratory the main piece of equipment is a coffee maker), or "experimental science" (done in a laboratory) may be valued more highly than "observational science."[2] Symbolic value is created in relation to the marked and furnished territories, for instance:

In many social sciences, the laboratory reduces to the provision of a one-way mirror in a room that includes perhaps a table and some seating facilities. In fact, experiments may be conducted in researchers' offices when a one-way mirror is not essential. But even when a separate laboratory space exists, it tends to become activated only when an experiment is conducted, when, given the short duration and special 'entitivity' of such experiments, happens only rarely. *The laboratory is a virtual space* and in most respects coextensive with the experiment. *Like a stage on which plays are performed from time to time, the laboratory is a storage room for stage props that are needed when social life is instantiated through experiments.* (Knorr Cetina, 1992, pp. 124–5, emphasis added)

The similarity of the laboratory and the stage is important: In both cases what is constructed is the *symbolic transformation of reality* for some specified audience. The latter varies, ranging from fellow scientists in the given area, to political or community leaders, and further to the laypublic. These different audiences require different kinds of

---

[2] It is interesting to note that many psychology laboratories have become transformed from being specially furnished places (for animal experiments) to offices furnished with one-way mirrors (supposedly for human observations). In our time, these mirrors need not be used, and "laboratories" often become offices furnished with computers – yet the symbolic label *laboratory* may be retained.

performances on the same stage. Thus, the public displays of posthypnotic suggestion in psychiatry clinics in France in the end of the nineteenth century (see Chapter 2) involved the selective presentation of some content material to the audience, while the same patients were investigated and demonstrated for different materials to psychiatrists and psychologists on non-public occasions.

At times, the valuation can overturn the privileged position of the special territorial units and lead the given discipline to different structuring of its situated activities. Thus, the "laboratory" may be abandoned for the sake of privileging of field research, or basic science can become subservient to applied research (and situated in applied contexts). Such reversals merely change the valuations-based dominance, rather than alter the nature of the territorial marking of the privileged scientific activity. Thus, in cultural anthropology the initiation of the researcher into fieldwork has been expected to take the researcher as far as possible from his or her familiar environments (e.g., we do not hear of an anthropologist doing fieldwork in his own kitchen, and doing it in the supermarkets of one's own society is a recent phenomenon).

Sciences and Their Self-reflexivity: The Role of History

The self-reflexivity of sciences depends heavily upon who is assumed to be the recipient of such reflexive messages. If it is meant for outsiders of science, presentation of one's image as forever productive and socially benevolent may be a frequent stance. Such presentations may not allow the construction of stories of intellectual stagnation of a field, even if it is the case. Sciences' storytelling is often similar to that of technology, and is using technological advancement as a proof of its own progress.

Interestingly, different sciences have attempted to deny their own history in the effort of being ever-modern. Together with moving away from its alchemical roots, Lavoisier's chemistry – at the end of the eighteenth century – underemphasized its history (Bensaude-Vincent & Stengers, 1996). Psychology has attempted a similar "cut-off" of its history in the twentieth century, in an effort to turn into an experimental science. That such effort has operated as a blinder for the development of the discipline may be obvious (Rosa, 1994). Instead of a careful reanalysis of how both successes and failures of past problem-solving efforts proceeded, sciences have often created mythical stories for their possible future advancement (e.g., "rhetorics of hope"; Mulkay, 1993). The function of such future-oriented rhetoric projections should certainly be seen against the background of the negotiation of specific science-society relations.

Intellectual Interdependency and "Blind Spots" in Self-presentation

The social organization of the activities of scientists is complemented by the enhanced subjectivity of scientists as persons. While recognizing the social-organizational factors that frame the activities of sciences as human contexts, we cannot overlook the primary relevance of the scientist's personal subjectivity. This starts from differences in thinking styles (e.g., Einstein's focus on imagination contrasted with Bohr's concentration on unambiguous language use; Kaiser, 1994). Different personal "sore spots" can be found to both sensitize and block scientists from particular research targets (Devereux, 1967).

Scientists themselves can be "blind" to their intellectual interdependencies without any hint of hiding such traces. Thus, tracing intellectual interdependency on the basis of admitted relations by author X with author Y (or paradigm W) may be complicated due to the natural existence of self-reflexive "blind spots" in the thinking of X. X may be so much involved in paradigm W that he or she is incapable of recognizing such involvement, and may deny it (or at least may find it difficult to explicate; Ross, 1908, p. 579).

Furthermore, the focus on the subjectivity of the knowledge constructor (a person who acts in the role of a scientist) becomes one of the institutionally set-up blind spots (Keller, 1996). This fits the notion of the institutional appropriation of constructed knowledge: The agency of constructors is replaced by ego-decentered abstract forms, such as "science has discovered A/disproved B." Science with a capital S takes the credit for successes, whereas the inevitable failures are attributed to individual scientists.

Summary: Multiple Dialogues of Intellectual Interdependency

The complex story of intellectual interdependency can be summarized with a relatively short set of claims:

1. Scientific ideas are created, and used, by individuals, who interact with one another, thus taking over each others' specific

ideas and general views, and transforming those to fit their personal-cultural worlds and their scientific idea complexes. Thus, the first version of the dialogical nature of knowledge construction in science is that of the scientist's dispute with himself or herself (the "scientific" and "personal" kinds of "voices," à la Bakhtin and Wertsch, creating the dialogue). In parallel, the scientist is in intrapersonal dialogue with the ideas of other scientists, known to him or her through interaction or through distal contact with their texts (i.e., the scientist's own "scientific voice" enters into dialogue with those of other scientists).

2. The intrapersonal dialogues described above are complemented by extrapersonal dialogues. Disputes, chats, and other forms of communication between scientists set the condition for symbolic movement of the encoded ideas, intentional persuasion, dis-persuasion, and negotiation efforts – all *constrained by the social role positions* that the given participating scientists are occupying at the given time. Communication between scientists is not that between equal members of the "scientific community," but between persons who are in some intellectual "kinship relation" with each other (e.g., the students of scientist X relate to him or her differently than to another scientist, with whom they have not studied), have moved into different social role positions of differential power (department heads, institute directors, members of granting agencies' decision panels, etc.). It is in these role-based and nonsymmetric dialogues that the symbolic material of institutional kind constrains the flow of ideas between scientists.

3. The interscientist dialogues are embedded *in the specific relations between the given social-institutional position of the given branch of science, and the realm of other branches of science* (and other sciences). Persons who carry out such dialogues move from the scientific to the meta-scientific level of organizing the dialogues. For instance, the talk by scientists in field X about their superiority (in "doing good science") over those in field Y belongs to this sociological level of science processes. Negotiations between different sciences about the "appropriateness" of whether science X can belong to some association of "sciences" is of such kind (e.g., the question of the acceptance of psychology into international boards of sciences; compare with the

possible question as to whether "leisure science," "pop music science," or "nursing science" are to be admitted to "clubs" having physicists, chemists, and astronomers as core members).

4.   The given scientist, assuming an institutional role (2) and carrying out his or her disciplinary objectives (3), can enter into dialogues between "the sciences" on the one hand, and "society" on the other. These dialogues are of meta-social kind, as these relate with power issues within the given society's multiplicity of institutions. The norms of "the scientific method" are often set up in a dialogue at this level (Shiva, 1988).

As a scientist, whose primary focus is on knowledge construction (level 1), is simultaneously relating in some way to issues of the levels 2–4, all intellectual interdependency is socially canalized. How scientists create new ideas is thus always socially canalized. Both successes and failures of scientists' efforts are socially embedded. Personal autonomy (i.e., relative distancing of level 1 from the other levels) is possible only under special circumstances and to a limited extent.

A more general question that arises from this multilayered notion of intellectual interdependence is the question as to which of the levels guides new developments in science. There will be "buffering mechanisms" available for reducing the excessive impact of any single one of the levels. Surely transformation at level 4 can have dramatic consequences at lower levels, yet the lower levels can resist sociopolitically instituted changes. We proceed to investigate these levels through our cultural-historical analysis of the notion of the social nature of the person. This analysis takes us to nineteenth century Europe, primarily to France, where the questions of mutual influences of human minds in everyday lay discourse, together with the social relevance of psychiatrists' opinions, led to the development of a social context (Chapter 2) within which the psychological analysis of Pierre Janet could emerge (Chapter 3). While the German thinking of the nineteenth century was occupied by issues of language in human thought, the French tried to get to the actions of human beings. Differently in different countries, the notion of the social nature of the personal mind became a topic of construction. We outline how that idea was constructed along parallel lines.

CHAPTER TWO

Social Suggestion and Mind

The notion that the human mind is social is deeply rooted in human fears about not being oneself and becoming controllable by other people. Not surprisingly, such fear has been part of the social role of the ruling or affluent social classes (who have the social or economic power to rule over others, and hence have something to lose). The possibilities that social suggestions might modify human personality was of ambivalent value in the nineteenth century European societies. That ambivalence found its playground in the psychiatric cases that demonstrated social suggestibility of human personality.

In 1892, Alfred Binet published his *Les altérations de la personnalité*, in which he gave an overview of the research into dissociation and fragmented or multiple personality. Having discussed the clinical investigations by, among others, Azam, Bernheim, Charcot, Gurney, James, Janet, Myers, Richet, and Weir-Mitchell, he reached the following conclusions:

In sum, we have seen . . . a veritable crumbling of consciousness; and from time to time, often with the help of a little suggestion, one of these consciousnesses has managed to reach the dignity of a veritable personality. . . . We must not, however, exaggerate the role of the subconscious personages. . . . The primitive fact, as we said, is not the secondary personalities, it is the desegregation of psychological elements; it is only afterward, and often through training, through suggestion, that these scattered elements organize themselves in new personalities. . . . We are used from way back, by the usages of language, by the fictions of law, and also by the results of introspection, to consider each person as if forming an indivisible unity. The present investigations profoundly modify this important notion. It now seems proven that if we accept the unity of the ego as very real it must get a totally different definition . . . this unity must be sought in the coordination of the elements which compose it (Binet, 1892, pp. 315–16).

Binet's conclusion, which echoed similar statements made by Ribot, is worthy of our attention for several reasons. First, his remark about the role of training and suggestion in the creation of multiple personality is sobering and contrasts markedly with the inflated claims about the nature and number of personalities in present-day patients. In his book, Binet discusses the evidence for spontaneous and experimentally induced dissociation and suggests that in the few cases that we can speak of truly different personalities in one individual suggestion (by the therapist?) played an important role (see below).

Secondly, Binet's conclusion points to the boundaries of the concepts of personality and consciousness. He suggested that the discovery of a fragmented consciousness or even separate "consciousnesses" does not necessarily imply the existence of various personalities.

Thirdly, he claimed that a unified ego, a coherent self, is not present at the outset but is at most a result, the result of an effort to synthesize the plenitude of experiences encountered by the subject (cf. Chapter 3). All three aspects are important in their own way.

Binet's book was published at a time that virtually every important psychologist dealt with issues of hypnosis and double consciousness. William James (1890), for example, carried out his own experiments with hypnosis and considered the "discovery of a consciousness existing beyond the field, or subliminally . . . the most important step forward that has occurred in psychology" (James, 1902, p. 233). Myers, Morton Prince, and Freud are some of the other international investigators who occupied themselves with these issues around the same time (cf. Boring, 1950).

In France, particularly, the phenomena of hypnotic suggestion and dual consciousness had caught the imagination of scholars, novelists, playwrights, and the general public. All sorts of reciprocal relationships between these groups existed and persons often combined different roles. Diderot, Flaubert, Proust, and Zola have often been mentioned as writers who dramatized the science of the time or served as a source of inspiration for new scientific models and theories. Cultural and medical-psychological history formed an incredibly complex whole that has been the subject of more than one book (see Carroy, 1993; Micale, 1995, pp. 221–39). The fact that most of the great cultural figures of that time (e.g., Bergson, Bernheim, Binet, Charcot, Durkheim, Le Bon, Lévy-Bruhl, Ribot, Tarde) knew each other personally contributed to the mutual influences and disciplinary transgressions. The psychologist Binet, for example, was involved in the writing and staging of drama (Carroy, 1993, pp. 147–70), while the philosopher Bergson participated in hypnotic séances and advanced a prosaic explanation for the "fact" that hypnotized subjects could read a book that was outside their field of vision (Bergson, 1886). In the 1890s the phenomena of dual consciousness were so well known that even what we now think of as mild forms of dissociation were phrased in its terms. Thus we can see the novelist Daudet complain about his "horrible duality" and exclaim: "*Homo duplex, homo duplex*! The first time that I realized that I was two was when my brother Henri died, and father exclaimed so dramatically; 'He is dead! He is dead!'. My first *me* was weeping and the second was thinking: 'What an appropriate exclamation! How nice would it sound in the theater!' " (Daudet, 1899, p. 1).

Many more examples from novels and plays could be given, but they would not suffice to do justice to the rich and complex culture of the time, a culture that had, once again (Crabtree, 1993; Gauld, 1992), become fascinated with issues of mesmerism and dual consciousness. As we will see, these issues briefly intersected with the study of hysteria, then emerged as variants or products of social suggestion, and finally served as stepping stones toward a sociogenetic account of mind (see Chapter 3).

Hypnosis, Double Consciousness, and Hysteria

There are no obvious links between the phenomena of hypnosis and double consciousness, on the one hand, and hysteria, on the other hand, but by the time Binet was writing his conclusions they had become inextricably linked in France, or, perhaps more correctly, in Paris. Gilles de la Tourette (1889, pp. 169–83), one of Charcot's students, "on the basis of *numerous* observations," considered sleepwalking in childhood to be the first stage of hysteria. He added that hysterics are very easily hypnotized, just like persons who suffered from sleepwalking in their youth. Hysteric somnambulism, which may occur in the stage of "passional attitudes" (see below), he considered to be a state that was very similar to both spontaneous and hypnotic somnambulism, mostly because of the subsequent amnesia and because of the suggestibility of the subject.

In sum, Gilles de la Tourette and other members of the Paris school considered sleepwalking and dissociation as pathological phenomena that were predictive of later hysteria if they were not its first manifestations.[1] This implies that hysteria was conceptualized as a disease of dissociation.

The phenomena of hypnosis (or "animal magnetism" or "mesmerism," as it was called in different periods) and double consciousness were more closely linked with each other than each of them with hysteria. In the early nineteenth century it was already common knowledge that somnambulists, upon waking, lose all memory of the sensations and ideas they had in the state of somnambulism, whereas they regain these memories when they again become somnambulistic. In 1826, Bertrand spoke of this phenomenon in terms of two separate memory chains, one for the waking state, and another for the somnambulistic state. Others (e.g., Braid) used such terms as "second memory" and "double consciousness" (Crabtree, 1993, pp. 283–5). Magnetizers sometimes noticed a similar phenomenon in magnetized subjects who would speak with another voice and say things of which they had no recollection afterward. It seemed logical to consider this state as a form of induced or experimental somnambulism. Finally, in the late eighteenth century, investigators began to notice a pathological condition in which someone would display alternating and entirely different personalities. Crabtree (1993, pp. 289–1) has argued that there is a connection between the rise of this alternating personality disorder and the discovery of a second, or alternate, consciousness in magnetic sleep. The discovery of a second stream of thought and memory in magnetic sleep made it possible to think of the disorder in terms of a divided consciousness, rather than in demonological or organic terms.

Many of the investigations into artificial somnambulism and divided consciousness were carried out with patients who had inexplicable pains, anesthesias, and other symptoms and who were diagnosed as suffering from hysteria. With retrospect we can say that a substantial part of these patients suffered from syphilis, others from epilepsy, still others showed symptoms (e.g., conversion symptoms)

---

[1] This view was contested by the Nancy school but also by Frederic Myers who often emphasized that French investigators tended to deal predominantly with the ill, especially hysterics, whereas the English, not having as many hysterics at their disposal, were forced to use persons who were basically healthy (Crabtree, 1993, p. 328).

that now have been grouped under other labels. Hysteria as such has disappeared from the pool of available psychiatric diagnoses.

Much has been said about hysteria, its demise, and the lessons to be learned for medical diagnostics from the historic period in which it flourished. According to Micale (1995), in ancient times, it was a disease that only befell women. Its cause was supposed to be a wandering uterus and the advised remedy for hysteric young women was to get married, which was a euphemism for having sexual intercourse.[2] Gradually this gynecological approach and the therapy that went with it disappeared, to be replaced by a demonological model in the Middle Ages. The highly dramatic symptomatology of hysteria was viewed as a sign of possession by the devil (see also Chapter 3). The demonological model was in its turn replaced by a neurological one in the seventeenth century through the works of Willis, Sydenham, and others. Micale (1995) then observes a re-eroticization of hysteria during the late 1700s and early 1800s for which no fully satisfactory explanation has as yet been offered. Finally, in the late nineteenth century we see a shift to a psychological model with the theories of Charcot, Bernheim, and Janet.

Before we briefly discuss Charcot's and Bernheim's psychological theories, we will make a few remarks about the sociocultural background of hysteria. The shifting symptoms of hysteria and the fact that its diagnosis disappeared in modern times suggest that the psychological model needs to be followed or complemented by a sociocultural model. Various overlapping accounts of the nature of hysteria have been advanced: It was the socially accepted way to be unhappy; it was a creation of doctors and patients who used cultural models made available through novels and the press; it was drawing on the symptom pool of the time; it was a curious way of making a career as a talented woman; it was a form of sexual suppression by medical doctors; and so on and so forth. Perhaps it was all of that and somewhat more.

It is certainly true that the thinking about hysteria and the doctor–patient relationships had at times strong sexual undertones (Carroy, 1993; Micale, 1995; see also below). Doctors were male, and before Charcot the overwhelming majority of hysteric patients were female. Stories about erotic doctor–patient relationships were quite common and Delboeuf (1892) advised his colleagues to hypnotize patients in

---

[2] This remedy was, curiously enough, again proposed by Freud.

public to avoid any rumors. In the Salpêtrière and probably elsewhere it was common practice to photograph nude female patients in characteristic, hysteric positions. It was a dubious practice and in 1864 Legrand du Saulle already voiced his reservations. One of his reasons was the fact that photographs of patients of an explicit pornographic nature were being sold outside the wards (Legrand du Saulle, 1864, p. 594).

It is also true that disease concepts vary across cultures (e.g., Payer, 1990) and it is likely that diagnoses come about in a more or less one-sided dialogue between doctor and patient. It is evident that patients feel miserable but how this feeling is conceptualized and expressed depends upon the available cultural disease models. Few Western men, as Showalter (1997) pointed out, will express their existential distress by claiming their penis is shrinking or receding into their body. Equally few will claim to be possessed by evil spirits. This means that somatic sensations are not just labeled but restructured or reconceptualized by fitting them into a plausible disease account or story and that subsequent sensations will tend to strengthen or confirm this account (cf. Valsiner, 1989). If we accept one of Janet's ideas (see Chapter 3), then the greater part of our mental life consists in attempts to synthesize the bewildering complexity of the environmental events. We continually attempt to create stories (*récits*) that make seemingly or actually unconnected events from our life into a coherent whole.

Suppose, to take a trivial example, that while walking in the street, you bump into another pedestrian. You make a verbal protest, but the other person just hits you on the head and disappears in the crowd. What now happens is that in your consternation, and while you continue your walk, you start constructing different stories that make some sense of the event you just experienced. In actual fact, you have perhaps seen very little and the little you saw is diminishing rapidly as the details fade away from memory. You don't know exactly what the stranger looked like, whether he was tall, whether he was wearing glasses, what color his coat was, and so on. All you remember is the collision, the exchange of words, the blow, and the emotion that went with it, or rather, followed it. But despite this indeterminacy – which is always there – or because of it, we try out different accounts of this same event, in a process that reminds us of Queneau's *Exercices de style*, until we have reached a version that can be presented to the social others and that makes sense to ourselves. The stranger may have become taller or faster, our own words sharper, and so on and so forth. In the end we settle upon an account that perhaps preserves our feelings of dignity but that in any case can be presented to important social others and to ourselves. In addition, this account or story is flexibly adjusted to the social other – we will tell it in a different way to a colleague and to a spouse (see Chapter 3) – and will tend to change over time as a function of our changing assessment of the event and the withering emotions. All this does not mean that some objective event did not take place, the collision was real enough and could have been videotaped (Hacking, 1995), but that our understanding and recollection of it is framed as a narrative, a story that has functions both for the social other and for ourselves.

It is likely that something similar occurs when we feel incomprehensible sensations or pain in certain parts of our body. We immediately begin thinking of explanations and are not satisfied until we have found a satisfactory candidate. In doing so we make use of the explanatory stories available in our culture and use these to estimate the seriousness of the experience. Few persons in America will attach any significance to a brief sudden pain in the head (few people even have a theory about headaches that last much longer, nor do they worry about them) or the left foot, but many cannot ignore a similar pain in the upper part of the left arm or in the chest. In a conversation with our doctor, such pains will either be found to fit in a certain acknowledged pattern and declared objectively existing, or they will be found incoherent (i.e., not fitting a known pattern) and not worthy of our attention.

In hysteria, things were even more complicated because of the high suggestibility of the patients. Hysterics were known to pick up any hints from their doctors or environment as to how to behave as a respectable hysteric. Thus doctors who were searching for a certain pattern of symptoms would very easily and against their intentions communicate these expectations to the patients. In this way certain patterns might be continued. But hysteric patients were also living in large wards with patients suffering from other diseases and easily adopted their symptoms (e.g., epileptic attacks). This caused part of the bewildering complexity and variety of the symptoms of hysteria. It can be seen, then, that the symptoms of this mimetic disease were socioculturally determined in multiple ways. In groping for an explanation of the widely varying and often bizarre symptoms, patient and doctor fell back upon available vignettes or cocreated these themselves. Often these did no more than provide a label or declare that the symptoms were common. Sometimes the symptoms and the patient herself were deemed fascinating and worthy of special study. That brings us to the theories of hysteria that were advanced by Charcot of Paris and Bernheim of Nancy.

Charcot believed hysteria to be disease entity that had a hereditary background but whose onset was caused by a physical or emotional shock (see Ellenberger, 1965; Gauld, 1992; Hacking, 1995; Janet, 1895a; Micale, 1995). Hereditary predisposition plus shock (the famous agent provocateur; see Chapter 3) caused a dysfunction of the central nervous system. He rejected the older gynecological theories and claimed that men too are susceptible to hysteria albeit in much lower ratios than women. According to Charcot, the most characteristic symptom of hysteria is the hysterical attack or *grande hystérie* which ideally consists of a number of well-ordered stages. Prodromi (e.g., hallucinations) are followed by an epileptic attack (Charcot's hysterics lived in the same wards as did the epileptic patients) which passes into sleep. Then the patients awake and enter a period of disordered movements beginning with the famous arched back position. This stage is followed by a period of "passional attitudes" in which the patients mimes or acts out erotic, ecstatic, or other emotions. The whole process may end in disorientation or delirium (Gauld, 1992; Micale, 1995).

In addition, Charcot's hysterics often suffered from chronic disturbances of sensibility and motor derangements. Many had hypersensitive "hysterogenic points or zones" on their bodies which could be pressed to induce a grand attack. Many suffered from anesthesias and hysteric paralyses (see Chapter 3). Hysterics were also prone to suffer from digestive, circulatory, and all kinds of other disorders (this is why it has been called a mimetic disease). And, of course, in Paris patients suffering from somnambulism or *dédoublement* were almost by definition counted as hysterics (Hacking, 1995).

Charcot's theory of hysteria brought order, perhaps too much order (see Janet, 1895a), to the bewildering complexity of hysteric symptoms. He rejected the earlier genital etiologies, democratized hysteria by making it into a disease for both men and women, and supplied excellent diagnostic descriptions. Although his theory was in principle neurological – in principle, because the alleged brain lesion was purely hypothetical and no neurological details could be given, – he accepted the idea that the occasioning cause of the disorder might be of a psychological nature. Strong emotions were "moral traumata" that could produce a number of the hysteric symptoms. Because of its neurological nature, Charcot did not believe that hysteria could really be cured and he made no attempts to develop some sort of therapy. Nor did he make the step to a largely or purely psychological theory of hysteria. Hacking (1995, pp. 187–8) has observed that in Charcot's thinking the occasioning cause for hysteria differed between men and women: Male hysteria was provoked by physical trauma ("railway spine") and female hysteria by psychological trauma. The final step towards a full-fledged psychological theory of hysteria was left to Bernheim and Janet.

Bernheim interpreted hysteria as an exaggerated psychological re-action that was potentially universal. In his view, more or less anyone might become hysteric and he did not believe in an innate neuropathic disposition. What caused the hysteric symptoms was a heightened suggestibility and Bernheim consequently developed a psychotherapy that was largely dependent on the use of hypnotic suggestion (Micale, 1995). Bernheim (e.g., 1903; 1995) demonstrated that he could move the so-called hysterogenic zones by simply suggesting to the patients that they did or did not feel pain (his favorite method was that of suggesting the absence or presence of sensations to the patient in the company of assistants or relatives saying, for example, "Now I will show you that the patient feels no pain *here!*"). He took great pleasure in showing that the hysteric anesthesias were purely mental. Using a crayon he marked the anesthetic zones of hysterics. He then blind-folded them, performed some impressive but nonsensical operations with magnets, and again marked the anesthetic zone. In doing so, however, he cheated the patient by moving the line some centimeters claiming that his operations had already achieved some success. Pa-tients now saw and felt that the anesthetic zone had indeed dimin-ished in size. Bernstein (1903; 1995, pp. 298–306) then again blind-folded the patient, performed his nonsensical magic operations, and shifted the line another couple of centimeters. Using such ingenious methods, Bernheim managed to cure many hysterics, although he confessed that they sometimes relapsed. He was more pessimistic about patients suffering from neurasthenia, melancholia, hypochon-dria, obsessive disorders, and the like. Fixed ideas were often more difficult to eradicate than pain sensations, Bernheim said, and he con-fessed that he had often tried to cure melancholia, hypochondria, obsessions, etc. – but had always failed (ibid., pp. 390–5).

This was exactly the field, of course, in which his contemporary

Janet would specialize after his first studies of double consciousness and hysteria. Contemporary hysteria experts view Janet as one the psychologists who elaborated on the psychogenic implications of Charcot's work. Janet shifted the focus of observations away from the physical symptoms and attacks to the altered states of consciousness associated with hysteria: amnesias, obsessions, dissociation etc. (Hacking, 1995; Micale, 1993; 1995). Janet's new psychogenic theory of hysteria and his gradually evolving sociogenetic theory of the mind are discussed in Chapter 3.

We may conclude that, at least in France, for many specialists the topics of double consciousness, hysteria, and hypnotic suggestion had become an inextricable whole. Laymen, novelists, patients, and medical doctors were all well aware of the standard models of hysteric patients, dissociation, and hypnotic séances. This knowledge undoubtedly codetermined the behavior of patients and doctors and the diagnoses they arrived at. It was Bernheim of Nancy who pointed out that many of the phenomena depended upon suggestion and were thus iatrogenic. But the opinions about the nature of hypnosis or suggestion differed.

Paris and Nancy Schools of Hypnosis

The distinguished neurologist Jean-Martin Charcot (1825–1893) founded what was called the Paris School of Hypnosis. Babinski, Féré, Gilles de la Tourette, and Raymond belonged to his school. In 1878 he and his students began seriously studying hypnosis, probably as a result of their interest in metallotherapy (Gauld, 1992; Micale, 1995). In trying to find out the basic characteristics of the hypnotic state Charcot followed a strategy that had earned him success and fame in neurology and the study of hysteria. He selected cases which showed a disease in its most developed form and considered these as "ideal types" from which other cases formed variations. He believed hypnosis to be a morbid state of three stages: the stage of *catalepsy* during which the subject is immobilized and reacts as an automaton to certain kinds of suggestion, the stage of *lethargy* during which the subject appears asleep and shows neuromuscular hyperexcitability, and the stage of *somnambulism* during which the subject reacts intelligently to verbal suggestions (Gauld, 1992). Charcot and his associates believed that hypnosis was strongly related to hysteria as defined above. Catalepsy, anesthesias, heightened suggestibility, and amnesia upon awakening, among other things, are found in both hysteric patients and hypnotized subjects. For these reasons, Charcot, Babinski, Binet, and, to a lesser extent, the early Janet (see Chapter 3) believed that in order to be hypnotizable subjects had to suffer from hysteria or at least from something that came quite close to it. In actual fact, the hypnotic experiments were carried out with a limited number of female hysteric patients from Charcot's wards. Charcot and his followers were criticized by colleagues who belonged to what came to be called the Nancy School of Hypnosis.

The Nancy School originated with the findings of the country doctor Liébeault (1823–1904) who was unknown to the scientific world of the time until he and his book on hypnosis (Liébeault, 1866) were discovered by the professor of medicine Hyppolyte Bernheim (1840–1919). Bernheim in his turn inspired Liégeois (1823–1908), a professor of law in Nancy, and Beaunis (1830–1921), a physiologist in the same city, and together these four persons constituted the Nancy School (Gauld, 1992; Voutsinas, 1960). Their basic claims were that hypnotism has nothing to do with hysteria and that fully normal persons can be hypnotized, and that the three stages of Charcot are merely artifacts which do not occur "spontaneously" but can be and are produced by suggestion. As Bernheim (1903/1995, p. 87) said, hypnosis is a purely psychological fact and suggestion is its key.

He defined suggestion as the act by which an idea is introduced into the brain and accepted by it (ibid., p. 37). Such ideas inevitably make themselves felt according to the *law of ideodynamism*, which says that "each brain cell stimulated by an idea stimulates the nervous fibers which must realize this idea" (ibid., p. 45). The concept that ideas, once implanted in the mind, tend to realize themselves in action, had been popularized by Fouillée (see Chapter 3) and was rather widespread in the 1890s (Nye, 1975, p. 65). Suggestion was seen by Bernheim as a centripetal process and its realization as the centrifugal process or the "exteriorisation of the idea" (Bernheim, 1903/1995, p. 62). More in general, he described the hypnotic state as state in which the subject is focusing his attention on an idea suggested by the hypnotizer. To be in this state is an ability of the subject (some are more talented than others) and Bernheim repeatedly stated that hypnosis does not exist, there are just suggestible subjects (e.g., Bernheim, 1903/1995, p. 99).

It is interesting that really mad people are not hypnotizable, according to Bernheim. Suggestibility requires a right mind and if such patients "were suggestible, they would not be mad" (ibid., p. 396). This claim was of course in almost perfect contrast with the claim of the Paris School that being hypnotizable is a sure sign of madness, although of a perhaps somewhat milder form than Bernheim had in mind, namely hysteria.

Bernheim's theory of suggestion was rather crude – his psychotherapy based on suggestion seems to have been quite effective, however – and his books were somewhat simplistic and testifying of a belief in scientific progress that now seems exaggerated. But in his criticism of the Paris School of Hypnosis he proved basically right. The three stages of Charcot could not be reproduced in independent investigations. Nor were they exhaustive. By 1890 it had become clear that the phenomena observed by Charcot had been wholly due to injudicious suggestion and to the involuntary drilling of patients. Several decades later, Janet gave Bernheim the credit he deserved:

It is possible that a few hypnotized hysterics may manifest natural modifications of sensibility, abnormal motor reactions giving rise to cataleptic states, and a remarkable inclination to develop contractures under the influence of trifling stimuli; but the regular arrangement of these modifications in successive phases, as demonstrated in the dozen Salpêtrière patients, was unquestionably due to an injudicious drilling (Janet, 1925, p. 186).

Janet (1925, pp. 188–92) also offered an explanation for the errors of the Paris School. In his view Charcot's cases had been precooked in several ways. First, Charcot dealt with his subjects in public, openly discussed their symptoms, and subjects may have picked up hints and suggestions as to how to behave. Second, Charcot's subjects had been selected and trained by his assistants who naturally strove for exemplary cases. Third, several of Charcot's subjects had previously been hypnotized by magnetizers who may have instilled and standardized the well-known "stages" (See Gauld, 1992, pp. 314–15).

In conclusion, we can say that Bernheim's theory of suggestion had inflicted defeat on the Paris school of hypnotism. In his efforts to present the most clear and intelligible cases to his audience (see Janet, 1895a), Charcot lost his customary cautiousness and created models of hypnosis and madness that could not be reproduced elsewhere. There was only one field in which the Nancy school was less successful: the field of suggestion and crime.

Social Suggestion and Crime

If one believes with the Nancy School that most normal people can be hypnotized or at any rate are highly suggestible then new possibilities for crime suggest themselves. The hypnotizer might take advantage of the hypnotized subject by sexually abusing her (most subjects were women and all hypnotizers men) or one might suggest to the subject to commit a crime in the hypnotic state or as a result of a posthypnotic suggestion. These possibilities did not escape the attention of the experts and the general public (e.g., Bonjean, 1890; Campili, 1886; Garnier, 1887; Ladame, 1888; Von Lilienthal, 1887). Some experts deemed these possibilities very real and argued that hypnotized subjects who committed crimes could not be held morally responsible for their behavior. Others flatly denied that it was possible to have someone do something against his or her own will. The issues of legal accountability or responsibility were interesting and lawyers were quick to exploit the possibilities for the defense. Things became even more complicated because of the emphasis on the more global issue of suggestion by the Nancy School. Almost anyone could come under the moral influence of some stronger personality and be brought to commit immoral deeds. And, of course, people might spontaneously reach the hypnotic state or dissociate and subsequently commit a crime and remember nothing of it. Indeed, the fact that a hideous crime was committed almost suggested that the criminal offender was mentally ill and could not be held morally (or even legally) responsible for his or her deeds. The concepts of pathology (mostly hysteria), hypnosis or suggestion, immoral behavior and crime were (and still are) very much entangled and authorities who worried about the moral hygiene of the public followed the scientific developments attentively and at times tried to regulate the course of events.

Not every follower of the Nancy School believed that hypnotized subjects could be abused or made to commit crimes. The Belgian Delboeuf (1892), otherwise faithful to the doctrine of the Nancy School, argued that there is no permanent submission to the will of the hypnotizer and believed the alleged cases of suggested crime were incredible. Perhaps some very few hypnotized subjects might be harassed but this was equally true for subjects who were intoxicated by alcohol so that at any rate no special legislation was necessary (Delboeuf, 1892, p. 47; cf. Babinski, 1910, for a similar argument).

Nor did all adherents of the Paris School believe that abuse of hypnosis was impossible. Féré claimed to have been the first to draw attention to the medico-legal importance of the subject and Binet and Féré (1887, p. 279) considered that a hypnotized subject might become "an instrument of crime of a frightening precision." Gilles de La Tourette (1889) and Charcot thought it possible to sexually abuse a hypnotized female subject, particularly in the lethargic state. Even at the Salpêtrière subjects were induced to commit staged crimes with phony knives, However, Charcot argued that in the real and prosaic lives of ordinary criminals it would be difficult to find suitable subjects (they had to be hysterics in his view; see below) and that the use of pathological subjects as instruments of crime was at any rate impracticable and unreliable (Gauld, 1992, pp. 495–6).

But on the whole members of the Nancy School were more inclined to believe in the use of suggestion and hypnosis for criminal purposes. Liégeois (e.g., 1884; 1889; 1892) was most extreme in his opinions. He extensively discussed case histories of crimes in which hypnotism supposedly had played a role (e.g., Liégeois, 1889, pp. 503–79). Several of his cases involved decent girls who claimed that their lover/abuser had first hypnotized and then sexually abused them. Sometimes the accusation was first raised when the girl found out she was pregnant. The possibility of sexual abuse of hypnotized subjects caught the imagination of the male experts in hypnosis and attempts were made to explore the area. Thus, one might hypnotize a subject and then suggest to her that it was time to take a bath and to undress. Or the hypnotizer might suggest to the subject that he was her legal husband and try to lift her skirts. Liégeois (1889, p. 549) claimed he had seen dozens of girls who reacted positively to such frivolous suggestions and he made the logical point that the counterexamples put forward by such experts as Brouardel and Delboeuf proved nothing (ibid., pp. 627–32). Absence of evidence is not evidence of absence. However, Liégeois' own proofs for the possibility of abusing hypnotized subjects were rather weak. The criminal case histories he discussed were sometimes very old (he interpreted events dating back to the 1830s, for example) and often very unclear. As a rule, there was no way of reliably sorting out where seduction ended and suggestion or hypnosis began nor to establish to what extend the subjects were will-less victims. And the standard procedure to reproduce the phenomena in the laboratory had its ethical drawbacks. Thus Liégeois was forced to count as evidence for his claims the fact that many hypnotized girls "in the presence of their mother" *verbally* accepted his suggestion that he was their husband. His strongest case was that of a girl who replied: "I am so happy, I have been wanting to marry for such a long time! Tomorrow we will *get up* late, won't we?" (Liégeois, 1889, p. 644; his emphasis). Liégeois' evidence for the possibility of hypnotizing old or dying people to make them change their will, another of his favorite topics, seems not to have been much stronger. Of all the dangers that he signaled in his book only "retrospective suggestion," i.e., the possibility of suggesting people they witnessed events that they in reality never witnessed, was corroborated by later findings. Liégeois and Bernheim seem to have been among the first who experimentally demonstrated this possibility (Liégeois, 1889, p. 651).

Several years later, and despite reservations raised in the scientific literature, Liégeois (1892) still maintained that deeply hypnotized persons become "a pure automation in the hands of the experimenter," although he now added the reservation that this was only true for 4 percent of the population (Liégeois, 1892, pp. 234, 236). But even that modest percentage was more than ominous: It would mean that in a city as large as Paris no less than 100,000 people might become the victim of vile suggestions. Liégeois clearly saw that the wider ramifications of this possibility. He considered it his duty (as a *"bon citoyen*, devoted to his country") to warn his compatriots that even the national defense was at stake. Listing several cases of soldiers and sailors who supposedly had been hypnotized against their will, he admonished his countrymen to face up to this "terrible danger." After all, soldiers might be suggested to defect or revolt and by cunningly hypnotizing every third or fourth soldier of each regiment one might render a whole army ineffective. As a remedy he proposed (Liégeois, 1892, p. 272) to check each and every person's suggestibility and to "morally vaccinate" the most suggestible ones by suggesting to them that in the future no one could ever by any means suggest anything to them any more. Liégeois' (1892, p. 262) fears that his colleagues might ridicule his worries were quite justified. Few people seem to have taken him seriously.

It is fair to say that other members of the Nancy school were less imaginative. Bernheim (1903/1995) realized that not all laboratory crimes formed convincing proof for the claim that real crimes can be committed under the influence of suggestion. He accepted that many subjects simulated or played the role expected of them but with Liébeault and Liégeois he insisted that 4 or 5 percent of all subjects really could be manipulated by the hypnotist. He claimed he managed to undress one such girl whom he had suggested that she was asleep and who felt nothing (Bernheim, 1903/1995, p. 178). But it was quite typical for Bernheim that he considered *all* moral and religious education to be based on suggestion. A person who had thus received the right suggestions in his youth had to an extent become impervious to immoral suggestions whether by hypnotists or ordinary people. Here he did himself and his colleagues Liébeault and Liégeois a bad service, of course. For if everything, including moral and religious education, is suggestion and if there is nothing special about suggestion by hypnotists, then the claim that 4 to 5 percent of the population can be made to commit a crime by suggestion becomes very weak indeed. It simply means that some persons will transgress the thin line between decent life and crime under the influence of some social others and despite contrary suggestions made by still others. This was certainly no new insight. By substituting the term suggestion for hypnosis and by making suggestion an ordinary fact of daily life, by stating that suggestion does not always imply the presence of someone who suggests (ibid., p. 206), by submitting the idea of subconscious autosuggestion (ibid., p. 311), by even talking about innate suggestions (ibid., p. 239), Bernheim had robbed the phenomenon of all its distinctive features. Hypnotic suggestion had become just another form of suggestion in the great sea of innate, moral, religious, and everyday suggestions. All cats are gray in the dark of some dominating principle or concept, as Vygotsky used to say in similar cases. This was of course exactly the criticism raised by Bernheim's adversaries from the Paris School (see above; cf. Binet, 1886a; 1886b).

We may conclude that the Nancy School had somewhat overstated the possibility of abusing suggestion or hypnosis for immoral and criminal purposes. Moreover, the discussions brought out a fundamental weakness of their conception, namely the tendency to inflate the meaning of suggestion to cover almost all human relationships. In doing so, they in a way returned to much older discussions about the influence of bad examples on the morality of the public. Legrand du Saulle (1864), for example, had warned against the tendency of newspapers to accord publicity to lugubrious stories out of fear they would be imitated. Despine (1870) likewise warned against this "moral contagion" by the yellow press. He listed many cases of published crimes which had given rise to a wave of identical crimes and formulated the "law" that sentiments give rise to similar sentiments in susceptible subjects. One can see why Janet (1925) found it so important to distinguish hypnotic suggestion from phenomena such as persuasion, imitation, and the like. If we do not distinguish these concepts, we are left with a global account of individuals who are being determined by various "influences," which is not very informative.

The tendency to fuse hypnotic suggestion with such phenomena as normal persuasion and imitation was there from the outset in the Nancy School. Liébeault (1889) devoted a chapter to the often subconscious imitation of ideas, feelings, and such phenomena as yawning and body posture and considered imitation to be a state analogous to "provoked sleep," that is, the hypnotic state. Here we see the issue of hypnosis/suggestion merge into more general questions about the role of suggestion in social and crowd behavior. Liébeault's description of imitation as a state analogous to hypnosis was in perfect symmetry with the ideas of Tarde and Le Bon who compared social suggestion and imitation to hypnosis (see Carroy, 1991).

Intercerebral Psychology: Tarde and Le Bon

Gabriel Tarde (1843–1904) was one of the figures who used the bewildering new insights about hypnosis, social suggestion, pathology, and crime to create a theory of society. His theory drew upon the most recent findings of psychology and he has been called a founder of both sociology and social psychology (Mucchieli, 1994a; Rocheblave-Spenlé, 1973).

Tarde's first writings were in the field of criminology and it was only gradually, in trying to understand the causes of crime, that he came to take an interest in what are now called sociological questions. In going through the files – he worked as a judge and was head of the office that studied crime statistics for the ministry of justice – he observed that only some criminals are truly creative and innovative and that most criminals simply imitate the examples made available by the press or through other channels (see Despine, 1870; Milet, 1973). This simple observation led him to posit what we may call the inventor-imitator dyad as the basic unit or molecule of any society. The basis of society is *invention* by creative individuals and its *imitation* by the social others (Davis, 1906). There are no external norms of collective representations à la Durkheim that constrain the individual (Dumas, 1924a) but just two or more interacting minds who freely and creatively imitate each other's inventions and internalize them. This is why Tarde coined his topic of study *intercerebral psychology* or *inter-mental psychology* or simply *interpsychology*. Adopting a genetic perspective, he argued that infants become part of different interpsychological relationships with the mother-infant dyad as the most important one. Such interrelationships contribute to form the personality of the child and Tarde stated that there is nothing in the child which is not the reflection of the social other (Rocheblave-Spenlé, 1973). Language facilitates imitation but is not indispensable for it. Tarde (1890, p. 231) speculated that language was originally "an order of the father to the child without any reciprocity . . . the chief alone had the right to speak" and that the imitation of ideas precedes the possibility of their verbal expression.

Tarde went on to elaborate his theory of society, to reformulate it in terms of the more abstract principles of repetition, opposition, and adaptation (e.g., Tarde, 1902). He investigated the factors that promote or prevent the spreading of ideas (e.g., Tarde, 1890), but in essence he stuck to his core idea that the process of socialization is a growth of similarity through a process of imitation (Davis, 1906) and that the basic unit of society is the inventor-imitator dyad. This forces us to consider the primitive terms *invention* and *imitation* in somewhat more detail. By *invention* Tarde understood any new idea or social form of adaptation. Such ideas can evolve as the result of the "fruitful interference of repetitions" (Davis, 1906, p. 11), i.e., when old ideas coming from different sources crossfertilize. Tarde sketched the dynamics of invention arguing that each invention makes other inventions possible while cutting off the possibility of still other inventions. It is as if the process of invention goes through a tree of possibilities and passes nodes or bifurcation points that allow no regress. It is the individual who does the inventing, because it is in the individual that the repetitions or imitations come together or intersect. Invention, then, is essentially the process of combining old ideas. By *imitation* Tarde understood something that was less defined. At times he would emphasize the selective and synthetic character of imitation arguing that we adopt this trait of this person and that trait of another to form new combinations or fusions. But often his idea of imitation came quite close to that of contagion, suggestion, or even hypnosis. Thus we find him saying: "To have but suggested ideas and to believe them to be spontaneous: that is the illusion proper to the somnambulist and also to social man" (quoted by Mucchieli, 1994a, p. 451).

This equation of imitation with phenomena such as somnambulism (see also Tarde, 1890, pp. 230–1) or with the more diffuse terms of suggestion (à la Bernheim) and contagion is quite characteristic of that period. Tarde was advancing his theory in that period (approximately 1878–90) when French intellectual circles were again fascinated with hypnosis and its relation to pathology, suggestion, and crime (see above). It may well be, as Mucchieli (1994a) has suggested, that the success of his *Les lois de l'imitation* (1890) in its turn was partly due to this renewed fascination.

In later years, Tarde (e.g., 1902) referred to Baldwin's notion of imitation as supporting his theory of society. The two men seem to have corresponded (Rocheblave-Spenlé, 1973, pp. 30–1; Van Ginneken, 1992, p. 225) and Baldwin used Tarde's writings in his attempts to make (circular) imitation the cornerstone of his own sociogenetic account (see Chapter 4).

We thus see the intimations of later sociogenetic accounts in Tarde's theory of interpsychology. We hear him saying that there is nothing in the child which is not the reflection of a social other. We see him laboring the point that imitation is the vehicle of social transmission. We read his statements that dyadic interactions of individuals constitute the core unit of society and that social psychology should study intercerebral rather than intracerebral events. And we are but one or several steps removed from the accounts given by Baldwin, Janet, and Vygotsky in which it is stated that mental processes take place twice, first on the interpsychological then on the intrapsychological plane. Baldwin greatly elaborated Tarde's notion of imitation and Janet's theory of language may well have sprung from Tarde's embryonic account of the origin of language. In the case of Janet we can discern the influence of Tarde both directly (see Chapter 3) and indirectly through the work of Baldwin. Tarde's interpsychology seems to have made a transatlantic detour (Rocheblave-Spenlé, 1973; Van Ginneken, 1992, pp. 226–7; see Chapter 4) before it returned to Europe and ricocheted in the work of Janet, Vygotsky, and others.

Gustave Le Bon (1841–1931) was still more involved with the French clinical pathological tradition than his friend Tarde. He was a medical doctor by training who became involved with physiological psychology and hypnotism in the early 1870s (Nye, 1975; Van Ginneken, 1992). It seems that Le Bon read Liébeault's (1866) book on 'sleep and analogous states,' because already in 1872, well before Charcot began experimenting with hypnosis in Paris, he referred to the concept of suggestion. In that year he published his *La Vie: Physiologie Appli-*

quée à l'Hygiène et à la Médecine, a textook of human physiology. In this book he claimed that, under hypnosis, ideas suggested by the hypnotist are accepted immediately and he compared this process with dreaming during sleep. He then made the connection with daydreams, or hallucinations, during which we focus our attention on certain ideas which we accept as realities, and concluded that hypnotic suggestion was common to all of us. It was, in fact, "the cause of the vast majority of our actions." As people also tend to imitate each other, we can see how hallucinations can become collectively shared (Nye, 1975, pp. 26–8). In this first book, then, we see elements of the Nancy conception of hypnosis: We are all suggestible, suggestion is everywhere and it plays a powerful role in the spreading of ideas.

In the years that followed Le Bon was a regular visitor of Charcot's public meetings, where the phenomena of hypnotism were demonstrated on hysteric patients. It was there that he met several figures who would have a decisive influence on much of his thinking and his career. Among them was the neuro-physiologist and hypnotist Jean Luys, one of the more bizarre followers of the Paris school who, among other things, managed to transfer disease symptoms from one person to another by use of magnets (cf. Gauld, 1995, pp. 334–6; Harrington, 1987). He also became acquainted with the physiologist and future Nobel prize winner Charles Richet, whose experiments with "provoked somnambulism" helped turn Charcot's attention to the issue of hypnotism (Gauld, 1995, pp. 298–302; Nye, 1975, p. 30). In the 1880s Le Bon began publishing in Richet's journal *Revue Scientifique*.

Perhaps most important for Le Bon, however, was his acquaintance with Theodule Ribot, who would become one of the central figures of French psychology. Through Ribot, Le Bon came to share the typical French approach to mental phenomena with its reliance on brain pathology and abnormal psychology (see Chapter 3). He would also regularly publish in the *Revue Philosophique*, founded by Ribot in 1876. Much later, Le Bon would become acquainted with Binet, and with Bergson with whom he made a major effort to disseminate William James's thinking in France (see Chapter 5).

Through his discussions with Luys, Richet, and Ribot, and his presence at Charcot's demonstrations, Le Bon's conception of hypnotic suggestion gradually changed, but in *L'Homme et les Sociétés* (1881) he still basically stuck to the Nancy model. With Liébeault, he posited that in the hypnotic state the attention is exclusively focused on an idea whose intensity is augmented markedly. The attention of the "sleeping" individual is at the disposal of the hypnotizer. Le Bon stated as his belief that

One is able to consider artificial somnambulism as the last term of a gradually rising series from simple suggestion to persuasion and to fascination in order to arrive finally at somnambulism itself . . . the fascinator exercises such an action over the attention of the fascinated individual that the senses of the latter soon become shut off from the exterior world and he will accept all the ideas suggested to him. (Quoted via Nye, 1975, p. 47)

We can see that Le Bon is, in the typically Nancy fashion, generalizing the hypnotist–subject relationship to cover all sorts of other human relationships. The relationship between the persuader and the persuaded person, or between the fascinator and the fascinated person, etc., have become comparable to the hypnotist-subject relationship. It would only be a matter of time before he compared the hypnotist–subject relationship to that which existed between a leader and the crowd. But that still required a few additional steps.

These steps were taken in *Lois psychologiques de l'évolution des peuples* (1894; dedicated to Richet) and his famous *Psychologie des foules* (1895; dedicated to Ribot). They marked the transition from Le Bon's racial psychology to the beginnings of a social psychology (Nye, 1975). To prepare the ground for his theory of crowd mentality, Le Bon posited that we are driven by unconscious forces. That unconscious or subconscious processes exist had by that time become common knowledge and Le Bon (1895, p. 16) was being only a trifle extreme in claiming that "conscious life represents but a feeble part in comparison to unconscious life." He also posited that these unconscious processes were primitive, hereditary, and make us all alike. Here he gave his own twist to the evolutionary thinking of Spencer and Ribot. To rely on unconscious processes meant in a way to regress to an earlier mentality that we share with the other members of our race. It is a mentality in which the brutal passions of aggression and sexuality rule. If education makes people different, then the unconscious is the great equalizer as we are all reduced to beasts again, or, to put it in Le Bon's (1895, p. 17) own words: "the heterogeneous is swamped by the homogeneous." It was Spencer who had claimed that evolution went from the homogeneous to the heterogeneous and Le Bon explicitly reversed the order of his terms to make clear that we are watching a regressive process.

Logically speaking, Le Bon then still had to make two additional steps. He needed to show that people can be reduced to the unconscious state and that this condition can spread from one individual to another. To show that people can be reduced to the unconscious state was easy: The experiments with hypnotic suggestion amply proved it and Le Bon was happy to make it into a general phenomenon characterizing human relationships. To show that this condition spreads from one person to another was equally easy: People imitate each other and are contaminated by each other's behavior. Here Le Bon was as vague and confusing as the members of the Nancy School and it is clear that he too was falling back on the notion of "mental contagion" of Legrand du Saulle and Despine.

Now all the elements for Le Bon's characterization of the crowd mentality are present: (1) Another person can reduce us to the unconscious state; (2) for all of us this unconscious consists of powerful and primitive passions; (3) as such we are reduced to a similar primitive state and become each other's equal; and (4) being in this primitive condition is contagious and spreads to other people. What was needed, in Le Bon's opinion, was simply one charismatic leader who could mesmerize one or more persons and then mental contagion would do the rest. The hypnotist–subject relationship had been transposed to the leader-crowd relationship in which the crowd was seen as some sort of organism (Nye, 1975, p. 71). The persons in a crowd become "absolutely like the cells which constitute a body" (Le Bon, 1895, p. 15) and each of them is:

in a particular state, which is very much like the state of fascination in which the hypnotized person is in the hands of his hypnotizer. Because the activity of his brain is paralyzed in the hypnotized subject, he becomes the slave of all the unconscious activities of his spinal marrow, which the hypnotizer directs as he pleases. The conscious personality has completely vanished . . . All sentiments and thoughts are oriented in the direction determined by the hypnotizer. Such is more or less also the state of the individual who forms part of a psychological crowd (Le Bon, 1895, p. 19).

Thus we see that in this conception the crowd had become a huge unconscious and primitive organism led by leaders-hypnotists and fully at their mercy. As Nye (1975) has pointed out, Le Bon's view was a curious and rather unfortunate mixture of the Parisian and Nancy views on psychology. He did not claim that being in the hypnotic state was pathological and confined to at most some 5 percent of the population (the Paris school), nor did he claim that this state was absolutely normal and attainable for the far majority of us (the Nancy school). Instead, Le Bon claimed that it was *both widespread and pathological* or regressive. To make things worse, he fully adopted the conceptual confusion caused by the Nancy school in which fascination, imitation, suggestion, contagion, and hypnosis become indiscriminate terms. Nye (1975, pp. 68–71) has argued that this confusion was quite general in the 1880s and persisted for decades despite attempts made by contemporaries (e.g., Dumas, 1911, and various writings by Janet) to introduce some conceptual clarity.

Tarde's intercerebral psychology and Le Bon's crowd psychology both emerged against the background of the tumultuous social events in the France of their time. There was the military defeat in 1870 by Germany, the Paris Commune revolt in 1871, frequent street battles, mass meetings, etc. (see Nye, 1975, pp. 72–8). These events stimulated their fascination with and worries about the way feelings and ideas travel through populations. We have seen how their sociological work was firmly rooted in the French psychological thinking of that time with its emphasis on suggestion and pathology and inherited several of its features. It now remains to say a few words about the way these various currents in French psychology affected the view on the human mind.

Conclusions

We have briefly surveyed the complex fabric of ideas about suggestion, hysteria, and double consciousness. It has become clear that the social roots of the twentieth century notion that human mental processes are social can be found in the interest that was widespread in the European societies of the nineteenth century in the domain of "mesmerism." The second half of this century was characterized by an increasing interest in the question of hypnotic suggestion, which for some demonstrated persons' vulnerabilities to social control by others. This interest often took the form of public display of hysterical patients who under hypnosis could be shown to act in accordance with the "anti-social" (e.g., aggressive) suggestions by the hypnotist. The possibility of hypnotic and posthypnotic social control over persons' "free will" fascinated both the experts and the lay public. On the one hand, these phenomena might constitute a major challenge to political ideals of freedom from social control. On the other hand, they might be exploited to reach some goals (e.g., education) that were viewed as noble. In a period of social turmoil, such possibilities naturally formed the topic of heated debates.

Having reviewed the various viewpoints, we are now in a position to see that Binet's conclusions at the beginning of this chapter constituted but one voice amid a sea of others and that his general position coincided with that of a particular school, namely, the Paris School (cf. Plas, 1994). However, the themes he addressed in the quote given above remain important and topical and transcend the debates between schools. We are still left with the question as to what extent the nature of the phenomena of dissociation and hypnosis is dependent upon suggestion. Neither have we fully resolved whether it is correct to speak of personality loss or multiple personalities on the grounds of amnesia or fragmented consciousness (cf. Hacking, 1995). Finally, his claim that a unified self is no primitive datum, but is the result of a synthesis, or perhaps a mere fiction, can be heard until the present day.

The psychological studies of the nineteenth century had uncovered that the original unity of mind could no longer be taken for granted. Evolutionary theory suggested that mind had a history and new layers of the mind were being detected. Hypnotic studies and dissociative phenomena suggested that mind was not unitary and different notions of the subconscious or unconscious conquered psychology. Social psychology suggested that mind was but the intersection of influences. In a way, then, the monadic mind had become transparent, permeable for the social environment, and moving through time. A unified mind was not the beginning but a possible result, the result of an effort to synthesize the baffling complexity of incoming and outgoing stimuli. Pierre Janet was one of those who tried to integrate these new findings and ideas into a coherent whole and who gradually moved from the field of hypnosis, dissociation, and hysteria to a sociogenetic account of mind.

CHAPTER THREE

Pierre Janet's World of Tensions

> Mesdames, messieurs! We have often remarked that fash-
> ion exists in scientific research as it does in the creation of
> ladies' dresses and hats. For no apparent reason a partic-
> ular, sometimes very tiny study becomes the order of the
> day in a certain epoch. Everybody feels obliged to write
> an article on this problem. Works, books, publications ac-
> cumulate during ten or fifteen years. Then, for no apparent
> reason, the wind turns, and this problem, which seemed
> exciting, rather quickly becomes uninteresting. In reality it
> has not been solved, but that does not matter. One loses
> interest, because in that epoch everything has been said
> that could be said with the existing methods and points of
> view. This does not mean that the problem is completely
> and definitively suppressed. It generally comes again into
> fashion twenty or twenty-five years later. This is the way
> scientific progress is made.
>
> Janet, in a lecture at the Collège de France; see his
> 1928a, p. 321

Today few Anglo-Saxon researchers have more than a faint knowledge of Janet's writings and one may only hope that Janet's dictum –
that there is a cyclic interest in scientific problems – holds true for the
study of scientific theories and their proponents as well. For Janet was
one of the major figures in psychology's and psychiatry's history and
his work deserves to be restudied by each new generation of researchers. Such a renewed study of Janet's writings and his significance for
psychological theory will yield new and different assessments of his
work, complement the existing literature (e.g. Allen, 1937; Barrucand,
1967; Ellenberger, 1970; 1978; Horton, 1924; Mayo, 1952; Prévost,

1973a; 1973b; Sjöwall, 1967), and reflect our present-day understanding of psychological issues in interesting ways.

The current lack of interest in Janet's theories and the scant knowledge of his writings stand in sharp contrast with the situation sixty to eighty years ago. At the beginning of this century Janet was well known outside France and was regularly invited to give lectures abroad. Many of his works were translated into other languages, such as English, German, Spanish, and Russian (e.g. Janet, 1894c, 1903b, 1911, 1913b, 1925, 1926a). Making lecture tours and attending conferences, Janet traveled widely. In the period from 1904 to 1936 he visited the United States (Atlantic City, Boston, Baltimore, Chicago, New York, Niagara Falls, Philadelphia, Princeton, Springfield, St. Louis), Latin America (Argentina, Brazil, Mexico), and different European cities (Amsterdam, Geneva, London, Oxford, Rome, Vienna, Zurich). Janet thus was well known and generally respected outside his homeland (Ellenberger, 1978).

Given that today outside France Janet's work is little known and in view of the fact that in the available literature he is mostly seen as one of the founders of dynamic psychiatry (e.g. Ellenberger, 1970; Van der Hart and Friedman, 1989; Van der Hart and Horst, 1989; Van der Hart, Brown, and Van der Kolk, 1989) it is of interest to highlight another crucial aspect of Janet's work, namely his sociogenetic ideas. For Janet was – together with Royce, Baldwin, Mead, Vygotsky, and the other figures analyzed in this book – one of the co-creators of the sociogenetic view in psychology (Van der Veer, 1994; Van der Veer and Valsiner, 1988; 1991a). In this chapter we will give an overview of the sociogenetic themes present in Janet's writings preceded by a short description of his life. It will be seen that Janet's sociogenetic theory involved the key notion that higher human mental functioning gradually develops – thereby becoming both more socialized and individualized – as individuals act in socially embedded contexts.

Janet's Life Course

Pierre Janet (1859–1947) followed the typical career of a French intellectual. After the Ecole Normale Supérieure (1879–1882), which he attended together with Durkheim and one year after Bergson, Janet went teaching at different Lycée in Châteauroux (1882–3) and Le Havre (1883–9). This period was part of the ten years of teaching to which the students of the Ecole Normale Supérieure pledged themselves (Ellenberger, 1970, p. 336). Janet taught philosophy at the Lycée in Le Havre but apparently had plenty of time left to pursue his other interests. During his stay at Le Havre he regularly traveled to Paris, where he used to see patients together with his brother Jules, who initially shared his interest in neuroses and hypnotism (Jules Janet, 1888; 1889) but after some years turned to urology and microbiology (cf. Janet, 1910b). In Le Havre he worked as a volunteer at the local hospital. There are some interesting parallels with Vygotsky's biography here (see Chapter 8). Just like Vygotsky, Janet started his career working as a teacher in a provincial town (Janet, 1946, p. 82) which, however, had a cultural life of its own and where one was well informed of the newest scientific and cultural events in the capital. In the cases of both men this activity left ample time for doing little scientific investigations. Just like Vygotsky, Janet's education was mainly in the field of philosophy and literature, yet his interest soon switched to psychology. Finally, like Vygotsky would many years later, Janet soon realized that a medical training was indispensable both for intrinsic reasons and for reasons of academic prestige.

It was in 1886 in Le Havre that Janet first pursued his psychological interests, undoubtedly inspired by the writings of his uncle, the philosopher Paul Janet, who had discussed the issue of double personality (Paul Janet, 1876) in connection with Azam's (1876a; 1876b; 1876c) famous papers on Félida X and who had dealt with the subject of suggestion in the hypnotic state in a series of articles in a literary magazine (Paul Janet, 1884a; 1884b; 1884c; 1884d; 1897). Paul Janet took a vivid interest in the issue of hypnotic suggestion, acquainted himself with the available literature and witnessed many of the hypnotic sessions in the Salpêtrière held by Charcot, Binet, and others. His attitude was that of the positivist scientist who, after careful investigation, took many of the facts to be indisputable but doubted their interpretation. Paul Janet (1884d, p. 199) raised the question as to what extent the actions of the somnambulic subject can be considered automatic repetitions of older habits and memories but replied himself that this was a subject that went beyond the topic of his articles and which required a whole new study. One wonders what he held of his cousin's answer to this question given in the latter's dissertation published five years later.

Pierre Janet started his psychological career by investigating the case of Miss B., a young woman who repeatedly and spontaneously fell into the hypnotic (or somnambulic) state. Janet and the physician

Gibert subjected her to experiments and discovered that she was an extremely sensitive subject who could be hypnotized within seconds. Trying to find out what exactly in the hypnotist's attitude caused the patient to become hypnotized, Gibert and Janet soon found out that no specific verbal instruction was needed. In fact, it eventually proved possible to hypnotize the patient without using any words even without touching her. This, naturally, led them to the idea that, perhaps, even the physical presence of the hypnotist was not necessary. Rather surprisingly, Gibert and – with less success – Janet indeed succeeded in hypnotizing Miss B. from adjacent rooms (mostly suggesting her to fall asleep) and, finally, from larger distances up to about one kilometer. The publication of these somewhat bizarre findings in the *Revue Philosophique* (Janet, 1886a; 1886b) was well received by the experts in this then very popular field, who related similar – and even more spectacular – cases from their own practice (Beaunis, 1886; Gley, 1886; Héricourt, 1886; Richet, 1886).

In 1889 Janet presented his main thesis on psychological automatism at the Sorbonne (Janet, 1889a) as well as the required lesser one of sixty pages in Latin (1889b). His Latin thesis was on Bacon and the alchemists in which he pictured Bacon as an intermediary figure halfway between traditional alchemist thinking and the newer experimental science (Ellenberger, 1970, p. 339). In 1889 Janet moved to Paris and was one of the co-organizers of the International Congress for Experimental and Therapeutic Hypnotism; this allowed him to meet colleagues such as William James. Janet now taught at the Lycée Louis-le-Grand, where he studied medicine until 1893, when he graduated with high honors. During this period he divided his time between his teaching commitments at the Lycée, his medical studies, and examining hysterical patients in various hospitals and Charcot's wards at the Salpêtrière (Reuchlin, 1986).

Janet had now become an inhabitant of two worlds: On the one hand he was well versed in philosophy (he had been teaching it for years at various Lycée and published a philosophical textbook; see Janet, 1896b); on the other hand he had been trained as a natural scientist. In his own estimation, this circumstance played a decisive role in the development of his thinking. It was due to – as he himself wrote many years later (Janet, 1930c, p. 123; 1946, p. 85) – a curious combination of interests. On the one hand he always felt inclined toward the natural sciences, but on the other hand he had pronounced religious and mystical feelings (one is reminded of the combination of interests of both William James and George Herbert Mead). The reconciliation of reason and faith through philosophy was his ultimate goal, a goal that proved to be an unattainable miracle, as Janet himself retrospectively acknowledged. It did lead him, however, to study all sorts of higher psychological and at times very curious phenomena with the cautiousness and rigor of a natural scientist.

In 1893 Charcot opened a laboratory for experimental psychology at the Salpêtrière and asked Janet to become the head of this laboratory (Janet, 1895a). In that same year Charcot died but his successor, the neurologist Raymond, allowed Janet to continue his psychological work. Together they published several books and a dozen articles (e.g., Raymond and Janet, 1898, 1903, 1904) although Raymond's contribution seems to have been minimal. Five years later Janet became professor at the Sorbonne and in 1902 he became the successor of Ribot for the chair of experimental psychology at the Collège de France. His rival for the vacancy had been Binet, and Janet's candidacy was defended by Bergson with whom Janet proceeded to have frequent scientific and social contacts throughout his life and whose ideas undoubtedly influenced Janet's action-oriented approach. From that time on, the Collège de France became the center of his activities (see Ellenberger, 1970, p. 343). Many of his later books were based on the weekly lectures given at this institute. Janet retired from the Collège de France in 1935, at the age of seventy-five, but continued being active in the field of clinical psychology until his death in 1947.

In 1910 Raymond, Janet's superior at the Salpêtrière, died and his successor Déjerine, who for some reason didn't like Janet's work (possibly because Janet seemed a follower of Charcot, whose hypnotic studies by this time had fallen into disfavor), successfully maneuvered to get Janet out of his laboratory and Charcot's wards. Janet found refuge in the ward of his friend Nageotte, a neurologist and brain histologist, and a colleague at the Collège de France. However, this meant that from then on Janet had many fewer patients at his disposal (he had a private practice as well) and no possibilities to do clinical teaching. At around the same time, and possibly partially because of the events just sketched, Janet started developing increasingly complex hierarchical systems of mental functioning. The painstaking description of individual cases of madness gradually made way for hypothetical, speculative reasoning about the evolution of mind and the psychology of conduct. But at the background of these more or less speculative ideas was Janet's vast knowledge of individual case histories of patients he had followed over the years. By 1920 he had accumulated the records of about 3,500 cases (Janet, 1925, p. 15) and after his death no less than 5,000 patient files were burnt according to his will (Ellenberger, 1970, p. 352; cf. Prévost, 1973b, p. 35). He himself (Janet, 1930c, p. 124) compared this huge collection of case descriptions to the herbarium that he had started in his childhood and kept enlarging throughout his life.

The fact that Janet had no possibility of training his own students and the fact that he taught at the Collège de France, which was very prestigious but mostly drew a lay audience, contributed to the fact that Janet did not create a "school" of his own. No doubt his personality played its role as well. However, the fact that he may have been somewhat of a bystander in some respects did not make him an isolated figure (see Prévost, 1973b, p. 51). Throughout his career Janet was active in various scientific councils, journals etc., and in 1904, together with Georges Dumas, he founded the *Journal de Psychologie*. He also had close intellectual friends, among them Morton Prince, Hack Tuke, Macfie Campbell, Weir Mitchell, Frederic Myers, and James Mark Baldwin, and he corresponded with, among others, William James (see James, 1890/1983, p. 1,071; Janet, 1889a, p. 215; 1893d).

Janet's contacts with Baldwin seem to date from at least 1892 when Baldwin visited Janet in Paris (Baldwin 1892c; 1892d) and when Janet (1892c) gave a favorable account of the paper presented at the International Congress of Experimental Psychology in London by "professor Baldwin of the University of Toronto." The story goes that their first conversations were conducted in some sort of Latin, the only language they had in common at the time (Ellenberger, 1970, p. 352; see also Chapter 4). In later years, however, Janet seems to have learned a passable English (Ellenberger, 1978).

It appears that Janet was a shy, reserved man who did not easily reveal his own feelings but could be sharp-witted and a brilliant conversationalist (see Ellenberger, 1970, pp. 347–53 for Janet's biography and an account of his personality; cf. Ey, 1968; Germain, 1960; Minkowski, 1960). Above all he seems to have excelled in the art of listening: His books are chock full with detailed and empathic accounts of the sufferings of hundreds of patients (cf. Crocq and De Verbizier, 1988). Always taking meticulous notes, he was soon nicknamed "Dr. Pencil" by his patients (Schwartz, 1951). Janet's lectures at the Collège de France were generally liked and his books and papers are written in a very elegant and at times brilliant style, full of irony and wit. His criticism of Freud's psychoanalytic ideas (Janet, 1914a; see also 1919, 1925), for example, was a masterpiece of rhetoric in which he praised psychoanalysts for their adventurous and bold ideas and at the same time made abundantly clear that he found their play with symbols (cf. Lyman Wells, 1912), their methodology, and their supposed therapy scientifically totally inadequate. Naturally, this criticism was not well received by the psychoanalysts (cf. Barraud, 1971; Ellenberger, 1970; Perry and Laurence, 1984; Prévost, 1973b) – Janet (1914a, pp. 119, 121) had gone so far as to compare the psycho-analytic movement with a religious movement with the corresponding practice of excommunication of heretics – and as it was psychoanalysis which became the fashion of the day, totally eclipsing Janet's own "analytic psychology." Janet in later years became somewhat of an isolated figure in psychotherapeutic circles. However, this was a po-sition he was used to and which to an extent may have matched his personality. When he started publishing his hypnotic studies he was drawn into the struggle between Bernheim and Charcot (see Chapter 2 and below) but tried to maintain his own position. When the Charcot school was being defeated, he defended some of Charcot's ideas against Bernheim (Bernheim, 1892; Janet, 1892c; 1892d). Finally, when hypnosis fell into disrepute as a therapeutic means of intervention, he maintained his interest in it and boldly claimed that "the decline of hypnotism has no serious meaning. It has been due to accidental causes, to disillusionment and reaction following upon ill-considered enthusiasm. It is merely a temporary incident in the history of induced somnambulism" (Janet, 1925, p. 207).

Janet's superb knowledge of the history of philosophy and psychol-ogy must have helped him to arrive at this impassive assessment of developments in which he personally partook. Over the years he gath-ered a rich collection of old writings on magnetism, mesmerism, spir-itism, etc. that allowed him to see how many supposedly new contem-porary developments and inventions in psychotherapy were common knowledge in earlier times (see especially Janet, 1919; 1925). He men-tioned (Janet, 1889a, p. 397) that he once found an anonymous bro-chure in a second-hand bookshop that antedated many of his own ideas on dissociation by some forty years. His own account of his intellectual attitude is insightful and brings us back full circle to the quote at the beginning of this chapter.

It has been my tendency, my misfortune perhaps, to have a fondness for moderation, and to dislike the absurd exaggerations of extremists. That is why, twenty years ago, I exposed myself to contempt by saying that hypnotic suggestion was not everything; and that is why, to-day, I run the risk of making people laugh at me by saying that hypnotism counts for something after all. The contempt and the laughter leave my withers unwrung. Moderation is the best aid to the discovery of truth. If my book be ignored to-day, it will be read to-morrow, when there will have been a new turn of fashion's wheel, bringing back treatment by hypnotic suggestion just as it will bring back our grandmothers' hats (Janet, 1925, p. 151; cf. Janet, 1907a/1965, p. 138).

Sociogenetic Themes in Janet's Writings: The Beginnings

While we cannot claim that in his early works Janet defended the explicit sociogenetic point of view that will be outlined below and which he would adhere to later on in his career, certain features of these works are of fundamental interest for this book. His early hypnotic experiments with the subject L(éonie) illustrate this well. Janet was struck by the seemingly illogical fact that this subject had no memory for his instructions – and, moreover, seemed unaware of them – even during the hypnotic state, but nevertheless carried them out perfectly. He suggested to her to respond to some of his questions in writing and this she did while continuing her other activities, such as having a conversation with other people present. Using this method of "automatic writing" it appeared that the subject was perfectly aware of Janet's instructions, i.e., some part of her personality was aware and another part was not. The normal Léonie would say that she had heard none of Janet's instructions, while the writing part of her would admit she did. On Janet's suggestion this latter part was given a name (first Blanche, later Adrienne) and he proceeded to find out what differences existed between the answers of Léonie and her alter ego. In this way it was found out that Adrienne felt the pain that Léonie claimed not to feel and that Adrienne saw the objects that Léonie reported not seeing after a posthypnotic suggestion. Janet concluded that this was a case of a certain dissociation or *dédoublement* of the personality, which might have its roots in certain traumatic childhood experiences (Janet, 1886c; 1888). Different parts of the personality are perfectly aware of everything that is going on, but some events are not perceived/accepted by the normal "me" and relegated to another group of phenomena or personality. The normal subject seems unaware of various events, but in reality they are "simply separated from the ensemble of psychic phenomena of which the synthesis forms the idea of 'me' " (Janet, 1887, p. 471.).

Thus Janet antedated the much later work of Hilgard (1977) on the "hidden observer" and the current writings on the childhood origin of multiple personality. But more important for this book is that he demonstrated a deep insight into the complex and socially induced nature of personality. He (Janet, 1888, p. 248) was well aware of the fact that as a hypnotist he was the co-constructor of the events that took place and he soon (Janet, 1886c, p. 589; 1888, p. 257) realized that the so-called mediums in spiritualist séances might be persons with a dissociated mind who ascribe their "non-me" feelings, ideas etc. to some dead person, because this is what is socially expected in that situation. The subjects are, as it were, experiencing their own feelings and emotions in socially accepted ways. This led Janet to follow the events in these circles with some interest and amusement (e.g. Janet, 1889a; 1892b; 1895b; 1897b; 1909a; 1909b). Thus, we see him complain that somehow the utterances of famous historical persons become rather mediocre when speaking through the voices of mediums (cf. James, 1890/1983, p. 223). Philosophers such as Leibniz state mere platitudes and classic poets produce doggerel. When during a spiri-tualistic séance a table signaled that the essence of love is suffering, Janet (1889a, p. 390) commented that this observation was not new "but for a table it is nonetheless curious."

Secondly, Janet understood that personality is an exceedingly complex construction consisting of different layers with asymmetrical or hierarchical interrelationships that develop in the continual social interaction with other people. He was not at all inclined to attribute this complex whole to genetic factors or brain processes, because he saw no point in introducing "physiological fantasies that have less poetry, without having more certitude" (Janet, 1888, p. 278; cf. Janet, 1893a, p. 194; 1898, pp. 250, 283).

Thirdly, he assumed that the particularities of these constructions were due to specific events in the lifetime of the person and sometimes originated in traumatic childhood events. In other words, such socio-genetic features of the human mind as its social, complex, and developmental nature were, albeit implicitly, present in the young Janet's writings.

With these findings the young Janet posited himself firmly in the then immensely popular field of hypnosis, and attracted the interest of both foreign (e.g., Arthur and Frederic Myers) and French (e.g., Charles Richet, Charcot) scholars who came to visit Le Havre to witness his patients and their strange symptoms with their own eyes (Hinshelwood, 1991; Janet, 1946). The Society for Psychical Research in London (led by Frederic Myers) asked Janet to reproduce his results with hypnosis from a distance in the presence of an investigation committee from London. Curiously enough, Janet again managed to make his subject fall a sleep from a distance of 1 kilometer "16 out of 20 times." Since that time, Janet seems to have maintained close contacts with members of the Society for Psychical Research (which included among its members such notable figures as Max Dessoir, G. Stanley Hall, William James, Morton Prince, and Theodule Ribot; cf. Milne Bramwell, 1903/1956, p. 35) and in his works he regularly referred to their proceedings. Much later, in his autobiographical note (Janet, 1930c; 1946), he stated that he was a bit shocked by the publicity these findings aroused and didn't fully trust them. The fact is that he soon moved to the meticulous study of the various somnambulic states that can be reached in hysteric patients and the crucial role memory plays in these various states. In this connection he hit upon the largely forgotten history of Mesmerism or "animal magnetism." One day, when he produced a specific deep state of somnambulism in a subject, the subject declared that she had been in this state before. Upon investigation it turned out that twenty years before she had been the subject of a "magnetizer." On the one hand, this made Janet aware of the need to have "fresh" subjects and/or to have a detailed knowledge of the life history of subjects. On the other hand, it led him to undertake a historical study of hypnotism and suggestion that convinced him of the fact that to an extent he and his contemporaries were merely rediscovering phenomena that had been well known to Mesmer, Bertrand, and many others. Reading these historical writings, he retrospectively replicated and confirmed his own findings. The first results of Janet's historical studies as well as new interpretations of his findings with regard to somnambulism were published in his dissertation on "psychological automatism" (Janet, 1889a).

Automatic Behavior

L'automatisme psychologique is dedicated to Gibert and Powilewicz, the medical doctors in Le Havre who enabled Janet to conduct his investigations. The book was based on the study of twenty-seven patients, but Janet preferred to illustrate his findings with descriptions of four of them, namely Léonie, Lucie, Marie, and Rose. Possibly because of the exotic nature of his topic and the accusations of fraud that had been voiced in connection with hypnotism, throughout his book Janet claimed to have followed a rigorous empirical method, i.e., he claimed to have gathered facts by observation and to have explained these facts by hypotheses whose corollaries he subsequently verified to see whether they disproved or corroborated them. We further see him making use of concomitant variation to establish the link between, for example, memory and anesthesia. All in all, one gets the impression that he took the Baconian model of inductive reasoning (the subject of his lesser dissertation) to heart. Characteristic of his style is that even when reporting an apparently highly successful cure of a patient Janet added that he was not sure how long it would last, just like he constantly underlined the provisional and temporary nature of all of his findings. He ended his study by stating the importance of the principle of refutability for the empirical sciences:

Strange though it may seem, *one of the great merits of these novel psychological studies is that they are susceptible of error.* One can demonstrate in a rigorous manner, and one will undoubtedly do so for many of these studies, that this or that observation is unintentionally inexact, that this or that interpretation is mistaken. *This is a merit and an advantage*: it is satisfactory for the mind to establish that one was mistaken about a point for this gives the hope that one was or will be capable of detecting the truth about some other fact. The general hypotheses of philosophy are not susceptible of error . . . That is why we should not engage in these theories which are by their nature above and beyond any precise discussion (Janet, 1889a, p. 479; our emphasis).

It is interesting to see that Janet found it necessary to defend the indirect method in psychology, i.e., he argued that it is possible to infer the existence of psychological phenomena in other persons going by their gestures, words, etc. "like the chemist determines the elements of the stars by the rays of the spectrum" (Janet, 1889a, p. 5).

Here one is reminded of Vygotsky's words several decades later, who in a similar vein argued that historians and geologists do not so much directly observe but reconstruct their facts and that the psychologist "acts like a detective who brings to light a crime he never witnessed" (see Van der Veer and Valsiner, 1994, p. 44; see also Chapter 8). Janet also emphasized that his subjects were mentally ill persons (mostly women suffering from hysteria) who were very suggestible and that an interrogation in public of these patients would yield only artifacts. He therefore preferred to study them in isolation. He also stressed the need to conduct these studies during a lengthy period so that the psychologist gets to know the patient and her history in great detail. With these words he at once distanced himself from the Paris school of Charcot (where public interrogation of patients was the rule) and the Nancy school of Bernheim (which had stressed that all somnambulic states could be reached in any subject, not just hysteric women) (see Chapter 2; cf. Janet, 1886d, p. 586; 1889a, pp. 47, 456; 1895a, pp. 601–2).

Compositionally, the book consisted of two parts. In the first part Janet dealt with what he called fully automatic behavior (*"automatisme total"*) and described the phenomena of catalepsy, various somnambulist states, and suggestion. Characteristically, he described these states as requiring increasingly complex mental capacities and thus as stages in the origin of mind. We can again view this as a conception that opposed both the Nancy and the Paris schools. The Paris school had insisted upon the existence of three qualitatively distinct states of hypnotism whereas the Nancy school had argued that the three states were artifacts, that there existed an infinite number of states, and that these differed only in degree (see Chapter 2). Now, Janet argued that these three states exist, but that other intermediary states exist as well, and that these states can be interpreted as stages in the development of mind (see Janet, 1886d). Alternatively, these stages can be seen as layers which become superimposed upon one another and of which the lower ones can become independently active again when the higher ones are somehow "switched off." We can thus see how already at the outset of his career Janet defended a hierarchical, evolutionary point of view that enabled him to occupy an independent position in the debate between the Paris and the Nancy schools of hypnotism. In the second part Janet described different phenomena of partially automatic (*"automatisme partiel"*) behavior. These occur when the subject's mind is dissociated, i.e., when the subject is consciously aware of part of his mind and unaware of some other, automatic, part.

Janet argued that the most primitive form of fully automatic behavior is catalepsy. He described its characteristics in great clinical detail (he managed to produce it in the hypnotic state in various of his patients), compared it to a hypothetical state described by Maine de Biran, argued that it is a psychological state, and distinguished it from (other) somnambulic states. In his view, catalepsy is a mental state in

which the mind is fully dominated by isolated sensations or movements that can cause prolonged responses in the form of movements,
because there is nothing in the mind that can counterbalance or ob-
struct these movements. Catalepsy is a sort of nascent consciousness
comparable to a state one goes through after having fainted (Janet,
1889a, p. 54) and during which the idea of "me" is still lacking: "The
notion of me is, indeed, a quite complicated phenomenon that com-
prehends the memories of passed actions, the notion of our situation,
of our powers, our body, our name even, and that in combining all
these scattered ideas, plays a considerable role in the knowledge of
our personality" (ibid., p. 39). Janet claimed that in this rudimentary
state (and in early ontogenetic states as well, see pp. 60–1) sensation is
inextricably linked with movement or action. He argued that his findings confirmed Fouillée's (1884, p. 3) thinking and refuted Condillac's
famous thought experiment about the statue that is successively supplied with senses: Condillac forgot that the statue would start moving
(Janet, 1889a, p. 55). We thus find in this early description of the
cataleptic state several fundamental and persistent ideas of Janet's
thinking: the idea of evolution, the idea of mind as a complex, hierarchical system, and the idea of the predominance of action in (primitive) mind.

Janet now discussed the characteristics of the hypnotic (somnambulic) state. In his view, all former definitions were inadequate and he
proposed to define the hypnotic state by the following characteristics:
(a) amnesia for the (deeper) hypnotic state; (b) memory for earlier
similar hypnotic states during the hypnotic state; and (c) memory for
the normal waking state and for less "deep" hypnotic states during
the hypnotic state. He gave a detailed description of his finding that
subjects who are in the hypnotic state can as it were be hypnotized
again to reach a deeper state of hypnosis. Having defined the various
hypnotic states by the disappearance and reappearance of memory for
certain events Janet proceeded to venture an explanation for the phenomenon of alternating memory. In his view, memory is linked to
sensibility (cf. James, 1890/1983, pp. 368–9). The hysteric patients he
examined all showed various signs of reduced auditory, tactile, or
visual sensibility and Janet was able to show that this sensibility varied with memory, i.e., by manipulating sensibility (e.g., using mild
electric currents) he could produce other memories *et vice versa*. Complex memory is based on certain elementary images, which are in
their turn based on sensations that the subject either perceives or fails

to perceive due to hysteric anesthesia. The alternating memory, then, is due to a periodic modification of sensibility. When subjects repeatedly are in a certain hypnotic state these memories cluster to form a second or third personality. Their mind becomes dissociated, a fact that had already been described, as Janet remarks, by all magnetizers. We can thus see that for Janet the different hypnotic states are characterized by different sensibility and memories and that they form a hierarchical structure.

A third category of fully automatic phenomena (catalepticlike states, hallucinations, etc.) can be induced via suggestion. By suggestion Janet meant the exertion of influence by one person over another through verbal means and without voluntary consent of the person being influenced. He took great pains to distinguish suggestion from hypnotism, a thing that he would continue to do throughout his career. One of his chief arguments was that hypnotized subjects are not necessarily suggestible, a fact that made him very critical of the possibility of 'criminal suggestion', a topic hotly debated at the time (ibid., pp. 176–7; see Chapter 2). In this regard, he flatly opposed the cherished ideas of Bernheim who had insisted on the possibility of criminal suggestion and who claimed that hypnotism was nothing other than suggestion (cf. Bernheim, 1911–12). Rejecting contemporary theories but in accordance with an idea first advance by Lasègue, Janet proposed that suggestion is possible through some kind of natural and perpetual distraction that prevents the patients from noticing anything outside their immediate field of awareness. As their field of awareness is very much reduced, the suggestions are immediately and automatically seized upon and transformed into actions, hallucinations, etc. The same distraction causes subjects to have full amnesia for the things outside their narrowed field of awareness. Janet concluded that suggestion is a particular form of psychological automatism that is caused by language and perception (ibid., p. 218). Incidentally, it is very interesting to see how Janet, using Baconian methods, tried to rule out alternative explanations for the phenomena he is investigating. To give one example, in trying to determine the role of magnets in producing suggestion, he asked the professor of physics Rousseaux to switch an electric magnet on and off in the adjacent room. Neither Janet nor the patient knew when the magnet was working. The result of this double-blind experiment *avant la lettre* was that suggestion was in no way dependent upon the workings of the magnet (ibid., p. 156).

In the second part of his book, Janet discussed various phenomena (e.g. partial catalepsy, automatic writing, posthypnotic suggestion, anesthesia, spiritualistic mediums, fixed ideas) that can occur in the normal waking state and argued that we can account for all of them by assuming the existence of subconscious acts, by the existence of a consciousness that exists below or outside normal consciousness. His hypothesis was that a person experiences a multitude of sensations that have to be integrated or synthesized into meaningful, personal perception. The recurrent synthesis of sensations eventually gives rise to the development of memory and personality. If persons for some reason repeatedly ignore (i.e., fail to synthesize) a number of sensations, these may cluster to form a second personality, or self, with its own memory, feelings, etc. (ibid., p. 317; cf. Janet, 1894b, p. 217). Such an inability to synthesize all sensations or, in other words, such a reduced field of consciousness, may occur spontaneously or can be produced in the somnambulist state, e.g., when the subject is asked to ignore certain parts of the environment. The result is that the person's mind becomes dissociated, i.e., two or more personalities may exist simultaneously or alternatively in the same mind.

Although the failure to synthesize is very frequent in hysteric patients, it is not exclusively linked to hysteria, and Janet argued that other patients and normal people may at times also show symptoms of dissociation (e.g., in the case of fatigue or passion). In the end, the failure to synthesize is due to some weakness called "*la misère psychologique*," which Janet was inclined to view as caused by hereditary and/or constitutional factors. Strong personalities are capable of synthesizing the phenomena at increasingly high levels, whereas weak personalities cannot do this and become dissociated into various personalities and/or fall victim to different automatic behaviors. That a lack of synthesis leads to the upsurge of automatic actions that have been formed in the past, Janet (cf. 1898, p. 469) considered a "fundamental law of mental disease" attributable to Joseph Moreau de Tours (1859; cf. Delacroix, 1924). Striking a more philosophical tone, Janet (ibid., pp. 481–5) argued that his dissertation had shown (after Fouillée) that action and thought are inextricably linked and that psychology and physiology may some distant day converge. He also argued that subjects should try to find a balance between "conservative activity" (e.g., memory) and "innovative activity" (e.g., synthesis) in order to maintain mental health.

L'automatisme psychologique was very well received inside and outside France, and for many Janet would be known as the author of this one book. The experts in this field reacted on the whole favorably to Janet's description of the facts and his interpretations. Binet (1890), for example, wrote a lengthy and positive review for the *Revue Philosophique*, and in his *Principles of Psychology* William James (1890/1983, pp. 200–10; 222–4; 363–9) discussed Janet's (and his brother Jules') findings extensively and favorably and obviously accepted large parts of Janet's theory of dissociation.

The book and the papers that preceded and followed it also made him to be seen as one of the founding fathers of dynamic psychiatry, together with Freud, Jung, and Adler. In fact, in many ways Janet's ideas anticipated those of the early Freud (see Ellenberger, 1970, p. 539 for a list of Janetian ideas and their Freudian counterparts) and Jung (Haule, 1983; 1984) as is obvious to those acquainted with both the German and the French literature. Ellenberger (1970, pp. 539–40) approvingly quotes Régis and Hesnard who claimed that "The methods and concepts of Freud were modeled after those of Janet, of whom he seems to have inspired himself constantly." Janet himself seems to have been of the same opinion. However, at the same time, given his cautious experimental approach, he was very critical of Freud's more speculative ideas. This led him to suggest in a number of works throughout his career that Freud took several of his ideas and methods, perverted them, and fitted them into a system that was based on little more than pure fantasy. Quite naturally, such a presentation of the state of the affairs was very much resented by Freud and his followers, and a bitter and more or less hidden struggle with sudden eruptions ensued (cf. Perry and Laurence, 1984; Sulloway, 1992, pp. 474–6). This is not the place to trace the history of this priority struggle (in which Janet's irony was met with brutal aggression from the side of Freud's followers), but one of these eruptions and its followings is worth noting. It was caused by Janet's lengthy discussion of psychoanalysis at the 17th International Congress of Medicine on August 8, 1913. There he once again – and justifiably – asserted his priority in a number of matters and went on to discuss the later developments within psychoanalysis, with a great deal of irony (Janet, 1913a; 1914a; 1914b; 1915b; 1915c; cf. 1907b).

By all accounts (cf. Ellenberger, 1970; Prévost, 1973b), Janet's (1914a) presentation caused quite a stir among those present. He was immediately attacked by Carl Jung ("Unfortunately, it is often the case that people believe themselves entitled to judge psychoanalysis when they are not even able to read German"), by Ernest Jones ("a long series of misconceptions, distortions and misstatements"), and by several others (cf. Coriat, 1945, p. 4). Retrospectively, Jones claimed that his reply "put an end to his [Janet's] pretensions of having founded psychoanalysis and then seeing it spoilt by Freud." He immediately notified Freud of his intervention and the latter thanked him in a letter saying that "I cannot say how much gratified I have been by . . . your defeating Janet in the eyes of your countrymen" (see Jones, 1974, p. 112). In his autobiography Jones gives an even more glorious account of the meeting. He writes that

At the Congress Professor Janet used the important occasion to make a slashing and satirical attack on Freud and his work. Delivered with his inimitable theatrical skill, it made a visible impression, especially on those in the audience who were disposed to accept his assertions without criticizing them. With my practice in such debates, however, it was easy for me to demonstrate to the audience not only Janet's profound ignorance of psycho-analysis but also his lack of scruple in inventing, in the most unfair way, men of straw for his ridicule to play on. He feebly excused himself by saying he could not read German, but in the *Journal of Abnormal Psychology* I published my comments on his address, and I feel sure his reputation for objectivity has never been the same since (Jones, 1959, pp. 241–2).

More sober accounts of the events, however, do not confirm Jones' heroic role. His actual role during the debate that followed Janet's presentation seems to have been rather more modest (see Ellenberger, 1970, p. 819). It was only in a paper published shortly after the congress that Jones stated what he had wished to say impromptu (Jones, 1914–15). Quoting from Janet (1915c), he tried to argue that Janet had been deliberately unfair and "allowed himself to be betrayed into the grossest lack of objectivity." Jones was clearly much annoyed by Janet's ridicule of the psychoanalytic emphasis on the role of sexuality in mental pathology, and particularly by Janet's claim that Freudians affirmed that the essential and only cause of every neurosis is sexual troubles. This Jones regarded as an unfair distortion and he subtly retorted that according to psychoanalytic theory sexual disturbances are the *specific* cause, but that other causes may also be operative. Neither did Jones like Janet's claim that psychoanalytic interpretations are rather arbitrary and "can with the greatest ease be varied in infinity." Janet's (1915c, p. 179) additional claim that, by using psychoanalytic methods, he would be able to demonstrate "that tuberculosis

and cancer were the indirect and unforeseen consequence of mastur-
bation in little children," Jones found so ridiculous that he didn't
deem it necessary to reply. For Jones, it was obvious that "he [Janet]
simply does not know that the [psychoanalytic] interpretations are the
very reverse of this, being based on objective principles that have no
reference to individual opinion, but only to the evidence of the facts
themselves" (Jones, 1914–15, p. 406).

Having given a number of examples of what he saw as Janet's
biased account of psychoanalysis, Jones went on to correct Janet's
mistaken views about the origin of this theory. He argued that the
points of agreement between Janet and Freud's views were not in any
sense the result of Freud's assimilation and extension of several of
Janet's ideas. Janet's first communication, Jones (1914–15, p. 409) argued, indeed antedated Breuer and Freud's by seven years, but these
two authors had delayed their first communication by as much as ten
years. Janet's priority, then, resided merely in the *publishing* of certain
ideas while Breuer and Freud's priority was in the *discovery* of these
same ideas. Jones happily concluded his forceful but somewhat simplistic account with the statement that "the development of psychoanalysis both originated and proceeded quite independently of psychological analysis in Janet's sense, was entirely uninfluenced by it
throughout its whole course, and would not have been different in
one iota if Professor Janet's work had never existed" (Jones, 1914–5,
p. 409).

It seems that Janet's teasing address and the vehement reactions to
it made all attempts at reconciliation between Janet and the psycho-
analytical movement impossible despite the fact that Janet on several
occasions went as far as to defend Freud against his critics in the years
that followed (Ellenberger, 1970, p. 821; Janet, 1915b; Prévost, 1973b,
p. 86). At any rate, when in 1937 Janet's son-in-law Edouard Pichon,
who was himself a psychoanalyst, wrote to the eighty-one year old
Freud to suggest a conciliatory meeting at a specified date. Freud
chose not to reply. Jones relates that Freud reacted as follows to Marie
Bonaparte:

No, I will not see Janet. I could not refrain from reproaching him with
having behaved unfairly to psycho-analysis and also to me personally and
having never corrected it. He was stupid enough to say that the idea of a
sexual etiology for the neuroses could only arise in the atmosphere of a
town like Vienna. Then when the libel was spread by French writers that
I had listened to his lectures and stolen his ideas he could with a word

have put an end to such talk, since actually I have never seen him or heard his name in the Charcot time: he has never spoken this word. You can get an idea of his scientific level from his utterance that the uncon-scious is *une façon de parler*. No, I will not see him. I thought at first of sparing him the impoliteness by the excuse that I am not well or that I can no longer talk French, and he certainly can't understand a word of German. But I have decided against that. There is no reason for making any sacrifice for him. Honesty the only possible thing; rudeness quite in order (in Jones, 1980, pp. 228–9).

So, Freud deliberately did not warn Pichon that he would refuse to receive Janet. The result was that Janet, who was by that time seventy-eight years old, took the train to Vienna, rang the doorbell at Berg-gasse 19, only to hear from a servant that Freud on no account would receive him (Prévost, 1973b, p. 89). Priority debates indeed often end up with closed doors.

Studies of Hysteria

In the next several years Janet studied hysterical patients in differ-ent hospitals in Paris, and he published articles and books (Janet, 1890; 1891; 1892a; 1892e; 1892f; 1893a; 1893b; 1893c; 1894b) describing their symptoms in great detail. Once again his method was that of obser-vation and description, and he more than once explicitly described the merits of this approach and the disadvantages of other approaches.

We have not tried to make our study more profound by making use of higher mathematics or equipment of an often deceiving precision. To us psychology doesn't seem far enough advanced to be susceptible to such measures; the general nature of the phenomena, their countless variations, their changing conditions are not known well enough to claim that one can measure one of these facts isolated from the others. It is useless and even dangerous to take a microscope to do gross anatomy, one risks not knowing what one sees. For us, experimental psychology is yet much more simple: it consists above all in knowing one's subject well, in know-ing his life, his studies, his character, his ideas etc., and in being convinced that one never knows enough. We must then place this person in simple and well-determined circumstances and note exactly what he does and says. To examine the actions and words, this is still the best method to know a person, and we do not find it superfluous or tedious to write down the ravings of a lunatic word by word (Janet, 1891, p. 406; cf. 1893a, p. 3; 1930c, p. 126).

Janet summarized his preliminary findings regarding hysteria in two books. In the first book, he (Janet, 1893a) described what were called the stigmata of the hysteric patients. Those were more or less permanent, essential symptoms of the disease, which the patients regarded with indifference and from which they did not seem to suffer (e.g., abulia, amnesia, anesthesia; cf. Janet, 1895d; 1895e; 1895f). In the second book, he (Janet, 1894b) discussed what were called the mental accidents ("*les accidents mentaux*"), i.e., the accidental, temporary symptoms of the disease, which the patients do experience and from which they suffer (e.g., attacks, fixed ideas, deliriums). The distinction between stigmata and accidents itself was due to Charcot's classic conception of hysteria (Dumas, 1924b, p. 918). In both books, Janet proceeded from the assumption defended by the later Charcot that the hysterical symptoms are caused primarily by mental problems (Libbrecht and Quackelbeen, 1995; Janet, 1895a, p. 596).

In trying to explain the different hysterical symptoms Janet slightly elaborated his concept of "personal perception" or "personification" (Janet, 1893b). He argued (Janet, 1893a, pp. 38–44; cf. 1894b, pp. 38–9) that the words "I feel" denote a very complex phenomenon. At the basis of personal perception are the sensations which are registered in the brain. These correspond to the "feel" part of "I feel." Janet attempted to visualize the registration of sensations in the brain by evoking the image of the physiologist Herzen, who had compared the brain to a vast room filled with an enormous number of gaslights. From time to time certain gaslights will start burning, which corresponds with the "feeling" and "seeing" of objects. Interestingly enough, Janet (1893a, p. 38) traced back this comparison to a still older one by Beard published in 1881. The modern reader knows that Pavlov (1928/1963, pp. 221–2) in his turn would use the metaphor of a bright spot moving over the surface of the cerebral hemisphere as a result of nervous excitation to visualize the process of consciousness. But to Janet these flickering gaslights, these sensations, were only the very first and incomplete step of personal perception, because in order to be able to say "*I* feel" or "*I* see," these sensations or elementary psychological phenomena have to be linked to the idea of a personality:

personality, i.e., the reunion of sensations present, the memory of all passed impressions, the imagination of future phenomena; it is the notion of my body, my capacities, my name, my social situation, it is an ensemble of moral, political, religious etc. ideas; it is a world of ideas, the most considerable one we can ever know for we are far from having listed everything. We thus have two things in *'I feel'*: a small new psychological fact, a small light which flares up, *'feel'*, and an enormous mass of ideas that already form a system, *'I'*. These two things become mingled, combined, and to say *'I feel'* is to say that the already vast personality has grasped and absorbed this small new sensation which just took place. . . . This operation of *assimilation* and *synthesis* is repeated for each new sensation (Janet, 1893a, p. 39; original emphasis).

Janet went on to explain that hysterics are incapable of assimilating the numerous visual, tactile, muscular, etc. sensations, of clustering these sensations into one single whole, and linking them to the existing personality. However, this process is absolutely indispensable to enable the person to make these sensations his "personal property," to allow him or her to say "*I* feel." Characteristic of hysterical patients is that they have a "restricted field of consciousness," i.e., they are incapable of assimilating as much of the elementary sensations as normal persons do and consequently suffer from anesthesia, amnesia, etc. (ibid., p. 108, 120). Janet's analysis of the singular lack of will-power (e.g., the inability to take any decision, to undertake any action) that hysterics often display anticipated his later work in interesting ways. He observed that for such patients it is the beginning of the action that is most difficult.

By this I mean the formation of that complex ensemble of ideas and images one needs to imagine in order to be able to grasp a specific object. This synthesis is not exactly the same for each object and it is the formation of this synthesis which is difficult for Marcelle, whereas the repetition of this same synthesis, when it is already accomplished, is easy (ibid., p. 148).

In this way Janet explained why with hysteric patients automatic actions are normally preserved, whereas novel, voluntary actions, which require the active adaptation to new circumstances and a new synthesis of ideas and images, become excessively difficult. The automatic actions rely upon previous syntheses and do no longer require the involvement of the whole personality. Automatic actions do not require personal perception and as a consequence do not suffer in hysteria.

Being unable to undertake any voluntary action themselves these patients increasingly rely on the psychotherapist for advice and encouragement. They need someone to "direct" their lives and can become very fond of their "director" while at the same time making excessive demands on him. Janet noted that this phenomenon is especially strong when patients are hypnotized on a regular basis and he explicitly stated that this "somnambulist passion" for the hypnotist or "need of direction" is not to be mixed up with erotic passion. To illustrate this, he mentioned several cases of patients who were greatly dependent upon him, seeking his company all the time, while at the same time being passionately in love with someone else. He therefore (ibid., pp. 159–160, 226) warned against "hasty and childish interpretations" of this phenomenon, which obviously seems linked with the earlier notion of "rapport" of the mesmerists (Gauld, 1992, pp. 442–3) and the later notion of "transference" of psychoanalysts (Ellenberger, 1970, p. 539).

The Notion of Subconscious Fixed Ideas

It was Charcot who, following Brodie and Reynolds (cf. Janet, 1898, pp. 213–4), insisted upon the role of fixed ideas in hysteria. However, it was Janet (e.g., 1891, 1894b) who elaborated the notion of *subconscious* fixed ideas in hysteria and other syndromes. Janet defined fixed ideas as spontaneously developing ideas that gradually come to dominate the mind. The term "fixed idea" does not necessarily refer to obsessive ideas of an intellectual nature but may also designate persistent emotional states that rest unaltered for long periods (cf. Janet, 1898, p. ii). As hysterics seldom consciously know the fixed ideas that obsess them, one may say that these are subconscious. That subconscious fixed ideas really exist can be shown by listening to the words that the subjects speak during dreams, by observing them when they are suffering from an attack, in the hypnotic state, and through various other methods that tap the subconscious mind such as distraction, automatic writing, crystal gazing, etc. Janet presented many case histories to show that the patients' problems originate in specific real accidents from their life (e.g., a woman is told, by way of a bad joke, that her husband has died). After the first emotional shock has passed, she has no memory for this event but she subsequently suffers from terrible nightmares, hallucinations, and memory problems (cf. Janet, 1893b, p. 170), which then grow into subconscious fixed ideas. As such they co-exist with the subjects' normal conscious mind and cause many of the symptoms (e.g., various tics, loss of sight in one eye, etc.).

At times, during attacks, somnambulism, or deliriums, the fixed ideas invade the whole mind.

The events that caused fixed ideas to develop are nearly always accidents that in themselves didn't cause severe physical traumata but that were accompanied by a vivid emotion. The hysteric symptoms develop only after some time ("the period of meditation," Janet, 1894b, p. 115; or "period of incubation," Janet, 1898, p. 368) and may take many forms. In his analysis of the origin of hysteric paralysis, Janet (ibid., pp. 128–34) nicely summarized his model.

1. At first there is a real accident causing an emotion. Thus, a man may be hit by a car and may be temporarily unable to move his arm;

2. A fixed idea develops that maintains the symptoms. Thus, the man may develop the fixed idea that the nerves of his arm have been damaged and consequently feel unable to move his arm. Characteristic for such cases is that the demarcation of the paralysis follows the lines predicted by the lay conception of the nerve pattern in the arm, which greatly differs from the real innervation;

3. This fixed idea is mostly subconscious, i.e., the patients have no idea that they produce or maintain the symptoms themselves and the symptoms can be made to disappear under hypnosis. In the hypnotic state and by various other means the therapist can learn about the existence of the fixed idea, because some part of the patient's personality will reveal it;

4. The fixed idea in hysterical paralysis is mostly simply the idea of being powerless, exhausted, and paralyzed, but other fixed ideas may cause the same result.

Janet remarked that the "mental accidents" caused by fixed ideas differ in a number of ways from the stigmata (such as reduced vision, amnesia for certain events or time periods, or anesthesia of part of the body). For the stigmata a historical accident may not be apparent and stigmata need not be consciously realized even in the hypnotic state. Finally, the stigmata seem not to be historically or individually variable and exist earlier in the genesis of the illness. The fixed ideas nevertheless have an indirect influence on the stigmata. One can, for example, establish the influence upon amnesia for a certain time period by suppressing the fixed idea (say, in the hypnotic state) and watching memory come back (ibid., pp. 140–1). Janet surmised that hysteric amnesia develops because certain fixed ideas come to dominate the subjects' mind and prevent them from storing or retrieving relevant memories. Also, because of the fatigue from which most patients suffer, the fixed ideas can fully occupy the subjects' reduced field of consciousness. The fact that the patients' attention and volition are enormously reduced weakens the possibility of psychological synthesis (ibid., p. 187; cf. Janet, 1895g). As long as everything goes well the subject may experience no severe problems but the fixed idea leads its latent subconscious existence only to strike hard when the subject's resistance is lowest (cf. Janet, 1898, p. 346). Thus, a subject may not greatly suffer from a traumatic memory but after a disease or in a period of great fatigue the subconscious fixed idea may suddenly pop up in dreams, tics, etc., or normal consciousness. Subjects who have just started to develop fixed ideas are still susceptible of contagion, i.e., when living in a ward they will copy each other's idiosyncrasies, but older ones no more: Their symptoms have become fixed and are automatically repeated when normal consciousness becomes inoperative (ibid., p. 185). In this connection, Janet (ibid., p. 181) remarked that he was able to recognize a patient by her fixed ideas because these had remained exactly the same since they had been first described in the scientific literature fifteen years before.

We can thus see that Janet used the model he developed in *L'automatisme psychologique* to explain the various symptoms of hysteria and that he with Charcot (cf. Gauld, 1992, pp. 312–13) considered hysteria, hypnotism, and dissociation as intimately linked phenomena. He defined hysteria as a form of mental disintegration characterized by the tendency towards permanent and complete dissociation of the personality (Janet, 1894b, p. 301). Due to various factors, the hysteric patients become unable to synthesize all the phenomena they experience, and the phenomena that cannot be comprehended in "personal perception" cluster to form second or third personalities. What was added was the concept of subconscious fixed ideas. It was suggested that under some circumstances for some subjects events that cause a strong emotion may give rise to fixed ideas that start leading a subconscious life, which cause part of the symptoms hysterics experience during their relatively good periods. At times these ideas come completely to the fore to cause attacks or deliriums. The strength of the subconscious fixed ideas depends upon their being isolated in the subject's mind. Exactly because they are isolated and subconscious the patient cannot resist them and they continue to develop and bother the patient (Janet, 1898, p. 226). The retrograde analysis of fixed ideas in their successive forms may reveal the original emotional event and can be used for therapeutic purposes. Subconscious fixed ideas play a role in the hysteric personality which is very similar to that of suggestions. Charcot had advanced a similar idea (cf. Janet, 1895a, p. 599). As with suggestions, the therapist can use hypnosis or artificial somnambulism to try to lay bare and suppress the fixed ideas (cf. Janet, 1898, pp. 213–33).

Incidentally, it is ironic that the notion of fixed ideas was used by Nobel prize winner Egas Moniz in the 1930s and 1940s to justify his infamous prefrontal leukotomy. Reasoning that fixed thoughts are maintained by nerve pathways in the frontal lobes, he decided to destroy these "abnormally stabilized" pathways (Valenstein, 1986, p. 84). Janet, who did not tire of warning against premature and useless translations of psychological terms into physiological ones, would have been absolutely horrified.

The Case of Justine

It was at around the same time that Janet (1894a; cf. 1898) published a lengthy and fascinating case history that allows us to get a better impression of Janet the psychotherapist. The patient in question was Justine, a woman of forty years old who developed an intense fear of contracting cholera. Janet saw her for about three years, at first once every eight days, then less frequently, and then considered her situation sufficiently stable to warrant describing her case. He found that at the age of seventeen Justine saw two corpses of patients who died of cholera, was much impressed by this sight, and ever since had constant thoughts about death and disease. A typhoid fever in the next year worsened the symptoms and Justine now developed nervous attacks. Over the years, her symptoms did not diminish but even got more serious and by the time her husband first brought her to the Salpêtrière Justine had developed full-fledged hysterical attacks, shouting "The cholera will come and get me!," vomiting, suffering contractions, etc. for several hours. Afterward she had no memory of the attacks. Janet at first used her attacks to establish the hypnotic "rapport," e.g., when Justine shouted that the cholera was getting at her, he replied that it was grabbing her right leg, upon which the patient would have a violent reaction that showed that she had heard and understood Janet's remark. Having thus captured the patient's attention, Janet gradually managed to engage her in a conversation. In a later state of the treatment, he managed to hypnotize Justine in a more regular way.

Janet regarded the fixed idea as a very complex synthesis consisting of visual, olfactory, etc. components. During hypnosis, he first tried to decompose this complex whole by suggesting that the events had not taken place in the way the patient remembered. He thus followed the principle that fixed ideas can be destroyed by subdividing them into their composite parts and rendering these ineffective. Visual memories, however, proved very resistant and as he couldn't suppress Justine's visual memory for the dead corpses Janet spent several sessions dressing them. As a result of many of these sessions, Justine's intense fear and her attacks fully disappeared. Unfortunately, now the fixed idea of cholera constantly occupied Justine's *conscious* mind and she was consequently much more unhappy than before, when sudden violent attacks would interrupt an otherwise tolerable life. What obsessed Justine now was the conscious idea of cholera. However, as Janet had already robbed this idea of most of its concrete (olfactory, visual etc.) qualities it had become very abstract, little more than a word. He now proceeded to attack the word itself by decomposing it into neutral elements. Thus, in the hypnotic state Janet suggested to Justine that cholera was the proper name of a Chinese general Cho Le-Ra. He also had her write words such as chocolate, which begin with the same syllable but have a much more pleasant meaning. Using various such procedures, which Janet refrained from describing in detail as "they may seem somewhat childish" (1894a, p. 132), he managed to neutralize the word "cholera." In fact, the word now had ceased to evoke any emotions at all in Justine. Janet remarked that this result had taken him ten months but that for a fixed idea that had existed for more than twenty years this might be an acceptable time span.

Unfortunately, Justine proved to be still far from cured. She now developed a great number of *secondary* fixed ideas, which Janet classified into three groups:

1. Derivative fixed ideas, i.e., secondary fixed ideas that are somehow related to the original fixed idea. Thus, Justine suddenly refused to eat, which was linked with her original fear to con-

tract cholera. She also developed the fixed idea that she had some other horrible disease, etc.

2. Stratified fixed ideas, i.e., secondary fixed ideas that ontogenetically precede the primary ones and that only become apparent when one manages to remove these. Janet relates that with some patients he was forced to go through all their fixed ideas in reverse order until he reached the first, primordial fixed idea (cf. Janet, 1894b, p. 183).

3. Accidental fixed ideas, i.e., secondary fixed ideas that are in no way related to the primary fixed idea. Thus, Justine developed the idea to strangle her dog; she became afraid to change clothes; didn't want to switch on the light; was haunted by the idea that she had refused her husband a drink ten years before, etc., etc. The original fixed idea that had dominated her life for twenty years had now given way to countless little fixed ideas that each threatened to fully occupy her mind.

Janet hypothesized that patients like Justine are still very feeble when the original fixed idea (in her case that of cholera) is destroyed, and they are in constant danger of contracting other fixed ideas that easily take possession of their minds. Justine was extremely suggestible, which Janet attributed to her inability to synthesize what she experienced. As a result, she could hardly read, consciously memorize, had blurred vision, etc. Together with other more physical problems (e.g., with digestion, menstruation), these symptoms formed an intricate whole, which Janet characterized as "the dissociation of functions, the loss of unity, the diminution of this continual synthesis that makes up life and thought" (ibid., p. 150). This disintegration, or dissociation, of their minds makes the patients helpless against the fixed ideas that invade their organism like parasites.

It makes little sense, then, to suppress the fixed ideas one after another as this might well turn out to be an endless endeavor. How then to cure Justine? Janet observed that numerous treatments had been suggested and he dryly remarked that "their number doesn't prove their value" (ibid., p. 151), an observation that is at any rate less pessimistic than a similar one by Chekhov, who once wrote that when numerous remedies are prescribed for a certain disease we can safely infer that it is incurable. Janet himself resorted to what he called "mental training": Justine was asked to perform small intellectual tasks, e.g., read lines in the newspaper, explain phrases, do subtractions, etc. In two years of training, the sessions were gradually lengthened and in the end her mental health was restored. Justine's suggestibility diminished considerably and little attacks she now was able to fend off herself. Rather surprisingly, her physical symptoms disappeared as well. Janet added that he stopped all medication that Justine had been receiving for the last twenty years, except for the hydrotherapy (i.e., taking showers). He also made some revealing remarks about the value of hypnotherapy, claiming that we cannot suggest willpower and liberty and that there is a real danger that patients become dependent on the therapist.

In a word, suggestion, just like any dangerous medicine, is useful in certain cases, it can serve to reach and suppress fixed ideas that have become subconscious, over which the subject no longer has any power, and that preclude any restoration of his mental activity. But beyond its role it is extremely harmful, for it cannot but augment the mental disintegration, the principle behind all accidents (Janet, 1894a, p. 152).

After three years of treatment, Justine's condition had considerably improved but Janet made it quite clear that not all symptoms had disappeared. One thing was that she had developed a need to be hypnotized, a need Janet (ibid., p. 165; cf. 1898, pp. 429, 455) regarded as being as dangerous as the need for morphine. He considered this need for hypnotism to be the need for an authority who would guide her, a *"directeur de conscience,"* and related that only with difficulty he managed to reduce the number of sessions with Justine to one session per month. Longer intervals proved impossible as the patient then relapsed. These relapses made Janet suspect that genetic influences might play a role, and in searching her family tree he indeed found a terrible incidence of premature death and insanity. He ventured that some diseases last longer than the patient. When a "hereditary lesion" has been formed over the course of several generations, a complete cure may not be expected in one (ibid., p. 168; cf. Chapter 7 of Janet, 1898 in which he described that Justine after two years of relative well-being relapsed and again displayed hysteric, although milder, symptoms). Incidentally, it should be observed that Janet – who to all appearance seems to have been an excellent therapist – never claimed brilliant therapeutic results and frequently published accounts of unsuccessful cures in which he gave a detailed picture of the various treatments he tried and their modest results (e.g. 1895c; 1897c).

We thus see that for Janet a complete explanation of Justine's fixed idea entailed the search for hereditary factors, serious diseases (e.g., typhoid fever, meningitis), and other factors (e.g., puberty, seen as both a biological and a cultural phenomenon) that might work as catalytic agents or "agents provocateurs" (Janet, 1894b, p. 299), plus the search for the traumatic event that eventually caused the subject to develop her fixed idea in all its successive forms. The suppression of fixed ideas or, alternatively, their free and conscious expression, seemed – at least in some cases – to be relatively useless, because new and various fixed ideas are bound to pop up. This finding makes it quite understandable that Janet didn't fully agree with Breuer and Freud's "On the Psychical Mechanism of Hysterical Phenomena: Preliminary Communication" (1893, in Strachey, 1973) who, having corroborated Janet's (1889a; 1891) earlier studies concerning the role of subconscious fixed ideas, had argued that it suffices merely to consciously express and "work through" these subconscious fixed ideas in order for recovery to occur. Judging by the case of Justine and the other patients he treated, Janet had ample reason to doubt the general effectiveness of such a "cathartic" cure and he consequently remarked that Breuer and Freud's "somewhat theoretical remarks contain some points which seem to us to be fairly right . . . But unfortunately this is just the first and easiest part of the work; for a fixed idea is not cured when it is expressed, quite the opposite" (1894a, p. 127; cf. Janet, 1894b, p. 190).

Later analyses would, of course, confirm Janet's doubts as to the effectiveness of the cathartic cure. We now know that Breuer and Freud's best-known patient, Anna O. (real name, Bertha Pappenheim), about whom they claimed in their *Studies on Hysteria* (1895) that she had been effectively cured, had many relapses, and was eventually institutionalized. Breuer himself, after he had ceased his treatment of the case, expressed the hope that his patient might die and so be released from her suffering. Breuer and Freud nonetheless included the case of Anna O. among their successful case histories (Ellenberger, 1970, pp. 480–4; Sulloway, 1992, p. 57).

That Breuer and Freud realized that their case histories had much in common with those published by Janet is apparent from a footnote, in which they remarked that "in Janet's interesting study on mental automatism (1889), there is an account of the cure of a hysterical girl by a method analogous to ours" (in Strachey, 1973, p. 7). But this reference doesn't make the similarities between their views sufficiently clear. Like Janet, Breuer and Freud found the precipitating cause of hysteric symptoms in traumatic events for which the patients have no memory. Like Janet, they noticed that under hypnosis these memories emerge with undiminished vividness. Like Janet, they noticed that this finding implies the phenomenon of dissociation in such patients:

The longer we have been occupied with these phenomena the more we have become convinced that *the splitting of consciousness which is so striking in the well-known classical cases under the form of 'double conscience' is present to a rudimentary form in every hysteria, and that a tendency to such a dissociation, and with it the emergence of abnormal states of consciousness . . . is the basic phenomenon of this neurosis.* In these views we concur with Binet and the two Janets (in Strachey, 1973, p. 12).

Breuer and Freud offered no explanation for "the splitting-off of groups of ideas" (ibid., p. 12) but they used the same techniques as Janet to establish their nature (e.g., establishing "rapport" with the patient during an hysterical attack). These and other striking similarities are no doubt partially explained by the fact that Freud studied with Bernheim and Charcot. In fact, he often used the French terms to designate the phenomena of hypnotism, hysteria, and dissociation (e.g., *agents provocateurs, double conscience, condition seconde,* etc.). Yet it remains somewhat unsatisfactory that Breuer and Freud in their famous preliminary communication did not demarcate their own original contribution in more detail. For example, this could have been done by comparing it to those of Moritz Benedikt, Joseph Delboeuf, Paul Möbius, and Pierre (and Jules) Janet (cf. Andersson, 1962; Chertok, 1960; Crocq and Verbizier, 1988; Ellenberger, 1970, pp. 488–9; Hesnard, 1960; Libbrecht and Quackelbeen, 1995; Macmillan, 1979; Sulloway, 1992, pp. 67–8).

Some time later, in Chapter 3 of their later *Studies on Hysteria* (1895) Breuer did pay attention to Janet's thinking and acknowledged that the theory of hysteria owed very much to him. However, he rejected what he called Janet's emphasis on "congenital mental weakness as the disposition to hysteria." Neither did Breuer believe that hysterical patients lacked the capacity for synthesis and he expressed as his belief that "Janet's views were mainly formed in the course of a detailed study of the feeble-minded hysterical patients who are to be found in hospitals or institutions because they have not been able to hold their own in life on account of their illness and the mental weakness caused by it" (Breuer in Strachey, 1973, p. 232).

In contrast, Breuer's own observations "carried out on educated hysterical patients" led him to different conclusions. This is not the place to discuss Breuer and Freud's theories. We will merely say that Breuer's exposition of Janet's thinking left something to be desired, and one may surmise that the combination of, on the one hand, the insufficient account of the close affinity between psychoanalytic and French thought and, on the other hand, the somewhat superficial critique of Janet's thinking did not form the fruitful soil on which an interesting dialogue between the two developing systems of dynamic psychology might develop.

The Study of Neurosis

In the next several years, Janet kept studying hysterical patients and publishing detailed case histories (Janet, 1898; Raymond and Janet, 1898). However, he gradually broadened his expertise and began publishing on other pathological syndromes as well. He also began making increasingly general statements – especially in lectures for lay audiences – about the relation between normal and pathological behavior, about the proper method in psychology, about the nature of mental life, about the advantages and disadvantages of hypnotherapy, etc. While retaining the basic set of ideas set forth in "Psychological automatism," Janet now began building his own system of psychology, a system he would refine and polish throughout the remainder of his life. It is interesting to note that this system became increasingly metaphysical, while Janet at the same time kept warning against theoretical systems that are purely metaphysical and not based on a sound factual basis.

The two volumes on "neuroses and fixed ideas" had a different focus. Janet's (1898) volume contained several lengthy case histories and a theoretical paper on the need for guidance in mental patients. The volume published by Raymond and Janet (1898) is a collection of short descriptions of very many and varied cases without much emphasis on theoretical explanation. As the authors declared, the longitudinal and deep study of a number of cases is essential, because it allows us to penetrate the thought of the subjects, to get to know their intelligence and character, to find out what they really experience, and to follow the long-term results of therapeutic interventions. It is also true that such longitudinal studies may lead the researcher to attach too much importance to phenomena that are merely characteristic of some patients. Moreover, there is a real danger that observer and subject are in a sense educating each other: The more importance the observer attaches to a particular trait, the more the highly suggestible subjects will tend to display it, and the more the observer will find his original ideas confirmed. The role of the subject can also be more active. Several years before, Janet had already remarked that "the subject whom one interrogates is not, as in physical research, an inert object; it is a thinking person who examines her own psychological phenomena and who herself makes a theory out of it. She interprets her disease in her way, and does not describe to us the raw fact, but the way she conceives it" (1891, p. 263).

Thus, what may happen is that subject and observer begin sharing an implicit theory of the origins and nature of the disease that they will subsequently find confirmed in new facts. Unwittingly, the subject and the observer are thus creating and corroborating the same theory. To counter this tendency and out of fearing to create grand theories on a very limited number of cases, Raymond and Janet found it useful to also study a large number of varied cases in less detail (Raymond and Janet, 1898, p. vi).

One of the most interesting case histories discussed in Janet (1894d, republished in 1898) is that of Achilles, a young man who committed adultery while on a business trip away from home. After his return, he greatly regretted his deed and developed various and increasingly serious mental symptoms. First, he turned silent and lost his appetite, then he developed symptoms that suggested some heart problem, and finally he became psychotic and claimed the devil had taken possession of his mind.

When Achilles was referred to Janet, the devil was speaking through his mouth, swearing and cursing and resisting all attempts to cure Achilles. Janet mentioned that he at first asked the chaplain of the Salpêtrière to take care of this peculiar case but that the chaplain saw no chance to help him, because the patient was insane. Janet thus had to practice his own modern form of exorcism. The devil resisted any attempts at direct hypnosis, and Janet had to take recourse to the method of distraction that he had successfully used before in other patients. Standing behind the back of Achilles and speaking in a low voice, he established "rapport" with the devil. "Not everybody has had the chance to talk with a devil, I had to use the opportunity. To force the devil to obey me, I took him by the sentiment that has always been the weak spot of devils, vanity. 'I don't believe in your power, I said to him, unless you give me a proof' " (Janet, 1898, p. 387).

When the devil asked how he could prove his power, Janet asked him to make Achilles lift his arm. When this succeeded, he continued to give the devil other assignments. Janet remarked that his conversation with the devil was quite traditional, but that one difference betrayed the influence of the culture and historical time period they were living in. Whereas the medieval exorcists preferred to speak in a more or less correct Latin or in a sort of invented Greek that religious people in those times understood rather well, Janet quickly resorted to French: ' "I also succeeded in making the devil of Achilles some very simple suggestions in dog Latin, they succeeded not too badly: "da mihi dextram manum, applica digitum tuum super nasum', but after some attempts it was evident that the devil and I preferred to speak French" (ibid., p. 389).

Janet's next step was to ask the devil to make Achilles fall asleep ("The devil didn't know in which trap I had lured him"), after which Achilles was in a sort of somnambulist state in which Janet could start questioning him. He then found out that Achilles was being tortured by remorse and the memory of his behavior during the business trip. Janet used the same methods he used to cure Justine to help Achilles, i.e., he step by step destroyed the memory of this event by subdividing it during somnambulism. This procedure had an immediate beneficial effect on Achilles' waking state and after some time Janet also succeeded in destroying the fixed ideas that kept haunting the patient during sleep. The other signs of dissociation that the patient displayed, such as somnambulism and automatic writing, disappeared simultaneously and Janet was able to state that eight years after the cure there had been no relapse.

There was an interesting digression in Janet's account of the cure of Achilles that transcended the strict boundaries of a case history and that, by its style and topic, foreshadowed the ideas that were relevant for Janet later on. Janet now observed for the first time that a mild form of dissociation is prevalent in normal people as well. He stated his belief that every person continually tells himself a story, especially during the performance of tasks that do not require much attention. It is the sort of internal daydreaming that many people know: "Thanks to this subconscious work we find problems fully solved that we didn't understand some time before. It frequently happens that we are working on a book or lecture and one nice day it appears fully ready without us understanding this miracle" (Janet, 1898, p. 394).

Janet claimed that such stories (e.g., being famous, beloved) persons tell themselves change very little and very slowly over the years and that they are only vaguely conscious and half-automatic. As soon as the subject's mind is somehow weakened, one sees these reveries grow immensely and become more involuntary and subconscious.

Janet (1897a; republished in 1898) now also elaborated his ideas regarding the need for direction that many patients manifest so clearly. He observed that when a subject has been hypnotized repeatedly by one and the same hypnotist one can distinguish three different stages in the posthypnotic period:

1. A short stage of fatigue which may last from several hours to a day or so;
2. A much longer stage of well-being or "somnambulist influence" during which the patients display no symptoms and do not demand to see their hypnotist; and
3. A stage of what Janet termed "somnambulist passion," during which the patients feel increasingly worse and develop a growing need to see their hypnotist.

The length of the second stage of relative well-being varied enormously: Janet mentioned that some of his patients needed up to one lengthy session of hypnosis per day, while others could manage with one session every one or two weeks. Janet wondered what role posthypnotic suggestion played in causing the state of well-being. He noted that the length of the period during which posthypnotic suggestion was effective was equivalent to the length of what he called the period of somnambulistic influence, but in his view this state wasn't caused only by suggestion. Janet observed that during the stage of well-being many patients are persistently thinking of their hypnotist, who gives them advice as to what to do or not to do, to the point of having hallucinations of his voice or physical appearance. In fact, the end of this stage is characterized by the fact that the idea of the hypnotist in the mind of the patients loses its distinctive characteristics; the subjects now enter the third stage of "somnambulist influence" is characterized by the conscious or subconscious persistence of the idea of the hypnotist. Janet emphasized that these phenomena are not dependent upon suggestion; they derive by association from suggestions made by the hypnotist but presuppose considerable mental work. "It thus seems that the idea of the hypnotist plays a considerable role, that it directs the subject's conduct, exerts an inhibitory action on his fixed ideas, excites his activity and thereby indirectly determines the improvement of the health, the development of sensibility, intelligence and will that seem to characterize this period" (Janet, 1898, p. 455).

In trying to explain the phenomenon of somnambulist influence, Janet compared it to other, normal phenomena. He once more emphasized that the feelings of the patients are not necessarily or predominantly based on erotic love and that variations such as filial or fatherly love occur as well. Moreover, the feelings come and go in a rhythm of about one or two weeks and can exist alongside genuine erotic love for another person. Janet noted that other patients who are not hypnotized display similar behavior: After the consultation of their doctor, they may initially feel tired, then show improvement, and, finally, develop a need to see their doctor again. What these patients need above all, according to Janet, is a person who guides them, who summarizes and synthesizes their feelings, who confirms that they are justified in having this or that feeling, who makes decisions for them, etc. This makes them feel better for longer or shorter periods. A related phenomenon we find in those patients who suffer from loneliness (e.g., after having lost someone). They feel isolated and abandoned and need another's will, an authority to guide them. In a way, their symptoms resemble those of hypnotized patients.

Janet concluded that what is essential is neither suggestion nor hypnosis but the need for direction or guidance. The therapist can do what abulic patients cannot do themselves: to make the synthesis, to make the decision, to do the mental work the subjects are incapable of doing themselves. Hypnosis and suggestion are merely means, albeit powerful ones, to accomplish this goal. With and without hypnosis the subject can be thinking of his "director" and his advice and thus temporarily be able to solve his problems.

Why is it that this influence of the therapist is not lasting? Here, Janet first pointed to the destructive effect of strong emotions. In his view, the emotions that subjects are bound to experience have a dissociative effect that destroys the work of synthesis accomplished by the therapist. The elements of thinking remain, but dissociated, isolated and the "director" must resume his work of synthesis and scaffolding: "It seems to me that thought like the living body itself is perpetually oscillating between these two great phenomena: assimilation, organization, and growth and, on the other hand, disassimilation, dissociation and destruction" (ibid., p. 476).

However, the influence of the therapist is bound to be short-lived, even when no strong emotions are experienced by the subject. How can we explain this limited duration? Janet explained that it is impossible to continue existence without modifications of behavior, without the subject's adaptations to novel circumstances. Time incessantly brings novel situations and incessantly demands adaptations and new decisions. What the patients do not know how to do is to adapt to the changing world. This is why the subjects regularly require help from their therapist and why one patient aptly called Janet the "*remonteur de pendules*," or the "rewinder of clocks" (ibid., pp. 476–7).

These considerations led Janet to the statement that easy and quick cures are frequently impossible. The therapist virtually needs to reeducate the subject, a complicated two-step process that involves (1) a first essential step of taking complete guidance of the subject's mind, and (2) the equally essential step of subsequently reducing this guidance to a minimum (ibid., pp. 478–9). The first step is essential, because the beneficial influence of the therapist cannot come about as long as his influence remains superficial. The second step is essential, because patients obviously need to develop the capacity to lead their own lives. Janet regularly remarked that this second step was often a quite difficult one to realize and this led him to reflections about the need for guidance in normal individuals. In a passage that reveals much about Janet's own personality, he remarked that the need for advice and guidance from other people varies greatly in individuals: Some people cannot work alone, frequently need guidance, are imitators in science and art, cannot amuse themselves, and constantly need the company of others. Others do not seek social company, are independent, make their own decisions, and belong to the innovators in science and art. Janet was inclined to see the need for company as a sign of weakness or, at any rate, the ability to amuse oneself alone as a sign of strength. In his view, individuals who constantly seek the company of others in fact follow an urgent need to obey, to subject their will to the will of others (ibid., p. 479). What these individuals wish is to carry out more or less automatic patterns of behavior, leaving the more complicated synthetic mental work to others. It is as if the division between automatism and synthesis that Janet analyzed for the individual mind is continued in society and gives rise to the domination of some individuals by others. If this is true, remarked

Janet: "Then this tiny curious phenomenon of 'magnetic rapport' is not insignificant, it allows us perhaps to study an important element of social relationships, to understand the origin of dependency and hierarchy, to connect the need for obedience of some and the authority of others to the diminution and the growth of the vital power (*la puissance vitale*)" (ibid., p. 480).

We thus see that Janet remained faithful to his original analyses of the workings of the mind and to his emphasis on the importance of the phenomena of automatism, synthesis, and dissociation. He kept publishing detailed case histories that confirmed the fruitfulness of his approach both theoretically and in the domain of therapy. But he increasingly left room for reflections about phenomena in human beings who do not seek the advice of the therapist and about human society at large. He also kept rethinking such basic theoretical issues as the relationship between suggestion, hypnosis, and influence. Here his long-time opponent was Bernheim, and we will have occasion to come back to their theoretical controversy (cf. Bernheim, 1911–12; Forel, 1927; Janet, 1910–11; Ochorowicz, 1909; see Chapter 2). What allowed Janet to make increasingly general statements about methodological and theoretical matters and about the issue of mind and society at large was, firstly, his growing knowledge of mental pathology, and, secondly, his thorough training in philosophy. One may also surmise that the tendency to make broad generalizing statements about man and society was at first checked by the need to establish his reputation as a scientific thinker in a field that was fraught with bizarre phenomena and even more exotic theories.

French Roots of Janet's Theory of Conduct

Below we will show that in the second half of his career Janet, inspired by the work of American behaviorism and (to some extent) Russian reflexology, developed a theory of conduct that emphasized the objective study of the behavioral actions of the subject. It is important to realize that Janet was in a sense well prepared to accept some brand of "objective" psychology. A major current in French thought (Cabanis, Comte) had for some time been emphasizing the study of objective, positive facts, and such founding fathers of French psychology as Charcot and Ribot had both argued against the purely subjective, introspective psychology of former times. Charcot, Janet's one time superior, argued that

It is another psychology that we must create, a psychology reinforced by the pathological studies to which we dedicate ourselves. We are busy creating it with the help of psychologists who this time do not merely wish to consider what is called internal observation as did their predecessors. The earlier psychologist locked himself in his study, he looked at his own inner being, he was his own object of observation. It is a method that had some value, but that is totally insufficient. To check this observation by man of himself, we need an inverse observation, and in this inverse observation nervous pathology plays a considerable role (Charcot quoted in Janet, 1895a, p. 593).

Charcot posited that alongside subjective psychology we need an objective psychology based upon the scientific observation of other people. This objective psychology would consist of four branches:

1. psychophysics, which determines and measures the relations existing between physical phenomena and sensations we perceive;
2. comparative psychology, which compares Western adult man with animals, children, and other races;
3. physiological psychology, which studies the brain-mind links;
4. psychopathology, which reveals to us the secrets of the normal mind.

The latter two branches of objective psychology were very well developed in France, and Janet clearly stood in their tradition (Beauchesne, 1986). It is quite clear that Janet from the outset basically shared Charcot's perspective. Quite early in his career, for example, he claimed that a new objective psychology already existed side by side with the older subjective one:

Instead of limiting himself to the study and description of his own feelings, which is no doubt fundamental but not very exact and very incomplete, the psychologist has increasingly examined the persons who surround him and going by their attitudes, actions, words, writings, he has attempted to analyze their feelings and ideas. A more or less, *objective* psychology has thus become added to the purely subjective psychology of our old masters (Janet, 1894d, reprinted in 1898, p. 375).

In his "Neuroses and Fixed Ideas" Janet (1898, p. 406) emphasized that the older subjective psychology was still necessary for the beginning of the studies on human thinking and would in no way be suppressed by objective psychology, which has no metaphysical or religious ambition and attacks no respectable belief. He then went on to subdivide this objective psychology into the branches that Charcot had already delineated. Janet shared the interest in the pathological branch of objective psychology, believing with Charcot and Claude Bernard that pathological cases can teach us something fundamental about normal functioning, as in both cases the same laws are operative (Reuchlin, 1986, p. 63). To study the nature of personality, one must study its conditions, i.e., one must study its various and preferably its extreme forms in the other person (cf. Janet, 1896a). In this connection, Janet made the following interesting comparison: "These diseases show us singular exaggerations of normal phenomena and allow us to study the facts of the mind with a strong magnification as does the microscope for physical objects" (Janet, 1894d, in 1898, p. 376).[1]

The conviction that psychopathology can uncover the secrets of the normal mind has a typically French tradition which can be traced from Ribot, via Bernard and Comte, to Broussais and Maine de Biran (Delacroix, 1924; Dumas, 1924d; Janet, 1896a; 1926b). It is a view that is, indeed, outspoken in Ribot who claimed that "the morbid derangements of the organism that cause intellectual disorders, the anomalies, the monsters in the psychological order, are for us just like experiments prepared by nature." (Ribot quoted by Janet, 1917, pp. 276–7).

For Ribot and Charcot diseases served as instruments of analysis and dissection that uncover the hidden structure of the normal mind. In this connection Ribot arrived at his well-known law of psychological disintegration or dissolution:

The disease dissolves all psychological functions according to an order and a law . . . it is a well-known fact in the domain of life that the structures that have been formed last are the first to degenerate . . . in the biological order dissolution takes place in an order inverse to that of evolution, it goes from the complex to the simple: the older acquisitions are the simplest ones, they have every reason to be most stable (Ribot quoted by Janet, 1917, p. 277).

In itself this law of dissolution and its connected notions of Spencerian evolution, hierarchy, and regression are traceable to the work

---

[1] He was echoed by James several years later: "Insane conditions have this advantage, that they isolate special factors of the mental life, and enable us to inspect them unmasked by their more usual surroundings. They play the part in mental anatomy which the scalpel and the microscope play in the anatomy of the body" (James, 1902/ 1985, p. 22).

of Hughlings Jackson, whose work Ribot studied very well (Ey, 1960; 1968; Reuchlin, 1986, pp. 63–4). In Chapter 8 we will see how Vygotsky (and Luria) used a similar Jacksonian and Spencerian approach to explain the development of mature conceptual thinking and its dissolution in schizophrenia.

We thus see that Janet shared in a French tradition of psychopathology that emphasized the objective study of behavioral symptoms and actions. At the same time he made it abundantly clear that he didn't believe in a psychology that tries to appear objective by translating its findings into physiological terms ("the crude symbolic explanation by reference to the imaginary play of fibers and cells," Janet, 1917, p. 275). As we have seen already at several occasions, Janet frequently argued that such a translation was premature, as our knowledge of the brain is still very insufficient and, consequently, nothing is gained by the substitution of psychological findings by hypothetical brain mechanisms (cf. Janet, 1898, p. 440). Here, again, he was following Ribot, who had tried to demarcate psychology from on the one hand, metaphysics and, on the other hand, physiology. A particular clear expression of Janet's stance can be found in his review of Tuke's dictionary of psychological medicine:

if the physical and mental phenomena form two series of parallel facts, it will be necessary to study each series separately with the process adapted to it; we must study the former by physiological methods, and must endeavor to reach the psychological facts by introspection, by observation of actions and language, by time measurement, etc. It is only after a complete and independent investigation that these two series of facts should be brought into juxtaposition. A physiological fact that has been clearly demonstrated by suitable methods, may then be corrected and usefully collated with a psychological fact that has been equally well proved by the proper process. If there is an error that seems intolerable to us, it is to invent, to construct from imagination either of these two facts and to bring it into juxtaposition with the other. Some authors delight in explaining a moral fact by imagining some physiological process or other, which they then collate with a psychical phenomenon. Thus, in the case of an association of ideas, or another very definite psychological fact, instead of accurately describing its exact nature they speak of an intercommunication between nervous fibers that takes place at that moment, of contact between branches of nerve cells, of a nervous current that has been established, etc., etc. Has this communication, this contact, this current, been observed by them through the microscope at the time of its occurrence, or have they even ascertained the existence of an association of ideas? If not, then why do they mention it? Such modes of expressing oneself are mere, meaningless, verbal translations. The actual psychological fact is made to disappear by translating it into another language; nothing is added to our real knowledge, and it would be as well to speak in poetical metaphors as to indulge in this vainest and hollowest metaphysics (Janet, 1893d, pp. 297–8).

It would seem then that the type of behaviorism advanced by Thorndike and Watson, with its emphasis on the study of objective action and its abhorrence of references to unknown mental or neurological mechanisms, fell on fertile soil with Janet. However, the very same French tradition in psychology that would make whole-hearted acceptance of behaviorism seem logical also provided the weapons against it. French psychology, as defined by people such as Charcot, Ribot, and Renan, was, as we have seen, much broader in scope than behaviorism ever would be. It included the study of development, of animals, of primitive man, of children, and of mental pathology. The study of mental pathology, in particular, with its intricate interplay of hereditary and environmental factors, with its phenomena of development, loss, and regression, with its complex social phenomena of transference, suggestion, and rapport, safeguarded Janet from attaching too much value to the obsessive study of the countless adventures of the white laboratory rat, *Rattus norvegicus experimentalis*. As we shall see below, his own concept of "conduct" was much broader than the behaviorists' concept of "behavior" and included such higher mental processes as the "conduct of triumph" and other phenomena that we still need to discuss. Here we have restricted ourselves to a short overview of some of the French roots of Janet's psychology of conduct that should make it understandable why the later Janet could both readily incorporate American behaviorism's basic methodological approach and avoid its more extravagant claims and practices.

From Neuroses to Obsessions

Janet now worked in the ward of Jules Falret at the Salpêtrière, in Raymond's clinic, and he saw his own patients in his private practice at home. Naturally, not all of these patients were hysterics, and Janet gradually broadened his understanding of mental pathology. In two bulky volumes Janet described and analyzed the cases of no less than 325 patients who suffered from what he called psychasthenia (Janet, 1903a; Raymond and Janet, 1903; cf. Pitnam, 1987). The first volume was dedicated to the detailed study of five patients and to the presentation of Janet's theoretical ideas concerning their diagnostics, cure, and prognosis. The second volume was a collection of several hundreds of short descriptions of cases that served as the empirical background of the more theoretical ideas proposed in volume one. Books on obsessive-compulsive disorders, hypochondria, etc. are always interesting to read, if only because one recognizes so much of oneself and one's friends and acquaintances, and Janet's delightful books formed no exception to this rule. But what made the books important for our understanding of the evolution of Janet's thinking is that Janet now for the first time described a hierarchy of mental functions that went further than his original dichotomy of lower, automatic functioning versus higher, synthetic functioning (Janet, 1903a, pp. 476–7; Meyerson, 1947).

Janet (1903a) claimed that the many and diverse symptoms of psychasthenia can be classified and ordered in three different ways according to the 3 groups of symptoms that he discerned. These groups of symptoms were:

1. the obsessions proper, i.e., certain well-defined ideas (e.g., the fear that one will expose one's genitals in public);
2. the forced agitations, i.e., the ruminations, tics, or useless operations that patients suffer from (e.g., the need to check and recheck whether the door is closed, etc.);
3. the insufficiencies, i.e., the feelings of unreality, impotency, incompleteness, etc. The problem is to decide which of these groups is most important and can explain the other two.

Different theories result depending upon which group of symptoms one regards as primary and which as derivative. Janet was not very charmed by what he called the intellectual theories, i.e., the theories that regard certain well-defined ideas as primary. He claimed that he had met many patients with tics, anxieties, etc. without a single clear obsessive idea and he argued that the idea is but the final stage of the disease (ibid., p. 452). The so-called emotional theories that take the forced agitations as being primary, Janet regarded with more sympathy. However, he claimed that he knew of patients who were obsessive but had no emotional problems, nor did they have them in the past. Clearly, then, many of the obsessions have an intellectual origin (ibid., pp. 457–61). This leaves the group of insufficiencies as the group of primary importance from which we should be able to derive the symptoms of the other two groups. In Janet's opinion the feelings of insufficiency arise because the subject somehow loses the capacity to concentrate, synthesize his concrete experiences. The result is that the world feels somehow changed for the subject, or that the subject feels changed himself, which leads to feelings of estrangement, impotency, etc. It was in this connection that Janet introduced his hierarchy of mental operations reasoning that the mental operations are lost in disease according to their level of complexity: "In a word, the mental operations seem to be arranged in a hierarchy in which the superior levels are complex, difficult to reach and inaccessible for our patients, whereas the inferior levels are easy and remain at their disposition" (ibid., p. 475).

However, if we use the criterion of loss in mental disease as the sole criterion to judge the level of complexity of mental operations, we are led to counter-intuitive results. Actions commonly judged to be very complex, such as the performance of abstract mathematical operations, can be carried out by psychasthenics until their disease has advanced quite far, while seemingly very simple concrete actions, such as visiting another person, may become impossible at a very early stage. Janet well realized the paradoxical nature of his conclusions and he maintained that our intuitive notions about the level of difficulty of mental functions are mostly mistaken. Making a comparison with the history of biology in which the original arbitrary classifications of animals according to their supposed degree of perfection were replaced by the objective classification according to evolution theory, Janet proposed to redo the ordering of mental functions according to their frequency and order of disappearance in mental patients. This resulted in the levels displayed in Table 3.1.

Let us comment briefly on several of the functions mentioned in this preliminary hierarchy of mental operations. According to Janet, most easily lost and therefore most complex is the reality function (*la fonction du réel*), which involves the "apprehension of reality in all its forms," or Bergson's "*attention à la vie presente.*" It involves the ability to act upon external reality and to change it, which is most difficult when this reality consists of other persons. To eat in public, or to play an instrument in public, is much more demanding than performing the same activities in private. One of the most difficult of these social operations is sexual intercourse, in particular when practiced for the first time. According to Janet, many factors contribute to its difficulty: the fact that one doesn't know one's partner very well, the fear of the

Table 3.1. *Hierarchy of Psychological Phenomena (after Janet, 1903a, pp. 487–8)*

the
reality
function

- the action
  - effective action upon reality { social / physical
  - novel action with feeling of { unity / liberty
- attention in
  - perception with feeling of reality
  - certitude, belief
  - the perception of new objects
  - the perception of persons { with a feeling of reality / with a feeling of unity

presentification, enjoyment and perception of the present

---

disinterested activity
- habitual action
- action without the feeling of { the present / unity / liberty
- perception without the feeling of certitude
- with a vague feeling of the present

---

functions of the images
- purely representative memory
- imagination
- abstract reasoning
- reverie

---

visceral emotional reactions { systematic / diffuse

---

useless muscular movements { systematic / diffuse

---

consequences, preoccupation with the future, etc. It is only natural, then, that psychasthenics often have problems with this operation. Actions are also difficult when they require precise adjustment, as in professional manual activity, or when the activity is new, i.e., involves liberty. Somewhat lower in the hierarchy we find the attention that permits us to perceive reality and the belief (*la croyance*) that it *is* reality. We also find memory and the consciousness of our own internal states and perception of our own personality at approximately this level. Still lower we find the operation of "presentification," which has to do with the formation of the present in the subject's mind. The natural tendency of the mind is to roam through the past and the future, and it requires much effort to concentrate one's attention on present action. According to Janet, the psychological present is an act of some complexity that involves a certain duration but is felt as a single state of consciousness (cf. Ellenberger, 1970). Below the 1st level we find what Janet (1903a, p. 480) coined the 2nd level of so-called disinterested functions (*opérations désintéressées*). These are the same functions as before but now robbed of their perfection, i.e., the feeling of reality. This implies that they are not adapted to new facts, not coordinated, vague, distracted, indifferent to reality. Such actions are easier to complete, and that is why it sometimes helps to distract patients. This is also why psychasthenics can often give excellent advice to others concerning psychological problems: The problems of others are less real to them. It is not that such disinterested acts are not conscious, but they are less so and lack precision and concentration.

When the problems of psychasthenics become more serious, we arrive at the 3rd level of complexity, when patients still have the ability to reason about ideas. In this connection, Janet (ibid., p. 484) remarks that abstract reasoning is much easier than concrete action and that patients retain this inferior capacity of reasoning for a long time. At this level, we also find the capacity of self-observation and the representative operations connected with imagery, memory, and imagination. Psychasthenics are prone to continuous self-observation and Janet regarded "this aptitude for psychological introspection [as] . . . simply a consequence of the weakness of their mind." He added that this type of introspection does not require any precision, and borders on rumination and reverie. At the still lower 4th and 5th level, we can place emotions that are not adapted to the situation, such as vague anxieties and useless movements.

Janet (ibid., p. 487) noted that the psychological facts were now ordered according to what Spencer called their "coefficient of reality," but he realized that his schema was largely empirical (i.e., based on the phenomena of loss of function or dysfunction in pathology) and wondered what actually distinguished these various levels. What do the higher operations require that lower ones do not? Having discarded several hypotheses, he arrived at the conclusion that what mattered were concentration and the number of phenomena attended to: "The reunion of these two phenomena, a new synthesis, a strong

concentration and very many facts of consciousness constitute a character that must be essential in psychology and that one can conven-
tionally call *psychological tension*" (ibid., p. 495).

So, the ability to concentrate and the number of phenomena that
one can hold in consciousness define the psychological tension one is
capable of at that moment. Janet observed that such a concept of
tension was not unlike similar concepts advanced by Maudsley, Spencer, Höffding, and Bergson. Characteristic of psychological tension is
that it varies between persons and between various moments of the
life cycle of one person. Disease, fatigue, and certain emotions may
cause a diminishing of psychological tension, which in its turn causes
certain superior mental operations to disappear, because these require
a higher psychological tension. Tension may be enhanced by, among
other things, certain drugs, pregnancy, physical exercise, and certain
pleasant emotions, in particular those caused by satisfactory sexual
intercourse (ibid., p. 534). Janet noted that, paradoxically, even unpleasant emotional shocks, such as the news about the serious disease
of a parent, may allow persons to regain psychological tension or
strength. Persons who have long been depressive and lethargic and
unable to get dressed in the morning may suddenly find the strength
and stamina to take care of a parent who suffered a stroke.

Janet argued that the psychological tension of psychasthenics was
normally very low and that they were hardly capable of performing
the operations in the middle of his hierarchy. He realized, however,
that to at least some observers the endless obsessive ruminations of
psychasthenics seemed to require considerable energy. To explain this
seeming paradox, Janet (ibid., p. 557) posited that the loss of higher
operations leads to feelings of insufficiency that cause the patient to
suffer. This suffering in its turn is a source of energy (much like the
mishap of a close relative may free considerable spare energy; see
above) and feeds the endless deliberations and ruminations.

With the natural and not so natural oscillations of psychological
tension Janet thus seemed able to provide explanations for many of
the psychasthenic's symptoms. He added the notion of *derivation*:
When a force originally destined to be expended for some goal rests
unutilized, because this goal has become unattainable, it will be expended to produce other and useless phenomena. Janet cited researchers such as Cabanis, Spencer, Ribot, Jackson, Tuke, and Freud to show
that similar concepts were not uncommon, but he hastened to explain

that his notion of derivation was slightly different. Thus, he claimed that any mental operation that requires high tension and is frustrated in its execution, because the subject cannot mobilize enough psychological tension, will lead to derivation. This was contrary to Freud, who had claimed that it is sexual failure that leads to pathological visceral reactions subjectively felt as anxiety. In general, in discussing the phenomenon of derivation of psychological tension it becomes quite clear that for Janet psychological tension was equivalent to psychological energy. Thus, he draws a comparison with the voltage of electric lamps. An electric current of 110 volt may not be enough for one big lamp but suffices for many smaller lamps. This analogy explains why subjects incapable of performing an act from the top of his hierarchy (see Table 3.1) may nevertheless occupy themselves endlessly with acts belonging to the lower levels.

In sum, psychasthenics try to perform mental operations that require high psychological tension (e.g., social acts). They fail because they cannot mobilize enough tension, and then the mobilized tension or energy gets dissipated to produce ruminations, useless movements, feelings of insufficiency, tics, etc. It is, said Janet (ibid., p. 567), as if we witness "an excitation which must be expended one way or the other."

Janet realized that this account does not yet explain why psychasthenics are obsessed with *specific* operations, why they fear the specific situations, animals, etc., they fear. In his view, many people do not know they lack psychological tension until they try to perform a certain action with particular attention, because they somehow judge it to be very important. For example, many of Janet's patients suffered from religious obsessions, because, said Janet, they had been taught that religious rituals were extraordinarily important, and therefore did their utmost to perform them perfectly. Thus, low psychological tension becomes manifest only when culture, education, or specific circumstances require subjects to perform some mentally difficult operation, and the symptoms of the patients vary because their culture, education, and personal circumstances vary.

Speaking about the etiology of the symptoms, Janet noted that very many factors played a baleful role. Diving into his own records of some 170 cases, he found that heredity played an important role in the sense that many parents of patients manifested symptoms of mental instability. Women were overrepresented in his sample (75 percent), which led Janet to conclude that women are the weaker sex in terms of his own hierarchy. Certain character types may predispose to psychasthenia. In most cases the symptoms start before twenty or thirty years of age (with puberty as a dangerous age period), but Janet added that the age of onset is difficult to determine. Many and diverse diseases may play an aggravating role. Janet (ibid., p. 644) submitted that in most cases the disease starts with psychophysiological insufficiencies that are followed by crises of psycholepsy (i.e., sudden lowering of the psychological tension) and, finally, by obsessions proper. The disease may last an entire lifetime but in a good number of cases at least partial recovery is possible after the patient's youth ("the hardest period of life") is over (ibid., pp. 668–9).

Janet considered psychasthenia to be a serious disease with, as we have seen, a hereditary background and he wasn't overly optimistic about its possible cure. He believed that children who are somehow in danger of getting this disease should be encouraged to practice physical exercise, to avoid monotonous abstract intellectual tasks, and be taught to overcome obstacles and to struggle with their peers ("I believe it is extremely important to force our young psychasthenic to fight," ibid., p. 687). But if all this is in vain then the doctor should act swiftly and unhesitatingly. By nature, the psychasthenic will believe that his state of mind is extraordinary, completely unique and that nobody, least of all medical doctors, has ever seen such a curious syndrome. The task of the doctor is to counter this attitude by displaying great confidence and by giving the impression that the patient's disease is perfectly known and trivial and that its treatment and (partial) cure is a matter of routine. In order to convince the patient of his knowledge and the triteness of the disease, the doctor should preferably give a detailed description of several of the patient's symptoms before the patient has had the time to relate them to himself or herself, a task that is relatively easy, according to Janet, as the symptoms tend to follow standard patterns (ibid., p. 689).

Janet's therapy consisted above all in a veritable reeducation of the subject (ibid., p. 723): he prescribed a (vegetarian) diet, a fixed waking/sleeping cycle, cold showers, a simplification of the subject's lifestyle (which, as Janet noted, sometimes made a divorce necessary), and so on. He believed far less in medication but nevertheless used at times sedatives and (seldom) morphine. But most important, Janet considered to be what he called "moral direction": The patients have to be advised about the right course of action (which they almost invariably already know but cannot realize in real life), comforted, encouraged, made angry, etc., depending upon the particular patient. In addition, they have to be given tasks that they can (easily) accomplish, in order to heighten their self-confidence and train their will and attention.

Janet considered psychasthenia to be a distinct disease, which nevertheless was linked to several other diseases. He believed that to some extent it was related to epilepsy (which he believed to be caused by sudden changes of psychological tension) and even claimed that psychasthenia could be seen as a mild and chronic form of this epilepsy (ibid., p. 734). Discussing some similarities of psychasthenia and hysteria (see below) he concluded that psychasthenia lies somewhere between epilepsy and hysteria and like all psychoneuroses is characterized by problems with psychological tension.

The Theory of Hysteria Revisited

Meanwhile, Janet kept polishing and revising his theory of hysteria. In his *The Major Symptoms of Hysteria* (first edition 1907) we can observe the changes Janet made since he first posited his theory in 1889. Having discussed what he now saw as the major symptoms of hysteria – various forms of somnambulism, fugues, double personalities, attacks, fits, anorexia, bulimia, etc. – Janet came to discuss the stigmata of hysteria. By stigmata, however, he no longer meant the more or less permanent, essential symptoms of the disease that the patients regard with indifference and from which they do not seem to suffer, as discussed in Janet (1893a). Instead, he proposed to speak of stigmata to refer to (a) characteristics that either served to diagnose subjects as being hysteric, or to (b) characteristics that are causally connected with other symptoms of the disease and can explain them. He now stated that hysterical anesthesia could not pass the second, stronger definition of a stigma, and that he had formerly, "under the influence of la Salpêtrière," exaggerated its importance (Janet, 1907a/1963, p. 275). He still believed, however, that anesthesia was of great practical importance, as it was present in very many hysterical accidents. Janet also made a distinction between (a) properly hysterical stigmata specific for hysteria, and (b) common or general stigmata, which hysterical patients share with other mentally diseased. Using this classification, he discerned three properly hysterical stigmata: suggestibility, absent-mindedness, and alternation.

Janet (ibid., pp. 279, 292) regarded suggestibility as the most important mental stigma of hysteria but he hastened to explain what exactly he understood by suggestion and suggestibility. By suggestion he meant the complete, extreme development of an idea that takes place without any participation of the will or of the personal perception or consciousness of the subject. Defined in this way, it is a very rare phenomenon, which Janet observed only in hysteric patients and which disappears as soon as the patient is cured. Such patients vividly feel the heat of the sun, see the water of the sea, and hear the sounds of seagulls when asked to imagine a beach and are totally blocked off from their actual environment during suggestion. Their state represents a form of artificial somnambulism or hypnotism and as such it requires the diminution of personal synthesis and the preservation of certain automatisms.

Exaggerated absent-mindedness Janet (1907a/1963, p. 296) regarded as another properly hysterical stigma. He claimed that the exaggeration of this disposition will bring about the phenomenon of subconsciousness as a great many things will exist outside the personal consciousness. Janet emphasized that hysterical absent-mindedness is not inattention but an active suppression of all that is not looked at directly. The hysteric anesthesia, for example, rests on an "unconscious decision" by the subject not to feel stimulation in certain body parts, i.e., the subject must discriminate between various parts and to perceive the stimulation in order not to feel certain stimulations. Janet demonstrated this paradoxical fact several times by asking blindfolded patients to react with "yes" when they felt the stimulus and with "no" when they didn't feel it, which the subjects duly did.

The third and final properly hysteric stigma Janet (ibid., pp. 298–302) considered to be the phenomenon of alternation or transfer. By this he meant the tendency prevalent in hysterical patients to suddenly replace one accident by another, e.g., a therapist may believe to have "cured" a paralysis in the left arm only to find it replaced by an identical paralysis in the right arm on the very next day.

All three major symptoms of hysteria Janet explained on the basis of his old conception of the retraction of the field of consciousness first advanced in (Janet, 1889a). He again suggested that becoming conscious of a fact is a matter of assimilation or personal perception of outer excitations, which he now, however, no longer compared to gaslights but to electric lamps. This conception still admirably explained the three major stigmata of hysteria. The extreme suggestibility of the hysteric subject is due to the fact that the subject has no control over the ideas suggested to her that somehow overwhelm her. But according to Janet, this amounts to saying that the idea doesn't meet opposition from other ideas united in the same consciousness, because the mind is too narrow to contain several ideas opposing one another. Absent-mindedness, and in extreme cases anesthesia, likewise follows from the subject's inability to entertain several ideas in consciousness simultaneously. The subject must necessarily ignore certain excitations if she is to perceive others. Finally, alternation is explainable from the same conception of the reduced field of consciousness. What happens is that subjects become anesthetic in certain body parts, because they simply cannot retain enough excitations in the mind. Forced to concentrate on the anesthetic left arm, they lose the ability to feel the right arm, or, in the words of Janet (ibid., p. 311), "they lose on one side what they seem to have gained on another."

So far Janet's description and explanation of the symptoms of hysteria was basically unaltered. His understanding and selection of the major stigmata had changed but the basic conception of (lack of) personal perception, synthesis, and the resulting subconscious had remained unchanged. He now, however, added that it was not enough to describe and explain the properly hysterical stigmata, because hysterics share several common or general stigmata with other mental patients, notably with neuropaths, subjects who show diminished nervous strength. Among these general stigmata, he reckoned a lack of feeling and will, and the "sentiments of incompleteness" discussed above (cf. Janet, 1903a). He concluded that the relation between the symptoms of neuropaths and hysterics was as follows:

It is easy to summarize, in a word, these general disturbances of neuropaths. It is a mental depression characterized by the disappearance of the higher functions of the mind, with preservation and often exaggeration of the lower functions; it is a *lowering of the mental level*. So we may say, in short, that hysterics present us with the following stigmata: a depression, a lowering of the mental level, which takes the special form of a retraction of the field of consciousness (Janet, 1907/1963, p. 316).

In this way, Janet linked the properly hysteric stigmata to the retraction of the field of consciousness, while he linked the general stigmata to the lowering of the mental level or nervous strength. Hysteria was still (cf. Janet, ibid., p. 332) a malady of personal synthesis characterized by the retraction of the field of personal consciousness and a tendency to dissociation and emancipation of the systems of ideas and functions that constitute personality. But in addition it had become a special case of a nervous depression based on the exhaustion of the "functions of the encephalon." As Janet explained, it will be the more complex, higher, and ontogenetically newer functions that suffer most from such a lowering of nervous strength; the simple and older ones may function more or less normally. Our nervous strength presents oscillations, it is diminished by hereditary predisposition, disease, fatigue, and emotion. This diminution of nervous tension may bring about a general lowering of all the functions, but especially of the highest.

We may conclude, then, that the notion of nervous strength or mental level and its oscillations due to both internal and external factors became increasingly dominant in Janet's thinking. This notion allowed Janet to compare normal and mentally sick subjects on the dimension of nervous strength and to make increasingly general remarks about normal subjects. It also allowed him to regard hysteria as just one, albeit very special, case of the mental diseases characterized by a lowering of the mental level.

Incidentally, the fact that Janet discussed both anorexia and bulimia among the hysterical afflictions allows us to gain some insight into the historical nature of this disease, or rather its diagnosis. It can be seen that Sulloway's (1992, p. 59) remark that hysteria has mysteriously disappeared in the course of the twentieth century and that present-day neurologists see this disease only once or twice in a lifetime of medical practice is only partially right. No doubt, such symptoms as hysterical paralysis and fits have become increasingly rare, a fact that is difficult to explain (Libbrecht and Quackelbeen, 1995; Micale, 1995) and which Janet from a theoretical viewpoint might have deplored. For Janet (e.g., 1907a/1963, p. 185) always emphasized the analytic power of the disease, which dissolves complex functions into their composite parts, and he wasn't very far from Féré's claim that hysterics are "the frogs of experimental psychology." But the other side to the question of the virtual disappearance of hysteria is one of diagnosis and classification. Present-day medical doctors wouldn't readily classify subjects suffering from anorexia or bulimia as hysterics, nor would they regard a severe depression as being potentially hysterical. In Freud and Janet's time, however, such syndromes still classified as hysterical. It seems, then, that the older Janet (1930c/1961, p. 127) was at least partially right when he claimed that the mysterious clinical diminution of the disease is due to a reclassification of still existing pathological syndromes. The continuity between older theories and classifications of disease and present-day medical knowledge is, of course, a fascinating topic that we cannot possibly explore in the present context (cf. Alam and Merskey, 1992; Micale, 1993a; 1995; Pope, Hudson, and Mialet, 1985; Shoenberg, 1975). Suffice it say that on a very general level Janet's theory of hysteria utilizes much older ideas about the origin of disease that survived in some form in our contemporary conceptions. On the other hand, when Janet speaks of the lowering of the mental level, its causes (emotions, fatigue), and its corollaries (enhanced susceptibility for mental pathology), one cannot help but think of the present-day theories about the relation between various forms of stress, the immune system, and disease.

From Anxiety to Ecstasy

During the next two decades Janet (1910a) first published a book on neuroses (by which he meant psychasthenia and hysteria) in which he summarized some of his earlier views. Neuroses were regarded as a form of arrested development of a function or group of functions. In neurosis the highest aspect of a function, i.e., the adaptation of the function to momentary reality, is not reached or lost due to disease, stressful circumstances, etc. It is therefore a "disease of development" (Janet, 1910a, p. 387). According to Janet, this explained why anatomy cannot yet discover the possible cerebral basis of neurotic disorders:

Anatomy, in fact, studies particularly and necessarily the older organs, which are well delimited and identical in all men. In a word, it studies the organs of the functions that have reached a stable state; it cannot know the future organs, those which as yet exist only in a rudimentary form, which are still being formed, and which, consequently, are neither clearly perceptible, nor well delimited or identical in all men (Janet, 1910a, p. 389).

With this statement, Janet firmly opted for a functional and developmental view of mental disease. Higher mental functions are not necessarily located in specific organs, may be executed in various ways, and are the result of a development that may get arrested on particular occasions. It is a statement that would have appealed to Vygotsky, who espoused a similar view of the localization of higher mental processes (Van der Veer & Valsiner, 1991; see Chapter 8).

Janet's next project was a thorough study of (the history of) the various forms of existing psychotherapy, the basic ideas behind them, and their chances of success, which resulted in his lengthy, masterful, and witty book, *Les médications psychologiques* (Janet, 1919), translated, as *Psychological Healing* (Janet, 1925). This was followed by *La médicine psychologique* (Janet, 1923a/1980), which can be more or less seen as a summary of his historical work on various psychotherapies. These books were interspersed with a large number of papers that dealt with case histories (e.g., Janet, 1910b), realms of the mind (e.g., the subconscious; Janet, 1910c; 1910d; 1910e), theories (e.g., psychoanalysis; Janet, 1913a; 1914a; 1915c), and concepts (e.g., the notion of psychological tension and its oscillations; Janet, 1915a; 1920a; 1920b; 1921a; 1921b; 1921c; 1923b).

Finally, Janet published what can easily be regarded as one of the most remarkable books in the history of psychology: a 1,225-page study written to explain the symptoms of one patient, called Madeleine, published as *From Anxiety to Ecstasy* (Charpentier, 1927; Janet, 1926b; 1928b; Wallon, 1928). Janet had been following this case for twenty-two years, since the 1890s, and described the case in great detail. Madeleine had been a sensitive, timid, and sickly child who soon developed neurotic symptoms and obsessions about religion. As she grew older, these became more pronounced until she displayed all the symptoms of a full-fledged religious mystic. She went through states of ecstasy and bliss in which she felt united with God and identified herself with God, Jesus, and Mary. These states were alternated by less benevolent ones during which she felt deserted by God, had feelings of emptiness and utter boredom, or was eaten by doubts regarding all sorts of moral and religious issues. Finally, she knew periods of relative tranquility and equilibrium, when she was no longer obsessed by religious matters – although she stayed a profoundly religious woman – and showed more mundane and social interests. This is also the state in which she was finally able to leave the Salpêtrière, where Janet treated her for a number of years.

What Janet did in his book was to analyze the various mental states of the patient in great detail, to relate them to her physical problems, and to describe the evolution of her disease during her lifetime. During the state of ecstasy, for example, Madeleine displayed strong physical inactivity combined with much internal speech. She could not be reached ("woken up") by anyone except for Janet and showed symptoms of catatonia, i.e., she could hold her arms in fixed positions for very long periods. During this state she did not react to environmental stimuli but at the same time was completely aware of what was going on in this environment. The subject of her thought was God, or rather God and Madeleine. God spoke to her, gave her moral advice, and stated philosophical and religious ideas (which Janet found rather crude and naive). Her feelings of a complete union with God sometimes had rather explicit sexual undertones and also led her to adopt the position of someone who is being crucified, and to develop stigmata in feet and hands. She had religious visions and replayed scenes of the life of Jesus, feeling with great confidence that she was being inspired by God. More generally, there was a feeling of deep insight in ultimate truths and a sense of pureness and joy that was impossible in other states. In sum, Janet remarked, Madeleine showed all the phenomena known from the descriptions of the classic religious mystics such as Saint Theresa of Avila (Janet, 1926b; p. 197).

In his attempt to explain these phenomena (which he described in his characteristic dry and somewhat ironic manner, comparing them with the symptoms of various mental diseases), Janet first paid attention to Madeleine's beliefs (*croyances*). He argued that in her periods of ecstasy Madeleine was in a state of delirium quite common among other, nonreligious, patients and during which reflective belief is being replaced by (lower) assertive belief. On the level of assertive belief, subjects simply hold to be true what is being asserted without questioning it. Words such as "inspiration," "revelation, "miracle," and "magic" are "but the expression of an absolute belief that imposes itself without reflection and reasoning" (Janet, 1926b; p. 373). Fascinating was Janet's description of his attempts to detect the origin and nature of Madeleine's stigmata. For months in a row he tried to outrule the possibility of a causative role of external factors (e.g., Madeleine scratching herself, applying bandages, etc., until he finally resigned and concluded that for longer periods there is no way one can prevent a hospital patient from damaging herself). In the end, Janet concluded that Madeleine's stigmata were the result of a combination of external factors (the patient's exerting pressure on her limbs) and internal factors (differences in blood circulation connected with the menstrual cycle). As to Madeleine's union with God, Janet reached the conclusion that in the end it was a normal love affair. Neurotic people

are in need of love and guidance and certitude in love. The love that
Madeleine all her life was searching for was that of a person who
protects her, takes her decisions, comforts her, etc. Being very timid,
she craved for such a love but couldn't realize it. Here, the advantages
of God are quite clear: He is invisible and almighty and does what
Madeleine wishes Him to do. Madeleine doesn't have to adapt her
conduct to Him, as she would have to do with people of flesh and
blood. God requires no energy, gives love and truth, and knows all of
Madeleine's most intimate desires perfectly well. His advice is consequently perfectly adapted to her wishes, and His love is guaranteed
for ever. In sum, God satisfies all the needs of the psychasthenics of
this world, who lack the energy or force to join in the struggle for love
and a social position. He gives perfect guidance and comfort at very
little costs: One merely must sit still and contemplate His being. Madeleine, with her chronic lack of energy, her diseases and timidity, was
unable to confront the real world, which requires constant adaptation
and expenditure of energy. Her religious fantasies compensated for
her inability to establish social ties with genuine persons. In sum,
"Madeleine, who all her life has presented the aspiration to love and
the incapability to establish social relationships of love, has succeeded
to realize this love in a delirium" (Janet, 1926b, p. 519).

The different states (of doubt, of ecstasy, etc.) that Madeleine went
through, are all well known from different psychiatric diseases. The
state of religious ecstasy, for instance, is surprisingly similar to a state
of morphine intoxication (Janet, 1928b, p. 655). What made Madeleine
(and similar to other religious mystics) more or less unique was the
combination and succession of various symptoms. As always, Janet
argued that the most important causative role in the succession of
various mental states (such as in bipolar diseases) was the amount of
available psychological force or energy. The ecstatic state, for example,
invariably developed when the subject was considerably tired: All
energy-consuming movements and actions are suppressed, and the
subjects concentrate on very simple mental actions. Ecstatic states
occur in nonreligious patients as well and, in fact, it may be concluded
that although Madeleine's symptoms took a religious form, there was
nothing in them that was specifically religious. Nor can we say that
religious education in any important way contributed to her symptoms (Janet, 1928b, p. 665).

Implicitly, Janet's analysis of Madeleine's symptoms implied a view of religion, a view that was not received very favorably among believers (Ellenberger, 1970, p. 396). Horton (1924), who attended Janet's course on the "Evolution of Moral and Religious Conduct" at the Collège de France in the Winter of 1921–1922, has presented Janet's views on the origin of religion in the most elaborate form. Janet discussed forerunners of religion proper through all the levels of his mental hierarchy but situated the advent of the idea of invisible spirits or gods on the reflective level. Crucial was the fact that speech became disconnected from action (the case of "inconsistent language," discussed below). Duplicity, or double conduct, now became possible as people's actions no longer necessarily coincided with their words (Janet, 1926b, p. 252). In the words of Horton: "Animism springs up spontaneously at the moment when you first learn the necessity of distinguishing between the man who talks and acts as if he were your friend, and the invisible, inaudible enemy who lurks behind him. Previous to this there could be no conception of the human spirit as distinct from the human body" (Horton, 1924, p. 30).

Human beings wished to ally with these disembodied spirits as they tend to have a strong need for direction and love. Friends or therapists can satisfy this need to some extent but cannot generally compete with an ideal, all-powerful, all-comprehending director and friend.

However, at the still higher rational and experimental level of Janet's hierarchy (see below) different factors make for the decline of religion. Most harmful for religious belief were logic and philosophy, but above all experimental science, this "conscious cult of success, the effort to subject all beliefs to the impartial and stern judgment of external nature" (Horton, 1924, p. 43). Philosophy cannot take religion's place, as it leads to analysis and dissection and fails to meet the need for guidance and inspiration. But Janet claimed that spiritualism (conversations through mediums with spirits) and romanticism (the worship of certain emotions, nations, races, etc.) could satisfy people's basic needs to some extent. Psychotherapy as well would take the place of religion, as it is often more capable of remedying the states of mental depression for which religion was traditionally thought to be the best remedy. Another substitute of religion – popular among scientists – might become the worship of progress. The really strong and mentally well, however, do not need religion, they have confidence in themselves and in the world (Horton, 1924, p. 48).

Toward a Theory of Conduct

From Anxiety to Ecstasy was the last book in which Janet gave detailed and lengthy descriptions of the various symptoms of a mental patient. In the books that followed, he attempted to present the outlines of his general approach to psychology, the theory of conduct. Elements of this theory can be traced to the turn of the century (Ducret, 1984, p. 604; Janet, 1898; 1903a), but in its semidefinitive form it only emerges in the late 1920s (e.g., Janet, 1928a; 1928b; 1929; 1930a; 1932; 1935; 1936). Characteristic of Janet's theory of conduct are three interconnected themes that together form a sociogenetic account of the origin and nature of mind. By the late 1920s and early 1930s, these themes were present in virtually every book or paper Janet published, and for the study of his sociogenetic views it makes little difference to which publication one refers.

In the following we will first discuss these three general themes. Because of their intimate connection this will inevitably introduce a certain amount of redundancy. These themes are: (a) the idea that all mental acts are originally social; (b) the idea that all human conduct is originally related to actions; and (c) the idea of the developmental nature of conduct.

The Social Origin of Mental Acts

The idea that all private mental acts have a social origin figured very prominently in Janet's later writings (e.g., Janet, 1928, pp. 148, 172; 1935, pp. 71, 81; 1936, pp. 55–6). Throughout his career he had been dealing with the topic of social influence (e.g., the use of hypnosis, the debate about the role of suggestion), but he now – under the influence of Baldwin, Höffding, James, Royce, and others – began emphasizing that it is social others who play a constitutive role in the genesis of personality. In itself such a point of view is still of limited value. The important thing is to show how this general statement might be true and what are its implications.

Janet stated the theme in a variety of ways. Explicitly, in the form of a so-called law of psychological development and, less explicitly, in the form of statements about the origin of humans' higher mental processes, such as memory, thought, and language. The theme is also evident in his theory about the hierarchic structure of the human mind (see below).

In its explicit form, Janet's thesis becomes clear from the following quote from *The Evolution of Memory and the Notion of Time*:

Together we have studied the interior thought of man for a long time and we have arrived at conclusions that seem to me to be largely true and useful, although they somewhat diminish what is called the dignity of thought: Internal thought is a way of talking to oneself, a way to inform oneself. All forms of social conduct performed vis-à-vis others have their private repercussions. All things we do vis-à-vis others, we do them vis-à-vis ourselves; we treat ourselves as another (Janet, 1928a. p. 22).

The theme reappeared in *The Psychological Evolution of Personality*. One of the fundamental claims of this book is that one is not born a personality (cf. Levitin, 1982), but that personality is a human construct, or invention. On these grounds, Janet resisted any attempt at explaining personality by exclusive reference to biological, or associational, findings. He argued that personality develops as we attribute to ourselves exactly the same features and attitudes that we first attributed to others and that others attributed to us (cf. Janet, 1919, p. 268; 1935, p. 225). In Janet's own words:

The studies of two American philosophers, Josiah Royce and William James, have helped to establish that our personality is above all a social product. Their work consists particularly in showing that the notion of the personality commences chiefly with the personalities of others that we build before our own personality, or, to be more exact, that the two personalities are constructed together and that the one perpetually influences the other. The child first distinguishes its mother, its nurse, the persons who surround it, it gives them different roles, it expects different forms of conduct and it reacts to these forms of conduct in different ways. The separation of persons [i.e., the making of a distinction between persons; JV & RV] is at first social and it is only subsequently – applying Baldwin's law – that we apply to ourselves what we have first applied to others.

The persons we live among give us a certain social function and force us to fulfill it. They attribute a particular character to us and often educate us in order that we preserve this character. Finally, and most importantly, they give us a unique name, compel us to keep it, to distinguish ourselves from other persons who have other names, to connect to this name the actions and intentions that have their point of departure in our organism and to connect to the name of others the actions and intentions that depend on their organism, in the story that we construct of both them and ourselves (Janet, 1936, pp. 55–6).

In this quote we can distinguish three, mutually related, aspects that partially overlap with the three themes (the social, action-based, and developmental origin of the mind) mentioned above. First, there is a clear element of constructivism (see the quote on Kant, below). Persons are said to actively build or construct their own personality on the basis of the opportunities afforded by the social (in the sense of social-interactional) environment. Janet did not provide detailed descriptions of how this process might take place. It is clear, however, that he attached much importance to different forms of imitation that had been described in great detail by, notably, Baldwin, Guillaume (1925), and Tarde to whose work he time and again referred (e.g., Janet, 1926c; 1935; 1936; 1937a). Second, in many places – although not in the quote given above – he clearly suggested some chronology in the sense that the social comes first and is *followed* by the individual (e.g., "Let us not forget . . . the general rule . . . : it is that *after* having constructed the personage of our fellow-man we construct our person-age for ourselves in the same way," Janet, 1929, p. 334; our emphasis).

This was the view that would later become well known among psychologists as one of the views most typical for Vygotsky, although he himself clearly and repeatedly referred to it as "Janet's law" (see Chapter 8). Janet's view that individual higher mental processes originate in social interaction implied that even the most intimate private mental processes (e.g., fantasies, wishes) have a social origin and bear the mark of this origin (see below). Third, and intimately connected with the second point, Janet clearly implied that higher social functions such as memorizing are first carried out externally and only subsequently become available as internal functions (e.g., "all social psychological laws have two aspects: an exterior aspect concerning other people, an interior aspect concerning ourselves. Almost always . . . the second form is posterior to the first one," Janet, 1929, p. 521). Here the notion of chronology is combined with the outer–inner distinction. Higher mental processes are first carried out in the interpersonal, external plane, and only subsequently in the private (intrapersonal), internal plane. Young children cannot hide their feelings, are not capable of secrecy, wear their hearts on their sleeves. It is only gradually that they become capable of hiding their feelings, of keeping secrets, of developing a private, inner sphere of fantasies, wishes, and beliefs (cf. Elias, 1991).

These are still, however, very general claims, which ideally should be defended by way of theoretical or empirical arguments. As will be seen below, Janet most often relied on theoretical arguments – e.g., inventing mythical stories about the origin of actions in the history of mankind – but he did also at times refer to clinical findings to illustrate his point of view. This is evident, for example, in his discussion of the social nature of human memory. Time and again Janet stated that memorization is adapted to circumstances, it is a social conduct. Memory, he argued, is only needed when there are other persons to whom one can communicate the experienced events. Discussing the case of a patient called Irène, Janet stated that he had often noticed the way patients adapt their account of past events to the person of the listener. This is so because memory is a social event, it is a conduct of the patient toward the physician who is interrogating her. We know, argued Janet, that Irène will repeat to herself the conduct she displayed toward me, and likewise she will interrogate herself the way I did her before. He concluded that this patient's conduct was thoroughly social all the time: "although she may be alone, it is still a social conduct" (Janet, 1928a, p. 213; cf. 1935, p. 87; see Chapter 2).

The social nature of human memory does also follow from Janet's account of its ontogenetic development. As stated above, his argument was that there would be no need for memory if there were no other people to relate the memorized events to. In his view, children begin committing the experienced phenomena to memory because they wish to tell their mothers what happened. This is their primary motive for memorizing things, and it is a typically human one. It followed for Janet that human memory was not to be equated with the memory of animals, which he considered to be of a qualitatively different type depending heavily on the formation of associations (Janet, 1936, pp. 159–69; see also below). More generally, Janet argued that all development of human thought is above all directed by social needs, i.e., the needs to understand each other and to communicate. He repeatedly illustrated this theme by telling his story of the sentinel. According to this simile, a group of people is living somewhere in the wilderness, supposedly in some distant past of mankind. To protect themselves from predators and enemies, they have appointed some persons to act as sentinels. These persons are standing at some distance from the area where the people as a whole are living. Now, when the enemy approaches, two things can happen. If the sentinels are quite near their base, they will shout and, thus, warn their people. If, however, the sentinels are far away from their camp, shouting would be senseless suicide. Instead, they memorize what they see, and

silently run to their camp. In both cases, Janet concludes, social organization enormously extends the power of the senses. The sentinels
literally form the eyes and ears of their fellowmen. Thus, society is
able to overcome time and absence. Memory, specifically, is a social
invention to overcome time and absence (Janet, 1928a, p. 233).

Generalizing, one might say that all seemingly private psychological functions, such as language and memory, are originally and essentially social. They all evolved out of the need to communicate with
others. In the case of memory, children keep track of their own conduct in order to be able to relate it to their mothers. This track-keeping
in itself serves an important function for the child for it makes coherent and organized behavior possible in the individual domain (Janet,
1936, p. 121). This example forms another illustration of Janet's fundamental claim – made well known by Vygotsky (see Chapter 8) –
that all higher, typically human forms of conduct have a social origin:
They exist first between people, as social, interpsychological acts, and
only afterward become transformed to private, intrapsychological processes.

The Origin of Conduct in Action

The theme of action and its importance for psychology was present
in several of Janet's books (cf. Elmgren, 1967, pp. 74–86), but it was
most eloquently defended in his *The Evolution of Memory and the Notion
of Time* (1928a). In this book, Janet argued that human higher mental
functions, such as language, emotions, and memory, are intimately
connected to action: language, because it is originally a command to
perform some action; emotions, because they are actions, or regulators
of actions (cf. Janet, 1935, p. 100); and memory, because it is originally
a postponed action (*une action différée*). By actions Janet (e.g., 1938)
meant observable movements of the human body, and his aim was to
connect as many mental processes as possible with these objectively
observable processes. In this he sided with behaviorism, although he
rejected the behaviorist approach, because it was of no use for the
study of the specifically human, higher mental processes (Janet, 1926b;
1938; Subercaseaux, 1927; see above).

The case of language – or rather speech – is particularly interesting.
Why should speech be originally a command? Actually, this sugges-
tion was part of a longer discussion on the origin of social actions.
Janet considered the action of commanding one of the most important

social acts. In his view it had a peculiar character: In normal situations we perform all parts of the action (initiation, continuation, completion) ourselves. Referring to clinical findings, Janet argued that the initiation of any action is always the most difficult stage. It is generally characterized by special gestures, movements, and cries that betray the effort involved. Janet speculated that human orders developed out of these initial cries. In this respect humans differ from animals. The barking of dogs chasing their prey is the signal for other dogs to follow. When human beings give orders, they restrict themselves to the initial cry and do not perform the rest of the action. While the dog goes on running, the human chief gives the signal – the cry of initiation – but does not continue his action: His subordinates will take care of its continuation and completion. Janet claimed that this is typical of commands and, more generally, of all human social acts: They are actions shared between several individuals in which each of these individuals performs only one part of the action (Janet, 1929, pp. 182–9).

Human speech has grown out of these primordial orders, Janet asserted, and speech has retained its commandlike character. This is also the reason why Janet considered speech to be an important second source of stimulation. In his view, elementary forms of behavior could be explained by reference to external stimuli from the surroundings, but at a more advanced level of behavior speech interferes. Janet considered speech to be the most important form of social stimulation and he concluded that "our actions are determined by those two great sources: the stimulations that come from the external world and the stimulations that come from society" (Janet, 1929, p. 419).

More generally, Janet endorsed the view, also to be found in the writings of Claparède and Piaget, that we first perform actions and only afterward – post factum – become consciously aware of them. He claimed that he found this principle independently from Claparède, but borrowed the latter's terminology, because it had known more success in the scientific community. Thus, he used Claparède's term *prise de conscience* for the process of becoming consciously aware of one's own conduct (Janet, 1928a, pp. 163,234).

It is interesting to note that Janet defended his action-oriented approach partially on epistemological grounds. One might even argue (cf. Ducret, 1984, p. 609; Prévost, 1973, p. 33) that Janet's system was in a sense a reply to Cartesian epistemological thinking. While Descartes built his metaphysical system on the indubitable premise that the individual thinks (*cogito*), and deduced all other phenomena from this first principle, Janet's psychology began from the other side in claiming that the right first principle is not *cogito*, but *ago* (I act), and deducing consciousness. In Janet's own words this reasoning sounded as follows: "To begin the study of psychology with thought is ... taking the risk of becoming incomprehensible ... Psychology is no other thing than the science of human action. Thought is only a detail and a form of these actions" (Janet, 1928a, p. 23). One year later he elaborated this point:

Philosophers, I believe, have made a big mistake. Since Plato, they have always considered the mind as something complete that was formed once and for all and in which all phenomena had the same value and the same reality ... and I think that thought is not, as Descartes thought, the point of departure for intellectual life. Thought did not exist in the beginning; it existed in the end. It was a late development. (Janet, 1929, pp. 403–4; cf. 1936, p. 33)

Janet was by no means the first, of course, to claim that human mental functioning gradually develops as the individual is *acting* within a complex social environment, and it is not difficult to find both predecessors and followers of his point of view. Interestingly enough, various thinkers have invoked the Gospel by John – in which (following Greek mystical tradition) it is written that "in the beginning was the word" – as their point of reference. Goethe (1832/1975, p. 44), for example, was one of the first who tried to improve the Bible by retorting with the obvious "in the beginning was the act" (*Im Anfang war die Tat*).

In his turn, Goethe inspired such thinkers as Gutzmann (1922, p. 72), Vygotsky (1934, pp. 317–18; see Chapter 8), and Wallon (1942/1970, p. 5), all who developed versions of an action-oriented psychology. Prévost (1973, p. 55) argued that for Janet *agitur* (there is *being acted* – no subject) might possibly have been an even more appropriate formula than *"ago,"* as Janet saw conduct as being a common act of the person and the object (cf. Chapter 5). Objects as such he regarded as human constructions (Janet repeatedly doubted whether our classifications and denominations correspond to some real distinctions in reality) and the person (the "I" of *"cogito"* and *"ago"*) as gradually evolving. It seems that he did accept the existence of a reality "as such," but it was a reality whose qualities could be revealed only imperfectly by human actions (Subercaseaux, 1927). Janet realized that this position was akin to some form of Kantianism (and to Bergson's metaphysics) and at times he expressed this affinity explicitly:

Kant already said: Time and space are no things; they are forms of the mind . . . that are applied to things. I think we have to go a bit further. They are no forms . . . [but] constructions of the mind. Everything in our human knowledge is a construction of the mind . . . space and time are likewise constructions of the mind (Janet, 1928a, p. 619).

It thus seems that Janet opted for an active Kantianism in which the categories or forms of human knowledge – including space and time – are gradually invented by the acting individual in both phylogeny and ontogeny. As has been remarked by Prévost (1973), this epistemological position was echoed by Piaget in his theory of cognitive development (Atkinson, 1983; Kitchener, 1986). More recently, Ducret (1984, pp. 469–86; pp. 604–32) conclusively demonstrated that Piaget indeed heavily relied on Janet in this respect.

It can be concluded that Janet advocated an action-oriented approach in psychology that had strong roots in his epistemological viewpoints and was strengthened by his analyses of clinical cases and speculations about the origin of human acts. Historically, his emphasis on the action nature of mental processes was also due to his intimate knowledge of the philosophy of Bergson to whom he frequently referred and whom he called "one the greatest initiators of the psychology of action" (Janet, 1936, p. 151).

The Developmental Nature of Conduct

Janet repeatedly claimed that human mental processes have evolved over thousands of years and will continue to develop. For humans this mental development is culturally-based and independent of physiological structures. Talking about the transfer of information of one generation to the next, Janet stated that the most primitive form of transfer – characteristic of lower organisms – is heredity. Higher organisms developed the capacity to give examples and imitate them, and, finally, with the onset of mankind, language and instruction evolved (Janet, 1928a, p. 15). This "extracerebral" mental development was in principle open to the future as is obvious from Janet's words in the same book:

We are at the beginning of a revolution . . . our descendants . . . will have quite different psychological conceptions and display quite different phenomena. . . . The mistake of traditional psychology was to present . . . psychological forms of conduct as definitive facts, as an acquired state . . . which existed once and for all, which had always existed and would always exist (Janet, 1928a, p. 160; cf. p. 502).

As concrete examples of processes that must have taken thousands of years to develop Janet often mentioned the manufacture and use of tools (discussing the findings on animal tool use by Köhler [1921b], Brainard [1930], and Guillaume and Meyerson [1930a; 1930b] in great detail), speech (referring to the work of Cassirer [1929], Delacroix [1927], Head [1920], and Mourgue [1921] on aphasia), and the more general ability to use signs (Janet, 1928a, pp. 581–2), but he also claimed that emotions have become more complicated and intellectualized (Janet, 1928a, pp. 173, 238). Finally, consciousness as such he considered to be a relatively recent invention that consisted of several hierarchically organized layers of psychological phenomena (Janet, 1928a, p. 162). It is clear that Janet thought that in ontogeny as well the human child must go through various stages of development, or enculturation, in order to become a fully conscious person.

The theme of the developmental nature of mental functioning can perhaps best be illustrated by referring to Janet's discussions of the phylogenetic and ontogenetic origin of memory. Janet discerned several stages (or levels) in the development of memorization and asserted that it rested at first on the symbolism of body movements. In this first stage, remembering consisted of enacting the experienced event. Janet believed that this original form of remembering still had not fully disappeared in contemporary human beings and he claimed that these "images still exist for us. I fear they are no more than fossil remains . . . of ancient procedures that tend to disappear." The next stages in the development of memory were formed by remembering based on different levels of verbal "coding," such as (simple) description, narration, and, finally, fabulation (Janet, 1928a, pp. 240, 5).

Interestingly enough, Janet also discerned another line of development of human memory: that of memory based on material objects. Most probably inspired by his friend Lévy-Bruhl (1910; 1922), he suggested that the first human memories were memories of objects and the use of these objects. He mentioned the use of knots in handkerchiefs and the buying of material souvenirs by tourists as examples of material memory aids (Janet, 1928a, pp. 262–3; 1936, p. 204). He also referred to the habit of making special drawings of these objects (inspired by Flournoy) and suggested that here we should look for the origin of writing (cf. Vygotsky and Luria, 1930, for similar reasoning). In short, what we call memory, is a very complex whole of intellectual operations that become superimposed on one another (Janet, 1928a, p. 349).

In view of the above, it is not surprising that Janet claimed human memory to differ greatly from animal memory. Animals – and infants, and some of the mentally disturbed – are dependent on associations and their reminiscences are inflexible, not adaptable to varying circumstances (Janet, 1928a, pp. 213, 223). Janet coined this type of memory *restitutio ad integrum*, meaning that one stimulus triggers the other, associated stimuli, which leads to the restoration of the whole. All this, in Janet's opinion, had nothing to do with human memory, which can be flexibly adapted to circumstances and is based on the telling of a story (*récit*) to oneself and others. Memory, in its highest form, is the telling of a story about the past in the present, i.e., to some specific person with some specific goal in mind. It has nothing to do with the searching for a carbon copy of past events that were filed away in some store, nor is it simply a reconstruction on the basis of memory traces and present knowledge. It is a reconstruction in the form of a story for a specific person, from a specific perspective. As such it is a quite complicated social process that may fail under various circumstances. For these reasons, Janet was – like Bartlett (1932/1977)[2] – quite critical of Ebbinghaus' (1885) contrived experimental approach. What persons normally do – even when learning lists of words – is not memorizing by simple repetition, but making use of various intelligent procedures, such as grouping words with a related meaning, or making clusters that have a certain rhythm. Janet (1928a, pp. 260–2) concluded that even under real-life circumstances greatly resembling Ebbinghaus' tasks "repetition is only one procedure amidst a multitude of others."

Naturally, these different levels of memorization have to be learned by the child, and had to be learned by mankind. The higher and more powerful ways of memorizing are heavily language-dependent. This is also the reason that infants do not have memories, Janet argued, and he saw no need to invoke psychoanalytic theories about repression to explain amnesia for childhood events (Janet, 1928a, p. 224).

Although the nature and order of Janet's developmental stages

---

[2] Interestingly enough, Bartlett (1932/1977, p. 293) read Janet (1928a), noting that: "Many of the points made by Janet have a close resemblance to the general line of approach which I have adopted in this volume. Perhaps I may be allowed to say that on neither side was there any possibility of interchange of ideas on the subject, and that though, in common with all other psychologists, I have for long had the greatest admiration for the psychological work of Prof. Janet, I had completed this part of my study before Janet's volumes appeared."

generally seem to have sprung from his work with mental patients (cf. Ducret, 1984, p. 617), he often used three types of arguments to justify his account of the phylogeny of human mental conduct.

First, he referred to the comparative study of animal and man. He was well aware of the empirical work of his contemporaries (see above), but did not shy away from inventing fictitious stories to argue the origin of specific behaviors. Prévost (1973, p. 62) has sternly remarked that several of these stories are rather unrealistic – e.g., cows are unpleasantly surprised by tigers – and suggested that Janet took his inspiration from the fables of La Fontaine.

Secondly, Janet suggested – as had many of his contemporaries – that today's Western children, mentally disturbed, and "primitive" (i.e., non-Western) people testify of Western man's mental evolution (e.g., Janet, 1928a, pp. 210, 240–1). Janet (1935, p. 25) considered these categories to be our "living documents" of the phylogenetic development that had taken place.

Finally, he claimed that earlier stages of human mental evolution are embodied in tools (Janet, 1935, p. 205) and in what he called "mental objects" (Janet, 1936, p. 28). The mental objects were actually typical, culturally based behaviors, such as the conduct of the apple basket discussed below. For Janet (1935, p. 28) they exemplified the "lifeless documents" of human mental evolution that we have at our disposal.

We may conclude that in Janet's view higher mental development in both phylogeny and ontogeny takes place by the gradual acquisition of resources that in time become available in the specific culture or society.

The Hierarchic Structure of the Mind

Janet's analyses of the three interconnected sociogenetic themes accumulated over the years and finally culminated in his theory of the hierarchic structure of the mind. The books he published on general psychological topics in the late 1920s and early 1930s (Charpentier, 1935; Janet, 1926c; 1928a; 1929; 1932; 1935; 1936) all discussed these topics from the viewpoint of this theory. The books themselves were based on the lectures Janet had been giving the Collège de France for several decades. In discussing specific subjects, Janet time and again referred back to lectures he had given one or two decades earlier. There is no doubt that part of these claims were made to substantiate priority claims, but they also reflected a genuine historical fact: since about 1905 Janet had been working on an elaborate and hierarchically organized theory of mind. In the tradition of Charcot's notion of objective psychology, he attempted to situate specific forms of conduct in his evolutionary system by considering them from various viewpoints. These regarded their presence in animals (the phylogenetic viewpoint; here he repeatedly discussed Köhler's findings), their presence in children (the ontogenetic viewpoint, in later years primarily discussed through Piaget), their presence in "primitive" people (the allegedly "historical" – in reality cross-cultural – viewpoint; mainly through Lévy-Bruhl and Durkheim), and their loss in disease (the pathological viewpoint; mainly through his own case histories and the findings of Head, Cassirer, Sherrington, and others). Analyzing various forms of conduct from these specific viewpoints, Janet attempted to determine their evolutionary age and to design a system of ever more complex and evolutionarily advanced conduct.

In Janet's view, mind consists of several layers originating in different periods of human phylogeny. It is obvious from his writings that he thought that the typically human higher mental functions are transmitted through culture and have to be acquired anew by each child in a long process of enculturation. Janet distinguished between phylogenetically older psychological functions that are represented by definite organs in the body and phylogenetically more recent ones that lack such organs but are somehow represented in different centers of the nervous system (see above). Thus, psychological functions are not all of the same kind and value, and may be arranged in a hierarchy. The lowest, and oldest, functions – also called *tendencies* in Janet's terminology – do not disappear as organisms develop, but become subordinated to the later, higher functions and form the basis of our psychological structures. They may take over control again when, for some reason (e.g., fatigue, pathology), the higher functions are out of order (Janet, 1936, pp. 122, 213). The higher functions, however, can develop a relative independence. The fact, for instance, that a person may lose the elementary function of vision and still retain the superior function of reflection, Janet (1930b, pp. 371–2) considered to be evidence for this claim. This notion may have inspired Vygotsky when he formulated his ideas about the cerebral substrate of mental functioning (Chapter 8; cf. Vygotsky, 1934d/1960, pp. 364–83).

What, then, are the layers of mind? In what order are psychological functions acquired? This is a problem to which Janet devoted much time and energy. He constantly revised his system. We will give a short description of the different levels using various of Janet's writings (e.g., 1921b; 1926b, pp. 201–43; 1928a, 202–43; 1938; 1936, pp. 30–1).

Janet ultimately distinguished nine levels, or tendencies of the mind, grouped into three broad categories: the lower, middle, and higher psychological tendencies (see Table 3.2. For slightly different schemes, involving eight or ten levels, see Janet, 1938; Bailey, 1928; and Subercaseaux, 1927).

The lower psychological tendencies (*les tendances psychologiques inférieures*) are, respectively, (a) the reflexive tendencies; (b) the perceptive-suspensive tendencies; (c) the sociopersonal tendencies; and (d) the elementary intellectual tendencies. These tendencies Janet called "psychological" to emphasize that we shouldn't abandon them to physiology, and "lower" because the chronology implies a hierarchy.

Janet's "reflexive tendencies" were equivalent to what we would call reflexes, or chains of reflexes. According to Janet, they are characteristically triggered by one single stimulus and have an explosive character. They are global, explosive actions, where all available forces are used at once. As such, reflexes form fixed action patterns, i.e., the organism has no possibility to change or withhold the response when the eliciting stimulus is presented.

A somewhat higher form of behavior is formed by the "perceptive-

Table 3.2. *Hierarchy of psychological phenomena (after Janet, 1938)*

Lower psychological tendencies
1. Reflexive tendencies
2. Perceptive-suspensive tendencies
3. Sociopersonal tendencies
4. Elementary intellectual tendencies

Middle psychological tendencies
5. Immediate actions and assertive beliefs
6. Reflective actions and beliefs

Higher psychological tendencies
7. Rational-ergetic tendencies
8. Experimental tendencies
9. Progressive tendencies

---

suspensive tendencies," which require the presence of two stimuli in order to be completed: one to stir the tendency and the other for its completion. A typical Janetian example of the perceptive-suspensive tendency is that of a beast of prey that sees, hears, or smells its potential victim (the first stimulus), but suspends its action until the prey is near enough (the second stimulus). This suspension implies a division of the primordial unitary act: The perceptive and motor parts are becoming separated as the stimulations of smell, hearing, and vision become separated from the sensation of actually having the prey in the mouth. The division of the act carries with it a certain primitive sense of temporality and the possibility of tendencies becoming latent. This latency, this potential waiting period, Janet considered to be a first sign of primitive intelligence. In his view, the organism now had added an intermediate third option to its behavioral repertoire that until then had consisted only of primitive, explosive reflexes and the possibility of not acting at all.

Janet's "sociopersonal tendencies" are, of course, particularly relevant for the purpose of this book. Janet claimed that it is at this stage that individual and group become gradually distinguished and he discerned two types of conduct, that toward one's own body and that toward the other. It is at this level of mental development that subjects start adjusting their acts to those of the social other, or *socius*, which gives rise to "doubles acts" (*actes doubles*), such as imitating, commanding, and obeying. As has been related above, according to Janet the individual first learns to react to the acts of his *socii* and only afterward learns to apply the same forms of conduct to himself.

It is not always very clear what Janet meant by the term double act, or double conduct. He seems to have used the word "double" in various ways, sometimes meaning "reciprocal" (see below), sometimes meaning "dual," and sometimes meaning simply "complicated." In the present context, he explained the concept by referring to the fact that all social conduct requires two types of stimulations. Suppose, Janet (1928a, p. 221) said, I want to show a person a lamp. Then two conditions have to be satisfied: The lamp and the person must be present. Looking to either a person or an object in itself would be just a simple perceptive act, but in the presence of another person I may perceive the lamp and draw the other person's attention to it. My act then consists of two parts: an external physical part (perception of the lamp), and a social part (drawing the other's attention to it). It is also possible, Janet continued, to perform a social act in the absence of either lamp or person. One then either describes the features of the (absent) lamp to the person or memorizes them (for the absent other). Janet concluded that all social acts consist of two parts: an external physical part and a social part. Crucial for social acts, then, seems to be that the conduct toward objects is transformed by the present or absent *socius*. The subject performs his or her actions with the image of the social other in mind. Elsewhere Janet explained that imitative behavior is only possible if the person being imitated tolerates this fact, i.e., consciously behaves in a way that allows imitators to copy the behavior.

Finally, the fourth level of the lower group of tendencies is that of the "elementary intellectual tendencies" (see Janet, 1935; 1936 for extensive discussions and many examples). It is the level of preverbal intelligence and of the beginnings of speech during which individuals become capable of creating intelligent, intermediate objects or forms of conduct. Janet often related the story of the "apple basket" as an example of a very elementary intelligent act (e.g. Janet, 1928a, pp. 252–5; 1936, p. 14). The story of (the invention of) the apple basket is at the same time a fine example of his peculiar metaphorical way of explaining things (to the lay audience listening to his lectures at the Collège de France) and we will therefore discuss it at some length. The apple basket stands for any object in which one can gather and transport several objects. Janet reasoned that at a specific time point in history this object (or conduct) must have been invented by some person of genius and that it is specific for a certain level of intellectual development. What is so intelligent about the use of apple baskets? Crucial for the use of an apple basket, Janet argued, is that one first has to fill it with a load of apples that will be consumed only at some later point of time. This implies, firstly, the postponement of immediate consummative action and the use of an intermediate object. Secondly, one has to fill the basket in anticipation of its later being emptied, which requires an understanding of the concept of reversibility. For this reason, Janet coined this behavior "double" or "reciprocal" conduct. In his opinion, examples of other reciprocal conduct were to tie and untie a knot, to make and recognize a portrait, to memorize and remember an event, and to buy a two-way ticket. He claimed – and Piaget would try to empirically demonstrate it – that this reversible character of elementary intelligent acts is beyond the intellectual abilities of small children and animals.

The level of elementary intellectual acts is also the level of the beginnings of speech, which in Janet's (1936, p. 116) analysis is also a double act of speaking and being spoken to. To exemplify the singular power of speech Janet often told the parable of the sentinel, related above, and he claimed that all lower forms of conduct will be transformed, or "intellectualized," by speech (Janet, 1928a, p. 217). Like Potebnya and Vygotsky (see Chapter 8), he explicitly stated that speech has not just a communicative function but a generalizing one as well (in the sense that one word may refer to a whole class of – sometimes very different – objects).

The level of "immediate actions and assertive beliefs" of the group of middle tendencies is characterized by the full development of speech. Speech now becomes dissociated from action and subjects start speaking to the *socii* and to themselves. As related above, at first the spoken word formed part of the beginning of an action, but now speech emancipates itself from bodily conduct (Janet, 1928a, pp. 291–2). Janet referred to this type of speech – i.e., speech disconnected from action – with different terms, such as "the language of conversations," "the play of language," and "inconsistent language" (e.g., Janet, 1937b). For him, the fact that speech became dissociated from actions had both positive and negative corollaries. A positive result was that it entailed the possibility of subjects talking to themselves, which leads to the beginnings of inner speech and thought. Subjects become conscious of their actions and the *cogito* comes within reach. A negative result was that it led to the myth of "the ghost in the machine" (Ryle, 1949). Janet argued that "the idea of a double, a spirit, existing invisibly behind the visible actions of the individual" could originate because thought is "dematerialized" speech. Another effect of the dissociation of action and speech was that persons can start hiding their intentions and develop the capacity of secrecy. Individuals can now develop a "personage," i.e., they can begin acting according to the picture they made of themselves and that they present to their fellowmen. They are now, in fact, performing a role and ascribing roles to other persons.

The next level Janet considered to be that of "reflective actions and beliefs." Reflection, according to Janet, issued from overt discussions between an individual and several *socii* (cf. the similar views by Bakhtin, Piaget, Rignano, and Vygotsky). This collective conduct also leads to inner discussions.

Finally, human beings reach the level of higher tendencies. This means first – at the level of "rational-ergetic tendencies" – the capacity to work, i.e., to accomplish chores and to endure fatigue and boredom. Janet (1926b, p. 229; 1928a, p. 229) gave as his opinion that "the value of a man can be measured by his capacity to accomplish chores."

At the next level – that of "experimental tendencies" – the subjects start taking into account experiential findings. Subjects now can experiment in a deliberate way, taking into account the results of their experiments in a systematic fashion. This then, marks the level of mature scientific thinking, but the attitude is not restricted to scientists and can be found in any person.

At the third, and highest, level, subjects reach the stage of fullest individuality. At this stage of "progressive tendencies" they realize that human beings are open toward the future. Subjects try to accomplish their individual goals, respecting the individual goals of others. In this connection, Janet wrote that we cannot foresee how far human beings will be able to develop. He summarized his genetic theory of mind with the following intriguing words:

Plants limit themselves to growing in space, the first acts of animals have permitted movements, [and] after that the displacements of the body that have gradually triumphed over space. The forms of conduct connected to time have been much later and much less fortunate, for we still limit ourselves to growing in time like plants grow in space . . . Will not man one day make progress in time analogous to that he has made in space? Evolution is not yet finished and human action has been and still will be a source of marvel (Janet, 1926b, pp. 233–4).

In subsequent works, Janet clarified this intriguing statement regarding the human being's conquest of time. Considering the construction of human memory as a first triumph over time (Janet, 1936, p. 169), he speculated about the future invention of the "paleoscope": an instrument to look back in time and see the things of the past that our memory couldn't retain (Janet, 1936, p. 155). Finally, he ventured as his opinion that one day human beings will be able to go back and forth in time, to visit their youth, and see the ones they loved and left behind (Janet, 1935, p. 155).

In a later encyclopedia article, Janet (1938) added that knowledge of the levels of tendencies as given in Table 3.2 is not enough: We also need to know why particular tendencies rather than others are activated. Here he evoked the twin concepts of psychological force (cf. Janet, 1937c; 1937d) and psychological tension, which he had been developing in the preceding two decades. Janet freely admitted that such concepts are hypothetical, that we know nothing of their possible physiological background, but insisted that they refer to real, observable phenomena. He claimed that psychological force is unequally distributed among individuals and that it varies with time. The presence of some social others may require very much of our force, while the presence of others may give us new force. The execution of different tasks requires different amounts of force: Tasks that have been carried out many times require less force than new ones and higher tendencies require more force than lower ones. The expenditure of psychological force may take place within seconds, but there is also conduct that requires a sustained and controlled expenditure of force over fairly long periods. This sustained expenditure of force requires high psychological tension; low psychological tension would lead to the immediate expenditure of all available psychological force. Janet ventured that higher tendencies require both more force and tension, and his favorite example was that of work (see above; cf. Janet, 1937d). Low levels of psychological force lead to low psychological tension, but the combinations "much force-low tension" and "little force-high tension" can occur. In the first case, the force is discharged immediately in various convulsions, attacks, etc. In the second case, we see agitated subjects whose mental state deteriorates the more they are rested, and who, apparently, are not able to canalize their force (energy) in useful ways. The picture that arises from Janet's discussions of psychological force and tension is that normal mental functioning requires the careful maintaining of an energy balance (cf. Elmgren, 1967, pp. 64–73). Energy-consuming meetings with members of the university bureaucracy must be followed by less costly ones with neighbors and preferably by exiting, energy-producing meetings with beloved social others. Therapists must attempt to restore the energy balance by prescribing rest and by suggesting the patients simplify their life, to economize action (Janet, 1925; Subercaseaux, 1927). The mentally sound person knows how to balance his or her psychological costs and gains and controls his psychological budget just like he takes good care of his financial budget.

Discussion and Conclusions

Janet advanced a vast number of concepts (e.g., the narrowing of the field of consciousness, the function of synthesis, the role of psychological tension and force, the function of reality, the need for direction) and defended a specific view of psychology with the emphasis on objectively observable conduct, the role of the social other, and evolution. In the end he gave much preference to the concepts of psychological force and tension. It is subjects who for one reason or another lack this force or energy who regress to lower forms of conduct, who cannot cope with reality, who cannot entertain energy-consuming relationships with social others, and who are in need of guidance and direction. In this world of tensions, we need enough energy to maintain ourselves and fulfill our ambitions. It is for this reason that Janet's psychology has been called dynamic and energetic (e.g., Subercaseaux, 1927, p. 214).

As has become clear in the preceding paragraphs, Janet's sociogenetic ideas were intimately connected with those of his predecessors and contemporaries and their sometimes peculiar and exotic nature should not blind us to the fact that he owed much to them. Space does not permit us to present an exhaustive picture of Janet's intellectual roots (cf. Ducret, 1984; Ellenberger, 1970; Elmgren, 1967; Valsiner and Van der Veer, 1988), but several influences deserve mentioning in this context. The theme of the action nature of human conduct, for example, was clearly shaped by his reading of Bergson (1939; 1944a) as Janet repeatedly acknowledged. The other themes of the social and developmental nature of human conduct evolved in close intellectual interaction with, for example, Durkheim, Guillaume, James, Köhler, Lévy-Bruhl, Royce (e.g., 1898b, pp. 169–7; 1901, pp. 245–66), Tarde, and, above all, Baldwin (e.g. 1895, pp. 334–8; cf. Valsiner and Van der Veer, 1988).[3] Baldwin's developmental approach, his treatment of the role of imitation, and his concept of the role of the social other – the *socius* in Baldwin's terms – had a prominent place in Janet's writings. Finally, the concept of a hierarchical structure of the mind shows close affinity with the ideas of contemporaries such as Kretschmer (1929) and Werner (1925) and owes much to the older theories of Jackson and Head, and the still older ones advanced by Maine de Biran and Moreau de Tours (cf. Janet, 1895b, p. 453).

In his turn, Janet exerted a profound influence on several of the major thinkers of psychology's history. The action theme, for example, was absorbed by such diverse thinkers as Piaget (who called Janet his

---

[3] Asked by Piaget in 1942 how he had managed to read Baldwin's difficult books, Janet replied "Above all I have regularly dined with him for a sufficient period of time" (Prévost, 1973, p. 298).

"maitre" and adopted, among other things, his epistemological Kantian position; Bringuier, 1977, p. 17), Wallon (cf. Van der Veer, 1996), and Leontiev (e.g., his so-called activity theory). Janet's themes of the developmental and social nature of human mental functioning were assimilated by various thinkers, but perhaps most actively by Vygotsky, who made several of Janet's claims well-known in the scientific community (cf. Van der Veer and Valsiner, 1988). Recently, there has been a revival of Janet's early ideas on automatism in the group of researchers who study the multiple personality syndrome.

The fact that Janet profoundly influenced several of the major thinkers of this century testifies to the value of his work, but it does not imply, of course, that a modern sociogenetic view should accept all of his claims. Janet's comparisons across developmental domains, for example, – e.g., regarding non-Western people as "living documents" of our past – now have become unacceptable (cf. Van der Veer and Valsiner, 1991). Nevertheless, Janet's three basic themes of a sociogenetic psychology can still be defended on theoretical and empirical grounds (cf. Ratner, 1991) and this in itself makes the study of his work worthwhile.

Tracing the roots of modern scientific thinking in the writings of the classics of psychology, as we tried to do in this long chapter, teaches modesty and makes one wonder about the value of much of the empirical work that has been done in the decades since Janet developed his system. Judging by Janet's writings it would seem that clinical insight, bold speculation, and a sound philosophy are at least as important requisites for scientific progress – if it exists at all in psychology – as rigorous empiricist experimentation. It is a conclusion that would have appealed to Janet (1936, p. 285; cf. Janet, 1895a, p. 574), who considered "philosophy the thread that should unite the pearls of observation."

CHAPTER FOUR

James Mark Baldwin's Theoretical Heritage

James Mark Baldwin (1861–1934) was one of the crucial contributors to the sociogenetic perspective in the social sciences. His interesting life course and theoretically sophisticated ideas have fascinated several of the developmental psychologists of the present time (Broughton, 1981; Cahan, 1984; Cairns, 1980, 1983, 1992; Mueller, 1976; Wozniak, 1982). Yet, much of his contribution to psychology and biology (see Campbell, 1988, Simpson, 1953) remains to be carefully reanalyzed. For that, Baldwin's own retrospect on his life and work provides thematic hints – his contributions that are of relevance entail a theoretical system of the social origin of the self, a concept of "organic evolution," and a methodology for what he called "developmental science" – in the form of a "genetic logic" (Baldwin, 1930, p. 30).

Baldwin and America: Development of the Thinker in His Social Contexts

Baldwin's life course maps well upon the sensitive period in the development of psychology in North America. The new discipline was being established on the North American continent, based on the socio-moral value system of the society which itself was in a turmoil during the last quarter of the nineteenth century. The aftermath of the Civil War was still there, while changes in U.S. society were taking place at a quick pace. Rapid industrialization and urbanization created both the fertile grounds and the limits for the establishment of psychology in the New World (Dolby, 1977). Baldwin himself has given a concise participant observer's account of the context in which American psychology emerged:

In America the influences which have tended to control psychological opinion have been mainly theological on one side and educational on the other. The absence of great native systems of speculative thought has prevented at once the rationalistic invasions into theology, which characterized the German development, and the attempts at psychological interpretation which furnished a supposed basis of fact to the idealistic systems. In Germany various 'philosophies of nature' sought to find even in objective science support for theoretical world-dialectic: and psychology fared even worse, since it is, *par excellence*, the theater for the exploitation of universal hypotheses. But in America men did not speculate much: and the ones who did were theologians. So naturally psychologists were theologians too. (Baldwin, 1894a, p. 364)

The role of religious undercurrents in social organization has always been the underlying reality in the United States. That reality continues to guide secular social thought in implicit ways. Thus, the focus on the community *as if it is necessarily benevolent* (to individuals), is evident in the thought of major American sociogenetic thinkers (John Dewey, Josiah Royce, George Mead). Nevertheless, there also exists an opposing undercurrent of basic distrust in social institutions (as a formalized kind of "hypercommunity"). The tendencies to *belong to* a community while emphasizing one's *individual rights* and preferences – ahead of those of any social group – can be seen to be paradoxically linked in a complex of feelings about the person-in-society in the case of many who have grown up in the United States.

Baldwin's Intellectual Course

Baldwin's life, work, and fate are in some sense good examples of the social processes of the American society, internalized by an ambitious young man, and externalized in the form of the variety of activities with which he was involved (see Baldwin, 1926, 1930). Like many American men of the 1880s, who later became psychologists, Baldwin at a time was not far away from ending up as a Protestant minister. However, the influence of McCosh at Princeton during his undergraduate years guided him into psychology.

Serious study of psychology in those days required being educated in Germany, where Baldwin went for three semesters in 1884–5 (spending a semester in Leipzig in Wilhelm Wundt's laboratory; another in Berlin with Friedrich Paulsen, and a third in Freiburg with Carl Stumpf). Most of the American psychologists of that time made

such trips. However, differently from his countrymen, whose fascination during their trips to Germany was with the technical organization
of experiments in Wundt's laboratory, Baldwin's main intellectual
benefit from the study trip was the introduction to Spinoza's philosophy in Berlin (see Baldwin, 1926, chapter 3; also Baldwin, 1902a, chapter 2). The work of Hermann Lotze likewise became a general source
of inspiration for Baldwin's ideas.

Baldwin returned to the United States as an instructor at Princeton
in 1886, followed by an appointment in 1887 at Lake Forest University
in Illinois. The latter position was jointly in philosophy and psychology. Baldwin's intellectual affiliations developed a clearly Francophile
focus. He visited Paris (the clinic of Charcot) and Nancy (the center of
hypnotism à la Bernheim) in 1892 (see his accounts of the trip in
Baldwin, 1892c, 1892d). From that time onward, Baldwin's closest
intellectual partner was Pierre Janet, with whom he remained close to
the end of his exile life, in Paris. He also benefited from the work of
Alfred Binet (see Binet, 1896), Gabriel Tarde, Theodore Flournoy (see
dedication in Baldwin, 1906), Edouard Claparède, and Henri Bergson
(Baldwin, 1926, 1930).

The Toronto Period

The crucial period in Baldwin's theoretical development can be
located in his years spent in Toronto (1889–93). It was here that he
was introduced to psychic phenomena of esoteric kinds. These phenomena – "animal magnetism" and cases of hypnotic, posthypnotic,
and quasi-hypnotic suggestion – were widely discussed among late
nineteenth-century intellectuals (see Chapters 2 and 3). Baldwin was
less than enthused by the myriad of "cases of visions of phantoms or
ghosts, premonitions of death" (Baldwin, 1926, p. 45), which he was
asked to examine. Yet psychology received its public appreciation –
then as well as now – from the marvelous capacities of the human
mind to see ghosts, imagine what heavens and hells are like, and try
to predict one's happy future. Baldwin had to diplomatically deal with
these "real-life phenomena" that were brought to him for scientific
scrutiny.

Fortunately, the miracle of human reproduction overrides that of
the esoteric phenomena. The second major feature of the Toronto-
period in Baldwin's life that is worth mentioning as of relevance for
his ideas, is the benefit Baldwin gained from direct contact with psychological phenomena in the practical context of taking care of his

two daughters (Helen, born 1889; Elizabeth, born 1891). Baldwin could be considered as one of the forebears of our contemporary fashion of emphasizing the role of fathers in the child care process. On occasions at which he wrote about issues of child care, his style of writing starts to resemble that of an evangelist whose main mission is to persuade fathers to participate in child care (e.g., see Baldwin, 1895, pp. 365–6). In his characteristically self-presentational way, Baldwin rarely missed the opportunity to bring to his readers examples of his own successes in the domain of parenting.

On the substantive side, Baldwin's observations of his own children constituted his major reality base for the advancement of his theoretical views. Observations of his daughters' motor actions made it possible for him to arrive at the formulation of the "persistent imitation" notion, which constitutes the basis for his "organic selection" viewpoint. Baldwin thus joined in with the productive tradition of psychologists who studied their own children (that is, subjects to whom the investigator has access for the whole twenty-four hours' period, without need to sign the now fashionable North American "parental consent forms"). Undoubtedly, the small numbers of child subjects (i.e., the psychologists' own children) investigated by Darwin, Preyer, Baldwin, the Sterns, the Bühlers, Piaget, Vygotsky, and others have provided science with greater synthesis of empirical and theoretical lines of investigation than the large numbers of subjects studied by investigators of others' children.

The Years at Johns Hopkins

Baldwin moved to Baltimore in 1903 to lead the establishment of a psychology laboratory there (the third he established at different North American universities). By that time he had lost most of his earlier interest in laboratory research, and was moving increasingly towards the development of his genetic logic (Baldwin, 1906, 1908a, 1911a, 1915). He also was on his way towards administrative prominence in the university world, which was terminated by his efforts to study psychology in the real world.[1] After spending a few years in

[1] His exploratory expedition to a Baltimore brothel – recorded through a coincidental police raid – was too much for the hypocritically moralistic "good society" of his contemporaries to bear. It tainted his possibilities to move ahead in his academic administrative ambitions, and he was forced to resign from Johns Hopkins in 1908 (see Richards, 1987, for the story).

Mexico City, at the Universidad Autonoma de Mexico, Baldwin emigrated to France, where he remained intellectually and socially active until the end of his life (1934).

Sociogenetic Ideas in Baldwin's Work

In his prophetic statement about the future of psychology in 1905, Baldwin claimed that: "The thought of the unity of social content is a great step toward the breaking down of any associational or other 'privately conducted' science. The psychology of the future will be social to the core; and its results, we surmise, will be revolutionary in logic, sociology, ethics, aesthetics, and religion – the disciplines which are built upon psychology." (Baldwin, 1905, p. 163).

Baldwin's own contributions were filled with this ambition. Indeed, on the basis of a general sociogenetic standpoint, he developed the constructive part of his theory – that of genetic logic.

Active Cognitive Processes: Social Mediation of Selectivity

Heterogeneity of the Social Environment

The social world of the developing person is variable, particularly thanks to the personal construction of psychological phenomena by individuals who constitute that social world. Of course, there is sufficient extent of regularity in that social world, but it is the constant encounter with changes that force the person to be constantly ready for new challenges:

The child begins to learn in addition the fact that persons are in a measure individual in their treatment of him, and hence that individuality has elements of uncertainty or *irregularity* about it. This growing sense is very clear to one who watches an infant in its second half-year. Sometimes the mother gives a biscuit, but sometimes she does not. Sometimes the father smiles and tosses the child; sometimes he does not. And the child looks for signs of these varying moods and methods of treatment. Its new pains of disappointment arise directly on the basis of that former sense of regular personal presence upon which its expectancy went forth. (Baldwin, 1894c, p. 277; also Baldwin, 1895, p. 123)

Baldwin's observations of his two daughters show their productive basis here. Elsewhere (Baldwin, 1897c, pp. 37–9) he adds the structural-social context to it: not only are particular persons who make up the child's social environment irregular within their habits over time (and personal conditions), but the set of persons who make up the social environment is constantly changing.

Personally Internalized Social Selectivity

From the heterogeneity of the person's social environment follows the need for selective treatment of that heterogeneity by the person himself. It is only the person who remains continuous within himself or herself, across the myriad of constantly changing environmental conditions. A previously established "schema" (see Baldwin, 1908b, p. 184) allows the person to become selective as to the variety of presently actual environmental inputs. According to Baldwin, "the individual *gradually builds up internally* the criteria of selection; and as his experience extends even more widely afield from the brute resistances, strains, and contacts with things, he becomes a more and more competent judge for himself of the value of variations in his thoughts" (Baldwin, 1898, p. 17).

However, the person's internalization of social experiences entails development of autonomy and such autonomy is itself socially constituted in any form that it takes. Sociality of the self cannot be viewed in the similarity of the internalized result of the social experiences, but in all of the personal-psychological phenomena. Thus, the developing person

comes more and more to reflect the social judgment in his own systematic determination of knowledge; and there arises within himself a criterion of private sort which is in essential harmony with the social demand, because genetically considered it reflects it. The individual becomes a law unto himself, exercises his private judgment, fights his own battles for truth, shows the virtue of independence and the vice of obstinacy. But he has learned to do it by the selective control of his social environment, *and in this his judgment he has just a sense of this social outcome.* (Baldwin, 1898, pp. 19–20)

It is obvious that the social nature of a person is expressed in his personal individuality, rather than in the mere direct mirroring of the social world surrounding the person. The latter is already rendered impossible by its high heterogeneity (which triggers the need for "systematic determination" of the new knowledge by way of internalized selection mechanisms – cognitive schemata – see Baldwin, 1898, p. 10). Baldwin saw the person–society relationships as a process of *particularization* of general meanings by persons in specific contexts on the one hand, and *generalization* (of persons' thought-variations by society) on the other (Baldwin, 1897c, part V). Society is thus a complex of various specifications of general meanings by concrete individuals, and institutionalized generalizations of some of the ideas of some individuals (see also Chapter 2 on Tarde).

Centrality of Play

Consistent with the rest of Baldwin's viewpoint, the person is capable of the intra-personal selection of ideas by way of playful – creative – application of knowledge (and its organizing meanings; Baldwin, 1908a, pp. 145–7) to new experiential contexts that are characterized by uncertainty (and heterogeneity). Hence, "the instrumental meaning is always and everywhere *a re-reading imaginatively, purposefully, personally of an actual or truthful meaning,* and the truthful reading is always and everywhere *a re-reading as common, stereotyped, actual of an imaginative personal construction . . . We make-believe in order that we may believe!"* (Baldwin, 1908b, pp. 183, 184).

Here, again, we can discover a parallel with the later conceptualization by Vygotsky of the relationships between "meaning" and "sense," as well as of the role of play and fantasy in human development (Van der Veer & Valsiner, 1991). In his autobiography, Baldwin expressed the idea of structural interdependence of social, personal, and constructive sides of development:

From the start, the growing individual finds himself bound constantly more and more tightly in the bonds of the actual; his actual self makes constant effort and finds constant resistance in the actual world. The two domains, 'inner' and 'outer', grow harder and more opposed one to the other, as his life adjustments proceed. The dualism of substances grows fixed and rigid. His release from this tension, this very serious business, is found in play, in fancy, in illusion, in fiction – in short, in semblance or make-believe of all kinds. Here he has a sense of freedom, of don't-have-to, of detachment; he plays with symbols, erects fancies, lives the hero, the pauper, the prince, at his own sweet will. In play, as a child or man, he remakes the world, mixing himself with other persons and with things in a delightful chaos; similarly, in art the man and artist again remake the world having in view only his own creation of something – anything –

within the possibilities of the ideal reconstruction that the materials allow. (Baldwin, 1930, p. 20)

In respect to issues of "dualism," Baldwin was (self-admittedly; see Baldwin, 1905) a defender of the *inclusive* separation of the person and the social world (Valsiner, 1987). The duality of integrated phenomena – of the "inner" and "outer," or self and society – constituted a field that warranted analysis of how the opposing-yet-united parts of a duality actually relate with each other.

The Concept of Self

The self is mediated through the language-encoded inner experiences, judgments that are "already and always socialized" (Baldwin, 1908a, p. 145). The self is a bi-polar entity that includes "the ego" and "the alter" (each of which constitutes the *socius* for the other; Baldwin, 1897, Chapter 1).

Baldwin's sociopersonalistic and future-oriented functional standpoint makes the personal construction of immediate future experiences on the basis of (but without formal isomorphism to) social guidance the only reasonable theoretical idea for self development. Personal construction is the general mechanism of development that has emerged on the basis of the social environment, and hence the person is social, without losing his or her individual uniqueness.

In general, while watching his daughters' very ordinary motor behavior, Baldwin was theoretically addressing the most fundamental question of human psychology: the existence of "free will" (volition; in our days usually labeled "intentionality") in organisms that are in principle dependent upon their relations with their (physical and social) environments. Again, this concern of his was parallel to Vygotsky's later interest in the same issue (see Van der Veer & Valsiner, 1991), and was a widespread puzzle for many intellectuals at the turn of the century.

Play and Art: Where the "Inner" and "Outer" Meet

The dynamics of "inner–outer" relationships led Baldwin to two other relevant phenomena – those of play and art. Baldwin saw in the process of make-believe play the place where one can observe the coordination of previous experiences (through memory) and suggestions from the objects in the present moment (Baldwin, 1906, chapter 6).

Play was viewed by Baldwin as having the function of "education of the individual for his life-work in a network of social relationships" (Baldwin, 1897, p. 148). Like Vygotsky afterward, Baldwin relied heavily on the work of Karl Groos on play. The similarities in the *foci* of Baldwin and Vygotsky in matters of play are thus not surprising. They shared the sociogenetic world view and relied on the same background descriptive sources (see Lee, 1982). Thus, both viewed play as a context in which the child transcends his present state in development.

Baldwin's empirical examples were obtained from his daughters' make-believe play, like the following:

On May, 2 I was sitting on the porch alone with the children – aged respectively four and a half and two and a half years. Helen, the elder, told Elizabeth that she was her little baby; that is, Helen became 'mama' and Elizabeth 'baby'. The younger responded by calling her sister 'mama', and the play began.

'You have been asleep, baby. Now it is time to get up', said mama. Baby rose from the floor, – first falling down in order to raise, – was seized upon by 'mama', taken to the railing to an imaginary wash-stand, and her face washed by rubbing. Her articles of clothing were then named in imagination, and put on, one by one, in the most detailed and interesting fashion. During all this 'mama' kept up a stream of baby talk to her infant: 'Now your stockings, my darling; now your skirt, sweetness – or, no – not yet – your shoes first', etc. etc . . . Baby acceded to all the details with more than the docility which real infants usually show. When this was done, 'Now we must go tell papa good-morning, dearie', said mama. 'Yes, mama', came the reply; and hand in hand they started to find papa. I, the spectator, carefully read my newspaper, thinking, however, that the reality of papa, seeing that he was so much in evidence, would break upon the imagined situation. But not so. Mama led her baby directly past me to the end of the piazza, to a column in the corner. 'There's papa', said mama; 'now tell him good-morning', 'Good-morning, papa; I am very well,' said baby, bowing low to the column. 'That's good', said mama in a *gruff, low voice,* which caused in the real papa a thrill of amused self-consciousness most difficult to contain. 'Now you must have your breakfast', said mama. The seat of a chair was made a breakfast-table, the baby's feigned bib put on, and her porridge carefully administered, with all the manner of the nurse who usually directs their breakfast. 'Now' (after the meal, which suddenly became dinner instead of breakfast) 'you must take your nap', said mama. 'No, mama; I don't want to', said baby. 'But you must'. – 'No; you be baby, and take the nap.' – 'But all the other children have gone to sleep, dearest, *and the doctor says you must*', said mama. This convinced baby, and she lay down on the floor. 'But I haven't undressed you.' So then came all the detail of undressing; and mama carefully covered her up on the floor with a light shawl, saying, 'Spring is coming now; that'll be enough. Now shut your eyes, and go to sleep', – 'But you haven't kissed me, mama', said the little one. 'Oh, of course, my darling!' – so a long siege of kissing. Then the baby closed her eyes very tight, while mama went on tiptoe away to the end of the porch. 'Don't go away, mama', said baby. 'No; mama wouldn't leave her darling', came the reply. (Baldwin, 1895, pp. 362–3).

In children's role play, the "inner" (memory-based) experiences are brought together with the present external situation. The constructive nature of imitation takes the form of a transformation of immediately available objects into functionally different ones (even against the odds of availability of the real ones; e.g., making the column into "papa," instead of making use of the readily available real specimen). Furthermore, the roles in play can be changed at every moment. Yet, there exist limits to the constructivity in play: Some aspects of the "outer" reality can be made into insurmountable obstacles for func- tional re-definition (e.g., "you cannot be an earthworm, you have too many legs"; Baldwin, 1906, p. 114).

Centrality of Empathy (Sembling)

It is in the realm of discussing play and art that Baldwin connected his theorizing with the issue of *Einfühlung* of Theodor Lipps. Bald- win's translation of that term into English is a good example of his liking for terminological inventions: he translated it as *sembling* ("to semble" – to make like by imitation; Baldwin, 1906, p. 122). Of course, in the decades after Baldwin the competing translation (suggested by E. B. Titchener and J. Ward; Baldwin, 1911a, p. 167) of that concept – *empathy* – has become accepted in psychology, albeit with all the confusions that *Einfühlung* brought with it in the beginning of the century.

Originally focusing on the "feeling-into" an object, Baldwin's ver- sion of sembling translates the *Einfühlung* into his imitation-centered conceptual system: "Broadly understood, the process of Sembling con- sists in the reading-into the object of a sort of psychic life of its own, in such a way that the movement, act, or character by which it is interpreted is thought of as springing from its own inner life" (Baldwin, 1906, p. 124).

Sembling thus entails projection upon one another of the oppositions that persist within one's own inner–outer relationships, as those are construed within the mind's "inner imitation." It was claimed to be present in both play and art. The "self sembles itself" – the jchild takes on new roles, attaches its personal understanding to their external demands, and that leads to further development of the self.

Feel-Forward Mechanisms

Sembling is based on imagination, which is oriented toward possible future events. and is viewed by Baldwin in his characteristic prospective way, emphasizing directedness toward ideal goals:

The sort of meaning known as ideal, due to an imaginative *feeling-forward*, has an essential place in the development of the affective life. The entire movement of cognition and feeling alike has not only the interest and intent to conserve its data and preserve its habits, but also the interest and intent to achieve, to learn, to adapt, to acquire, to *feel-forward* (Baldwin, 1911a, p. 125).

Sembling is thus a mechanism of the feeling-forward process (it is interesting to note that here Baldwin comes close even in his terminology to the concept of "feed-forward" that decades later became used in cybernetics).

A similar psychological function was asserted by Baldwin to exist in art – as he moved to idealize the notion of "aesthetic synthesis" in his theory of *pancalism* (or, "constructive affectivism"; see Baldwin, 1911a, 1915). Yet, he claimed that art differs from play in some ways:

In art, the motives of the serious life are not reinstituted fragmentarily and capriciously, for mere recreation and amusement, as they are in play; but systematically and truthfully, in a system in which the judgments of value, appreciation, ideality, are semblantly reconstructed. Art thus becomes in its own sense serious. It is not a mere imitation of the actual; nor is it a caricature of it. It is a re-reading of the actual in the more systematic, perfect, and satisfying form which the abrogation of partial controls and the removal of their oppositions renders possible. The reality of the external is not lost; since the reconstructions preserves the gains of judgment and insight, both theoretical and practical. Nor is reality in the inner world lost or impaired; since the work of art is charged with its very spirit and life. (Baldwin, 1915, p. 243)

Here – as Baldwin was writing in 1915 – we can see how his thought had become quite different from his previous writing (e.g., about play in 1895). First, he reverts to the use of the common-language notion of imitation ("mere imitation"), although what he has in mind here is in line with his own persistent imitation idea. Further-more, differently from the vividness of the encounter that he as par-ent-psychologist had with his daughters' play, his encounters with art seem to be those of a recipient facing a finished art object (rather than an observer of the actual work/play of the artist). Probably moving along the road of German philosophers of the past who had been searching for the "absolute truth," Baldwin's system-building reached its maximum in the suggestion that aesthetic synthesis is the highest accomplishment of the human psychological organization.

The Invention of "Persistent Imitation": The Constructivist Breakthrough

The key concept for understanding Baldwin's efforts toward making psychology both developmental and social is that of "persistent imi-tation." The reasons for Baldwin's need to create this concept can be discerned in his efforts to explain the future-oriented developmental processes at the level of the individual:

Suppose at first an organism giving random reactions, some of which are useful; now for development the useful reactions must be repeated, and thus made to outweigh the reactions which are damaging or useless. Evidently if there are any among the useful reactions which result in immediate duplication of their own stimulus, these must persist, and on them must rest the development of the organism. These are the imitative reactions. Thus it is that *a thing in nature once endowed with the reacting property might so select its stimulations as to make its relations to its environ-ment means to its own progress*: imitative reactions, as now defined, being the only means to such selection. (Baldwin, 1894b, p. 29; emphases added)

Here the need for inventing *some* notion of imitation becomes ob-vious as a deductively created object of study. The functionalist and instrumentalist stance of Baldwin's is clearly visible (e.g., reference to "usefulness" in general). The developmental orientation helped him to extend the sequence of a stimulus and reaction into a time-extended "circular reaction" – in which the organism's reaction to a stimulus becomes the next stimulus for the organism, leading to the next reaction, and so on. The organism *begins to construct non-random experiences* on the basis of such circular reactions. The reactions become instruments, and thus begin to participate in the developmental process.

The imitative reactions are thus the key to understanding the process of development. Baldwin's analyses of those reactions was based on his observations of the motor action of his infant daughters (Baldwin, 1891; 1892a; 1892b) on the one hand, and the conceptual distinctions of automatic versus perception-based copying of models (Janet, 1889, p. 475) on the other. Janet's contrast was, of course, based on adult psychopathological evidence (see Chapter 3).

Baldwin's "Simple" and "Persistent" Forms of Imitation

Baldwin's conceptualization of imitation is a good example of his tendency to extend the meanings of common-sense terms. This neologistic habit of Baldwin's was disliked by his contemporaries (e.g., Sully, 1896), and it undoubtedly contributed to the later forgetting and misunderstanding of his ideas. Yet it is exactly within the realm of such terminological play that Baldwin addresses the single main issue of development: the creation and preservation of novelty (see also Freeman-Moir, 1982).

At the lower level of development, Baldwin recognized the realm of "pre-imitative suggestions," which covered much of the involuntary phenomena in the child-environment relationships:

Here we find many *Subconscious* and *Physiological* Suggestions akin to the subliminal suggestive reactions in recent hypnotic reports. Especially do suggestions of sleep, and of the personality of the mother, nurse, etc., take early hold upon the child. An important source of subconscious suggestion to the child is its dreams. Another class of suggestive influences in the pre-imitation period, we may call *Deliberative* Suggestions: cases in which two or more motor suggestions come into conflict. For example, the suggestion of a forbidden act and the memory of the pain of punishment give rise to apparent deliberation which is merely the balance of motor tendencies. (Baldwin, 1892a, p. 49)

The active role of the child is not evident in Baldwin's description of the pre-imitative phenomena (which, it should be noted, are not limited to early infancy or childhood; adult cases of emotional conflict or pathological aboulia are other examples of those phenomena). The world of pre-imitative kind is filled with numerous influences on the person, and does not emphasize the future-oriented feed-forward role of the reactions of those influences.

In contrast, the phenomena of "imitative suggestion" – subdivided by Baldwin into *simple imitation* and *persistent imitation* – go beyond the here-and-now reactivity of the organism to the external influences. For Baldwin, "an imitative reaction is one which *tends normally to maintain or repeat its stimulating process*" (Baldwin, 1895, p. 350, added emphasis). Here we can see an effort to describe a process that entails continuity in time (and over multiple acts of interchange with the environment as opposed to a simple one-time stimulus–reaction juncture). This continuity in time leads to the question of the *double nature* of the copy to be imitated: on the one hand, such a copy is available from the external world (immediately through the perception process), on the other hand, it is available from the previous experiences via internal memory. Here, again, we can point to a parallel with the later elaboration by Vygotsky of the "method of double stimulation," the innovative nature of which is based exactly upon the inevitable duality of the immediate experience and semiotically encoded earlier life experiences.

The duality of the copy (mapped upon the duality of the intrapersonal and extrapersonal sources of experience) creates the basis for continuity of the imitation process. It is exactly here that Baldwin's notions of imitation transcend the common-language meanings of the term "imitation," and for good reason. The function of human language can be viewed to be the relative temporary stabilization of the flow of life experiences. Furthermore, most of the common-sense accounts of child development have relied upon the unidirectional culture transmission model (see discussions in Valsiner, 1988; 1989; 1993b). Hence, it is not surprising to discover that the common-language meanings of the term "imitation" did not fit Baldwin's developmental theoretical needs.

Baldwin was faced with a dilemma: either to invent a new term (which he did on multiple other occasions and much to the dismay of his contemporaries), or to redefine "imitation" in ways that would fit his developmental orientation. He opted for the second solution – obviously since much of his contemporary scientific discourse was already filled with examples of the use of that term in scientific discussions (e.g., Tarde, 1884; 1895; see Chapter 2).

The Meaning of "Simple Imitation"

For Baldwin, simple imitation amounted to "sensori-motor or ideo-motor suggestion, which tends to keep itself going by reinstating its own stimulation" (1895, p. 352). His efforts to explain the meaning of this version of imitation may be more understandable: "The child imitates a word, gets it wrong, and repeats its own mistake over and over. Physiologically we have a "circular activity"; the stimulus starts a nervous process which tends to reproduce both the stimulus and the process again. In Simple Imitation the channels of association are sufficient for the discharge, and there is no effort" (Baldwin, 1892a, p. 50).

This kind of simple imitation is in fact equivalent to what both common sense and post-Baldwinian psychology have habitually considered imitation to be (i.e., a version of the external model is replicated, in full or in some less-than-accurate form, in the child's behavior, where it may persist). In contrast, for Baldwin this form of imitation was clearly of secondary importance, for the reason that *simple imitation is incapable of producing novelty beyond the model* provided externally. It is reproductive (rather than productive), automatic (i.e., effortless), and lacks orientation on the future (as it is explainable by past associative links). After the first act of imitation of the external copy, the "circular process" of simple imitation enters a loop of repetitive status quo, which could be described as:

Model A–> Imitation A' = Model A'–> Imitation A'–> etc.

The Meaning of "Persistent Imitation"

As Baldwin described the persistent imitation process, it involves the "trying, and trying again" phenomenon of experimenting with the features of the model:

In persistent imitation the first reaction is not repeated. Hence we must suppose the development, in a new center, of a function of co-ordination by which the two regions excited respectively by the original suggestion and the reported reaction coalesce in a common more voluminous and intense stimulation of the motor centre. A movement is thus produced which, by reason of its greater mass and diffusion, includes more of the elements of the "copy." This is again reported by eye or ear, giving a "remote" excitement, which is again co-ordinated with the original stim ulation and with the after effects of the earlier imitations. The result is yet another motor stimulation, or effort, or still greater mass and diffusion, which includes yet more elements of the "copy." (Baldwin, 1892b, p. 287)

In terms of contrast, persistent imitation entails increasing experimentation with different aspects of the model, and going beyond the model as given by way of producing imitated versions that deliberately modify the model:

$$\text{Model A} \rightarrow \text{Imitation A'} = \text{Model A'} \rightarrow \text{Imitation A''} =$$
$$\text{Model A''} \rightarrow \text{Imitation A'''} = \text{Model A'''} \rightarrow \text{etc.}$$

It is through persistent imitation that construction of novelty on the basis of social suggestions becomes possible at all. On the one hand, this is made possible by the "overproduction" of actions and the accompanying effort; on the other, by intraorganismic emergence of some "coordination center." Here is the duality of "making the reacting property into an instrument" – it occurs both in relation to the external world (i.e., actions as instruments) and to the intrapsychological world (i.e., new "functional centers" as psychological coordination mechanisms). Persistent imitation leads to the hierarchical organization of psychological mechanisms, and the control of the voluntary actions is given over to these higher psychological functions (e.g., see Baldwin, 1895, p. 379). Furthermore, the function of persistent imitation is oriented towards future encounters with the world: "Imitation to the intelligent and earnest imitator is never slavish, never mere repetition; it is, on the contrary, *a means for further ends*, a method of absorbing what is present in others and of making it over in forms peculiar to one's own temper and valuable to one's own genius (Baldwin, 1911b, p. 22).

Even if this strong and seemingly exaggerated generalization about the constructive nature of imitation seems dismissive of the nature of simple imitation, it need not be so. Aside from Baldwin's emphasis on persistent imitation, it is not difficult to see that *simple imitation is a special case of the more general persistent imitation* – it is a special case in which the constructive nature of the subsequent imitations is fixated upon the exact replication of the first imitation. If that fixation (or perseverance) is overcome, the imitative process returns to its normal (i.e., persistent) mode. Furthermore, it becomes clear that persistent

imitation is the mechanism by which individual uniqueness is constructed under the flow of social suggestions.

From Persistent Imitation to "Fossilized Behavior" and Internalization

The concept of persistent imitation introduces into developmental
psychology the constructive perspective (i.e., the role of the imitator
in the active modification of the models via experimentation). It builds
upon the constant generation of variability by organisms.

A consistently developmental perspective needs not only to explain
the continuity between the external and internal worlds, but also to
explain phenomena of discontinuity. The notion of persistent imitation
implies constant creation of such discontinuity: A process of such
imitation starts from an external copy, but transforms it drastically in
the process of "trying, and trying again." The original model that set
the given developmental process into motion may soon become unrec-
ognizable. Baldwin was well aware of that implication, which later in
Vygotsky's texts became known as the "fossilization of behavior":

We see how it is possible for reactions which were originally simple
imitative suggestions to lose all appearance of their true origin. Copy-
links at first distinctly present as external things, and afterwards present
with almost equal distinctness as internal memories, may become lost in
the rapid progress of consciousness. New connexions get established in
the network of association, and motor discharges get stimulated thus
which were possible at first only by imitation and owed their formation
to it. A musician plays by reading printed notes, and forgets that in
learning the meaning of the notes he imitated the movements and sounds
which his instructor made: but the intermediate copies have so fallen
away that his performance seems to offer no surface imitation at all. His
sound copy system, of course, persists to the end to guide his muscular
reactions. But a musician of the visual type goes further. He may play
from memory of the printed notes; that is, he may play from a trans-
planted visual copy of notes which themselves are but shorthand or substitute expressions of earlier sound and muscular copies, and finally the
name only of a familiar selection may be sufficient to start a performance
guided only by a subconscious muscular copy series. (Baldwin, 1894b,
p. 34)

We here get a glimpse of the role of persistent imitation in the
internalization of (previously) external experiences, including the de-

velopment of the self (Baldwin, 1894b). That internalization is a process of constructive differentiation of the social and the personal: The inwardly oriented persistent imitation results in the intramental construction of psychological phenomena that are transformations from (rather than simple-imitative replicas of) the social experiences of the person. Through the persistent imitation and "fossilization" of behavior in the course of development, Baldwin could explain how increasingly personal psychological phenomena are of social origin. The process of persistent imitation makes it possible to construct novelty in both the interpersonal and intrapersonal spheres of human existence. Those spheres may develop in directions of increasing separateness from one another, and yet exactly their becoming separate is made possible by their unity in the social nature of development. The more detached a particular personality at a given time might be from the immediate social context, the more its developmental roots can be located in some personal relationship context of the past (cf. Elias, 1991). Baldwin, on the basis of his general dialectical view, had no difficulties reconciling the personal (intrapsychological) and the social (interpsychological) facets of human development. Vygotsky, decades later, was similarly unworried about the person-society "dualism" (see also Baldwin's polemics with Dewey and Mead, in Baldwin, 1904).

Baldwin's Conceptualization of the "Inner–Outer" Relationships

At first glance, Baldwin's numerous statements about the social nature of psychological phenomena seem overwhelming in their declarative generality (e.g., of "personality-suggestion"; Baldwin, 1894c). Some of these statements look deceptively similar to the arguments in favor of "appropriation" as discussed in our time (e.g., Harré, 1984), like: Imitation is . . . the method by which our living *milieu* in all its aspects gets carried over and reproduced within us. Our consciousness of the relationships of the elements of this reproduced world is our sense of sufficient reason" (Baldwin, 1894b, p. 37).

Of course, as should be clear from the discussion above, the centrality of the process of persistent imitation in the person-world relationships renders invalid the reading of Baldwin as a mere proponent of the appropriation notion. However, it is clear that the "inner is not the outer" (Baldwin, 1906, p. 92), and that the duality of the "inner" and the "outer" constitutes the source of development of both.

Development of Interests

The imitation process leads to the creation of a personal psychological world that is rooted in external experiences, but is not an exact copy of those (see also Baldwin, 1911a, p. 23). Furthermore, neither are the objects in the external world psychologically separate from the person's already established (i.e., internalized) orientation toward them. Baldwin labeled that orientation "interest":

The object itself varies throughout the entire gamut of cases possible in the respective arrangements of a more restricted or a more amplified body of psychic contents. The bird's object "earth-worm" is a certain group of sense experiences taking on a determination as an edible whole; that is, it is determined by what we may call the gustatory interest. The naturalist's earth-worm is a group of anatomical and morphological data and relationships which are determined as a biological specimen; that is, it is determined by the "scientific" interest. The same variations arise also in successive "objective" determinations within the same consciousness; the bird determines the earthworm differently when its gustatory interest is compounded with its maternal interest, that is, when the worm is to be carried to the nest to feed the young. So the naturalist's worm is very differently determined if perchance it prove to be an edible snail to be carried home for luncheon. (Baldwin, 1906, pp. 42–3).

Interests undergo change. For the establishment of such "interests," the functioning of memory as a link between the many past events and the current experiences, is obligatory. Development of memory functions moves from involuntary tyranny of memory to person's active control over it (Baldwin, 1906, p. 68). The interdependent nature of the "inner and outer" duality leads to the development of other united oppositions ("self and not-self" – Baldwin, 1906, p. 91).

Baldwin's Role in the Development of the Idea of "Organic Selection"

It is this prospective developmental orientation that made it possible for Baldwin (1896a; 1896b; 1897a; 1897b; 1902b) to join with C. Lloyd Morgan (1896) and Henry Osborn (1896) in suggesting an alternative theoretical model for evolutionary thought that attempted to overcome the artificially exaggerated "Darwinist" versus "Lamarckian" fights of evolutionists. His notion of "organic selection" was based on the idea that selection at the species level operates upon individual organisms after the latter have proceeded to generate new forms of adaptations (see also Vonèche, 1982). Furthermore, Baldwin's ideas served as a relevant input for Henri Bergson's philosophy of creative evolution (e.g., Bergson, 1944, p. 32), whose role in the history of developmental science should not be underestimated.

Adaptation and Organic Selection

Many developmental scientists adhere to a time perspective that entails a past-to-present focus on emergence (i.e., a retrospective view). Their answer to this question is in analyzing different kinds of imitation. Few – Baldwin as well as Vygotsky among them – have taken an explicitly present-to-future oriented stance, as is well explained by Baldwin himself as he addressed the issue of adaptation:

Considering the state of an organism at any moment, with its readiness to act in an appropriate fashion, – say a child's imitation of a movement, – the appropriateness of its action may be construed in either of two ways: either *retrospectively* or *prospectively*. By construing it retrospectively, I mean that an organism performs its appropriate function when it does what it has done before – what it is suited to do, however it may have come to be so suited. The child imitates my movement because his apparatus is ready for this movement. This is Habit; it proceeds by repetition. But when we come to ask how it got to be suited to do this function *the first time*, or how it can come to do a new function *from now on*, – how the child manages to imitate a new movement, one which he has never made before, – this is the prospective reference, and this question we must now try to answer. (Baldwin, 1895, p. 171)

Baldwin's "organic selection" notion borrowed from his observations of infants' sensori-motor actions. It entailed ejecting into the notion of adaptation the orientation of time, moving from the present to the immediate future. This notion is certainly similar to Henri Bergson's adaptation idea, i.e., that of the construction of adaptive resources with an eye to future possibilities.

Methodology for the Study of Development: "Genetic Logic" and Its Implications

The equivalent of psychologists' methodological "gold standards" at the turn of the century was logic. Different thinkers paid careful attention to issues of logic, both in the sense of its philosophy and its formalization (e.g., John Dewey, C. Sanders Peirce). Hence it is not surprising that Baldwin made an ambitious effort to build a developmental version of logic. That version of logic was expected to consist of

tracing out the movement of the function of cognition- in this case, the logical mode of it as such – in its great typical movements or 'progressions,' with the attempt to determine the 'how,' 'why,' and 'whereunder' of each stage in the advance. Thinking is thus considered in the light of an *effective function*, working upon the objects of cognition, having adequate motives for its passage from one stage to another, and pursuing its characteristic method in achieving each successive stage. It is this general conception of a logic that is genetic. (Baldwin, 1906b, p. 388)

Baldwin's genetic logic can be considered a version of what in our times has gained extensive recognition, i.e., the so-called "cognitive science." Baldwin's efforts to formalize the processes of cognitive development have largely passed into the oblivion of science – for perfectly wrong reasons. The difficulty of discovering explicit laws in the implicit flow of developmental phenomena is an intellectual challenge yet to be taken and successfully solved, rather than a reason for abandonment of the phenomena of interest. The latter has been usual in psychology – and has contributed to the crisis in its conceptual and methodological sphere.

Baldwin's "Genetic Developmental Science"

Psychology has been in a methodological crisis ever since its establishment as a separate social institution. It is particularly the the case of the study of development, that is, the investigation of real (but yet – at the given time – ephemeral) emerging phenomena that brings to the attention of developmentalists the full extent of that crisis. It was clear to Baldwin that developmental science (or, as he termed it, "genetic science") could not develop using the inferential tools of non-developmental sciences. Thus, he understood the futility of the acceptance of quantitative methodology in psychology:

The . . . quantitative method, brought over into psychology from the exact sciences, physics and chemistry, must be discarded; for its ideal consisted in reducing the more complex to the more simple, the whole into its parts, the later-evolved to the earlier-existent, thus denying or eliminating just the factor which constituted or revealed what was truly genetic. Newer modes of manifestation cannot be stated in atomic terms without doing violence to the more synthetic modes which observation reveals. (Baldwin, 1930, p. 7)

Likewise, Baldwin did not find much value in the behaviorist ways of analyses of "objective" phenomena, criticizing that orientation for its elimination of consciousness from consideration (Baldwin, 1930, p. 29). Needless to add, that in both of these evaluations (made more than a decade after his active work in psychology), Baldwin's criticism paralleled that of Vygotsky (see Van der Veer & Valsiner, 1991). Both of these thinkers used the same general argument (i.e., the nonreducibility of the properties of a molecule, say, water, into its atomic components[2]; a defense of the view of "analysis-into-units") in their methodological claims in favor of the study of psychological synthesis. However, Baldwin in his productive years had gone further, pointing to the uselessness of importing the nondevelopmental notions of causality into the new "genetic science":

We must be free from all constructions drawn from the strictly a-genetic sciences in which the causal sequence is the typical one. The birth of a new mode in the psychic life is a *"progression" from an earlier set of conditions, not the effect of these conditions viewed as cause*; and this is equally true of any new genetic mode, just so far as the series in which it appears is really genetic at all. (Baldwin, 1906a, p. 29; emphasis added)

The social model for scientific rigor at the turn of the century was formal logic. Hence it is not surprising that Baldwin's efforts to build a developmental science took the form of creating a general system of thought that would constitute developmental logic – a system of deductive kind that could guide our expectations about how development takes place. In his system, he addressed questions of three kinds of logic: functional logic (Baldwin, 1906), experimental logic (Baldwin, 1908), and reality logic (*logique réal* – Baldwin, 1911). Genetic logic for Baldwin implied the study of emergence, rules of use in bringing by further emergences, of meanings. In this respect, Baldwin's genetic logic can be viewed as an effort to develop a system of developmental semiotics. The principles of development that were elaborated by

---

[2] That example can be dated back to J. S. Mill's *Logic of the Moral Sciences* (cf. Sidgwick, 1886, p. 212). It was widely used in the beginning of the twentieth century discussions about the whole being not equal to the sum of its parts (see Chapter 7)

Baldwin in this work in the 1890s (and laid the foundation of the "organic selection" theory of evolution), were taken and applied to the realm of the philosophy of language in general, and of language use in particular. Any general system of such a kind needed explicit basic axioms.

Axioms and Postulates of the Genetic Science

Baldwin formulated four "axioms" of genetic science (1902, p. 323; 1906a, p. 20), which fortified the irreducibility of the developmentally more complex phenomena to their preceding (less complex) counterparts. This effort can be viewed as a counteraction to the reductionist habits that were coming into vogue at his time.

Baldwin made four basic claims:

[Axiom 1]. . . . the phenomena of science at each higher level show a form of synthesis that is not accounted for by the formulations which are adequate for the phenomena of the next lower level. ["lower" here denotes a developmental antecedent, "higher" an emerging subsequent]

[Axiom 2]. . . . the formulations of any lower science are not invalidated in the next higher, even in cases in which new formulations are necessary for the formal synthesis that characterizes the genetic mode of the higher.

[Axiom 3]. . . . the generalizations and classifications of each science, representing a particular genetic mode, are peculiar to that mode and cannot be constructed in analogy to, or *a fortiori* on the basis of, the corresponding generalizations or classifications of the lower mode.

[Axiom 4]. . . . no formula for progress from mode to mode, that is, no strictly genetic formula in evolution or in development, is possible except by direct observation of the facts of the series which the formulation aims to cover or by the interpretation of other series which represent the same or parallel modes.

(Baldwin, 1906, p. 20)

By assuming the existence of qualitatively different levels of knowledge construction in sciences, Baldwin had to clarify the relations between them. Hence, Axioms 1 and 2 specify the nonreducibility of the newly emergent levels to the previous ones. They also specify the continuing viability of the previously existing levels, after the novel level has emerged. In a concrete example: the consciousness of *Homo sapiens* is an emergent new level of phenomena that cannot be explained by reducing it to physiological principles that governed the functioning of the nervous systems of prehuman species. Consciousness requires explanation in terms of its own principles, even as the phenomenon itself is an outgrowth from the previous ("lower") physiologically regulated processes. At the same time, the new level of explanation, which fits consciousness, does not invalidate the physiological mechanisms that keep regulating the continuously existing lower processes.

Axiom 3 restricts the transferability of scientific models by way of analogy. It is consistent with the other axioms – if each new level of phenomena is a new, unique emergent, then surely a model that fits that uniqueness is not transferable to other phenomena (and levels) *merely* on the basis of analogy. Rather, the principles (the models) need to be constructed from the study of the emergent phenomena themselves (Axiom 4).

Following these axioms, specific elaborations of the methodology of the developmental science were in order. Baldwin specified two "postulates of method." The first (or "negative") postulate emphasized the irreversibility of time in development:

The logic of genesis is not expressed in convertible propositions. Genetically, A = (that is, *becomes*, for which the sign ((is now used) B; but it does not follow that B = (becomes, (( ) A. (Baldwin, 1906, p. 21)

The first postulate specifies the realm of possible relations that are allowable among the formulae of genetic logic, namely, each proposition includes a temporal directionality vector. Thus, the reversal (i.e. B ((A) is not implied by the notion of A becoming B. If we were to use a better known terminology (from Piaget's talk about operations), Baldwin's genetic logic is set up using nonoperational terminology. The symmetry of transformation between A and B is broken by the irreversibility of time, and of the very transformation.

Such a symmetry-breaking process (see also Prigogine, 1973) leads to the question of *loci of accessibility* to developmental phenomena for Baldwin's designated "developmental science." These loci were charted out in the second (so-called "positive") postulate: "that series of events is truly genetic which cannot be constructed before it has happened, and which cannot be exhausted backwards, after it has happened" (Baldwin, 1906, p. 21).

The "positive" nature of this postulate is in its focusing the study of development on that of the *unfolding novel processes*, rather than their prediction, or retrospective explanation. The phenomena of *emergence, becoming,* and *transformation* become the objects of investigation. Such investigation would entail *preserving the irreversible time sequence* in the data.

Elaborations: "Canons" of Genetic Logic

Baldwin translated the "postulates of method" into a series of "canons of genetic logic." These "canons" were expected to "regulate the method," especially in the sense of the avoidance of "fallacies," which were set up as counterpoints to each of the given canons.

Continuity. All psychic process is continuous. The fallacy of discontinuity "consists in treating of any psychic event as *de novo*, or as arising in a discontinuous series" (Baldwin, 1906, p. 23). Baldwin had a biological scenario of his time in mind – that of "divergence" of change. In the case of the diverging phenomena X and Y, which emerge from the same antecedent (Z), the temptation is to trace one of the two (opposing) forms, X or Y, to Z, and to "say that the other is without antecedents, or is de novo" (ibid., p. 23). Thus, here Baldwin uses de novo in the sense of absolute novelty (which is not rooted in any previous state – an idea he rejected), rather than in the sense of the construction of novelty on the basis of previously constructed foundations (which he accepted).

Progression. All psychic process is genetic, not a-genetic, expressed by the formula A becomes B whether or not it is ever true that B becomes A. The birth of a new mode (B) is a progression from the previous state (A), which entails specific conditions. However, the latter are not "causes" for the new mode (B); causality is a way of discussing phenomena that is fit for a-genetic sciences. The opposite Fallacy of Composition (or "Cause and Effect Fallacy") "consists in treating a psychic event as compounded or made up of or caused by other psychic events: So the fallacy of treating the sensation purple as made up of the sensations blue and red, or as caused by them" (Baldwin, 1906, p. 23).

In this canon, the contrast between developmental phenomena (which operate in irreversible time, hence the reversal of development – B –> A – is not possible), and nondevelopmental phenomena (where one can, time-freely, assume reversibility of A $\rightarrow$ B and B and B $\rightarrow$ A) is played out. In the case of dynamic, organismic processes, the developing novel state cannot be reduced to causes that are conditions of the immediate past. Neither can the complexity of the new state be reduced to elementaristic causes. Baldwin here opened the door for a theoretical system where discussion about specific (independent) causes is replaced by analysis of the process of emergence (of B from the set of conditions A).

Quality. Every psychic event is qualitatively different from, not equal to, the next antecedent and the next succeeding event and also from its own earlier or later case. This canon emphasizes the constant emergence of novelty within the developmental process. If a developmental series of events entails a sequence of A $\rightarrow$ B $\rightarrow$ C, then there exists a qualitative difference not only between A and B and B and C, but also within each of the states (A, B, C, i.e., the formulation of difference "also from its own earlier or later case"). The fallacy of this canon – "Fallacy of Equality" – entails treating any two psychic events as equal, or any one as identical with itself when repeated.

The Canon of Quality brings the uniqueness of the lived-through psychological events to the core of method construction for developmental science. Any aggregation of similar events over time and space constitutes a captivation by the Fallacy of Equality. If such aggregation is accomplished, it leads to the construction of a fuzzy category of similarity, which cannot be interpreted as that of sameness. There is no sameness (other than our mentally constructed illusion) in the world of developmental phenomena, and all similarity is of a fuzzy kind.

Modal Relevancy. No psychic event can be taken out of its mode and treated as belonging in or with events of another mode. This is opposed by the Fallacy of Modal Confusion, i.e., treating an event or meaning characteristic of one mode as remaining what it was, when it is used in a synthesis of another mode.

Modal Unity. No psychic event or meaning can be treated as being what it is except in the entire context of the mode in which it arises. Here the context-specificity of development is emphasized: any developmental event emerges only in the given context, and none other. The opposing Fallacy of Division or Abstraction consists of treating an event or meaning as a static and separable "element" or "unit."

Through the modal unity canon, Baldwin attempted to keep the research effort focused on the unique psychological phenomena united with their context of emergence. Yet the whole research process entails abstraction.

Actuality. No psychic event is present unless it be actual. A corollary from this Canon requires us to identify first the clear and unambiguous case, rather than the "first case" at which the given state can be said to have evolved in some minimalist form. According to Baldwin, this canon "checks the rage for the "simplification" of what in its concrete occurrence is rich with shadings of complex meaning" (Baldwin, 1906, p. 24).

A fallacy of this canon (Fallacy of the Implicit or Potential) consists of treating something as implicitly or potentially present when it is not actual (e.g., claiming that implicit logical processes are present in the prelogical mode of thinking, or the "potential self" is present in the impersonal mode of thought). The focus here is on *being* present, as contrasted with *becoming*. Thus, if a psychologist claims that "intelligence" is implicitly present in a child who fails to solve a given mental task (e.g., as implied by "production deficiency"), then this kind of a statement exemplifies the fallacy. If, instead, a claim is made that "intelligence" emerges from the failures to solve a problem, then the canon is upheld (since talking of emergence does not entail projection of a hidden ontological state onto the present phenomenon).

Revision. No psychic event or meaning is to be treated as original or unrevised except in its first appearance, since its reappearance may be in a mode in which it is essentially revised. This canon is another way to emphasize the uniqueness of each observable phenomenon. Its fallacy – that of Consistency – consists of holding the psychic process to any consistency except what it shows. This is a basic call for perceptual reality to be trusted, and application of static, predetermined categories upon the flow of phenomena to be considered suspect. For instance, the researcher's interpretation of the subject's meaning system remaining the same over the course of participation in a study constitutes a case of this fallacy: the researcher expects the subject's statements to remain the same (consistent) over the session, while in actuality the subject has changed his or her understanding of the whole situation, and answers in accordance with this changed understanding (yet possibly using the same words). In our contemporary terminology, Baldwin's canon here prescribes a recognition of the hypergame nature (see Harsanyi & Selten, 1988) of the encounter of the researcher and the person in the role of the subject.

Baldwin's formulation of the canons of the method was an effort to overcome the tendencies that existed in his contemporary sciences to reduce all phenomena to static, causal explanatory entities. Thus, he claimed:

We have all been hypnotized by the thought of cause of the type of impact, transfer of energy fixed in quantity, with a formulation of effect in terms of an equation . . . We are told that nothing can be in the effect that is not already in the cause. All this is a partial and forced interpretation of nature. If science deals only with such causation series, then the great body of what we may in the large case call, "conditioning," or "sequence," remains uninterpreted. The Adaptations, Growths, Novelties, in nature are as much in evidence to the scientific observer as are the Identities, Conservations, and Effects.

The genetic progression recognizes *all the characters* of the event, allows the causal interpretation as an abstraction, but attempts to reconstitute nature in the fullness of her processes of change from the mode that conditions to a richer mode . . . that succeeds. The psychology that does not do this makes a fetish of physics, and sells her birthright for a mess of pottage. (Baldwin, 1906, p. 25)

Baldwin's effort was in direct opposition to his contemporary efforts to reduce psychology to physics, especially through the use of the notion of energy (propagated by Wilhelm Ostwald; see Hakfoort, 1992). The use of concepts similar to those of energy was prominent in Baldwin's time (e.g., Vladimir Bekhterev's rooting his reflexology on the notion of energy, e.g., Bechterev, 1932; Strickland, 1994; the obvious energy allusion in Freud's "libido"). It continues to proliferate at the end of twentieth century (e.g., the notion of cognitive "processing capacity"). The transfer of the energy concept from physics to psychology has created a conceptual obstacle for the latter, similar to the role "phlogiston" notions in earlier physics.

Baldwin's fight for the preservation of developmental processes is evident in the case of each canon. Thus, instead of viewing an event as without predecessors he insists upon its continuity with previous states (Canon of Continuity), while the continuity entails constant transformation of the state of the event (Canon of Revision). This state of affairs is brought about by irreversibility of developmental processes (Canon of Progression), and that entails transformation of the qualitative reorganization of the events (synthesis; Canon of Quality). Finally, all the uniqueness of developmental psychic events is context-bound: hence, Baldwin demands that scientific analysis maintain the linkages with the context (Canon of Modal Relevancy) and is not transposed to another context (Canon of Modal Unity).

For a contemporary sociocultural developmentalist all these canons may look very familiar, as our modern discussions return constantly to themes of "context-dependency," "continuity/discontinuity" in development, and to the irreversibility of development. However, there is somewhat illusory comfort in thinking that Baldwin's canons fortify our present-day quests for a novel methodology in the study of development. This becomes evident if we address the question as to whether Baldwin developed his imperatives any further (into productive methodology). The unfortunate answer to this question is that he did not: After declaring the relevance of "genetic science" he continued his general philosophical system-building (ending in the absolute synthesis of everything human, i.e., in the theory of Pancalism). Canons of "genetic logic" were not developed further as a formalized logical system that would be a foundation for a consistently developmental methodology. It may have been that Baldwin's general direction of intellectual pursuits at the time of formulating the canons of genetic logic was already such that productive further development of that logic was impossible.

Singular Phenomena and Community of Experience

Any developmental logic has to face the difficult problem of referential generalizability. In principle (given the irreversibility of time) each and every particular phenomenon can occur only once, in its absolute individual uniqueness. Nevertheless, any general formal system needs to refer to phenomena in general, as the general laws for the phenomena transcend each and every special occasion. This generalization is in some way performed by any user of language in everyday contexts, as well as by scientists in their categorization of phenomena. Yet that generalization occurs within the mental construction by a person. In order to obtain understandability it needs to be communicated to others. Baldwin formulated two principles:

Identity of indiscernibles – "in the absence of discernible difference two or more objects are judged to be one and the same recurrent experience . . . we have here the process of individuating as one, objects which do not give experience of difference." *Difference of discernibles* – "A single object is rendered, by reason of differences discerned in its several appearances, as more than one." (Baldwin, 1907a, p. 399)

The process of generalization operates at the opposition between the identity and difference principles, always moving away from the absolute objectivity of being (i.e., that of the singulars as such). Baldwin describes different moves of generalization in his rather colorful way:

A paranoic declares that everybody is persecuting him, because he generalizes recurrent experiences as all fit to excite his fear of others; he is working under the principle of 'identity of indiscernibles'. At the other extreme we may cite the individual we call 'subjective,' who sees always in our conduct, however uniformly kind, new and varied signs of change. He in turn is magnifying the 'difference of discernibles'. (Baldwin, 1907a, p. 400)

As Baldwin pointed out, human language provides its users vehicles to assist the generalization in either directions. With language, knowledge becomes relational and communicable. Fuzzy quantifiers are always available to create indeterminate (yet realistic) reflections upon the reality:

'This woman is always vain' is a universal in appearance; it is quantified in community; just as 'women are always vain', equivalent to 'all women are vain', has universal quantity in extension. Proposition in 'sometimes' are particular in community (as 'this woman is sometimes vain') or in extension (as 'women are sometimes vain') or in both (as 'some women are sometimes vain'). (Baldwin, 1907a, p. 400)

A critical issue in Baldwin's conceptualization of sameness of phenomena lies in the equalization of intrapersonal and interpersonal spheres of application of the principles described above. Thus, he claimed:

The process whereby the meaning of 'sameness' attaches to an object is the same whether the recurrences of the meaning thus identified as the same be in one mind or in more; for there is either actual reference [or: conversion] or the presupposition of it, from one experience to another in both cases alike . . . a judgment of singular identity is possible on the basis of a single person's recurrent experience; and . . . it is a judgment in community, having the force of commonness for all thinkers alike. (Baldwin, 1907a, p. 397)

According to Baldwin, there exist three modes of quantity that can be attached to judgments: quantity *in extension* ("men are sometimes irritable"), quantity *in community 'for whom'* ("John is sometimes irritable"), and quantity *in community 'by whom'* ("we all find John irritable"). This differentiation leads Baldwin to the question of social representations – yet from a specific person-centered angle of *how do social representations become personal* (and vice versa).

The discourse about social representations (a more modern notion of our times, see analysis of Moscovici's work in Chapter 9) was framed in Baldwin's time in terms of *collective* representations. This concept was introduced in the work of Durkheim and amplified by Levy-Brühl. Baldwin focused on the issue from his internalization-oriented perspective, within which active persons reconstruct social suggestions to become their intra-mental psychological system. Largely taking over the contrast of "primitive" and "developed" cultures (which was widespread at his time), Baldwin introduced his specific terms "syndoxic" and "synnomic" to characterize the internalization process:

Primitive interpretation, considered as common meaning or *représentation collective*, is "syndoxic": that is, it is apprehended by the individual as being the common possession of the group, accepted by others as by himself. He makes no claim to have discovered or even have confirmed it. It is a body of commonly accepted teachings – rites, observances, prescriptions, prohibitions, and so forth – for which he is not responsible, but which he accepts as being already established and binding. He is brought up from infancy in this body of syndoxic beliefs and apprehensions, just as the civilised child is reared in a body of socially recognized truths and usages. The difference is that at the logical stages of social culture, the individual comes sooner or later to criticise in some measure the social formulations, conforming or rejecting them in some detail, by the use of his own individual judgment. In this way the syndoxic becomes personal and "synnomic." (Baldwin, 1915, pp. 47–8)

Baldwin was explicit in his uncritical takeover of the "primitive" – "civilized" societies contrast – denying the individuals' "breaking through the social crust" (ibid. p. 48) to happen in the case of persons from the former kind of societies, and accepting such developing individuality in the "civilized" case. His acceptance of this contrast need not surprise us, since this value-laden contrast was clearly syn-doxic (in Baldwin's own sense) in the discourse of the time. Yet, Baldwin was cautious in spelling out that contrast. If we were to pay attention to his quantifiers (social formulations are said to be con-firmed or rejected in *some* detail; the individual criticizes *some* social formulations), it seems that the picture he painted of the "civilized" societies was not that of a simple takeover of logical modes of thought due to the active questioning of the established social system. Rather, the picture that emerges is that of *selective regionalization* of the do-mains of synnomic thinking: Within the field of socially promoted (syndoxic) "truths and usages," the developing person establishes his or her exploratory (i.e., experimenting) relationship with some sub-areas of that field, within which the constructive internalization of the syndoxic, by transforming it into the synnomic, then takes place. Nev-ertheless, the loci of these regions of personal experimentation are themselves dependent upon the syndoxic field, and effectively set up by it. For instance, a person may be guided to establish a completely idiosyncratic (maximally synnomic) way of thinking about the politi-cal system of the given country, yet the very same person would never question his or her own patriotic feelings toward the country as a whole. The latter domain remains outside of the promoted region of synnomization, and is appropriated by the person "on the side" from the active questioning and experimentation with ideas within the syn-nomization region.

The Focus on Experimental Logic

Baldwin's focus was on logic – yet on something different from classical logic. Namely, he emphasized the experimental logic, by which he tried to emphasize how thought proceeds by experimenta-tion, which "consists essentially in the *experimental* erection of an ob-ject already made up in consciousness, and its treatment as having a meaning or value which *it has not yet been found to have*, with the expectation and intent that in the result it may be found to have it" (Baldwin, 1908, p. 4).

Thus, the cognitive activity entailed in the logic is oriented towards further construction of meanings. He made a conscientious effort to redefine many of the crucial terms of classical logic (e.g., disjunction, proposition, implication, inductive and deductive inference; Baldwin, 1908). Nevertheless, his elaboration of logical concepts can be seen as a frivolous step in the area of language philosophy, and is not well connected with the foundations of genetic logic as outlined above.

Baldwin's Introduction of the Notion of "Schema." Baldwin's focus on the functional role of construction of meanings led him to the formulation of a schema notion. Its foundations are in the person's constant movement of *what is* (= is made to be, by creating a given meaning), toward *what-is-not-yet*. The latter is inevitable, given the uncertainty of the context in which a person is attempting to make the next "move" at construction. In that, imagery, fantasy, and *Einfühlung* ("sembling") play an important role. An external object is put into some constructed, desired imaginary role, and leads to the establishment of its internalized counterpart – the schema.

The semblant or make-believe use of an object having merely inner character as image or fancy, whereby it is treated for playful or other personal purposes as having further meaning or reference. The object thus becomes a "scheme", a *Schema*, charged with further meaning which it has not as yet been found in its own right. (Baldwin, 1908, p. 5)

The actual thing, passes into the instrumental image, becoming a mere "schema" of the further intent read in and through it, to be again 'tried-on' in the actual struggle with the world. (Baldwin, 1911, p. 6)

It is through further experimentation that the person builds up the cognitive schemata – the present *content* (presently established schema) is set up in a tensional relation with present *intent for the immediate future state* of the thinking process. The schema is *anticipatory* as to the desired future state. Thus, "The different stages of experimental meaning called, from the psychic point of view, schematic, are those in which an established recognitive context, accepted for what it is, *is also read for what it may become*" (Baldwin, 1908, p. 11).

It is clear that Baldwin's conception of the schema follows conceptual traditions that he had applied to the development of infant self-control over ever-novel motor actions in the early 1890s. If Baldwin was talking about the establishment of new, internal "control centers" in the sensori-motor system, then by the time of his *Thought and Things*, the notion of schema became the equivalent when applied to internalized mental processes. The former focus on persistent imitation is paralleled with the latter focus on experimental logic. Similarly to a child who is involved in persistent imitation of some motor action model, the adult involved in the cognitive inquiry using experimental logic is experimenting with the properties of the external object (of cognition), and modifies the schema by way of feedback from this experimentation.

Developmental Stages: Prelogical, Logical, and Hyperlogical

The development of human cognitive functions, according to Baldwin, entailed three stages: prelogical, logical, and hyperlogical. This sequence fits the notion of differentiation and hierarchical integration (e.g., that of Werner, 1957), or of a system of dialectical synthesis. First, from the undifferentiated field (captured by the notion of a prelogical stage) there emerges a set of differentiated oppositions (which are described by formal logical forms). The tension between these logical opposites leads to the emergence of dialectical synthesis, which provides the nature of the highest, hyperlogical stage. In the latter, the former opposites become united in a complex in which a newly emergent feature of the situation – a higher-level organizer – comes to unite the opposites.

Superficially, the hyperlogical stage phenomena may resemble the undifferentiated state of the prelogical stage. However, the defining characteristic of the third stage is the emergence of affective generalization.

Affective Logic. Baldwin (similarly to Vygotsky later), was eager to solve the problem of relations between human affective and rational sides. Without trying to eliminate the duality between them through the notion of fusion (as suggested by Dewey, see Chapter 5, and by his many followers in years to come), Baldwin was eager to look at processes *of affective generalization, ejection*, and *idealization* (as parts of the affective processes) in relation to their rational-logical counterparts. He warned his readers that his affective logic "is distinctively French in its origin, as the theory of *Einfühlung*, "also accepted and utilized in its fundamental meaning, is distinctively German" (Baldwin, 1911, p. x). He was building actively on the heritages of Ribot and Lipps.

Affective processes are teleological, i.e., they express desired values and beliefs in ways that relate the presently established belief with one desired for the future, or that are simply considered true. This teleology can occur through processes of affective generalization, ejection, and idealization.

Affective generalization entails the distribution of a particularly established emotional tone from the object (or context) of its original emergence, to other objects (and contexts). This process is complemented by ejection: "the self . . . embodied in . . . mass of general interests, ejects itself semblantly or imaginatively into other selves, and so establishes meanings of common interest, conformity and practice" (Baldwin, 1911, p. 94).

Idealization is a by-product of constructive internalization. In the process of establishing personal meanings of objects, the object becomes "charged with further unfulfilled meaning" (Baldwin, 1906, p. 233). Persons always create ideal meanings of objects, aside from their common meanings. These ideal meanings orient the person in relation to the given object, as well as to other objects: "The ideal meaning resides (1) in the objects constructed out of certain materials – these materials . . . *not allowing any construction which does not have something of the ideal meaning* – and (2) in the treatment of other materials in the same way, that is, *as if they also had the characters which normally take on this meaning*" (Baldwin, 1906a, p. 235).

The person establishes an idealized view of one object in his or her encounters with it, and then transfers it to further encounters with other objects. In its function, the idealized meaning limits the set of possible affective relations to these objects. It serves as the mediating device that imbalances any equally-valenced disjunctive situation ("X is equally either Y or Z"), turning it into a case of affective dismissal of one of the options ("X *must be* Y, even if it can be both Y or Z").

It becomes clear that affective logic is closely intertwined with the cognitive logic, at the level of particular content-filled versions of those operations. Baldwin's elaboration of the operation of disjunction illustrates that connection very well:

We customarily say, 'It is this or that', meaning 'It may be this, *but is probably that*'; and often also, 'It may be either of these, *I have no means of deciding*'; and sometimes, again, 'It may be that, *but let us try this*'. While, that is, the circle of determinateness closes around the entire group of alternatives, it does not in just the same sense hold aloof from each of them. On the contrary, *it has its points of emphasis, its selections, its preferences, due to the attitude – the selective interest, the dispositional character, etc., – of the thinker.* Some disjunctions should read, 'It may be that, *but I hope it is this*'. (Baldwin, 1908a, p. 50, emphases added)

The subjective future-orientation, as well as personal volition at the given time ("let's try this" and "I hope it is this") link the affective and cognitive sides in the logical form of disjunction. In reality, Baldwin's efforts to elaborate logical terms amounted to construction of a synthetic philosophy of language (on the basis of schemata of the classical logic), where the meanings entered into logical forms have both representational semantic structure, and personal-desire or preference quality. In this, Baldwin was moving along an intellectual trajectory that was later – in the 1920s and 1930s – used by Karl Bühler in the development of his speech theory (Bühler, 1934/1965; 1990), particularly in respect of Bühler's three levels of "fieldability" of meanings (the *Darstellungsfeld*). Bühler's primary level corresponds to the cognitive side of Baldwin's logic, his secondary field (that of linkages with personal life history) covers much of the affective side of Baldwin's logic. Finally, the tertiary field (later used by the "speech act theory") – that of the communicator's intentionality in saying something – would fit with Baldwin's focus on the teleology of thinking.

Real-life phenomena where the logical and teleological sides of human psychological functioning relate exist everywhere. Yet phenomena of religious (or any kind of ideological) thought may bring these phenomena to our attention with greatest force. As Baldwin remarked,

The logical erects classes and establishes facts and truths, by its methods of proof; the teleological issues in affective interests and defines ends and values. Now, in the religious life we find the object, God, looked upon as *really existing, as if* established by processes of knowledge, while, at the same time, it is determined by the religious interest *as an ideal or end*. Religion claims to present both a system of truth and a system of personal and social values. God is *both fact and ideal*; not merely in the common way of a value attaching to a fact or truth, as utility attaches to my inkstand, but in the peculiar way in which a meaning attaches to that which symbolises it. (Baldwin, 1915, p. 108)

Baldwin himself saw the solution to human social (and personal) problems in the realm of aesthetic synthesis. Again, one is reminded of Vygotsky's interests – Baldwin ended his career in psychology by elaborating a system of affective-cognitive development that was built on the notion of aesthetic synthesis (Baldwin, 1915). Approximately at the same time, the young Vygotsky began his complicated travels into the understanding of mind in society from an explicit interest in the phenomena of affective generalizations that are triggered in the recipients at theater performances, or in reading poetry or short stories.

Pancalism

Baldwin's final synthetic solution to the problem of the social nature of human psychological functions took the form of an aesthetic synthesis. He labeled this focus "pancalism," or "constructive affectivism," as it was claimed to unite aesthetic feeling with a distanced view of the object. Aesthetic synthesis entails retaining the object-subject differentiation (i.e., the subject does not "fuse" himself with the object), yet it simultaneously entails the emergence of a novel feeling that overwhelms the subject. In Baldwin's terms:

What we are justified in taking the real to be is that with which the free and full aesthetic and artistic consciousness finds itself satisfied. *We realise the real in achieving and enjoying the beautiful.* (Baldwin, 1915, pp. 276–7)

The object of art does not tolerate any strictly private motives or purposes; it is detached from the individual self, at the same time that it embodies what is common and essential to the life of all. (Baldwin, 1915, p. 298)

In aesthetic experience, the singular event (a person's encounter with a particular art object in a here-and-now situation) becomes generalized by the person to represent something at the level of great abstraction. The aesthetically operating person relates to the object in terms that are generic, even as the actual encounter is not different from a mundane one. Thus, an external observer watching a person who faces the Mona Lisa with admiration, need not distinguish that observation from seeing persons watching food staples in supermarkets. However, the former setting can entail an aesthetic synthesis (of the person) that "leaps" from the immediate encounter to notions of "art" and "beauty," while the supermarket scenario is unlikely to reveal such an emergence of the highest affective generalizations. Such episodes of aesthetic synthesis are necessarily singular (in psychologists' terms, these are N = 1 case studies). No appreciator of aesthetic experiences looks for a "representative sample" of such encounters prior to "jumping" to the aesthetic generalization. Rather, it is exactly the uniqueness of the occasion that allows such generalizations to emerge.

The person's arrival at the aesthetic synthesis is made possible by the process of tension between the aesthetic and mundane areas of reflection. Thus, for instance in watching a theater performance,

There is a certain vibration of the mind between the ordinary and prosaic system of actualities and the dramatic situation depicted on the stage. The

mind's eye, open in turn to each of the two spheres of actual and semblant, prosaic and ideal, enhances the value of the latter by allowing itself
from time to time to lapse into the former. And after the play is over, after
the intense concentration of the mind on the depicted situation, there is a
violent return, a reaction amounting sometimes to a shock, to the partial
interests and concerns of every-day life . . . it is simply the return from the
ideal completeness of a fully organized aesthetic whole to the sphere of
relativeness, opposition, incompleteness. (Baldwin, 1915, pp. 281–2)

Pancalism retains the structure of the generalized affective (aesthetic) process, and constitutes (for Baldwin) the highest form of psychological synthesis. Even within the pluralist set of aesthetic experiences, some of them serve as anchoring points.

Conclusions: Sociogenetic Ideas and Logic of Development

James Mark Baldwin's contributions to developmental science at the
beginning of the twentieth century still await adequate evaluation and
elaboration as we are moving into the next millennium. Even as he at
times tried all too hard to invent solutions to unsolved problems, and
failed, it is a rare case to see an author undertaking such an ambitious
effort as to create a full system of the logic of development. Maybe the
idea of a logic of development was ill-conceived (i.e., perhaps development defies any logic, except for whatever may be mentioned under
the label of *abductive* logic, or "*il*logical" logic. Yet the effort was
commendable. Baldwin served as a crucial starting point for the study
of child development undertaken by Jean Piaget in the 1920s and
1930s. He was an influential source for Vygotsky. And he was directly
indebted to Pierre Janet, as was described in Chapter 3.

Baldwin's ideas emerged at the intersection of intellectual influences – uniting the American cultural quests of the time with the
European tendencies of psychology's separation from philosophy. Although American himself, Baldwin's intellectual quest – like that of
any scientist and serious thinker – had no national boundaries. It is
only by an unfortunate series of sociomoralistic events that Baldwin
vanished from his leading position in American psychology after the
1910s.

However, it is possible that Baldwin's work could have stopped
anyway: As in Mead's case (see Chapter 6), Baldwin's intellectual
advancement proceeded quite contrary to the prevailing ethos of pragmatism and its practical outgrowth – behaviorism. Baldwin's evolu-

tionary thought and developmental philosophy was antithetical to behaviorism, and it was an opponent of the development of pragmatism (at least Dewey's version). Probably he would have felt out of place if he had been accused for taking a "soft" or "subjectivist" stance in psychology. Together with the advent of one or another popular perspective in psychology, previous thinkers are easily forgotten in the fervent of the (self) declared "revolutions" – be these "behaviorist," "cognitive," "ecological," or any other. The demonic battlehorse of Progress in Psychology usually gallops ahead, leaving the elderly wise men and women of previous times flabbergasted by its terrifying sounds. Yet the slogans of various "revolutions" in psychology that have succeeded one another leave the discipline relatively empty of substantive progress. Retrospects on Baldwin have at times pointed to his rhetoric constructions (of new terms, or of grand general systems of thought), yet it is precisely these starting efforts that have remained without further development. In developmental psychology, Baldwin was *the* most relevant American contributor to the science at large. Ironically, the social context of development of psychology in the United States has turned his developmental theoretical ideas into unwelcome (or at least unnoticed) visitors in their own native land.

CHAPTER FIVE

Pragmatism and the Social Mind: An American Context

> The test of truth is utility: It's true if it works. Hence the final philosophical wisdom: if you can't have what you want, don't want it. For man is the measure of all things. The universe ultimately is a joint-stock affair: We participate in the evolution of reality. Our action is a real factor in the course of events. In the search for truth, we must run the risk of error. Lies are false only if they are found out: a perfectly successful lie would be tantamount to absolute truth. We must 'will to believe'.
>
> Bowden, 1904, p. 421

American philosophy of pragmatism emerged from the social context of the end of the nineteenth century. The credo of utility became its core, which was emphasized with a fervent of restless eagerness. Its opposing ideological stance was the notion of the given (to be more precise: God-given) nature of things, propagated through churches. Yet the men who were active in creating this focus were themselves products of the religious contexts in the United States. So it is not surprising that the advent of pragmatism at the end of the 1890s had the flavor of a new creed.

Overcoming the confines of one belief system often requires creating another. The philosophical side of this new creed was an appendix to the call to action in the rapidly changing society. This social turmoil of the late nineteenth and early twentieth centuries made social sciences in North America a fertile ground for the growth of social ideas.

The Puritan Roots and the Tension between Individualism and Collectivism

The emergence of the pragmatist perspective in America was an appropriate escape from the religious orthodoxies that pervaded the United States. However, as it often happens, opposition to one orthodoxy leads to the construction of a new one. Escaping and overcoming religious orthodoxies has always been a complicated process for any science. In America, where the puritan religious tendencies historically found an appropriate and free land for proliferation, this issue has plagued the thinking in the social sciences into our present time. The roots of American perspectives on the social nature of individuals are found in seventeenth and eighteenth century Europe (see Tufts, 1904 for an analysis of the ideas of Shaftesbury, Butler, Hobbes, and Mandeville). The American independence gave these root tendencies a trajectory of new development in a society that combined commercial exploration with religious piety. The result was a general feeling of optimism: Through community actions any problem could be solved (Ross, 1907). The fact that the exact meaning of community was not questioned indicates the strength of that faith.

The U.S. is a unique descendant of the English colonial domination that the enterprising organizers of the Boston Tea Party successfully revoked, and which developed by its own inherent social trajectory during the past two centuries. In the nineteenth century the U.S. society was primarily rural, and given its vast territory, allowed for various social, religious, and ethnic groups to set up their particular communities in different locations. By and large, the relationships between these communities displayed the characteristic of tolerance at a distance, which may be the core of American democracy.

Efforts to control others go along with a focus on freedom for oneself and others. Tolerance of others' freedom has limits when these others are geographically close, and enter into the social organization of the local community. In the United States, examples of social actions of intervention in the activities of sub-groups of people abound. Most of these remain local actions, even if they become nationally known. Efforts to eradicate pornography have surfaced in the United States throughout its history (e.g., the Comstock case in 1887; Beisel, 1993), and the censorship of texts for public consumption has recurred at the level of local communities (e.g., DelFattore, 1992).

Describing societies in terms of unitary traits is a conventional creation of simple solutions to complex problems. Surely the United States cannot be described in terms of homogeneous, and positively flavored traits like "melting pot" or "land of freedom," even if these are desirable social presentations for institutional discourse. Rather, a description may be adequate through systemic combining of opposite social tendencies, such as tension between "freedom" (individual's constitutional rights) and "unfreedom" (e.g., sociomoral regulation of people by local community). The opposites in the United States, like in any other society, exist in unison. Their tension may lead to the excessive focusing on one of them in social presentation (e.g., the American public presentation of the United States as the heaven of unlimited freedom), while legitimizing acts limiting freedom (e.g., forcing smokers out of public areas) through the notion of the needs of the wider community. The same is true of other societies. For example, neither would the Russian society be adequately described by assumed traits of "collectivism" or "submission to authority." Along with such tendencies are their opposites – of "individualism" (sometimes taking the form of anarchism) and insubmissiveness. Opposite characteristics coexist in a given society are mutually linked. The crucial question then is: In what ways can that mutuality be conceptualized?

Mutuality of Individualism and Collectivism

A description of any society is possible in terms of mutually united opposites. Overlooking that leads to conceptual impasses. Yet the latter are widespread in psychology. A good example of the latter are the efforts to classify societies into "individualist" and "collectivist" ones (e.g., Triandis, 1995). This leads to empirical cross-cultural research that is rooted in a theoretically unproductive assumption of uniformity. At the conceptual starting point, empirical researchers often begin with an exclusive definition of the opposites. For example:

Individualism pertains to societies in which *the ties between individuals are loose*: Everyone is *expected to look after* himself or *herself and his or her immediate family*. Collectivism as its opposite pertains to societies in which people from birth onwards *are integrated into strong, cohesive ingroups*, which throughout people's lifetime continue to protect them in exchange for unquestioning loyalty. (Hofstede, 1991, p 51, emphases added)

This contrast compares different levels of social integration as if they were not different. The description of the individual's relation (of taking care) to one's immediate family is not contradictory to the notion of strong cohesive ingroups (which in this case are nuclear family ingroups – made strong and cohesive through individuals' efforts). In contrast, the "collectivistic" scenario applies to groups of differing complexity (including the immediate family group, but extending outward to a kinship group, community, etc). The immediate family in its cohesive form is present in both, while the collectivistic scenario emphasizes cohesiveness (and loyalty) to a larger social unit.

Hofstede's differentiation is interesting also in its overview of the relations between the opposites. Persons in any society necessarily unite in themselves both sides: While making strong "we" versus "they" distinctions (as in collectivist societies; cf. Kim, 1994), the persons who make such distinctions look after themselves in the midst of the given we (in-group). During different historical periods, the socio-institutional guidance toward making the *we* versus *they* distinctions can become exaggerated (e.g., see descriptions of Fascist Italy – Malvano, 1997; of Nazi Germany – Michaud, 1997; of China – Chan, 1985; and of the former Soviet Union – Valsiner, 1984), precisely through an emphasis on the individual's active looking after him or herself in accordance with the collectivist emphasis. Furthermore, a society can organize human lives in dynamic ways, which render the exclusive distinction of the opposites unrealistic (e.g., the case of India, Sinha, & Tripathi, 1994).

That the distinction between individualism and collectivism as mutually exclusive entities is untenable becomes understood in cross-cultural psychologists' efforts to transcend the theoretical limitations (see Kim, 1994; Triandis, 1994, 1995; see also the critique by Branco, 1996). Here we can formulate a notion of mutuality of individualism and collectivism by viewing one of those as enabling a supportive structure for the other. Thus, to be individualistic, a person needs to be collectivistic first, and vice versa. This linkage amounts to a terminology of individualistic collectivism or collectivistic individualism, thus uniting the opposites into a functional whole, rather than treating them as exclusive (either–or) poles.

Unity of individualism and collectivism would be the normal case in any society, since any society encompasses both the foci on stability and on change. Surely change is possible only if some individuals (as persons, or in coordinated groups) break away (or through) the social status quo of a particular collectivistic system. Without letting some individuals take such an (individualistic) emphasis, the society cannot change (i.e., the only scenario for such change would be a social-consensual mutation of its rules – an unlikely or very slow way toward change).

Furthermore, the united opposites of individualism and collectivism may exist in different domains, in parallel, and yet be separate. The individualistic ethos of commerce for a trader may be paralleled by an ethos that accepts collectivism in his personal world of attachments – to his family, religion, political cause, etc. This solution to the unity of opposites – their separation into parallel activity domains, and as a consequence, co-existence of the two extremes – characteristically exists in the fragmented (or modularized) life-worlds of human beings.

Whether we look at feudal autocracies or contemporary democracies, we see that the personal actions by some leaders (kings, presidents, or re-electable parliament members) are coordinated with collective units (masses, social interest groups, parties, etc.). The individual in a role of a leader is interdependent with the collective "social other" of the given society. It is merely the forms of such interdependence that may vary between societies. In the context of European history,

Frequently in very despotically ruled groups individuality may develop itself very freely, in those aspects particularly which are not in participation with the mass. Thus began the development of modern individuality in the despotisms of the Italian Renaissance. Here . . . it was for the direct interests of the despots to allow the largest freedom to all those aspects of personality which were not identified with the regulated mass, i.e., to those aspects most apart from politics. Thus subordination was more tolerable. It is one of the highest tasks of administrative art to distinguish properly between those characteristics of men with respect to which they may be included in a leveled mass, and those other characteristics which may be left to free individual development. (Simmel, 1896, p. 175)

This focus on the simultaneous assurance of social role taking, (making persons into a leveled mass described by their prescribed roles – such as parents, employees, taxpayers, women, men, adolescents), and the creation of possibilities for individual actions (e.g., risk taking in business, personal accomplishments in sports, dieting, or piety) further fortifies the notion of the unity of individualism and collectivism. From that point of view, any classification of societies into the exclusively separated categories of individualistic (e.g., the United States is often attributed to this category) and collectivistic (e.g., many oriental societies are referred to by this label) obscures a basic organizational issue in our understanding of society in a generic sense.

Idealizing Community: An Anglo-American Cultural-Historic Construction

The key to making sense of the unity of individualism and collectivism in the United States is in the understanding of the relations between persons and communities. The latter term is ill defined as it applies to any size or form of social unit. At least during the past two centuries, two major oppositions that organize human activities in their social lives can be found in the United States. First is the unity of individualism and associative collectivism (i.e., individuals' dependence upon flexibly formed, and re-formed associations). Individuals are free from external bondage, but suggested to construct their own collective identities which then take the place of superordinate social control units. The second relevant opposition that may be built upon the first is the unity of active transformation of the environment (individuals' boundless freedom of action) and dutiful following of social norms (mostly of religious kinds or origins, fortified by the social consensus).

American's strong focus on the generic community may be rooted in the "Christian socialism" of England and the United States (Monroe, 1895). In the community orientation, the ideal of harmony between person and society is expressed. Yet this ideal is an ideal, rather than reality. Consequently the community's imperative to its individual members is to channel individual, uncontrollable zeals into that ideal action in favor of community.

The healthy affections and emotions of men should not be curbed but should be directed into useful channels. Zeal and ardor are precious gifts if only they tend in the right direction, and society may profit by every human attribute if only it has the wisdom to utilize it. The principle involved in attraction . . . is simply that of inducing men to act for the good of society. It is that of harmonizing the interests of the individual with those of society, of making it advantageous to individuals to do that which is socially beneficial; not merely in a negative form, as an alternative of two evils, as is done when a penalty is attached to an action, but positively, in such a manner that he will exert himself to do those things that society most needs to have done. (Ward, 1897, pp. 808–9)

This call for the positive direction of persons to serve their society is certainly reminiscent of the goal of attaining conscious discipline in the case of Soviet education during the latter part of the twentieth century (Valsiner, 1984), and takes new forms when a U.S. president teaches his subjects to: "Ask: not what your country can do for you, but what you can do for your country." Roots for this suggestion can be found in the changes that the Protestant Reformation brought with it, in terms of the locus of social control over the acts of individuals. Once the persons themselves were delegated the social role of making sense of the rights and wrongs, they needed to be taking in the social control mechanisms over their conduct, into their individual consciousness. Much of the recurrent story telling in sociogenetic and sociocultural psychology, (for example "human psychology is social"), continues this tendency of viewing persons as required agents of social control over their own selves.

By the nineteenth century, the United States was operating with success in this channeling of the positive kind – that of active participation by individuals – yet remaining punitive on the other. In this orientation toward community, the active role of persons in establishing, maintaining, and reorganizing such collective units is taken to an extreme in the United States. Alexis de Tocqueville's – even if at times skeptical – insights into U.S. society during the 1830s remain interesting to the present time:

Americans of all ages, all stations in life, and all types of disposition are forever forming associations. There are not only commercial and industrial associations in which all take part, but others of a thousand different types – religious, moral, serious, futile, very general and very limited, immensely large and very minute. Americans combine to give fêtes, found seminaries, build churches, distribute books, and send missionaries to the antipodes. Hospitals, prisons, and schools take shape in that way. Finally, if they want to proclaim a truth or propagate some feeling by the encouragement of a great example, they form an association. In every case, at the head of any new undertaking, where in France you would find the government or in England some territorial magnate, in the United States you are sure to find an association. (de Tocqueville, 1969, p. 513)

Hence the focus on the role of the social embeddedness of individual activities is already embedded into the texture of the U.S. society. The forming of an association is an act by some (or many) persons who subsequently begin to follow the association's norms. Hence the personal actions and their immediate embeddedness in the social lives of people are intimately intertwined. They are intertwined through the participation in communal goal-directed actions. A community is goal oriented – it is constantly in the process of transforming or maintaining the life conditions of individuals that belong to it (as well as that of others, who do not). Ideologies operate as superordinate value systems for a community's goal. The contemporary dominant social stratum in the United States – the 'middle class' – was a historically emerging new social order in the middle of the nineteenth century's American religious and economic transformations (see Ryan, 1981).

The tendency to form associations leads to the co-existence of many different associations in the United States at any given time. All different social groups – from religious orthodoxies to alternative lifestyle movements – operate through the same formation of active embedding of the individual in the constructed social context. These processes work when the society is in a relative state of stability as a whole; while in specific loci within the society heterogeneous forms of social units may exist.

The United States during the nineteenth century was filled with the upsurge (and later decline) of various utopian communities. Examples of these included communes with socialist equality (Robert Owen's society of New Harmony, 1825–7), "perfectionist" procreation in the society of Oneida (see Fogarty, 1994), evangelistic New Awakening (Charles G. Finney); or socio-religious reformation of marriage (by the Mormon Society in Utah). Many ideas on the social nature of individual psyches were put to practical tests, and were expressed in religious messages. For example:

Evolution through the social passion and its life of humane service, transmutes the individuality from naturehood into humanhood. It transfigures the private self from the low, base, serpentine thing, crawling on its belly and feeding upon dust, to the majestic creature of God; its attitude upright; its radiation beauty; its movement harmony; its aspect benignant, intelligent, divine. The mission of Collectivity is 'not to destroy but to fulfill.' (Harris, 1891, p. 10)

The fate of social heterogeneity in the United States is ambiguous. Often it is possible for the different alternative societies or lifestyles to co-exist with majority values and beliefs. Yet there are examples (like in the case of Mormon society and the Federal government) that have led to direct conflicts. And of course the impacts of the Civil War and its latter memories demonstrated how a fight between two 'loyal communities' can come into being on U.S. soil. The prevailing tensions around the issues of slavery were sufficiently heterogeneous as well. Yet these tensions have been institutionally forgotten in cases where American history is presented as a monologic master narrative (see the analysis of history narratives by Wertsch, 1997). The social functions of such an univocal presentation are those of a goal-oriented community control over the potential emergence of deviations from the community norm.

To summarize, two basic social strains could be seen in the United States during the nineteenth century: the Enlightenment-based focus on building a new empire of liberty (Thomas Jefferson) and the anti-Enlightenment evangelicalism. However, "Both viewed the American past and future in utopian terms: The United States was destined to establish a new society, based upon the dignity and brotherhood of man and the fatherhood of God, an example to the rest of the world" (Hugins, 1972, p. 5).

Thus the common denominator of different, mutually opposite, social ideologies could be found in the focus on the primacy of belonging to a social group. Such belonging to group takes place by individual choice, and all that under the banner of God. The latter belief creates an overarching context for the individuals' striving toward community membership.

The parallels of the U.S. and Russian societies may be found in the focus on community: the community of participants believing in a cause in the U.S. context, and that of a village community in the Russian context. The crucial question for America was the transformation of the rural community into that of a town – thus, the question of trustability of city municipalities was a concern for publicly minded urban reformists (Addams, 1905). A solution to make municipalities trustworthy was found in practical action (Addams, 1902).

Despite all the heterogeneity within the United States during the nineteenth century, until the last two decades, it could be considered to be in a steady yet heterogeneous state. The vast territory, the kaleidoscopic social organization of state governments, and the generally limited (and distrusted) powers of the Federal government create a social system that is unique in the world. Efforts to imitate it by other countries are either doomed to fail, or have turned out to be failures already (e.g., the exportation of the U.S. kind of social system to Liberia).

Mechanisms of Social Reformism

What are the mechanisms on which the social reform movements are based? First, there exists a tendency to create boundaries between the subject and the objects that create a disturbance in the subject's state. This amounts to a version of ingroup ↔ outgroup, we ↔ they distinction, onto which a specific valuation is projected. Under ordinary circumstances, the valuation can be within a neutral range (e.g., "They are just different from us."), or can entail subject-centered value assertions (e.g., "They are different from us, and have their right to be so, yet we are in the right way of being.") The reference to basic right is usually sufficient to re-evoke such an acceptance of "the other" in terms of tolerance. The subjective preference, and belief in the adequacy of the self's own point of view, remain intact.

This tolerance changes if the object is perceived as threatening the status quo of the subject beyond the limits controllable through the semiotic mediating device of rights. The overly disturbing object now becomes subjected to either segregation from the subject by removal (e.g., moving the vices away from a community), by eradication, or other means; or it becomes subjected to change into a form no longer threatening to the subject (see Royce's discussion of the need to teach loyalty notions to immigrants as will be discussed in this chapter). The opposites of acceptance (paired with missionary reformation) and rejection (possibly involving expulsion) of outsiders are united in any society. The historical uniqueness of the United States has led to a solution where the relations between these opposites have been dynamic and hence neither tendency has become fixed. That dynamic nature of the opposition has granted the society with its wave-like pattern of movement in the positive and negative orientations toward immigrants, and the unity of social inferiority and superiority complexes (see Phillips, 1947).

Rapidly Changing Society: Unity of Openness and Rigidity

The social changes in the United States at the end of the nineteenth century and at the beginning of the twentieth were remarkable; both in the realm of industrialization and urbanization on the one hand, and increases in immigrant population on the other. The same society that had previously been in a steady state entered into a turmoil, within which novel social tendencies were mixed with efforts to maintain the previous status quo. The latter tendency included efforts toward racial (Haller, 1984) and moral (Rosen, 1982) purification of U.S. society during the Progressive Era (1900–18). While rapid urbanization and industrialization brought with them new ways of living for many, there were others who made it their task to control the actions of the new urbanites, re-educate (or save) them if they appeared wayward, and select the kinds of "desirable" immigrants. The active socio-moral missionary effort was put to work at home.

During the 1890s, heightened stress and storm in the U.S. society – wrought by the immense immigration (e.g., New York City's population grew twelve-fold during the 1890s) and industrialization – marked the emergence of numerous tensions. The immigration wave of this time was different from earlier ones. While the earlier immigration had led to the spreading of immigrants over vast rural landscapes, now the industrialization at the end of the century kept them in the growing cities. City life was – at the turn of the century in the United States – almost the equivalent to work in modern industry (see Henderson, 1909), with all the implications of such a vocational niche.

Urbanization created substantial stress: many of the issues could have been solved easily in the rural agricultural life. For example, the issue of what would children do during their summer vacations (in rural contexts they participated in agricultural labor on the farms) required new attention when treated in urban environments (e.g., children loitering in city streets, participating in the crime scene). This led to questions about the value of vacation schools (summer vacation time school activities – interestingly, without books – with the orientation of taking children back to nature; American, 1898b; Milliken, 1898), and to the creation of children's playgrounds in urban environments (American, 1898a; Zueblin, 1898). Social guidance of children's play into "wholesome" directions was part of the efforts to cope with the social stress, through training children to work together. Kindergartens were viewed as the training ground for community participation (O'Shea, 1906). It was assumed that in children's joint play good will and cooperation may be learned, while tendency to crime will not be given an opportunity to emerge.

Interestingly, the major themes at the turn of the century have continuity. In general, the creation of public parks in urban areas – a behavior setting where features of a rural environment are brought into a controlled city context – were advocated as miraculous solutions to the problems of the new urban crime of adolescents (Addams, 1912; Hamilton, 1900). The worries about urban conditions for children of one hundred years ago sound much like our contemporary talk of inner city conditions in the United States:

Where small parks have been made, the verdict of the police is unanimous that they have changed the character of the neighborhood. Give the children adequate playgrounds, and the same spirit and imagination which form rowdy gangs form baseball clubs and companies for plays and games and drills of various kinds. Children's imagination is vivid and must be satisfied. It will satisfy itself, whether we wish it or not. Feed it properly, and it will blossom into beautiful fruitage; starve it and throw it back upon itself, and we have all the ugly excrescences, deformities, and depravities of crowded-city life. (American, 1898a, p. 167)

The social context of the rapidly urbanizing, industrializing, and overly immigrant-filled country in the United States provides the context for understanding how American social science at the turn of the century was both open to new ideas, and rigidly closed about issues of social policy. Aside from the ideological voice of making a problem out of the new urban industrialization processes in accordance with a regressive narrative framework, (downfall of the old mores and values, due to immigration, overcrowding, and poverty), voices of revolutionizing the society through exactly the same processes could also be heard. Without denying the social problems in the urban life, it still became a positive utopia to view new urban communities rising where currently social stress could be viewed. This ideological voice played with the connotations of the urban-rural contrast:

The words civil, urbane, and politic indicate that men soon realized how good manners and diplomacy were promoted by city life. In contrast, the terms rustic, pagan, and heathen connote a certain backwardness among country folk . . . It may be granted that the proverbial "smartness" of the city chap is superficial, but the fact remains that ambitious country boys seek the stirring life of towns and are apparently stimulated by it. (Woolston, 1912, p. 608)

The opposition of both problematizing and idealizing voices created a tension in American life at the turn of the century that in

Europe had proceeded earlier. The tension carried over to the intellectual life.

Tensions in American Intellectual Life

Of course the intellectual life in the United States moved historically in a slightly different course than that of the industrializing society. Nevertheless, some aspects of the social demands of industrialization amplified the themes that intellectuals thought about. There has been an inherent tension that historically dominates U.S. society: The contradiction between the action orientation, which is emphasized in politics and business, and speculation. The latter is oriented toward the interpretive tradition that stems from the social-religious history of this unique country.

This contradiction has led to the unique form of independent dependence of the social sciences in the United States. The latter depend upon the society's immediate needs to fix its problems at a quick speed, and thus are intellectually guided by that. Since improving society is a complex and inherently contradictory process, rarely do the campaigns of such a quick fix lead to success. Oftentimes, they have given rise to rhetoric efforts to accomplish the unaccomplishable, and to declarative persuasion that the latter has indeed been accomplished.

On the side of speculation, fashionable ideas which claim to be socially useful are turned into theories, without much ado about their philosophical underpinnings. Many of the ideas that became fashionable have been of European origin, yet adjusted to the American conditions. That contradiction continues to fuel the discourse in the social sciences, along the lines well described by one of its participants, pertaining to the turn of the century:

America's native culture accepted the forms and standards of European culture. It was confessedly inferior, not different. It was not indigenous. The cultivated American was a tourist even if he never left American shores. When the American felt the inadequacy of the philosophy and art native to the Puritan tradition, his revolt took him abroad in spirit if not in person, but he was still at home for he was an exponent of the only culture the community possessed. (Mead, 1930a, p. 218)

Nevertheless, the creative social turmoil in the United States did produce substantial extensions of the basically European ideas of sociogenetic perspectives on human development. These ideas arrived at their Euro-American synthesis that has in many forms continued to dominate the social sciences of this century. Thus, John Dewey's version of pragmatism lives on in the sociogenetic traditions of psychology and education in the present time (see Chapter 9), and themes of the behavioristic creed live their new life under "cognitivist" labels. And, after all, psychology's glorious return to the uses of the label "cognitivism" is traceable to the ethical perspectives at the beginning of the twentieth century (see Green, 1996), rendering the question of the innovation of the core of the discipline to be episodic and jumpy.

Why Psychology Prevails

Proliferation of psychology in America during the 1890s was a relevant social tendency, catering mostly to the social strata that could find in it a way out from the traditional religiously flavored authoritarian social context. The themes of importance at the time seem familiar to the modern reader:

Middle-class culture of the late nineteenth century, especially for youth, consisted of anxieties as well as ambition, self-doubt as well as self-control and knowledge, and fragmentation as well as order. If the 1890s are seen only in terms of the professionalization of the sciences, vertical mobility, and progressive attitudes, then we can see how the new psychology served the citizens of this culture by way of offering a utilitarian and reformist as well as scientifically grounded profession. (Morawski, 1996, p. 149)

The American social setting at the turn of the century was pregnant with an upsurge of new intellectual efforts, most of which quickly became canalized into practices that were viewed as useful by communities, or profitable by their business applications. The notable tendency of institutionalization of psychology in the service of social-ideological agendas has been the mark of American psychology all through this century (Danziger, 1990; Herman, 1995). It is the dominant substratum of U.S. society – the recognized but almost always ill-defined middle class – that has created the need for psychology in the United States, has fed it by accepting different social constructions of psychological problems, and has paid for their treatment. The result is a constant tension in the participation of academic psychology –

aimed at constructing a basic science – in the local social discourses of communities (such as mental health, prediction of outcomes, detection of at risk cases, and prevention of socially undesirable outcomes, or eradication of social vices). In a society of a strict religious background, the advancements of secularized knowledge are brought back to bear upon solving practical moral issues, obtaining the halo of scientific truth, while being used as weapons for moral crusades. Social histories of different diseases, such as anorexia nervosa (Brumberg, 1988) or AIDS illustrate the social nature of focusing attention by way of labeling diseases.

The American context at the beginning of this century was filled with the campaign of social hygiene against venereal diseases, within the wider context of purification of the socio-moral realm of the society as a whole (Hooker, 1915; Snow, 1915). Missionary campaigns raged over the vast country, building up their community of followers, and crushing or discrediting their opponents on the way. Yet, at the same time, knowledge about the morally reproachable aspects is limited, and the campaigns may themselves disappear as the focusing power of the moral rhetoric is worn off.

Summary: The American Focus of Attention on Community and Participation

This tension between "social control" (over issues of conduct and morality) and "individual choice" as a glorified right, is reflected in American thought about the social nature of human individuality. Different thinkers at the end of the last century (as well as of this century) invented slightly different ways of thinking about the issue. Yet the notion of the primary relevance of the community, and that of the person's active participation in it, seem to mark the American folk construction of the issue. The theme of the immersion of the person in a community seems to be shared by many American thinkers.

Given that the intellectual locus of gravity was on the community, it is not surprising that theoretical concepts that build on the assumption of the persons' immersion in the community find preference among American social scientists. Thus, appropriation by persons fitted the theoretical constructions of the social scientists at the turn of the century (e.g., Duff, 1902) as well as today (Rogoff, 1990; Wertsch, 1997). When the notion of the community is made into a conceptual departure point, the role of the persons within this community becomes that of participation in it, rather than that of any loose or distant relationship that the persons might establish with the community. Ironically, urbanization and industrialization created exactly the latter situation – a case where immigrant laborers, or non-unionized sweatshops (e.g., MacLean, 1903) became involved in loose social groups in their American context. These immigrants had their own social groups in which they were participating. These may have been their background kin groups – in the countries of origin or in equal immigrant status within the United States. Yet these groups were their communities – and no move from the control by these groups to the local community in the American sense could be established.

While recognizing the variety of impacts a social context can have for individuals, the American thinkers who used community as an anchor concept were usually presenting it in an idealized form. The notion of community for America is an utopia of socially constructed salvation of secular souls through their loyalty to some form of social unity. Hence it is defended vigorously against any efforts to replace it by another axiomatic standpoint. Likewise it remains a nebulous concept of inherently benevolent connotations. It could be argued that the focus on community in American social thought has been itself a reflection upon the challenges upon genuine rural social structures turning into urban governance vehicles.

The Role of the Philosophy of Josiah Royce within the Sociogenetic Tradition

The idealist sociogenetic philosophy of Josiah Royce (1855–1916) can be viewed as a transitory phenomenon from the nineteenth century's philosophy to its successors. Royce came from a fundamentalist background in California, and through his brilliance and hard work found a way to be one of the foremost philosophers at Harvard. The question of community was of interest to him during his childhood in California:

My earliest recollections include a very frequent wonder as to what my elders meant when they said that this was a new community. I frequently looked at the vestiges left by the former diggings of miners, saw that many pine logs were rotten, and that a miner's grave was to be found in a lonely place not far from my own house. Plainly men had lived and died thereabouts . . . The log and the grave looked old. The sunsets were beautiful . . . What was there then in this place that ought to be called new, or for that matter, crude? I wondered and gradually came to feel that part of my life's business was to find out what all that wonder meant. (McDermott, 1995, p. x)

Like most other educated Americans at the time, he made a short study trip (in 1875–76) to Germany, where he worked with Wilhelm Wundt and Wilhelm Windelband in Leipzig, and Hermann Lotze in Göttingen. Noteworthy was Royce's encountering of Wundt's psychology before its official separation from philosophy (in 1879). Back in the United States, Royce finished his dissertation: "Of the Independence of Principles of Knowledge" at Johns Hopkins University in Baltimore during 1878. After some time in California, Royce moved to Harvard in 1882, where he stayed until the end of his life. While becoming one of the two (William James being the other) notable philosophers at that small college, Royce never established a "school of thought" of his own, which would have meant having disciples carry around his message to the uninitiated. Such a lack of missionary endeavor was as un-American then as it would be nowadays. Furthermore, he actively discouraged an intellectual following. As the story goes, "One of his doctoral oral students thought to improve his chances by parroting the ideas of his mentor. Royce was displeased and threatened the student with an R.D. (Doctor of Royce) instead of a Ph.D" (Hine, 1991, pp. 118–19).

In the words of his interlocutors, Royce was free of conventions in everyday interaction, ready to engage a person in a substantive conversation without any preliminary niceties. He was "a benevolent monster of pure intelligence, zigzagging, ranging, and uncatchable" (John Jay Chapman in Hine, 1991, p. 123). A misfit into the refined society of New England because of his rough west coast manners and red hair, he left the refinements of that society far behind by his intellectual productivity. As is usually the case, the "nice" society entails pride in the triviality of interaction, and surely the better thinkers of all periods have had to find their individual ways to ignore the social-consensual pressures that are imposed upon them. Royce resisted the fundamentalist religious teachings of his parents as a young man, and would not let any cult or sect catch him into their bosom. In his later years, he described himself as finding his religious satisfaction: "In being the sole member of a religious sect. You need not propagate the faith, you are relieved from all the rivalry of fellow-worshippers, you enjoy alone the sacred fountains" (quoted in Hine, 1991, p. 42).

Even if he did not propagate his particular form of personal religion, Royce was adamant about propagating the idea of personal commitment to some belief system. Toward the end of his life (in 1911) Royce glorified the personal living in loyalty as an example of an "invisible church" (Royce, 1912, p. 280).

Royce's intellectual interdependence with William James and C. Sanders Peirce was notable, yet his philosophy was his – perhaps better connected with Continental European thought than with that of his native land. The Hegelian roots of his thought were reflected in his treatment of the social nature of human being. Royce's idealist philosophy of a Hegelian kind was a relevant intellectual addition to American intellectual life at the turn of the century (Mead, 1917). Combining his indebtedness to Hegel with influences from Spinoza, Fichte, and Schopenhauer (Royce, 1892a), Royce was interested in questions of selfhood and spirit in the context of community (see Collins, 1968).

The Issue of Loyalty: Self in the Middle of the Social World

Royce was adamant about loyalty in its generic sense – loyalty to loyalty (a principle of relating to the community in a general sense). The social realities at the time (the early 1900s) undoubtedly provided a good contrast to this general ideal: the loyalty. The many immigrants to the United States were usually far from the general principles of loyalty, but their practical loyalties were often with their social contexts of origin, rather than with the new country. Thus, Royce himself described his dispute with a "very earnest youth, the son of a Russian immigrant," sometime around 1907:

I was trying to tell . . . how much we all need some form of loyalty as a centralizing motive in our personal lives. I was also deploring the fact that, in our modern American life, there are so many social motives that seem to take away from people the true spirit of loyalty, and to leave them distracted, unsettled as to their moral standards, uncertain why or for what they live . . . My words had awakened my young friend's righteous indignation. 'Loyalty,' so he in effect said, 'has been in the past one of humanity's most disastrous failings and weaknesses. Tyrants have used the spirit of loyalty as their principal tool. I am glad,' he went on, 'that we are outgrowing loyalty, whatever its forms or whatever the causes that it serves. What we want in the future is the training of individual judgment. We want enlightenment and independence . . . ' (Royce, 1995, p. 29)

Royce had no difficulty subsuming his young opponent's call for the abolition of loyalty under the label of loyalty in his terms (i.e., loyalty to the fight of eliminating loyalty). Royce's 'loyal community' emphasized the centrality of the individual person, and the constructive nature of the individual's development of one's intricate self (Royce, 1893/1966; 1898). Yet that construction was not left to the individual himself, especially when the U.S. socio-moral texture of discourses was under the influence of massive foreign influences. The rapid immigration at the turn of the century created a perceived need to convert them into the belief system of the recipient society:

the task of teaching millions of foreign birth and descent to understand and to bear constantly in mind the value of loyalty, the task also of keeping our own loyalty intact in the presence of those enormous complications of social life which the vastness of our country, and the numbers of our foreign immigrants are constantly increasing. The problem here in question is not merely the problem of giving instruction in the duties of citizenship to those to whom our country is new, nor yet of awakening and preserving patriotism. It is the problem of keeping alive what we now know to be the central principle of the moral life in a population which is constantly being altered by new arrivals, and unsettled by great social changes. (Royce, 1995, p. 99)

Thus the development of the intra-psychological loyalty system in the newcomers (and maintenance of it in the hosts) was a social engineering task at the beginning of the twentieth century. The need for loyalty emphasized religious feelings, yet in their absolute, personal, rather than denominational, or institutional, sense. Thus, "Loyalty is the will to manifest, so far as is possible, the Eternal, that is, the conscious and superhuman unity of life, in the form of the acts of an individual Self" (Royce, 1995, p. 166).

Loyalty was seen by Royce as the center for individual personal integrity (or an "invisible church"). In terms of personal conduct, loyalty was to mean: "The willing and practical thoroughgoing devotion of a person to a cause. A man is loyal when, first, he has some cause to which he is loyal; when, secondly, he willingly and thoroughly devotes himself to this cause; and when, thirdly, he expresses his devotion in some sustained and practical way, by acting steadily in the service of his cause" (Royce, 1995, p. 9).

The center for such loyalty is personal devotion. The objects of loyalties can vary, as they are often external to the person, taking the form of social institutions. The latter can lead to contradictions. The divided nature of loyalty objects was quite clear to Royce – party, labor union, and national loyalties were often seen as mutually disagreeing (ibid., p. 107). Yet the social contradictions between loyalty objects did not mean for Royce a fragmentation of the issue. It was the person's loyalty to the selected loyalty object – even if (or maybe especially when) that loyalty results in social clashes – that indicated to Royce the basic functioning of the loyalty as a generic mechanism. In his terms, the person remains devoted to his or her devotion to a selected cause: There is something like "loyalty to loyalty."

Loyalty to Loyalty

It is to be expected from an absolute idealist philosopher to center the issues of a person's social embeddedness on the person's own subjective constructions of participation. Thus, loyalty was one of the personal psychological phenomena to relate with social units or ideologies. Loyalty to loyalty was a meta-attachment of a personal kind – loyalty to the very principle of loyalty. The notion was propagated by Royce almost as a catechism:

The conscience is the ideal of the self, coming to consciousness as a present command. It says, Be loyal. If one asked, Loyal to what? the conscience, awakened by our whole personal response to the need of mankind, replies, Be loyal to loyalty. If, hereupon, various loyalties seem to conflict, the conscience says: Decide. If one asks, How decide? conscience further urges, Decide as I, your conscience, the ideal expression of your whole personal nature, conscious and unconscious, find best. If one persists, But you and I may be wrong, the last word of conscience is, We are fallible, but we can be decisive and faithful, and this is loyalty. (Royce, 1995, pp. 91–2)

Loyalty to loyalty here becomes translated into the imperative to act, making decisions as they seem fitting for the person at the given time. Thus even acting in error is an act of loyalty, whereas a refusal to act is not. The person's inner dialogue between conscience and consciousness leads the latter into acting upon his or her own decision, yet under the control of the conscience. This happens in two ways: (1) to act (rather than not act) is prescribed, and (2) the realm of the possible actions is limited by the meanings created by conscience. Royce viewed social control as internalized; the "social other" has become the conscience, whom the person consults and from who he or she expects guidance in making his or her immediate decisions mediated via consciousness.

Royce's View on the Ego ↔ Non-Ego Dialectics

Royce set out his specific view on the self: as a dialectical unity of Self and Non-Self. The emergence of Ego depends upon the differentiation of the habits of guiding oneself, and remembering from the flow of the stream of consciousness. The subject-object differentiation allows the person to construct his Ego in terms of a contrast with its dialectical opposite (non-Ego). There are different possibilities for such a construction. According to Royce,

If a man regards himself, as this individual Ego, he always sets over against his Ego something else, viz.: some particular object represented by a portion of his conscious states, and known to him as his then present and interesting non-Ego. This psychological non-Ego, represented in one's conscious states, is of course very seldom the universe, or anything in the least abstract. And, for the rest, it is a very varying non-Ego . . . If I am in a fight, my consciously presented non-Ego is my idea of the opponent. Consequently I am then conscious of myself as of somebody fighting him. If I am in love, my non-Ego is thought of as my beloved, and my Self, however much the chord of it pretends . . . is the Self of my passion. (Royce, 1895a, p. 443)

The development of the self takes place through constructive imitation that builds new oppositions on the basis of social experiences. The origin of the process of the differentiation of Ego/non-Ego is social, and its vehicle is the use of language (Royce, 1895a, p. 449). Internalization is the process by which the social experiences become functional in the self system, which always entails dialectical oppositions. For instance,

If conscience is aroused . . . to act, one has, purely as a matter of social habit, a disposition to have present both the tendency to the action, and the disposition to judge it, standing to one another in the . . . relation of Ego and non-Ego. Which of them appears as the Ego, which the non-Ego, depends upon which most gets possession, in the field of consciousness, of the common sensibility . . . (Royce, 1895a, p. 454)

The ego and non-ego are thus competing for "possession" of "sensibility" – allowing for a variety of scenarios for such possession to emerge. The flexibility of the distribution of the roles of the Ego and non-Ego in Royce's self theory is crucial for development. This temporary tendency of dominance of one aspect of the self over the other resembles quite notably our contemporary interest in discourse analytic views on the self that apply Bakhtin's idea of "voices," their dialogue, and temporary prioritization of some voice over another (Wertsch, 1991, 1997; see also Chapter 9). Such a construction of asymmetrically dominant units in a pair guaranteed a view on the mental world in terms of dualities (Royce, 1894a, p. 543), quite differently from the anti-dualistic declarations of the Chicago School of thought, of John Dewey and his colleagues.

Voices in the Mind

For Royce, the phenomena of an internal dialogue were valuable sources of evidence for the demonstration of his self-system. Royce had access to the phenomena of self-work of a young student (reported in Royce, 1895a, pp. 574–84) which demonstrated richness of the internal dialogues, with self-analyzed different selves (or voices) marked, e.g.:

So I say to myself, I give myself up to you to make what use of it you can. The personal self – the narrowest – cries for recompense – says I am foolish – even in saying this 'foolish' foolish – says I may be ridiculed – The more impersonal steps in and says, What then the difference? You (that is I) may be foolish but he (you, Professor Royce) makes use of it – and he understands – you wish to be understood – you have no object – not much object even in this – but let the writing go to him. (Royce, 1895a, p. 583)

This excerpt – even as it was reported by Royce as an "anomaly of self consciousness" – is nevertheless usual for the intra-mental multivocality of "voices" and parallels descriptions of extra-mental voices in social interaction. Scenarios of different selves' perspective taken within the intra-psychological dialogue emerge in the stream of consciousness, the different "voices" begin to negotiate their relationships within the self, at times making reference to extra-mental (social) events. Differentiation of the perspectives of different selves amounts to the emergence of hierarchical organization, personally constructed meanings begin to act upon one another (e.g., the application of the notion of "foolish" upon saying "foolish" about something else). The parallel of this idea of the functioning of action control hierarchies and Pierre Janet's thinking is obvious (see Chapter 3). Royce's focus on how "voices act upon voices" is a forerunner to our contemporary efforts to explain the flexibility of human language Josephs & Valsiner, 1998). Through a hierarchy of voices, abstracting meaning from a given context becomes possible.

Infinite Potential for Abstraction: Meta-Voices

The emergence of meta-levels in the intra-self discourse has in principle possibilities for "infinite progress" into ever-more abstract and context-free talking about the different perspectives, as well as value-flavoring of any of those. This reflexivity of reasoning has rarely been considered in psychological analyses, yet it constitutes a relevant process in human symbolization, both in its adaptive and maladaptive (pathological) cases (e.g., a reanalysis of the religious fixation of John Bunyan; Royce, 1894b). As always, serious literary figures have provided psychology with a richness of intrapsychological dialogues, yet very few psychologists have made use of them, or recognized literature as data, like Royce did (Royce, 1892b).

Nevertheless, the sociogenetic nature of human self-reflection remains in force all through human lifetime, requiring at least episodic embeddedness in the social world. Although Royce's main interest was in the intramental subjective world, he recognized its dependence upon the social realm: "Self-confidence is always a dependent affair. We can only choose whether our dependence shall be rational or capricious. Self-consciousness needs constantly renewed draughts of that water of life, the imitated authority of other minds" (Royce, 1894a, p. 541).

Royce considered psychological terms as opposites united within the cycle of interdependency inside the mind, between the mind and the society, and between social units within a society:

It is only in abstraction that I can be merely egoistic. In the concrete case I can only be egoistic by being also voluntarily altruistic . . . I can aim, for instance, to be a political 'boss'. That appears to be a very egoistic aim. But the political 'boss' exists by the suffrages of interested people, and must aim at their conscious, even if illusory, sense of advantage in so far as he wills them to be sincerely interested. I can will to be a flattering demagogue, admired for vain show by a crowd of fools. The end is selfish; but it also involves wishing to be agreeable in the eyes of many people. (Royce, 1895c, pp. 468–9)

The dialectical unity of opposites focus of Royce provided numerous theoretical advantages, none of which were productively advanced either in American or international psychology (see the discussion above of individualism and collectivism). Perhaps this was partly due to the philosophical stance of Royce's so-called "synthetic idealism" (Royce, 1892a), in which subjective idealism was explicated in the form of a constantly self-searching individual mind. The phenomena of loyalty would be an example of such ideal synthesis. Yet it remained one of the voices in the wider American "epistemic market of ideas" of the time.

Royce's work has not been notably followed. During at the era of suspiciousness to intramental phenomena that captured psychology in North America with the advent of behaviorist beliefs, Royce's unabashedly subjectivist description of the personal worlds vanished from the focus of social attention. However, his fate of being forgotten was shared with his contemporaries (W. James, C. S. Peirce), and may have a sociological explanation. During the early decades of the twentieth century, there entailed a social discourse setting whereby philosophers were allotted the role of "public men" – their ideas were propagated through the whole of society, and scrutinized for their fit with the current public ideologies. After World War I, that public role of American philosophers disappeared (Kuklick, 1995, p. 145), only to return after World War II, and to disappear, again into the squirmishes for public attention governed by journalists at our time.

William James: A Stream of Ideas Leading to Pragmatism

William James (1842–1910) was moved by the end of the 1890s to elaborate a pragmatist standpoint – first in his presentation at the University of California in 1898 (Myers, 1986, p. 299), followed by a full treatise propagating this direction (James, 1907a). It created a new social movement, with large crowds of followers. During the 1890s, the intellectual orientation of the audience was already turning toward acceptance of the notions of practical relevance, utility, and dynamic actions, well prepared by James himself and others (Dewey and C. Sanders Peirce). The movement of pragmatism may have fitted the needs of the public at the time (Hollinger, 1995).

Despite being talked about as a "school," pragmatism was a general orientation that can be seen in the thinking of a number of scholars, each retaining their individual identities. The beginnings of pragmatism as a uniform movement go back to James himself. He credited the founder role of pragmatism to Peirce, whose article in *Popular Science Monthly* in 1878 ("How to Make Our Ideas Clear" was hailed as the birthdate of the movement. Peirce's actual work was closer to later logical positivism than to James' pragmatism (Wilson, 1995, p. 125), yet he remains one of the progenitors of the movement. Dewey's philosophy differed from James' in many ways, and the two men had been involved in a crucial dispute of the 1890s, yet James found it appropriate to consider himself together with Dewey (and all of the Chicago School; see James, 1904a) in one social movement. Internationally, James himself credited similar ideas to have been expressed by Karl Pearson in England, Ernst Mach in Austria, Henri Poincaré in France, and Georg Simmel in Germany.

James' claims for pragmatism as being "radically empirical" (James, 1904c) were immediately recognized as being close to the "critical realism" of Wilhelm Wundt. By acting upon objects, the person appropriates the relevant functions of these objects, thus turning the objects into both subjective and objective in relation to person (James, 1905, p. 179).

Pragmatism was meant to be an alternative to intellectualism – the belief in the finite existence of the mind. As such, it constituted a general belief system which made the notion of utility the core for the determination of the truth or falsity of ideas. In the middle of human personal experience (characterized by James as "quasi-chaos"; James, 1904c, p. 543), practical consequences of action lead to the possibility of establishing truth value of facts.

The Pragmatist Notion of Truth

In the efforts to distinguish itself from the ideological orthodoxies of his time, James' pragmatism needed to redefine the notion of "truth." This concept could not be reflected upon along the lines of an immanent status (i.e., the "truth" of X exists independently of us, whether we know it or not). Instead, James separated the "truth" issue from the "factness" issue: "True ideas are those that we can validate, corroborate, and verify. False ideas are those that we can not. . . . The truth of an idea is not a stagnant property inherent in it. Truth happens to an idea. It becomes true, is made true by events. Its verity is in fact an event, a process, the process ... of its verifying itself, its verification. Its validity is the process of its validation" (James, 1907b, p. 142).

The process of verification can certainly be varied, ranging from direct testing of an object, to interpersonal establishment of a common language referent. James' example was a clock on the wall. He claimed that if he would consider that object a "clock" and his interlocutor would agree that it is a "clock," that this indirect verification can be sufficient because it works for the given purposes. The usefulness of consensual validation of names was seen by him as "true" (or "false") as any mental pictures would be – depending upon the utility of the present use of these names (James, 1907b, p. 147). The penetration of the world of commerce (based on the notion of "utility") into James' "radical empiricism" is evident in his uses of the notion of "cash value" as applicable to ideas (e.g., James, 1904d, p. 563).

James saw truth emerging at the intersection of belief-> verifica- tion-> new belief cycle. Yet much of human knowledge is mediated via symbolic means, and not immediately available. For example, the act of reading about "tigers in India" in a here-and-now setting pro- vides the immediate access to the qualities of the paper on which the text is written (e.g., to a molecular architecture "beneath" the smooth whiteness of the paper). Yet the meaning of tigers in India is available to the reader only via representative or symbolic knowing (James, 1895, p. 107). The latter is fully dependent upon the trustability of the writer of the text. The possibility that there might be no tigers in India is not considered by the reader, as the story is created by the writer.

Treating the Problem of Intersubjectivity

If the cases of mediated verification depend upon communication between persons, the issue of intersubjectivity is of prime relevance for any standpoint that claims usefulness to be the core criterion of truth. After all, any claim about usefulness of anything is an act of labeling, and such labeling can occur in accordance with the personal goals of the labeler, even if claimed to be so from the viewpoint of the common good. This possibility makes the application of pragmatism's utility-centered criterion of truth infinitely open-ended, since the rhet- oric construction of "usefulness" can take an infinite number of forms.

James recognized this open-endedness of the communicative validation of truths, and tried to solve the problem of the indeterminacy of the pragmatic view on truth via a moralistic imperative of avoiding falseness. Thus, "A truth must always be preferred to a falsehood when both relate to the situation; but when neither does, truth is as little of a duty as falsehood. If you ask me what o'clock it is and I tell you that I live at 95 Irving Street, my answer may indeed be true but you don't see why it is my duty to give it. A false address would be as much to the purpose" (James, 1907b, p. 154).

All in all, the pragmatist doctrine depends upon the axiomatic assuming of a particular position of what "usefulness" is. Interpsychological communication situations of purposeful and effective deception of the other are not assumed to be the basis for the verification of truth. The role of the "social other" in the process of the mediated verification of truth is assumed to be that of a benevolent seeker of the same truth (only from a different starting point).

Yet the problem of intersubjectivity is not soluble via moralistic imperatives for communicative interchanges. Behind these interchanges is the inevitability of different persons' necessarily different perspectives upon the same object, and their different personal life histories. This difference is overcome by way of communication about shared referents – yet overcome via an approximation of the "sharedness" of the personal experiences. James was aware that:

Your objects are over and over again the same as mine. If I ask you where some object of yours is, our old Memorial Hall [at Harvard], for example. You point to my Memorial Hall with your hand which I see. If you alter an object in your world, put out a candle, for example, when I am present, my candle ipso facto goes out. It is only as altering my objects that I guess you to exist. If your objects do not coalesce with my objects, if they be not identically where mine are, they must be proved to be positively somewhere else. (James, 1904d, pp. 565–6)

The crucial question for intersubjectivity is whether the "shared object" – be this the Memorial Hall or a candle – is actually the "same" for the communicating persons. That the object – taken separately from the perceivers – can be characterized as "the same" (for itself, over time) may be accepted as a starting point. James was clear that the two different consciousnesses, referring to the "same" object, cannot be the same. Instead, the communication process establishes a space of an approximately common reference field, within which the persons maintain their distinctive personal vantage points. This is best illustrated by James' example of one person touching the body of another:

'There' for me means where I place my finger. If you do not feel my finger's contact to be 'there' in my sense, when I place it on your body, where then do you feel it? Your inner actuations of your body also meet my finger there: It is there that you resist its push, or shrink back, or sweep the finger aside with your hand. Whatever farther knowledge either of us may acquire of the real constitution of the body which we thus feel, you from within and I from without, it is in that same place that the newly conceived or perceived constituents have to be located. (James, 1904d, p. 568)

James' solution to the intersubjectivity problem remains centered on the coordination of personal subjective experiences: Rather than beginning from social experiences to explain individual consciousness (as most sociogenetic thinkers have tried to do), he generates an analysis of social experience out of the personal subjectivities (see Cronk, 1976). As such, James' version of pragmatism remained true to his person-centered psychological analysis expressed earlier (i.e., in his *Principles of Psychology*), rather than becoming social along the lines that emerged in the work of John Dewey.

The Fallacy of Social Pragmatism

It is tempting to locate an analogue to James' "psychologist's fallacy" in the realm of sociogenetic persuasions. The crucial feature of the social pragmatist perspectives in America, which we will see repeated in the thinking of Royce, Dewey, Mead, Cooley, and others, is the assumption of the ideal benevolence of the social community. Different directions of thought framed that assumption differently, yet none of them relativized it so as to accept the possibility that the social community can be malevolent toward persons, or at least ambiguous. This is all the more surprising as it was exactly the potential "moral-decline" themes – of particular individuals who might belong to an alien community (of prostitutes, or of Italian immigrants) – that were circulating in the Anglo-Saxon (and more widely white European) dominated U.S. society at the turn of the century. It is almost as if the social scientists were narrowing their scope to a particular social utopia of their preference, treating it as if it really existed, and trying to treat issues of the social origin of the human mind in the light of the positive social scenario. The socially oriented pragmatism of John Dewey has been a core of sociogenetic thought for later generations.

John Dewey's Pragmatism: Dynamic Relatedness

John Dewey developed his version of pragmatist thinking by moving from his own (Cahan, 1992; Goetzmann, 1973; Mead, 1930a). The role of the ideas of Wilhelm Wundt and G. Stanley Hall was present for early Dewey (Shook, 1995). Aside from moving out of Hegel, Dewey moved (from the University of Michigan) to the University of Chicago where he established his "school of thought" through a vigorous group of disciples (James, 1904a).

There were major differences between the two lines of pragmatist thought – James', and Dewey's. James' (and Peirce's) was clearly personal, whereas Dewey's was clearly social. Furthermore, it was goal-orientedly social: Dewey's activities in Chicago included the establishment of an experimental school. Dewey's version of pragmatism had the question of experience at its center. Yet his notion of experience differed from the person-centered philosophy of experiencing that would dominate Continental Europe (see Chapter 7). In his early writings Dewey explained that:

Experience begins when intelligence projects something of itself into sensations. We have now to recognize that experience grows, or gets more meaning, just in the degree in which intelligence reads more ideal content into it. The adult has more experience than the child – the Englishman than the Bushman – because he has more ideas in his intellect to bring to bear upon his sensations and thus make them significant . . . it is . . . the supplying of meaning through sensations, and not of sensations, that makes the experience more significant. (Dewey, 1887, p. 395)

It is the eclectic mixing of quantified notions of the process described ("experience . . . gets more meaning," adult "has more experience") with qualitative structural-dynamic process mechanisms (projection by "intelligence" onto "sensations," supplying "meaning through sensations") that qualifies the still-Hegelian Dewey of 1887 as an American thinker. It is from that viewpoint that Dewey expanded upon James' theory of emotions. The qualitative process mechanism he implied to generate experience – the projection of intelligence upon sensations, through which meaning emerges – is a step in the direction of his emphasis on the pragmatic dynamics of the relation between an organism and the environment.

Although embracing pragmatism as a general label, Dewey's thought constituted a special version of it – one that emphasized the dynamics of experience, its ethical and prospective side (e.g., Dewey, 1908, p. 97) – in contrast with James' person-focused and eclectic version of that general philosophy (James, 1907a; also Allport, 1943). Dewey's fight with dualisms in psychology seems to have resulted in the permanent incapacity of psychologists to think in terms of dualities (i.e., inclusively separated parts of the system, between which functioning processes can be specified). Dewey himself perhaps cannot be viewed as the sole producer of such a casualty in ideas, because in conjunction with the notion of emergence traces, the notion of dialectical synthesis seems to come through:

In any organized system . . . there is no dualism of self and world. The emergence of this duality is within the conflicting and strained situation of action; the activities which subtend purpose and intent define the 'me' of that situation, those which constitute the interruptive factor define its 'external world'. . . . It is precisely the process of rationalization by which a brute practical acceptance-rejection gets transformed into a controlled directed evaluated system of action, in which the duality of me and object is again overcome. (Dewey, 1907, p. 255)

Dewey made a step forward in the direction of conceptualizing the process of development in his textbook *Psychology* (1st ed. in 1886). Building upon the Hegelian notion of dialectical synthesis, Dewey claimed that "activity of mind never leaves sensuous elements isolated, but connects them into larger wholes" (Dewey, 1891, p. 90). The mechanism of such an establishment of wholes of experience was seen as a unity of integration (of different present sensations) and reintegration ("extension of present sensory elements by distinct revival of past elements"; Dewey, 1891, p. 96). However, it is remarkable that the linkages between present and past sensations were conceptualized by Dewey in associationist terms (similarity, contiguity), rather than building into the process of reintegration a Hegelian dialectical scheme. It could be claimed that Dewey was already on his way toward the elimination of structural notions and toward an emphasis on the process over its participating components which later became the key for his thinking. Dewey explicitly considered integration to be synonymous with fusion – the latter being clearly free from the notion of dialectical tension between opposites:

We have . . . a continuous whole of sensation constantly undergoing modification and constantly expanding, but never parting with its unity. This process may be termed fusion or integration, to indicate the fact that the various elements are continually entering into the whole in which they lose their independent existence. Professor James illustrates this intimate union by the taste of lemonade. This does not retain unchanged the tastes of sugar and of lemon, but is itself a new sensation into which the old ones have passed as elements. What association gives us . . . is not loosely connected aggregate of separable parts, but a new total experience. (Dewey, 1891, pp. 94–5)

James' example of the taste of lemonade (James, 1895, pp. 105–6), which Dewey used here, is utilized as an example of how fusion of substances leads to the holistic new taste as an outcome, rendering the process of the fusion itself de facto into a "black box." Yet in James' original version, it was not fusion but making of a whole based on bringing together the different components. Thus, a glass of lemonade (for James) did not equal lemonade as a fused new term that would be equal to its components (lemon, sugar). Instead, it gave James a superordinate notion: While tasting "lemonade" the person tastes lemon and sugar at once. Lemon remains lemon and sugar sugar, only they become united to a new whole-quality ("lemonade"). The actual drink may of course be a result of mixing of the substances (lemon becomes "fused" with "sugar" in the water). James' thinking was recognized as influential for the German *Ganzheitspsychologie* (see Chapter 7) precisely because of its recognition of the hierarchy of qualitatively different levels. Dewey's idea was in tune with efforts to eliminate hierarchical models from the social sciences, which are in vogue in our times as well (see Chapter 9).

The irony of Dewey's constant insistence on the process nature of experiencing is that by that emphasis it was exactly that process that was left out of the investigation itself. By giving the process of entering into the whole of total experience a label (integration), and especially creating its synonym by the notion of fusion, Dewey successfully eliminated the process of emergence of that holistic experience (i.e., the process of synthesis) from the focus of investigation.

Here we can trace an example of the canalization of scientists' thought by the concepts they use. On the one hand, Dewey successfully ruled out an atomist account of experience as a mere separated "count of elements" of the objective world or subjective state, and antedated the Gestalt psychological traditions in his youthful propagation of the primacy of the "experiential whole" (see Allport, 1951, p. 266). However, on the other hand, his emphasis on the fusion of the subject and object constrained his focus to intellectual fights with

"dualisms," and away from solving the conceptual problem of the
very processes that he successfully kept in focus through the use of
the fusion concept. Dewey led the path for many other sociogenetic
theorists who came after him and who – willingly or unwillingly –
took over the defocusing on emergence by an emphasis on the fusion
of the person and the social world (e.g., Rogoff, 1990; Werner &
Altmann, 1997).

The Discussion about Emotions

Undoubtedly, for psychologists, issues of emotion are emotional issues. It was around the question of emotions that a major intellectual
dispute emerged in the 1890s, leading to the question of reflex arc
concept. It was the catalytic mind of William James whose efforts to
make sense of emotions (James, 1884; 1890; 1894) served as the basis
for the emerging pragmatist discussion. Furthermore, James' emotion
theory served later, in the 1930s, as a target for Lev Vygotsky's intellectual quest (Van der Veer & Valsiner, 1991; and Chapter 8).

James' theory has become well-known through many reiterations
in (text)books on the history of psychology and – perhaps because of
this – has been shown to have been inadequately understood (Ellsworth, 1994; Lang, 1994). Confusions about his theory started from the
very beginning, as the description of the debate below shows. Furthermore, James' own expression of his ideas about emotions varied over
the decade (1884–94); inclusive was his changing of the claim of the
theory as theory. It is the speculative argumentation where philosophical ideas, introspection data, and claims for the establishment of the
status of his ideas are intermingled, which characterized James' writing.

A First View: James of 1884

James recognized from the very beginning that his emotion theory
goes contrary to the common-sense belief about feelings:

The bodily changes follow directly the PERCEPTION of the exciting fact,
and that our feeling of the same changes as they occur IS the emotion.
Common sense says, we lose our fortune, are sorry and weep; we meet a
bear, are frightened and run; we are insulted by a rival, are angry and
strike. The hypothesis here to be defended says that this order of sequence

is incorrect, that the one mental state is not immediately induced by the other, that the bodily manifestations must first be interposed between, and that the more rational statement is that we feel sorry because we cry, angry because we strike, afraid because we tremble. . . . Without the bodily states following on the perception, the latter would be purely cognitive in form, pale, colourless, destitute of emotional warmth. We might then see the bear, and judge it best to run, receive the insult and deem it right to strike, but we could not actually feel afraid or angry. (James, 1884, pp. 189–90)

Perhaps it was exactly here that James' rhetoric (see James, 1894, p. 519 for an explicit claim of this kind) led to the simple interpretation of his viewpoint as the reversal of the usual belief (i.e., from perception – feeling – action to perception – bodily reaction – feeling – action). It is that notion that has found its way into numerous popular and textbook re-tellings of the James-Lange theory of emotions. In reality, James' focus was different – he saw emotion as feeling (Izard, 1990).

What James emphasized is the interposing of bodily manifestations in the process of perception; it is clear from the above quote that his example is used to emphasize the "purely rational" (or cognitive) action as contrasted with felt-through ones. In the latter case, the bodily manifestations of the feeling through provide the emotional character to the event. The tension between the chain-like nature of the emotional reaction processes, and their view in terms of unity (interposing) of visceral and subjective experiences in the process of perceiving is already visible here. The dynamic unity versus structural order opposition became the theme for Dewey's dispute with James (Dewey, 1895).

James' View Extended: Anno 1890

In his *Principles of Psychology* (James, 1890, Chapter 25), James continued to make sense of the issue of emotions. However, now the issue was set up in a context of James' system of psychology as a whole. The chapter on emotions followed the one on instincts, and preceded the one on will. Already such a compositional placement of the issue is indicative of James' efforts: Indeed feelings are part and parcel of the organism's perception and bodily behavior (as instincts would include), and precede the emergence of volitional action. Thus, in his textual transition from the preceding chapter, James emphasized that instinctive reactions and emotional expressions "shade imperceptively into each other" (James, 1890, p. 442). Emotional reaction "usually terminates in the subject's own body," while the instinctive reaction was seen to "enter into practical relations with the exciting object" (ibid.).

In the chapter, James expanded the coverage to emphasize the work of Carl Lange. Hence the well-known "James-Lange theory" was set forth in the English-speaking psychological world. James claimed that his theory should not be called "materialistic" (James, 1890, p. 453), despite its obvious reliance on the bodily processes that generate emotion. Emotions are "embodied" (ibid., p. 452). While making preemptive counterclaims to different possible challenges to his theory, James considered the most central positive proof for it to come, possibly, from the clinical evidence. It is in this connection that he considered Pierre Janet (whose hysterical patient L. from *Automatisme psychologique* (Janet, 1889a) is described on p. 456), in support of his perception notion of emotion, yet finding the case to be inconclusive for his purposes.

Of course the crucial distinction that James could not avoid was that between "coarser" and "subtler" emotions. The latter were viewed as emerging from the former, thus proving James' theory (James, 1890, p. 470). James claimed that all emotional phenomena can be traced to some reflex circuit, in which the perception of the stimuli becomes interposed with bodily processes:

Quick as a flash, the reflex currents pass down through their preordained channels, alter the condition of muscle, skin, and viscus; and these alterations, perceived, like the original object, in as many portions of the cortex, combine with it in consciousness and transform it from an object-simply-apprehended into object-emotionally-felt. No new principles have to be invoked, nothing postulated beyond the ordinary reflex circuits, and the local centers admitted in one shape or another by all to exist. (James, 1890, p. 474)

This insistence upon the "reflex pathways" in the uniting of perception of the triggering event and the bodily reactions is interesting because it is the intermediate step between instinct and will. Note that in the case of emotions, no new neural circuits are supposed to develop. In James' account of the development of volition, it is exactly the emergence of new "command centers" that would indicate the emergence of will (e.g., James, 1890, pp. 581–92). This idea at least paralleled (if not preceded) Baldwin's explanation of the development of "circular reactions" (as was elaborated in Chapter 4).

Of course, emotions themselves undergo development and James was not trying to avoid that question. Over repeated experiences, different feelings attenuate, and their initial reaction components may drop out (James, 1890, p. 478). The result of this developmental process is the existence of so-called "idiopathic" effects of the stimuli. All in all, James attempted to bring all emotional phenomena – including the "subtler" emotions and "idiopathic" phenomena – under his perceptual-bodily reactive viewpoint. It is not surprising that this generalization met with counter-arguments from his contemporaries.

Criticisms of James' Theory

James was quite right in his estimation that his view on emotions would not fit the common-sense viewpoint where emotions are primary psychical entities that can be viewed as being expressed. The dispute about James' ideas culminated in the period 1893 to 1896, with numerous participants (e.g., Baldwin, 1894; Irons, 1895a, 1895b, 1895c; Worcester, 1893).

Worcester's critique concentrated on the generality of James' theory – the "discharge theory" was viewed as if it could not explain emotions that are part of complex, intentional actions. In an ironic twist upon James' most remembered example, Worcester elaborated:

If I see a shower coming up, and run for a shelter, the emotion is evidently of the same kind, though perhaps less in degree, as in the case of a man who runs from the bear. According to Professor James, I am afraid of getting wet because I run. But supposing that, instead of running, I step into a shop and buy an umbrella. The emotion is still the same. I am afraid of getting wet. Consequently, as far as I can see, the fear, in this case, consists in buying the umbrella . . . Anger, again, may be associated with many other actions than striking. Shylock's anger at Antonio's insults induced him to lend him money. Did the anger, or revengefulness, or whatever we may call that passion, consist in the act of lending money? (Worcester, 1893, p. 291)

Although Worcester's criticism was obviously based on James' examples rather than on the general idea of the interposing of action and emotion (and James' response to Worcester pointed that out; James, 1894, pp. 518–19), it brought to the discussion a relevant idea.

Namely, there can exist multiple structural relationships between feeling and acting, as the same action (fused with feeling) can be substituted by another one. Worcester's argument fits the ethos of the cultural mediation of emotional phenomena. However, the idea of multiple ties later disappeared as the dispute became a battleground for the emerging pragmatism (and its emphasis on the fusion of structural units under the banner of usefulness).

David Irons (1895a, p. 81) criticized James' logic of argument, claiming that he moved from a realistic notion of, emotions' not being dissociable from bodily feelings, to equating emotions with bodily feelings. He consistently defended the psychological (spiritual) nature of emotions, and in this emphasis moved to criticize Dewey's elaboration of the discharge theory (Irons, 1895b) by pointing out that it does not consider voluntary actions. James' answer (1894) triggered Irons (1895c) to point out changes in James' viewpoint, yet insist upon the centrality of emotions as functional aspects of human psyche (rather than outcomes of bodily sensations).

James' Viewpoint Modified

In his response to his opponents, James (1894) clarified his previous position, and introduced some disclaimers about the nature of his viewpoint on emotions. He claimed that his (and Lange's) viewpoint should "no longer be treated as a heresy, but might become the orthodox belief" (p. 529), and he claimed that it has no theoretical status at all: "In my own mind the theory has no philosophical implications whatever of a general sort. It assumes . . . that there must be a process of some sort in the nerve centres for emotion, and it simply defines that process that consists of different currents. It does this on no general theoretic grounds, but because of the introspective appearances exclusively" (James, 1894, pp. 522–3).

Of course this claim about a lack of philosophical implications was merely a rhetorical defense. All through the emotions chapter in the *Principles,* the use of "theory" as a term occurs in the context of uniting different existing phenomena through his main core idea: that of perception interspersed with bodily reactivity.

However, James' claim for "no theory" diffused the discussion, leaving relatively little to be discussed. It triggered an angry surprise from his opponents (see Baldwin, 1894; Irons, 1895c), as James' eclectic reconstruction of his theory – including his claim that it is no theory –

left rather little to be discussed. James' turn to his "claim for ortho-doxy" brought the discussion to its end – his opponents could surely not have a worthwhile discussion with a fixed authoritative declara-tion.

The notion of emotions was not clarified, and most of the argu-ments involved vanished from the focus of attention of psychologists. However, in the domain of emerging pragmatism in American philos-ophy and psychology, the debate showed the making of the anti-structuralist ethos that was idealizing the persons' involvement in their situated activity contexts.

Reflections by Baldwin and Janet

James Mark Baldwin took up a critical analysis of James' emotion account from an explicitly developmental perspective. He pointed out James' lack of distinction of the origins and nature of emotion pro-cesses. In a return to the example of the child who puts his finger in a candle flame, he wrote that:

The inhibiting effect and the pain are brought about by the burn, and the recurrence of that – that is the thing to be prevented. The thrusting movement is a mere incident. Suppose the candle is brought up against the child instead of the reverse: it then shrinks from it just the same. The movement of the former case is inhibited, to be sure; but only because that is the way the developed organism has learned to escape damaging stimulations in general. . . . The real question is how did the organism learn to withdraw? And the answer must be: The pain must have origi-nally preceded the adaptive movement – as a signal of an injury. . . . We cannot simply leave the organisms to the risks of getting repetitions of stimulus by accident; for that means that the organism waits the second time for the lucky chance, just as it did the first time. (Baldwin, 1894, p. 616)

The organism's future-oriented extrapolation, rather than experi-ence (or perception), triggered visceral reaction, and was thus impor-tant for understanding emotions. Pierre Janet's reaction to the emo-tions discussion became available a decade later (Janet, 1905), and followed the lines of his general focus. Without denying the impor-tance of the visceral excitations in the emotions, he still cautioned against the reduction of emotions to these reactions:

We must not confine ourselves to the peripheral manifestations of emo-tion. The weak point of the famous theory is to be found in the dictum that: 'We are sorry because we cry'. . . . Side by side with these motor phenomena, which have quite correctly been called extra-motions, there occur infra-motions which constitute retroactive modifications of consciousness; and these psychical resultants are no less important than their physiological concomitants. Emotion is attended by a mental agitation, just as it is attended by a physical agitation. A multitude of ideas surge into consciousness and disturb the equilibrium. (Janet, 1905, pp. 105–6)

Possibly part of the "emotions discussion" was the exclusive focus on emotions as such, forgetting the larger scheme of processes in which they are enclosed. Thus, while explaining issues of volition, James' coverage (see James, 1890, p. 501 on "anticipatory images" and pp. 535–7 on "feeling of effort") need not have been in contradiction with Janet's retrospect on the emotions discussion. Of course, the issue of the inclusiveness of emotions in the ongoing action process was the major extension of James' theory that John Dewey contributed to the discussion.

From Hegelianism to Pragmatism: John Dewey on Emotions

We cover the discussion about the nature of emotions in great detail not just because of its value for understanding how psychology has had conceptual difficulties with feelings and emotions, but because it constituted part of the context of intellectual interdependency in the development of Dewey's version of pragmatist thought in America.

Dewey's two articles (Dewey, 1894, 1895) that pertain to the emotions discussion are interesting because they reveal the structure of his thought from a neo-hegelian to a pragmatist standpoint. In his dispute with both Darwin's emotional expression viewpoint (which Dewey rejected), and James' "discharge theory" (which he accepted with amendments), he arrived at a developmental theory of emotions, which he summarized as follows:

Certain movements, formerly useful in themselves, become reduced to tendencies to action, to attitudes. As such they serve, when instinctively aroused into action, as means for realizing ends. But so far as there is difficulty in adjusting the organic activity represented by the attitude with that which stands for the idea or end, there is temporary struggle and partial inhibition. This is reported as Affect, or emotional seizure. Let the coordination be effected in one act, instead of in a successive series of mutually exclusive stimuli, and we have interest. Let such coordination become thoroughly habitual and hereditary, and we have Gefühlston (Dewey, 1895, p. 32).

How did Dewey arrive at this differentiation notion of the affect-within-act? Dewey's rejection of Darwin's idea of emotional expression was necessary because he was trying to overcome the intramental/extramental duality by an emphasis on the dynamic relatedness of the two within the stream of goal-directed movements, or act:

The very word 'expression' names the facts not as they are, but in their second intention. To an onlooker my angry movements are expressions – signs, indications; but surely not to me. To rate such movements as primarily expressive is to fall into the psychologist's fallacy: it is to confuse the standpoint of the observer and explainer with that of the fact observed. Movements are, as a matter of fact, expressive, but they are also a great many other things. In themselves they are movements, acts, and must be treated as such. (Dewey, 1894, p. 555)

It is here that Dewey's emphasis on "treating movements as acts" and James' effort to see feelings and bodily reactions emphasize the unity of the processes. Yet Dewey's treatment of the issue allowed him to advance a consistent developmental perspective on emotions, which was absent in the case of James. Furthermore, Dewey rejected Darwin's idea that certain expressive behaviors exist for the purposes of emotional expression. For him, the solution for how all emotional phenomena are possible was to view them as emerging from the flow of the act.

Crying and Laughing

These two behaviors were of importance to Dewey in the elaboration of his argument, since both of them could most directly be claimed to prove the "expressionist" viewpoint on emotions. Dewey claimed to have performed observations on himself (the science of psychology at that time did not deny the value of introspection), on children, and on other adults. His argument about laughing exemplifies his act-centered idea:

The laugh is by no means to be viewed from the standpoint of humor; its connection with humor is secondary. It marks the ending (that is, the attainment of a unity) of a period of suspense, or expectation, and an ending which is sharp and sudden. Rhythmical activities, as peek-a-boo, call out a laugh at every culmination of the transition, in an infant. A child of from one and a half to two years uses the laugh as a sign of assent; it is his emphatic 'I do' or 'yes' to any suggested idea to which he agrees or which suddenly meets his expectations. A very moderate degree of observation of adults will convince one that a large amount of laughter is wholly irrelevant to any joke or witticism whatever. It is a constant and repeated 'sign' of attaining suddenly to a point. . . . It is a divided activity, party of the kinaesthetic images being fixed upon the immediately present conditions, part upon the expected end. Now let the end suddenly 'break,' 'dawn,' let one see the 'point' and this energy discharges – the getting the point is the unity, the discharge. This sudden relaxation of strain, so far as occurring through the medium of the breathing and vocal apparatus, is laughter. (Dewey, 1894, pp. 558–9, emphasis added)

As is obvious, Dewey sees the physiological bodily processes – especially rhythmic activities like breathing – as the birthplace of the emotional 'bursts' in the course of a goal-directed act. The opposition that leads to such outburst is the contrast – as exemplified in kinesthetic "images" – between the present state and the expected future. The unity emerges through the discharge. Hence the outburst of emotion – be it laughing or crying – is an example of dialectical synthesis that emerges in the course of the dynamic act. Parallels here with Lev Vygotsky's thinking about the nature of aesthetic experience some decades later are remarkable (see Van der Veer & Valsiner, 1991). In answering the question of emotional synthesis when reading a short story, Vygotsky similarly emphasized the unity created by the opposites of descriptive text (text as it is) and its meanings' implications. Furthermore, Vygotsky's first interest in the psychology of emotions was related to the study of breathing rhythms while reading poetry and prose. Henri Wallon's ideas are similarly close to Dewey's (cf. Van der Veer, 1996b).

Dewey saw unity in diversity, from his act-centered perspective, opposite emotional outbursts were viewed to be the same. Thus, "Both crying and laughing fall under the same principle of action – the termination of a period of effort. . . . Crying is either a part of effort to expel an intruder, an effort so general as to engage spasmodically the lungs and vocal organs . . . or, as we see so often in children, an explosion of energy, accumulated in preparation for some act, suddenly discharged in vacuo upon the missing of the essential part, the finishing factor of the act" (Dewey, 1894, pp. 559–60).

Dewey's act-based perspective entails a consistent focus on processes that occur between the person and the environment, within which tensions are built up on the basis of oppositions, which then lead to discharge. The category of idiopathic movements needed to be explained within his perspective.

James had acknowledged – in his critical view of Darwin (James, 1890, p. 482) – that a number of physiological reactions and bodily movements that are feeling full are not directly and unequivocally linkable with specific eliciting stimuli. Such idiopathic movements were viewed by Dewey (1894, p. 561) as a result of some previous (and by the time of observation – disappeared) process of the act. In a similar vein, Dewey rejected Darwin's "antithesis principle," viewing it as a superfluous explanatory principle. Instead, Dewey proposed the explanation in terms of coordination of movements that has led to the establishment of particular habits.

Cats and Dogs

Surely Darwin's illustration of the behavior of cats and dogs is classic in its influence on biological and behavioral sciences' efforts to explain the complexity of animal behavior. Dewey, however, saw the crucial weakness in Darwin's example: The latter had used examples of domesticated animals without considering the use of processes of domestication in his explanation.

Interestingly, at this point Dewey used the argument of George Mead (whose role at the University of Michigan at the time was that of an instructor in physiological psychology; see Chapter 6), preannouncing Mead's own theory of emotions as being in the making (cf. Dewey, 1894, p. 568 footnote). In Dewey's terms (with Mead's thought involved), it is made clear that the case of domestic animals like cats and dogs differs cardinally from that of their wild relatives:

Wild animals have, speaking roughly, just two fundamental characteristic attitudes – those connected with getting food, including attack upon enemies, and those of defence, including fight, etc. A domestic animal, by the very fact that it is domestic, has another characteristic attitude, that of reception – the attitude of complete adaptation to something outside itself. This attitude is constituted, of course, by a certain co-ordination of movements; and these are antithetical to those movements involved in the contrary attitude, that of resistance or opposition. . . . The attitude of 'humility' and 'affection' [in dogs] consists, as Mr. Darwin well says, in continuous, flexuous movements. These movements are precisely those of response and adaptation. (Dewey, 1894, p. 567)

It is interesting, that Dewey's emphasis on the process of emergence allows him (and Mead) to view Darwin's examples of "antithetical behaviors" as resulting from the coordination of movements in the process of adaptation (to conditions of domestication). Mead's explanation of cat behavior was along similar lines – only emphasizing the cat's assuming of "more passive contact" or "less active adjustment" in the process of domestication. In sum, Dewey emphasized that the expressions of emotions are actually resultant reductions of originally useful movements into attitudes.

Transformation of Movements

Dewey emphasized the unity of excitatory and inhibitory processes in the regulation of the act. Habits, thus viewed, consisted of the limitation of the "certain average range of fluctuation" of movements, inhibiting the excesses of possible movements (Dewey, 1894, p. 564). Furthermore, in the process of development acts that originally were complete became abbreviated (Dewey, 1895, p. 26). In the realm of emotions, the original full feelings of excitement may disappear under repetition, and are given over to the control of habit. However, when this transition is not possible, then we can observe tension emerging from coordination of movements – resulting in emotional outburst. Dewey returned to James' "bear story":

In psychological terms, this tension is always between the activity which constitutes, when interpreted, the object as an intellectual content, and that which constitutes the response or mode of dealing with it. There is the one phase of organic activity which constitutes the bear as object; there is the other which would attack it, or run away from it, or stand one's ground before it. If these two coordinate without friction, or if one immediately displaces the other, there is no emotional seizure. If they coexist, both pulling apart as complete in themselves and pulling together as parts of a new whole, there is great emotional excitement. (Dewey, 1895, p. 27)

Thus, coordination can be of a harmonious or disharmonious kind, and only the latter results in emotional outbursts, which emerge in the process of constructing a new whole. Dewey's Hegelian background and his (still only) emerging pragmatism created the tension in his thought that resulted in a developmental revamping of James' "discharge theory" of emotions. Interestingly, the advent of pragmatism led to the diminishing of the emphasis on dialectical synthesis, yet it retained the complex of thought of unity of opposites in a whole, their inseparability, and dynamicity. These themes constituted the core of the discussion of the "reflex arc" concept, which has been marked as substantial in the history of psychology.

The Nature of the Reflex Arc

Dewey's reconceptualization of the notion of the reflex arc follows closely from the discussion on emotions. In fact, the classic paper (Dewey, 1896) contains reverberations of the issues from the emotions discussion. Thus, one can find examples used from the former, e.g., the burn by candle (pp. 358–60 and p. 364), and running away from beasts or robbers (pp. 362–3). The main opponent to Dewey in the reflex arc discussion is Baldwin (p. 361 ff), whom he – quite mistakenly (see Chapter 4) – singles out as the exponent of the dualistic stimulus-response model of the reflex arc. Dewey's whole text is an effort to replace the supposed dualism of the reflex arc notion by his focus on the dynamic processes of the circle of the reflex. That effort was remarkably similar to Baldwin's focus on "circular reactions."

For Dewey, the reflex arc concept was important because it came close to his desired working model of a functionalist scheme, yet it carried the separation of parts of the functioning system ("center" versus "periphery") that he found to be unproductive. Hence his relabeling of the reflex arc as a "circuit" of "mediated experience" (Dewey, 1896, p. 363). The continuous unity of the process of acting does not allow a separation of parts of the process into independent units, but only to temporarily distinguish parts from the whole. The relations between thus inclusively-separated (yet linked) parts were described as coordinations – another term referring to a process:

The reflex arc idea, as commonly employed, is defective in that it assumes sensory stimulus and motor response as distinct physical existencies, while in reality they are always inside a coordination and have their significance purely from the part played in maintaining or reconstructing the coordination; and (secondly) in assuming that the quale of experience which precedes the 'motor' phase and that which succeeds it are two different states, instead of the last being always the first reconstituted, the motor phase coming in only for the sake of such mediation. (Dewey, 1896, p. 360)

In another terminological effort, Dewey argued that the response is not to be that to a stimulus, but into it (1896, p. 359). The parts of the arc were to be viewed not as separate entities in themselves, but as divisions of labor within a single dynamic whole. Stimulus and response are viewed as "teleological distinctions" (Dewey, 1896, p. 365), that is, distinctions of functions with reference to reaching or maintaining an end. Interestingly, Dewey borrowed Baldwin's "circular reaction" idea, yet claimed that he expanded it beyond the notion of imitation (cf. footnote in Dewey, 1896, p. 363). However, since Baldwin's focus on imitation was already widely extended to many forms of experiences, such a claim by Dewey may be merely a token describing the intellectual opposition of the two.

From the Psychologist's Fallacy to Coordinations

Dewey expanded James' idea of psychologists' fallacy to cover the historical features of the act:

A set of considerations which hold good only because of a completed process, is read into the content of the process which conditions this completed result. A state of things characterizing an outcome is regarded as a true description of the events which led up to this outcome; when, as a matter of fact, if this outcome had already been in existence, there would have been no necessity for the process. (Dewey, 1896, p. 367)

For Dewey, the sensation meant a function. What the sensation might be at a given time depends upon the activity being used. It has no fixed quality. For instance,

Take a child who, upon reaching for bright light (that is, exercising the seeing-reaching coordination) has sometimes had a delightful experience, sometimes found something good to eat and sometimes burned himself. Now the response is not only uncertain, but the stimulus is equally uncertain; one is uncertain only in so far as the other is. . . . The question of whether to reach or to abstain from reaching is the question what sort of bright light have we here? Is it the one which means playing with one's hands, eating milk, or burning one's fingers? The stimulus must be constituted for the response to occur. (Dewey, 1896, pp. 367–8)

The dynamic nature of the act, for Dewey, always links the sensation and movement (into sensori-motor coordinations). His argument against the reflex arc notion entailed the criticism of turning the dynamic process of the act (exemplified by coordinations), into a static and disjoint separation of "stimuli" and "responses," hence eliminating their dynamic interdependence. In his reformulation of the terms, Dewey emphasized:

The stimulus is that phase of the forming coordination which represents the conditions which have to be met in bringing it to a successful issue; the response is that phase of one and the same forming coordination which gives the key to meeting these conditions, which serves as instrument in effecting the successful coordination. They are therefore strictly correlative and contemporaneous. The stimulus is something to be discovered; to be made out; if the activity affords its own adequate stimulation, there is no stimulus save in the objective sense already referred to. As soon as it is adequately determined, then and then only is the response also complete. (Dewey, 1896, p. 370)

Coordination thus is seen as the holistic unit which relates the two mutually constituting phases (of sensation and movement, or stimulation and response). It is interesting to see similar efforts in Vygotsky's development of the "method of double stimulation" some decades later. His original scheme – of stimuli being turned into functional ones by the subject via acting upon them – fits well with Dewey's functional scheme (the similarity was sensed by Jean Piaget, cf. Van der Veer, 1996c). Of course Vygotsky added the role of semiotic mediating devices to the scheme. Semiotic mediation was of no relevance to Dewey in his fight with dualisms.

Pragmatism and Its Excesses: The Behaviorist Manifesto

Dewey's circle gave rise to a number of elaborations, among which the turn to redefine psychology in functionalist terms and relate it to the natural sciences was one of the most far-reaching ones. John B. Watson's (1913) call for a revolution was applauded by pragmatists like Dewey and James (Hollinger, 1995). The vigor of the revolutionary call was comparable to other "social purification" efforts that were occurring at the time in the U.S. society. It fitted well with general notions of the inherent modifiability of the world and society.

Pragmatism was a welcome voice in this effort. Its extension into psychology – behaviorism – was a natural outgrowth from that parentage of Mother of Religious Morality and Father of Business Enterprise. Behaviorism would probably have remained an American idiosyncrasy in psychology, had not the historical circumstances surrounding the two world wars propelled the United States into a leadership position in many areas of the world. Psychologists all over the world succumbed to the newest fashions from America in much the same way as the international audience proved receptive to the mythical world of the Hollywood movies. The latter were fussed about; each new movie was treated with curiosity and fascination, and used as a model for one's own production.

Loyalty to Behavior – Whatever It Is

Watson's behaviorist manifesto can be viewed as a radical step toward the eradication of the consciousness-oriented traditions in psychology:

Psychology as the behaviorist views it is a purely objective experimental branch of natural science. Its theoretical goal is the prediction and control of behavior. Introspection forms no essential part of its methods, nor is the scientific value of its data dependent upon the readiness with which they lend themselves to interpretation in terms of consciousness. The behaviorist, in his efforts to get a unitary scheme of animal response, recognizes no dividing line between man and brute. The behavior of man, with all of its refinement and complexity, forms only a part of the behaviorist's total scheme of investigation. (Watson, 1913, p. 158)

Statements about science are not necessarily scientific themselves (like a statement about a pipe is not a pipe that one could smoke; Foucault, 1983). Watson's use of the notions of "scientific value" and "pure objectivity" constituted a rhetoric play with these value-laden labels. The central turn proposed by Watson was the elimination of the assumption of species specificity of behavior, and the notion of qualitative levels of psychological functioning within species. Hence he could redirect the investigation toward the study of behavior – a term widely used and never defined. Eradication of species' and levels' boundaries made it legitimate to study any animal and claim to study principles that equally apply to humans.

Watson's focus on the immediate observability of behavior (as contrasted with the full dependence upon introspectionist observers) certainly fitted with the pragmatist focus on truth as obtainable by looking at the utility of consequences. The crisis in the empirical work of the introspectionist kind was certainly there, as Watson remarked:

Psychology, as it is generally thought of, has something esoteric in its methods. If you fail to reproduce my findings, it is not due to some fault in your apparatus or in the control of your stimulus, but it is due to the fact that your introspection is untrained. The attack is made upon the observer and not upon the experimental setting. In physics and in chemistry the attack is made upon the experimental conditions. The apparatus was not sensitive enough, impure chemicals were used, etc. In these sciences a better technique will give reproducible results. Psychology is otherwise. If you can't observe 3–9 states of clearness in attention, your introspection is poor. If, on the other hand, a feeling seems reasonably clear to you, your introspection is again faulty. You are seeing too much. Feelings are never clear. (Watson, 1913, p. 163)

Watson here makes his attack on the imprecision in the calibration of the introspectionist "research instrument": the introspecting "observer" (=subject). The boundary is created between the trustworthiness of the person as an instrument, and of the "objective" instruments of the experimental setting. The positive halo of physics and chemistry is set up in contrast with the introspectionist method. At the same time, the presence of similar imprecision in the calibration of the state of the animal subjects (e.g., the exact extent of hunger of laboratory rats prior to an experiment) is not mentioned as it pertains to the experimental conditions. The reproducibility of learning curves in animal experiments in the decades to come created a situation of unclearness that is similar to the one Watson attributed to the introspectionist results.

The "behaviorist turn" in psychology fitted well into the *Zeitgeist* on which pragmatist philosophy thrived. All in all,

The pragmatists emerge as reflectors of, and powerful agents for, a distinctive cluster of assertions and hopes about how modern culture could be integrated and energized. The particular elements in this cluster were often articulated singly and in relation to other ideas by other moralists of the period, including some critical of pragmatism, but the combination of elements found in the writings of the pragmatists and their popularizers was nowhere else advanced more persistently and with more notice from educated Americans. (Hollinger, 1995, p. 20)

The advancement of the behaviorist tradition in America led to the narrowing of the discipline of psychology to the study of selected animal species, and to treating them as if these species could be analogues of basic human ways of functioning. The issue of the "social nature of the mind" disappeared from the discourse of American psychologists together with the disappearance of the focus on the mind (and other cognitive terms). It took American psychology about sixty years of successful stagnation to return to the flexibility of asking research questions of a cognitive kind.

The history of American psychology during the twentieth century is a good example of uneven historical processes in different disciplines under the social conditions of different countries. After the initial period of intellectual storm and stress (during the 1890s and early 1900s), American psychology moved away from dispute to social practices of an applied kind. The advent of behaviorism had a similar effect on American psychology as Stalinist ideology had on Russian psychology in the middle of the century. Psychology developed extensively, but the ideas in psychology were limited to specific realms of discussion. A similar early openness to innovation was seen in American sociology.

American Sociology and the Social Nature of the Mind

Given the advent of the behaviorist belief system in American psychology, most of the sociogenetic thinking became "exiled" into other areas of social sciences where its theoretical sophistication was tolerated. Thus, G. H. Mead's work moved increasingly toward the domains of sociology and philosophy. Apart from him, sociogenetic ideas were worked through by the efforts of several of his contemporaries, but again, in sociology rather than in psychology.

American sociology had its own (Spencerian) roots in the work of Lester Frank Ward (1841–1913), whose work in both the applied and basic domains of sociology was classic for the social sciences (Ward, 1883, 1903). The recognition of Ward's role in the writing of the history of American social thought has gone through curious periods of silence and fascination (Burnham, 1956; Scott, 1976), despite the prominence of his contribution to sociology during the twentieth century (Gillette, 1914, cf. eulogies in Lester Frank Ward, 1913).

During the 1890s, the development of American sociology became closely intertwined with John Dewey's version of pragmatism at the University of Chicago, where – aside from notable efforts of social reformism by sociologists – the first department of sociology and its first journal (*American Journal of Sociology*) was established. Just like psychology in the United States during the 1890s, sociology was notably international in its scope. Largely due to the efforts of Albion Small, sociologists in America were well informed about the development of the sociological system of Georg Simmel in Germany – at times when Simmel's countrymen paid scarce attention to that Berlin freethinker. Simmel was perhaps one of the most translated German authors in the intellectual field of Chicago Sociology. Parts of his *Soziologie* appeared in English translation as a series of articles: "The Philosophy of Value" (Simmel, 1900; also Altmann, 1903), "Of Secrecy" (Simmel, 1906), "The Sociology of Religion" (Simmel, 1905), "The Organization of Social Groups" (Simmel, 1989; 1902), "The Sociology of Conflict" (Simmel, 1904), "Superiority and Subordination" (Simmel, 1896), and "Society as an Organism" (Simmel, 1909, 1910). These articles were all in the American sociological mindscape.

American sociology was actively working through different directions of European thought. The "crowd psychology" of the French tradition (see Chapter 2) got special attention (e.g., King, 1990). Issues of reforming society through biological selection – Francis Galton's eugenics movement – were heatedly debated at the beginning of the twentieth century. Galton's work was published in the *American Journal of Sociology* (Galton, 1904, 1905). Yet the role of the active person in the context of a community remained the birthmark of American sociological thought. This was obviously an outgrowth of the changes in the American society at the time. The paradoxes of the rapid urbanization and industrialization led to reflection about society and persons in its bosom:

Late nineteenth – and early twentieth-century social science was obsessed with the problem of alienation. Its unifying theme was the destructive result of industrialization, which, in eliminating the traditional small town, destroyed the moral community based on personal ties ... When sociologists agreed that the. . . . 'group' rather than the individual should be the primary datum of their discipline, this was a choice premised on the prevailing notion that human beings were moral persons only as members of groups, to which they owed obligations and from which they derived rights. (Kuklick, 1980, p. 213)

The concern with community was obviously central to sociologists. Yet the individuals were not considered to be fully subordinate to the community. They were viewed as active agents who would change it. This sentiment was well expressed by James Leuba: "Individuals do more than reflect social life; they modify it, for they are centers of creative energy. Identical circumstances acting at the same moment upon two persons will not produce identical effects" (Leuba, 1913, p. 338).

Of course, this focus on the agentive role of human individuals had its counterpart in the form of a belief in the positive role of the socio-institutional control of individuals. The result of the tension between the individual agency and the institutional counter-agency roles led to the recognition of the impossibility to predict effects of social reform efforts (Mead, 1899, p. 369). Yet such efforts were undertaken, and many of the American sociologists lived their lives in the process of active participation (Deegan, 1996). Such a life obviously led toward the overcoming of the simple *society suppresses person* versus *the individual is unboundedly free* opposition. Hence the focus is on looking at how the society constitutes the basis for the development of individual autonomy (see Chapter 4, for a similar focus in Baldwin's thought). Our contemporary discussions about appropriation or internalization do not look particularly new when we consider statements like the following:

The individual as well as society has been brought into existence through the development of human civilization. The results of that process are at once socialization and individualization. On the one hand appear progressive differentiation of function, complication of relations and integration in a system of continuously increasing mutual dependence. On the other hand appears an individual life which grows endlessly more manifold and significant through the progressive enrichment of its own inner content. (MacDonald, 1912, p. 14)

In American sociological thought at the beginning of the twentieth century, community and individual were viewed as interdependent – each supported the particular qualities of the other. The individual developed beyond the social expectations of the community, creating his own psychological world, and acting accordingly within the community, transforming the latter. This interdependence surfaced clearly in the thinking of the leading sociogenetic thinkers at the time.

The atmosphere in the North American world at the turn of the century facilitated the play with sociogenetic ideas in a number of versions. Few are of importance in the present context, but there were certainly others whose ideas were sufficiently close to the ones briefly outlined here. The relevance of Charles Horton Cooley was emphasized by Mead (1930b) as well as others (Perinbanayagam, 1975).

The Sociogenetic Thought of Charles H. Cooley in Its Context

As a master of the method of "sympathetic introspection," Cooley provided accessible narrative accounts of persons within their social worlds (see Schubert, 1998, for a thorough overview). The belief in the positive ideal of "sharing" within a community is immediately evident to the reader of Cooley's work:

All mankind acknowledges kindness as the law of right intercourse within a social group. By communion minds are fused into a sympathetic whole, each part tends to share the life of all the rest, so that kindness is a common joy, and harshness common pain. (Cooley, 1925, p. 40)

[The sentiment of mutual kindness] flourishes most in primary groups, where . . . it contributes to an ideal of moral unity of which kindness is a part of. Under its influence the I-feeling becomes a we-feeling, which seeks no good that is not also good of the group. And the humanism of our time strives with renewed energy to make the we-feeling prevail also in the larger phases of life. (ibid., pp. 189–90)

For Cooley, the "self" and "social other" did not exist as mutually exclusive phenomena (Cooley, 1902, 1907). They were united via the notion of sympathetic introspection – a person puts himself

into intimate contact with various sorts of persons and [allows] them to awake in himself a life similar to their own, which he afterward, to the best of his ability, recalls and describes. In this way he is more or less able to understand – always by introspection – children, idiots, criminals, rich and poor, conservative and radical – any phase of human nature not wholly alien to his own. (Cooley, 1907, pp. 67–8)

The mind is inevitably social, since it is interdependent with the world of others. In ontogeny, that sociality comes into being. In his only adventure into the empirical study of child development (the recording of the emergence of a self-reflexive lexicon in the speech of his third child (Cooley, 1908), he demonstrated the intricate interdependence of the child and the social world. This interdependence led Cooley to favor thorough case analyses for the accumulation of data (Cooley, 1929). His "sympathetic introspection" fits with his general theoretical stance. It was also reflected in his remarks on how he preferred sociology to be taught at universities (Report of the Committee of Ten, 1912, pp. 622–3).

Cooley appropriated the notion of the fusion of the person and the social world. George Mead's perceptive reflection on Cooley may fit as a summary on his work: "His approach was that of objective introspection. The community that he discovered, so to speak from the inside, was a democracy, and inevitably an American democracy. . . . Finding it in living, it was a process. Its organization was a manner of living. Its institutions were the habits of individuals. . . ." (Mead, 1930b, p. 694).

However, Cooley's notion of interdependence of person and society was not unstructured. He emphasized the importance of feelings of personal "ownership" of activities of the community in which the given person is a member, and made a plea against application of economic thought to human values (Cooley, 1913).

For Cooley, human knowledge was viewed as both behavior-oriented (i.e., viewing the world as it behaves) and sympathetic (empathizing with the world). Thus, the same person may at times treat another person as an external object (i.e., without any identification with him or her), and at other times move to share his or her internal selves, via empathic fusion (Cooley, 1926). The individual mind is a kind of mental-social complex that includes all the socially developed sentiments and understandings. At the level of social organization, a corresponding social-mental complex (or "group mind") can be conceptualized. The basis of common (shared) social perceptions is the general similarity of mental-social complexes throughout the human species. Persons become aware of this similarity by watching the behavior of others and realizing that the behavior of others can be attributed sentiments characteristic of one's own. This leads to the construction of the complex individual (which is social at the same time) self which – figuratively – has got the label of "looking-glass self." Yet, again, the basic trust in the community is evident in Cooley's sociology.

Forms of Social Participation: John Boodin's Elaboration of Lévy-Bruhl

John Boodin was a philosopher in Kansas, with close – and critical – ties to William James and Josiah Royce. In fact, Boodin's criticism of James led the latter to the writing of his basic pragmatist essay "The Will to Believe" (James, 1896; for specific description of the incident: James, 1979, pp. 311–12). Boodin also provided a cognitive criticism of Bergson's philosophy (Boodin, 1913). Starting his work from an interest in the time concept (Boodin, 1904, 1908), he elaborated the notion of "social minds" (Boodin, 1913) and "social systems" (Boodin, 1918). He furthered the sociogenetic thought in the context of looking at social participation (Boodin, 1921).

Boodin's main focus was on the social embeddedness of human

behavior – in order to understand human beings the researcher needs to understand their participation in social life. That participation is highly variable, specific to the particular contexts. Yet that variability is guided by social meanings – collective representations in the sense of Durkheim. In accordance with Lévy-Bruhl, the "law of participation" entailed the "primitive minds" direct participation in the essences (symbolic worlds) of objects, through which the "mystical essence" of being could be revealed.

Boodin was obviously not alone in criticizing Lévy-Bruhl for the insistence on "primitive mentality." He pointed out that much of the social life of persons of the Western world – clearly not attributable to the "primitive" category – is also imbued by such magical constructions. Thus,

Human beings do not live unto themselves nor die unto themselves, as the non-social animals do, but in their science and in their illusions, in their virtues and in their vices they are influenced by the fact of association. The group sentiment . . . must have emblems to focus the common consciousness, and these emblems thus become part of the association. It may be a totem sign or an institutional name or a flag or a constitution. In any case the emblem is invested with the collective life of the group. And in turn the emblem becomes an independent source of group sentiment, so that we worship the name of France or Britain or the United States of America; we pay homage to the flag and die for it as a thing having value in itself; we come to regard the constitution as the source of our rights and liberties; the religious ritual itself becomes a means of salvation. (Boodin, 1921, pp. 33–4)

For Boodin, the "law of participation" was a general methodological imperative: In order to understand the beliefs and conduct of human beings, we must look at them within their social matrix, i.e., by analyzing the social group and the historical period in which the given person lives. However, the participation of an individual in a group can occur in various degrees. Some causes of the group lead to conflicting orientations by persons. Secondly, some forms of participation can be hidden under ordinary circumstances: "Loyalty is likely to be merely dormant until the common cause is challenged. The devotees of a religion may be comparatively indifferent until persecution, the violation of the religious conscience, sets in . . . People may speak indifferently and even critically of their nation until its life is threatened; and then the flood tide of emotion and heroism rises to meet the crisis" (Boodin, 1921, p. 35).

Boodin distinguished three types of social participation. In "automatic participation" the individual accepts unquestioningly and unthinkingly the customs and beliefs of the group. In "dogmatic participation": "The individual recognizes the authority of the group as supreme, and the individual 'devoutly strives to understand and interpret the meaning of the group' " (Boodin, 1921, p. 41).

Finally, "critical participation" entails personal meaningful understanding of the world of social institutions. Each meaning of the group or institution is evaluated – and sometimes accepted – by the person through his or her own meaning system. Thus, "We accept theories, not because they are the collective judgment of the past nor because some distinguished individual may have held them . . . but because the facts of human experience vindicate them. Sometimes one man of great vision may be worth all the rest. Galileo was right and the ecclesiastical tribunal that forced him to retract was wrong, in spite of the authorities of the past and the authority of the church" (Boodin, 1921, pp. 44–5).

Boodin's view of the social matrix would not fit well with either pragmatism nor behaviorism, since the meaningful separation of the group and the individual is implicated here. In the realm of philosophy and sociology, it was reasonably possible in America to critically participate in the community of behaviorism. Yet boundaries were necessary there as well. The general framework of communally accepted "cloud of behaviorism," but could not bypass sociogenetic thinkers outside of psychology.

Charles Ellwood's Efforts to Delineate Social Psychology from Sociology

Charles Ellwood was a sociologist in Chicago (Ellwood, 1901b), who developed the notion of social training of instincts (Stocking, 1962, pp. 246–7). Habits can become instincts, yet this process has its limits, and many innate tendencies prevail over the social training efforts (Ellwood, 1901a). The relevance of the social nature of psychological functions was set by Ellwood to reflect a developmental (which was labeled "genetic," in the usual terminology of the 1890s) facet of both persons and societies:

When conceived as social philosophy . . . sociology in its genetic aspects may be regarded as the philosophy of history . . . social psychology in its genetic aspect has also to do with the philosophy of history on its subjective side. Group psychical processes are the historical processes on their subjective side par excellence. When the genetic aspect of social psychology is fully worked out, therefore, it should yield a philosophy of history. (Ellwood, 1899a, p. 660)

Social psychology is a section of the genetic psychology of the individual (Ellwood, 1907, p. 336). The life process is what gives rise to the new forms of psychological kind. Ellwood followed John Dewey's idea of the centrality of functional coordination (Ellwood, 1910), providing an account of development that would not have been foreign to developmental psychology of the later decades – especially that of Jean Piaget:

All the phenomena of psychical life group themselves about these two fundamental forms [coordination and adaptation] – are the outgrowth of them, and are functionally explained by their reference to them. Thus a coordination which has once been successfully established tends to persist, or becomes a habit. The necessity of adjustment . . . arising from some variation in the organism or environment, causes the old coordination or habit to break up, and sensation results. Sensation . . . is the sign of the interruption of a habit, and represents the point at which an activity is reconstructed. The old coordination in breaking up . . . must yield the material for the new coordination . . . must be used as means for the construction of new coordination. (Ellwood, 1899b, p. 809)

While the person's coordinations are constructed by the life worlds of individuals, they become socially selected for their survival. The specific needs of the social system at a given time set up the criteria for such a selection. The analogy of society to organism was crucial for Ellwood. He emphasized the processual view of the "social mind," in contrast to the "soul": "Just as in the most recent individual psychology the term 'mind' has come to mean, not an entity, but a process, so in social psychology the term 'social mind' must mean, not a societary 'soul' but a societary process" (Ellwood, 1899c, p. 224).

It is in the realm of such processes that social intervention becomes possible. Ellwood called for the development of "social pedagogy," which could adjust the persons to the demands of the society. Yet he rejected the socioeconomical determinism of the psychical by the socio-economic class, as his contemporary Marxists were propagating (Ellwood, 1911). He kept emphasizing the need for a historical perspective on the social phenomena in psychology (Ellwood, 1924), and arguing against the "objectivist" dogmatism in psychology (Ellwood, 1916). The historical process in any society was not viewed by him as an economic process, but as a sociopsychological one, in which the social conditions were leading human acting and thinking, yet not determining it. Historically formed social institutions play a central role in that (e.g., religion; Ellwood, 1913). Cultural evolution was viewed by him as produced by human groups, who jointly perfect different ideas and cultural tools, then switch to new ideas or implements (e.g., technology). The social world is organized by "pattern ideas" (Ellwood, 1918).

Sociology, according to Ellwood (1907, p. 303) was "the science of the organization and evolution of society," with a focus on processes of change. American sociology at the beginning of the twentieth century was attentive to Francis Galton's eugenicist efforts to purify the society. While entering the practical dispute about "biological purification" of the human race (i.e., the social reform movement of the eugenicists), Ellwood continued to emphasize the developmental and transactionist perspective on recognizing both heredity and environment as mutually related in human lives. He cautioned against simple social engineering solutions to the eugenic problems (Ellwood, 1914, p. 226).

Conclusions: America's Booming and Buzzing Community Orientation, and Sociogenetic Thought

In this chapter we have looked at the relevant intellectual background of the sociogenetic ideas that existed in American intellectual thought during the late nineteenth century, and which gave rise to the new philosophical credo of pragmatism in its different versions. The pressures of immigration and urbanization led to both the opening of the U.S. society to new ideas, and to a further tightening of the reins on all novelties that emerged in the society. The tendencies toward anarchism and totalitarian control worked together in a society that was based on a humanistic ideal, yet which needed to be surrendered to the powers of the capitalist production system.

Ideas of development were a natural part of the scene. The catalytic roles of William James and John Dewey in this background became evident. James Mark Baldwin's ego-cosmopolitan tour-de-force through developmental thought guided different further developments in Europe (e.g., Janet, Piaget, Vygotsky). There was of course a direct intellectual impact from the booming and buzzing confusion of American psychology during the 1890s – followed by the vicissitudes of the progressive era – upon the European intellectual scene during the following decades. The 1920s in Europe may have continued the efforts of the 1890s in America – a time when American psychology itself became increasingly oriented toward applied demands and behaviorist phraseology.

A crucial peculiarity of the American vision of the role of the social world in the psychological lives of persons was the assumed implicit benevolence of the social units. Thus, even crowds – viewed as potentially unruly and disruptive in European social thought (see Chapter 2) – were seen as the basis for the build-up of democratic institutions (King, 1990). The idea that some individual force (an elite agent) might begin to dominate the social masses was alien to American thought. Surely the dangers of the manipulation of public opinion by journalists did not go unnoticed, yet the principled belief in the checks and balances inherent in American democracy seemed to frame the belief in the benevolence of the society.

The seminal work of George Herbert Mead was one of the results of the social-intellectual context in America during the 1890s. Mead's productive career started then and there, and continued into this century, ending unfinished. In the following chapter, we will consider the history of his ideas in detail.

CHAPTER SIX

George Herbert Mead's Development of the Self

George Herbert Mead is a major contributor to the history of sociogenetic thought in this century (Cook, 1977, 1993; Joas, 1985), as well as
a carrier of progressive social reform ideals between Europe and the
United States (Shalin, 1988). His contributions have led to various
controversies around the "real" and "reinvented" versions of Mead's
thinking, largely concentrated on issues of the movement in sociology
called "symbolic interactionism" (Fine, 1993; McPhail & Rexroat,
1979).

In the usual class society of the social sciences, Mead has been
difficult to locate. His alleged intellectual closeness to behaviorism
(see Baldwin, 1988, 1989; Cook, 1977; Farr, 1983), to the cultural-
historical thought of Lev Vygotsky (Glock, 1986; Leudar, 1991; Valsiner & Van der Veer, 1988; Vari-Szilagyi, 1988; Winter & Goldfield,
1991), to the phenomenology of Alfred Schütz (Wiley, 1979), and the
contemporary fashions of cognitivism (Schwalbe, 1987), has been intensively discussed. Certainly, these discussions have been flavored
by efforts to appropriate Mead's thought for different contemporary
agendas, rather than to represent the synthetic individual thinker.

Such disputes about what Mead "really" or "possibly" meant by
his often difficult texts are not surprising. Mead's intellectual heritage
is not easy to put into a special framework or school of thought, as
our contemporary history writing of the social sciences sometimes
desires. His intellectual interdependency with other thinkers of his
time – Baldwin, Dewey, James, Bergson, and later Whitehead – provided productive thought material for his construction of a sociogenetic picture of the self in its social world. The same sources complicated his tasks by creating intellectual impasses that Mead had to
work through carefully and slowly. The slowness in the development

of Mead's ideas is usually attributed to his personality, yet – as we will try to demonstrate in this chapter – certain guiding axioms that Mead took from his contemporaries (such as Dewey), or from the social processes raging around him (the advent of behaviorist discourse), complicated his conceptual advancement. Mead was working on the major question of sociogenetic thought – in what ways is the human mind actually related to the social world?

Mead's contribution was remarkable in that he preserved the duality in the dynamic relation of the person and the social world, while fighting dualisms in that relation. The distinction between those two phenomena is not usually clear in modern social sciences' discourse (nor was it at Mead's time). Dualism amounts to the exclusive separation of the person and society, and their treatment as static opposites. It is certainly true that no sociogenetic perspective can make productive use of such static oppositions, since those eliminate the possibility to make sense of development from the very beginning of the theoretical construction. Thus Mead had perfectly good reasons to follow Dewey in the fight with the very real windmills of dualism. However, in case of an emphasis on dualities – that is, dynamically linked opposite functioning parts of the same whole – developmental issues could be considered. Mead's emphasis on how the duality of self and society is actually organized in its dynamic flow was his major contribution to sociogenetic thought.

Mead's Life

George Mead was born on February 27, 1863, in Massachusetts, into the family of a Puritan minister (see Cook, 1993 for biographical details). His father's academic activities (he was to become the chair of the preaching science at Oberlin Theological Seminary) led to George's home being filled with the classics of literature, philosophy, and theology, as well as experiences of observing his father engaged in intellectual debates. His mother's side complemented the home environment. She was educated in a seminary, had been a schoolteacher prior to her marriage, and after her husband's death (in 1881) became a college teacher and finally the President of Mount Holyoke College (1890–1900). Thus, from both parents, George Mead was provided with a religious, academic-growth environment at home, closely associated with life at college.

George entered Oberlin College in 1879, taking an interest in philosophy. He was at odds with the ways in which philosophy was taught at Oberlin: The young man was exposed to a selection of English psychology and Scottish philosophy. The social context of Oberlin was aimed at the appropriation of the Puritan theological views; the questioning of basic values was discouraged, and the "right ways" were expected to be internalized. Yet these right ways were not necessarily those of the main tendencies of American society at the time. The Oberlin atmosphere entailed a remarkable amount of religious dissension that itself remained, of course, religious and dogmatic in its implications for human life.

It was during his college years at Oberlin that George Mead was working through his complex relations with religious dogmatism. Mead lived through a liberating conversion:

I remember the time and place – the spring of 82, on the way to the class in *Porter* [COMMENT: i.e., the class in which Noah Porter's *The Elements of Intellectual Science*, 1871, were studied] – when and where I demonstrated to Henry's [Castle] and my satisfaction that no dogmatic philosophy was possible. The statement is dry enough; but the sudden awakening to an inner consciousness that could know no law that was not its own, was an experience that was as profound as any religious conversion could be. (Cook, 1993, pp. 3–4)

In some ways, the effect of this liberation can be sensed in all of Mead's work; there seems to be a dispute against the dogmatism of any theoretical system, possibly including his own.

Starting from his college days when he and his close friend Henry Castle (see description of his role in Mead's life in Wallace, 1967) edited a college newspaper, "*The Oberlin Review*," George became active in what would be life-long activities involving open intellectual debates. In the process of their editorial activities on the paper, the two young men displayed their active intellectual resistance to the local expectations for politically correct thinking. Castle wrote in 1882: "We have our own notions as to what a college paper should be, and are very uncompromising in carrying them out. We do not trouble ourselves to cater to the popular taste, and with our lofty transcendental ideas, and superlative scorn of all things practical, it will be strange indeed if we do not have the whole establishment in the ditch" (Wallace, 1967, p. 403).

The uncompromising stand of the young newspaper editors indeed stirred a controversy in which "a few unguarded remarks made lately ... were most outrageously construed into an attack on religion" (ibid., p. 404).

After graduating from college in 1883, George Mead became a schoolteacher in an effort to earn an income and to contribute to the society (as well as his mother's well-being). However, the realities of teaching in a high school soon brought him to desperation (see Cook, 1993, pp. 7–9 for a description of its dynamics). He moved further in his job search in the real world, and in April 1884 he joined a land surveying team in Minnesota. The social context of such work – being associated with an engineer and an axman who "smoke, drink, and swear like troopers" – was not encouraging the young man of twenty-one to concentrate on the studies of philosophy. By January 1885, George was finished with this healthy outdoor activity, settled down in Minneapolis, and started working as a private tutor. In early September 1887, he left the Midwest to study philosophy at Harvard, while continuing his private tutoring in order to make ends meet. After his first year at Harvard, George was approached by William James to be the tutor to his son and live with them during the summer of 1888. As Mead himself explained (in a letter to Castle):

I shall here have very little work to do, just see to the arithmetic and United States History of a small docile boy ['Harry' James, age 8]. Otherwise I am my own master. The family is a pleasant one consisting of Prof. and Mrs. James, four small children, Mrs. James' sister and mother. Mrs. James is about 40 I should [think], pleasant and devoted to her children. The sister may be 28 or 30, pleasant, very well informed I should judge, a teacher I think, not pretty but with a good complexion and character in her face. (Cook, 1993, pp. 15–16)

Mead's romance with that not pretty but very well-informed girl in the James' family led to an effort to distance him from the idyllic family atmosphere, and encouraged him to further his philosophical studies in the country of his greatest dreams: Germany. From the fall of 1888 to the fall of 1891 Mead studied in Germany, first in Leipzig and then in Berlin.

In Leipzig, George joined the crowds who wanted to learn the latest of psychology from Wilhelm Wundt. He considered specialization in physiological psychology – a widely popular but ill-defined subject – which nevertheless could open a way for thought upon his return to America. Henry Castle (who was with Mead in Germany) explained:

George thinks he must make a speciality of this branch, because in America, where poor, bated, unhappy Christianity, trembling for its life, claps the gag into the mouth of Free Thought, and says 'Hush, hush, not a word, or nobody will believe in me any more,' he thinks it would be hard for him to get a chance to utter any ultimate philosophical opinions savoring of independence. In Physiological Psychology, on the other hand, he has a harmless territory in which he can work quietly without drawing down upon himself the anathema and excommunication of all-potent Evangelicalism. (Cook, 1993, p. 21)

Even if Castle's description is his personally exaggerated version of how Mead was thinking of his life's work in 1888, it explicates the intellectual context of the United States during that time. In many ways, Mead's (later) slow and tentative expression of his ideas in writing may be linked to the recognition of the viciousness and negativity that the "excommunicating all-potent Evangelicalism" could entail.

After settling in Germany, Mead experienced "something akin to conversion" (Shalin, 1988, p. 922) in his sociopolitical views. He was enthusiastic about the European kind of socialism, and was eagerly speculating on its possible transplantation to the United States. It is around this time that Mead's conviction about the central role of cities in the social reform in the United States formed. Thus, Mead's own later practical activities in the politics of Chicago were antedated by his ideal reconstruction of European socialist thought for the contexts of the New World, at the age of twenty-five.

One could return to the significance of the conflict that both Castle and Mead had with the religious powers at the time of their editing of *The Oberlin Review*. Experiences of such a kind could lead the young American intellectuals to have an ambivalent relationship to the role of the community in guiding thought. Years later, Mead himself expressed his view on the role of the community in the American mental life. Without being unpatriotic with respect to the United States in any way, Mead put the cultural history of the country into its dynamic context. Thus, the history of the colonial past of the United States was built on the immigrant mentality, which colonists carried from their background country:

It was a mind that brought with it from Europe habits already formed of ecclesiastical and political self-government. The dominant habits were those of Puritanism and the democracy of the town meeting. The philosophy of the Puritanism is indicated in the phrase 'thrift and righteous-

ness.' Calvinism had found a place for business within its spiritual econ-
omy. . . . God had given men property and blessed them in its increase,
and punished the unprofitable steward by taking away even that which
he had. (Mead, 1930a, p. 211)

At the same time, the political self-government system underwent
a substantial change in the New World, in contrast with its beginnings
in the context of British society, especially as a result of the independence of the United States. By liberating the country from its colonial
status, the new U.S. society led to the development of a new form of
self-government, which was an exaggerated (liberated from social-
class constraints, one might say) and generalized version of the centrality of community. The new citizens of the United States

had changed the character of the state which gave the former colonists
their political consciousness. When they recognized themselves as citizens
it was no longer as members of the English social hierarchy. For this they
had substituted a political national structure which was a logical development of the town meeting. The state has never impressed itself upon
the American citizen. It is nothing but the extension in representative
form of the political habits of the town meeting. . . .
    The habit of self-government in local affairs was an inherited English
method, but the creation of a national state out of these habits was purely
American. (Mead, 1930a, pp. 212–13)

As will be seen later in this chapter, Mead was committed to the
purely American social dominance of community-centered thinking
(which goes beyond the community itself) in both his theoretical ideas
and practical efforts to mediate in the process of social reforms in
Chicago (see also Cook, 1993, Chapter 7, and Shalin, 1988). Interestingly, it was the same societal context that created the tensions for his
own life – both at the time of his intellectual development during his
university years, and at the end of his life, being in the middle of
the arbitration for the preservation of his department at the University
of Chicago (see Cook, 1993, pp. 183–94, for the "Hutchings controversy"). The credo of a personal fight with dogmatism in thought, and
social suppression of the underprivileged that often coincides with it,
created an unavoidable controversy for Mead's own career development, which he solved over decades in his persistently unexcessive
ways.
    After the move to Berlin in March 1889, Mead continued to read
with weary regularity into the complexities of anatomy and physiol-

ogy, as relevant parts of his possible specialization in physiological psychology. Yet his heart remained with the philosophical topics – he took Friedrich Paulsen's seminar on the history of recent philosophy, as well as ethics with Wilhelm Dilthey. As to his psychology studies, Mead studied with Hermann Ebbinghaus. His experiences in Germany seemed to have freed his thought from the constant fight with American pietism. Instead, he became inspired by developmental psychology and European socialism, and he was filled with a spirit for secular social reform (Cook, 1993, p. 22). The German intellectual context prepared Mead for a lucky reentrance into the social world of the United States, which was made possible by the remarkable job offer from John Dewey in the summer of 1891. As a part of his new opening career, in October, 1891 George married Henry Castle's sister Helen.

From Berlin to Ann Arbor

For Mead, the entrance into the issues of the social nature of psychological processes can be dated to his return from Berlin during the fall of 1891, when he became a lecturer in psychology at the University of Michigan. In Ann Arbor he joined the small group of intellectuals who were about to change American social sciences, as well as the society as a whole. Mead was twenty-eight-years-old at the time, his immediate superior John Dewey was four years older. In Dewey's department he met and made friends with Charles H. Cooley (who was twenty-eight). He missed the previous members of Dewey's group: James R. Angell (a student – twenty-four-years-old), who had just moved to Harvard to study with William James, and James Tufts (then twenty-nine-years-old) who had just moved to the University of Chicago (and whose teaching position Mead took over in Ann Arbor). Closeness to Tufts continued through Mead's lifetime, as they continued to be colleagues in the philosophy department at Chicago.

During his years in Ann Arbor (1891–94), and thanks to the close contact with John Dewey, Mead's focus on the issue of the unity of the social and the personal began to emerge (Cook, 1993, pp. 27–36). During the early 1890s, Dewey was in the process of change himself, after moving away from George Wallace's idealistic background and getting closer to a kind of pragmatism he created for himself (see Chapter 5). His move from a Hegelian to a functionalist perspective was taking place concurrently, so the mutual intellectual sharing guided both of the thinkers in Michigan, and later on in Chicago (Raphelson, 1973).

Mead and his family settled down in Ann Arbor and was pleased intellectually and familywise (his son was born there in 1892). Living next door to the Deweys was a pleasant context and not just in a philosophical sense; Mead was full of admiration for the personal style of Dewey outside of academic tasks. Intellectually, Mead continued his search, mostly along the direction charted by Dewey, but building upon it with his own dynamic perspective on the interdependence of self and society.

In his eulogic retrospect at the beginning of their intellectual interdependency, Dewey recognized Mead's "original haunting question" of the relations between subjective consciousness and social interaction. In a way, the difficulties Mead experienced in his efforts to solve that problem are unsurprising:

The power of observing common elements, which are ignored just because they are common, characterized the mind of George Mead. It accounts for the difficulty which he had in conveying what he observed to others. . . . Mr. Mead's philosophical thinking . . . springs from his own intimate experiences, from things deeply felt, rather than from things merely thought out by him, which then seek substantiation in accepted facts and current concepts. His interest in the concept of emergence is, for example, a reflex of that factor of his own intellectual experience by which new insights were constantly budding and having then to be joined to what he had thought previously, instead of merely displacing old ideas. He *felt* within himself both the emergence of the new and the inevitable continuity of the new with the old. (Dewey, 1932, pp. xxxviii–xxxix)

In turn, Mead expressed his utmost fascination with his friendship with Dewey, and confessed that in many ways he had attributed to Dewey the role that had previously been carried by his tragically deceased friend Henry Castle (Cook, 1993, p. 36).

Unity of Opposites in the Scientific Mind

Mead's empathic treatment of intellectual issues may be one of the best demonstrations of William James' emphasis on the primacy of introspection in the construction of knowledge in psychology (James, 1890, p. 185). Yet Mead emphasized the opposite – the relatedness of the person with the social world, in terms of interdependent participation in the latter.

Mead's actual living and thinking through mutually related opposites proved to be a hurdle for later interpreters of his thought. A similar difficulty has been eminent in understanding Vygotsky (Van der Veer & Valsiner, 1991), and seems to stem from the interpreters' urge to fit a dialectical thinker into a categorization system that disallows viewing the systemic complexity of the thought of the target person. Intellectual interdependency entails a number of systemic relations between ideas, from which novel ideas may emerge. Thus, in the case of Mead, he was neither an "introspectionist" nor a "behaviorist" (see also Cook, 1977, 1993), nor a "social psychologist," nor an "interactionist." Each of these labels is necessarily misleading because they try to reduce to a label-associated homogeneity the richness of thought that emerged in a dialogue between self (Mead's own self, here) and society, or in the tension between static and dynamic aspects of experience, external and intramental. The habit of label assignment to persons in science leads to the displacement of the analysis of that thought system into the realm of social classification of the author. In Mead's case, such classification has persistently failed (e.g., see Glock, 1986, p. 142 on Mead being a "sophisticated behaviorist"), despite the recurrent efforts in the literature.

Mead's Mind in Society

Mead's own quest for social progress entailed the belief in the improvement of society by social means, leading to a synthesis of the materialism and spiritualism that coexisted in American society. As Mead continued to move further away from his theologically embedded family background, he (in a letter to relatives, written in 1892) expressed his belief that: "The body and soul are but two sides of one thing, and that the gulf between them is only the expression of the fact that our life does not yet realize the ideal of what our social life will be, when our functions and acts shall be not simply ours but the processes of the great body politic which is God as revealed in the universe" (Cook, 1993, p. 31).

The theme of the continuous working through of his relations with religion surfaced during the Michigan years in the form of themes he took interest in, outside of his main work on teaching physiological psychology. Thus, he delivered a talk "The Psychology of Jesus' Use of Emotions," in February 1893 to a meeting of the local Students' Christian Association. In that lecture, as Cook shows, Mead argued that:

The gospel of love taught by Jesus . . . was a call to a kind of life that went beyond mere conformity to traditional religious forms and rituals. . . . Christian love . . . had to be a sort leading to activity deeply rooted in our social nature. Such love 'must have back of it the instinctive actions of the whole social, in other words religious, nature,' and it must lead us to identify with the shared interests of all those involved with us in a common social life. (Cook, 1993, p. 33)

In that address, Mead preemptively covers his sociogenetic theme of the decades to come, yet in a framework that is emerging from the realm of theological discourse. The turn from religion to science was of course a complicated one for all science, as it entailed the displacement of ideas from religion to the secular world in ways that recreated new religionlike movements.

Energetism: A Secular Religion for Science

The unity of the universe was constructed from the turn-of-the-century science in terms of the extension of the concept of energy beyond the bounds of physics. Wilhelm Ostwald's energeticism was on its rise during the 1890s (see Hakfoort, 1992), and Mead's intellectual dispute (during his Michigan years) with that direction took the form of emphasizing the evolution of organisms over the atomism of physics and psychophysics (Mead, 1894a, 1894b). Notably, these very first scientific publications were in the form of book reviews, or short abstracts (Mead, 1895). Mead was certainly not eager to proliferate his contemporary literature on psychology with a never-stopping flow of empirical papers.

Nevertheless, these early texts reflecting Mead's thinking during the Michigan period are of substantive interest. In no uncertain terms did Mead elaborate the need to analyze psychological processes as systemic entities, without their being reduced to their atomistic components. This beginning point in Mead's rejection of associationist psychology has its counterpart in Vygotsky's thinking in terms of "units as minimal wholes" (see Van der Veer & Valsiner, 1991). The impossibility of atomistic reduction was built by Mead on the claim that psychology as a science cardinally differed from the natural sciences, especially physics. Obviously relating with Dewey's position, Mead claimed (1894a, p. 172) that psychology has to treat dynamic phenomena as such and analyze them in terms of their process nature, while physics could take a static view of its target phenomena.

How, then, could psychologists study these dynamic processes, and explain them? Mead gave an answer to that question that largely followed the "circular reaction" idea of James Mark Baldwin in his claim, saying that:

An object which is *a co-ordinated group of activities* must have developed in the process of evolution under the same law which governed the development of the whole organism. This can be stated in terms of a food-process – involving the assimilating of food, its expenditure in motion which brings the organism in contact with new food, a negative reaction upon non-nutritious or dangerous environment, and an overflow in reproduction. *The same process must serve as a formula for the development of the psychological object, constructed as it is out of the activities which the search for food in an increasingly complicated environment has called out.* (Mead, 1894a, p. 174, emphases added)

The emphasis on coordinated activities and the unity of the processes that operate in organisms (i.e., alimentary and psychological processes expected to operate in similar ways) is certainly a Dewey-based view on the evolution of consciousness (see Chapter 5). The selective nature of the activities, their change being triggered by environmental pressures, and the overproduction of activities resembles Baldwin's scheme of organic evolution (see Chapter 4). The psychological processes are – as novelties – built upon their physiological foundations, even if the principles of their organization are unified. Thus, we have the emergence of qualitative novelty (surely a Hegelian idea, mediated by Dewey) based on the unity of the principles (or "energy" in the world belief of the energeticists at the time (see Chapter 4).

Mead's description of the actual processes of the emergence of novelty is particularly interesting in its nuances. It was expressed in terms of physiological processes of emotions, and linked clearly to the debate on the nature of emotions during 1894–5 (see Chapter 5). Whereas it is clear that Mead was providing a supportive voice in that dispute for Dewey, it is his specific claim that deserves closer attention. After describing the circular process involved in the vasomotor system, he explained:

The act must commence before the flow of blood can take place. It is in connection with this increased flow of blood that we have to assume the emotional tones of consciousness arise according to the discharge theory. Within the act it would answer only to interest. It is in the preparation for action that we find the qualitatively different emotional tones, and here we find increased flow of blood before the act. *We find also what we may term symbolic stimuli which tend to arouse the vaso-motor processes that are originally called out only by the instinctive acts.* These stimuli in the form in which we study them, seem to be more or less *rhythmical repetitions of those moments in the act itself which call forth especially the vaso-motor response.* In this form they are recognized as aesthetic stimuli, and may best be studied in the war and love dances. It is under the influence of stimuli of this general character that the emotional states and their physiological parallels arise. *The teleology of these states is that of giving the organism an evaluation of the act before the coordination that leads to the particular reaction has been completed.* (Mead, 1895, pp. 163–4, emphases added)

We can see here the expression of the idea that about a decade later became famous under the label of conditional reflex. Careful consideration of Mead's statement allows us to see that the symbolic stimuli (or conditional stimuli that have become established in their regulatory functions of the unconditional physiological processes) begin to stand for some expected (teleological) next state, and produce emotional states in the process of anticipating the future. While Pavlov was working upon his experimental demonstration of how certain stimuli may be made into conditional provokers of physiological reactions that otherwise proceed by unconditional automatic reflex schemes, Mead was on his way to build up his emphasis on the significant symbol, starting from the web of the emotion discussions during the mid-1890s.

As far as is known, Mead himself did not put into practice the ingenious idea of studying the rhythmic nature of love or war dances. Instead, he followed his friend and mentor John Dewey to Chicago in 1894, where he could be seen as a very central – even if not outwardly productive – member of the whole intellectual circle that was soon labeled the Chicago School of Thought.

Mead and The Chicago School

The core of Dewey's intellectual nucleus that was established in Ann Arbor recongregated at the University of Chicago from 1894 onward.

Dewey and Mead moved there that year, Angell followed in 1895. Mead's construction of social psychological ideas continued in Chicago during the following decade.

Chicago was a productive place for the young and socially active intellectuals of Dewey's circle, where they became involved in vigorous discussions and put their ideas into social practice. Being newly established, the University of Chicago provided the young intellectuals an environment that the old and established major universities of the United States could not – there was a free environment for their social and intellectual growth. They made the most of that advantage, leading William James to exclaim:

Chicago has a School of Thought! – a school of thought which, it is safe to predict, will figure in literature as the School of Chicago for twenty-five years to come. Some universities have plenty of thought to show, but no school; others plenty of school, but no thought ... Professor John Dewey, and at least ten of his disciples, have collectively put into words a statement, homogeneous in spite of so many cooperating minds, of a view of the world, both theoretical and practical, which is so simple, massive, and positive that, in spite of the fact that many parts of it yet need to be worked out, it deserves the title of a new system of philosophy. (James, 1904a, p. 1)

Under the "new system of philosophy," James was of course referring to the philosophical orientation of pragmatism that through the activities of Dewey reached numerous areas of thought, ranging from education to psychology (including behaviorist movements) and sociology. Of course, James was himself an important participant in this construction (James, 1904b; 1907), so that in a way, his laudatory exposure of the Chicago School was also a version of a rhetoric presentation of a major change in all American thought. What emerged alongside pragmatism (or in its intellectual womb) is the ideological takeover of American psychology by the behaviorist creed (see Angell, 1961, p. 26). It eventually blocked serious intellectual efforts in the domain of the study of human higher mental functions as dogmatically as the previously dominant religious-moralistic kind of thought had done.

Among Dewey's disciples (there were at least ten mentioned by James) were George Mead, James Tufts, Addison Moore, and Edward Scribner Ames. Even after Dewey's resignation from the University of Chicago, in 1904, most of his disciples continued to provide a direction to the social thought at the university. Furthermore, the early pragmatist orientation at Chicago was paralleled by a substantial sociological tradition (Charles Henderson, Charles Ellwood, William Thomas, Robert Park) to which the anthropological efforts of Edward Sapir were added in the 1920s. The intellectual tradition started by Dewey during the 1890s has lived its innovative life course, and now a century later the social sciences at the University of Chicago retains its productive uniqueness.

One of the important features of the Chicago School was its effort to put theoretical ideas into social practice. Thus, pragmatism did not remain only in the minds of philosophers, but found its outlets in educational practices. Dewey's Experimental School at the University of Chicago was established as a condition for his move to Chicago. His applied pragmatism would allow for educational reforms locally and in city politics. The latter was the practical action domain for Mead – he became involved in a lifelong participation in the complex affairs of the city and its (mostly immigrant) inhabitants (Deegan & Burger, 1978, Shalin, 1988).

Mead as a Mediator in the City Context. Even when fully immersed in his academic work, Mead remained active in social action, and devoted much of his life to the progressivist social-action efforts in Chicago. Indeed, Chicago was filled with social problems, and it was an ideal ground for Mead to try to put into practice his ideal of "city hall socialism" that he had created during his study years in Germany. His main idea was to alter the interdependence process between the opposed or opposing parties, thus hoping to create "silent" and "noviolent" revolutions, or the gradual betterment of human conditions. In that, Mead's position has been viewed as close to that of Marx (Shalin, 1988, pp. 929–38).

Mead's social activities in Chicago were based on his belief that the modification of the environment could lead to the overcoming of human social problems. The employers were seen to become individualistic because they opposed the trade unions, the latter because they overlook the employers' needs. Such direct opposition creates a vicious circle, where one side's acts lead to further escalation of the individualistic stance of the other, and so on. In contrast, if the process of interdependency were to be emphasized by mediators of a social conflict, the vicious escalatory cycle could be reversed. Of course, Mead saw in the priority of external conditions a starting point for such a deescalatory pattern: "If the community educated and housed its members properly, and protected machinery, food, markets, and thoroughfares adequately, the problems at present vexing the industrial world would largely disappear" (Mead, 1908a, p. 318).

Mead himself was a lifelong mediator who tried to bring about social reforms through increasing mutual understanding and improvement of conditions. He was seriously devoted to the improvement of the lives of the underprivileged, which at that time meant the European immigrants. Interestingly, however, Mead's concern was not in any explicit way extended to the historically American problems of the underprivileged status of different racial groups (Shalin, 1988, pp. 946–7). Mead followed the ideology of progressivism which "tended to confuse the normative and the descriptive in their accounts by, on the one hand, criticizing contemporary democracy and, on the other, insisting that the institutional framework of democracy necessary for social reconstruction was already in place" (Shalin, 1988, p. 946).

Surely it was not in place, and perhaps that miscalculation has hindered a number of social reform efforts in the United States. Hence Mead's active social mediation efforts, even if consistent with his general world view, were largely of limited success. In his focus on social improvement, we can again see parallels with the personal concerns of Lev Vygotsky (who was devoted to the ideal of providing all children and adults with opportunities for further advancement; see Chapter 8).

Mead's Educational Reform Ideas

Along the lines of progressive educational ideas, Mead called for improvements in the process of school learning and teaching. Certainly here we can observe strong influences of Dewey's thought (e.g., that instruction should be an "interchange of experience" between teacher and child). However, Mead called for the recognition of the child's self in the educational process in ways that the intraself interaction of the child and the social interaction with the teacher form a mutual feedback loop:

If the lesson is simply set for the child – is not his own problem – the recognition of himself as facing a task and a task-master is no part of the solution of the problem. *But a difficulty which the child feels and brings to his*

parent or teacher for solution is helped on toward interpretation by the conscious-
ness of the child's relation to his pastors and masters. Just in so far as the
subject matter of instruction can be brought into the form of problems
arising in the experience of the child – just so far will the relation of the
child to the instructor become the natural solution of the problem – actual
success of a teacher depends in large measure upon this capacity to state
the subject matter of instruction in terms of the experience of the children.
(Mead, 1910a, p. 691, emphasis added)

The child's self can become productive in the educational process,
or remain unconnected with it. In the latter case, it may easily happen
that the child's opposition to the efforts of educators in highly authoritarian school settings, where discipline and rule and reign, creates a
situation very similar to the fights between employers and trade unions. This eliminates the active self-involved participation of the
learner from the educational process.

The parallel here with Vygotsky is again noteworthy (see Chapter
8, and Van der Veer & Valsiner, 1991). The focus on the "zone of
proximal development" was in Vygotsky's thought similarly calling
for the unification of the children's experience of challenges with the
teachers' efforts to create them. However, it is more important to
emphasize the consistency in Mead's thought between the domain of
the mediation of social conflicts and the domain of educational processes. Productive results in both domains can be achieved only if the
intrapsychological (self) system is continuously interactive with social
others, and the novelty created in social interaction feeds into reorganization of the self system.

In his academic teaching, Mead moved from his previously established secure path of physiological psychology to the new world of
social psychology. Starting from his personal search of social problems, Mead gradually introduced a course on social psychology at the
University of Chicago from 1900 onward (Cook, 1993, pp. 46–7) – first
in the institutional context of the psychology department and later
within the department of philosophy. From 1919 onward the course
was labeled advanced, because the introductory part was covered by
his former student Ellsworth Faris in the sociology department. The
contents of the last few years of Mead's advanced course (during 1927
and 1930; see Morris, 1934, p. vi) have been partially preserved in the
composite edited text of *Mind, Self and Society* (Mead, 1934). Mead's
death in 1931 interrupted this continuous rethinking of his philosophy

of the social living of the active person. Mead's lifetime work could never have reached a completed state beyond which there would be no possibility for further construction.

Nevertheless, there are basic themes that continued to interest Mead throughout his life. Aside from the general sociogenetic orientation (which resulted in numerous claims about the social nature of the mind), it is his philosophy of dynamic processes that unite the self (in itself) and society (with the self). Talk about the self was not exactly the major pastime of pragmatic psychologists at the turn of the century. In a way, it was beneficial for Mead's development in Chicago that he moved increasingly away from psychology as an institution, and toward philosophy. This self-encapsulation in American society resulted in a similar domain of free thinking that Mead had been longing for when he considered an escape from philosophy into physiological psychology during his study years in Germany. He thus became an obscure figure in the scene of American psychology. The latter had its own developmental course. During Mead's four decades in Chicago, American psychology moved away from the line of thought that Mead advanced. The proliferation of the excessive focus on behaviorist objectivity in psychology was certainly on a course quite opposite to Mead's efforts to find a solution to how intramental processes are dynamically united with the extramental ones, and how that interaction results in psychological novelties.

Mead's increasing misfit with the development of psychology in North America during the early 1900s led both to his minimal contribution to psychology and to his fame in sociology and philosophy. Of course, he did not fit into the mainstreams of these other disciplines either. In many ways, George Mead may be the first American thinker to whom the label "interdisciplinary" can be applied without trepidation. He did not intend to present an eclectic mixture of ideas from different disciplines as if they were consistent. In his search for solutions to basic problems, Mead built an inherent consistency of ideas – slowly and with a great deal of hesitation – which left our contemporary social sciences with a challenge to understanding its complexity.

Mead's Personal Style

It could be said that Mead himself lived according to his slowly emerging theory. In his own life, external social events guided the reconstruction of his self-system, which then fed into his interaction with others. Again in an astounding parallel with Vygotsky, Mead in his personal style was by far more comfortable with speaking than with writing, and his course on social psychology was always new in its specific renderings. In the words of a participant observer and later colleague,

George Mead developed his views on social psychology in a course of oral lectures, delivered without notes in a conversational tone. He always spoke while seated, and to some of us seemed to be more concerned with the development of his thought than with the response of his audience. He would sometimes go over again as much as half of what he had said the day before, so that his presentation resembled a sort of spiral. The reaction he received was not uniform. Some students failed to get the key and found the presentations unsatisfying, while others became enthusiastic disciples and considered that he had given them what they had long and vainly sought elsewhere. (Faris, 1937, p. 391)

A similar "spiral advance" of ideas can be detected in Mead's writings, when analyzed in their historical sequence. His writings constituted a slowly progressing spiral of disputes with a number of interlocutors in his intellectual field. Mead's thinking was extremely interdependent with the community of scholars of his time. Linkages with Dewey played a major part, but simultaneously one can trace direct intellectual interdependencies with Wundt, James, and others (Valsiner & Van der Veer, 1988). It could be said that Mead was in continuous conversation with his "social others," and advanced his own ideas via constructive participation. In his spiral argumentation scheme in those conversations, Mead produced novel nuances of seemingly well-known ideas. He cautiously argued the expression of novel ideas, often taking the form of complicated written constructions, which may be explained if we look at Mead's main intellectual dispute, i.e., his disputes with dogmatism of any kind that had emerged through his own life experiences. The opening of conversation and keeping it going is a precursor to overcoming dogmatism, but the solutions to the problems that are thus put into focus did not emerge overnight.

Mead's Intellectual Search

Mead's social philosophy brings together three interweaving factors. In each, the protestant Anglo-Saxon recurrent themes of discourse in

U.S. society are visible: a sense of wholeness, the glorification of the community (and the axiomatic assumption that persons strive towards unity with the community), and a focus on action (Barry, 1968, pp. 188–9). Nevertheless, George Mead was acting – starting from his college years and through his educational sojourn to Germany – in opposition to the existing social context of U.S. education, which was described (by his closest friend Henry Castle, in a letter from Germany in February 1889) as follows:

I am merely attacking the preposterous system by which the sects in America have taken possession of the higher education everywhere, so that no mathematical, chemical, or mineralogical fact can get into the world, and come into contact with susceptible youth, without having received the official methodistical or congregational pat on the back . . . How often has the church been found in this. . . . melancholy situation, fighting the truth to the death. (Wallace, 1967, p. 406)

Thus, the tension between the individual's self and the expectation for belonging to the community that Mead himself reflects upon later in his work (Mead, 1930a, 1930b) was a relevant part of his formative years as a psychologist, social reformer, and philosopher. He was also caught in the tension between a view on the highly dynamic nature of social and psychological processes, and the necessity to communicate about them through static expressions afforded by language. The stylistic obscurity of Mead's writings may have suffered from that tension, as it did in the case of other thinkers who tried to capture the dynamic (e.g., Heraclitus). Likewise, the emphasis on belonging to the community may explain why Mead joined in the different intellectual discussions of his times, rather than rushing to propose his own innovative solutions. In this, he seems the complete opposite of Dewey, whose preference for writing never seemed to end. It is exactly in the context of the major dispute about functionalism – initiated by Dewey – that Mead was a rather silent participant.

It was during the period prior to World War I that Mead's sociogenetic perspective was firmly established. Certainly Mead never finished updating his system, and kept adding further aspects to it (e.g., the connections with Whitehead after 1921). Later, his ideas suffered from social transformation by his followers, where his best-known work (*Mind Self, and Society*; Mead, 1934) as well as other posthumous publications (Mead, 1936, 1938) were published with the help of editorial interventions. It was necessary to turn students' lecture notes into written texts.[1] As such, these texts cannot bear proof of authenticity. Nor can they represent the development of Mead's own thought in full, since these were oral conversations (with himself, aside from his audience) that Mead delivered in his course. Perhaps the most authentic representation of Mead's thought, written just before his death, is *The Philosophy of the Present* (Mead, 1932), which, however, includes his draft lectures (Carus Lectures at the meeting of the American Philosophical Association, at Berkeley in December 1930).

Mead combined the intellectual heritages of Dewey, James, Wundt, Whitehead, and Bergson. His efforts to build his own theoretical understanding of the sociality of the person is evident in his definition of the psychical (Mead, 1903), which largely followed the lead of Dewey's criticism of the concept of the "reflex arc" (see Chapter 5). Mead created dialogues with his contemporaries who emphasized the centrality of the individual (e.g., with Warner Fite; see Fite, 1911; Mead, 1911), or with Lloyd Morgan, who would not grant the social nature of the human psyche its central role (Mead, 1895a). In a similar vein, he critically analyzed sociological views (e.g., those of Draghiscesco, 1904) that tried to downplay the role of the self in relations with the social world (Mead, 1905). In cases in which the development of the self was viewed in terms of static representations – as Mead saw present in McDougall's social psychology – he argued for the view on the dynamic side of the development of the self (Mead, 1908b, p. 389). Mead also defended the ideas of socialism against attacks by Gustave LeBon (see Mead, 1899) in ways that laid the foundation for his latter elaboration on the issue of time in development (Mead, 1932).

We can find a number of basic themes in Mead's intellectual discourse over his life. From the issue of the physiological psychology of emotions (during the mid-1890s) his interests moved toward the general notion of the social genesis of the self (and to the role of gestures). This led Mead into the realm of social psychology, and to disputes with individual-centered or society-centered reductionism of the basic social process of the person-world transaction. As a side problem to this, Mead had to deal with the nature of the environment. Apart from that, ethical questions continued to worry him all throughout his life.

---

[1] A similar event happened with Vygotsky, of whom several posthumously published books were also based on lecture notes, and with Janet, of whom many books were based upon the – sometimes rewritten – lecture notes made by Miron Epstein. See Chapters 3 and 8.

Perhaps the most constructive general theme in the development of his thought during the early (i.e., pre-1904) and middle periods (from approximately 1904 through the end of the 1910s) of Mead's thought is the issue of gesture. On the basis of this issue, Mead worked through both the complex topic of internalization (see Glock, 1986), as well as that of the systemic organization of the self <-> other relations (Dodds, Lawrence, & Valsiner, 1997). The analysis of gesture in dialogue with Wundt can be seen as a crucial point (*Knotenpunkt*) in Mead's transition from the physiological to social psychology, or to general philosophy of the sociogenesis of the self.

The Role of Gesture in Mead's Thought

The notion of gesture as a means of interaction as well as relation to oneself is central to Mead's thinking. As was discussed earlier in this chapter, the beginnings of the notion of the relevance of "symbolic stimuli" were there at the time of the emotions discussion during the mid-1890s. The emphasis on gesture became further advanced in Mead's conversation with Wundt's *Völkerpsychologie* (Mead, 1903; 1904; 1906).

Obviously, Mead's knowledge of Wundtian thought in general relates to his years in Leipzig, where he listened to the grandfather figure of psychology during 1888–9. The notion of gesture (borrowed from Wundt) for Mead becomes related with that of the self. In the latter, Mead built upon the self-concepts system from James (1890, Chapter 10), advancing the system of selves in the sociogenetic direction (Mead, 1908a; 1909; 1910a; 1910b; 1912, 1913, 1918). Bergson's emphasis on the irreversibility of time was also of importance to Mead (1907; especially 1925), even if he was wary of the intuitivist excesses at which Bergson arrived as a consequence of his philosophical system (Mead, 1936, Chapter 14).

Mead was trying to create a theory of meaning that was more action-oriented than that of the introspectionist views, and more mentalistic than that of the then emerging behavioristic thought (Wiley, 1979). In his thinking, Mead made ample use of Wundt's gesture theory as the latter formulated it in the first volume of his massive *Völkerpsychologie*. Wundt discussed gestural communication among deaf mutes, primitive people, civilized people, and hypercivilized people, such as monks. His fundamental claim was that: "Gestures are nothing more than movements of expression which have been given special qualities by the urge to communicate and to understand" (Wundt, 1973, p. 73).

Wundt distinguished between demonstrative, imitative or descriptive, and symbolic gestures. Gestural communication is a natural product of expressive emotions and constitutes a specifically human product, insofar as the range and extension of its developmental forms can be compared to those of speech. The demonstrative gesture, which appears to be the very earliest among human beings and whose spontaneous origin may be observed in infants, hardly ever occurs among animals or, at most, has stopped at an intermediate stage between the most primitive grabbing motion and the demonstrative gesture (ibid., p. 127). However, a more sophisticated developmental process takes place in the human case:

The mimed gestures are most closely related to the imitative expressions. What separates them from each other is merely the development which they undergo due to the influence of reciprocity on the part of the individuals. Returning from the one in which an affective expression is directed back to its originator, the expression changes its contents. Since this change also bears upon the conceptual contents of the affect – and this to an even higher degree because of the greater complexity of these contents in one and the same basic mood – *the back and forth motion of gestures gradually becomes an exchange of those concepts which are prominent in the consciousness of the individuals.* These concepts are maintained at first in one and the same basic mood. Then they acquire the power, by a retroaction of the conceptual change, to give the affective content an altered character. The 'communicative drive' is, thus, no more than a unified psychic power than the 'imitative drive,' but is rather an inevitable product of two-way communication between individuals. If, in the 'imitative drive', the expressive motion of one individual is confused with someone else's feelings, from which the same motion stems, *then the 'communicative drive' proceeds directly from the emotive effect which accompanies the perception of the sympathetic affect.* For the emotive effect becomes an impulsive motivation, stimulating the same effect in the other person. Communication is thereby closely connected with the concepts accompanying the affect. *Through repetition of the process, this communication can itself become a motivation. The more this happens, the more are mimed gestures associated with demonstrative ones.* In such a way, the former are probably just as much products of the developing gestural communication, for, on the other hand, in their fuller development, they make gestural communication possible. Thus, instinctive communication is derived from an expression of a concept flowing unintentionally from the affect in any two-way communication.

From this, finally, comes the arbitrary gesture as the actor *lets the result of his action work back upon itself.* The border remains blurred, however, between the original, self-sufficient expression and the one which originated later from the will to affect others. (Wundt, 1973, p. 129; emphasis added)

The emergence of demonstrative gestures from the affective-imitative process occupies a central position in different ontogenetic perspectives on how semiotic means come into being (e.g., Vygotsky, Mead). The intellectual core of these perspectives is in Wundt's thinking. However, what Wundt did not explain is the process of emergence itself – i.e., by what process does emotive effect become impulsive motivation to trigger the same affect in the other person remains unclear. Surely a reference to repeated experiences – as well as that of finding an imitative drive a product of communication – is a crucial background for the process of emergence. Wundt posited the line of development from repetition of communicative experiences to communication itself becoming motivation, and the subsequent experiential overlay of associated and demonstrative gestures. Furthermore, the arbitrariness of gestures eventually emerges from the distancing of the symbolic gestures from their original emotive roots, and the acquisition of concepts that "act back on themselves."

Wundt was quite explicit about the affective basis of the communicative complexity:

The primary cause of natural gestures does not lie in the motivation to communicate a concept, but rather in the expression of an emotion. Gestures are first and foremost affective expressions. Essential as it be that gestural communication rise above this level, *it could never have come into being without the original affective motivation.* Only secondary, *insofar as every affect contains strong emotional concepts, does the gesture become a conceptual expression.* In the further psychic effects associated with this aspect of affective expression, however, lies the origin of the whole development of actual gestural communication . . . the gesture of the addressee is no longer just a simple reflex of the original movement; *rather it has involved from a co-gesture into a responsive gesture. . . .* Thus, *the private sign is transformed by the continual reciprocity of gestures to a general one of constantly changing affect . . .* the commonly experienced affect becomes shared thought, set in motion by the interaction of gestural expression. (Wundt, 1973, pp. 146–7; the same quote is used in Mead, 1904, pp. 380–1)

The direction of development is thus clear: From affect it proceeds to expression, its repetition, and to triggering of a similar affect in others, feeding back into oneself. At some moment concepts emerge to organize the psychic life, which then again is entered into the loop of relations with others (becomes "co-gesture"). The private affective world is constantly being transformed through such signs.

An occidental culturally accepted hierarchical relation between the rational and the affective is set up here as a developmental sequence, implying a leap to a higher level of functioning. Even as the initial starting state for psychological phenomena is affective, the rationality in the form of concepts will emerge to supersede it. Wundt's law of *psychic effects* or *creative synthesis* (see Chapter 7) is somewhat similar to the Hegelian conception of development (as the synthesis of thesis and antithesis) that Mead (and Vygotsky; see Chapter 8) espoused. Thus, he claims that "The basic law of all mental development [is that] what follows always originates from what precedes and nevertheless appears opposed to it as a new creation . . . every stage of [this] development is already contained in the preceding and is, at the same time, a new phenomenon" (Wundt, 1973, p. 149).

It need not be in any way surprising to find developmental and dialectical ideas in the voluminous writings of Wundt. The crucial feature that unified those ideas was the notion of synthesis – be it by way of structural reorganization that produces a new quality in the aggregate (as in chemical synthesis, or in Gestalt psychology), or by way of conflict and the overcoming of it in the case of dialectically united opposites.

Internalization, Dramatization and Autonomy

In ontogeny, language develops from the outer toward the inner direction. It is the person's inner speech that creates the autonomy of the self, through the capacity for imagination. The development of inner speech was viewed by Mead to pass through the state of self-oriented dramatization of conduct. It is in that conduct that the two parallel processes of communication – with oneself and with the other – participate in intrasubjective growth:

The young child talks to himself, i.e., uses the elements of articulate speech in response to the sounds he hears himself make, more continuously and persistently than he does in response to the sounds he hears from those about him, and he displays greater interest in the sounds he himself makes than in those of others. We know also that this fascination of one's own vocal gestures continues even after the child has learned to talk with others, and that the child will converse for hours with himself, *even constructing imaginary companions, who function in the child's growing self-consciousness as the processes of inner speech – of thought and imagination – function in the consciousness of the adult.* (Mead, 1912, p. 403, emphasis added)

Thus, the self's movement through social roles plays a central part in the coordination of the social and the personal in development (Mead, 1925, pp. 271–3). We could summarize Mead's model to entail a *double* (i.e., intrapersonal and extrapersonal) *feedback loop of constructive relations*, where the social action upon the environment (the extrapersonal loop) – which constructs novelty in the social world – feeds back as "input" to the internalization system of the person and leads to the construction of novelty in the intrasubjective sphere, which is then the basis for further external action (i.e., the intrapersonal loop). The primacy in this double-loop system is decidedly in the hands of the extrapersonal loop (which serves as the basis for the establishment of the other feedback loop in ontogeny). Hence we can observe Mead often making claims about the social nature of psychological functions. However, such claims merely state the sociogenetic primacy of the personal consciousness, rather than eliminate their difference. The social world operates differently from its physical counterpart.

The Social and the Physical Realms: A Basic Difference. Hegelian dialectical notions are present in Mead's conceptualization of the self (Wiley, 1979). The need to address the dialectics of the self emerges from the distinction of the physical and social worlds that Mead clearly drew: "The other selves stand upon different basis from that of physical objects. Physical objects are merely objects of perception, while the other selves are perceiving subjects as well as perceived objects" (Mead, 1905, p. 403).

In essence, probably any conceptualization of the self that includes the notion of development has to confront the question of qualitative structural transformation. That latter issue can, in principle, be resolved by either some notion of inherent harmonious "growth" (to another form of complexity), or by some indeterministic notion that entails a reference to a chaotic or fuzzy intermediate state, from which qualitatively novel structures may emerge via some "leap." Dialectical models of any kind are a version of the latter, as they specify that (a) some contradictions exist between parts of the previous system (hence, the system may produce a chaotic-looking outcome for a while), and (b) the contradiction leads to a "break" with the past in the form of the emergence of a qualitatively novel form of the system. Mead tried to make sense of the dialectics of the human self by viewing the internalization process in inherently dialectical terms.

Autonomy of the Self. It is through the movement into, through, and out of the roles of other selves, that construction of inner autonomy becomes possible:

Response to the social conduct of the self may be in the role of another – we present his arguments in imagination and do it with his intonations and gestures and even perhaps with his facial expression. In this way we play the roles of all our group; indeed, it is only so far as we do this that they become part of our social environment – to be aware of another self as a self implies that *we have played his role* or *that of another with whose type we identify him for purposes of intercourse.* The inner response to our reaction to others is therefore as varied as is our social environment . . . the child can think about his conduct as good or bad *only as he reacts to his own acts in the remembered words of the parents. Until* this process has been developed *into the abstract process of thought,* self-consciousness *remains dramatic,* and the self which is a fusion of the remembered actor and this accompanying chorus is somewhat loosely organized and very clearly social. Later the inner stage *changes into the forum and workshop of thought.* The features and intonations of the dramatis personae fade out and the emphasis falls upon the meaning of the inner speech, the imagery becomes merely the barely necessary cues. But the *mechanism remains social,* and *at any moment the process may become personal.* (Mead, 1913, pp. 377–8, emphases added)

The roles are constantly being constructed as they are being assumed by the person – the self-processes construct both the external bases for social dramas, and the internal models of assuming such constructed roles. The dialectic opposition exists in the relationship between the "outer" and "inner," and takes the form of internalization. That allows the self to construct its own functioning structure, based on its social roots. The I $<=>$ ME structure entails the internally hidden nature of I that can only be captured by way of a (META – ME reflecting on another ME (Mead, 1913, pp. 374–5).

Mead's Conceptualization of the Self

Mead's self-system was a slowly built theoretical construction, following the eclectic – yet synthesis-oriented – (see Allport, 1943, p. 112) system that was elaborated by William James. Furthermore, other versions of self conceptualizations that made use of the "self"; "other" distinctions were circulating during the 1890s (e.g., Baldwin's *ego* and *alii* – see Chapter 4; Royce's *self* and *not-self* – see Chapter 5).

James on Self. James' conceptualization of the self was all-inclusive (man's self is the "sum total of all that he can call his"; 1890, p. 291). That totality was divided by James into its constituents (material, social, and spiritual selves, and "pure ego"), which lead to *self-feelings* and prompt actions (of *self-seeking* and *self-preservation*). The material self expands the personal identity outward from one's body: "We all have the blind impulse to watch over our body, to deck it with clothing of an ornamental sort, to cherish parents, wife, and babes, and to find for ourselves a home of our own which we may live in and 'improve' " (James, 1890, pp. 292–3).

James' social self entails recognition from other persons. As a personal reflection upon these relations, the person "has as many different social selves as there are distinct groups of persons about whose opinion he cares" (ibid., p. 294).

The internalized role-taking notion of Mead borrows from this notion. Furthermore, James' dependence on the community (groups) which – as we emphasized repeatedly – has been a recurrent social representation among North American thinkers, surfaces here. Persons' identity is being viewed through the angle of group membership (rather than group memberships resulting in participating persons, i.e., the person-centered reverse view on the phenomenon). Of course, the qualification (about whose opinion he cares) reintroduces the personal agency to the functioning of social selves. Nevertheless, the core of the social self is an existing social unit – group or community – and not a person's subjective invention of it. Personal meanings of identification merely follow the lead of the community, rather than the community being subjectively constructed by way of the development of such identification.

However, meanings-based personal identification with social-institutional organization of life remains subjective in its execution in real-life practice, and thus the subjective lived-through life events are constantly and dramatically set up by the institutionalized roles of the social self. Thus,

A man's *fame*, good or bad, and his *honor* or dishonor, are names for one of his social selves . . . a layman may abandon a city infected with cholera; but a priest or a doctor would think such an act incompatible with his honor. A soldier's honor requires him to fight or die under circumstances where another man can apologize or run away with no stain upon his social self. (James, 1890, pp. 294–5)

What was excluded from the focus of attention in the case of the social self, became central in the spiritual self. The spiritual self for James was a felt-through reflection of the inner sanctuary of the personal subjective world. Recognizing the irreversible flow of experiencing, James charted out the relations between *me* and *not–me* as aspects of the process of reflection, as "objects which work out their drama together," but which do not yet include the contemplating of one's subjective being (James, 1890, p. 304). It is thus clear that the different kinds of selves for James were parts of the whole of personality, within which questions of relationships between different selves (e.g., between social and spiritual selves) were worthwhile to ask.

However, the structure of the selves was not to be viewed in static terms. The relations between the selves entail their present-future differentiation:

In each kind of self, material social, and spiritual, men distinguish between the immediate and actual, and the remote and potential, between the narrower and the wider view, to the detriment of the former and advantage of the latter . . . the potential social self is the most interesting, by reason of certain apparent paradoxes to which it leads in conduct, and by reason of its connection with our moral and religious life. When for motives of honor and conscience I brave the condemnation of my own family, club, and 'set'; when, as a protestant, I turn catholic; as a catholic, freethinker . . . I am always inwardly strengthened in my course and steeled against the loss of my actual social self by the thought of other and better *possible* social judges than those whose verdict goes against me now. (James, 1890, p. 315)

It is here where the personal subjectivity is brought back to be the core of the selves system: The person is constantly moving away from some social self, toward some other (possible, yet often indeterminate) one. The personal core of the selves system is fortified through this constant readaptation – the selves are there not to keep, but to constantly abandon, in the sense of novel versions of the selves system.

Mead's Elaboration of the Self System. The concepts used by Mead in describing the self system are of course ideal mental constructions that cannot be located in the brain or mapped upon the functioning of the nervous system. Displeasing as that fact may be for the insecure psychologist who wants to see objectivity in terms of human "hardware," it is exactly the heuristic value of general scientific concepts that can allow for a general understanding of material reality. Mead's self conceptualization entails the constant construction of a dynamic structure of ME-s, including some that are reflecting upon others (here we call them meta-me-s). This highly dynamic interactive process is paralleled by the constructive system within the self. In this, Mead synthesized both Dewey's insistence on the dynamics of relation with the world and James' differentiated self system.

The themes of heterogeneity and dynamicity of the self structure are present in Mead. Nevertheless, Mead went beyond James, being close to Dewey's functionalism, he set a more pointed focus on the emergence of novel psychological phenomena within the self system. Thus, in one of his earliest statements on the process structure of the self, he wrote that:

There appears to be . . . a field of immediate experience within reflection that is open to direct observation, this does not have to be approached from the standpoint of parallelism . . . For this functional psychology an explicit definition of its subject-matter seems highly important. That suggested in this paper is as follows: That phase of experience *within which we are immediately conscious of conflicting impulses* which *rob the object of its character as object-stimulus,* leaving us in so far in an attitude of subjectivity; *but during which a new object-stimulus appears* due to the *reconstructive activity which is identified with the subject 'I'* as distinct from *object 'me'.* (Mead, 1903, p. 35, emphases added)

What Mead accomplishes is an act of internalization of the subject ↔ object contrast into the whole of the self. He sets those two components up in a constantly reverberating circuit of experience (in a way similar to Dewey's of the reflex circle – Dewey, 1896). Mead makes the I ↔ ME circuit to generate novel subjective experiences, as well as new acts that transform the person's environment (see especially Mead, 1908, on the development of environments). Mead expressed his surprise at Bergson's unwillingness to view consciousness as an emergent phenomenon (Mead, 1907, p. 384), and made declarations of the usual sociogenetic kind (e.g., "consciousness of meaning is social in origin"; Mead, 1909, p. 406). In criticizing Baldwin (for the latter's simplification of the *ego* ↔ *socius* relations), Mead claimed that:

There must be other selves if one's own is to exist. Psychological analysis, retrospection, and the study of children and primitive people give no inkling of situations in which a self could have existed in consciousness except as the counterpart of other selves. We can even recognize that in the definition of these selves in consciousness, the child and primitive man have defined the outlines and the character of the others earlier than they have defined their own selves. (Mead, 1909, p. 407)

Aside from the emphasis on internalization as construction of the self in consciousness on the basis of social experience, the external world, for the developing person, depends upon the generalized other. Mead's criticism of the traditions of formal education – pointing out that the children's experiences and teachers' personalities are considered unimportant – is built on the assumption that the specific organization of the social experience serves as the basis of children's self-construction (Mead, 1910a). The process of interselves' action is guiding the process of intraself construction of consciousness. The feel of one's own attitude arises spontaneously within the self to meet the gesture of the other. As interaction guides development, novelty emerges both in the interaction and intraaction domains of social conduct:

Social conduct must be continually readjusted after it has already commenced, because the individuals whose conduct our own answers, are themselves constantly varying their conduct as our responses become evident. Thus our adjustment to their changing reactions take place, by a process of our own responses to their stimulations. In these social situations appear not only conflicting acts with the increasing definition of elements in the stimulation, but also a consciousness of one's own attitude as an interpretation of the meaning of the social stimulus. *We are conscious of our attitudes because they are responsible for the changes in the conduct of other individuals.* . . . Successful social conduct brings one into a field. . . . within which *a consciousness of one's own attitudes helps toward the control of the conduct of others.* (Mead, 1910b. p. 403, emphasis added)

The flow of social experiences in irreversible time (*à la* Bergson's duration notion) makes it inevitable that the person is constantly confronted with the practical need to adjust to the changing conduct of other persons. This triggers self-reflexivity (consciousness of attitudes), which leads into further efforts to control the conduct of others. Language emerges in this two-sided process (oriented toward the consciousness of the self, and toward the conduct of others) as a highly specialized form of gesture (Mead, 1910b, p. 404), or an instrument that makes both intra- and intermental acts possible in their human form. However, it is the intramental cyclical process of the self's reflection upon one's own conduct toward the gesture by the other, the strain of indeterminacy in that reflection, and its constructive openness that allows for the emergence of consciousness (Mead, 1910b, pp. 400–1). Yet Mead avoided the provision of an explicit structure of the self. For him, the self system operated in terms of a dynamic field (Petras, 1973). It is this tension between the dynamism of fields and the necessity of having a nonfluid description of the self that may have made Mead's self-theory rather cumbersome to comprehend.

Contemporary uses of the self concept. Psychologists in modern times often use the self concept, yet they usually fail to give it any substantial concreteness, except a few elaborations along the lines charted out by James (Markus & Nurius, 1986; Markus & Wurf, 1987; Markus & Kitayama, 1991). Certainly there is no lack of use for the term as a general umbrella label to legitimate a never-ending flow of empirical studies of self-esteem or self-identity, most of which bear no relevance for a conceptual enhancement to the field beyond the intellectual sophistication of James or Mead.

In a stark contrast to this inadequate use of the term in contemporary psychology, the concept of self (obviously in a different meaning than in Mead and James) has been productive in modern immunology, exactly as it allows for the general knowledge of potentially endlessly novel biological adaptations (Löwy, 1992). Thus, it is not a breach of the scientific nature of Mead's self concept that parts of it – especially that of the I – remain transcendental for psychologists' direct research efforts.

The inaccessibility of I in Mead's self system is probably a major conceptual problem for contemporary psychology, where nonoperational theoretical concepts are met with almost paranoic fear. Mead's need to create the concept of the I was based on the irreversibility of time: The I addresses a ME but as the latter becomes transformed as a result, any reflection upon that "by-I-transformed-ME" necessarily involves a new (meta)-ME emerging as a consequence. Hence, the reflection by the meta-ME upon the by-I-transformed-ME occurs within a time lag that renders any effort to catch the initially functioning I, impossible. In our recent literature, Schwalbe (1987, p. 121) has introduced the notion of "meta-act" (an act that can succeed in its objective only by the consummation of constituent subacts). The notion of "meta-ME" would be the internalized counterpart of such meta-acts; both together would restore the notion of a hierarchical organization of the intra- and extramental self processes to Meadian thought (where it was inherently present, yet not elaborated). This direction of thought would bring Mead's self system close to the thinking of Pierre Janet (see Chapter 3). However, any action-linked view on the self requires some conceptualization of the environment within which the self functions.

The Role of Environment in Evolution

It is obvious from our analysis of Mead's views of gesture, internalization, and self that the key role in human existence is played by the environment. The latter is social, and its role is to trigger the social interaction and intraselves interaction. Yet what are the characteristics of that environment? Obviously, Mead could not derive a dynamic concept of the social person from a static notion of the environment.

Mead saw environments as constantly changing or developing (together with the conduct of the person). Thus, he claimed: "An environment can exist for a form only in so far as the environment answers to the susceptibilities of the organism; that the organism determines thus its own environment; that the effect of every adaptation is a new environment which must change with that which responds to it" (Mead, 1908, p. 312).

By acting upon its environment, the organism (in biological evolution) and the person (in social conduct) change that environment, and through it, change themselves. In the domain of social thought, this is a reiteration of a well-known Marxist statement. However, in the case of biological evolution discourse, Mead's emphasis on the development of environments is akin to Baldwin's organic evolution notion, where the organism is constantly involved in the construction of novel forms of behavior that then become targets of selection.

The same theme of mutual reorganization under conditions of constant interdependence comes through in Mead's thinking years later:

What is peculiar to intelligence is that it is a change that involves a mutual reorganization, an adjustment in the organism and a reconstitution of the environment; for at its lowest terms any change in the organism carries with it a difference of sensitivity and response and a corresponding difference in the environment. It is within this process that so-called conscious intelligence arises, for consciousness is both the difference which arises in the environment because of its relation to the organism and its organic process of adjustment, and also the difference in the organism because of the change which has taken place in the environment. (Mead, 1932, p. 4)

Here we can again see Mead's preferred use of the dynamic interaction loop – that produces changes in both of the parts of the system – which stems from Dewey's coordination notion, but within which the idea of dialectical synthesis is preserved. A very clear similarity with Vygotsky's conceptualization of the environment exists (see Van der Veer & Valsiner, 1994, Chapter 9).

It is important to focus on the emergent nature of environments, as that notion is not usually emphasized when psychologists talk profusely about environment. If we assume the theoretical perspective of Mead, then the view on environment that sees it as constantly being revamped fits the general thought construction. Likewise, when we look at the products of natural evolution, Mead's strict separation of physical and social environments is a necessary sequitur to his dynamic-constructionist idea. Mead's example of a stone (boulder) is of interest here, as we can observe the advancement of his thought:

A boulder is a definite thing with its own mass and form, but its relations to things about it do not give rise to qualities in them which through the contacts, weight, or momentum of the boulder conserve the boulder. The boulder has no environment in the sense in which the animal has an environment. The background of the inanimate object is that of conservation – in our present day formulation, of the conservation of energy. No transformation affects the reality of the physical system . . .

Plants and animals, however, present to science objects *whose essential characters are found not in that which undergoes transformation but in the process itself and in the forms which the object assumes within that process.* Since the process involves the interaction of animal or plant with surrounding objects, it is evident that the *process of life as really confers characters upon the environment as it does upon the plant of the animal.* (Mead, 1932, p. 34, emphases added)

Now it becomes clear that Mead's boulder versus plants (and animals) contrast is a figurative explanation of the closed versus open-systems nature of physical and living systems, correspondingly. From the very outset of his intellectual productivity, Mead understood the open-systemic nature of the biological, psychological, and social phenomena. This understanding is the axiomatic starting point of any developmental perspective (see Valsiner, 1989), yet little of the psychology or sociology that appreciated Mead's claims about the social nature of the self has assumed this developmental perspective. The latter, unfortunately, is often confused with that of child psychology in our contemporary labeling practices within psychology. As Mead was not directly interested in children's psychology, his actual developmental standpoint has largely been ignored by his later interpreters.

Within Mead's own thought system, however, the dynamic-transformational nature of both the animal and the environment are consistent with his emphasis on the processes between opposing parts of the integrated system. In that systemic process, exchange relationships (i.e., the defining feature of open systems) between the organism and the environment are taking place, resulting in the transformation of both parts. Structured differentiation of both parts of the system is the result – entailing both structuring of the here and now and of the distanced consideration of the time-based events of the past and possible future. Consciousness emerges in evolution

when the animal passes from the system in which it formerly existed to an environment that arises through the selectiveness of its own sensitivity, and thus to a new system within which parts of its own organism and its reactions to these parts become parts of its environment. The next step is reached with the dominance of the distance senses and the delayed responses to these. The selection and organization of these responses, together with the characters of the objects which they have selected, now become objects within the environment of the organism. *The animal comes to respond to an environment consisting largely of possible futures of its own delayed reactions,* and this inevitably emphasizes its own past responses in the form of *acquired habits. These pass into the environment as the conditions of his acts. These characters of the environment constitute the stuff out of which values and meanings later arise,* when these characters can be isolated through gestures in communication. (Mead, 1932, p. 84, emphases added)

The exchange relation thus leads to the structuring of the system in space and time. The acquired habits (undoubtedly involved in repetition, as Wundt emphasized for the emergence of gestures) act upon the environment, transform that accordingly, and through that become parts of the environment that guide later actions of the organism toward its further change. By constant modification of the environment the organism sets up sleeper conditions that could trigger a certain kind of an act later on. The similarity of this idea with Baldwin's "feel-forward" notion (see Chapter 4) is noteworthy.

It would also be interesting to imagine Mead in dispute with a number of our contemporary ecological psychologists who view the organism ↔ environment relation in terms of the former's never-ending "pick-up" of affordances of the latter (they claim indebtedness to J. J. Gibson). Following the line of argument elaborated earlier in this chapter, Mead would have tried to explain the construction of affordances by the active role of the organism in the environment. The affordances could not exist as pregiven entities, but would emerge in the feedback loop of interaction. The organism acts upon the environment, changes it in line with some goal, and thus new affordances of the environment result from the organism's actions. Surely these newly constructed affordances are then ready to be "picked up" by the perception/action systems instantaneously. Of course, such emphasis on construction would recognize its limits:

Great geological changes, such as the gradual advance and disappearance of the glacial epoch, are just superinduced on the organism. The organism cannot control them; they just take place. In this sense, the environment controls the form, rather than being controlled by it. Nevertheless, in so far as the form [i.e., the organism belonging to a species] does respond it does so in virtue of its sensitivity. In this sense it selects and picks out what constitutes its environment. It selects that to which it responds and makes use of it for its own purposes, purposes involved in its life processes. It utilizes the earth on which it treads and through which it burrows, and trees that it climbs; but only when it is sensitive to them. (Mead, 1934, p. 245)

We can see here that the domain of mutuality between the environment and organism that has been captured by the affordance concept in modern ecological psychology would be seen by Mead as the background – or the initial field – upon which the active efforts by the organism (selection of appropriate contexts, and active transformation of those) is then immediately built. Environments can change in ways uncontrollable by the organism (e.g., in the case of earthquakes), yet the immediate process that follows such sudden changes is that of the reconstruction of the environments. It is here that the qualitative difference between humans and animals is emphasized by Mead (1934, p. 249): An animal is constituting its environment by its sensitivity, or by its movements toward objects, while the "human form" constitutes its environment in terms of "products of our own hands." That construction of environments has led human beings in their history to build up increasingly complex environments, with an effort to control them:

The human form establishes its own home where it wishes; builds cities; brings its water from great distances; establishes the vegetation which shall grow about it; determines the animals that will exist; gets into that struggle which is going on now with insect life, determining what insects shall continue to live; is attempting to determine what microorganisms shall remain in its environment. It determines, by means of its clothing and housing, what the temperature shall be about it; it regulates the extent of its environment by means of its locomotion. The whole onward struggle of mankind on the face of the earth is such a determination of the life that shall exist about it and such a control of physical objects as determine and affect its own life. The community as such creates its environment by being sensitive to it. (Mead, 1934, pp. 249–50)

Of course the effort to control the environment leads to new unpredictable transformations within that environment, which lead to further control efforts, and so on without an end. In some ways, Mead's description here entails a social constructionist (yet realist) repetition of the old "Achilles and the tortoise" paradox. In that classic Greek paradox, Achilles, trying to compete in locomotion with that obviously different locomotor, the tortoise, still cannot overtake his slow competitor. Within a same unit of time, Achilles' (obviously quicker) move can only reach the previous time-unit position of the tortoise. The latter is, by the present time, moved ahead (in an infinitely small way) from the previous location. As this situation repeats itself from moment to moment, Achilles cannot overtake the tortoise (who is always moving one step ahead, so to say, relative to his competitor). Mead's version of this classic paradox would entail the human beings undertaking a present effort to control the environment, thus creating its immediate future state (its new present), which then constitutes novelty for the agents of the previous effort in its newly transformed form, as a challenge for their next step. It follows that exactly because of the efforts to control the environment, the environment will forever remain uncontrollable. The control efforts lead to the emergence of a new environment that requires further control efforts, etc. This paradoxical obstacle has been facing all sciences that deal with environment-organisms relations, from its macroscopic (e.g., the evolution of organisms, histories of societies) to intermediate (e.g., coping with the emergence of new viruses in immunology), to microscopic forms (e.g., child development, microgenetic cognitive problem solving).

Human community invents its own structure as a means to continue controlling the uncontrollable (environment) and it is here that social institutions emerge. Mead saw the emergence of these institutions as a build up on the notion of the generalized other:

The institution represents a common response on the part of all members of the community to a particular situation. This common response is one which, of course, varies with the character of the individual. In the case of theft the response of the sheriff is different from that of the attorney-general, from that of the judge and the jurors, and so forth; and yet they are all responses which maintain property, which involve the recognition of the property right in others. There is a common response in varied forms. And these variations, as illustrated in the different officials, have an organization which gives unity to the variety of the responses. . . . One does take the attitude of all these different officials as involved in the very maintenance of property; all of them as an organized process are in some sense found in our own natures. When we arouse such attitudes, we are taking the attitude of what I have termed a 'generalized other'. Such organized sets of responses are related to each other; if one calls out one such set of responses, he is implicitly calling out others as well. (Mead, 1934, p. 261)

Mead's thought is consistent within itself. Through the construction of a control-effort system in the form of heterogeneous roles, a super-individual organizational form of the community – the institution – emerges. It can emerge as it "feeds through" the self-systems of the persons in the community. Thus, both in the direction of personal and institutional development, the need to control the environment lead to ever-increasing reorganization and new structure buildup. In sum, the complexity of the self and the society is a result of the construction of a means for the efforts to control the environment through psychological and social processes. However, since the environment constantly changes as a result of these efforts, the development of selves and institutions is a never-ending process in the course of irreversible time.

Mead and Time: Irreversibility of Emergence

Not only are organisms involved in the immediate transformation of themselves through changing the environments, they also build their own set of possible future developmental trajectories through embedding goal-oriented changes in the presently transformed environment. This is the only possibility of creating some stability for the future in the course of irreversible flow, where the organism can encounter directly only the present, and never the future itself (unless it has already become the next present). Mead's dynamic perspective on development faced the challenges that time brings to any dynamic-developmental account.

Any construction of a dynamic self-system necessarily has to take into account the issue of time. As Mead was guided by Dewey's pragmatic dynamism, he had to conceptualize the issues of time. Starting from his criticism of LeBon's antisocialist stance (Mead, 1899), Mead wandered into a life-long concern about time. Time, from the viewpoint of a constantly developing individual, entails a sequence of constant yet changing presents:

No one knows what he is going to do, judged by results, for the result is too wide and far-reaching for him to estimate, but he may know that he is reacting rationally. We may depend upon our interpretation of the present in terms of the past, so far as method is concerned. The engineer does not know the full value and meaning of the bridge he is building; no elevation will tell him that. But he knows *how* to build it. While we are perfectly willing to have the unexpected happen, we expect science, physical and mental, to tell us how to behave in its presence. Furthermore, we state the law, the universal, in terms of society, and its infraction, the exception, the particular, in terms of the individual. But that is only till we can either modify the law or enlarge the individual. Thus, while reason is bridging over the chasm between society and the individual, it is forming a new society or a new individual. (Mead, 1899, p. 409)

Traces of Mead's belief in the changeability of society and of the individual are visible here, along with curious questions he had to ask about the use of stabilizing inventions (for instance, science performs such function) in human coping with the inevitable novel uncertainties. The interdependent development of both individual and the environment is the basis for unceasing dependence upon novelty challenges in irreversible time. Furthermore, the constant construction of novelty makes it impossible to recover any "true" (i.e., unaltered by the life experiences in between) picture of the past. Just before his death, Mead wrote: "When one recalls his boyhood days he cannot get into them as he then was, without their relationship to what he has become; and if he could, that is if he could reproduce the experience as it then took place, he could not use it, for this would involve his not being in the present within which that use must take place." (Mead, 1932, p. 30).

Thus again paraphrasing Baldwin (see Chapter 4), development cannot be predicted before it has happened, nor explained after it has taken place. It is the inevitability of existing in a "string of presents" that never repeat themselves, that this open-systemic nature of organismic reality entails.

Mead's treatment of the question of the present led him to critically analyze Henri Bergson's time philosophy which was of course a relevant transition point from the nineteenth to twentieth centuries for many a scientist of his time (Valsiner, 1994). Mead had a consistent view of Bergson – on the one hand, he appreciated much of Bergson's emphasis on *dureé* (e.g., see his review of Bergson in Mead, 1907). Mead was working on that concept a week before his death (Murphy, 1932, p. viii), and the role of language in relative stabilizing of dynamic reality. On the other hand, he rejected Bergson's attribution of causality for dynamics of development to the *élan vital*, as well as the general intuitivism in which Bergson arrived at his philosophy (Mead, 1936, Chapter 14). It is Mead's pragmatist self that would not accept Bergson's absolutization of the flow of the existing, and its result in intuitiveness:

The anti-intellectualist attitude of Bergson represents a failure to grasp the import of the scientific method, especially that it puts the environment under the control of the individual. It is always true that we get ahead and keep going without knowing what the goal is toward which we are moving. But we are free to work out the hypotheses that present themselves and test them and so solve the immediate problems that we meet. (Mead, 1936, p. 294)

For Mead, the scientific method thus performs a relative stabilizing function in scientific thought, along the lines of language in the common experiencing. Mead resisted the implications of intuitivism, which could easily turn into a dogmatism of highly subjective kind (see Mead, 1936, p. 303). It was in this matter that Mead turned to Whitehead (Mead, 1936, p. 315; 1938, pp. 523–48).

In the case of irreversible time involved in life processes,

Past, present and future belong to a passage which attains temporal structure through the event, and they may be considered long or short as they are compared with other such passages. But as existing in nature, so far as such a statement has significance, the past and the future are the boundaries of what we term the present, and are determined by the conditioning relationships of the event to its situation. (Mead, 1932, p. 24)

Our present is the fusion of both the past and the present going-on (Mead, 1936, p. 300). The focus on the ongoing event is crucial in this focus on past, present, and future, which entails the emergence of novelty. That novelty stems from the constant interaction with the environment:

We orient ourselves not with reference to the past which was a present within which the emergent appeared, but in such a restatement of the past as conditioning the future that we may control its reappearance. When life has appeared we can breed life, and given consciousness, we can control its appearance and its manifestations. *Even the statement of the past within which the emergent appeared is inevitably made from the standpoint of a world within which the emergent is itself a conditioning as well as a conditioned factor.* (Mead, 1932, p. 15, emphasis added)

Mead's double-constructive feedback loop core of the idea of person-environment relations makes this statement understandable – any present reflection upon an emergence of some new state in the past is in itself a move toward the emergence (by way of a constructive act) of the future, and thus feeding into the creation of the next present.

The Context of Meaning

Any extraction of the emergent events of the past takes place within some meaning-framed context of the present, which may be static, yet changeable:

The past in passage is irrecoverable as well as irrevocable. It is producing all the reality there is. This meaning of that which is, is illuminated and expanded in the face of the emergent in experience. . . . To say that the Declaration of Independence was signed on the 4th of July 1776 means that in the time system which we carry around with us . . . this date comes out in our celebrations. Being what we are in the social and physical world that we inhabit we account for what takes place on this time schedule, but like railway time-tables it is always subject to change without notice. Christ was born four years before AD. (Mead, 1932, p. 27)

The arbitrary nature of our constructed meaning systems is itself a potential tool for creating another context for the use of past distinguishable events (emergents) in the present construction of the future.

Mead's flexibility of meanings as context-setters is paralleled by the inclusion of such arbitrary meanings (which may "jump" or "leap" to another state, thus redefining a context) in the actual psychological process that evokes interesting parallels with Paulhan's and Vygotsky's "meaning" ↔ "sense" distinction:

Since the symbols with which we think are largely recognized as word images, ideas and images have a very close consanguinity. The relationship is of course the same as that between a spoken or written word and its meaning; but since auditory or visual image of a word seems to be in the mind where the idea is placed, it is not uncommon, when we desire to distinguish between words we use in speech and the meanings which they connote, to identify the meaning with the inner words with which we carry on our thinking. (Mead, 1932, p. 75)

The "inner words" can be viewed as Vygotsky's (borrowed from Paulhan) emphasis on "personal sense," which is guided by word meanings (see Van der Veer & Valsiner, 1991). Or, in Mead's words: "Meaning is that which can be indicated to others while it is by the same process indicated to the indicating individual" (Mead, 1938, p. 545). Meaning requires participation and communicability. The individual participates in the worlds of others through similar ways of relating to the world. The result of this participation "is communicability, i.e., the individual can indicate to himself what he indicates to others. There is communication without significance where the gesture of the individual calls out the response in the other without calling out or tending to call out the same response in the individual himself" (Mead, 1938, pp. 546–7).

Here, the possibility of disconnection of the intrapsychological feedback loop is recognized, yet such disconnection leads to "communication without significance." In contrast, of course, there was Mead's constant emphasis on the significant symbol that operates both in the intra- and extramental worlds. Here one is reminded of Vygotsky's similar emphasis on symbols as stimuli that stimulate both the social other and the self.

General Conclusions: Mead's Legacy

We have seen that the fundamental questions that haunted the thinking of George Mead amounted to a relatively small – yet persistently worked-through – set of issues. It could be said that Mead's most fundamental theoretical core was in the emphasis on the construction of novelty in the irreversible life course of organisms. In that focus, his explicit assuming of an open-systemic perspective on the lives of developing organisms provided the basis for his unification of the organism ↔ environment and organism ↔ itself relations in a dynamic constructionist double-feedback loop, where changes in environments and in the habits of organisms dynamically feed into one another. Certainly, Mead's greatest interest was in understanding how human psychological processes work. Humans as social organisms are constantly involved in a novelty-constructing relation both with their environments (which they constantly transform) and with their personal worlds (which they also constantly transform via social experiencing). Substantial parallels with the thought of Lev Vygotsky and James Mark Baldwin can be demonstrated.

Mead consistently brought together the main themes on which his sociogenetic philosophy was based: the dynamic coordination of organism and environment, the transformation of both of them in the process, the emergence of novelty in the coordination process, and the constant emergence of the self through assuming roles. It is through the haunting problem of the irreversibility of time that Mead recognized the unity of the personal and the social, and avoided the theoretical pitfall of ontologically reducing the one to the other. In fact, he could not describe the self ontologically at all (i.e., he could not make statements about what the self as such is), because his ontological reflection would have had to be translated into a microgenetic one, and thus entails a direct effort to specify functioning processes of the mind in the social context. That process was allo- and auto-communication. It is in the former case that:

The individual is an other before he is a self. It is in addressing himself in the role of an other that his self rises in experience. The growth of the organized game out of simple play in the experience of the child, and the organized group activities in human society, placed the individual then in a variety of roles, in so far as these were parts of the social act, and the very organization of these in the whole act gave them a common character in indicating what he had to do. He is able then to become a generalized other in addressing himself in the attitude of the group or community. In this situation he has become a definite self over against the social whole to which he belongs. (Mead, 1932, p. 168)

Here we see a resolution to the haunting problem of self-society relations: The self rises above the society exactly through a construction process that requires being part of the community. Through internalization new knowledge and values are constructed on the social basis, but not through a simple takeover of ready-made models from the community. Mead's sociogenetic perspective on human subjective agency can be summarized in his own words:

The order of the universe that we live in is the moral order. It has become the moral order by becoming the self-conscious method of the members of a human society. We are not pilgrims and strangers. We are at home in our own world, but it is not ours by inheritance but by conquest. The world that comes to us from the past possesses and controls us. We possess and control the world that we discover and invent. And this is the world of the moral order. It is splendid adventure if we can rise to it. (Mead, 1923, p. 247)

CHAPTER SEVEN

Striving Toward the Whole: Losing Development in the Course of History

The history of the idea of the social nature of the psyche is intertwined with the cultural-historical trajectories in the fate of psychology in different countries, and on different continents. It constitutes an interesting case of a global historical migration of ideas. Born in Germany during the 1860s and 1870s, psychology as a discipline[1] became quickly an "export article" for ideas and instruments to move to other countries. As we showed in Chapter 5, much of the social sciences in the United States had a heavy German "accent." This was the case not only in the sense of ideas, but even in the use of the German language in U.S. universities (Josiah Royce's seminars at Harvard being an example). Yet that fitted both the topics, and the multilingual nature of the country that at the time was captured by intense immigration from various areas of Europe. To discuss German philosophy in English translation would have been a travesty from Royce's perspective, and because the interested American students could follow him in German, the problem was solved. The academic community in America at the time was well acquainted with German, as many of its members had been studying in Germany. It was only as an aftermath of World War I that the central relevance of Germany as the source of knowledge began to diminish.

---

[1] We deliberately wish to include both directions in the emergence of psychology – that of experimental psychology (Wundt in Leipzig in 1879) and that of *Völkerpsychologie* (Lazarus in Bern in 1860) in this designation. The fact that historians of psychology have overlooked that the institutional establishment of *Völkerpsychologie* was earlier than that of experimental psychology is a good example of psychology's efforts to deny its humanities-oriented roots in favor of the ideals of the physical sciences.

The Continental European Mindset: The Spirit of the Whole

Probably the geographic dividing line between the worlds of associationism and holism is the English Channel, rather than the Atlantic Ocean. While the Anglo-American *Weltanschauung* has easily become involved in reducing complex wholes into their constituent elements, the Continental European mindset has equally habitually emphasized the qualities of the wholes ahead of their parts. The whole consists of parts, and each part is subordinated to the whole. Eclecticism can be a sign of freedom in Britain or the United States, but it would be seen as breaching against the aesthetics of the whole if it concerned architectural styles. Matters were different in psychology.

Of course, psychology's architectonics is less visible than architectural ensembles. In the 1910s, the socially constructed directions in the United States and in Continental Europe began to diverge. While the new creed of behaviorism became consolidated in the United States (see Watson's "manifesto" of 1913, analyzed in Chapter 5), in Europe, different philosophical approaches led to the consolidation of a number of directions in psychology, all in one or another way emphasizing the holistic nature of psychological phenomena. The German-speaking psychology of the beginning of this century suddenly abounded in holistic directions.

In general, the otherwise quite varied intellectual currents in German psychology seem to have shared a set of common features (Metzger, 1965, p. 110):

(1) an inclination to phenomenology;
(2) a deep-rooted distrust of purely empiristic views;
(3) a reserve against elementaristic assumptions; and
(4) a reserve against 'suicidal objectivism.'

In the history of psychology in Germany, there has been no repression against philosophical speculation (or thinking) as a primary means for knowing (*Wissenschaft*, or science). Strong belief in the objectivity of the data can be labeled "suicidal" (for psychology) indeed (see Chapter 1 on pseudo-empiricism). Yet the German alternative – of complex speculative philosophizing – may constitute a similar hazard. It makes no difference for knowledge whether it is drowned in the excesses of uninterpretable empirical data, or in thick volumes that include imprecise (and hence widely interpretable) general ideas. In both cases, the relationship of the whole system of thought and its parts (empirical, or abstract) is violated.[2]

The German philosophizing tendency has its historical-religious roots. A similar tension – between religion and science – was present in North America (as we showed in Chapters 5 and 6). In Continental Europe, the tension between the parts and the whole in science was different – it took the form of opposition between the analytic and holistic general theoretical orientations. A complex phenomenon could be seen as a simple sum (or combination) of its constituent elements, or as a whole that is qualitatively different from each of its parts.

In European intellectual history, the notion of the whole as possessing qualities that transcend those of its parts has been emphasized in a multitude of ways. There are some national differences in that focus between different countries (and languages) – the holism of the French language area (France, Switzerland) may differ from that of the German speaking area (Metzger, 1965; Reuchlin, 1965; see also Chapters 2 and 3). Yet, the unifying feature in the Continental European tradition has been the dominance of the whole over its parts, and the focus on the relationships between the parts and the whole. This direction of theorizing expanded from Continental Europe in various directions – to North America on the one hand, and to Russia on the other. Its reception differed profoundly. Much of Russian sociogenetic thought became and remained closely intertwined with its German and French counterparts (see Chapter 8). In contrast, most of these perspectives died out or changed their quality when they entered into the Anglo-American social contexts.

Historical Bases for Holistic Thought

The roots of European holism are multiple, deriving from both the natural sciences and romantic deliberations about the human soul. The work of Johann G. Herder and Giambattista Vico in the eighteenth

---

[2] The social institutional status of psychology in Germany at the turn of the century made the tension between psychological and philosophical approaches complicated – the conflict between philosophers and psychologists in 1912 about the appointments of psychologists to professorships in philosophy (see Ash, 1995, Chapter 3) created a rivalry in which psychology continued to be in a subservient role.

century set the stage for viewing the person as social (White, 1979). Johann Wolfgang Goethe's writings, as well as the work of Johann Friedrich Herbart and Wilhelm von Humboldt, constituted further impetus for the holistic/dynamic thought perspectives of the nineteenth and twentieth centuries. Neither should we underestimate the relevance of the dialectical philosophies of Hegel and Marx. In the case of sociogenetic ideas, the question of the holistic nature of persons in society first became elaborated in different directions of *Völkerpsychologie*. Subsequently, it took a developmental perspective in Germany and in Russia.

All of psychology borrows its conceptual system from common sense and ordinary languages. Thus it is not surprising that the origins of *Völkerpsychologie* are firmly rooted in the meaning complexes emphasizing the notion of spirit and soul (*Geist, Seele*). If persons have souls, so can social units (groups, nations; as was shown in Chapter 5). By carrying a meaning that is consensually accepted for individuals to supra-individual units, psychology has arrived at complex explanations for complex phenomena.

Both ordinary and scientific reasoning are constrained by language. Hence from the beginning of psychology – or of *Völkerpsychologie* – researchers paid attention to differences between languages in conceptualizing aspects of human perception and expression. From Wilhelm von Humboldt (1767–1835) to the present day, (e.g., extensions of the "Sapir-Whorf Hypothesis," and discourse analysis) the question of how language mediates psychological processes remains an issue for investigation. Contact between persons of varied language backgrounds increased, together with the colonization of the rest of the world by European countries. Discrepancies in mores and understandings that emerged at the boundaries of cultures brought the questions of social formation of the mind to the forefront of psychological issues.[3]

---

[3] Jahoda (1993, p. 142) describes how Johann Friedrich Herbart (1776–1841) discussed (in 1816) the consequences of educating a young Maori in Europe – he would neither become completely European nor remain entirely Maori. Discussions of this kind exemplify the need to make class distinctions (European versus "savage") and then try to overcome these (by turning the savage into an European, or by idealizing the "becoming native" idea for Europeans. Differences are either opposed or eliminated – they can't be accepted. Acceptance can exist in case of philosophical minds (e.g., W. von Humboldt), but not in institutional practices.

Fateful and Faithful Sciences: Labeling and Its Impacts

It could be argued that the demise of *Völkerpsychologie* was already encoded in its beginning. The notion of *Völkerpsychologie* was introduced by Moritz Lazarus (1824–1903) in 1851 (Jahoda, 1993, pp. 145–6) as an explicit labeling effort that was meant to create a new discipline (rather than mark one that already existed). Having spent his childhood in the multicultural East Prussian context (which meant, in his case, a mixture of German, Polish, and Jewish cultural heritages), Lazarus moved into studies of theology, and became the first holder of a *Lehrstuhl* in psychology in 1860 in Bern. For Lazarus, the task for *Völkerpsychologie* was to determine the psychological nature of the "folk spirit" that is expressed in both human minds and social worlds of art, science, and other forms of life organization. In this quest, he was joined by Hajm Steinthal (1823–99). Yet this quest was first based on the label, and did not advance any special knowledge base (other than provide an organizational, labeled framework that unified existing language and ethnological investigations). By introducing the concept of *Völkerpsychologie* no theoretical advancement was achieved.

The notion of *Volksgeist* can be seen as the German nineteenth century antecedent to the notion of "collective representations" (introduced by Emile Durkheim in 1898), which reaches our contemporary psychology in the form of social representations (see Chapter 9). As Jahoda explained.

Lazarus and Steinthal stated explicitly that the *Volksgeist* 'lives' within the individual and has no separate existence. Yet they also referred to the *Volksgeist* as though it were a distinct superordinate entity that exerts power over the individual . . . there is no escape from the implication of their claim that the *Volksgeist* is governed by laws analogous to those governing individual minds. Since they also defined the *Volksgeist* as 'the inner activity common to all individuals' (*das allen Einselnen Gemeinsame der innerem Thätigkeit* – Lazarus & Steinthal, 1860, p. 29), it is hard to avoid the conclusion that they fell into the very trap they had been anxious to avoid. (Jahoda, 1993, p. 152)

Jahoda's pointing to the inherent inconsistency in the discourse about the *Volksgeist* basically fits all of the rest of sociogenetic discourse. All through this book, the same tension surfaces in many different terminologies: The person is simultaneously individual and social, yet how the relationships between these two facets become theoretically crafted remains a major conceptual stumbling block for all efforts. As a result of this, the literature is filled with repetitive claims about the social nature of the person (or the folk-spirited nature of the person – to use the terminology of Lazarus and Steinthal). While the power of the social over the personal is implied (rarely would it be assumed to be in the reverse direction), the particular forms of this power relation are not elaborated. In 1860, Lazarus and Steinthal established the first journal on psychology, the *Zeitschrift für Völkerpsychologie und Sprachwissenschaft*. This publication continued until 1890, and presented comprehensive systematic investigations of human cultural phenomena.

It is important to emphasize a cross-language distinction between German and English for the understanding of the scientific status of *Völkerpsychologie*. While the English-language contrast between science and the humanities denies the latter the halo status that science carries, in German the distinction of *Naturwissenschaften* and *Geisteswissenschaften* does not carry the same folk-psychological denigration of the latter. Both deal with the issue of knowing, and of knowledge – albeit with knowledge about different objects (Dilthey, 1895/1924).

Even if the one is prioritized over the other (e.g., a particular German scientist may consider *Naturwissenschaft* to be clearly the source for knowledge about the human psyche), *Geisteswissenschaft* is not denied the status of an enterprise that seeks to achieve knowledge (in its own ways). *Geisteswissenschaft* has its own – even if secondary – role in human knowing. A similar differentiation of values does not exist in the English science/humanities distinction. For the German language, both are *Wissenschaft*.

Lazarus and Steinthal's journal had a distinctly Continental European flavor – many of the articles published in it dealt with the European historical heritage in classic Greek and Roman cultural institutions. Part of the *Völkerpsychologie* was to be a historical analysis of the development of cultures (the "genesis of the folk-development"; Lazarus & Steinthal, 1860, pp. 19–20). On the nonhistorical side, Lazarus and Steinthal envisaged the study of the "personality of a nation, of a city, of a society" (ibid., p. 28), in direct parallel with the study of human individual psyche. This unity of the developmental and ontological facets of folk psychology was lost later in twentieth-century psychology, and is currently being reinstated in cultural psychology.

The *Zeitschrift* included a number of notable works that antedated the developments in the early twentieth century. Early work of Georg Simmel (on Dante's psychology – Simmel, 1884; on the psychology of women – Simmel, 1890) was published there. Adolf Bastian's discussion of comparative psychology (Bastian, 1868), and Flügel's (1880a, 1880b) on the self in the life of peoples and the history of morality and custom (*Sitte*) are examples of relevant scholarship published in that source. The beginning of the twentieth century, however, became dominated by the massive nature of Wilhelm Wundt's narrative efforts to make sense of *Völkerpsychologie*.

Wilhelm Wundt's *Völkerpsychologie:* History, Development, and Synthesis

The role of Wundt in psychology has been covered by many layers of myths. As the initiator of a major experimental psychology laboratory, his work has been hailed for administrative and substantive efforts to turn psychology into an independent science. This led – already in Wundt's lifetime – to a partial emphasis on some sides of his contributions, and to the selective forgetting of other facets that would undermine the scientific hero myth constructed around him.

It has been demonstrated (Jahoda, 1993; Krueger, 1922; Van Hoorn & Verhave, 1980; Volkelt, 1922) that Wilhelm Wundt's contributions to psychology entailed in parallel the foci on elementary psychic processes (experimental psychology) and on complex phenomena of the human psyche (which came to be subsumed under the *Völkerpsychologie* label). In the latter, Wundt was – all his life – trying to create a historical-cultural system of knowledge (Volkelt, 1922) that both separates and unites the elementary and complex psychological functions, through consideration of their development. It is the separation aspect that has been emphasized in most stories about Wundt. This is evident in accounts of the history of Wundt's work that claim that he only became interested in the "soft" (folk) side of psychology in his old age. In reality, Wundt was interested in *Völkerpsychologie* all through his career (beginning from an illness at the age of twenty-five; see Volkelt, 1922).

Despite these two parallel lines of interests, Wundt had two central ideas (Van Hoorn & Verhave, 1980 p. 72) that unified these two: those of psychological causality (*Psychische Kausalität*) and creative synthesis (*schöpferische Synthese*). When psychological causality would operate at both elementary and complex levels of analysis, then the notion of creative synthesis explains the transition from one to the other level. As will be seen below, it is the latter that formed both the connection and dispute point between Wundt and the Second Leipzig School. The latter insisted upon the primacy of the whole over the process of synthesis. The issue of psychological causality was the basis for a break between Wundt and his former assistant Oswald Külpe (who is known as the main figure in the Würzburg School).

Wundt's focus on *Völkerpsychologie* developed in both continuity and opposition to the Lazarus/Steinthal version. The individual and historical focus was central for Wundt. He was interested in creating a story of the "developmental history of the soul" (*Entwicklungsgeschichte der Seele*; Volkelt, 1922, p. 82).[4] The crucial material for Wundt's thought was the history of human religions, and anthropological descriptions of the customs and morals (*Sitte* in German) of people from non-European societies. The latter were viewed in Wundt's time by a widespread social consensus as being less developed than the European "cultured person" (*Kulturmensch*). Yet at the same time, Europe was filled with a fascination with the ways of living of the "natural peoples" (*Naturvölker*). Many projections of the Europeans' psychological constructions into the "primitive people" were evident in the nineteenth century (e.g., Mason, 1996; Mitter, 1992). It is not surprising that Wundt (and many psychologists in the twentieth century; see Van der Veer, 1996a, 1996d) took over the consensual evaluative opposition between "culture" and "nature" as applied to Europeans' "we–they" distinction.

Wundt gave a series of lectures on *Völkerpsychologie* in Zurich in 1875 (Jahoda, 1993, p. 173), and gradually worked that direction into his system of general knowledge. By 1887 (in the 3rd ed. of *Grundzüge der physiologischen Psychologie*), he was claiming that the experimental and *Völkerpsychologie* approaches belong together in science, even if they have different goals. This message was extended in 1893 (in the 4th ed). Thus the preparation of his ten-volume monograph *Völkerpsychologie* (published in two editions during the years 1900–1920) was continuous with the rest of Wundt's life work.

In Wundt's own words, *Völkerpsychologie* is "The area of psychological investigations of these psychic processes which in their conditions

---

[4] The allusion here is to Karl Ernst von Baer's *Entwicklungsgeschichte der Thiere* (von Baer, 1828) which was the foundation for all embryology and developmental biology at large.

of origins and development [*Entstehungs- und Entwicklungsbedingun-gen*] are tied with mental communities [*geistige Gemeinschaften*]" (Wundt, 1921, p. 224).

The developmental orientation in this delineation of *Völkerpsychologie* is obvious. The notion of development runs through the lengthy volumes of his monograph. Writing extensively about speech, morality, customs, and history, Wundt was trying to make sense of complex phenomena that were of interest to his younger contemporaries – for instance, to James M. Baldwin and to George H. Mead. At the same time, Wundt's own efforts to build the system of *Völkerpsychologie* were informed by the knowledge base of his time (e.g., William James' *The Varieties of Religious Experience*). It may be the psychologists' hero myth that was constructed around Wundt's image later, and some aspects of Wundt's own personality (e.g., the critical downplay of differing ideas), that have contributed to the image of an old man who, already slightly senile, was writing a *Völkerpsychologie* without any connections with his contemporary science. In fact, Wundt's connectedness with his contemporary science was probably similar to George Herbert Mead's – both were being revered, and not much understood by students, and intellectually massacred by disciples who tried to surpass the imposing father figure.

It is therefore not surprising that some crucial examples usually assumed to have been introduced by others (e.g., Vygotsky's story about the development of "pointing to oneself" out of the child's indicative gesture; the same idea was used by George H. Mead, using the same source) can be traced back to Wundt's *Völkerpsychologie*. There are many hidden connections between Wundt's thinking and actual ideas developed further (or at least pondered about) by subsequent sociogenetic thinkers. Yet, given the Wundt myth that has circulated in psychology, it is true that new movements in contemporary psychology (first cognitive psychology during the 1950s, then cultural psychology during the 1990s) avoided admitting their roots in Wundt's *Völkerpsychologie*. Later, these currents recreated some of their ties to Wundt, after becoming sufficiently self-confident (as shown by Jahoda, 1993, p. 184). In a way, Wundt has been the liked, feared, and dismissed father figure for a number of approaches in psychology.

Wundt's creative synthesis notion was his answer to the question of how the elementary and complex levels of psychological phenomena (and their analysis) could be connected. Wundt saw a parallel between psychological synthesis and chemical processes of synthesis

(Wundt, 1921, p. 267). Elementary constituents can combine, arriving at synthesized new compounds. Complexity here emerges – so to speak – from elements "upwards."[5] This point was rejected by the Second Leipzig School of Krueger, Sander, and Volkelt who insisted that creative synthesis takes place in transformation of one whole to another whole (and not from elements to a whole; see Volkelt, 1922, p. 88).

Wundt's recognition of the mutuality of the elementary and complex levels was soon to be overtaken by the primacy of the whole over its parts, in the Leipzig context where Felix Krueger gained control in 1917. Holistic perspectives start from different assumptions, and are constrained by those. The avalanche of different holistic schools of thought in German-speaking intellectual realms gathered momentum from the 1880s onward, and reached its climax during 1920s and 1930s in the form of the *Ganzheit-* and *Gestalt-*psychology traditions.

The Basic Focus: Wholes are Not Reducible to Elements

The core issue of all holistic perspectives is the decision to recognize differences in quality between different levels of analysis of phenomena. If such differences are denied, it becomes possible to reduce complex phenomena to their elementary components, and assume that such reduction gives the investigator a key to making sense of the phenomena. In contemporary psychology, for instance, the belief exists that the complexity of the human psyche can be reduced to one or a few genes. Such belief entails the reduction of the hierarchical complexity of organisms' functioning to one level (thus denying that different levels exist), and the establishment of simple cause-effect relations. In contrast, holistic perspectives begin with the assumption that there exist levels of organization of phenomena, and that the quality of these levels differs. Thus, the chemical composite H_2O has the

---

[5] As Volkelt (1922, p. 88) pointed out, Wundt used the notion of creative synthesis in two senses. One of these was the capacity of psychological elements to combine into wholes, and to decompose. This was a formal, timeless, abstract solution to the issue of levels (elementary, complex). The second meaning involved locating that synthesis in a real developmental process. This could have led to a developmental theory of culture (*Entwicklungstheorie der Kultur*), on a par with developmental theories of the person. Wundt's focus on creative synthesis in his *Völkerpsychologie* could be an example of the beginnings of general developmental science (Cairns, Elder, & Costello, 1996).

characteristics of water, ice, and steam, which are qualities not present in its chemical subcomponents hydrogen and oxygen.

The dispute between holistic and elementaristic perspectives was (and continues to be) an ideological fight between different axiomatic systems. Each of them highlights one area of investigation while keeping others out of focus. The holistic direction maintains the complexity of a whole in the center of attention, but remains inarticulate about the organization of the whole. The latter may be available if both the analysis of the whole into its parts (not elements) and their joint work within the whole (synthesis) is organized. The elementaristic orientation eliminates the nature of the whole in the analysis – yet is clear about how to perform the analysis, thanks to that. Yet the analytic elements can no longer be viewed as parts of the whole, and the question of how to synthesize a whole from its elements is not answered.

The Austrian Tradition of Holism: Meinong and von Ehrenfels

In Continental Europe at the turn of the century, the orientation toward wholes (and holistic approaches) was "in the air." It was perhaps similar to behaviorism (and its basis-pragmatist philosophy that was becoming widespread in the United States at the same time. The flow of holistic perspectives intensified in the sciences during the early twentieth century (see overview by Herrmann, 1976).

The holistic tradition in psychology the end of the nineteenth century was largely of an Austrian sociocultural background, with Graz as its main location. In that little town, starting from 1882, Alexius Meinong (1853–1920) – a student of Franz Brentano from Vienna – created the Graz School of psychology. This direction included among others Vittorio Benussi and Stephan Witasek (Fabian, 1993). The first psychology laboratory in Austria was established by Meinong in Graz in 1894; Christian von Ehrenfels received his doctorate from the University of Graz in 1885.

The intellectual roots of this approach go back to Franz Brentano (see Heider, 1970), yet Meinong's relations with Brentano ceased as he developed his holistic realism (Findlay, 1972). Meinong's main contributions included treatises on assumptions (Meinong, 1902/1983) and emotional presentation (Meinong, 1917/1972).

Branching out from the Graz tradition, holism developed in Vienna and then (after 1897) in Prague – where Christian von Ehrenfels (1859–1932), aside from studying musical harmonies with Anton Bruckner and chatting with Freud, launched his key holistic claim (*Über "Gestaltqualitäten"*, Ehrenfels, 1890/1960). The year was the same as William James' *Principles of Psychology*. The context was very different however – Ehrenfels' primary object of investigation was music (rather than the personal "stream of consciousness"). This gave the basis for a focus on time-wholes (*Zeitgestalten*) – a melody is a structured whole that cannot be reduced to its component tones but unfolds in a particular time pattern. The other side of wholes – structures existing in space (*Raumgestalten*) – would later become the main topic for the Berlin direction of Gestalt psychology.

The crucial argument in favor of Gestalt-based thought is the transposability of a structure from one absolute state to another – if the relationship between the parts in the whole remains constant, the whole survives – even if its actual physical manifestations are new. Thus, a musical tune can be played in different keys, still remaining recognizable as that particular tune. In contrast, if a particular relation between two parts of a whole is changed, the whole can immediately cease to exist.

The philosophy of von Ehrenfels became the ideological cradle for Gestalt psychology as it is usually known in the history of psychology (i.e., the direction represented by the Berlin School of Köhler, Wertheimer, Lewin, and others). Gestalt psychology supported its scientific status by linking with its contemporary physics (Köhler, 1920) – yet its beginnings were firmly in the Diltheyan tradition of thought, supported by Carl Stumpf (see Ash, 1985, 1995). Prior to the "official" emergence of Gestalt psychology of the Berlin kind (dated usually to Max Wertheimer's two papers, published in 1912 – on the thinking of *Naturvölker*, and on phi-movement in perception – Wertheimer, 1912a, 1912b), there were a number of years (from 1906 onward) when all the to-be Berlin Gestaltists did their doctoral work in Berlin, under the advisorship of Carl Stumpf.

Stumpf's work on musical/acoustic tunes – based on his dedication to performing music – further fortified the dependence of the emerging holistic research directions on the phenomena of acoustic complexes (Sprung, 1997). The focus on ethnomusicology (and the collection of examples of music from different non-Western societies) was crucial for the hatching of Gestalt psychological ideas (see Ash, 1995).

Most of the would-be Berlin Gestaltists who later turned to experiments with visual perception were first initiated into Stumpf's acoustic and musical perceptual environment. Efforts were made to analyze the structural patterns of music of other peoples (Stumpf & von Hornbostel, 1911; von Hornbostel, 1913).

The holistic environment of ethnomusicology was enriched by Stumpf's administrative roles (one time chancellorship at University of Berlin) and provided institutional framing for that direction. Stumpf was attempting to build up the Berlin Psychological Institute in competition (and constant comparison) with the most developed institute in Germany – that of Wundt's in Leipzig. He carefully groomed his successor, Wolfgang Köhler, to continue in that administrative role.

Given the philosophical starting ground for holism, the developments in psychology in Europe during the beginning decades of the twentieth century were paralleled by similar foci in biology. It is in biology that the notion of symbiosis was created (by Anton de Bary in 1878; see Sapp, 1994). Von Bertalanffy's general systems theory was developed in this century on similar bases (Müller, 1996), having received an impetus both from physics and embryology. Field theories proliferated in the thinking of social scientists, and entered medicine (von Weizsäcker, 1927/1957). Last, but not least, Jakob von Uexküyll's theoretical biology was a holistic effort to relate the animal with its world. Complex organized systems needed to be understood in terms of their complex processes of functioning, rather than reduced to their constituents.

The Second Leipzig School: A Focus on Sociogenetic Synthesis

The core idea of the post-Wundtian tradition in Leipzig – expressed by Felix Krueger – was to unify the social and developmental approaches to phenomena, through the notion of wholes that need not have explicit form (structure), but may nevertheless constitute the core of psychological phenomena (e.g., generalized affect, or feeling – *Gefühl*). In the focus on affect, Krueger rightly viewed his approach to be richer than the nondevelopmental (yet dynamic) Gestalt psychology of the Berlin tradition.

The tradition of *Ganzheitspsychologie*[6] in Leipzig was based upon (and positioned itself against) Wundt's psychology. Given the two tendencies (elementarism and holism) co-present in Wundt's experimental and folk psychologies, it made sense for Krueger to develop the notion of creative synthesis (*schöpferische Synthese*) further within a holistic theoretical framework (Sander, 1922). The holistic focus of the Krueger tradition linked with German psychology. Yet it fit with the complex treatment of subjective psychological phenomena.

Krueger's *Ganzheitspsychologie* was indebted to the holistic ideas of Hans Cornelius (1897), and the whole personal-phenomenological focus of his tradition is indebted to William James' stream-of-consciousness focus (Volkelt, 1954). The whole is not just more than the sum of its parts (Ehrenfels' version), but it is primary to its parts. This includes the temporal organization. Furthermore, in the process of organizing in time, the whole changes its quality (i.e., reorganizes). That process allows the uniting of holistic ethos of the theoretical system with the general notion of development.

Krueger called for the construction of an explicitly developmental sociogenetic theory. He emphasized the historical nature of psychological phenomena:

It seems to me one of the most general and important results of experimental analysis that every psychic phenomenon, even the most simple, depends not only upon actual conditions, but also upon the after-effects of determinable *past* experience. Thus already the classical methods of psychological experimentation themselves are leading to the systematic limitations of experimental psychology. The ever changing *genetic* [i.e., developmental] conditions of all psychic processes and the intimate fusion of their effects with those of actual circumstances, constitute a characteristic trait of all psychic life. Herein lies the essential reason why the psychic can not be reduced to constant and qualitatively equal elements such as physical atoms. (Krueger, 1913a, p. 260)

The comparative psychological study of the human mind must be carried on at all stages of mental and cultural development. The genetic structure

---

[6] This term is difficult to translate. It can be translated as "holistic psychology," but that term would cover all of the different holistic traditions. Another translation effort by Suzanne Langer rendered it into English as *integrational psychology* (Klemm, 1961, p. 169). When referring to the Krueger tradition, we here continue to use the German term.

of human consciousness is really a historical one, that is to say, fundamentally dependent upon every individual's interrelations with other individuals and upon the past of their civilization. These social-genetic or cultural conditions admit still less of experimental method than do those of the individual. (ibid., p. 261)

At the intersection of *Völkerpsychologie* (with its emphasis on the holistic nature of complex phenomena) and the psychology of music (with the necessary acceptance of the dynamic unfolding of acoustic form, created by the person), Krueger was in a unique position to create a new sociogenetic direction in psychology. Krueger's notion of structure and its transformation was very similar to Goethe's morphogenetic ideas (Wellek, 1954, p. 53). Possibly because of the romantic undertones to his psychological theories, Krueger succeeded only partially in the *Umwelt* of a psychology that would prioritize physics discourse over that of poetry.

Krueger's Life course. Felix Krueger (born in 1874 in Posen, died in 1948 in Basel) studied philosophy in Strassbourg, Berlin, and Munich. He studied with Windelband (in Strassbourg) with Dilthey, Simmel, and Paulsen (in Berlin), then with Lipps and Cornelius (in Munich). He was active in the Bavarian Academic Psychological Society (which was set up by Theodor Lipps in an effort to make Munich a formidable center of psychology in Germany) as its secretary. As a twenty-two-year old student he published an essay: "Is Philosophy Possible without Psychology?", based on a discussion in the Academy (Wirth, 1961, p. 292) with a clearly negative answer to the posed question. This was in line with Theodor Lipps' philosophical orientation, yet Krueger was by far more closely related to Hans Cornelius who worked in Munich in parallel with Lipps. From Cornelius came the focus on the feeling tone (*Gefühlston;* Cornelius, 1897, pp. 74–6).

After finishing his doctoral studies in Munich in 1898 (on values and moral philosophy) he moved to Leipzig (to Wundt's Psychological Institute) and became an assistant at the Psychological Institute. After a short sojourn in Kiel University during 1899–1902, Krueger returned to Leipzig. His work during these years on the acoustic perception of musical wholes led to his consonance theory (which was the topic of his *Habilitationsschrift* in 1903; see Krueger, 1906). Simultaneously, he was interested in the phylogenesis of human activities. He analyzed the capacity to work as a new emergent characteristic of the species (Krueger, 1903).

The consonance theory was the basis for Krueger's general focus on the holistic units of experience. In Krueger's case, we can observe that the phenomenon of music – which was widely practiced in the German middle and upper classes – constituted a phenomenological framework for a clear emphasis on a holistic perspective. Analysis of a musical composition into its acoustic elementary constituents loses the holistic character of the given musical whole.

During 1906–9 Krueger was a professor of psychology at the University of Buenos Aires, establishing the Psychological Laboratory there and traveling widely in South America. In 1910 he received a professorship at Halle. During his professorship there, he was a visitor at Columbia University during 1912–13. It was from Halle that he moved to Leipzig to take over Wundt's Institute in 1917 (Hammer, 1993). It is in conjunction with the latter position that the Second Leipzig School of developmental holistic psychology (*genetische Ganzheitspsychologie*) entered onto the German psychological landscape of ideas (and social infights). The Second Leipzig School included among its main participants Hans Volkelt, Friedrich Sander (who developed his own experimental, microgenetic "school" at Giessen from 1928 onward, as well as in Jena and Bonn), Albert Wellek, and others. At the beginning of the 1930s, researchers working in the *Ganzheitspsychologie* tradition were doing numerous empirical studies, describing phenomena on their holistic organization, mostly in laboratories, and with perceptual stimuli.

Krueger's academic career continued at the University of Leipzig during the 1930s; he served as the chancellor of the university during the mid-1930s. Given his relatively conservative-nationalistic yet humanistic orientation, he was both appointed the chancellor of the university by the Nazis, and dismissed by them in 1936 for his "too liberal" attitudes. He was pensioned in 1938, lived in Potsdam during the war, and in Basel for the last years of his life (1945–8).

The Notion of *Komplexqualität* (Complex-Quality)

Krueger's framework undoubtedly benefited from nearness to phenomena – of inner psychological experience (*Erlebnis*). In that realm, ill-defined phenomena abound. All personal experience has holistic quality; it "flows through" different realms of the person's construction of his or her psyche. In general terms, Krueger's theoretical efforts were to develop a developmental theory of psychic life, in conjunction with a philosophy of value (*Entwicklungstheorie des Lebens und Philosophie der Werte*). In that effort, he was paralleled by William Stern (Stern, 1908, 1918, 1924).

The framework of *Ganzheitspsychologie* became one of the ideological parties in the German holistic psychology environment at the beginning of the century. Its core term – *Komplexqualität* (introduced by Krueger during the period 1903–6; Wellek, 1954) – found itself opposed to Theodor Lipps' *Gesamtqualität* (or "form of a whole"; Lipps, 1926, p. 177), and to Gestalt psychology's *Gestaltqualität*. Much of this intra-German controversy was a sociopolitical dispute between rival groups, who at times used each other's terminology (e.g., many *Ganzheit* psychological texts included discussion of Gestalt qualities). Krueger wrote,

In reality, the experience of a normal individual (and also all joint experience [*gemeinsame Erleben*]) consists in its main bulk of indistinctly bounded, diffused, slightly and not at all organized complexes in whose genesis all organs and functional systems take part. It is significant and not at all obvious that, at least in adult human beings and higher animals, the total state of their experience often unfolds into a multitude of relatively closed part-complexes. But even in the highest stages of development, this is not always the case, e.g., in states of the highest, permanent excitement, great fatigue, most complete self-subservience. Even where we observe experience in relief, its organization, as a rule, does not correspond at all . . . to 'stimulus'-relations. Never are the differentiable parts or sides of real experience as isolated from one another as the parts of physical substance, i.e., its molecules or its atoms. All things which we can differentiate there . . . always grip into one another and around one another in the greatest elaboration. And every time it is . . . imbedded within a *total whole* (*Gesamtganze*), by which it is penetrated and more or less completely enclosed. *Feelings are the Qualities of the Experiences of This Total-Whole.* (Krueger, 1928b, p. 67; 1928a, p. 104)

The notion of complex quality (*Komplexqualität*) covers the nature of the whole that penetrates the specific realms of phenomena. *Komplexqualität* is more general than the notion of Gestalt quality. While Gestalt implies that the whole has a form (configuration), Krueger's complex could be general, holistic, and include formless wholes alongside Gestalts. The focus on formless – but still organized – wholes was the critical positive contribution of Krueger's tradition (see Krueger, 1926). Without any doubt, theoretically the idea of "organized formlessness" seems like a contradiction in terms. Yet in the case of human psychological functions such phenomena are not difficult to find. For instance, in the realm of human affect such nebulous phenomena exist in abundance – a field or sea of undifferentiated anger or drowning in happiness. These feelings are holistic, but lack any Gestalt-like configuration. It is in the realm of ill-formed (yet organized) phenomena that Krueger's thinking benefited from that of William James. And it is probably unfortunate that the fascination with fuzzy sets and chaos[7] models that is so much a part of our scientific discourse during the 1990s was not a reputable scientific interest during the 1920s. Krueger's thinking was influential in the perceptual psychology of Wolfgang Metzger and the personality psychology of Philip Lersch.

It is clear that Gestalt quality is a form of complex quality – but not vice versa. *Ganzheitspsychologie* thus was aiming to include Gestalt psychology as one of its parts (which obviously did not appeal to the Berlin Gestalt tradition – all the more as the two schools inherited the Berlin versus Leipzig rivalry from the Wundt versus Stumpf opposition). Krueger's effort to conceptualize holistic human affective phenomena in terms of *un*organized fields was a bold attempt to revolutionize psychology's theoretical system. Any analytic effort applied to a phenomenon implies some form of organization – yet in the case of developing phenomena the researcher needs to make sense of the becoming of some form of organization from its absence (see Bergson, 1907/1944b, Chapter 4).

Krueger's effort failed in the middle of social infighting with the Berlin Gestalt school, and because of limited elaboration of the holistic terminology. Yet it was linked with other German holistic systems, e.g., that of the Hamburg School of William Stern and Heinz Werner (Wellek, 1967, pp. 388–91). The effort, however, had its distant echo. Lev Vygotsky's interest in "thinking in complexes" (and his use of the terminology "pseudo-concepts") was linked to Krueger's and Werner's ideas. Another linkage is with our contemporary focus on social representations. Social representations are complexes that unite generic meanings between personal and social levels (Farr, 1998).

Yet it is the developmental focus that was most notably present in Krueger's conceptualization. The assumption that all soul-complexes (Krueger did use the word "soul" – *Seele*) strive toward wholeness ("*Drang nach Ganzheit*"; Wellek, 1954, p. 32) makes it possible to unite

[7] Interestingly, "chaos" was explicitly mentioned as an example of *Komplexqualität*; see Sander, 1927, p. 186.

the developmental and holistic sides of the phenomenon. Yet it creates a difficulty for analysis – when it is assumed that the phenomena themselves tend toward the synthesis of some holistic unity, then how can one analyze that process of synthesis? It is not preknown which unity it is – it is only possible to detect it after it has emerged (by way of researchers discovering that A is no longer A but B). These methodological difficulties were similar to the ones Baldwin faced (see Chapter 4).

Krueger's main theoretical contribution to sociogenetic thought was his *On Developmental Psychology* (Krueger, 1915). In that book he outlined the conditional-genetic analysis (later utilized by Lewin, 1927) – the analysis of the sets of conditions under which the developmental process reorganizes itself in some – rather than another – direction. These directions or developmental lines (*Entwicklungsreihen*) may proceed in parallel, at times integrated with one another, at times not. The general idea seems similar to the later thinking by Vygotsky about "parallel lines" of development (in his case taken from Vagner; see Chapter 8). Under some social conditions, parallel lines may become integrated into a holistic state. These conditions in real human life are social (hence the sociogenetic locus in Krueger's thinking, which is repeatedly stated, but not elaborated). He called for the conjoint investigation of the persons who experience, and of their community (*"der Erlebenden und seiner Gemeinschaft"*; Krueger, 1915, p. 118), viewing this kind of study to be possible in various domains of phenomena (psychopathological cases, studies of children, etc.). Similarly to Wundt, Krueger recognized the inevitability of using nonexperimental methods for the study of cultural (i.e., historically self-organizing) phenomena. This brought Krueger into the realm of his contemporary German ethnography, and particularly to the work of Richard Thurnwald (see Melk-Koch, 1989, for a substantive overview of Thurnwald's contributions). It is interesting to note that Thurnwald's work was later of crucial relevance for Vygotsky (see Van der Veer & Valsiner, 1991).

The phenomena Krueger considered worthwhile for study naturally followed his axiomatic holism. Thus, ethnography provided many examples of musical melodies from other societies (note the personal background of Krueger's in the study of acoustic wholes in melodies). These melodies can be very different from the European hearer's patterns of understanding, yet they have their own organizational history (of being human-made cultural phenomena, depending upon human cultural instruments). Analysis of the history of musical tunes in a society gave a developmental picture of the development of that culture through concrete meaningful and functional objects (see similar efforts by Ernst Boesch, 1993, 1997; see also Chapter 9). The cultural meaningfulness and functions can only be guaranteed by the holistic nature of these objects, a melody that is part of a relevant religious ritual in some society cannot obviously be reduced to its constituent sounds (losing the *Gesamtqualität*), and still remain functional. Further parallels between Boesch's cultural psychology and that of the Krueger tradition can be seen in the interest of longing for home (*Heimweh:* discussed in Boesch, 1997, and in Fischer, 1928).

A similar holistic nature made the issue of the phylogenetic emergence of human labor interesting for Krueger (1913b). The move from nonhuman behavior to human activities was viewed by Krueger as being mediated by emotional tension (a formless, yet functional, all-encompassing whole) which led to the organization of action (religious ritualisms, dancing, etc.). Emotional tension – as well as its turn into organized religious forms – was a central concept of Janet's perspective (as described in Chapter 3). Krueger applied the centrality of affect to the explanation of phylogenesis. Religious-magical regulations of human actions were supposed to "teach self-restraint, growing independence of momentary stimuli, self sacrifice, – all of which are essential conditions of a man's *capacity* to work" (Krueger, 1913b, p. 258).

Our contemporary holistic emphases of different kinds of activity theories (see Chapter 9) seem to follow in the footsteps of Krueger, when they emphasize the molar units of analysis (e.g., activity or actions). Other complex qualities, created by human cultural activities – such as art (Sander, 1932) – were also appropriate targets for analysis along the lines of *Ganzheitspsychologie*.

The Battlefields of Germany: Mutuality of Intolerance

German intellectual life at the beginning of the twentieth century was filled with geographic and ideologically marked regional divisions. Such parochialism guaranteed a rather difficult time for some innovative scientists in their German contexts (e.g., Georg Simmel's fate – being well known in American sociology, while almost not at all at home – see Chapter 5). Different regionally based leaders of psychology were fighting for prominence of their school in Germany, by expanding their local facilities and by pushing forward their doctoral students as candidates for professorship in other German universities.

The social context of Krueger's approach in Germany was thus part of the political fights before the Second Leipzig School took over from Wundt the leadership in Leipzig in 1917. Some of the rivalry between the Leipzig and the Berlin holistic directions, which became evident during the 1920s, was already historically set up (by the efforts of Wilhelm Dilthey and Carl Stumpf in Berlin) to overtake the prominence of Wundt's Leipzig research center. In fact, the Berlin Gestalt tradition (of Köhler, Koffka, Wertheimer, and Lewin) emerged from Stumpf's background that was decidedly anti-Leipzig already at the beginning of the century (see Ash, 1995, on Stumpf's explicit buildup of the Berlin Institute in contrast to Leipzig). Wundt's Institute in Leipzig was certainly the best in Germany at the time, although not perfect.[8] However, Stumpf was trying administratively to keep up with and surpass the developments in Leipzig. The dramatic increase in the space of the Leipzig Institute in 1897 was followed by a similar one in Berlin during 1900 (Ash, 1995), and surpassed the Leipzig case during 1920 when the Berlin Institute moved to the former Imperial Palace (Berliner Schloss) and was directed by Wolfgang Köhler who had proven his administrative capacities in his work with chimpanzees on Tenerife during World War I.[9]

The fights between "the Berliners" and "the Leipzigers" antedated the emergence of the Berlin Gestalt tradition. The fight started from the very beginning, as Krueger later (1928b, p. 65) complained. Already, in 1897, the first expressions of holistic ideas by Hans Cornelius were met by scorn, and in 1906, Carl Stumpf "declared incomprehensible" Krueger's ideas about Gestalt quality. Without doubt, Krueger's writing was not simple (see Krueger, 1928a, discussion of his chapter). The issues he tried to explain – complexes of semiformed kind – were

---

[8] The German tradition – now used widely in other countries – of using an offer from another university to upgrade the conditions in one's home university was utilized by Wundt, who in 1883 received a call to Breslau, which resulted in a 40 percent salary rise in Leipzig (Bringmann, Bringmann, & Ungerer, 1980, p. 149).

[9] This phrasing is intended. Köhler's difficult task as the administrator of the Tenerife primate colony was to maintain it under difficult economic circumstances (speedy loss of value of the German currency during wartime). He succeeded well (see Ash, 1995, for further details).

(and are) not easy for any theoretical system to eschew. Yet the opponents often used the supposed unclearness of the writings of the not-so-revered author as a good excuse to pay no attention to them.

Picky infighting between the Berlin Gestalt movement and the Second Leipzig School continued during the 1920s (see Ash, 1985). There was a clear difference in scientific credos – the Berlin direction idealized physics, while the Leipzig direction expressed romantic or poetic ideas, and other kinds of inexact formulations. The Leipzig direction was explicitly developmental, while the Berlin tradition was an addendum to the general Gestalt principles.

Both directions hailed the unity of the whole (Gestalt), yet they had very different ideas about how to conceptualize the processes that underlie the wholeness of the Gestalt. Nor were they alone in building and propagating a holistic theoretical perspective in the Germany of that time – William Stern's personology developed in Hamburg; Erich Jaensch's holism developed in Marburg. Georg Elias Müller (1850–1934) developed his own *Komplextheorie* (by 1923) in Göttingen, in counterbalance to the Gestalt movement (Behrens, 1997). Thus, holism of different kinds was the consensually accepted starting point for German researchers at the time. Within that intellectual climate, different researchers were building their differing theoretical castles, and making distinctions between those accepted in these castles and others who were left outside the gates.

Yet there was a social side to the dispute as well. It was situated in the historical regional conflict between Prussia (where Berlin belonged) and the Land of Saxony, which – with Leipzig as its major metropolis – was decidedly attempting to be the major German town at the end of the nineteenth century. Furthermore, the Prussian bureaucracy was not exactly appreciated in other German lands. A letter written to Wundt (by a friend in 1883) testifies to the mutual distrust that reigned between the different regions: "Everyone here is of the opinion that the Prussian government does not like to call anyone from Leipzig . . . because in Prussia the system of academic calls seems to have been replaced by bureaucratic promotions" (Bringmann, Bringmann, & Ungerer, 1980, p. 149).

The issue here was Wundt's possible "win over" to Breslau during 1883 (which did not happen). It clearly indicates the basic interregional distinction and stigmatization. Contrary to the belief in German unity that was introduced by Bismarck, that country has remained divided internally along both religious and regional lines. Such social divisiveness is a facet of the unique German history, and its impact upon the intellectual interdependency of scientists is of importance.

The social fights (i.e., discursive battles) between the Gestalt and *Ganzheit* psychologies in Germany during the 1920s needs to be distinguished from the substantive theoretical constructions of both directions. Furthermore, strong egos were involved. The complexity of Wilhelm Wundt's character, openness and supportiveness on the one hand, but intolerance of disciples' differing viewpoints on the other, led to rifts between him and his previous disciples (e.g., breaks with Külpe and Münsterberg; a dispute with Karl Bühler). Such breakdowns of intellectual relations between teachers and disciples abounded in the German-speaking academia: e.g., Franz Brentano broke with Alexius Meinong after the latter's move away from Brentano's basic ideas; the Freud/Jung separation is well known. The social movements of intellectual kinds were undoubtedly led by vigorous and complex people who "engaged in propagating their faith" (Hartmann, 1935, p. 78). Yet the concepts developed by them advanced psychology's knowledge constructive potential, and stayed alive long after their deaths.

Productive Research Directions

As is usual in psychology, a new theoretical system is made into a domain of empirical research in order to prove itself in the middle of the discourse about psychology as science. Krueger's disciples found their places at the universities of Leipzig (Hans Volkelt), Kiel, Giessen (Friedrich Sander), Jena (also Sander), Mainz (Albert Wellek), Heidelberg (Johannes Rudert), and Bonn, and the 1920s and 1930s these institutions were filled with productive empirical work.

Ganzheitspsychologie's empirical research program included a huge variety of investigations of different phenomena. Although processes of visual perception were the chief domain for empirical research, other domains were also well represented – such as the formation of the understanding of art works (Mantell, 1936; Sander, 1932b), music (Schmidt, 1939; Wellek, 1935), speech reception (Ipsen, 1926, 1928), social-psychological wholes (Beck, 1953; Dürckheim-Montmartin, 1954), and complex action structures (such as javelin throwing – Klemm, 1938; or diving – Rüssel, 1944). As a general framework, *Ganzheitspsychologie* served to interpret several efforts of ethnographic analysis (Gutmann, 1923, 1926, 1932, 1935).

Aside from the work of Friedrich Sander (see below), two other members of the Second Leipzig School are of importance in the context of our story. First, Krueger's closest disciple, Hans Volkelt (1886–1964), should be noted for his elaboration of *Ganzheitspsychologie's* ideas in the areas of animal and child psychology. As the son of the German aesthetic philosopher Johannes Volkelt (1848–1930), Hans received his doctorate in Leipzig in 1912 (on representations in animals; Volkelt, 1914). In the area of child psychology, Volkelt further developed Krueger's ideas of feelings-imbued holistic experience worlds. Thus, the child's life in a family is fully covered by the emotional field that the mother and the others create. Yet the particular orientations introduced by the parents with the best feelings for the child (e.g., luxurious, child-oriented environments) may become "enemies" for the child (Volkelt, 1938), as the latter can create a different affective field for the same conditions. Furthermore, the child's feeling field is embedded in mutually overlapping contexts, both spatially (home, yard, neighborhood, city, country) and socially (family, kinship network, society at large). The "we-experience" (*Wir-Erlebnis*) is a complex that can be modified to include a wider (or narrower) sphere of persons, environments, and social organizations. In a general sense (see Volkelt, 1963, p. 34), striving for creating the whole (*Gestaltungsdrang*) governs all of human life, and takes the form of a culture-creative (*kulturschöpferisch*) synthesis.

Volkelt's emphasis on the function of emergent (and vanishing) contours (Volkelt, 1963, pp. 28–31) resembles the basic premises of co-genetic logic (Herbst, 1995), and is in line with Kurt Lewin's application of topological concepts to psychological phenomena (Lewin, 1933). Volkelt's emphasis – in line with the dynamic and developmental focus of *Ganzheitspsychologie* – on the semiorganized and organizing boundaries surpasses that of Lewin's. This was possible as Volkelt emphasized the affective nature of the constantly made and emerging boundaries, on the basis of the person's *Einfühlung*. *Einfühlung* was not the notion of empathy (as it has been translated into English, since Titchener's introduction of the term, which was described in Chapter 4). It involves the experiencer (who "feels into") and the experienced field (to which the "feeling into" is oriented). The experiencer and the experienced are mutually interdependent, but not fused. The experiencer inhabits the experienced object with some subjective character (*Beseelung*), and treats it from his or her own perspective, without fusing that perspective with that attributed to the object. *Beseelung* involves a dynamic attribution of bodily sensual powers to the object ("Durchkraftung mit ungeschieden-ganzheitlich somato-psychischem Leben," Volkelt, 1959/1962, p. 154).

The roots of the notion of *Einfühlung* were clearly seen in the work of Johann Gottfried Herder (his work *Plastik*, 1769; see Volkelt, 1959/ 1962, p. 149; 1963, p. 67), even if Herder did not use that term itself. The question was very ordinary – how do viewers make sense of statues or sculptures? Why would a classic statue depicting a human body (e.g., Michelangelo's "David") be of any affective relevance, so that human beings may enjoy looking at the statue, may go on long pilgrimages to look at the statue, etc. Herder emphasized that this is possible through human embodiment of the statue by attributing meaning to its subjective characteristic. The statue-appreciating person is involved in a process of "living through and in oneself" (*Durch- und-Inunsleben*) that object of experience. This Herderian idea was the basis for Lipps' and Johannes Volkelt's aesthetic focus of *Einfühlung* at the turn of the twentieth century.

Albert Wellek's (1904–72) work entails a parallel extension of Krue- ger's basic direction. He was perhaps the most active preserver of the whole tradition through the turbulent years of the 1930s and 1940s. His work after World War II at the University of Mainz carried the tradition almost into contemporary German psychology.[10] During the late 1930s, the high time of German psychology's fulfilling of the Nazi social demand for methods to study differences between types of people, Wellek developed a dynamic idea of the systemic holistic functioning of any type.

The main Zeitgeist of the Nazi-era psychology was the diagnosis of race-linked psychological types. Many of the German psychologists were ready to fulfill this state-mandated requirement. Diagnostic tests of typological kinds flourished. In that environment, Wellek proposed his theory of a systemic view on types. A type as a class concept was

---

[10] It may be fair to say that *Ganzheitspsychologie* is one of the undeserved victims of German history since 1933. Although the major authors of the post-Krueger genera- tion (Sander, Volkelt, Wellek, Rudert, Rüssel, and others) continued their work in West German academia after World War II, they did not leave a new generation that could have maintained German intellectual traditions in the otherwise increasingly self-Americanizing German psychology of the 1950s and 1960s. They continued to exist in a neutral or perhaps relatively hostile intellectual environment, in which their (e g , Sander's) episodes of documented Nazi-era statements were at times recollected as morally reprehensible signs.

viewed by him as functioning through inherent polarity (tension between type and counter-type) transitions from one pole to the other. He introduced the concept of approach (*Annäherungsbegriff*: The "ideal type" is not yet reachable as "real type") and multiple conditional determination of the type (Wellek, 1938, p. 477). Psychological typology here is no longer a diagnostic scheme (to which one would fit different persons), but a personal functional system that by its inherent tensions (between type and counter-type, ideal and real type) moves the person forward in his or her life experiencing.

Friedrich Sander's Theory of *Vorgestalten* and *Aktualgenese*

Probably the most important contributor to the developmental side of *Ganzheitspsychologie* was Friedrich Sander. Sander (1889–1971) studied in Leipzig (he finished his dissertation with Wundt on the perception of the geometric figure in 1913; Tinker, 1980, p. 277), and worked with Krueger after that. In 1928 he moved to the University of Giessen, and in 1933 to the University of Jena. After World War II, Sander continued his work at the University of Bonn.

It is thanks to his work – mostly in the area of perception – that a new methodological focus, *Aktualgenese*, became established (Sander, 1927, 1928/1962, 1930). Sander's focus was built upon the notion of development, in continuation with Krueger's ideas:

Elements do not develop. They may aggregate in varying numbers, and according to the frequency of their associations arrange themselves in variously complex patterns – but real development, in the full sense of the word, means something more than this. Hence the non-genetic character of the old phenomenalistic element-psychology, which was based almost exclusively on the description of the consciousness of adult subjects without any inquiry into genetic and social conditions. (Sander, 1930, p. 189)

As the wholes establish new forms, and lose old ones, the whole task of psychology is located in the study of Gestalt origination (*Entstehung*) and Gestalt decomposition (*Gestaltzerfall*; Sander, 1962a). The core of psychology is the study of genesis, not of the status quo. Phenomena of speech (Sander, 1934) and art (Sander, 1932b) provided examples of the making and breaking of the experiences of the whole.

Microgenetic Methodology: Looking at the Processes of Unfolding

The research direction of *Ganzheitspsychologie* was productive in creating a new methodological focus – that of the empirical analysis of psychological processes in the course of their formation. Three authors have been credited for setting the stage for microgenetic methodology: Friedrich Sander, Günter Ipsen, and Heinz Werner (Graumann, 1959). The year was 1926 (Ipsen, 1926; Sander, 1926, 1927; Werner, 1927).

This developmental methodology was fitting Krueger's and his co-workers' theoretical needs (Sander, 1926, 1928, 1930, and Werner, 1927). The extinction of the methodology began from terminological problems. Sander's notion of *Aktualgenese* was originally translated into English (by Susanne Langer) as "genetic realization." Thus, Friedrich Sander explained the general idea:

The presentation of figures by a very brief exposure in the tachistoscope, in twilight vision or indirect vision, or in extreme miniature, all have this trait in common, that a constellation of stimuli operates under unfavorable conditions, too briefly, etc. The less the perception [more precisely: perceptive experience – *Wahrnehmungserlebnis*] is decisively influenced by the physical condition, the stimuli, the more freely will the dynamic structure come into play and mold the phenomenal content in its own interest. The transition from maximally unfavorable to normal circumstances gives the raise to a whole series of sense experiences, whereby the evolution of configurations is exhibited in logical order. [For this process of gradual configuration [*Gestaltentstehungsprozess* in the German version] I have suggested the term "genetic realization" (*Aktualgenese*)]. In this configurative process the emergent perceptual constructs are by no means mere imperfect or vague versions of the final figure which appears under maximally favorable conditions, but characteristic metamorphoses with qualitative individuality, "preformulations" (*Vorgestalten*). These properties, which certainly are not determined by the constellation of stimuli, may be traced back to structural causes, and let us deduce the direction toward which they tend in forming the objects of experience. (English version; Sander, 1930, p. 193; German version; Sander, 1932a, pp. 244–5)

Sander's methodological focus was in tapping into the microprocess of development. In an experiment, the presentation of an altered stimulus involved the emergence of a whole succession of Gestalt experiences. In that successive emergence one can analyze the process of becoming.

Aktualgenese is in effect the process of the emergence of the actual (out of uncertain potentialities, in real time). The actual was conscious reflection (*Bewusstsein*) in the process of development (Sander, 1927, p. 187). This focus narrowed needs of Sander's experimental methods, on the side of the subject's response; it involved one or another form of descriptive interpretation of the object phenomenon. Thus, Sander had no need to worry about the possible formation of the subconscious (as was the question for the researchers dealing with hypnotic and posthypnotic suggestion; see Chapters 2 and 3). Empirical elaborations of Sander's *Aktualgenese* are in many ways the forerunners of the "thinking aloud" protocol analysis (Ericsson & Simon, 1993).

The focus of *Aktualgenese* as a methodological orientation was on the description of emerging novel forms in time. This fits well with a Baldwinian theoretical perspective (of persistent imitation; see Chapter 4). However, it does not fit at all with the focus on measurement of the nondevelopmental tradition that came to dominate all of psychology after the 1930s (built on misunderstood notions of "operationalism"; see Koch, 1992).

Sander's orientation led to empirical analyses of different kinds. First, of course, was his focus on the experimental limitation of the stimulus presentation conditions – bringing those from a nonoptimal to an optimal state while registering the *Vorgestalt* emergence process. In the process of introducing the *Vorgestalt* notion (see Sander, 1926, p. 127), Sander relied upon Heinz Werner's early work on optical rhythms (Werner, 1919a, 1919b).

The sequential emergence (and disappearance) of the *Vorgestalten* was an important phenomenon for gaining access to the process of *Aktualgenese*, whereas the end-Gestalt merely introduced a final point. The experiential periods of living through the stage of *Vorgestalt* were psychologically central. The experience in that stage "pulls" the person's psychological system further. For artists and writers that is the locus for creative synthesis. The *Vorgestalten* are imbued with *Drang nach Gestalt* (Sander, 1926, p. 127).

If the empirical focus of researchers is set upon the sequences of *Vorgestalten* emerging and decaying, many different empirical tasks can be generated. Yet the value of such empirical descriptions depends upon the theoretical goals of the investigation. Two issues were crucial – the "richness" or "poverty" of the *Vorgestalten* (in comparison with the final form), and the dynamic movement from one to another configuration of the *Vorgestalten* in time. Thus, Sander remarked:

The formation of the successive stages [of visual percept], which usually emanate one from the other by sudden jerks, has a certain shading of non-finality; the intermediaries lack the relative stability and composure of the final forms; they are restless, agitated, and full of tensions, as though in a plastic state of becoming . . . The peculiar mode of presentation of these prefigurations that are simplified relative to some final form is in no wise comparable to that of the final forms of similar outline; *it is considerably richer in quality*. (Sander, 1930, p. 194, emphasis added)

The feeling-tone of tension detected in the *Vorgestalten* sequence is an indicator of the process of development. Here a crucial distinction in looking at theoretical accounts of stages in the formation of a final Gestalt needs to be made. Two models of such stage accounts are possible:

Model 1: *Vorgestalt* sequence: A → B → C → leads to final → X
Model 2: *Vorgestalt* sequence: A–ab–B–bc–C → leads to final → X

In Model 1, the sequence of intermediate forms (A, B, C) is treated as if these forms were mutually independent, and merely are evoked in a given sequence. These kind of models are widely used in contemporary psychology in cases of time-series analyses, where the independence of the units in a sequence is necessary to construct formal (probabilistic) relations between them. Such models do not reflect development (as transformation of one unit in a sequence into another). Transitions become reconstructed in terms of the formal probabilistic sequential order of independent units.

In contrast, Model 2 entails a focus on the transformation from one unit (A, B) to another (B, C), through an inherent transformative process that binds both the previous and the subsequent unit (ab, bc). These intermediate forms in the process reflect *development as it is taking place* (see Baldwin's ideas about development in Chapter 4). The *Aktualgenese* tradition unified both a theory of development and a methodological direction for how to empirically study that development.

For Krueger and Sander, that connection was clearly set – the study of *Aktualgenese* equaled the study of development of holistic structures. Yet with the separation of methods from theory in the psychology of the second half of the twentieth century, that connection gradually became lost. While Sander was building his *Aktualgenese* as a method along the lines of Model 2, subsequent alterations of the method led to its translation into a version of Model 1. It is therefore not surprising that the end product of such a reconstruction is not of wide use. Without the developmental theory behind it, *Aktualgenese* (as a method) has no innovative power amidst the myriad of other nondevelopmental methods in psychology.

From *Aktualgenese* as a Narrow Method to Microgenesis as a General Perspective

The label of microgenesis (introduced by Heinz Werner; Werner, 1956) is in some ways synonymous with *Aktualgenese* – after all, Heinz Werner was one of the originators of the idea – but in other ways it was different because it was embedded in a different theoretical matrix. Werner introduced his parallel version of the developmental method simultaneously with Sander (Werner, 1927, 1940), but the term microgenesis went into English-language practice only after 1956 (Flavell & Draguns, 1957; Werner, 1956). For Werner, microgenesis referred to "Any human activity such as perceiving, thinking, acting, etc. is an *unfolding process*, and this *unfolding, or 'microgenesis'*, whether it takes seconds or hours or days, *occurs in developmental sequence*" (Werner, 1956, p. 347).

Werner's focus on unfolding interestingly differs from Sander's focus on the emergence of a rich variety of forms (*Vorgestalten*). The notion of "developmental sequence" here refers to Werner's orthogenetic principle (Werner, 1948, 1957), which includes the notion of the construction of organizational order (like Sander's or Krueger's developmental axioms). Yet at the same time, it entails the generic similarity of developmental processes at all levels, from microgenesis to ontogenesis, and from there to phylogenesis, pathogenesis, and ethnogenesis.

Werner (1890–1964) was a contemporary of Sander, and a quasi-competitor as a member of the Stern School in Hamburg (from 1917 onward, see Wapner & Kaplan, 1964; Witkin, 1965). Like many of his contemporaries in Europe, Werner's early experiences in Vienna included music as a realm of lived-through and trained experience. Like many German psychologists at the beginning of the twentieth century (Krueger, Lipps, etc.), Werner was interested in issues of aesthetics (on which he did his dissertation at the University of Vienna in 1914). After completing his dissertation, he worked in Munich while continuing to study two to five-year-old children's spontaneous construction of melodies. He was interested in issues of meaning construction, emphasizing the roots of metaphor (published in Krueger's mono-graph series; Werner, 1919), and in lyrics.

Before joining William Stern's Psychological Institute in Hamburg, Werner was already a notable researcher. The intellectual atmosphere in Hamburg facilitated the further growth of his ideas. The Stern tradition was not in a direct social fight with the Second Leipzig School, but was actually quite close in ideas to the latter. Stern's personology could be viewed as standing somewhere between the Leipzig and Berlin traditions (see Witkin, 1965, p. 310) It was close to the former in the emphasis on lived-through experience, yet did not make the holistic developmental concentration its full focus. At the same time, it was distant from the Berlin Gestalt tradition by focusing on the person, and by refusing to insist on the absolute nature of organisms' striving toward a "good Gestalt." In that refusal, Stern assumed a position quite similar to the Krueger direction. As Werner himself explained, in an effort to present Stern's ideas to the American readership:

The person is not only a gestalt, but a *non-gestalt* as well. Vagueness, non-gestalt, equivocality are not to be evaluated in any negative sense. They are a positive characteristic of the person. Equivocality and vagueness constitute a fundamental condition, a field of potentiality, to be realized in the future. Person is not only defined according to what it is now in its present state of being, but also according to what it would become in the future. (Werner, 1938, p. 113)

On the one hand, the latter focus unifies the Stern-Werner tradition with that of Vygotsky, and on the other hand, with Mead and Bald-win's thought. Time as a constituent part of the living process is brought into the center of the theoretical focus. The issue of impor-tance becomes the question of how, in which ways, the *unitas multiplex* (Stern's term for the person being a heterogeneous psychological sys-tem) of the given time transforms into a new state, given the organ-ism's set goal orientation for the future. This was shared with the Sander-Krueger tradition as well.

Werner's theoretical orientation entailed the unity of various levels of developmental processes. First, Werner's joint teaching with Johann Jakob von Uexküll promoted the issue of phylogenesis in his thought. At the same time, his interest in symbolic construction led him to think of the cultural faccts of the human psyche. Looking at humans in their life course added the ontogenetic focus, and interest in clinical phenomena entered into his system in terms of pathogenesis. All these were united through the general, abstract, orthogenetic principle of differentiation (Werner, 1956, 1957).

Werner had two parallel, life-long interests. First, he was eager to find out how human perceptual systems are holistically organized. The second was to inquire into the role of signs (symbols) in human psychological functioning. This focus was rooted in his interest in aesthetics, from where follows his physiognomic thinking (Werner, 1927, 1931). In his work on micromelodies he used the terminology of the Krueger/Sander tradition (e.g., *Gliederung*; Werner, 1926, p. 82). Furthermore, in conjunction with his interest in aesthetics, Werner emphasized the process of *Gestaltschichtung* (future-oriented organization of a whole; Werner, 1931).

The notion of the process of differentiation and de-differentiation that was relevant during the 1950s in his work and Bernard Kaplan's formulation of the orthogenetic principle was well prepared by Werner's experiences with music and poetry. The turmoils of German history forced Werner to emigrate to the United States, where from 1947 until his death in 1964, he brought the psychological research at Clark University once more to excellence (Witkin, 1965). In that context, he outlined his explanation of differences between fusion, differentiation, and separation in connection with the notion of rigidity (Werner, 1946, p. 50). Both the *un*differentiated and *hyper* differentiated (parts of a system that has become isolated from one another) states of the organism can show rigidity of action, while it is only the differentiated system – with its distinction of parts and their relations – that allows for flexibility of conduct.

Werner wanted to find out about the holistic features of the person-environment relationship (e.g., danger). His work on symbolic representation led to the elaboration of the microgenetic method. An example of the latter was the Word–Context test (W–C test; Werner, 1954) The W–C test was directed at determining the processes involved in arriving at a decision about the meaning of a particular unknown word, which is inserted in a sequence of mutually unrelated sentences. After each sentence (on a card) that included the word was read by the subject, he or she had to give a meaning for the word, and explain how the word fitted into the sentence. After an answer, the subject looked at the next card, and gave a new guess. Thus, for example, the word POSKON was embedded in the following sequence:

1. You should try to give POSKON to other people.
2. If you believe in POSKON, you are a good person.
3. The children will like that teacher because she believes in POS-KON.
4. People will always be afraid when there is no POSKON.
5. Some bad people do not like POSKON because they don't want to be punished.
6. There is no POSKON when a thief is not punished [POSKON was expected to mean justice]. (Werner, 1954, p. 189)

Notice that in this method, two aspects of psychological methodology credos are combined. The sentences selected are assumed to be independent from one another (like any items in a questionnaire, or test). No conceptual ordering of the particular sentences from one to six is made explicit. In this respect, the sentence contexts utilized in this method are treated as mutually independent.

In contrast, the artificial word inserted into the sentences remains nominally the same, and is expected to grow in its meaning (constructed by the subject) in the direction expected by the investigator (who sets the rule that POSKON = justice). At the intersection of the formal sequence of contexts (see Model 1 above) and developmental continuity of the word, the latter is expected to grow under the impacts of the contexts (and provide information along the lines of Model 2 above). Without doubt, this situation is part of everyday life (learning the rules for contextual insertion of new words), yet the setting is very different from the experimental tasks in the *Aktualgenese* tradition. There is a similar moment (the end goal is pregiven), but in the case of Sander's preferred techniques the stimulus remained the same while the perceptual conditions were gradually changed (to the better, or to the worse). In the W–C test, the latter is not the case. Hence the continuity of intermediate forms (the subject's interpretations of what POSKON means after each sentence) becomes de-emphasized. Even as it necessarily exists in the constructive activity of the subject, the empirical record need not reveal it in full.

Changing Focus: The Drop–out of Intermediate Forms from Attention

As can be seen, Werner's emphasis in the meanings guessing task speaks about retaining the sequential order of the complex (and every time modified) stimulus presentation. Even as the words embedded in the sentences were artificial, the experimenter created "the right" answer and expected the subject to arrive at that answer. In this the "poskon story" differs from the tachistoscopic examples used by Sander, and by Werner himself. While introducing the notion of microgenesis, he used a clinical example of tachistoscopic meaning recognition. A subject was presented the same word combination ("sanfter Wind" = gentle wind) with increasing exposure time, with the following report:

1. "— ? Wind." What stood before "wind" *feels like an adjective specifying the nature of wind*, feels like "warm" or something similar. Definitely not a word defining direction.
2. "— ter Wind" Know now that *the word is "heavier" than "warm"* . . . somehow more abstract.
3. "— cher Wind". Now it looks more like an adjective of direction.
4. "— ter Wind". Now again somewhat more concrete, *it faces me and looks somewhat like "weicher Wind" (soft Wind)*, but "ter" is in my way.
5. Now very clearly: "sanfter Wind". Not at all surprised. I had this actually before in the characteristic feel of the word and the looks of it. (Werner, 1956, p. 348)

The "sanfter Wind" case can be seen as a direct analogue to Sander's *Aktualgenese* experiments. In contrast, the word meaning guessing technique introduced a novelty – a change in the actual nature of the stimulus (by inserting it in different contexts). Werner explained the rationale for the method: "We were predominantly interested in the nature and variety of the processes involved in giving meaning to words – not in the meanings *per se*, i.e., we sought to determine how children of different developmental stages handled the artificial word for each and every one of the six contexts comprising a series" (Werner & Kaplan, 1954, p. 135).

Here the ontogenetic comparison overrides the microgenetic one, and the focus on outcomes de facto overshadows that on the processes. The processes are analyzed in terms of specifiable replacement types (synecdoche, displacement, juxtapositioning and chaining; Werner, 1954). These types describe the variety of trajectories of meaning construction, yet all of these are merely illustrations of the general principle of development: differentiation and dedifferentiation. The latter was assumed to apply universally at all developmental levels.

Generic equation of different levels of analysis (e.g., treating ontogenetic and pathogenetic foci as generically equivalent, under the aegis of the orthogenetic principle (see Werner, 1957, pp. 142–3), moved Werner away from a focus on discovering different forms of the process (the study of which he had called; Werner, 1937). The processes can be described in the data (as in the W–C test), yet the theoretical relevance of such descriptions remains merely illustrative. At the same time, the social pressures in the United States led psychology to turn increasingly toward a hyper-empirical and outcomes-reporting orientation. The inferential tool of statistics became canonized as an orthodox scientific method (Gigerenzer, 1993).

This focus on the reporting of empirical outcome evidence (from experiments which were oriented toward underlying processes in person-environment relations) also occurred in Werner's work – within the cycle of studies based on the sensori-tonic field theory of perception (Werner & Wapner, 1949, 1956). Ironically, exactly when Werner introduced the notion of microgenesis into English-language psychology (Werner, 1956), his own empirical research program was leaving behind the strict process orientation of both Sander's *Aktualgenese* and Werner's own earlier convictions. In the empirical work, the intermediate forms (*Vorgestalten*) reported by subjects in the microgenetic experiments were recorded; but there was no corresponding middle level theoretical scheme – explicit conceptual construction between the orthogenetic principle and the empirical evidence – that would make use of these recordings. The orthogenetic principle did not need empirical evidence (because it was set up as an axiomatic principle), and there were no theoretical constructs between it and the phenomena that were studied. Yet experiments were conducted to demonstrate the functioning of the principle. Demonstration experiments, however, do not develop the theoretical scheme any further. They merely allow the general principle to be restated.

Werner's research program became one of the European-based hostages to the social transformation of the North American social sciences during the 1950s and later. General theoretical frameworks were transformed from their previous role as intellectual tools that help generalization from empirical data, into self-standing belief systems. Henceforth, such systems have even become labeled "theoretical systems" (and are taught in U.S. colleges to undergraduates in courses labeled Theories and Systems). Such systems started to function as "umbrellas" for normatively determined ways of getting empirical data. The notion of methodology became a synonym to methods, and the realm of "right methods" became the criterion for science in empiricism-driven psychology. Methods became autonomous tools that could be transported from one theoretical umbrella framework to another – without worry about the conceptual fit between phenomena, methods, and theory. For Werner, it was not difficult to adjust to such a conceptual climate. After all, he was primarily an experimenter and interpreter of empirical phenomena who combined that – in the best European tradition – with general theory building. Yet he never turned into a pure theoretician.

Werner and Kaplan's metatheoretical orthogenetic principle was set into place as the golden rule of development – thus fitting the umbrella function now allotted to theories. When Sander's methodological innovations grew out of Krueger's (at times vague) theorizing, a new focus (on the dynamics of *Vorgestalten*) in investigation became possible. This was not the case during the 1950s for Werner – the orthogenetic principle turned into a general umbrella for many different empirical research efforts using different versions of the microgenetic methods without the necessity of constructing a theory of microgenesis (separately from onto-, phylo-, patho-, or culturo-genesis). Hence there was no need for further analysis of *Vorgestalten* that were emerging in the experiments.

Transformations of Microgenesis in North America

While the origins of the *Aktualgenese* and microgenesis ideas can be located in the German context of the 1920s and 1930s, the further development of these notions was a phenomenon of mostly American context,[11] from the 1950s onward. Although Heinz Werner was one of its initiators, its further development beyond the late 1950s filled it with the dominance of nondevelopmental explanatory systems. The concept of learning – originally used for description of the nature of specific processes (e.g., classical or instrumental conditioning were mechanisms explaining learning) – became an explanatory concept itself. Thus, claims like "X is established by learning" became explanatory, rather than requiring explanation themselves. Furthermore, psychology since the 1950s has been losing interest in the study of

---

[11] The other relevant extension took place in Sweden, where Gudmund Smith and Ulf Kragh developed a specific set of methods to study personality on the basis of *Aktualgenese*. Their percept-genetic analysis includes a variety of differential psychological methods (see Kragh & Smith, 1970)

psychological processes, and has moved toward treating outcomes of these processes as if these entail explanations themselves.

A key publication for the dissemination of knowledge about microgenesis was an article published in 1957, co-authored by John Flavell and Juris Draguns, which provided a substantive overview of the work of the Sander tradition of *Aktualgenese* as well as Werner's microgenesis (Flavell & Draguns, 1957). Flavell had been at Clark University, where he got his Ph.D. in 1955. There he could get a close view of Werner's ideas, whereas Draguns joined him with his interest in the phenomena of perception as studied *Aktual* genetically. In their explanation, "The term 'microgenesis,' first coined by Werner [Werner, 1956], as an approximate translation of the German word *Aktualgenese*, will refer here to *the sequence of events which are assumed to occur in the temporal period between the presentation of a stimulus and the formation of a single, relatively stabilized cognitive response* (percept or thought) to this stimulus" (Flavell & Draguns, 1957, p. 197, emphases added).

It is obvious that Flavell and Draguns attempted to translate the developmental notion of *Aktualgenese* into language understandable to the American psychologists at the time (stimulus, response, sequence of events). They tried to limit the notion of microgenesis to brief cognitive acts, emphasizing two directions within these acts (microgenesis of perception, microgenesis of thought). They failed to see the historical connection with Krueger's theoretical system for microgenetic methodology.[12] More importantly, the constructive developmental orientation – central to Krueger's theory and relevant for Sander's construction of the *Aktualgenese* notion – was diminished by Flavell and Draguns' account. Sander's empirical focus was replaced from the construction of *Vorgestalten* to their mere sequential recording – as a case of a cascade of intermediate responses to the stimulus that merely need time to become recordable. In terms of the models outlined above, relevant features of the developmental focus, Model 2, became replaced by those of Model 1. Growth as an organic process became de-emphasized, while the sequential nature of phenomena remained in its place. In their words,

Sander . . . did develop an explicitly microgenetic theory of perception. . . . He believed that perception is a developmental *process consisting of a*

[12] E.g., they stated (Flavell & Draguns, 1957, p. 198): "Krueger developed a *complicated and somewhat esoteric* general theory *which is of only tangential relevance to microgenesis.*" (emphasis added)

number of conceptually distinct phases. . . . He granted that the precursors of the final percept are not observable in the normal, perceptual process. However, he argued that if one experimentally blocks the formation of the clear, complete percepts by presenting stimuli very briefly, in bad lighting, in peripheral vision, etc., *one can elicit these perceptual precursors.* (Flavell & Draguns, 1957, p. 198, emphases added)

The precursors here are not viewed as novel constructions, but merely as a sequence of stages that lead to the correct outcome. Of course the *Vorgestalt* phenomena were not forgotten, but instead of being viewed developmentally, these were presented as examples of how affect disrupts the process of unfolding, rather than how it functions as a resource for development of a new understanding:

Of particular interest to Sander and his students *was the stage just preceding the formation of the final, stable percept.* In this *Vorgestalt* or preconfiguration phase the *S has constructed a tentative, highly labile Gestalt which is more* undifferentiated internally, more regular, and *more simple in form and content than is the final form* which is to follow it. The construction of this initial, fluxlike pre-Gestalt is said to *be accompanied by decidedly unpleasant feelings* and unrest which later subside when a final, stable configuration is achieved. (ibid., p. 199, emphases added)

In Sander's understanding, *Vorgestalten* could be richer in form and content than the final percept – a point that is decidedly overlooked here. Although Flavell and Draguns spoke of construction here, their reference was limited to the construction of simpler, incomplete, hypotheses about the final percept. Their notion was that of selection between available options (for *Vorgestalt* formation), rather than construction of novel forms. They did not emphasize the holistic reorganization of the forms in the process of microgenesis (while that reorganization was crucial for *Aktualgenese*).

It is interesting to note that the work of the other relevant European developmentalist, Jean Piaget, underwent a similar translation by the recipients in North America (and promoted by the same person – John Flavell): Piaget's constructionist developmental emphasis was viewed as providing a stage theory. This translational shift was one of relocating emphases, yet it resulted in the loss of the developmental nature of the investigation. Piaget's stages have become a target of diagnosis in the most nondevelopmental sense, and Sander's microgenetic method was made into yet one more method to study perception as it is. A similar story was present in the efforts to turn Vygotsky's and

Sakharov's (and Ach's) concept formation method – which focused on the processual side of concept construction – into an intelligence test (and having to accept that it does not fit; see Van der Veer & Valsiner, 1991, pp. 282–3). In the latter half of the twentieth century, psychologists have worked productively to eliminate developmental theoretical and methodological ideas and techniques from their thinking. The social reasons for such a systematic eradication remain to be investigated.

Some of the social reasons for looking down at Sander's research program were evident in Flavell and Draguns' own evaluation. Thus, they claimed that "Many of these studies [of perceptual microdevelopment] *would be considered quite poor* by present-day methodological standards. This is especially, although not exclusively, true of research done by Sander and his school. *Few Ss were used* and *these were seldom experimentally naive, statistics were inadequate or absent*, and methods of measuring and evaluating perceptual responses were *informal* to say the least" (Flavell & Draguns, 1957, p. 200, emphases added).

It is quite interesting to look back at this evaluation with a forty-year hindsight. Since 1957 psychology has indeed become a mechanistic application of standardized methods of the study of outcomes based on large samples of subjects, whose naiveté is seen as a proof of purity of their value as research subjects. Ironically, the criticism by Flavell and Draguns was made in one of these few areas (perception research) where intense single-case experimental analyses still prevail. Most curious is the use of Werner's developmental thought in the process of eliminating the study of development from the microgenetic analysis.

Microgenesis subsequently did not gain wide popularity in U.S. psychology (in the 1960s and 1970s), even though Draguns (1983, 1984) attempted to propagate it. His account of it by the 1980s is worth a closer look. For instance, in 1984 he claimed:

Microgenesis is *an adaptive act* that involves the various *resources* of the person. Traditionally, it has been studied on the basis of the person's verbal report, which, however, provides glimpses into only one of the several response systems involved. The theoretical stance of the pioneers of microgenetic investigation (Sander ... Werner) helped them conceive of these progressions as instances of a self-fueled and self-propelled development with a specific direction and a predetermined outcome. *By the same token, their theoretical perspective caused them to underplay the role of experience and learning in these microgenetic experiences.* That learning plays an important role in microgenesis is demonstrated by the observation of a great many microgenetic investigators that the presentation of a stimulus sequence can be effectively accomplished one time per subject. Microgenetic studies lend themselves poorly to the establishment of test-retest reliability! More subtly, the subject learns the features of specific subjects presented and also learns how to learn – by establishing more efficient and effective strategies of information extraction. If the subject learns, or attempts to, then the question arises, What impels him or her to learn? Why does the person not sit passively and wait for the termination of the progression of the series from ambiguity to clarity. (Draguns, 1984, p. 10, emphasis added)

Thus, the crucial issue of development is seen not as construction of novelty in lifetime experience, but merely development with a specific direction and a predetermined outcome. Development becomes explained by the concept of learning, rather than learning by some theoretical system of development. By the 1980s, Draguns had completely reversed the original (Krueger-Sander) emphasis of *Aktualgenese*. Microgenesis is no longer viewed as genesis, but merely as a process of a search for a solution. True, some nuance of "heuristic activity" is mentioned:

What is fundamental to microgenesis is a *process of search* that is triggered by the discrepancy between the information inherent in the stimulus and the activity, task, or solution demanded by the observer. Microgenesis . . . is *necessarily a heuristic activity* . . . that is triggered by the demand or challenge of going beyond the information given . . . or of completing the incomplete. The operations typically require time and provide the opportunity for observing the *alteration of stages* in the formation of a percept, the attainment of a solution, or the development of a stabilized, automatized response. Thus microgenesis cuts across the domains of functioning into which psychology is so neatly divided – perception, cognition, motivation, and the rest – and may last from seconds to days, or longer, provided that it unfolds in observable time. (Draguns, 1984, p. 4)

Elsewhere (Draguns, 1983), an effort was made to explain microgenesis through the use of cognitive heuristics (*à la* Tversky & Kahnemann). This completes the cycle of first translating the developmental theoretical focus on phenomena (*Aktualgenese* as both a phenomena-based approach, and method) to method per se; then finding that the method produces data that does not fit well with the data from the uses of other methods (created on nondevelopmental bases); and then summoning an essentialistic explanatory label as if that could explain the data.

In contemporary U.S. psychology, microgenesis as a method has a minuscule share (Catan, 1986). As described above, that is not surprising – stripped from its original developmental theoretical backing, and viewed in comparison with other methods, it has little use for contemporary psychological discourse. It can be (and has been) picked up only in cases where the investigator's target phenomenon gives it a priority over other methods. The result of the transformation of the microgenesis concept is visible in the work of Robert Siegler (Siegler, 1996; Siegler & Crowley, 1991) on children's arithmetic problem-solving strategies, as well as in discussions that it engendered (Fowler, 1992; Pressley, 1992; Siegler & Crowley, 1992).

Siegler's substantive interest has been in revealing the discovery of strategies of arithmetic operations. As strategies can be viewed as means to an end, they can be viewed as processes unfolding in time. As such, the microgenetic line of methodological thought becomes relevant again. Yet for Siegler, the intensive analysis of aspects of change need not include a focus on how a new cognitive strategy is emerging (that would entail Model 2, see above), but rather a description of the sequence in which a child takes over (discovers) a strategy that already exists (but has not been utilized by this child yet). This focus equals Model 1, described above. For Siegler, the ideal technique equals that of a movie (rather than a sequence of still pictures; cf. Siegler & Crawley, 1991, p. 607). Yet no movie is possible independently of the viewer – the movie emerges in the process of looking at a sequence of still frames that are tied together through the viewer's perceptual synthesis of the whole event.

Siegler and Crowley's (1991, p. 613) concrete examples allow further scrutiny of the ways in which the notion of microgenesis has survived in contemporary psychology. They describe a five-year-old girl who is documented to use the "min strategy" of addition for the first time in a longitudinal follow-up:

E: OK, Brittany, how much is 2 + 5?
B: 2 + 5 – [whispers] 6, 7 – it's 7.
E: How did you know that?
B: [excitedly] Never counted.
E: You didn't count?
B: Just said it – I *just said after 6 something* – 7 – 6, 7

E: You did? Why did you say 6, 7?

B: Cause I wanted to see what it really was.

E: OK, well – so, did you – what – you didn't have to start at one, you didn't count 1, 2, 3, you just said 6, 7?

B: Yeah – smart answer (Siegler & Crowley, 1991, p. 613, emphasis added)

In this example, there is limited access (see emphasis) to the reflection by the child about the process that actually led to the strategy discovery. Trying out "just saying something" after 5 is a glimpse of *Aktualgenese* in Sander's sense. Yet that information is limited, and is basically unnecessary for Siegler's goal – that of diagnosing at what precise moment in the longitudinal course the new strategy is in its place for the first time. This goal is a regular nondevelopmental question asked usually about outcomes of children's development. The nature of the adding strategy as verifiable through looking at (coding) process information becomes translated into an outcome category. In this respect, Siegler's study necessarily used the Model 1 type of sequential information (see p. 305, above).

However, the phenomena of administering simple addition tasks to young children provide evidence for the interdependence of the social and cognitive lines of psychological experiences (for both the subject, and the experimenter). A five-year-old girl (Whitney) was found to utilize an interesting complex of cognitive and social constructions (with the participation of the investigator) in a simple addition task:

E: How much is 4 + 3?

W: 5, 6, 7, I think it's 7.

E: 7, OK, *how* did you *know* that?

W: Because *I am smart* and *I just knew it.*

E: You can tell me. *I heard you counting. I heard you.* Tell me how you counted.

W: I just–*I didn't count anything*–[long pause] I *just added numbers onto it.*

E: Can you tell me how you added numbers?

W: No.

E: *Come on, Whitney – come on, we have to do this*, OK?

W: OK [in a bored voice]. 3, add one makes 4, add one makes 5, add one makes 6, add one makes 7, add one makes 8.

E: *Wait,* but how did you know what 4 + 3 was?

W: Cause *I did what I just showed you*. I *just used my mouth* to figure it out. (Siegler & Crowley, 1991, p. 613, emphases added)

Perhaps the microgenetic focus here adds little knowledge about the emergence of arithmetic operations, but it certainly illuminates the sociogenetic nature of experimentation with children.

The traditions of both Sander and Werner were relevant for the development of Lev Vygotsky's "method of double stimulation," which in its focus is a microgenetic one. Other research on the emergence (microevolution) of children's mathematical representations (Meira, 1995; Saada-Robert, 1992a, 1992b, 1994) has linked the social-interactive and cognitive processes. Such a widening of the scope of the process-oriented empirical studies brings investigators back to look at the levels of different qualities.

As was evident above, the fate of the notion of microgenesis – both theoretically and as a method – has been quite unfortunate over the last sixty years. The notion widened (and then disappeared, or was translated into a nondevelopmental concept). It is in the widening of microgenesis in the direction of sociogenesis that a need for organization appears. Madelon Saada-Robert has suggested that

A *distinction* must be made between problem solving situations, *where the objective is explicit and fixed at the onset* (even though there is always some degree of interpretation by the subject who appropriates the situation) and more *open learning situations, without a defined goal given at the beginning*. In this second case, the goal is defined by the subject; either an explicit overall goal's initially specified, or more implicit goals are progressively defined in the course of the resolution activity. In all situations, there are goals and sequences of resolution, even without solutions. *In this context, the microgenesis of resolution can be viewed as a change of meaning for the subject.* (Saada-Robert, 1994, p. 57)

She suggested two levels of analysis: microgenesis and mesogenesis. The latter was meant to accommodate Siegler's studies (which focus on the transfer from discovered strategies to new contexts), while "Microgenetic study . . . aims at understanding knowledge construction in context, from several perspectives: it emphasizes the mechanism of internalization by procedure sequencing in relation to the subject's intentions (his goals and meanings)" (Saada-Robert, 1994, p. 63).

So, after a long wandering in the field of empirical psychology, the microgenetic orientation seems to return to its sociogenetic roots, similar to the ones charted out by Felix Krueger and Friedrich Sander. Yet what that return tells us about the progress of psychology during the twentieth century is still an open (and perhaps somewhat disturbing) question.

Conclusion: Intellectual Interdependency and Socially Constructed Forgetting

The history in psychology of holistic perspectives and their corresponding interest in the study of complex psychological functions provides us with an intricate story of how socially guided intellectual interdependency can lead to the extinction of a possibly productive direction for investigation. As we have seen, all levels of the social organization of intellectual interdependency participated in it. The social and regional rivalries inside Germany, and political conflicts between countries, set the stage for different holistic thought complexes in German psychology. Domineering professorial egos of the persons who invented and propagated these complexes further specified the rhetoric disputes about ideas, and their empirical elaborations. Last (but not least), the social history of psychology at large – linked with the relocation of its geographical origins in Europe to the United States during the 1930s – guided the transformation of ideas.

In our story, we saw the disappearance (or at least the reduction of their relevance) of two important ideas in psychology. First, the Austro-German holistic perspectives on the complex nature of psychological phenomena became transformed into complex procedures for the analysis of elementaristic data. The complexity of the phenomena became forgotten – and hence the question of different levels of organization of the phenomena (Cairns, 1986).

Second, the initial focus on development which was present in Wundt's *Völkerpsychologie*, Krueger's *Ganzheitspsychologie*, Sander's *Aktualgenese*, and Werner's and Kaplan's orthogenetic principle was eliminated from both the theoretical and empirical attention fields of psychologists. The sociogenetic idea that was so evident in the German holistic perspectives disappeared together with the focus on development.

More important than the documentation of such socially guided changes in psychology is the analysis of the specific mechanisms through which these changes happen. Sociopolitical rhetorics lead historians of psychology to either silences about once existing perspectives (e.g., German psychologists of the 1990s probably know as little about Krueger and Sander as Soviet psychologists knew about Vygotsky during the period 1936–56), or toward reevaluations. Both hero myths and dismissal stories about scientists or schools of thought are constructed by others for current social needs. Thus, Vygotskian thinking may be claimed to be ahead of Piagetian thought; or Gestalt psychology may be claimed to be more important for psychology at large than *Ganzheitspsychologie*. Such statements have no scientific value by themselves. They may reflect – as Janet suggested (see the motto of Chapter 3) – a particular fashion change in general psychological discourse (e.g., Vygotskian talk has come into fashion, Piagetian is vanishing), or a sociopolitical stance (after all, the Gestalt psychologists ended up being on "the right side" in World War II, while the case for *Ganzheitspsychologie* was unclear), or some other short-term perspective. But, in a curious parallel to the story told in this chapter and to the art of photography, they can do no more than temporarily freeze psychology's development, i.e., present a more or less subjective picture of the state of art in psychology from the vantage point of that particular time.

At the substantive level, psychology has lived through a process of separation of theoretical and empirical domains of inquiry during the twentieth century. As a result, the "old grand" theories have become general "systems of ideas" which are followed by believers and converts, rather than used as means for further intellectual elaboration. At the same time, empirical investigations are conducted under the rigor of consensually established (and institutionally sanctified) sets of "right methods" – in ways distanced from general theories. That practice of accumulating empirical evidence through socially accepted methods is legitimized by the general ideological claim that psychology is an empirical science. Under such conditions, it is no surprise that specific methods (e.g., studying microgenesis) became historically distanced from their conceptual frameworks of origin, and abandoned because they did not quite fit with the present toolbox psychologists use to evaluate the objectivity of research and methods.

Interestingly, intellectual interdependency appears in different ways as scientists from different countries, and countries, interpenetrate one another's intellectual worlds. While in the case of the migration of Continental European holistic ideas to North America, one can observe the systematic disappearance of both the foci on integral wholes and on development, the very same ideas migrating into East-ern Europe and Russia show us an almost opposite tendency. Devel-opmental ideas fared well in Russian psychology (until the crack down during the mid 1930s), and holistic speculations have always found a home in Russian intellectual interchanges. In Chapter 8, we will cover the development of Lev Vygotsky's ideas in his social and intellectual contexts. This is meant to complement our previous anal-ysis of Vygotsky's quest for a psychology that emphasizes the notion of creative synthesis as its core (Van der Veer & Valsiner, 1991). Maybe it is exactly that desire to make sense of the emergence of new per-spectives that makes the historical scrutiny of ideas fascinating.

CHAPTER EIGHT

Vygotsky's World of Concepts

Early specialization is not an essential requirement for outstanding academic achievement. In applying their knowledge to new fields, outsiders have often realized major scientific breakthroughs. Such cross-fertilization, or "bisocation" (Tweney, Doherty, and Mynatt, 1981), has been the rule in the history of science, and it may be a particularly fruitful strategy.

In psychology, we have the examples of, among others, Pavlov, Freud, and Piaget. Pavlov was a physiologist who only turned to the study of conditional reflexes when he was about fifty-two years old (Mecacci, 1979). Freud originally specialized as a biologist and neuroanatomist and began developing psychoanalysis when he was about forty years old (Sulloway, 1992). Piaget trained as a biologist, specialized in mollusk taxonomy, and did his first work with children several years after he had finished his dissertation on mollusks (Vidal, 1994).

The principal figure of this chapter, Lev Vygotsky, is yet another example of such an outsider who changed the psychological landscape. Throughout his life, he was fascinated with literature and art. He studied law, history, and philosophy; and during the first seven years of his career, he combined work as a teacher at different schools with that of an art critic for various local newspapers. He only formally became a research psychologist when he was twenty-eight years of age (Van der Veer & Valsiner, 1991b, Vygodskaya & Lifanova, 1996).

Unlike Pavlov, Freud, and Piaget, however, Vygotsky died young, at the age of thirty-seven. At that age, Pavlov was still working on the digestive system. It would take fourteen more years before he began developing his theory of conditional reflexes, a theory that he refined and elaborated during another thirty-four more years of research. At that age, Freud had not yet written a single word on psychoanalysis, the theory that he would be revising and elaborating for approximately forty-four more years. At that age, Piaget had published his first psychology books, but he worked for another forty-five more years to develop and change his ideas.

Both the fact that Vygotsky came as an outsider to the field of psychology and the fact that he died young are crucial for the understanding of his works. We will see that his psychological ideas were enriched by notions coming from linguistics, biology, philosophy etc., and that these notions continued to influence his thinking until the end of his life. It will also become clear that he left us with a legacy that is open to many and diverse interpretations. Vygotsky died when his theoretical ideas were still in a flux, and when no finished, coherent system of ideas was yet in sight. In no sense can we say that his ideas had crystallized and stabilized. Even within the decade that he worked as a professional psychologist, researchers have been able to distinguish several different periods. What we have, then, is a body of work, a collection of hypotheses and ideas, which is basically unfinished, and that defies easy classification. However, what we can do is to attempt to situate his activities and theories in the complex fabric of the social and scientific culture of his time, and show in what ways he contributed to the sociogenetic account of mind. It is to such an analysis that we now turn.

Vygotsky's Life Course

Little is known of Lev Vygotsky's childhood and youth. The recently republished reminiscences by his youth friend Semyon Dobkin (Levitin, 1982; 1990; Feigenberg, 1996), which until recently formed virtually the only source of information, have been enriched with detailed memories by Vygotsky's oldest daughter Gita Vygodskaya and the fine archival research of Tamara Lifanova (Vygodskaya & Lifanova, 1996). Kozulin (1990) and Van der Veer and Valsiner (1991b) have contributed some historical background information.

Lev Semyonovich Vygodsky[1] (1896–1934) was born in Orsha and grew up in Gomel near Chernobyl. He was the second child of Semyon L'vovich Vygodsky (1869–1931) and Cecilia Moiseyevna Vygodskaya (1874–1935). He had an older sister, four younger sisters, and two younger brothers. The youngest brother died of tuberculosis at

---

[1] He later changed his name to Vygotsky.

the age of fourteen; the other brother died about one year later of typhus. It was while taking care of his mother (who also suffered from tuberculosis) and his youngest brother that Vygotsky contracted the disease from which he would eventually die (Vygodskaya & Lifanova, 1996).

Semyon Vygodsky was a bank employee and a representative of an insurance company in Gomel who ended his career as the branch manager of the Industrial Bank in Moscow. He seems to have been a respected citizen in Gomel who actively participated in societal activities and helped, among other things, in creating the excellent local public library. In 1903, he played a major role in a political event, although it remains a bit obscure what exactly his role was. According to his granddaughter (Vygodskaya & Lifanova, 1996, p. 26), he played an active role in the organization of the Jewish self-defence during the pogrom, which occurred during that year. The attackers lost almost as many men as they managed to kill Jews (Feigenberg, 1996, p. 15). Kozulin (1990, pp. 13–14), however, showed that Semyon Vygodsky played an important role as a witness for the defense at the subsequent trial. During this trial, which – characteristic for the anti-Semitic stance of the authorities at that time – was organized to convict the successful defenders, Vygodsky senior pleaded the democratic rights of the Jews. Somehow, the role of active participant and witness seem difficult to combine.

Vygodsky senior is remembered as a very intelligent and cultivated person, disposed to bitter irony, (Feigenberg, 1996) with a difficult, harsh character, who left the upbringing of the children to his wife (Vygodskaya & Lifanova, 1996). At an early stage, he gave his eldest son a copy of Spinoza's *Ethics*, which would remain the latter's favorite book throughout his life, and would fundamentally determine his world view. Semyon Vygodsky financially supported the family of his deceased brother, which explains why the Vygodskys, in principle a middle-class family, lived a rather modest life (Vygodskaya & Lifanova, 1996).

Cecilia Moiseyevna is said to have been a totally different person. She is described as a sensitive, gentle, meek person who formed the heart and soul of the family. A teacher by training, she devoted all her time to the household and her children; she created a warm and loving atmosphere. Like her husband, she was a very cultured person. She was proficient in several modern languages and seems to have been infatuated with Heinrich Heine's poetry. With her husband, she created an intellectual and emotional atmosphere where the reading and passionate discussion of books were the most important family activities. Every night the parents and all the children would gather around a large table to read aloud poetry or prose, to discuss recently seen theater performances, and to talk about anything else that came up. Perhaps Tolstoy was mistaken after all, in claiming that all happy families are alike.

Lev Vygodsky (or Vygotsky as we will from now on call him) is remembered as a lively, sensitive, essentially normal but intellectually precocious child. He loved to play chess, collect postmarks, and ride horses. During the summer, with his many friends, he often went swimming and boating in the local river. He soon showed unusual intellectual abilities and received his first education at home from a gifted private tutor, a mathematician named Solomon Markovich Ashpiz. Ashpiz had as a student been expelled from the university and exiled to Siberia, because he had participated in the student democratic movement. After his return, he earned his living by giving private lessons to gifted children in whom he tried to develop the ability to think independently. He taught all subjects but had a predilection for Latin and mathematics. Lev Vygotsky he reckoned among the two best pupils he ever had. After five years of study with Ashpiz, Vygotsky finally entered one of the two local gymnasia – the private Jewish gymnasium for boys headed by a certain Dr. Ratner – to go through the last two years of study and to receive his diploma. Even among the Ratner students, who seem to have reached a rather high level, Vygotsky excelled (Feigenberg, 1996, pp. 26–8). He finished the gymnasium with a gold medal for having obtained the highest grade for all subjects (which included Latin, German, French, physics, mathematics, religion). At home he had added the study of English, Greek, and Hebrew (Vygodskaya & Lifanova, 1996). In addition, he probably knew Yiddish as well, like his private teacher Ashpiz and many others (although there is no indication that the Vygodskys among themselves spoke Yiddish). In later years he would write reviews of theater performances of Jewish groups presented in Yiddish (e.g., Vygotsky, 1923a, 1923b, 1923c). Vygotsky's childhood friend Dobkin has suggested that a local literary magazine, edited in the years 1911 to 1913, by students of Ratner's gymnasium and university students, may have published Vygotsky's first articles (Feigenberg, 1996, p. 28).

In those years the Esperanto movement still flourished. Part of the discussions about proper psychological terminology at the Sixth International Congress of Psychology in Geneva, for example, were conducted in this *internacia lingvo* (Claparède, 1910; see Chapter 1). In Russia, the movement was actively supported by Lev Tolstoy and led by N. Kabanov, a *privat-dozent* at Moscow University (e.g., Kabanov, 1913). Through his cousin David, the young Lev Vygotsky became acquainted with Esperanto, and for a number of years he collected foreign postmarks by corresponding with other enthusiasts of unhampered international communication. The cousin was a gifted and remarkable person himself. David Isaakovich Vygodsky (1893–1943) was a linguist and philologist who had studied at St. Petersburg. Three years Vygotsky's senior, he exerted a considerable influence upon him. He wrote countless literary articles for the same journals that Vygotsky had published in (perhaps one of the reasons why Vygotsky changed his name) and for foreign journals. He earned his living as a translator of poetry and prose and was a minor poet himself. He translated from Spanish, Portuguese, Italian, German, French, English, and Hebrew into Russian. He was close to the members of the OPOYAZ group, a branch of the formal school in Russian literature, with Viktor Shklovsky and Roman Yakobson as its major representatives (Feigenberg, 1996). During the civil war in Spain he served as the intermediary between the Soviet authorities and the anti-Franco movement. He was arrested in 1938 and died in the Gulag Archipelago in 1943. His arrest led to an unprecedented and courageous protest by his Leningrad friends (with Zoshchenko and Shklovsky among them), who turned to Stalin and other authorities to demand his release (Van der Veer & Valsiner, 1991b). David Vygodsky's apartment was a meeting place for writers, poets, and students of literature, and it may have been here that Vygotsky first met members of the formalist school and the acmeic poet Mandel'shtam, one of his favorite poets, whom he would quote much later in *Thinking and Speech*.

One might ask to what extent Vygotsky identified himself with the Jewish religion and the Jewish people. The Vygodskys were not religious (Vygodskaya & Lifanova, 1996, pp. 289–90; see also Vygotsky, 1931, p. 163, where he writes: "in peoples developing under the influence of religious prejudices, for example, the Jews") but held to the Jewish traditions. Thus, Vygotsky received a traditional Jewish education, reading the Torah in Hebrew, delivering a speech at his Bar Mitsva, and so on. He grew up in a Jewish milieu, had a Jewish private tutor, and went to a Jewish private gymnasium. If he had not realized that he was a Jew, external circumstances would have made him conscious of it. The latent anti-semitism in Russia often became manifest and was used by the Tsarist authorities for their own goals. Actual pogroms were infrequent (Vygotsky experienced two of them, however) but various harassments were the norm. At any rate, already at an early age, Vygotsky developed an intense interest in Jewish history. When he was fifteen years old, several of his sisters, their friends, and some classmates got the idea to study Jewish history together and asked him to preside over their meetings. The topic soon led the group of young adolescents to regard more abstract questions like "What makes a nation a nation?," "What is the role of personalities (of statesmen) in history?," and so on. These questions they discussed for the historical period covered by the Bible, using the Bible and historical books as their source. Dobkin remembered that Vygotsky played a major role in these meetings and that he defended a Hegelian, historic, and dialectical method. He also made the interesting remark that Vygotsky's own style of speaking, which like his writing was full of repetitions and paraphrases, was possibly influenced by the biblical texts he studied (Feigenberg, 1996).

Five years later, we find the first papers in which Vygotsky explicitly addresses Jewish topics. In a journal article, on the occasion of the seventy-fifth anniversary of Lermontov's death, he discussed the stereotyped image of the Yid in Russian literature. Such writers as Pushkin, Gogol, Dostoyevsky, and Turgenyev had confirmed the cliché of the greedy, ridiculous, and treacherous Yid, worthy of contempt. According to Vygotsky, Lermontov was the first to divert, albeit incompletely, from this cliché by writing a piece in which Jews play a more worthy and tragic role (Vygotsky, 1916a). In one of his two (strangely divergent) reviews of Belyj's astonishing novel *Peterburg*, he pointed out the implicit and explicit anti-Semitic traits of the book, and remarked that Belyj continued the tradition of the Russian authors mentioned above (Vygotsky, 1916b). Finally, in a paper published shortly after the revolution, he welcomed the liberation from the oppressive power, but evocatively argued that the Jews were not yet ready for this painful freedom, full of choices. They were like the Israelites who left Egypt: accustomed to slavery, unprepared, paralysed, and frightened for the future. Nevertheless, the Jews must take their fate in their own hands, their consciousness must be raised. But this could not be accomplished by the decrees or resolutions of one or the other political party. The people's will, its consciousness (cf. Hegel's *Geist*) is deeply rooted in history, and therefore has its own inertia. Politicians cannot create it overnight but can only hope to lay bare this will and to see the renaissance of this consciousness (Vygotsky, 1917).

In sum, then, Vygotsky grew up in a secular Jewish milieu and acquired a thorough knowledge of Jewish history, the history of the Jewish religion, etc. He also published on these matters, but mostly from a philosophical, Hegelian angle. There is no doubt that he identified himself with the Jewish people, but, as far as we know, he kept aloof of practical, political matters connected with the question of Jewish identity. He probably did not develop the intense involvement with Judaism that his later acquaintance Kurt Lewin manifested (cf. Lück, 1993).

University Years

The fact that Vygotsky finished the gymnasium with a gold medal did not guarantee that he could enter the university. Formerly, three to five percent (depending on the university) of the student population were allowed to be of Jewish origin, and Jewish gold medal winners were sure to be admitted. However, just a few months before Vygotsky was to take his examinations, it was decided by the authorities that Jews were no longer to be admitted on the basis of previous results, but were to be enrolled by casting lots. Fortunately, Vygotsky belonged to the lucky few, and he started taking courses at Moscow University and the private Shanyavsky University. At Moscow University, he began studying medicine but quickly changed to law. Neither of these studies particularly attracted him, but they were the only ones that guaranteed Jews relative freedom and a reasonable income (Van der Veer & Valsiner, 1991b). He did not hesitate, however, to attend other courses in other faculties, and for a time attended a seminar given by the famous Humboldtian scholar Gustav Shpet, who together with Chelpanov founded the Faculty of Psychology at Moscow University. At Shanyavsky University, Vygotsky followed courses in philosophy, psychology, and education (taught by Pavel Blonsky). It was around this time that his interest in psychology became more evident. Characteristically, his growing interest in psychology was at least in part connected with the theater and literature. Dobkin has suggested that Vygotsky grew interested in psychological matters through his reading of novels by authors such as Dostoyevsky (Feigenberg, 1996). We will see that he also eventually became fascinated by the way pieces of art and literature establish an emotional reaction in the person watching or reading them.

We have seen that Vygotsky grew up in a family that revered literature and the theater. It is only natural, then, that he and his sisters acquired a penchant for literature. Throughout his life, Vygotsky attended the newest theater performances, read the latest poetry and prose, and even to the Russian standards, his literary expertise was exceptionally good. He knew dozens of fragments of poems and novels by heart, and he would often quote appropriate lines in daily conversation and in scientific writings. Literature was his first love, and he would never betray it. As a student he became fascinated with Shakespeare's *Hamlet,* and he spent years studying the literature about this play and in writing his own analysis of it. Eventually, this resulted in his master's thesis (Vygotsky, 1916) and part of his doctoral dissertation (Vygotsky, 1925). With his older sister, who had joined him in Moscow, he went to all major performances.

The information about Vygotsky's university years is scarce, but we may safely assume that he exploited these years to the best. He attentively followed the literary scene, missed no theater performance and, quite probably, published more reviews in literary journals than are so far known. In addition, he attended seminars and courses on various topics (including psychological ones) of his liking. According to his daughter (Vygodskaya & Lifanova, 1996), he managed to graduate from both Moscow University and Shanyavsky University. That would mean that, apart from his master's thesis on Shakespeare written at Shanyavsky University, there would somewhere be another thesis on, perhaps, Roman law, or the concept of natural and civil rights in Spinoza's *Tractatus Politicus.* Be that as it may, the final months of Vygotsky's studies must have been turbulent: He graduated at the end of 1917, the year that shook the world.

Revolution and War

We know little of Vygotsky's political convictions and it seems that politics, in the narrow sense of the word, did not interest him (Feigenberg, 1996). It is likely, though, that he welcomed the October Revolution in 1917. Only fools believed everything the new authorities promised, and only inveterate cynics and political opponents believed that absolutely nothing would come of it. Vygotsky was neither, but he was young (and thus more of a fool than of a cynic) and, as we saw above, realized the great advantages of reform for the many. Years later, Vygotsky (1923d) would write a positive review of Reed's (1919/1977) simplistic and severely biased account of the October Revolution, *Ten Days That Shook the World*, and concur with its author that the communist leaders did no more than canalize the heroic will of the masses. But even in that unquestioning review for a local newspaper, he managed to touch upon a philosophical question, i.e., that of the relative contribution of leaders and masses in bringing about historical change, the problem that he had discussed in his adolescent days, using Tolstoy's well-known essay in *War and Peace* as a source of inspiration.

Quite likely, his own private ideal was close to that of the Enlightenment. Reason would bring tolerance, progress, and social improvement (cf. Mead's similar goal in Chapter 6). Emancipation of Jews, workers, and farmers would come by way of free education for everybody. His father had been active as the president of the Gomel branch of the Society for the Dissemination of Enlightenment among the Jews of Russia (Feigenberg, 1996, p. 16), and in this capacity helped to found the local library. After the Revolution, Vygotsky would continue along the same line by giving innumerable lectures at a labor school, a trade school for metal workers, for example. It was his conviction that uneducated people and physically or mentally handicapped children could be lifted to a higher level by gaining access to cultural attainments and knowledge. Indeed, one of the reasons for his immense involvement with the education of handicapped (deaf, blind) children was his fear that they would be cut off from the treasures of civilization.

Dobkin (in Feigenberg, 1996, pp. 52–3) remembered that, in the first months after the February Revolution in 1917, Vygotsky wrote several brochures in which he objectively summarized the views of one of the many revolutionary political parties (e.g., the Socialist Revolutionary Party). No one has as yet unearthed these brochures, but if the story proves true, then it would testify to the fact that Vygotsky was more of a sympathetic bystander, i.e., he welcomed the idea of major reforms but was relatively indifferent as to which political faction would eventually carry the day.

It seems true that the philosophy of Marxism (rather than its practical application in the Soviet Union) appealed to Vygotsky. In his work we find the standard stock of quotes from the writings of Marx, Engels, and Lenin – we also find this in the work of most of his

progressive contemporary psychologists, which had become something of a shibboleth of the right world view at the time – but we also
find passages that show that he had studied and assimilated the works
of, above all, Marx and Engels. His excellent knowledge of Hegel's
work formed a good preparation, of course, for the reading of Marx
and, to an extent, Lenin. In addition, he managed to integrate part of
the Marxist anthropology in his theoretical thinking; i.e., the theses
that human beings are tool using and tool making animals, and that
man is a social being. We will see, however, that such notions were
far from exclusive to Marxism and, in fact, it would be an interesting
intellectual exercise to investigate to what extent Vygotsky's theories
are dependent upon the Marxist legacy. In this sense, the modern
ahistoric trend to ignore the Marxist, leftist elements of Vygotsky's
thinking can be understood, although not justified. Historically, leftist
students of psychology fought hard to get Vygotsky's ideas accepted
by mainstream psychology. Ironically, now that Vygotsky has finally
become accepted by textbook writers as a towering figure of developmental psychology, it may turn out that he lost some of his distinctive
features in the process.

Working in Gomel

After his graduation, and stay of several months in Kuybishev
(called Samara before and after the communist reign), Vygotsky returned to his native Gomel. The living conditions in Gomel were quite
difficult. World War I continued and the treaty of Brest-Litovsk in
March 1918 brought no substantial improvements. The Germans controlled large parts of Byelorussia and had installed a puppet regime
in the Ukraine. Gomel was occupied and looted by German and
Ukraine troops. In addition, after the October Revolution of 1917, Red
and White troops fought each other. In January 1919 Gomel was
liberated from the Germans by the Red troops. Even then, the situation in the country as a whole did not much improve. The fighting
continued, the famine peaked at around 1921–2, and many children
roamed the country without their parents. It is estimated that these
homeless children (*bezprizorniki*) totaled about seven million in 1921
(Stevens, 1982). They caused the authorities many problems (e.g., de-
linquency, prostitution) and eventually Vygotsky would be involved
in finding a solution for this major social problem. However, during
the period immediately after the Revolution, Vygotsky could not find

a permanent job, and he temporarily earned his living by giving private lessons (Vygodskaya & Lifanova, 1996). During this period, he changed his name to Vygotsky, not so much because he felt dissatisfied with the root *vygod* (from *vygoda* = profit, or advantage), but because he traced the origin of this name to the name of a Jewish quarter in a small Byelorussian town.

In 1918, Vygotsky made a dangerous trip to Kiev with his mother and younger brother Dodik. The plan was to travel to the Crimea, where the climate was beneficial to the health of his brother, who suffered from a progressive form of tuberculosis. However, when they arrived in Kiev, having covered about one fourth of the route, the doctors decided that Dodik's condition did not allow further travel. The Vygodskys had to stay in Kiev for several months while Dodik was being cared for in a medical clinic (Vygodskaya & Lifanova, 1996). This situation did not prevent Vygotsky from meeting interesting people and making new acquaintances. Dobkin (Feigenberg, 1996) remembered that it was during his stay in Kiev that Vygotsky became friends with the poet Ilya Ehrenburg and the philosopher Makovel'sky; and Dobkin surmised that during his forced stay in Kiev, Vygotsky may have published literary reviews in the local journals and newspapers. Be that as it may, after several months the Vygodskys returned to Gomel because the doctors feared that Vygotsky's younger brother would not survive the long and dangerous trip to the Crimea.

In Gomel, where his brother would soon die, Vygotsky still had no permanent work. It was only during the spring of 1919, after the liberation of Gomel, that the town slowly came to life again. Frantic attempts to recognize the system of education began, and in the next years Vygotsky gradually became one of the most active and visible local public figures. He and his cousin David began working as teachers of literature and history at various schools and institutions (e.g., labor school, trade school for metal workers, people's school of music). There were many vacancies in the field of education because many opponents of the communist regime refused to continue working and because new groups (e.g., workers, farmers) were admitted to higher education.

In 1920, Vygotsky suffered his first serious attack of tuberculosis, and he was admitted to a sanatorium. Fearing death, he arranged for the posthumous publication of his writings (Van der Veer & Valsiner, 1991b). Incidentally, this fact again suggests that the number of literary reviews thus far found (which together with his masters thesis on *Hamlet* comprise no more than ninety pages) is not complete. During the years that followed, Vygotsky also taught subjects such as logic, psychology, psychoanalysis, aesthetics, and philosophy. At the same time, he was appointed to promote the theater and to enhance the general cultural level of Gomel. In this capacity, he traveled all over Russia to bring the best theatrical companies to Gomel. He also wrote weekly reviews of their performances for the local newspapers. Some seventy of these have been unearthed and many more are likely to be found (but none of them have been published in other languages). He was one of the founders of the short-lived literary journal *Heather (Veresk)*, and he worked for the Press Museum (*Muzej Pechati*), which made books and newspapers available to readers and organized evening lectures on literary subjects. He also worked as an editor for various local publishers. With some friends he founded his own publishing house, *Ages and Days (Veka i Dni)*, which until it was closed because of a shortage of paper, published several books by poets (Ehrenburg, David Vygodsky) and prose writers (Feigenberg, 1996).

Vygotsky's turn to psychology, which can be traced to his university years, was most visible in his work at the Gomel Teacher College, which aimed to educate the future elementary school teachers. Here, in 1923, Vygotsky installed a small psychological laboratory, where he and his students applied mental tests, did pilot experiments, and carried out investigations. In this laboratory, Vygotsky carried out the empirical study on breathing rhythms. He summarized the results of his investigations in three papers presented at the Second Psychoneurology Congress in Leningrad in 1924, and soon afterward he was appointed as a junior psychologist at the Institute of Experimental Psychology at Moscow University (Van der Veer & Valsiner, 1991b).

It is safe to state that the immense number of professional activities Vygotsky displayed during these five years (1919–23) were at first primarily in the area of literature and theater (e.g., lecturer of Russian literature, critic for a newspaper) and that he gradually made the switch to psychology, primarily while teaching at the Gomel Teacher College and lecturing elsewhere. Vygotsky was now twenty seven years old, and his primarily linguistic and literary training was certain to have a lasting effect on his psychological writings.

Turning Into a Professional Psychologist in Moscow

In Moscow, Vygotsky started work as a "scientific coworker of the second rank" in Konstantin Kornilov's collective at the Institute of Experimental Psychology of Moscow University. One year before, in 1923, Kornilov had replaced his mentor Georgi Chelpanov, who had refused to fully embrace the communist world view and had been fired with part of his staff. Kornilov recruited new personnel from different locations and it must be said that the new research collective formed a motley crew. It consisted of fanatic psychoanalysts (e.g., Luria, Fridman), physiologists (e.g., Bernstein), leftovers from Chelpanov's staff, students of animal behavior (e.g., Borovsky), applied psychologists (e.g., Shpilrejn), Marxist activists (e.g., Zalkind), and all sorts of hybrids of these varieties (Van der Veer & Valsiner, 1991b). Very different by training, they shared a belief in the possibility of creating a "Marxist psychology," although nobody had very clear ideas about what it would look like, and quarrels about its definition and outlines would soon begin.

At about the same time, in November 1924, Vygotsky began teaching at the Moscow Institute of Pedology and Defectology. He also was appointed head of the subdepartment for anomalous children at the Ministry of Education (*Narkompros*). These appointments show that he was immediately drawn into the institutions that dealt with disabled and difficult children. This is of interest because it points to one of the enigma's of Vygotsky's professional life: By all accounts, he developed a very early interest in the diagnosis, treatment, and education of physically (deaf, blind) and mentally handicapped children. Moreover, contemporaries claim that he was a very skilled clinician and a veritable virtuoso in diagnosing children. The enigma is that we do not know when and where Vygotsky's interest in these problem areas developed, nor how he developed his alleged superb diagnostic skills. Be that as it may, the fact is that Vygotsky's interest in handicapped children became manifest around this time and that throughout his life, despite his many other activities, he would remain involved with the diagnosis and treatment of these children. This does not mean that he had no other, broader interests. On the contrary, judging by the talks he gave during that year, Vygotsky's interests were very broad indeed. Thus, he lectured on the education of physically handicapped children, and also on the theories of psychoanalysis and behaviorism, and the concepts of dominant reactions and consciousness.

In 1925, Vygotsky began teaching Introduction-to-psychology courses at different faculties of the First Moscow State University. He also began teaching and doing experimental research at the Krup-skaya Academy of Communist Education. In July of that year, Vygot-sky made his one and only journey abroad. He presented a talk at the International Conference on the Education of the Deaf (Vygotsky, 1925b) and visited several schools for the deaf. On his way to London, Vygotsky visited the University of Berlin, and the Netherlands, and he stopped in France. Historians of science will perhaps be able to retrace his footsteps in these countries.

During September 1925, possibly as a result of the fatiguing train journey through Europe, Vygotsky suffered his second major attack of tuberculosis. He spent six months in a hospital and in bed for several more months. He was declared partially incapacitated ("inva-lid of the second degree") on June 8, 1926. He was so weakened by a right-side pneumothorax and pleuritis that he could no longer walk independently. It was only in January 1927 that he was declared able to work again (Vygodskaya & Lifanova, 1996). Despite his illness, during October 1925 he was elected to a commission of the Scientific State Council, in which he would be active until his death. After his recovery, at the end of 1926, he organized the laboratory for the study of anomalous (i.e., disabled and difficult) children in the Medical-Pedagogical Station in Moscow. This station had evolved from a pri-vate prerevolutionary school sanitarium into a complex of schools, clinics, and laboratories (Knox & Stevens, 1993). He would head the Medical-Pedagogical Station from December 19, 1927 until October 1, 1928 (Vygodskaya & Lifanova, 1991).

During the late 1920s and early 1930s Vygotsky reached the summit of his career. He worked for several publishing houses and functioned as the editor of translations of books by international psychologists such as Köhler, Koffka, Bühler, Lashley, Piaget, and Thorndike. He joined the editorial broad of the scientific journals *Voprosy Defektologii, Psikhologija, Pedologija, Pediatrija*, and *Psikhotekhnika i Psikhofiziologija Truda*. In 1929 he began working as an assistant, later as the head, in the laboratory at the Sepp Clinic for Nervous Diseases of the First Moscow University. In April of that year he went to Tashkent to teach for several months at the Central-Asian State University (SAGU). Dur-ing that year, he also replaced Kashchenko as the scientific leader of the Experimental Defectological Institute of the Ministry of Education (EDI). This institute was the result of the reorganization of the Medical-Pedagogical Station. It included, among other things, a school for the deaf, a school for mentally disabled children, and a clinic where children were diagnosed. In 1933, the decision was made to study children with speech disorders (Vygodskaya & Lifanova, 1996).

Meanwhile, state control over science was increasing and in 1931 several decisions were issued that directly and indirectly influenced Vygotsky's career. The journal *Voprosy Defektologii (Questions of Defectology)* was closed down, possibly as a result of a decree published in that same year, which stated that schooling was guaranteed for all, including handicapped children. Special schooling was to become an integral part of the broad mass educational system, and institutes that specialized in the study of disabled children were reorganized. In addition, Kornilov's Institute of Experimental Psychology came under attack and Vygotsky, who was still working there, was criticized in talks and papers by Talankin (1931a; 1931b) and Anan'ev (1931). There were talks about making Vygotsky's cultural-historical theory the subject of one of the regular so-called public debates, a threat that would be in the air until Vygotsky's untimely death (Van der Veer & Valsiner, 1991b).

In essence, the authorities were following the very efficient divide-and-rule principle, i.e., they attentively followed the vehement discussions between the different research groups within psychology (almost all of whom claimed to be in line with the communist party principles) and then suddenly and capriciously decided in favor of one or the other group. As it was in constant flux, no one could be sure what the party line was, and this unpredictability caused a feeling of uneasiness and fundamental insecurity that demoralized the discipline and led people to cast stones at colleagues in desperate attempts to save their own career (or even their skin in the period that followed). Thus, the ideological pressure was mounting and Vygotsky, who was very active in the fields of special education (defectology) and general education (pedology), could not escape criticism. However, despite setbacks and despite ferocious attacks on his ideas in the scientific press, he remained very active, and was even appointed to various new positions.

In February 1931, he became vice-director for scientific matters of the Institute for the Protection of Children's and Adolescents' Health OZDiP). He also became chairman of a section of the All-Union Association of Workers in Science, Art, and Technology to Further the Socialist Construction (VARNITSO) at the Bubnov State Pedagogical Institute in Moscow, and he was elected deputy in the section concerned with education of the Frunze Soviet (Frunze being one of Moscow's districts). He received the rank of full professor in the various institutes where he was teaching. Finally, in November 1931, he was appointed head of the Department for Genetic Psychology of the State University for the Preparation of the Cadres of the Ukrainian Ministery of Health (Vygodskaya & Lifanova, 1996). This latter appointment was connected with the fact that Vygotsky was now gradually moving his activities to Kharkov and Leningrad. In 1930, the Ukrainian Psychoneurological Academy in Kharkov was founded and a substantial part of Vygotsky's research collective, headed by Leontiev, was lured to Kharkov by the prospect of excellent research facilities and relative freedom from ideological pressure (Van der Veer & Valsiner, 1991b). Vygotsky retained close ties with his coworkers by traveling on a regular basis to Kharkov. During short stays in Kharkov, he combined research meetings with his colleagues and students with teaching, and with the study of medicine. He began this study during the fall of 1931. Now, eighteen years after his first short-lived attempt to study medicine, he deemed it necessary to study medicine in order to deepen his understanding of the pathology of mind and to enhance his professional possibilities.

During 1932 and 1933, Vygotsky's situation became still more precarious. Various journals he was involved with (e.g., *Pedologija*) ceased publication and the Psychological Laboratory of the Krupskaya Academy of Communist Education, where Vygotsky had done much of his experimental work, was closed. He also suffered severe and ignominious attacks in the scientific press by Feofanov (1932), Abel'skaya, and Neopikhonova (1932). The effect was that Vygotsky felt forced to move still more of his activities outside Moscow. In December 1932, he began teaching at the Herzen Institute of Education in Leningrad, where he rapidly formed a new research collective. However, there was no way to escape the mounting ideological pressure, and it seems that Vygotsky suffered endless interrogations in 1933. At the end of that year, he also had a major clash with Leontiev, who, under the increasing pressure of the circumstances, had decided that Vygotsky's ideas were obsolete and had to be replaced by his own concepts (Van der Veer & Valsiner, 1991b).

Death

Under these circumstances, the offer to head the Psychological Department of the All-Union Institute for Experimental Medicine (VIEM) in Moscow at the beginning of 1934, must have been very welcome. It provided Vygotsky with a new location to carry out experiments, to do clinical work, and to form a research collective. Unfortunately, after several months of preparatory work, Vygotsky suffered a fatal attack of tuberculosis. On May 8, 1934, while working at the VIEM, he had a hemorrhage in the throat and was brought home. On May 25 he had another hemorrhage, and on June 2 he was hospitalized. He died during the night on June 10, 1934. Experts claim (e.g., Keizer, 1994) that most dying people say something quite trivial, like "Can I have some water?," or "Where's John?" Only some mortals (e.g., Franz Kafka ten years earlier) say something that we, under the circumstances, find remarkable. Vygotsky is said to have said *"Ya gotov"* (Feigenberg, 1996), which is in that context a fundamentally ambiguous utterance as it can mean "I am ready" (With the things I did? For what is to come?) or "I am finished/done with." Then he died of tuberculosis, like Barukh de Spinoza, another brilliant Jew, had done some two-and-a-half centuries before.

Theoretical Development

It is often believed that Vygotsky was a child psychologist who investigated cognitive development in the framework of mother–child interactions. Hence, the frequent comparisons with Piaget, who is believed to have studied cognitive development in an abstract, socially isolated child. These beliefs do justice to neither Vygotsky nor Piaget. In regard to Vygotsky, it can be argued that he was (1) no child psychologist; (2) did not exclusively study cognitive development; and (3) never studied mother–child interactions.

He was no child psychologist but a psychologist who became increasingly interested in the theoretical problem of development, which led him to study cultural diversity, brain pathology, and other disciplines. By inclination he was a theoretical psychologist. In practice, his applied work was mostly in clinical settings.

He did not exclusively study cognitive development, but devoted much time to an analysis of emotional development and was convinced that emotions and feelings are crucial. Apart from that, he was much interested in the processes of loss and disintegration that may occur in the (mentally) diseased.

He never studied mother–child interactions, and it must be said that his account of the way cognitive development is socially co-constructed always remained rather abstract. In the background was always the Humboldtian idea that people "change their minds" by appropriating linguistic tools and that these tools change in the process of being mastered and used. He plausibly argued that education was important to development, that instruction by adults or more knowledgeable peers was essential, that children appropriate or master cultural tools in the process of learning, and so on and so forth. Yet he carried out few experiments to show how these processes of teaching and mastering might take place. He never studied genuine parent–child or teacher–child dyads to check whether parents and teachers played the scaffolding role attributed to them, and he never tried to operationalize a concept such as the zone of proximal development, nor did he check whether it has the prognostic value attributed to it. He advanced plausible and fruitful hypotheses but left it to his students and modern research to give flesh and bones to these general ideas.

Thus, the historic Vygotsky is rather different from the popular textbook version. Without pretending to be comprehensive, in the following sections we will pay attention to the genesis of the major ideas of the historic Vygotsky (cf. Van der Veer & Valsiner, 1991). The focus will be on Vygotsky the sociogenetic thinker and his relevant scientific predecessors and contemporaries.

From Drama and Language to Psychology

As we have seen, Vygotsky's interest in psychological matters originated with his fascination with literature and drama. Among the dramatists, he particularly favored Shakespeare whose play *Hamlet* he analyzed in great depths in his student years. Elsewhere (Van der Veer & Valsiner, 1991b) we have given a detailed presentation of Vygotsky's fascination with this play. Here it will suffice to say that he was trying to make sense of the Hamlet tragedy as a myth, i.e., he wished to capture the mysterious moment, while at the same time paying attention to its compositional structure. In this structure, he found tensions between opposing forces (activity–inactivity; day–

night) that by the end of the play result in a new quality in a Hegelian fashion. Through *Hamlet*, Vygotsky became fascinated with the way certain affective experiences are generated by the structure of literary texts. Analyzing the general structure of the fable and that of a short story by Bunin, he concluded that:

> Over the course of centuries aestheticians have claimed the harmony of form and content, and that the form illustrates, complements, accompanies the content; and suddenly we discover that this is the greatest misunderstanding. Instead, the form is at war with the content, fights with it, overcomes it, and in this dialectical contradiction between content and form the real psychological sense of our aesthetic reactions lies hidden. (Vygotsky, 1925/1986, p. 204)

Here Vygotsky followed a dialectical approach: A new emotional quality is created as a result of the struggle between form and content. It was also Bunin's short story that led him to conduct his first experimental psychological study. His hypothesis was that different stories would lead to different breathing patterns that in their turn would lead to different emotional experiences in the reader. He found that hypothesis confirmed in his study of nine subjects (cf. pp. 31–2 of Van der Veer & Valsiner, 1991b; cf. Dewey's similar analysis in Chapter 5).

We can see then, that Vygotsky began with an interest in the aesthetic qualities of works of literature, then gradually became fascinated by the question of how works of art can generate aesthetic feelings in their recipients, and, finally, was led to carry out empirical studies to check whether specific structural qualities of texts can produce specific emotions in the reader.

Using Potebnya

In his first analyses of *Hamlet*, Vygotsky referred to the writings of the great Russian linguist Aleksandr Potebnya (1835–91). He had read Potebnya in his student years and throughout his psychological career would make use of Potebnya's ideas. Potebnya worked in the tradition of Humboldt and saw the study of language as being of the utmost importance for psychology. In his view language, or articulate speech, does not only serve as a means of communication it also shapes our own thinking (Budagov, 1988).

One of Potebnya's main themes was that of the relation between words or concepts, on the one hand, and ideas or thoughts, on the other. In his book *Language and Thought*, Potebnya (1926/1989) argued that ideas are not simply expressed in words (as if ideas lie ready-made in our mind and need only to be stated aloud) but are born together with the word. Language or speech adds something to the idea; it is an instrument that creates or shapes our ideas, it is the creative organ of thought, as Humboldt put it.

The relationship between speech and thinking would become a fundamental theme in Vygotsky's work as well (cf. Vygotsky, 1934b/1990), and it is quite clear that Vygotsky shared Potebnya's general view that language or speech shapes our mental processes in fundamental ways. Vygotsky was inclined to regard the linguistic tools we inherit from our culture as being of the utmost importance, and like Potebnya, he regarded the word as a tool of progress; without progress, no civilized life would be possible.

Potebnya argued that what language does is to objectify our ideas. This idea has several interconnected repercussions. First, by stating my ideas in the language of some culture, they become accessible to the whole community and thereby stop being my own private ideas.

Second, if I wish to communicate my ideas, I must make use of the available words of my native or some foreign language. Potebnya argued that we are confined within the boundaries of our language, and we can only step out of it by stepping into another language. We are forced to use the heritage of the past embodied in the language. Because words necessarily refer to classes of similar events or objects, by describing my ideas in existing terms, I necessarily make my private ideas comparable to the existing ideas of that culture and thereby objectify them. In other words, to speak is to connect one's own special ideas with existing ideas (Potebnya, 1926/1989, p. 149).

Vygotsky referred to these ideas when he repeatedly argued that by using concepts we not only communicate with others (*obshchenie*) but generalize (*obobshchenie*) as well (cf. Janet's similar claim in Chapter 3). A substantial part of his research was dedicated to the investigation of concept formation in children, and in this connection he showed that at different age levels, the words children use mean different things but that genuine communication is fortunately possible because of the joint reference class. He argued that one of the fundamental advantages of academic concepts (rather than everyday concepts) is that they form part of a system of interconnected concepts that allow the subject to link up with existing knowledge and to draw conclusions based upon this system.

Third, once I have given form to my idea in words, it becomes an object for myself, because words are audible and in this way are returned to the speaker. By stating a certain idea, I not only communicate that idea to the listener, but I also make it audible for myself and thereby influence myself. Man understands himself only when he has tried the intelligibility of his words upon the social other. This led Potebnya to state that the word is as much a means to understand the other as it is a means to understand oneself. Articulate speech is a means to understand oneself due to the fact that it is returned to its source as an object.

Vygotsky likewise explicitly and repeatedly dealt with the fact that words are "reversible stimuli," i.e., they are heard by the speaker himself. Vygotsky (1925/1997) dealt with this issue in reflexological terms and stated that words are reversible reflexes which lie at the basis of consciousness. The uttered word (a reflex or response) is returned to the speaker (as a stimulus) for further processing. In this connection, Vygotsky argued that deaf-mutes' vocal speech remains unconscious and nonsocial as the "reversibility of the speech reflex is paralyzed by the absence of hearing" (Vygotsky, 1925/1997, p. 78). More generally, he defended the view that we are conscious of ourselves "only to the extent that we are *another* to ourselves, i.e., to the extent that we can again perceive our own reflexes as stimuli" (Vygotsky, 1926a/1997, p. 42).

It was a view that came close to several of the ideas of Royce, Baldwin, Mead, and Janet, and it was in the spirit of Humboldt's antinomies: It is only by operating upon the social other (i.e., by speaking) and by becoming the social other to some extent (i.e., through the use of accepted terminology, etc.) that we can become our own conscious selves (i.e., through reflection upon our own utterances, and the effects they produced).

These few remarks make it quite clear that Vygotsky shared many fundamental ideas with Potebnya. Throughout his psychological writings we find references to Potebnya's work, and it is significant that in his very last writings (i.e., the last chapter of Vygotsky, 1934b/1990) the influence of Potebnya is again very evident.

The Crisis In Psychology

By moving to Moscow and starting to work at the Institute of Experimental Psychology, Vygotsky had formally moved into the area of psychology. He immediately began publishing important theoretical papers (cf. Van der Veer & Valsiner, 1994), and by 1926 had acquired such complete knowledge of psychology that he felt able to write an analysis of the contemporary state of art in this discipline. This became his *The Historical Meaning of the Crisis in Psychology: A Methodological Investigation* (Vygotsky, 1926b/1997), which was not published during his lifetime but acquired justified fame among the selected group of people who had access to it. It was in a sense the prelude to his own cultural-historical theory of the higher psychological processes. In the following, we will highlight some of its central tenets and again point to the influence of Vygotsky's earlier literary and linguistic studies.

One of the major themes in *The Crisis* was that of method or methodology. It is a theme that can be analyzed at several levels. Vygotsky was concerned with the choice of appropriate research methods and techniques, with the selection of a general approach to psychological phenomena, (e.g., objectivating or subjectivating), and with more general problems of epistemology. Thus, we can see him discuss introspection and the method of double stimulation as a specific research technique to disclose the development of mind (the most concrete level), the drawbacks and advantages of the behavioristic approach in psychology (the intermediate level), and the merits of general philosophical views such as materialism and empiricism (the most abstract level). *The Crisis* dealt mainly with the latter two levels. From this essay, but also from his earlier and later writings, it became quite clear that Vygotsky advocated an objective, deterministic, causal psychology that uses objective means which yield replicable results. He argued that no third way, besides objective and subjective psychology was possible; he sharply criticized subjective approaches and seemed to opt for a psychology inspired by the natural sciences. Whether psychology itself might be called a natural science, he did not discuss because he felt that this is "a special and very deep problem, which does not, however, belong to the problem of the meaning of the crisis as a whole" (Vygotsky, 1926/1997, p. 303).

Vygotsky made it quite clear, however, that there can be no such thing as an atheoretical psychology (or science at large) as the behaviorists seemed to imply. There is no such thing as the objective registration of facts (this he regarded as a sensualistic prejudice) because our epistemological principles always co-determine our scientific facts. The positivistic idea that we merely have to register the objective facts, and then through induction and mathematical elaboration, we can arrive at genuine scientific theories was as foreign to Vygotsky as it was to someone as Janet (see Chapter 3). He strongly condemned such an approach and argued that we need interpretation, abstraction, and analysis as the *salto vitale* for psychology. The psychologist may act as a "detective who brings to light a crime he never witnessed" (Vygotsky, 1926a/1997, p. 49).

The influence of theory or interpretation begins with the words we use to designate the facts or phenomena discovered in our research, and it is for this reason that Vygotsky attached such tremendous importance to the choice of a proper terminology in scientific research. It is here that we can trace clear links to the linguistic work of Potebnya (and Von Humboldt) and his emphasis on the importance of words as prototheories. Similarly, it is quite interesting to see how Vygotsky's analysis of the role that words play in the production of scientific facts (i.e., at the level of methodology) is transposed to the domain of ontogeny during the early 1930s when Vygotsky gradually seemed to realize that words or word meanings can be viewed as the vehicle of mental development (cf. Van der Veer, 1997).

Vygotsky elaborated his critique of the exclusive use of induction in psychology by comparing it to theoretical analysis. Again, his argumentation showed clear traces of his earlier literary work. He argued that: "The domination of induction and mathematical elaboration and the underdevelopment of analysis substantially damaged the case of . . . experimental psychology" (Vygotsky, 1926b/1997, p. 317).

In his view, what was needed was the analysis of single phenomena and the deduction of laws based upon such analyses. To exemplify his idea of an analytical method, he referred back to his earlier work concerning the psychology of art:

I have tried to introduce such a method into conscious psychology and to deduce the laws of the psychology of art on the basis of the *analysis* of one fable, one short story, and one tragedy. In doing so I proceeded from the idea that the well-developed forms of art provide the key to the underdeveloped ones, just as the anatomy of man provides the key to the anatomy of the ape. I assumed that Shakespeare's tragedy explains the enigmas of primitive art and not the other way around. Further, I talk about *all art* and do not verify my conclusions on music, painting etc. What is even more: I do not verify them on *all* or the majority of the *types* of literature. I take *une* short story, *one* tragedy. Why am I entitled to do so? I have not studied the fable, the tragedy, and still less a *given* fable or a *given* tragedy. I have studied in them what makes up the basis of all art – the nature and mechanism of the aesthetic reaction. I relied upon the general elements of form and material which are inherent in any art. For the analysis I selected the most difficult fables, short stories and tragedies, precisely those in which the general laws are particularly evident. I selected the monsters amongst the tragedies etc. The analysis presupposes that one abstracts from the concrete characteristics of the fable as such, as a specific genre, and concentrates the forces upon the essence of the aesthetic reaction. That is why I say *nothing* about the fable as such. And the subtitle 'An analysis of the aesthetic reaction' itself indicates that the goal of the investigation is not a systematic exposition of a psychological theory of art in its entire volume and width of content (all types of art, all problems etc.) and not even the inductive investigation of a specific number of facts, but precisely *the analysis of the processes in their essence*.

Abstraction and analysis does all this. The similarity with the experiment resides in the fact that here, too, we have an artificial combination of phenomena in which the action of a specific law must manifest itself in the purest form. It is like a snare for nature, an analysis in action. In analysis we create a similar artificial combination of phenomena, but then through abstraction in thought. This is particularly clear in its application to art constructions. They are not aimed at scientific, but at practical goals and rely upon the action of some specific psychological or physical law. Examples are a machine, an anecdote, lyrics, mnemonics, a military command. Here we have a practical experiment. The analysis of such cases is an experiment with finished phenomena. Its meaning comes close to that of pathology – this experiment arranged by nature itself – to its own analysis. The only difference is that disease causes the loss or demarcation of superfluous traits, whereas we here have the presence of necessary traits, a selection of them – but the result is the same.

Each lyrical poem is such an experiment. The task of the analysis is to reveal the law that forms the basis of nature's experiment. But also when the analysis does not deal with a machine, i.e., a practical experiment, but with any phenomenon, it is in principle similar to the experiment. It would be possible to prove how infinitely much our equipment complicates and refines our research, how much more intelligent, stronger and more perspicuous it makes us. Analysis does the same. (Vygotsky, 1926b/1997, pp. 319–20)

In this lengthy quotation we see an interesting plea for interpretation and analysis in psychology, rather than the blind accumulation of facts and their subsequent elaborate mathematical or statistical processing (cf. Janet's similar argument in Chapter 3). It is a plea that, sadly enough, has lost nothing of its topicality and still deserves to be read in its entirety. The quotation also shows to what extent Vygotsky's methodological and psychological writings were rooted in his earlier work as a literary critic and theorist of art. For almost a decade (i.e., 1915–23), Vygotsky devoted most of his attention to the area of literature, drama, and art. He never lost his interest in these topics, and throughout the decade of his work as a psychologist (i.e., 1924–34), he kept referring to literary examples, and theorists of literature, art, and language.

Vygotsky and Comparative Psychology

In his efforts to understand the development of the human mind, Vygotsky turned to the findings of child development, ethnography, pathology, and comparative psychology. Or, in other words, he hoped to find the key to the understanding of what is specifically human in the study of phylogeny, ontogeny, and pathological regression. In this respect he essentially followed the research strategy advocated by Jackson, Spencer, Ribot, Janet, and others (see Chapter 3). However, while Janet in his forays into the alleged phylogeny of human behavior mostly relied on the findings of Köhler (1921b), the French school of sociology, and his own imagination, Vygotsky drew more extensively on the findings of his contemporary comparative psychologists, several of whom were his compatriots. It is not generally known that evolutionary biology (to which we may reckon comparative psychology) was quite strong in Russia at the beginning of this century, and therefore we do well to pay some attention to several of its principle figures and their connection to Vygotsky's thinking.

Vygotsky himself referred most extensively to the discipline of comparative psychology and its Russian representatives in a little brochure written for the lay public called "The Behavior of Animals and Man" (Vygotsky, 1929c). For unknown reasons it was never published. In this work he discussed such questions as whether animals have a mind, whether animals can be said to have intellect and speech, what can be said about the evolution of brain size and its relation to intelligence, and whether acquired characteristics can be inherited. Making use of this brochure and related scientific writings of the same period (Vygotsky, 1929a; 1929b; 1930) one can get a reasonable impression of Vygotsky's ideas on comparative psychology and his position relative to other Russian scientists of the time.

Vygotsky made it quite clear that he believed that comparative psychology can only be practiced from an evolutionary point of view. In his opinion, the forerunner or father of scientific comparative psychology was Darwin (1872) with his *"The Expression of the Emotions in Man and Animals."* It was Darwin who pointed out that certain behaviors can become inherited just like morphological aspects. He demonstrated, in the words of Konrad Lorenz, that:

Behavior patterns are just as conservatively and reliably characters of species as are the forms of bones, teeth, or any other bodily structures. Similarities in inherited behavior unite the members of a species, of a genus, and even of the largest taxonomic units in exactly the same way in which bodily characters do so. The conservative persistence of behavior patterns, even after they have outlived, in the evolution of a species, their original function, is exactly the same as that of organs; in other words, they can become 'vestigial' or 'rudimentary', just as the latter can. (Lorenz, 1965, p. xii).

Vygotsky embraced the evolutionary point of view as a useful antidote against two approaches in the study of animal behavior which he found inadequate. The first approach was the tendency to give anthropomorphic accounts of animal behavior (of the "clever Hans" type). In such an approach animals are ascribed human behavioral capacities (e.g., language and intelligence) on the basis of anecdotal evidence. It was an approach that was typical of the work of Romanes, but that to an extent can be seen in the work of Darwin as well. The second approach claimed that animals display no intelligent behavior whatsoever and in a way returned to Descartes in considering animals as little more than machines that run on the principle of reflexes or instincts. Vygotsky considered Thorndike (who tried to reduce the feats of animals to the operating of the principle of trial and error) to be a representative of this approach.

To Vygotsky both views (anthropomorphism and behaviorism) were unacceptable. The first view ascribed higher forms to lower animals and thereby essentially denied the evolution of mental properties. After all, if lower organisms display higher mental capacities such as language and thought, then no further evolution is needed to arrive at the human mental processes. The second approach could not even discover the rudiments of higher forms in lower animals, and thereby made the appearance of these forms in higher animals and man something of a miracle. It was, in essence, the Cartesian approach which left an inexplicable gap between human beings and animals, and which essentially denied evolution as well (cf. Walker, 1983, for a similar contemporary view). Historically, of course, one has seen a third variant in the study of comparative psychology – equally unacceptable to Vygotsky – which said that animal behavior is explicable on the basis of a few basic principles (e.g., classical conditioning) but that the same is true of human beings as well. Human beings are just more of the same. It is an approach that goes back to at least the work of La Mettrie (1748/1981) and was defended in various forms by Pavlov and American behaviorists.

Vygotsky rejected these approaches because he favored an account of phylogeny and ontogeny which stresses both continuity in development and the emergence of qualitative changes. In fact, the problem of continuity and change (whether in ontogeny or in phylogeny) was one of the few major themes of his writings (cf. Van der Veer, 1997). It was especially prevalent in his discussion of the various writings of the Gestalt theorists and in his analysis of Karl Bühler's conception. The key question can be formulated as follows: How is it possible that continuous development results in intermediate products or stages that are nevertheless fundamentally distinct? The question recurs time and again and takes various disguises, e.g., how can we explain continuity in phylogenetic development without taking the viewpoint of either mechanism (which reduces all qualitatively distinct forms to the workings of some primordial mechanism) or vitalism (which creates a gap between lower and higher forms of development by introducing a mysterious principle that is only applicable to the latter)? How can we explain that the immediate evolutionary predecessors of humans, the anthropoid apes, seemingly have almost all of the prerequisites necessary for intelligent behavior (such as tool use and tool manufacture) but nevertheless seem fundamentally less intelligent than humans? How can we explain the development from instinct to intellect without either creating an unbridgeable gap between the two forms of behavior or invoking some mysterious purely mental acts? These are questions that date back to pre-Socratic philosophy and are still very much on the agenda of contemporary psychology (Van der Veer, 1997).

Vygotsky's own view of emergent levels of mentality developed against the background of the writings of Severtsov, Vagner, Khotin, Pavlov, Bekhterev, Köhler, Yerkes, Koffka, Bühler, and others. Some of these writers defended views that came quite close to Vygotsky's (e.g., Severtsov, Vagner, Khotin), others defended views that he found clearly unacceptable (e.g., Pavlov, Bühler), while still others provided empirical material that served as a constant source of reflection (e.g., Köhler, Yerkes). In addition, we must not forget that Vygotsky's own views (on, for example, the meaning of Köhler's findings) underwent gradual changes.

Comparative Psychology in Russia

Vygotsky's assessment of Köhler's findings and their value for developmental psychology must be seen against the background of the work of the Russian comparative psychologists and biologists of his time. The work of these researchers was at the international level, and they all followed and interpreted the prominent research projects of the time. In doing so, they provided commentaries and interpretations that were of fundamental importance for Vygotsky's own project. Russian developmental psychology and Russian psychology at large cannot be viewed in isolation from the work of Russian evolutionary biologists (cf. Valsiner, 1998, pp 40–8).

Potentially most relevant for Vygotsky were the writings of, respectively, Ladygina-Kohts, Borovsky, Severtsov, and Vagner. The writings of these researchers were instrumental to Vygotsky in that they clearly distinguished different levels of mentality (e.g., reflexes, instincts, intellect) and tried to trace their origin in phylogeny, viewing them as (slowly) changing means of adaptation to the environment.

Ladygina-Kohts

The work of Nadezhda Ladygina-Kohts (1889–1963) is no longer well known internationally, and perhaps it never was. Working at the Darwin Museum in Moscow founded by her husband A. F. Kohts, she began studying the behavior and mental capacities of chimpanzees and lower apes (*Macaca mulatta*, the rhesus monkey) (Ladygina-Kohts, 1923; 1928a; 1928b; 1930; 1982). In a typical experiment, Ladygina-Kohts showed a model, say an object of some specified color or form, to a chimpanzee and then required the animal to pick the same object (discrimination) or a similar one (abstraction) from among a collection of available objects. In this way she managed to show that chimpanzees were relatively good at discriminating colors and forms but bad at abstracting. She also claimed that chimpanzees were virtually unable to learn to react to objects by their names. These findings were somewhat similar to those of Yerkes who claimed that the ape's visual imitation is much better than his auditory imitation (cf. Mecacci, 1992; Misiti, 1982).

In her monograph on the rhesus macaque, Ladygina-Kohts (1928b) described how she confronted her subject Desi with countless boxes that had to be unlocked by means of bolts, chains, keys, latches, etc. She summarized her findings by saying that "Inasmuch as every labour process is in the first place an act tending toward a clearly realized goal . . . *we must say* on the ground of the present research mainly devoted to the monkey's manual labour (which labour, in fact underlies every working process) *that the monkey, such as it is today, is incapable of work*" (Ladygina-Kohts, 1928b, p. 351).

As Ladygina-Kohts (ibid., pp. 323–4) pointed out, this conclusion was completely in line with the ideas of Marx and Engels about the relevance of labor for the origin of mankind, and she concluded that her research had provided the experimental confirmation of Engels' (1925) claim that labor is the defining characteristic of man. Incidentally, the phrase "such as it is today" in the quote given above refers to Ladygina-Kohts' belief that *Macaca mulatta* had known better, more humanlike times and was now undergoing a regressive evolution.

Perhaps most relevant for Vygotsky's purposes, however, was a voluminous book (596 pages of text plus hundreds of drawings and photographs) in which Ladygina-Kohts gave a careful and fascinating account of the psychological development of Joni, a chimpanzee, and her son Rudy during the first four years of their life (Ladygina-Kohts, 1935; 1937; 1982; Mitisi, 1982). Against her own expectations, Ladygina-Kohts had to conclude that Joni's mental capacities in many ways lagged far behind those of Rudy's. Years after Thorndike and Vygotsky, she noted the surprisingly limited aping ability of apes (cf. Aronovich & Khotin, 1929). Published just before the Pedology Decree, Ladygina-Kohts' book disappeared from the field of attention (only 775 copies were printed), and the author resumed publishing on the comparative study of the behavior of chimpanzees and human children in the late 1950s (e.g., Ladygina-Kohts, 1959; cf. Ladygina-Kohts and Dembovskii, 1969; Misiti, 1982), when Stalin was dead and gone.

The books of Ladygina-Kohts (which contained lengthy German or English summaries) drew the attention of specialists working in the same field, such as Buytendijk and Yerkes. Yerkes wrote a sympathetic review of Ladygina-Kohts (1923) in which he voiced some doubts concerning her method but nevertheless concluded that "Mrs. Kohts' work constitutes an almost unique and a highly valuable contribution to our knowledge of the behavior of the chimpanzee" (Yerkes & Pe-trunkevich, 1925). In the preface to his *Almost Human*, Yerkes (1925) thanked Ladygina-Kohts and claimed that her work on chimpanzees contained "some of the best pictorial and verbal descriptions of the animal ever presented." He apparently corresponded with his Russian colleague, and in June 1929 he visited her laboratory at the Darwin Museum in Moscow.

It would seem, then, that Vygotsky had every reason to discuss Ladygina-Kohts' work. It was clearly relevant to the assessment of the work of the Kellogs (Kellog & Kellog, 1933), Köhler, Yerkes, Revesz, and other prominent researchers at the time. Moreover, Ladygina-Kohts' laboratory was not far from the Institute of Experimental Psychology where Vygotsky worked, and he surely knew her work, if not the author herself. Finally, he knew that Ladygina-Kohts was in contact with Yerkes, whose work Vygotsky positively discussed more than once, as is evident from his published correspondence in which he mentions that Yerkes visited Ladygina-Kohts and her husband (Vygotsky, in a letter to Vagner, dated June 25, 1929; Vygodskaya & Lifanova, 1996, p. 374). Nevertheless, to our knowledge, Vygotsky never once referred to the work carried out by Ladygina-Kohts (and he never referred to the work of the Kellogs). We can offer no satisfactory explanation for this rather surprising fact, and we do not know whether Vygotsky's silence about Ladygina-Kohts' work reflected the fact that he shared a negative appraisal of her work with close colleagues, such as Borovsky (1927b, pp. 183–4), who worked with Vygotsky at the Institute of Experimental Psychology, and dismissed Ladygina-Kohts' work as being subjective and in the anthropomorphic spirit.

Borovsky

Vladimir Borovsky headed a small section for the study of animal behavior (his collaborators were V. V. Troitsky and V. N. Belyaev) at the Moscow Institute of Experimental Psychology (Luria, 1926). Borovsky did empirical work on the reactions on monochromatic stimuli in invertebrates, and on delayed reactions in guinea pigs, and he was quite well informed about international comparative psychology (cf. Borovsky, 1927b). In judging the claims made in the investigations of Lloyd-Morgan, Hobhouse, Yerkes, Köhler, Hunter, Ladygina-Kohts, and others, he seems to have followed the line advocated by Vagner, i.e., while resisting the reductionist approach of physiologists such as Pavlov (e.g., Borovsky, 1927a), who claimed that all behavior of lower animals, higher animals, and human beings is based on the reflex, he at the same time opposed the tendency to ascribe humanlike abilities to animals. Thus, he was very critical of Yerkes who claimed to have observed "ideation" in apes, he denied that Köhler had positively proved that chimpanzees display insight, and he dismissed Ladygina-Kohts' claims as being ill founded. These viewpoints, which were always well argued, eventually brought him into conflict with the ideological authorities. In 1930, Borovsky was still able to attack Pavlov for his claim that reflexes are the basic units of behavior, for his "reflexes of freedom and purpose," and for his shaky neural fantasies. However, in 1934, when venturing ideologically acceptable scientific ideas had become as difficult as coming back in one piece after a walk through a minefield, his work was slaughtered in the press by the infamous Razmyslov (who in the same year also viciously attacked Vygotsky and Luria, see Van der Veer & Valsiner, 1991b), and some time later he left Moscow for a provincial teacher-training institute.

All in all, Borovsky's theoretical position and scientific fate show similarities with that of Vygotsky. Just like Borovsky, Vygotsky took an active interest in the work of the American behaviorists and the Russian physiologists Pavlov and Bekhterev, and just like Borovsky he resisted their imperialist tendencies. Unconditional or conditional reflexes could not serve as the ultimate explanatory unit of behavior, nor did it make sense to introduce such terms as "reflexes of freedom and purpose," which clarified absolutely nothing (Vygotsky, 1926b/1997). With Borovsky, Vygotsky (1929c) criticized the anthropomorphic approach in comparative psychology, and like him, he tried to steer in between two forms of "reductionism": that of reducing complex human behavior to elementary principles valid in the explanation of the behavior of elementary, lower animals, and that of lifting animal performance up to the human level by ascribing it human qualities.

Their main difference was in the judgment of Köhler's work: While Vygotsky at first believed that Sultan and his colleagues showed humanlike abilities, Borovsky from the very beginning contested this claim. As we will see, it would be Vygotsky who would eventually change his opinion. Undoubtedly, Vygotsky's later viewpoints concerning comparative psychology developed under the influence of his growing friendship with Vagner.

Severtsov

Before he became increasingly fascinated with Vagner's ideas, however, Vygotsky toyed with the ideas of Aleksey Severtsov (1866–1936). Severtsov taught as a professor at Moscow University until 1930 and offered courses in, among other things, the theory of evolution. He has been called "the most original and productive Darwinian scholar in Russian" (Vucinich, 1988, p. 176), and his writings in foreign languages gained him an international reputation as a leading scholar in evolutionary morphology (Severtsov, 1927; 1929; 1931). His so-called theory of phylembryogenesis (*filembriogenez*) provided important new ways to look at the relationship between phylogeny and ontogeny (Gould, 1977; Valsiner, 1988, pp. 43–8; Vucinich, 1988, pp. 220–30). There are good grounds to argue that Severtsov's many biological writings exerted an important influence on Russian developmental psychology (cf. Valsiner, 1988). He did write, however, a book that was specifically devoted to psychological issues in relation to evolution (Severtsov, 1922). In that book he discussed the role of behavior in the evolutionary process, in the case of environmental conditions that are themselves undergoing constant change. He emphasized that animal behavior may serve as a means of adaptation to quickly changing environmental conditions. In his opinion evolution biologists had so far concentrated on hereditary changes of organs and had neglected the role of nonhereditary changes. Severtsov emphasized that successful organisms should be able to cope with rapid environmental changes and argued that adaptation works in four different ways:

First, the structure or build of the organs of an animal will change in certain ways under the pressure of environmental selection. Severtsov somewhat hesitantly acknowledged the role of mutation, but nevertheless insisted that this sort of adaptation is exceedingly slow. By its nature this type of change is hereditary.

Second we can distinguish what Severtsov called functional changes of organs. By this he meant the rapid change of organs, such as muscles, under the influence of repeated practice during the life time of the organism. Despite Lamarck, this type of change is nonhereditary.

Characteristic of these first two types of change is that the structure of the organ changes (either rapidly and temporarily, or slowly and lastingly). In addition to these changes, Severtsov (1922, p. 23) distinguished two types of adaptation that do not involve changes in the structure of the organ. These were:

Third, reflexes and instincts that are expedient, adaptive behaviors characterized by their automatic, inflexible nature, by the fact that they are elicited by specific environmental stimuli, and by the fact that they are inherited. The differences between reflexes and instincts is that the latter are more complex, according to Severtsov.

Fourth, there is intellectual activity that is also expedient but not hereditary, and not machinelike. What is inherited is the capacity for activities of this type but not the activities themselves. They have to be learned and do not follow automatically upon certain stimuli.

If we now group these four types of adaptation according to their capacity of being inherited, we get the following schema (Table 8.1; cf. Severtsov, 1992, p. 46):

Severtsov (1922, pp. 52–4) argued that in human beings behavior of the type 2b is most prevalent and added that: "From a very early stage of his evolution, man begins to replace new organs by new tools. Where the animal, to adapt to new life conditions, elaborates new structural capacities . . . man invents . . . new tools . . . man creates for himself so to speak an artificial environment, – the environment of culture and civilization" (Severtsov, 1922, pp. 52, 54).

All in all, Severtsov's ideas on different forms of adaptation, which were much more elaborate than can be presented here (cf. Valsiner, 1988; Vucinich, 1988), provided an interesting account of the role played by individual behavior in evolution. His emphasis on the qualitatively new level of existence in the case of human beings, because of their ability to change their environment with the help of tools, fitted in well with the ideas of Engels (1925), which were to become the dominant philosophy of Soviet science. It comes as no surprise, then, that Vygotsky repeatedly referred to Severtsov when discussing issues of evolution.

However, while Severtsov presented a useful general account of human evolution, the role of individual behavior, and tool use, he did not discuss the finer details of specific forms or levels of behavior. His "reflexes and instincts" (level 1a), for instance, are grouped together indiscriminately, and Severtsov seems to have regarded instincts simply as more complex forms of reflexes. Neither did Severtsov discuss in sufficient detail how we can distinguish behavior of the intellectual type (level 2b) from other types of behavior. It is exactly these issues

Table 8.1. *Forms of Adaptive Behavior According to Severtsov.*

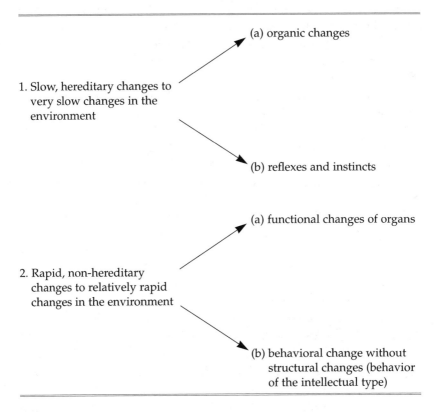

1. Slow, hereditary changes to very slow changes in the environment
   (a) organic changes
   (b) reflexes and instincts

2. Rapid, non-hereditary changes to relatively rapid changes in the environment
   (a) functional changes of organs
   (b) behavioral change without structural changes (behavior of the intellectual type)

which increasingly came to dominate the international psychological debate, in particular after the publication of Köhler's findings. Behaviorists and reflexologists claimed that animal behavior was ultimately based on no more than reflexes. Others claimed that higher animals such as apes operated at the level of instincts but certainly did not show the rudiments of intelligence. Still others acknowledged the existence of three levels of behavior (reflexes, instincts, intellect) but maintained that intellect was not the exclusive possession of human beings. The question as to how to distinguish between these different forms of behavior became increasingly important for psychology, and several of the actors on the scene (although not the behaviorists and the reflexologists) realized that only detailed comparative study of the behavior of many different species could answer this question. What was needed, in sum, was what we now call ethological studies. It is here that the writings of Vagner became of the utmost importance.

Vagner

Vladimir Vagner (1849–1934) was a prolific writer in comparative psychology and has been said to be "one of the most original and productive Russian evolutionary biologists of his age" (Vagner, 1992a; Vucinich, 1988, p. 184). He regarded animal psychology as a comparative or evolutionary discipline and, like Vygotsky, rejected both anthropomorphic subjectivism and physiological objectivism. He advocated the comparative study of closely related species, the introduction into psychology of a natural-science methodology, and a consistent historical perspective. Vagner argued that every stage in the evolution of animal behavior represents a distinct adaptation to changes in the struggle for existence. He wrote about, among other things, spiders and city swallows and showed, for instance, how city swallows changed their nests from a hanging type (attached to a wall) to a sitting type (made on a horizontal surface such as a roof) (Vagner, 1896; 1898; 1901; 1904; 1910; 1913; 1923; 1925; 1928; 1929).

In many ways, Vagner's work laid the foundation of Russian ethology (Krementsov, 1992), which, however, never got a real chance from the authorities (Joravsky, 1992; Vagner, 1992b) and came to an end when Vagner's pupil Boris Khotin (1895–1950) was exiled to Central Asia in 1935 (Malakhovskaya, 1992a; Mecacci, 1992; Sokolov and Baskin, 1992). Khotin himself had done interesting work on imitation in a variety of species (carps, doves, cats, wolves, reindeer, monkeys, etc.) (Malakhovskaya, 1992b) and had introduced interesting methodological novelties (Aronovich and Khotin, 1929). An unpublished paper from about 1934 (Khotin, 1992), which probably aimed to convince the authorities that Vagner's approach was worth pursuing, can be read as the testament of the founders of Russian ethology. In this paper Khotin advocated the observation of different species in natural conditions. Essential was the study of organisms within the environment and with one another in natural habitats, although Khotin did not totally exclude physiological experimentation (e.g., extirpation of brain parts, etc.). Through such studies one should be able to establish the phylogeny of a certain phenomenon (e.g., nest-building behavior). The next step was to proceed to the ontogenetic study of the same phenomenon studying it in different age periods of the organism. Finally, the findings of both domains should be synthesized, taking care to avoid the crude identification or confusion of findings from these domains. Such a historical approach Khotin opposed to the simple-minded physiological approach in which phenomena of very unequal nature are reduced to reflexes and in which the findings in one species are declared relevant for another species without further argument or study.

Vucinich (1988, pp. 184–5) has argued that Vagner's influence on his contemporary thought was rather limited. Working as a *privatdozent* at Moscow University and as a professor of general biology and comparative psychology in Leningrad (Varshava & Vygotsky, 1931, p. 36) he formed no scientific school and it can safely be assumed that the little influence he had was declining in the late 1920s, when he first began corresponding with Vygotsky.

This correspondence and their subsequent friendship was remarkable in itself. In 1928, when they exchanged their first letters, Vygotsky was a young thirty two years old, ambitious associate professor of paedology, with an interest in clinical, developmental, and theoretical psychology, and with excellent connections in the ministry of education. At that time, Vagner was an old man of seventy-nine, who occupied the only chair in comparative psychology in the Soviet Union, which ceased to exist when he retired in 1931. Vagner actively continued to pursue his interests, finding in it "the source and sense of life," but felt that his cause had been frustrated by the authorities (Vagner, 1992a; 1992b).

At first sight, the young pedologist and the old biologist made an odd pair. But the fact is that, in December 1928, after Vagner invited Vygotsky to participate in a workshop on comparative psychology, they started corresponding and continued doing so until the death of Vagner, which was followed shortly thereafter by Vygotsky's. As is evident from the correspondence published in Vygodskaya & Lifanova (1996), they became close friends. Through his contacts in bureaucratic and scientific circles, Vygotsky helped his older colleague in all possible ways. When, for example, Vagner complained about the low amount of his pension, Vygotsky made inquiries at the ministry of education and learned how Vagner could increase his pension. He also attempted to arrange for the publication of a book written by Vagner. Vygotsky was not very successful in his efforts on Vagner's behalf, and could he not do anything about the ideologically inspired bureaucratic machinations which had become the rule. Moreover, he himself became increasingly ideologically vulnerable as well. But through his contacts with editorial boards and publishing houses he managed to find out why manuscripts got delayed.

In the field of theory, Vygotsky and Vagner grew closer. They at first differed about various subjects, but they gradually came to understand and accept each other's viewpoints and to an extent reached a shared perspective. Rather soon, Vagner came to see Vygotsky as the person who could continue his cause, the cause of introducing the idea of the comparative study of animal behavior into psychology (or, in other words, the creation of what we now call ethology). Vygotsky, however, was reluctant to do so, because he felt he lacked the required training and experience in the field of animal psychology and because his main interest was in the application of comparative psychological findings in the field of child psychology and eventually nothing came of it (Vygodskaya & Lifanova, 1996, p. 375). Some years later, Vagner would find Khotin and Roginsky as persons who could continue his line of research (Vagner, 1992b).

Theoretically, Vygotsky had been interested in Vagner since at least 1925, when we find his first references to Vagner's work. From the beginning he seemed to have shared Vagner's antireductionist view. Thus, he quoted Vagner approvingly when the latter criticized reflexology by stating that reflexes may be the foundation of behavior, but that a foundation says little about the building to be built on it. Reflexologists (read: Bekhterev and Pavlov) could not pretend to give an explanation for all human – or even animal – behavior (Vygotsky, 1925/1997; 1926b/1997). Vygotsky (1926c) also accepted Vagner's view that reflex, instinct, and intellect are qualitatively different levels of behavior that cannot be reduced to each other, and his claim that instinct and intellect developed in parallel from the common basis of reflexes (cf. Van der Veer & Valsiner, 1991b, pp. 194–7). Vagner's notion of "parallel lines" in development was also clearly relevant to Vygotsky's endeavor. Vagner had argued that: "The change of morphological and psychological characteristics *can take place independently of each other in two parallel lines*: In that the changes in these lines may coincide or not coincide with each other; new features can appear separately, i.e., morphological ones remain unchanged and psychological ones change, and vice versa: Psychological ones change and morphological ones remain unchanged" (Vagner, 1913, p. 235).

This was rather similar to Severtsov's notion of behavior of level 2b (see Table 8.1), i.e., behavior that is unaccompanied by gross structural or morphological changes. It also resembled Janet's functional approach that stated that higher mental functions need not be located in specific organs and can be executed in various ways (see Chapter 3). Such an approach enabled one to think of behavioral changes that were not necessarily accompanied by structural changes. In sum, it allowed Vygotsky to think about the influence on the behavioral development of learning and the culture at large within a framework of accepted biological science.

To be sure, during that period Vygotsky did not share all of Vagner's views. He was, for instance, critical of Vagner's remedy for the crisis in psychology, and he argued (Vygotsky, 1926b/1997; just like Ladygina-Kohts, 1923, pp. 23–4) that Vagner's biological approach was of limited value for human psychology. But in other respects, Vygotsky clearly thought along the lines indicated by Vagner, and we can see obvious parallels in their writings (Van der Veer & Valsiner, 1991b). More generally, we can say that Vygotsky fell into the camp of Russian comparative psychologists in that he (1) found the comparative (phylogenetic) study of animal behavior very relevant for psychology; (2) concurred with their view that different animals functioned on qualitatively different levels of behavior; and (3) rejected the reductionist approach of the physiologists who believed that all behavior – whether animal or human – was ultimately based on reflexes. Russian comparative psychologists opposed Russian reflexologists much like Western ethologists would later oppose Western behaviorists (Roëll, 1996). In practice, this meant that Russian comparative psychology disappeared for several decades after the authorities embraced Pavlov's new doctrine. During the 1930s, it became gradually more difficult to criticize Pavlov's ideas – let alone to state, like Borovsky, Ladygina-Kohts, and others had done, that his supposedly objectively existing brain processes, such as irradiation, were very hypothetical (cf. Joravsky, 1992) – and comparative psychologists took great care to make themselves invisible until comrade Stalin died.

The one major theoretical difference of opinion that Vygotsky had with Vagner was associated with their appraisal of the work of Wolfgang Köhler and Gestalt psychology at large. Vagner believed Köhler was over-interpreting his data and tried to persuade Vygotsky to take his point of view. Vygotsky at first accepted part of Köhler's claims and only gradually came to share Vagner's skepticism.

Gestalts and Developmental Psychology

There is no doubt that Vygotsky felt a great affinity for Gestalt psychology, and he was highly impressed and influenced by many Gestalt psychologists. During his only trip abroad, in 1925, Vygotsky visited Berlin University, where he probably met the major Gestalt psychologists and established long-lasting contacts. Luria also visited Berlin University on several occasions. Gestalt psychologists such as Gottschaldt, Koffka, and Lewin visited Moscow during the 1920s and 1930s, and Koffka participated in one of Vygotsky's major research projects. The fact that Russian psychologists such as Gita Birenbaum, Tamara Dembo, Maria Ovsiankina, and Bluma Zeigarnik worked for long periods in Berlin testifies to the close personal ties that existed between the Berlin Gestalt School and Russian psychology *à la* Vygotsky (Birenbaum and Zeigarnik returned to Moscow and became Vygotsky's collaborators). Vygotsky actively promoted Gestalt psychology in the Soviet Union by organizing the translation and publication of Gestalt psychological articles and books (e.g., Koffka, 1926; 1934; Köhler, 1930) and by writing overviews of and critical introductions to their ideas (e.g., Vygotsky, 1929b; 1930a; 1930b; 1934e). He also – following Köhler, Bühler, Brainard, and others – replicated Köhler's experiments with children and, like all great developmental psychologists, he used his own children as experimental subjects. As his oldest daughter remembers:

This was the period [1931, JV & RV] when father was very fascinated by Köhler's experiments. He wanted to replicate with children some of the things Köhler did with animals. . . . From various objects father made a labyrinth on the floor of the small part of the room that was available. I remember well, in particular, that long narrow boxes with index cards were used for that purpose. In the center of the labyrinth daddy put a mandarin, which means that the stimulus was for us very significant. Near the labyrinth a stick was lying which we had to use as a tool. If we managed to 'lead' the mandarin through the labyrinth, we ate it with pleasure . . . because this was for us a delicacy which we only seldom got. (Vygodskaya & Lifanova, 1996, p. 131)

This account, by the way, inadvertently shows the cultural context of psychological experimentation. Köhler's chimpanzees were motivated to act by the sight of bananas, Bühler's child subjects by the incentive of a piece of biscuit, the American psychologist Brainard

(1930) carried out Köhler-like experiments with his daughter by sticking chewing gum to the ceiling and, finally, Vygotsky enticed his daughter with a precious tangerine (*mandarin*).

Vygotsky considered relevant the findings of Gestalt psychology for both the genesis of human intelligence in phylogeny and the growth of intelligence in ontogeny, i.e., child development. In the domain of phylogeny, Vygotsky claimed that Köhler showed, in the best Darwinist tradition, that animals and man do not merely show anatomical and physiological similarities, but psychological ones as well. He amply discussed Köhler's investigations of the chimpanzees' problem solving behavior and concluded that they "threw a bridge over the abyss which divided intelligent and non-intelligent behavior; they showed a truth which from the viewpoint of Darwinism is undisputable: That the rudiments of intellect, the rudiments of intelligent activity are already present in the animal world" (Vygotsky, 1929c, pp. 420–1).

Vygotsky's fascination with Gestalt studies did not go unnoticed by his contemporaries, and when Gestalt psychology became suspect during the mid-1930s (because of its bourgeois, "foreign" nature), critics (e.g., Talankin, 1931a) were quick to point to the Gestalt influence in Vygotsky's work. Judging by Vygotsky's correspondence, even sympathetic researchers now and then identified him with the Gestalt movement. In a letter to Vagner (dated May 30, 1929), we find him saying that Vagner doesn't fully understand him, and that he is "not a Gestalt psychologist" (Vygodskaya & Lifanova, 1996, p. 374).

However, despite his high estimation of Gestalt psychology, Vygotsky always retained an independent view, and over the years he grew more critical of the key notions of Gestalt psychology (Van der Veer & Valsiner, 1991b; Van der Veer, 1997). Also, on the basis of his replication of Köhler's experiments with children, he came to see crucial differences between human problem solving and animal problem solving. In essence, he made three claims: (1) The ape's problem solving ability is limited; (2) The ape's semiotic activity is limited or nonexistent; and, most importantly, (3) In the ape, semiotic activity and problem solving are never connected (Vygotsky, 1929a; 1929c).

As to (1), Vygotsky pointed out, following Köhler and Bühler, that intelligent problem solving involving tool use or tool manufacture never is an important feature of animal life. That is, the chimpanzees show tool manufacture and tool use now and then but that it never becomes an important feature of the animals adaptation to the environment. This implies that without their "tools" the chimpanzees would live just as well as with them. For human beings, this is, of course, quite different.

As to (2), Vygotsky argued, following Köhler, that the chimpanzee's utterances are always subjective expressions of emotions and never signify something objective. He was inclined to attribute this lack of speech not to peripheral causes (e.g., inadequate vocal apparatus) but to some basic brain incapacity. In this connection, Vygotsky criticized Yerkes who had hypothesized that anthropoid apes have "higher ideation," i.e. the capacity to think with the help of representations and concepts. According to Yerkes, the apes failed to speak because they lack auditory imitation (cf. Ladygina-Kohts above). Vygotsky couldn't not believe this, as every known fact pointed to the ape's inability to signify something, but he reasoned that if Yerkes were right it should be possible to teach apes sign language such as is used by deaf and dumb people.

The principal fact, however, was in Vygotsky's view that (3) in animals language capacity (if at all present) and problem-solving activity are never connected. This important fact, which somehow received little attention in much of the later work on animal and human intelligence, Vygotsky amply discussed in a special paper (Vygotsky, 1929a), which subsequently became chapter 4 of *Thinking and Speech*. Following Köhler, he argued that the chimpanzee's problem solving (or practical intellect) is determined by the optical situation: Tools lose their "toolness" when they are not in the vicinity of the goal or when they become part of another Gestalt. A box used many times as a "platform" from which to reach a banana attached to the ceiling loses this quality as soon as another ape is sitting on it; it has become a "chair." In no way can it be said that the ape's attempts to reach a solution are connected to its vocal expressions. As said before, these simply serve to express or communicate emotions. Vocal speech, on the other hand, can in no way be said to depend upon the optical situation because it is an intellectual function. Vygotsky (1929a, p. 118) concluded that anthropoid apes display humanlike intelligence in some respects (the rudiments of tool use) and humanlike speech in quite different respects (phonetics, emotional expression, and rudiments of the social function). What they lack is the intimate connection between thinking and speech that is typically human. Thinking and speech thus have clearly distinct roots, and one can distinguish a preverbal stage in the development of intellect and a preintellectual stage in the development of speech. The theory developed to explain how lower (practical problem solving) and higher (speech) mental processes became merged was the so-called cultural-historical theory.

The Cultural-Historical Theory of Higher Mental Functions

Vygotsky's fascination with comparative psychology and Gestalt psychology should be seen against the background of what had become his main goal: to formulate a theory that gives an adequate account of the development, function, and structure of specifically human mental processes. From about 1927 he worked on this theory, advancing different versions, carrying out many experiments, and reading the contemporary literature. In 1931, he wrote *The History of the Development of Higher Mental Functions*, which can be seen as the most complete version of his so-called cultural-historical theory of the higher mental functions (Vygotsky, 1931/1983; 1931/1997). This theory offered a peculiar and controversial account of children's mental development based on the findings of the anthropology, clinical psychology, comparative psychology, and developmental psychology of the time.

Vygotsky's basic idea was that human ontogeny differs from animal ontogeny and human phylogeny in that it combines two "lines": the lines of natural and cultural development. In his view, human phylogeny consisted of two "stages," a stage of slow biological evolution and a stage of accelerated development after the "invention" of tools and language. Biologically, he reasoned, the human species has not changed much during the last few hundred thousand years. Human natural capacities have essentially remained the same. However, the development of tools and language made rapid cultural growth possible, which resulted in radically changed mental processes. The mental processes of modern human beings are fundamentally different from those of hominids who had only the rudiments of speech and tool use. Thus what we observe in human phylogeny is Vagner's and Severtsov's psychological development without gross morphological change.

Human ontogeny differs from phylogeny in that biological, natural development (maturation, growth), and culture (language, tools, cultural artifacts) are present at the same time. The biological, natural newborn grows up in an environment replete with cultural signs, tools, and other artifacts. The result is a merging of two strands of development, the natural and the cultural one, into a specifically human, unique form of development. Nevertheless, it is still important to distinguish between a natural and a cultural line in child development; if only because an adequate understanding of their intricate interplay may allow us to help handicapped children for whom the standard cultural means may often be inappropriate, and who need circuitous routes.

The concept of cultural development can be elucidated as follows. The older S – R psychology described persons as beings who passively reacted to environmental stimuli. The S – R schema is valid as a general principle but cannot do justice to what is specifically human. Specific to human beings is that they create stimuli to determine their own behavior. Such stimuli-means have a social origin, and we usually call them "signs". Vygotsky's favorite example was that of a situation in which two equally strong stimuli call for a response. Suppose that a girl cannot make a choice between two equally attractive lovers. According to the S – R doctrine, if the lovers are really equally attractive, the girl cannot make a choice and will not act. In reality, however, she will introduce a totally new stimulus into the situation which will decide the situation in favor of one of the lovers. She may decide that the first one who calls is her favorite. She may toss a coin. She may translate the letters of the first names of her lovers into numbers, and decide that the one with the lowest sum total has won. And so on. There is an infinite number of methods to decide such a theoretically balanced situation. Characteristic is that the person herself introduces a fully arbitrary stimulus into the situation and reacts to that stimulus. Vygotsky emphasized that the S – R principle remains valid, because the girl will react to the new stimulus in a prearranged way, if she plays honest. Thus, if John calls first, he will be her man. However, the fact that persons themselves introduce these new stimuli-means into the situation to steer their own behavior makes it a special, specifically human one that transcends the S – R analysis.

This analysis is peculiar and paradoxical because it describes the person as deciding to be a slave to the situation. Unlike animals, human beings can alter the environment and thereby master their own behavior. In this new environment, however, they are subject to the S – R laws. To be genuinely free is to know the natural laws that hold and to make use of this knowledge. This master–slave view echoed similar views by Hegel, Engels, Spinoza, and Bacon. The latter's dictum "Nature to be commanded must be obeyed" (Bacon, 1620/1960, p. 39), Vygotsky used to quote approvingly.

Vygotsky's idea was that all higher mental processes involve such arbitrary or conventional stimuli-means. To the extent that such stimuli-means, or signs, are cultural and social products, we can say that higher mental processes are culturally and socially determined. Thus cultural development is that part of development that makes use of cultural stimuli-means, or signs, or instruments.

The concept of natural development was left somewhat undefined at this stage of Vygotsky's theorizing. In analyzing his experiments, he was inclined to call that type of behavior natural if it does not involve the use of stimuli-means or instruments. Thus, if subjects are supplied with cards in a paired-associates memory task and are not capable of using these cards to improve their performance, their behavior is considered natural. In this sense, natural clearly meant preinstrumental, and the period of natural development presumably varies depending on the cultural instrument to be mastered. In this sense, seven or eight-year-old children can still be said to display natural behavior. Natural behavior is behavior that does not make use of specific, task-related cultural means, e.g., a child does not yet know how to use dice to force a decision.

We might define natural behavior broader by saying that it is behavior that does not make use of any cultural means. However, if we accept this broader definition, then it immediately becomes clear that the behavior of seven or eight-year-old children cannot be natural in this sense. For, as Vygotsky repeatedly emphasized, the pre-eminent cultural instrument is the word (conceived as sign during this period of Vygotsky's development; conceived as concept in the final stage of his theorizing). But children of that age surely use words and conceive of the experimental task in words. Therefore, it is impossible to consider their behavior to be natural. To find natural behavior one would have to go back to the preverbal period in child development, which is what Vygotsky implies in other parts of his work. Proceeding from such a broad definition, several psychologists have criticized Vygotsky's conception of natural development (Van der Veer & Van IJzendoorn, 1985).

Vygotsky emphasized that the distinction between natural and cultural development was a conceptual, theoretical one, and in actual practice the two lines could hardly be distinguished. However, under specific circumstances, these lines could be shown to be different.

First, we can try to study the merging of cultural and natural lines in vivo by supplying subjects with the cultural means that they can use to enhance their natural performance in some experimental setup. According to Vygotsky, such experiments quite probably do not yield an accurate account of how this merging takes place in actual child development, but they can provide a model for how it might take place in principle. Thus, he carried out many experiments in which he confronted children with tasks that surpassed their natural abilities, and then he supplied them with the cultural means that made better performance possible. This constituted his method of double stimulation, so-called because the subjects are confronted with both stimuli (stimuli-objects) and means (stimuli-means) to control their reaction to these stimuli (cf. the intimations of this concept by Baldwin and Dewey in Chapters 4 and 5). For example, children might be asked to memorize lists of twenty or thirty words that were read to them. Naturally, they would be incapable of reproducing such a list after one trial. Performance improves dramatically, however, if we now supply the children with pictures that can be associated with the words to be memorized. At a certain age, children become capable of making effective picture-word links and reproducing the words by looking at the pictures laid in front of them. Vygotsky and his associates carried out dozens of such experiments to find out, among other things, whether the ability to use such aids is dependent on age (it is); whether it comes spontaneously (mostly not); whether children of different ages use them in different ways (they do); whether the use of external aids is replaced by the use of internal aids (it is); and so on. On the basis of his findings, he concluded that the merging of natural processes (in this case, natural memory) and cultural means (in this case, pictures) is a process of internalization. Subjects originally rely on material, external means but gradually learn to replace them by internal means (mostly verbal means, e.g., the ability to enhance performance by grouping words into categories).

Second, Vygotsky argued that historical, anthropological, and developmental findings showed that his account of the genesis of higher mental functions was indeed plausible. Take the example of counting. According to cultural-historical theory this should be an ability that first proceeds by making use of external means and then becomes internal. Historical findings do indeed show that earlier in history counting systems existed that made use of external means such as body parts or strings with knots. Anthropologists have shown that such systems exist in non-Western cultures. Vygotsky interpreted this finding developmentally by positing that such systems still exist, thereby suggesting that the development of counting somehow got arrested in these cultures, and that such systems are remnants of the past. Finally, developmental psychologists have pointed out that younger children often prefer to make use of external means – such as their fingers – in counting. As they grow older they can increasingly do without these external means. Of course, adults do rely on external means (e.g., agendas, lecture notes, secretaries) but Vygotsky again interpreted this fact developmentally. In his view, the usage of such means was again a remnant of the past. For example, when a person ties a knot in his or her handkerchief to remember a certain event, he or she is making use of a method that developmentally speaking belongs to an earlier period. Such phenomena Vygotsky called rudimentary processes or functions, and in his view they betrayed the origin and development of our mental processes. One feels that ideally, then, for Vygotsky, all mental processes should proceed completely internally, relying on internal means. For a person with a perfectly organized memory – Vygotsky is known to have performed as a memory artist for his students, memorizing and recalling long lists of words in chronological and reverse order – it was a plausible assumption to make.

Third, in certain clinical cases we can see that what we take for natural processes and abilities are in reality cultural conventions. Thus such cases serve as natural experiments (see Chapter 3) and allow us to distinguish between the natural and cultural line in development. For example, in normal, sighted people, reading is a visual process, and one is inclined to forget that visual reading is a cultural convention. However, learning to read is learning how to connect certain conventional signs with certain meanings or words, and there is no need for these signs to be visual. Thus, in the case of blind people, finger reading using the Braille characters proves perfectly possible. Such examples show that processes that we take to be natural may rely on cultural conventions. They also show that if regular development of a process is blocked because of pathological disturbances or handicaps, adequate functioning may still be possible by way of other, circuitous routes. The existing conventions for reading, speaking, etc. are perfectly adapted to the normal healthy person, and that is why we fail to fully appreciate their cultural origin. Nature's experiments allow us to unravel the natural and cultural lines of development.

Above we have used such terms as higher, cultural, social, medi-ated, and internal, on the one hand, and lower, natural, unmediated, and external, on the other, rather indiscriminately. It is useful to dis-cuss them in somewhat more detail. This will allow us to see what meaning Vygotsky attached to these terms and whether they are fully equivalent or have different shades of meaning.

Often Vygotsky would distinguish between higher and lower psy-chological functions or processes. Higher processes are called higher because they are lower processes that have been transformed in cer-tain ways. Specifically, they have become cultural, social, mediated, and internal. Let us try to elucidate these terms by discussing some of Vygotsky's examples of so-called lower and higher psychological pro-cesses.

Why are higher processes cultural? Higher mental processes are called cultural because they involve the use of cultural procedures and means that vary across cultures. Thus, if asked to memorize a long list of unrelated words we might simply look at them carefully (a type of strategy that we presumably share with animals, although in animals recognition is of course more easily demonstrated than recall) and hope to be able to reproduce them afterward. Such a procedure is not very effective. We might also try to make use of mnemonics such as the method of loci. However, such mnemonics have been developed within specific cultures and vary across cultures. In this sense, the higher and typically human memory strategy of using mnemonics is cultural.

Why are higher processes social? Higher mental processes are social because they have a social origin. Here, two of Vygotsky's examples are particularly interesting. The first example is that of the pointing gesture. In Vygotsky's analysis, the pointing gesture is originally no more than the infant's unsuccessful attempt to grasp an object. How-ever, the adults surrounding the infant interpret its movement as a pointing gesture and react accordingly. Gradually, the child will real-ize the (social) effect of its movement and, finally, it will begin making use of it deliberately. Thus, it is the social others who initially attach meaning to the child's movement, and the child is the last to realize the meaning of its gesture. The pointing gesture exists first for others and only then for the child. In this sense, the pointing gesture can be said to have a social origin. The second example is that of words. Vygotsky accepted and repeatedly quoted what he saw as Janet's law (see Chapter 3):

In general we might say that the relations between higher mental functions once were genuine relations between people. I relate to myself like people relate to me. Just like verbal thinking represents the internalization of speech, just like reflection is the internalization of argument, precisely so the mental function of the word, according to Janet, can only be explained by taking into consideration a system broader than man himself. The original psychological function of the word is a social function, and, if we wish to trace how the word functions in the person's behavior, we must examine how it previously functioned in the social behavior of people . . . every function in the cultural development of the child appears on the stage twice, in two planes, first, the social, then the psychological, first between people as an interpsychological category, then within the child as an intrapsychological category. (Vygotsky, 1931/1983, p. 142/145)

A simple example would be that of a child learning to cross the street. At the first stage, the parents will tell the child to watch to the left and to the right, etc., and the child will simply follow these instructions. At the next stage, the child will tell himself or herself aloud to watch to the left and to the right and thus instruct himself or herself. At the final stage, he or she will think only these instructions. Thus a process that was originally shared between two persons, an interpsychological process, has become an individual, intrapsychological process. The child is applying to himself or herself what first was applied to him or her by others.

The example of the pointing gesture and the example of verbal instructions seem to deal with cases that are rather different. In the example of the pointing gesture, the child spontaneously displays behavior that is subsequently interpreted in a specific way and only then acquires this meaning for the child itself. This is the way spontaneous behavior might become socialized. In the same way, the infant's affective states expressed in global motor behavior are continually interpreted by the social others, viewed as the externalization of certain internal mental states and thereby become expressions of mental states, if we must believe Wallon (cf. Van der Veer, 1996b). In the example of verbal instruction, there is no spontaneous behavior but imitation or mastery of the instruction to steer the self. No such self-instruction or autostimulation is apparent in the pointing gesture example. What we see here is that the notion of the social origin of higher mental functions acquires different meanings, meanings that can be traced to the different traditions from which Vygotsky synthesized his own view.

Why are higher processes mediated? Higher mental processes are mediated because they involve the use of a means or medium in the sense of an intervening thing through which a force acts or an effect is produced (cf. Webster's dictionary). As shown above, the basic idea is that the original S – R link is broken by the introduction of an intermediate procedure or stimuli-means. The meaning and force of the new stimulus is determined by convention. There is no intrinsic reason why heads would mean staying home, and tail visiting Aunt Annie, but if the subject decides so then heads and tails acquire this meaning. The possibility of introducing stimuli-means of our own making allows us to master our own behavior in a roundabout way.

Why are higher processes internal? Vygotsky reasoned that all higher mental processes are internal because they have undergone the process of internalization. Initially we perform calculations using various body parts, etc., later on we learn to do it by heart. But of course many complex mental processes are still and will always be carried out with the help of external means. Abacuses, slide rules, pocket calculators, and computers make the performance of complex operations much easier, and their usage sometimes requires complex thought. In Vygotsky's theory, it is not always clear what is being internalized, nor why complete internalization of some complex process would be recommendable (higher).

It is important to see that the various ways to designate higher mental functions (cultural, social, mediated, internal) do not fully overlap and may not always be entirely consistent. Thus, the pointing gesture does not seem to be cultural in the sense of cross culturally variable. Nor does it become internalized unless we consider it with Vygotsky (1931/1983, p. 323) to be a precursor of words, which is doubtful. The terms mediated and internal do not have the same meaning. It is an interesting question whether mediated processes need to be social in the sense of having an interpersonal origin. Likewise, one might ask whether all cultural transmission requires mediation in the Vygotskian sense (Van der Veer, 1996a). There are, we think, still many unexplored issues here. Vygotsky adduced massive evidence from a variety of sources for his sociogenetic view and used a plethora of examples to illustrate it. It is one of modern psychology's tasks to see whether the data makes a coherent unified theory.

The cultural-historical theory was strongly developmentally oriented. Vygotsky's pathos was to unravel the synthesis of natural and cultural lines in development, and all of his investigations during this

372   THE SOCIAL MIND

period were designed toward this goal. Investigation should be developmental, genetic investigation, because the true nature of a phenomenon can only be established by tracing its origin and development. Ideally, as stated above, development should be caught in vivo in specially designed experiments. Vygotsky criticized existing research for its almost exclusive concentration on what he called finished, fossilized processes, and he argued that we need to liquify them by returning to their origin (cf. Baldwin's remark that reactions may "lose all appearance of their true origin" in Chapter 4). If we want to analyze the skill of reading, for example, it is much more instructive to study children learning to read than to study adult readers. For adults, the development of reading skills has been completed and the whole process has become automatic. To analyze a skill in such static cases can be quite difficult. Just like a hare in a field becomes practically invisible when it no longer moves, the true nature of mental processes is difficult to discover when they no longer develop. "It is only while moving that a body exhibits what it is," Vygotsky (1931/1983, p. 63) said.

What, then, is development? What is the relationship between lower and higher mental processes? Development is the continuous restructuring of natural processes and abilities by mastering cultural instruments (which can subsequently be replaced by more powerful instruments and so on). Natural processes and abilities are subject to growth and maturation themselves, but they undergo a much more crucial transformation, in Vygotsky's view, when they intersect the cultural line of development. For example, infants clearly show memory abilities in that they can recognize faces and objects. This type of memory may develop and become much stronger to the extent that children acquire a truly eidetic memory. Insofar as this type of memory is nonverbal and, more generally, unmediated, Vygotsky would consider it natural. However, at a certain age children learn to use cultural means such as words (e.g., category names) to enhance their memory performance. Certainly, for certain material, this constitutes a definite improvement (the recognition of faces may be a special case). It doesn't mean, however, that the child's natural memory has disappeared. The natural memory capacity is still there but now has come under the control of language. It is not replaced but preserved in a subordinate form or superseded, as Vygotsky (e.g., 1931/1983, p. 113) used to say. Like Janet (see Chapter 3), he was inclined to compare lower and higher mental processes (e.g., nonverbal and verbal memory) with lower (older) and higher (younger) layers of the brain and to discuss the process of development in geological terms. Like Janet he suggested that lower processes might take charge again if higher processes are somehow disturbed.

One may distinguish two conceptions of the relationship between lower and higher processes here. A radical conception (transformation) says that lower processes, in the process of mastering a cultural skill, undergo a fundamental alteration that cannot be undone. For example, a person having learned how to play chess would never again be able to see a configuration of chess pieces in a naive fashion. A less radical (superseding) conception says that the lower function is controlled by the higher one but can function in its original form if this control is somehow relinquished. Like Janet, Vygotsky opted for the less radical version, and like Janet he referred to studies of aphasia by Cassirer, Goldstein, Head, Hughlings, and Jackson, and others to argue this view. In this view, a person who loses the capacity to use abstract terms, for example, is essentially reduced to the state he was before he acquired these terms. It is a view that seems as debatable as it is difficult to test.

Vygotsky's view of development and his cultural-historical theory at large borrowed many concepts and findings from the investigations of his predecessors and contemporaries. Many things that now seem original and truly innovative were quite commonplace at the time Vygotsky advanced them. His genetic approach, for example, with its study of the phylogenetic and ontogenetic domain and comparative psychology (cf. Wertsch, 1985) had been a usual one for some time.

In 1922, an APA committee led by Howard Warren had already defined genetic psychology as the "systematic study of mental phenomena in terms of the origin and development of mental life in the individual, in the race, or in any part of the animal series" (Calkins, Dunlap, Gardiner, Ruckmick, & Warren, 1922). In other chapters of this book, notably Chapter 3, the reader can find many concepts that sometimes are seen as Vygotskian by modern psychologists. Elsewhere (Van der Veer & Valsiner, 1991b) we have made a major attempt to trace some of the roots of Vygotsky's thinking and have argued that his cultural-historical theory should be seen as a synthesis of more or less known ideas from different sources.

The theory is truly unique in its emphasis on and elaboration of certain concepts. And it is quite easy to recognize a text as having been written by Vygotsky. If we were to mention some elements that would allow the lay reader to recognize a text as Vygotskian, then the following things come to mind. First, there is Vygotsky's singular elaboration of the issue of mastery or control. Cultural instruments allow us to master our own primitive behavior in a roundabout way. By using these instruments we are both master and slave, and to the extent that cultural instruments are transmitted to us by the social other, we are both the other and ourself, alter and ego. In short, Vygotsky concluded, we are a homo duplex (cf. Daudet's observation in Chapter 2). Second, there is Vygotsky's internalization theory that emphasized the transition from reliance on external means to reliance on internal means. Debatable as it may seem, this allowed Vygotsky to investigate (a model of) the internalization process empirically. Ironically, his often criticized and vaguely described experimental investigations of internalization were the first of their sort. Finally, Vygotsky made his own use of nature's experiments. The idea of studying pathological cases to understand normal development was traditional (see Chapter 3), but the idea to use the case of handicapped (deaf and blind) children to illuminate the conventional, cultural nature of such processes as reading and speaking was distinctly Vygotskian.

The cultural-historical theory was a grand attempt to elucidate the nature-nurture issue in child development. The assumption was that one may distinguish lower and higher mental processes and that higher processes develop in ontogeny under the strong influence of culture. To argue this view, Vygotsky and his associates investigated both pathological (e.g., mental disturbances following brain damage) and developmental evidence. The developmental evidence was gathered in three branches of research. The first branch of research was meant to investigate whether different cultures indeed yield different higher mental processes as cultural-historical theory predicts. To investigate this issue Vygotsky's associate, Luria, organized several expeditions to Uzbekistan (Van der Veer & Valsiner, 1991b). The second branch of research involved a longitudinal study of homozygotic and dizygotic twins. The study of these diverse twins helped to unravel the contribution of nature and nurture. Finally, the study of normal and handicapped children allowed Vygotsky and his associates to distinguish the natural and cultural lines of development and to see which alternative routes development can take. Taken together, pathological and developmental data yield a picture of mental development that one may find convincing or not, but it did give rise to a research tradition that continues to this day.

Concepts in Education

During the final years of his life, Vygotsky's thinking underwent several important changes, and he developed several of the concepts for which he would become most well known. One of the major shifts in his thinking was his growing emphasis on word meanings or concepts. Previously, in his cultural-historical theory, he had discussed the process of the mastering of lower natural functions in terms of the mastering of cultural signs. Signs could be material means or they could be words, but they were conceived of as something static, as solid stimuli-means that themselves did not undergo development. Cultural development was seen as the mastering and discarding of instruments (see Vygotsky & Luria, 1930). By 1932, Vygotsky realized, in the case of words, the stimuli-means themselves might be seen as undergoing development, and the somewhat discrete, mechanistic image of children who stimulate themselves with ever new stimuli-means (as if they themselves were operating the switchboard in Pavlov's famous switchboard analogy) was replaced by a more fluid image of children who acquire concepts or word meanings that gradually change as the child acquires new experience. In a way, this new emphasis on changing word meanings was a return to Vygotsky's earlier fascination with Humboldt and Potebnya.

Important was Vygotsky's realization that word meanings do change, a fact that had been empirically demonstrated in the research of Ach, Uznadze, and others (Van der Veer & Valsiner, 1991b). Children use the same words as adults do to designate specific objects, but the meaning of these words may be quite different. Thus, the word "farmer" may evoke romantic images in the child of a person taking care of animals and growing crop, while adults may think of an entrepreneur who, within certain constraints, tries to maximize his profit. Using various strategies, Vygotsky tried to prove experimentally that a mature understanding of many concepts is only reached in adolescence. In this connection, he introduced a distinction between mature, academic, or scientific concepts, on the one hand, and immature, or everyday concepts, on the other. Supposedly, the academic concept expressed the true state of affairs and was linked to other similar concepts. Together they formed a coherent network covering a field of knowledge. Academic concepts are taught at school. Everyday concepts often focused on irrelevant features of some subject and together formed a disconnected whole. Everyday concepts children acquire in an informal setting and more or less independently.

Vygotsky's basic idea was that academic concepts and everyday concepts mutually enrich each other. The everyday concept of farmer is enriched because the child now learns the nonapparent fact that farmers form part of an economic market in which they try to realize certain goals. The academic concept of farmer is enriched because the abstract notion of entrepreneurs dealing with cattle and crop is filled with concrete facts of daily farmer life; it gets body and flesh. Thus, academic concepts presuppose everyday concepts, build upon them, but once acquired they alter the everyday concepts in fundamental ways. The result of the interplay between the everyday and academic concept is an elaborate and rich notion of the concept of farmer. Vygotsky speculated that the introduction of systems of academic concepts in school would restructure the child's whole style of thinking, i.e., he assumed that the introduction of such concepts in specific subject areas would generalize to other areas. Investigations by his student Shif (1935) were designed to prove this hypothesis but remained inconclusive (Van der Veer & Valsiner, 1991b).

Although Vygotsky discussed the interplay between academic or scientific and everyday concepts in terms of mutual enrichment, it is quite clear that he attached far more importance to the academic concepts. Academic concepts embodied the latest scientific knowledge about a certain topic, and it was of the utmost importance that students were introduced to them in school. Without this knowledge and understanding of scientific concepts, their understanding of reality would remain inadequate. Thus teaching scientific concepts in the formal setting of a school is essential because it fundamentally restructures the child's whole way of thinking that becomes more in accordance with the scientific point of view. Education leads development, as Vygotsky used to put it. Instruction in the school setting propels child development along lines that are each time specific for a certain culture or society.

The fundamental role of word meanings or concepts in all higher mental processes had now become a major theme in Vygotsky's thinking. In his view, concepts formed the key to understanding both cognitive and emotional development, and mental disintegration.

Mastering mature conceptual thinking was not confined to the cognitive domain, but will also lead to more mature aesthetic reactions, and a more refined emotional life. In case of serious pathology, such as in schizophrenia (Vygotsky, 1934f) or Pick's disease (Samukhin, Birenbaum, and Vygotsky, 1934), the thinking in concepts was thought to be influenced adversely, and several of the symptoms of these diseases were interpreted as the result of a breakdown of conceptual thinking.

Vygotsky's view of conceptual development was not received favorably by his Soviet contemporaries. The idea that children's concepts of material objects gradually change in the interaction with adults who have other concepts of these same objects was branded philosophical "idealism." True knowledge was based on and determined by interaction with, or rather action upon, objects, mental development. Interaction of free-floating minds could not yield such true knowledge. And Vygotsky's earlier experiments in which he tried to show that all mediational means are originally external or material were happily ignored by his comrades who zealously participated in the autos-da-fé organized by the authorities (cf. Van der Veer & Valsiner, 1991b).

From the present viewpoint, the emphasis on (scientific) concepts as the prime movers of mental development seems to imply a somewhat static and peaceful view of (scientific) thinking. In this view, scientific approaches crystallize into generally agreed upon scientific concepts (such as "energy" and "mammal"), which subsequently must be transmitted to the next generation. Such an approach should be complemented with an approach in which science is depicted as less uniform, and in which children are taught certain more content-free heuristics, skills, rethorics, and practices that may be flexibly used in broad contexts (cf. Van der Veer, 1992).

The Zone of Proximal Development

In 1933, in a number of lectures for various audiences, Vygotsky introduced the concept of the so-called zone of proximal development. Many interesting interpretations of this concept have been advanced (cf. Valsiner & Van der Veer, 1993), but these need not bother us here. It will suffice to say a few words about its context, its nature, and its usefulness as an instrument of a sociogenetic approach.

The first thing to realize is that Vygotsky's thinking about the relationship between instruction or education, on the one hand, and mental development, on the other, proceeded within the context of Russian paedology. *Paedology*, or child study, as it was known in English-speaking countries, had known better times in the West, but still flourished in the Soviet Union during the late 1920s and early 1930s. Its supporters advocated the massive use of mental tests to fit education to pupils, or, perhaps, to fit pupils to available schools. Following the work of Western investigators such as Burt and Terman ("What pupils shall be tested? The answer is all"; cf. Terman et al., 1923), attempts were made to compose ideal groups of pupils, the assumption being that pupils should have the same mental age (e.g., "The mentally old and mentally young do not belong together"; Terman, 1921, p. 27). Western journals such as *Journal of Educational Research*, *Journal of Educational Psychology*, and *Pedagogical Seminary*, were filled with methods to use IQ tests to improve classroom composition, to construct optimal curricula, to optimize the choice of textbooks, and so on. Russian pedologists, such as Blonsky and Vygotsky, followed these developments attentively and tried to use them to their advantage. It can be said that Vygotsky was actively participating in the testing movement.

However, Vygotsky had always been critical of IQ tests. Working as a clinical psychologist with deaf, blind, and backward children, he was in need of truly diagnostic instruments that allowed one to make a prognosis and to devise prosthetic means. The apodictic numbers of the Stanford-Binet test were of little value in this context. He also vehemently opposed the idea (equally vehemently advocated by Burt and Terman) that mental tests measured pure genetic endowment.

However, the Russian educational system was confronted with millions of pupils of very diverse economic and cultural backgrounds (e.g., whose parents were illiterate or did not have Russian as their native tongue). It was an issue of great practical significance to find the right educational route for the right child; in his work at the Herzen Institute, Vygotsky could not ignore these problems. We can see, then, why Vygotsky would be extremely anxious to find the optimal student-education fit, and why he would be looking for methods to optimize this fit.

It was in this context that he hit upon the concept of the zone of proximal development. We have seen that Vygotsky subscribed to the sociogenetic law that "every function in the cultural development of the child appears on the stage twice, in two planes, first, the social, then the psychological, first between people as an interpsychological

category, then within the child as an intrapsychological category."
This law described a fundamental law of human ontogenesis. It seems
Vygotsky transposed this law to the domain of prognosis. He interpreted the interpsychological process and the intrapsychological process as two stages (first – then) and concluded that, if the one preceeds
the other, then the one may be used to predict the other. Hence his
claim that we should measure what the child is able to do in cooperation with someone else (interpsychologically) in order to be able to
predict what the child can do independently (intrapsychologically)
later on. At any given moment, we can measure both the child's
independent and its dependent performance. The difference between
the two performances gives us the child's nearest mental trajectory. In
his own words: "The zone of proximal development of the child is the
distance between his actual development, determined with the help of
independently solved tasks, and the level of the potential development of the child, determined with the help of tasks solved by the
child under the guidance of adults and in cooperation with his more
intelligent peers" (Vygotsky, 1935, p. 42).

Thus asking a child to perform a series of tasks twice, first independently and subsequently in cooperation with an adult, was another
means to externalize development, to make cultural development visible. As such, it was comparable to Vygotsky's earlier experiments in
which subjects first learned to make use of external means and subsequently switched to internal means. And we meet with a similar
difficulty. In the case of the use of external means (e.g., cards in a
memory task), we can reconstruct (memory) development until children begin making use of semiotic means. We then have no longer a
means to externalize the process other than the age-old one of introspection. And the use of material cards is not predictive of these
semiotic means. Children may rely on different semiotic means. Thus
the final stage of development remains elusive and unpredictable. The
same is true for the repeated measurement of intelligence in the context of determining the zone of proximal development. We may conceive of the interpsychological performance (performance in cooperation with an adult of more able peer) as a stage, we may claim that
this way we have externalized part of development, but there is no
reliable way of fully externalizing or predicting intrapsychological
development. The problem is that we cannot know what use the child
will make of the guidance and assistance. The problem is that the
child will creatively and idiosyncratically transform the assistance

given, and therefore the attempt to capture the future by determining the zone of proximal development is misguided.

These problems also touch upon the issue of the transformation of cultural instruments or means. During the final period of his life, Vygotsky discussed the issue of inner speech and, on the basis of the existing linguistic theories, argued that inner speech differs fundamentally from external speech. In the internalization process (which goes from external speech, via egocentric speech, to inner speech) speech acquires very different properties. He also argued that words or concepts may acquire a different personal sense for different individuals. But if we take his arguments seriously, and we should, then it follows that mediational means undergo a process of fundamental transformation that makes all prediction hazardous and inconsistent with Vygotsky's whole approach (cf. Valsiner & Van der Veer, 1993, for a more elaborate discussion).

Emotions

In Chapter 5, ample attention was paid to James' theory of emotions and its reception by Baldwin, Dewey, Irons, Janet, and others. No definite conclusions were reached, and the subject of emotions remained a lively topic of discussion throughout the 1910s and 1920s. In 1927 the first international symposium on feelings and emotions was held at the Wittenberg College, in Springfield, Ohio (Reymert, 1928). Among the psychologists who presented a paper, we find such experts as Adler, Bekhterev, Karl Bühler, Cannon, Claparède, Janet, McDougall, Prince, and William Stern. In 1928 Janet published the second volume of his *From Anxiety to Ecstacy* and amply discussed the peripheral theory, i.e., the James-Lange theory, and the critique it received from both European (e.g., Binet, Courtier, Sollier) and American scholars (e.g., Dewey and the Chicago School with Dearborn, Gardiner, Stanley Hall, Irons, and others). He particularly singled out the "remarkable paper" by Irons (1895d), entitled "Descartes and Modern Theories of Emotion." In discussing Nahlowski's intellectual theory of emotions, he remarked that its ideas could be traced back to Spinoza's discussion of passions (cf. Janet, 1928b, pp. 17–43).

These few remarks do not adequately describe the developments in the contemporary debate on emotion theories, but they are mentioned here because far away, in distant Moscow, Lev Vygotsky made his own attempt to think through the topic of emotions, and the proceedings of the Wittenberg symposium, and Janet's chapter formed his major sources of inspiration. From about 1930 onward, he wrote different versions of a manuscript on theories of emotion and their deficits. The final variant survived in his private archives and was recently published (Vygotsky, 1933/1984; cf. 1932/1984).

Drawing on Irons (1895d), Vygotsky argued that James' theory of emotion was largely equivalent to Descartes' (1649/1985) theory presented in his *The Passions of the Soul*. He then proceeded to show that the psychology of emotions and psychology at large were hampered by the Cartesian legacy of mind-body dualism. Finally, he argued that a study of Spinoza's work might yield a way of overcoming mind–body dualism in emotion theory.

Vygotsky argued that both James' emotion theory and Descartes' theory of passions provided a deterministic and causal account of emotions and that they emphasized their bodily part, However, such an approach has an unfortunate consequence, that is, it becomes difficult to conceive of the development of emotions as the child grows older. After all, if an emotion is taken to be a process of becoming aware of bodily changes, as James' theory seemed to suggest, then one would have to argue that these bodily processes change in ontogenesis, which seems unlikely. In any case, it is difficult to see how primitive emotions (e.g., fear, anger) develop into more refined emotions (e.g., spite). In the Cartesian view, primitive emotions (and the bodily states that give rise to them) continue to exist or decay and are replaced by other more refined emotions.

Vygotsky was not satisfied with such an account of emotional development. He argued that adults have a more refined emotional life than children, and demanded that psychology should sketch the transition from the first primitive emotions to higher emotional experiences (cf. Averill, 1986). In his view, development was not a process of replacement but a process of transformation (cf. his critique of Piaget in Vygotsky, 1934c/sh1987). The reason that James could not show how lower emotions develop into higher ones, Vygotsky argued, was that the first belonged to the realm of the body and the latter pertained to the realm of the soul. In fact, James (1884/1984, pp. 127–8) distinguished the "standard" emotions, for which his theory would hold, from intellectual, or "cerebral," emotions that supposedly had no bodily correlates and for which his theory, consequently, would not hold. The latter he preferred to call "judgments," or "cognitions," rather than emotions, but he realized that this "solution" still implied "an antagonism . . . between the spirit and the flesh" (James, 1884/1984, pp. 138–40).

Vygotsky was not impressed by James' distinction between standard emotions with bodily correlates and cerebral emotions without such bodily correlates. He stated that James concurred with Descartes (1649/1985, p. 381), who had likewise posited "internal emotions which are produced in the soul only by the soul itself," and concluded that James continued Cartesian mind–body dualism. In his view, James' theory of emotions did nothing to explain how higher, specifically human, emotions develop from lower ones.

Vygotsky's analysis was interesting but could he offer an alternative? He could not. In his vain efforts to find a satisfactory, nondualistic, developmental, approach of emotions, he turned to what had been one of his favorite books since his adolescence, Spinoza's (1677/ 1955) *Ethics*. Yet he never managed to develop a theory of emotions on the basis of his reading of Spinoza, and it is easy to see why. Spinoza's work was useful to Vygotsky insofar as it advocated that there is no principal distinction between lower emotional processes and higher intellectual processes and defended a monistic, causal-deterministic approach. The problem was that it entirely lacked a developmental perspective, and thus was of no use in the attempts to devise a developmental theory of emotions. Thus Vygotsky's manuscript offered an interesting analysis of James' theory of emotions and its deficits, but failed to offer an alternative.

Conclusions

Looking back to Vygotsky's work and its echoes in this chapter, one can see that much of his efforts went into devising a psychology that was at once truly human and based on sound biology. He wished to show that humans share emotions with animals but that they, in addition, have higher emotions. He acknowledged that animals have a memory but added that humans can master their memory by making use of instruments. He accepted that animals make use of tools but argued that humans dispose of the very special tool of speech which fundamentally alters their mind. He wished to show that humans have consciousness but emphasized its biological function and wanted this phenomenon to be causally explicable. In sum, he wished to show animal–human being continuity in the spirit of Darwinism and human uniqueness in the spirit of Marxism. He wished to show that human beings had somewhere in human history made the dialectical leap from biological necessity to human self-mastery and freedom. In essence, then, his was a very optimistic theory that emphasized that humans can master their own fate by making use of the instruments of civilization.

This general theme is behind several of the key features of Vygotsky's work: his consistent developmental approach, his anti-reductionism, his interest in comparative psychology, his emphasis on dialectical synthesis (cf. Van der Veer & Valsiner, 1991b). During his final years, he became convinced that the preeminent cultural instruments are word meanings or concepts. From then on, in a curious return to his earlier fascination with linguistic theory, he described mental development in terms of the acquisition of concepts, and mental structure in terms of mental functions that become interlocked by the dominant function of speech, i.e., the acquisition of concepts. The prime mover of mental development had now become the mastery of academic concepts in education. Hence the title of this chapter.

To argue his view, Vygotsky drew upon many contemporaries and predecessors. We have seen that he owed much to Janet and Gestalt psychology, criticized James, made use of Baldwin's ideas, and so on. Elsewhere we have shown that Vygotsky had an intimate knowledge of all the major psychological and philosophical theories of his time and was well-versed in the history of these disciplines. His major feat was to have synthesized many of the existing ideas into his own version of a sociogenetic theory. To have done this in that time in that country was no minor accomplishment. It should not be forgotten that his work was composed under unusual circumstances. Vygotsky always held several positions at a time; he had a "teaching load" that many of us would find entirely unacceptable; he was a member of the board of several journals; he worked for several publishing houses and edited translations of foreign works; he served as a clinical consultant for maladapted children; and he wrote most of his books and papers at home in a tiny room amidst playing or sleeping children (Vygodskaya & Lifanova, 1996). In addition to that, Vygotsky was seriously ill during the 10 years that he worked in an academic position and, in fact, wrote several of his works (e.g., *The Historical Meaning of the Crisis*) while being treated in hospitals. The least one can say is that this demonstrates an unusually high level of energy and concentration.

If James was right in saying that psychology "is no science, it is only the hope of science" (Burkhardt, 1984, pp. 400–1), then Vygotsky may be credited for giving us new hope, for having provided a flash of insight, a brief flickering of genius, before he disappeared in the maelstrom of his time.

CHAPTER NINE

The Social Person Today: Continuities and Interdependencies

The main goal of this book has been to look at intellectual interdependencies between thinkers on the theme "persons are social beings" in the history of the social sciences between the 1880s and 1930s. Yet all this digging of ours into the intellectual heritage of various authors (and their contexts) was motivated by the very contemporary need to take stock of actual evolution of ideas about sociality of persons as such are expressed in our present time. Within the field of possible ideas, there are not too many directions in which to look for a solution to the problem of how human beings are social. As we have shown all through this book, these few roads have been traveled by different thinkers at different times. At each time the intellectual landscape for these travels has been slightly different. Still, the travelers have arrived at roughly similar destinations, finding the road beyond that to vanish, or to be impenetrable. The history of different constructions of sociality of persons might tell us something about how to proceed beyond where the social sciences have reached.

There are multiple levels to this task. The grand generic idea that persons *are* social beings is of course not difficult to document. Yet a more subtle – and more constructive – question is: *What are the different ways* in which the social *nature* of the person and his or her social *development* have been crafted out in theories of sociality of human beings? As our contemporary social sciences in the 1990s undergo a revival of the sociogenetic focus, it is of interest to look briefly into different ways in which that question has been answered at the end of the twentieth century. Have we learned from the past? Are we capable of doing so?

The latter decades of the twentieth century in psychology entail fierce fights between the "social constructionist" and the "traditional" directions. The latter – which is never well defined – is often linked with the notion of "being positivist" and attacked fiercely as being the main enemy of all progress in the social sciences. Since the 1970s, social constructionism has been creating havoc in social psychology (Gergen, 1985, 1994). While building upon a reasonable claim about the socially constructed nature of psychological phenomena, social constructionism can easily be taken to an extreme that becomes applied to all acts of social scientists.[1]

The major difficulty for contemporary social sciences begins with the recognition that psychology (and other disciplines) are intertwined with moralities (they "secrete moralities" – Much & Harré, 1994). This social interdependence leads to both extremes – its denial (which has repressed the person-as-social idea from the surface discourse of psychology at times); or its reification (Shotter, 1993). From here it is one step to assuming an activist (or "revolutionary" or "rebellious"; the label depends on one's point of view) in the given society at the given time. As a result, social sciences may become ideological credos for different social interest groups.

We claim here that turning the morality *dependence* of psychological conceptual systems into a moral *imperative* for actively taking (and following) a specific stance has all the dangers of replacing general knowledge creation (as an epistemological enterprise of science) by applied actions. No doubt that the latter extension is desired by different social institutions (which may try to utilize psychological know-how in competition with their counterparts). Yet a direct and doubtless acceptance of these desires by psychology may eradicate science under the banner of its practical usefulness in a society.

The Web

Contemporary scientific discourse about the social nature of human beings is an active epistemic marketplace (Rosa, 1994) – albeit one where it is no longer clear who is doing the selling or buying, what is being sold or bought, and for what purposes. It seems that our contemporary social sciences have been caught in the world-wide web of

---

[1] With the interesting exception of stopping short of applying the notion of social constructedness to the constructions by advocates of social constructionism themselves. It is the others' (opponents') views that are pointed out to be socially constructed (thus assuming no correspondence with any reality, if reality is accepted to exist at all).

concrete implications of the so-called post-modernist ideology. A large part of such ideology is an emphasis on the local (context-specific) nature of human knowledge. This has led to two paradoxical tendencies:

(1)   The post-modernist tend to cover legitimate empirical descriptions of local phenomena, with a good excuse against any effort of generalization from the empirical phenomena toward abstract knowledge. Researchers are caught by the claim that if all knowledge is context bound, no generalization effort is in principle possible. The result of this tendency is the continuation of 'galloping empiricism' in the social sciences – only now it is the qualitative orientation to description that takes over from the quantitative one. Yet both are atheoretical. As a result, scientific (generalized) knowledge vanishes in the qualitative, context-specific, descriptive empiricism at a speed even greater than it vanished in the proliferation of quantified, context-forgetting "psychological measures" of the kind which have often been labeled, with the assumed negative connotation of the term "positivist."

(2)   The post-modernist belief system brings out to the open all the ambiguities of the researcher's role in creating descriptions of local phenomena. The researcher is faced with the understanding that she or he is an author of *an account*, rather than being an *analyst* of the 'true state' of the target object. This tension leads to quasi-novelistic accounts in the social sciences (primarily in anthropology), where the researcher is no longer intimidated by reflecting about the world through the subjective prism. Yet, instead of making the analyst's knowledge rich, such personal subjectivity often constitutes an additional obstacle towards general understanding. The author may express one's personal moral stance together with the description of the object of investigation. As a result, the notion of researcher-independent knowing becomes impossible. All knowledge becomes fused with the constructor of the knowledge, and the constructor of the knowledge vanishes in the ocean of socially nonneutral phenomena in which she or he is necessarily a participant.

The problem that has been actively unsolved in post-modernist social sciences is the necessary distancing between the scientist and the object of investigation without exclusively separating one from the other. This notion of *being distanced while being part of the system* has been foreign to social sciences. Yet, that is the very same difficulty the sociogenetic discourse has had in considering a person to be simultaneously individually unique and socially embedded. Only in the social sciences the issue is played out on the role of the researcher – the researcher is simultaneously a separate researcher and a part of the system that is under investigation.

A solid foundation for the solution of the problem was laid by C. Lloyd Morgan in 1894, who suggested that in research "two inductions" – those of introspection and extrospection – are constantly coordinated (Morgan, 1894, pp. 47–8). First – and foremost – the social scientist uses introspection to arrive at plausible research questions to ask and hypotheses to test. The scientist is a subjective meaning maker. This subjectively constructed perspective is then used extrospectively – to observe external phenomena. The result of the observations is subjectively compared to the initial introspectively assembled expectation, which is then corrected, abandoned, restructured, or maintained. The scientist is the human agent who integrates the results of extrospective and introspective inquiries. Thus, all scientific, objective, knowledge is created through an inevitable and necessary subjective process of the knowledge-constructing scientist. In this respect, any claims about the social nature of human beings are based on the personal construction of the idea.

Two Generic Models and Their Synthesis

In our contemporary social sciences, the question of the social nature of the person continues to be solved by either of two archetypal models. First, there is a grand urge for scientists to demonstrate the fusion, or merging, of persons and their social contexts. From that perspective, persons are social because they relinquish their personal individuality in favor of either participating in the activity of a social unit, or in favor of affective and mental communion with others. The second, opposite, archetype presents persons as being captivated by the social world, and forced (or obligated) to follow its rules and regulations.

There is a third model as well – which emphasizes both the individual's uniqueness and (simultaneously) relatedness with social units. This model – which could be considered *coconstructionist* (Valsiner, 1994c, 1996) – attempts to overcome the one-sidedness of the other two models. The latter direction finds its place under the label "cultural psychology," which has become a focus of attention in the 1990s.

Cultural Psychology: Unity of Dialogue, Activity, and Symbolic Thought

The past decade is one of rebirth of cultural psychology in its different versions (Valsiner, 1995), and proliferation of different directions of the analysis of discourse and narratives (Edwards, 1997). It is obvious that cultural psychology is nothing very new in psychology – if it is traced to issues of language philosophy and folk psychology. Rather, the cultural side of psychology (as science) has been repressed by the social presentations of psychologists of their activities as science. That human psychological functioning is inevitably cultural has thus been a re-emerging theme that at each next time of surfacing *became presented* as a new invention. In reality, it may be that merely the particular terminology that presenters use is a novelty, while the basic structure of thought has continuity with similar efforts in the past.

However, such historical connections – in our framework presented in this book – are the basis for further progress of ideas. Within cultural psychology, we can – by way of some gross approximation – distinguish three directions. First, there exists a class of *dialogical perspectives* upon human psychological phenomena. These perspectives emphasize the notions of discrepancy, opposition, negotiation, and conflict as productive (rather than destructive, or "abnormal") aspects of the theoretical constructions. Second, with partial overlap with the former, we can delineate perspectives that set up human *socially situated activity* as the location where human sociality is displayed. Finally, we have a number of directions – again partially overlapping with the activity orientation – that emphasize symbolic construction by human minds as the locus for the social being of the person.

Dialogical and Dialectical Perspectives

Different dialogical perspectives have found their place in the social sciences (Hermans, 1994, 1995, 1996; Hermans & Kempen, 1993; Josephs, 1998a; Linell, 1992, 1996; Markova, 1990, 1994; Wertsch, 1991, 1997; and others) largely under the impact of reading into the literary theories of the 1920s and 1930s – particularly in conjunction with the spread of translations of the work of Mikhail Bakhtin into English. Yet Bakhtin was a literary scholar with marginal interests in psychology. Appropriating his ideas has enriched contemporary social sciences theoretically, while leaving them baffled as to the kind of empirical work that needs to follow. The latter makes use of the processes of communication.

The process of communication between human beings is not a case of simple transmission of information. Instead, people who communicate do so from a certain position, having particular objectives in mind (which they may, or need not, achieve), and construct messages that are necessarily and purposefully ambiguous (Rommetveit, 1972, 1992). Negotiation of positions between persons who communicate is the essence of communication (Robinson, 1988; Rommetveit, 1998). In the process of negotiation of positions, the participants assume a state of mutually shared field of meanings (intersubjectivity) which is merely a temporary state to create a basis for coordinating the position differences (Josephs, 1998b; Rommetveit, 1979). There are multiple possible goal orientations to assume within the field of intersubjectivity, which makes any communication process necessarily open ended.

Ivana Markova's dialogical approach integrates the cognitive and language functions, as these appear in the process of communication. She relies upon the traditions of the Prague Linguistic Circle (Markova, 1992). Markova brings the notion of Hegel's dialectics home to the reality of analysis of dialogues (both interpersonal and intrapersonal). Within her analytic scheme, the concentration on the emergence of novelty in dialogue becomes highlighted, as she develops a three-step analytic unit (at time 1 two opposites, A and B, are in a relationship that leads to the transformation of at least one of these into a novel form – e.g., A becomes C – at time 2). Hers is a good example of how dia*logical* perspectives can relate to dia*lectical* conceptual models (Markova, 1990).

Hubert Hermans' dialogical approach to the self constitutes an example *at the vicinity* of dialectical perspectives. Building on the notion of traditional research on motivation, and on the dialogical approaches of Martin Buber and Mikhail Bakhtin, Hermans has formulated a view on the self which builds upon the relationship between different meanings (or "voices") that take different forms (e.g., those of agreement, disagreement – Hermans, 1995). His theory of dialogical self is connected with phenomena of psychotherapy, and with his *valuation theory* (Hermans & Kempen, 1993), in conjunction with a measurement system for personal valuations. Yet the relations between different "voices" are not formulated to be directly relating with one another through the concept of valuations.

Dialogical perspectives can be based on the phenomena of human social interaction (Smolka, Goés, & Pino, 1995). Social interaction as a phenomenon (and dialogue as such) can be conceptualized in different ways – in terms of synchrony, harmony, polyphony (of voices), etc. – none of which requires the notion of dialectics. On the other side, dialogical approaches have needed a careful focus on dialectical schemes (Rychlak, 1995) that have been underemphasized and in many ways ideologically stigmatized in psychology of recent decades.[2]

Thus not all dialogical approaches are dialectical. Rather, some of the dialogical perspectives incorporate into themselves the construct of *unity and contradiction of opposites within the same whole*. Only these approaches are dialectical in their nature. Furthermore, of these approaches only some may emphasize the *process of synthesis* (as emerging from contradictions) as a device for emerging of novelty. In the strictest sense, it is only the latter that could be considered dialectical.

James Wertsch's Dialogicality: Voices of the Mind in Texts

Wertsch's general theory of "voices of the mind" clearly belongs to the class of dialogical perspectives. Wertsch took off from the thinking of Vygotsky in his focus on semiotic mediation (Wertsch, 1979, 1983). In parallel, he relied on Leontiev's activity theory (Wertsch, 1981). Wertsch consistently built his theoretical ideas on the central axiom of all sociogenetic approach – that all psychological functions are social first, and become personal by a process of developmental "ingrowth." The latter is conceptualized in terms of appropriation (rather than internalization). His efforts to work in parallel at the level of

---

[2] The ideological excesses of monopolization of dialectical thought by Soviet and other former Eastern-European social institutions necessarily led to an ambivalence by the international scientific community in regard to such models. The few psychologists who emphasized the notion of dialectics – Klaus Riegel in North America and Klaus Holzkampf in Germany – were largely single voices of not much impact on the wider scene. Yet the ideological appropriation of an idea by a social institution does not discredit the idea itself, but only its concrete application.

activity and at the level of semiotic mediation led him to prefer the concept of appropriation precisely because it eliminates the difference between those levels.

Wertsch has been looking upon the *dynamic process of situation redefinition* as the primary means by which persons involved in joint activity context guide one another's conduct. Communication partners are constantly in some relation of intersubjectivity (sharing similar situation definition), which they transcend by the process of situation redefinition (Wertsch, 1984, pp. 7–13). Communication about the situation definition (and redefinition) takes place by semiotic means, while the structure of the activity in which the persons are involved guides the process of redefinition (Wertsch, Minick, & Arns, 1984). Semiotic means can operate at different levels of indexicality, ranging from the most simple (simple indexical sign use) to common referring expression, and finally, to context-informative expression (see Wertsch, 1985, pp. 78–81).

Wertsch borrows Bakhtin's emphasis on voices and makes it work in ways that afford the treatment of the complexity of communicative messages. The result is a consistent return to the study of ambivalences embedded in communicative messages – in the form of "polyphony of voices" or "heteroglossia." Different voices can be seen in the utterances in ways that "interanimate" or dominate each other in the act of speaking in situated activity contexts. Bakhtin's legacy allows Wertsch to advance his theory of communication into the realm of conceptualizing *processual relations* between the components in a dialogue (i.e., different voices). "Privileging" in relation between voices (i.e., the "foregrounding" of voice X while voice Y is simultaneously being "backgrounded") is a central issue for Wertschian analysis.

Wertsch is interested in society's macrolevel dialogues (such as the dialogicality involved in school history textbooks leading to different forms of national identity). Dialogicality here is constituted through the co-existence of different narrative versions of history of the same social entity (nation, ethnic group, etc. – Wertsch, 1997). Some of these versions can (at times) be privileged over the other(s), or even eradicate the others in which case the dialogicality disappears. Dialogicality in the case of national identity construction is viewed by Wertsch as the process through which reorganization of previous identities takes place.

Activity-Based Theoretical Elaborations

In the 1980s and 1990s, the sociocultural direction of research in psychology became fascinated by a focus on activity. Probably a number of factors have fed into this. First, the hope to transcend the elementaristic analytic schemes of behavior analysis led researchers toward a look for molar-level analytic schemes. This amounts to a continuation of the tension between holistic and elementaristic perspectives that were evident a century ago, and which were not productively resolved. Second, the proliferation of the "activity theory" of A. N. Leontiev – beyond its original confines of Moscow University in the former USSR – could have added some mystique of the unknown "Russian power."[3] In the context of U.S. psychology, it took on an oppositional stance to cognitivist perspectives, and carried a latent continuity with John Dewey's pragmatism, as well as showing a need to attack the "mainstream psychology" for its positivistic sins (see Ratner, 1991, 1996). In the European context, activity-theoretic perspectives have allegiance with French (Janet, Wallon) roots as well (Del Rio, 1990).

Klaus Holzkampf was a promoter of Leontiev's activity theory in German-language psychology. Activity-theoretic ideas of Franco-German origin were exported to the East and West, where they have developed in their peculiar ways, at times returning to their places of origin.

The concentration upon activity leads contemporary psychology into a field of complexity of observable activity settings. Without doubt, for empirically oriented researchers this provides for a lifetime of descriptive task-solving, yet in the theoretical vein it entails decisions that are of a rather complicated kind. The fluidity of activities may lead to the need to see them as examples of syncretic phenomena (Del Rio & Alvarez, 1995). It becomes relatively easy to demonstrate lack of expected (strict, logical) organization of observable activity patterns. Yet it is no easy task to create conceptual systems that could be general theoretical frameworks for making sense of the syncretic

---

[3] It is only ironic – and a good example of our focus on transmigration of ideas between countries and the intellectual interdependency of scholars – that Leontiev's "activity theory" was rooted in the social demands of the Soviet society in the 1930s, and when it was developed by Leontiev in the 1970s, constituted a combination of Pierre Janet's action theory with selected Marxist viewpoints. The "Russian mystique" was not so indigenously Russian, on a closer look.

phenomena. Metaphoric expressions like "external brain" (Del Rio, 1990) or even "external soul" (Lang, 1992) may at times be used to organize our conceptual spheres – yet use of such metaphors does not amount to theoretical innovation. It is only in a few cases that systematic elaborations have been attempted. Barbara Rogoff's system of guided participation notions is one of these few.

Guided Participation and Persons' Immersion in Activity Contexts

Barbara Rogoff has worked on issues of socially situated activities over the recent decade (Rogoff, 1982; 1986; 1990; 1992; 1993; Rogoff & Lave, 1984). Her focus has been mostly ethnographic, which allows her to take into account intricacies of complexity of activity and its context (Rogoff, 1990, 1991, 1993). Rogoff has been emphasizing the unity of persons and their sociocultural contexts, refusing to separate them theoretically from one another. She provides a solution to the problem of the context – it is the *sociocultural activity* that involves *active participation* of people *in socially constituted practices* (Rogoff, 1990, p. 14). Within that activity, persons are interacting on problem-solving (rather than being involved in lengthy intrapersonal contemplations or soul searching). The active (but not always persistent) social guidance by the others to the person is complemented by the person's own constructive role in one's own development. The person who is always an *active* apprentice *participates* in the *socially-guided activity settings*.

Rogoff's research program could be characterized by three features: (a) recognition of the holistic nature of human development; (b) viewing development as it proceeds through *appropriation* of cultural practices in contexts of *guided participation*; and (c) prioritizing qualitative methodology for the study of persons in situated activity contexts.

Rogoff is not a builder of grand theoretical schemes of high level of abstraction. Instead, her theoretical credo permeates her empirical, phenomenological, and educational discourse in small "takes" on general issues. Oftentimes these takes have a concrete addressee (interlocutor) in the field of contemporary psychology and education. She moves thoughtfully between descriptions of phenomena, different folk models existing in psychology and education, and her own theoretical claims (and counter-claims). Theory, for Rogoff, seems to participate with other aspects of research (ethnographic description of phenomena, experimentation in real-life contexts) in the knowledge construction process in equal standing. In this respect, Rogoff's general methodology constitutes a rich and potent complex of ideas, phenomena, and actions. That complex defies any effort to be turned into a hierarchically ordered structure.

The exclusive emphasis on persons-in-contexts has led Rogoff to counteract claims that persons can have autonomous (psychological) existence. This is a heuristic stance (Rogoff does not deny the existence of persons per se), but in order to explicate her basic theoretical premise, she explains:

Studying human events or activities contrasts with the more traditional approach of examining the individual in isolation or in interaction with a separate environment. In our approach, individuals' efforts and sociocultural practices *are constituted by and constitute each other* and thus *cannot be defined independently of each other* or studied in isolation. We may focus on the contribution of one or another individual or a cultural tradition, but *always in relation to the whole activity rather than extracted from it.* (Rogoff, Baker-Sennett, Lacasa, & Goldsmith, 1995, p. 45, emphases added)

For Rogoff, the central issue is *mutual constituting* of persons and activities. From that standpoint, efforts of describing either part of the whole separately makes no sense – even if in fact it could be possible to look at the individual separately from the context (e.g., if the "contributions" by a particular person to the activity in fact are distinctively overwhelming). Yet such possibility is not to be used, precisely because Rogoff is interested in the process of mutual constituting between person and activity. Rogoff's theoretical system is hence holistic, and her refusal to separate individuals is substantiated by her definition of *where* (in activity) and *how* (through guided participation) human development proceeds.

For Rogoff, there is no distinction possible that specifies "inside" and "outside," there is no framework for the concepts of internalization and externalization. Instead, the process of mutual constituting becomes elaborated through two concepts – *appropriation* (Rogoff, 1990) and *participation* (Rogoff, 1996, 1997).

Appropriation is conceptualized as creative process. According to Rogoff, (1990, p. 197) information and skills that are present in socially shared activity settings are not transmitted as given, but *become transformed* in the process of appropriation. Participation in social activity involves selectivity on behalf of the participants. Communication partners in social activity become "propelled ahead together" and develop new social means. Within the field of participation, Rogoff recognizes the role of individuals: "Individuals transform culture as they appropriate its practices, carrying them forward to the next generation in altered form to fit the needs of their particular form and circumstances. The shifts in societal practices over decades and centuries result from the transformation of institutions and technologies to fit current needs" (Rogoff, 1990, p. 198).

Thus, Rogoff's answer to the question of development is that of active *individuals-who-are-participants* in an ongoing social activity, transforming the complex of *themselves-and-activity* into a new form through active, constructive appropriation.

Rogoff combines the notions of appropriation and participation. The result is the concept of *participatory appropriation*, which involves individuals changing through their own *adjustments* and *understanding* of the sociocultural activity (Rogoff, 1993, p. 141). Furthermore,

Participatory appropriation refers to how individuals change through their involvement in one or another activity, in the process of becoming prepared for subsequent involvement in related activities. With guided participation as the interpersonal process through which people are involved in sociocultural activity, participatory appropriation is the personal process by which, through engagement in an activity, individuals change and handle a later situation in ways prepared by their own participation in the previous situation. This is a process of becoming, rather than acquisition. (Rogoff, 1995, p. 142)

It is obvious that the personal mental world is not denied (Rogoff, 1992), but merely left outside of the focus of empirical ethnographic analysis, while the main emphasis is put on individual change through activity through which participation takes place. This emphasis follows Dewey's focus on coordination (as was described in Chapter 5).

Tools for a New Dimension: Semiotic Mediation within Activity

Michael Cole's work – his *cultural practice theory* – has been historically indebted to the thought of Alexander Luria, and through him to Lev Vygotsky. Cole's activity-oriented, yet semiotic sociogenetic stance emerges from his studies of cultural tools, paired with an explicit interest in the historical nature of cultural processes (Cole, 1992, 1995, 1996). The role of Dewey's pragmatism is also present in Cole's work.

The problem of relationships between microgenetic and ontogenetic phenomena in human development is central for the cultural practice theory. The main mechanism by which culture and person are related is that of *mutual interweaving*. This interweaving reflects the general process in which the culture becomes individual and the individuals create their culture – the culture and cognition are *mutually constituted*.

It is through the socially organized context selection and creation processes that human beings develop knowledge, and thus the relation of culture and cognition becomes an *intersubjective* phenomenon. The whole world of the developing child is culturally organized in a number of ways:

1. Culture arranges the occurrence or nonoccurrence of specific basic problem-solving environments embodied in cultural practices.
2. Culture also organizes the frequency of occurrence of these basic practices.
3. Culture shapes the patterning of co-occurrence of events.
4. Culture regulates the level of difficulty of the tasks within contexts (so that the balance between learning successes and failures is regulated)

(Laboratory of Comparative Human Cognition, 1983, p. 335)

Analysis of everyday activities can be accomplished in many different ways. It can be used to legitimize the empirical description of an increasing variety of developmental contexts in which a child partakes. Whereas undoubtedly development takes place in (and through) experiences within such contexts, scientific explanation of development cannot be reduced to the description of these contexts. Somehow, the general processes that make it possible for the developing person to create knowledge in ever new (even if formally repetitive) contexts need to be conceptualized. In psychology, that issue has usually been addressed in terms of transfer, conceptualized as if taking place from the vantage point of the person. In contrast, Cole's cultural practice theory deemphasizes transfer as a central process occurring within the minds of individuals and emphasizes movement of information across contexts as a social accomplishment. The tuition of young children by adults, their direct intervention, especially when a mistake is about to be committed, and adults' practice of embedding learning in everyday experiences, are some of the ways in which environments are arranged for events to reoccur. There is redundancy and repetitiveness in learning situations that makes the occurrence of new situations less effective. When people are confronting new situations, the physical features of those environments, the social distribution of social knowledge, and the presence of a number of cultural resources assist in providing bridges between contexts (Laboratory of Comparative Human Cognition, 1983, p. 342).

The emphasis on socially organized transfer between contexts leads Cole to the emphasis on the concept of appropriation (Newman, Griffin, & Cole, 1989, pp. 62–5), along the lines emphasized by Leontiev. The culture provides a range of cultural mediating devices (tools or signs) to the developing child in specific activity contexts; the child actively takes over (appropriates) those cultural means, reconstructing them in the process of activity.

Symbolic Constructionist Perspectives

A number of contemporary sociogenetic perspectives have been emphasizing the socially based construction *in* the human mind, and *by* the human mind. Discourse about "meaning making" (cf. Bruner, 1990) has become appreciated in the social sciences. The profoundness of symbolic meaning construction and its role in everyday life is oftentimes dramatically visible (Kakar, 1996). In cultural anthropology, one can find Gananath Obeyesekere (1981, 1984, 1990) actively trying to free his thinking from the prescriptions of Freudian psychoanalysis, yet to retain the complexity of phenomena in their vivid reality.

It is precisely the phenomenological richness of the symbol-constructive side of contemporary cultural psychology that may lead the way for finding productive solutions to the person-as-social being problem. Oftentimes, psychological phenomena from the Hindu sociocultural universe have been used for this.

Speaking through India: Richard Shweder's Intentionality in Context

Richard A. Shweder's version of cultural psychology is based on his experiences with moral reasoning of persons in Orissa, India. Among the recent efforts to make psychology culture-inclusive, Shweder's prolific claims to write the history of an interdisciplinary and integrative discipline of cultural psychology (Shweder, 1984; 1992; Shweder & Much, 1987; Shweder & Sullivan, 1993) bring the theoretical and methodological limitations of psychology into the focus. Shweder accepts the sociomoral basis of cultural phenomena – persons in any society are "members of a moral community who work to coconstruct a shared reality and who act as though they were parties to an agreement to behave rationally within the terms of the realities they share" (Shweder, 1996a, p. 20).

Theoretically, Shweder has claimed interdependence of both the person and the social world for cultural organization of human conduct. His cultural psychology relates the *intentional worlds* of human cultural environments, with the actions, feelings, and thinking of intentional persons. Persons and their cultural worlds *interpenetrate* each other's identities, and set the conditions for each other's existence and development, while jointly undergoing change through social interaction (Shweder, 1990, p. 25).

The notion of interpenetration is in the process of being developed as an actual empirical research practice. This would entail interpretive study of the *sanctioned* social discourse and praxis (Shweder, 1996a, p. 26). This interpretation includes recognition of personally differential knowledge about the sanctioned discourse and praxis – not all members of a "moral community" are experts about their own way of life.

The latter is partly due to the immediate obviousness of cultural organization of human lives. According to Shweder, *psyche* and culture are "seamlessly interconnected" – a person's psychic organization is built on culture, in relation to which (i.e., the intentional *worlds*) the intentional *persons* "continually and continuously make each other up, perturbing and disturbing each other, interpenetrating each other's identity, reciprocally conditioning each other's existence" (Shweder, 1990, pp. 26–7).

Such seamlessness of the connection would create a situation where the persons do not explicate the cultural knowledge that they use. The problem here is similar to that addressed by *Ganzheitspsychologie* (Chapter 7) – the most relevant psychological phenomena are so obvious in human lives that they cannot be easily made into an object of investigation.

Much of the research by Shweder's research team is devoted to moral reasoning in Hindu religious contexts in Orissa, India. Shweder recognizes both the heterogeneity and culture inclusiveness of moral reasoning by human beings (Shweder, & Much, 1987; Shweder, Mahapatra, & Miller, 1987). This complex mosaic of persons who live within their cultural worlds – yet remain persons rather than "clones" of the "culture" – who are inconsistent from one context to another, and yet demonstrate cross-situational continuities, and who hold strong and unalterable personal opinions (e.g., see the Babaji interview, in Shweder & Much, 1987, pp. 235–44) that are "seamlessly" related to the culture – all that requires a fresh theoretical attack on the issues raised in psychology, anthropology, and linguistics.

Shweder does not explicate the different possible forms that this *reciprocal construction* or *conditioning* ("making each other up"; or "affording each other" – see Shweder & Sullivan, 1993), or interpenetration, can take. There exist "dialectical feedback loops" and "dynamic nonlinear relationships" in person-society relations (Shweder, 1990, pp. 31–2; also Shweder & Sullivan, 1993). Yet there is little elaboration of how such perspective could be constructed within research methodology. His own empirical extensions of theoretical ideas either use traditional techniques (e.g., Guttmann scales – Menon & Shweder, 1994) or interview interpretations (Shweder & Much, 1987 – Babaji interview). His research credo is refreshingly qualitative, recognizing the unity of quality behind quantity (Shweder, 1996b). Locating his empirical work in the area of moral reasoning led him into dialogue with psychology's stage-theoretic analyses of "moral stages" of Lawrence Kohlberg. Shweder and his colleagues demonstrate the cultural relativity of moral reasoning patterns, which often take the form of dramatizations of hypothetical scenarios.

Symbols in Formation: Bernard Kaplan's Genetic Dramatism

The story of the migration of Heinz Werner and his ideas – from Europe to America – provides a good example of how interpersonal and societal factors become coordinated in the development of ideas. Werner's work at Clark University from 1947 onward (until his death in 1964 – see Chapter 7) included two directions, that of experimentation on issues suggested by the sensori-tonic theory, and on issues of symbol formation (Werner & Kaplan, 1963). Both of these interests coexisted in Werner's thinking long before he arrived at Clark. The focus on the physiognomic nature of human psychological functions was evident already in the 1920s (Werner, 1919, 1929).

It is the latter direction that is of relevance as an advancement of the sociogenetic ideas. The main developer of these ideas was Bernard Kaplan, who first studied with Werner at Clark, and then became his colleague and one of his successors. Kaplan is the coauthor of the final formulation of the "orthogenetic principle" (published as Werner & Kaplan, 1956, p. 866).

It is due to Kaplan's efforts that the orthogenetic principle was given a status of an overriding general perspective – a reference frame for researchers – by which to look at a variety of human psychological phenomena. For Kaplan, the developmental view was a generic look at progress in any area of human knowing. He had to face the same difficulty about which Wundt (1917) warned his successors (Krueger) – that a generic developmental approach would be interpreted by others as a narrow look at children. Children, indeed, develop, and this is precisely a conceptual difficulty for developmental psychology as a science. As children are not only persons but persons-to-be-cultivated, a science of development cannot be based on the study of children, at least not exclusively so.

In Kaplan's case, however, his major opponent is the idea that development must be narrowly linked with time-dependent pro-cesses. His philosophical orientation guided him against it. So, in his characteristically forceful way of speaking, Kaplan argued:

I have several times ... and not a few would say ad nauseam, insisted that development be distinguished from *change, history*, and *evolution*; that it be recognized as a *normative* concept, in terms of which one discrimi-nates between more primitive and more advanced, lower and higher, worse and better; that is, I take it that the concept of development ought to be, as it has typically been in the past, intimately linked with the idea of *progress*. (Kaplan, 1994, p. 5)

He insists strongly that:

I see no point or value in collapsing the idea of development into that of mere change over time, whether in the sociocosmos or in the microcos-mos, in collective history or individual history. Although it was once widely believed that an *imminent law of progress* informed change, history, and evolution ... we should realize, I urge, that neither progress nor development can be read off from the mere facts of change over time, either in the actual social order or in the individual member of a social order. (ibid.)

This generalization of the notion of development into a timeless moral concept effectively concludes the loss of the productivity of the generalized concept. This fate has been shared by many specific concepts in the sociogenetic tradition (G. H. Mead's "me," Vygotsky's "zone of proximal development," etc.).

Instead of the focus on development as time-bound, Kaplan has suggested drama as the root concept to encapsulate development. The intention here has been that of unification of complexity:

> How often in the past have attempts been made to bridge the eternal and the temporal, the transcendent and the immanent, the ideal and the actual, the perfect and the imperfect, the normative and the positive, the ought and the is? How inevitable that these attempts, in subsequent periods, have appeared partial and parochial? How inescapable that these "failures" have not forestalled later attempts, but indeed have acted as a stimulus for a never-ending quest?! (Kaplan, 1983, p. 68)

Kaplan's Genetic Dramatism – A Holistic Solution to the Problem of the Person

Kaplan's solution – philosophy of genetic dramatism – is a holistic-dynamic effort to create a concept even more abstract than the earlier orthogenetic principle. This striving toward complexive abstraction is on the one hand similar to Krueger's efforts to capture complex wholes (compare the "feeling-tone" with the wholeness of "genetic dramatism").

Any theoretical construct needs an anchor point, or field. In Kaplan's case, the anchor point is societal morality and social practice. The notion of striving for perfection acquires the role of centrality. In defining developmental psychology, Kaplan considers it to be "a practico-theoretical discipline, a policy discipline, concerned with the perfection (including liberation or freedom) of the individual and the perfection of those modes of operation promoting the perfection of the individual" (Kaplan, 1986, p. 96).

He is careful to point out (ibid, p. 101) that by "freedom" lack of constraints is not implied. Rather, socially constructed moral rules are viewed as superordinate regulators of the *telos* of individual. Here Kaplan synthesizes the physiognomic holistic general idea of Heinz Werner with the philosophy of Kenneth Burke. In the background for this synthesis are also the philosophies of Ernst Cassirer and John Dewey, as well as the work of George Herbert Mead (Kaplan, 1983, p. 56). Kaplan's philosophical synthesis has led him to an ideologically positioned view on development:

In many societies, the process of *development*, in contradistinction to the process of mere change, is a movement towards *perfection*, as variously as that idea may be construed. Among hermeticists and occultists, this view of development is embodied in the maxim, 'Become what you are.' One is said to develop only insofar as one moves in the direction of realizing one's full potentialities. 'Development', so to speak, is the 'curse' or obligation placed upon 'souls' or 'selves' incarnated in bodies to become the God, in whose image they were made. Had we not had to suffer incarnation, there would be no need for 'development.' Once embodied, however, we are under the obligation to struggle *in time* to attain whatever degree of perfection we can. (Kaplan, 1983, p. 57)

Obviously, by equating perfection with the end goal of any effort to develop, Kaplan creates a humanly appealing, but scientifically fuzzy, context for looking at human *psyche*. He is himself aware of the shock value of his claims to the audience (ibid, p. 57 – claims that the idea above "is too theosophical for your taste"). His theoretical move overgeneralizes the "orthogenetic principle" into an idea complex which could be conveniently relabeled "the principle of striving for perfection." This reminds us of the holistic claims of "striving for the whole" (see Chapter 7). In both cases of formulating such general principles, the prevailing question remains – do these principles generate new ways of knowing? If that is the case, then they are semiotic tools for starting a progressive research program (in the sense of Lakatos). If they do not – then they lead to a new reified meta-theoretical "black box" which resists being opened by further inquiry. Without doubt, a generalized concept can do either. Yet the social sciences are filled with many black boxes the opening of which is usually vigorously defended by their owners keepers.

In other terms, how would the striving for perfection be put to practice? Kaplan elevates the notion of social participation to the main way by which perfection can be attained. Taking the roles of the others (*à la* G. Mead) – through imagination, cognition, and affect – a person can come closer to the "telos of development" (perfection) – yet remaining always at an "infinite distance" (Kaplan, 1983, p. 60). This actualization of the ideal is thus always relative – resembling Piaget's notion of never-fully-reachable harmony in *progressing equilibration*.

Personal psychological phenomena in their sociocultural contexts are captured by the notion of "dramatism" – *the idealization of the actual*. Dramatism "is a critical and self-critical method for making us aware not only of the remarkable range of 'worlds' we inhabit, but also of the symbolic ways in which we constitute such 'worlds' and ourselves within those worlds" (Kaplan, 1983, p. 67).

What is then genetic about genetic dramatism? By considering symbolic action constructive and creative, all episodes of dramatism are unfolding in time (see the example of redramatizing the affective reaction of a boy getting sutures – Cirillo & Kaplan, 1983, pp. 237–8). Yet for Kaplan's genetic dramatism, time is merely the dimension within which the episode becomes symbolically constructed. The notion of genetic here is merely a marker of the fact that the dramatism has been created – obviously unfolding in time. Yet it is analyzed in its ontological state, *as-it-is*, not as it *came-into-being*. The *Aktualgenese* idea (see Chapter 7) is foreign to Kaplan's extension of Werner's principle.

This move (toward symbolic construction and de-emphasis on time) was evident already in the 1950s when Kaplan took over and perfected Werner's earlier (Werner, 1929) physiognomic idea of translating verbal concepts into pictograms (Werner & Kaplan, 1963). The activity of representing a sentence (e.g., the sentence "He catches a [fly/lion/criminal]" – see Werner & Kaplan, 1956, p. 876) by way of line drawing has precisely the same time-losing properties which later are perfected in the theory of genetic dramatism. The process of drawing inevitably takes place over time. Yet once it is finished, the drawing is now a symbol which *includes* time *in a timeless fashion*. There is a parallel with the act of speaking a word, and the resulting word. The process that was involved in the drawing (or speaking) effort can be observed through its intermediate products (e.g., through copying a pictogram, or repronouncing the word). Yet in the graphic or acoustic image as it is perceptually available to us, that time-bound process is replaced by the simultaneous visual access to the pictogram, or the word. The spoken word written down becomes a product from which the process of its generation is distanced.

In a similar way, any soap opera created in our everyday life unfolds in time through the actions of its participants, and entails a step-by-step joint construction of roles and counterroles. In this respect, genetic dramatism may be the ultimate form of constant coconstruction of social phenomena in interpersonal communication (see Oliveira & Valsiner, 1997). Yet in a *description* of the whole episode of a soap opera or any theatrical act, time can be abstracted out from the plot.

By resisting the role of time as part of development – and replacing it by accent on perfection – Kaplan has effectively closed the door to the question: how do people construct their dramatisms? What remains is the detection of such dramatisms once they are created, and reflection upon them. Nevertheless, Kaplan's notion of genetic dramatism constitutes a step ahead in his (and other holistic psychologists') interest in capturing the "atmospheric character" of physiognomized phenomena (see Kaplan, 1955, p. 22). However, it still needs dramatic improvements to reach perfection as a scientific concept.

Representing Socially: Human Beings and Socially Constructed Dramas

The research field of *social representations* is a characteristically European (originally French, since the 1960s) tendency to make sense of the social belongingness of human beings. Started by a Romanian-Jewish immigrant to France who reached international fame in social psychology, Serge Moscovici, the social representations orientation has proliferated in the 1980s and 1990s in other countries in Europe (Flick, 1995b; Wagner, 1994) and in Britain (Farr, 1987, 1998). By the 1990s, the discourse of social representations has acquired its own social organization, and internal heterogeneity (DeRosa, 1994).

The notion of social representations continues the European holistic conceptual tradition (Chapter 7), by making the complex notion of *social* representation into the core of the theoretical system. This creates two tensions, first with the cognitive focus on representations (which are not conceptualized as social), and, second, with the narrow focus of mostly North American experimental social psychology (which focuses on social *behavior* – at times relabeled "action" – rather than representations). Moscovici's efforts to elaborate his ideas of social representation are not part of a dialogue with these interpretations. He wanders through the multifaceted intellectual landscape of societies – often using his contemporary French society for evidence – for the sake of making sense of human fate in the middle of the socially constructed psychological worlds. The tradition of investigation into social representations is usually dated back to the appearance of Moscovici's (1961) book on the appropriation of psychoanalysis in French society. At first the research tradition was observational in its nature, with qualitative descriptions dominating over quantified accounts or experimental applications. However, in line with psychology's prestige orientations, the empirical research world easily took over the wide and often ill-defined "umbrella" realm of social representations.

The process of embedding the notion of social representation in the social meaning system of psychologists has been a slow one, filled with many conceptual confusions. It has been complicated by the specific audiences to whom Moscovici's writing has been directed (Farr, 1987). Differently from the English-language psychology sources (which have traditionally been read by specialists in the area, rather than lay public), the French language psychology communicates with a wider audience (see also peculiarities in other French scholars' writings – Chapters 2 and 3).

Antiempiricism in Moscovici's Construction

From the very beginning, the focus for creating the social representation notion was a synthesis which

was conceived outside the sphere of influence of American social psychology [of the 1950s–60s – JV & RvdV], which has dominated the scientific style of most of our colleagues. It is a direct product of the classical tradition, according to which a theory *is both an approach, a way of looking at social phenomena, and a system describing and explaining them.* (Moscovici, 1988b, pp. 212–13, emphasis added)

The unity of the perspective (of looking) and description is crucial here. It fits with the cyclical model of scientific methodology (Branco & Valsiner, 1997), and is completely nonunderstandable (or vague) from a perspective that enforces an exclusive separation between theories (as perspectives) and methods (as descriptive devices). Most of contemporary empirically based psychology has adopted the latter stance. Moscovici retains the classical view.

He has good reasons for sticking to that view – both epistemological and practical. In any science, methods are oriented by the theoretical background, thus are not separable from the latter. Most of the social life phenomena Moscovici is interested in are not reducible. The aspects of the social world that need such perspective are the complex ones – those of the reflection of mental illness in laypersons' minds and activities (Jodelet, 1991), notions of democracy in changing societies (Moody et al., 1996), war and peace (Wagner, Valencia, & Elejabarrieta, 1996). In contrast to the social psychology of the empirical kind which looks for causal linkages between assumed "influences" and the constructed "data," Moscovici's theory of social representations "takes as its point of departure the diversity of individuals, attitudes and phenomena, in all their strangeness and unpredictability. Its aim is to discover how individuals and groups can construct a stable, predictable world out of such diversity" (Moscovici, 1984, p. 44).

The diversity becomes organized by social representations that carry with them past constructed meanings, and make these available for new applications. Phenomena that demonstrate the power of such representations in social life are profound. Thus,

The German or Russian citizens who saw their Jewish or subversive compatriots sent to concentration camps or shipped to the Gulag Islands certainly did not think they were innocent. *They had to be guilty since they were imprisoned.* Good reasons for putting them in prison were attributed (the word is apt) to them *because it was impossible to believe that they were accused, ill-treated and tortured for no good reason at all.* Moscovici, 1984, p. 45, emphasis added)

Phenomena of this kind – persons' willing acceptance of suggested verdicts about others, or themselves, or persons' active construction of meanings-based life-or-death scenarios for others (e.g., the history of construction of witchcraft and punishments of witches) – provide evidence for social unity in the construction of *psychomorphic universe* (Moscovici, 1987, p. 164). This is a social realm akin to the Shakespearean recognition of "all the world is a stage." The same notion was captured by Bernard Kaplan in his notion "genetic dramatism." Human beings create their dramatized worlds, create their roles and counterroles in it, and attribute to their game the notion of truth, justice, or necessity.

Much of Moscovici's writing has been dedicated to questions of human biological and cultural history (Moscovici, 1968, 1974, 1976, 1985). This is not coincidental – the story about the assimilation of psychoanalysis into French society (Moscovici, 1961) is but a very special case of historical-constructive processes that must have taken place all through the history of *Homo sapiens* as a species. These processes operate on the basis of distinctions – the separation of "society" from "nature," and on the "natural" (=savage) / "cultural" distinction. Human beings become social through self-domestication (see Moscovici, 1974, chapter 1). The act of domestication of other species becomes possible once human beings have domesticated themselves –

so the first pet of a pet owner is the pet owner oneself (or the best pig for a pig farmer is he himself).

Most importantly, Moscovici has concisely formulated the nature of the social processes that are in operation for domestication of *Homo sapiens*. These entail unavoidable unity of opposites:

Our society is an institution which inhibits what it stimulates. It *both tempers and excites* aggressive, epistemic, and sexual tendencies, increases or reduces the chances of satisfying them according to class distinctions, and *invents prohibitions together with the means of transgressing them*. Its sole purpose, to date, is self-preservation, and it opposes change by means of laws and regulations. It functions on the basic assumption that it is unique, has nothing to learn, and cannot be improved. Hence its unambiguous dismissal of all that is foreign to it. Even its presumed artificiality, which might be considered a shortcoming, is taken, on the contrary, for a further sign of superiority, since it is an attribute of mankind. As for all other societies, they are nothing but the product of environmental and organic influences. (Moscovici, 1976, p. 149, emphases added)

The ways in which such social creation of distinctions is possible are presented by Moscovici through the notion of social representation, (implying both the process of representing and its vehicle). Moscovici has been interested in such constructed complex events and the complex social representations that make these possible.

We argue that the main source of confusions in understanding Moscovici's concept is the question of the function of social representations in contemporary social sciences. Moscovici's seemingly inconsistent, often declarative and at times polemic discourse about social representations cannot be understood as failure to operationalize the concept, but as an act that renders psychologists' unreflexive quest for operationalization obsolete. It seems that Moscovici's quest is for general human understanding of the simultaneous sociality and nonsociality of personal psychological phenomena. He suggests a general meaning complex, (which is poorly definable, as many a critic of the concept of social representations has shown) as a meaning-making device for the general relation of person and society. He is not interested in creating a concept which allows simple, reductionist operationalization (see Moscovici & Marková, 1998). In this respect, Moscovici continues along the lines of *Ganzheitspsychologie* (cf. Chapter 7 – Krueger's notion of *Gefühlston* and *Komplexqualität* are complexes comparable to that of social representation). Recognizing this general function of Moscovici's concept, a number of ordinary confusions can be bypassed.

The first confusion worth mentioning is the issue of continuity from Durkheim's notion of collective representations to Moscovici's social representations. Despite the fact of Moscovici's recurrent claims for such continuity (e.g., Moscovici, 1981, p. 184; 1995) – with stipulation of clear differences – it can still be argued that a more appropriate predecessor for his concept is either Max Weber or Wilhelm Wundt (Farr, 1981; 1989; 1998) and it can have linkages with the work of Frederic Bartlett and Fritz Heider (Moscovici, 1990). These connections are crucial for the actual historical interdependency between Moscovici and the Austrian-German (as well as Hamburg) traditions (Chapter 7). Heider is a person whose work unites the Viennese, Hamburg, Würzburg, and Berlin (Lewin) traditions, remaining productive in his exile in the United States (Heider, 1958).

Social Representing: Anchoring and Objectification

The crucial point in understanding social representations is to view them as molar-level meaning complexes that do not simply exist in some "as is" form, but regulate human conduct as personal guides. They exist for that function. Social representations include encoded information about something that is to be utilized in some (rather than another) socially prioritized direction. Hence, social representations link the existing, socially constructed and values-directed knowledge, with the necessities of reconstructing the socially meaningful world of the actors.

The notion of social representation reflects the *linked* nature of information (see Moscovici, 1982, p. 140) that a person works within his or her social world. Any information is (or could be) linked with a prior generalized and socially widespread "knowledge template." These templates – folk ideas, or social representations – guide meaning construction by persons in their individual worlds. Persons anchor their understanding of something in the system of social representations, and such anchoring leads them to objectify these representations *in* that something thus anchored. The anchoring process can become fixed, automatized (or rigidified). In this case, the use of social representations guarantees the *socially guided personal resistances* to new information. In Moscovici's own example,

Galileo's telescope taught and made visible new phenomena only to the proponents of the heliocentric representation of the world. All the others who maintained the geocentric representation, could see nothing but strange appearances – and the reason was not that they were catholic or obtuse. *To make someone responsive to new information, there is no need to overwhelm him with large quantities of it nor to 'rectify' his thinking. All that is needed is to connect it by modifying the representation of the object to which the information is related.* Despite everything, psychoanalysis has colored common sense, and more than common sense, without offering any measurable data, without any confirmed fact. Facts were gathered only after the theory had gained acceptance, in order to persuade oneself and others of its correctness. (Moscovici, 1982, pp. 140–1, emphasis added)

Here we can see that social representations *are complex wholes of signification* that provide the direction for constructive interpretations of life events by individuals. Personal interpretations take the form of objectification, which "saturates the unfamiliar concept with reality, changing it into a building block of reality itself" (Moscovici, 1981, p. 198). This can happen in various ways – persons in "traditional" societies may objectify the surrounding physical world through the social representing of various spirits (e.g., Horton, 1993), while in the "modern industrialized" world there is a case of "reverse animism" (attributing machine-like characteristics to living beings) that is an accepted form of objectification (Moscovici, 1981, p. 202). Both cases are functionally the same. Moscovici's notion of objectification provides substance to what Mikhail Bakhtin has labeled "populating the word with one's own intent." In the widespread quote from Bakhtin,

The word of language [*slovo iazyka* – in Russian] – is half alien [*chuzoye* – not belonging to me and unknown – in Russian] word. It becomes "one's own" *when the speaker inhabits* [*naselit*, in Russian] *it with his intention*, with his accent, masters [*ovladeet*, in Russian] the word, *brings it to bear upon his meaningful and expressive strivings.* Until that moment of appropriation [*prisvoenie* in Russian] the *word is not existing in neutral and faceless language* (as the speaker does not take the word from a dictionary!), but [it exists] *on the lips of others, in alien contexts, in service of others' intentions*, from here it has to be taken and made into one's own. (Bakhtin, 1934/1975, p. 106)

Here "word" (Bakhtin used *slovo* which is both *word* and *utterance*) can be filled in by social representation *à la* Moscovici, and the process of objectification is that of inserting one's own intention into the word through its contextualization.

The difficulty for Moscovici's (and any others') discussion of the notion of representation is the objectlike nature of the complexes-as-entities. When X is described to be a social representation that functions in a given society at the given time, it becomes a de facto object, and loses its dynamic, functioning properties. This inevitable result of language use makes restoration of the generative, directive potential of social representations difficult to recapture in scientific discourse. This may be particularly a problem in the English-language rendering of the notion of representation, which focuses on the object (entity) and defocuses from the process (i.e., the process of representation, or represent-*ing*).

Social representations do not just reflect, but *direct* interpretations that are made by oneself, or suggested to others. For instance, the notion of "debriefing" in psychological experiments has the function of directing the subject's emerging meaning of what happened in an experiment, in a direction desired by the researcher (Moscovici, 1991, p. 256). For productivity in science, it is necessary for the individual to brush aside the implications of particular social representations and transform the latter into a novel form (Moscovici, 1993). That novel form is a new (or modified) social representation, which serves as a further guide for future process of social representing.

Thus, one could emphasize the dynamic, constructive nature of social representations over their ontological status (which undoubtedly can be spoken of as well). As Wagner has pointed out,

> *As soon as a pool of tradition and representations exist more or less consensually in a group*, social actors do *not* engage in their social interactions with others and with the somethings in their world because they *want or intend* to construct an object. . . . Social construction is always an *unintended* process. Constructing a socially significant "object" is what a group or its members do and what they intend to do after having contemplated about it; construction *happens*, it is an event . . . A *constructive event* is an event in the course of which a something in the world is named, equipped with attributes and values, and integrated into a *socially* meaningful world (Wagner, 1996, p. 110).

Wagner indicates a vantage point that is easy to overlook in discourse about social representations. The phenomena of social representations are embedded in the happenstance realities of everyday life events (and should best be viewed as such). Yet our focus on the social representations as "target entities" frees them from that context, and makes them into "pure things" that can be described as if they can be separated from their contexts (and from their constructors).

Perhaps an example is due from our current efforts. All through this book, we have tried to trace the history of reconstruction of the *person-as-separate individual* social representation into *person-as-social (yet autonomous) individual*. We have demonstrated how many scholars in the social sciences have struggled with that transformation, and how progress in this has been slow, at best. It could be said that the history of the sociogenetic idea is a case of a history of reconstruction of a social representation. Once reconstructed, however, the social representation changes the way the human *psyche* is being understood.

Social versus Collective Representations: Generativity versus Ontology

Durkheim's paper (Durkheim, 1898) that outlined his concept of collective representations entailed a contrast between persons and society on the one hand, and between societies ("European" versus "primitive") on the other. Moscovici's focus on social representations was explicitly oriented toward the functioning of the representations in the middle of current, ongoing social life (Moscovici, 1981, p. 185; 1988b, p. 218). Moscovici differentiates himself from Durkheim's sociology (Jahoda, 1988). Social representations are not "given to" the persons from their society, but have become inherent in the human psyche (e.g., they have "objectified for so long that we no longer notice them" – Moscovici, 1988b, p. 220). Interestingly, Moscovici claims close ties to Gananath Obeyesekere's (1981, 1984) analysis of cultural symbols. Social representations are persons' ways of "world making" (ibid, p. 231), which integrate both the mental and affective spheres of that process. Phenomenologically, social representations are distinctive psychic phenomena. Moscovici provides a description of the microgenesis of social representations:

When a representation emerges, it is startling to see how it grows out of a seeming *repetition of clichés*, an *exchange of tautological terms* as they occur in conversations, and a *visualization of fuzzy images* relating to strange objects. And yet *it combines all these heterogeneous elements into one whole and endows the new thing with a novel and even cohesive appearance.* The key to its method of production lies in the anchoring and objectivation process. (Moscovici, 1988b, p. 244, emphases added)

Here we can observe a number of connections of relevant ideas from the beginning of the century to Moscovici's notions – albeit *not* from Durkheim. The focus on clichés, images, and tautologies is reminiscent of the focus of the Würzburg School of Oswald Külpe and his associates (including Karl Bühler). The focus on emergence of unification of the elements into a whole is close to Wundt's creative synthesis as well as to *Ganzheitspsychologie's* "strive for the whole" notion. Of course the socially shared ontological aspect of the notion of social representation remains close to Durkheim's collective representation idea. Yet Moscovici needed his concept precisely for the purposes of looking at constantly emerging socially communicable phenomena, rather than fixed entities projected into the abstracted realms of society or culture. Hence his insistence upon the critical difference between his and Durkheim's concepts.

Methodologically, Moscovici takes a developmental stance by locating where one can investigate social representations:

It is during the process of transformation that phenomena are more easily perceived. Therefore we concentrated on the emergence of social representations: either starting *from scientific theories* – so as to follow the metamorphosis of the latter within a society and the manner in which they renewed common sense – or from *current events*, experiences and 'objective knowledge' which a group had to face in order to constitute and control its own world. (Moscovici, 1984, p. 57)

This methodological credo applies well to the two main research projects Moscovici has carried out himself (the establishment of psychoanalysis as anchored in religion and medicine in French society – Moscovici, 1961; and making sense of social "crowds" – Moscovici, 1985). However, it does not fit very well with many empirical studies conducted under the umbrella label of "social representations research" in the 1990s. The popularity of the notion of social representations in current social psychology may be linked precisely with the nonfollowing of Moscovici's methodological credo. Usual, outcomes-oriented methods are used to reveal subjects' relatively stable and *already existing* notions about some relevant issue in the social world. Statistical analysis results of such studies then become interpreted as if the notions involved have the status of social representations. Through such separation of the phenomena from their contexts, the contribution that Moscovici's version of the concept could bring to empirical research becomes lost. It becomes anchored in the established empirical practices of the very same psychology that criticized Moscovici for the undefined nature of his concept, and its lack of operationalization. No surprise that Moscovici himself feels close to the developmental orientations of Piaget and Vygotsky (Moscovici, 1998), and could perhaps feel comfortable in the company of contemporary holistic activity theoretic discourse.

Ernst E. Boesch's Symbolic Action Theory

Boesch's focus is in many ways parallel to the explanation of conduct through the notion of social representations by Moscovici, yet builds new concepts of a personal subjective kind (e.g., *Heimweh* or longing-for-home – Boesch, 1997c). It could be perhaps said that Boesch's work constitutes a bridge – created in the Saarland, which is an area of both French and German cultural backgrounds – between the French and German holistic orientations in psychology. The French orientation of Boesch (reliance on the work of Pierre Janet, fortified by his studies in Geneva with Piaget, see Boesch, 1997a) could explain his efforts at the rightness of traditions. The holistic side was prepared by Boesch's aestheticism and psychoanalysis. Through his holistic orientation, Boesch laid the foundation for the Saarbrücken School of psychology (see Baltes, 1997; Eckensberger, 1997).

Another aspect in the birth and growth of the Saarbrücken School of psychology that could have contributed to its development was the sociohistorical nature of the Saarland. Being at the border of French and German language areas, and having the history of constant moves between the two countries, the aftermath of the Second World War need not have had the same impact on the intellectual life as in the rest of Germany. In the latter, universities survived under hardships. In Saarland, Boesch was building up a new research tradition (Boesch, 1997a, p. 262). This tradition was facilitated by his experiences within another society: Thailand, from the 1950s onward.

Boesch developed his symbolic action theory in ways that integrate concepts from developmental constructionism of Jean Piaget and Pierre Janet with basic psychoanalytic insights. It occurs in clearly personological ways, yet with an emphasis on the symbolic construction of the person by the person himself (Boesch, 1991, 1997b). Boesch's theory includes a basic focus on complex psychological phenomena (e.g., aesthetic objects such as violins – Boesch, 1993) that guide personal experiences in socially charted out directions. In a way, Boesch's emphasis on actions with objects can be viewed as an actions-centered parallel to Moscovici's social representations. Boesch's focus on poly-valence of symbols (see Boesch, 1997b, p. 424) is similar to Moscovici's use of the representations as guides for social being.

A person experiences herself through personal generalized symbols (*fantasms*), which are based on socially available *myths*. Boesch's focus on the symbolic nature of action allows for analysis of the ways in which persons move from myths to actions via personally relevant fantasms. For Boesch, fantasms can include person's general meanings of "love," "justice," "happiness," etc. (Boesch, 1991), or *Heimweh* (longing-for-home, Boesch, 1997c). These fantasms – complex mean-ings – could qualify as social representations in Moscovici's terminol-ogy – if their social roots are indicated (e.g., the representing of "love" in nineteenth-century French society, or that of "madness" in the twentieth century; Jodelet, 1991). Boesch's distinction fantasm <–> myth – along the lines of person–society distinction – would not be represented in Moscovici's social, representation notion. The latter would capture both in one complex.

Like most holistic psychologists before him, Boesch's interest in understanding the social nature of the person-in-society is based on personal moral philosophy. His own self-organizing fantasm is human dignity. In his words, "Dignity can mean many things, certainly au-tonomy and responsibility in one's bearing, but does it not, above all, also include an ability to withstand and transform evil? In other words, transforming misery into fulfillment, drabness into light, cold into warmth, it is committed to goals which lead to humane life. Such an ability constitutes *creativity*, in the genuine sense of the word" (Boesch, 1997b, p. 429).

Here we see the telos of striving for perfection (*à la* Kaplan), yet with the twist of sociorepresentational kind (use of representations of "genuine," "evil," "misery," "fulfillment").

Boesch's cultural-psychological emphasis has continued in two di-rections. First, in the semiotic ecological psychology of Alfred Lang (1992, 1993, 1997) one can find a synthesis of American semiotic prag-matism of C. S. Peirce and Boesch's focus on symbolic action. Second, in Lutz Eckensberger's action-theoretic perspective exists an extension of the dynamic side of Boesch's ideas. Originally formulated within the crosscultural psychology perspective, Eckensberger has moved on to construct a dynamic theoretical perspective of cultural psychology of human action and thinking (Eckensberger, 1990, 1992, 1997). The

emphasis on persons' goal-directed actions and their emerging reflexive abstraction are the cornerstone of Eckensberger's view of psychological processes.

Conclusions: Open and Closed Nature of Social Construction of Scientific Concepts

All of the contemporary efforts to make sense of the social nature of
persons are firmly rooted in the intellectual interdependencies with
core authors from the past. For most North American sociogenetic
thinkers, the spirit of John Dewey (see Chapter 5) emanates from
behind either semiotic or activity-based constructions (Rogoff,
Wertsch, Cole, and Kaplan). Dewey has also fed into contemporary
American philosophy (e.g., Richard Rorty). Shweder's "intentional
worlds/intentional persons" notion can be viewed as a tentative reconstruction of Edmund Husserl's ideas in a cultural context. Boesch's
(and Eckensberger's and Lang's) perspectives relate to Pierre Janet
and C. S. Peirce.

What seems to emerge from this overview of our contemporary
thought is the basic lack of serious intellectual breakthroughs, paired
with a number of promising starting points that are not taken to their
full potentials by their authors. Possibly the following (rather than
transcending) orientation – in respect to the predecessors – that might
be a reason for not proceeding further. The general notion of polyphony of voices from Bakhtin should easily allow for many concrete
elaborations of the idea (yet has produced very little "ventriloqua-
tion"). The notion of guided participation could lead to a rich range
of versions of both guidance and participation, yet that direction has
not been developed. There is of course Kaplan's genetic dramatism
notion that does transcend Werner's ideas in specific ways. Yet it also
has not opened a wide range of opportunities for innovative research
that its meaning entails.

Hypothetically, we could locate the obstacle to the unleashing of
creativity in contemporary social sciences in the change in the nature
of the epistemic market over the twentieth century. While in the beginning decades of psychology as a new discipline, the creation of new
ideas (on old bases) could proceed with support of that "market
demand." Psychology then needed to demonstrate its autonomy from
philosophy, and in order to accomplish that, was openly accepting for
new ideas that could be linked with newly developing empirical in-

vestigations. By our contemporary time, these market demands are almost reversed: Now the autonomous discipline of psychology depends upon economic support from the rest of society by selling its services to the world dominated by social institutions. Instead of increasing the wide variety of ideas by deriving from some root source, for the contemporary social sciences it becomes sufficient (and necessary) to *create the prominence of a particular idea complex* in both the epistemic and economic markets of the social sciences. This is accomplished by way of anchoring a particular notion upon other (laypersons,' rather than sciences') social representations, and filling the notion "in" by empirical research conducted by way of methods that are similarly positioned on their corresponding "market of methods." At times we hear psychologists talk about the "right" ("objective," "standardized") methods separately from concerns about the issue of what the research question is. This entails the overshadowing of the epistemological issue of research. Psychologists often rely upon the "utility for society" of one or another kind of research themes.

Here we are getting evidence of the disconnected functioning of the different markets. Under conditions of such disconnection, symbolic material that seems to belong to one realm becomes transposed to another, and de facto operates within the other. With this transposition, elaboration of theoretical ideas can become unnecessary if the discourse takes place on the market of selling the given perspective to social users. Theoretical constructs become packaged like consumer products, their black-box nature is not to be revealed on that market. It is therefore not surprising that social scientists often take colleagues' criticisms of their expressed ideas for personal attacks that undermine their activities. Such comments undermine the success of the well-packaged product on the market, rather than open novel alleys for redesigning the present state of knowledge.

If this hypothetical picture of the social processes in contemporary social sciences is adequate, then it is not surprising at all that the sociogenetic orientations in psychology have not demonstrated profound conceptual breakthroughs. The multiplicity of the markets in which the ideas and practices operate may stand on the way toward innovations, and guide social scientists toward repetitive promotion of core meanings that are polysemic. These have their meanings in both lay thinking and in science. A concept like "attachment" operates simultaneously in the laypersons' world, as well as in that of psychologists. The latter can rely on the former in promoting the idea that "attachment theory" is of central relevance for child psychology (in contrast with a possible opposite "detachment theory"). Moscovici's focus on anchoring new social representations among the previous ones acquires here additional structural properties. A scientific concept is validated through the intuitive appeals of laypersons' ordinary language uses, and then using that appeal at the level of scientific language uses, situates the same social representation in between the levels. Nominally, the concept belongs the scientific language, but its use is that of common language.

An additional feature of such anchoring may be important for creating the closed nature of the concepts. The questions in the laypersons' world that are asked about the meaning complex that is proven in this way to be relevant need not require further decomposing of the attachment concept itself. Thus, the feedback loop between scientists' and laypersons' queries guarantees the establishment of the given meaning as a consensual black box.

Last, but not least, the fragmented aspects of social (mass) communication systems can be a reason for why most of the sociogenetic generic concepts, once expressed, quickly assume the status of black boxes. If focus on brand names, or appealing labels, begins to overtake a focus on the systemic functioning of the mechanism that is named by the label, there is no necessity to develop elaborate versions of scientific concepts. An appealing label is enough – it can be put on any complex social phenomenon, and utilized as a consensually validated explanation. It takes either a doubting young scientist, or a dramatic change in the phenomena subsumed under the label, to throw the given discipline off balance, and to search for more sophisticated explanations.

Conclusion: Social Mind in Action, the Socially Guided Intellectual Interdependency in Science

We have covered a substantial array of knowledge in this book. When we started our effort to make sense of the different ways in which the *mind* has been declared to be *social*, we did not expect to discover such a multitude of approaches to the issue. Furthermore, these approaches have surfaced in the thinking of scientists in a number of countries. We limited our coverage to the United States, France, Germany, and Russia, knowing all too well that this is an artificial self-limitation.

Nevertheless, the picture that emerges in this book reveals three features about the construction of the mind as a social entity. First, we discovered *how slow the progress is* in the development of a basic idea. Over the slightly more than the past one hundred years that we cover, the notion that the human mind is social has been reiterated many times, and in different countries. Yet we find our contemporary social sciences in the 1990s making claims – and fighting rhetoric battles – that are very similar in nature (and in their lack of elaborations) to those that were made in the 1890s. Why so? We claim that socially guided intellectual interdependency of scientists may give us an answer.

Second – and this may seem a paradoxical statement – we could *discover a multitude of specific elaborations of the basic idea of social nature of the mind*. Different theorists – Baldwin, Mead, Janet, Vygotsky – tried in their particular ways to suggest at least general solutions to the question *how to study* the social nature of the mind. Slowly, but surely, did each of them arrive at their solution, yet by a time when none of them could personally put the solutions into practice. Janet's (or Vygotsky's) "sociogenetic law" was formulated by the end of his long carreer, and well after he had moved out of the clinic where his "fountain pen psychology" provided him with rich empirical basis for the law. Baldwin developed his "genetic logic" at around the time of his exit from the academic world. Mead was incredibly slow in elaborating his I–ME self-system ideas in the last two decades of his life, and Vygotsky died young. The history of sociogenetic thought is thus filled with a number of productive starting grounds from which appropriate methodology could have been launched. Instead, the ideas stayed in the public domain, semiforgotten, and were later resuscitated as objects of admiration and following, rather than as bases for further development.

Third, our analysis revealed the socially guided nature of the ideas of sociogenesis. The wider societal contexts in the four countries we looked at in this book seem to have guided the thinking of social scientists towards an emphasis on the social nature of the psychological functions at some historical epochs, while suggesting forgetting or denial of the idea at other times. The main arenas for the development of the sociogenetic idea moved around in the geopolitical realm. Starting from continental Europe (Germany, Austria, France) in the mid 1800s, the intellectual center of gravity of this process quickly moved to the United States at the turn of the century. It was tamed with the pragmatist/behaviorist avalanche, and reappeared in Germany and Russia in the 1920s. The horrors of European history again made the United States the fertile field of these ideas during World War II. After some decades of dormancy, 1950–1970s, the sociogenetic direction again reemerged in American social sciences in the 1980s, largely through rediscovery of Soviet psychology. But some of that rediscovery amounted to reimporting ideas that originally were developed in the United States, e.g., the role of John Dewey in Russian activity theories, or that of Baldwin in the developmental ideas of Jean Piaget and Lev Vygotsky.

Two Views on Sociogenesis: Troubles with the Notion of Development

The notion of sociogenesis has two alleys of interpretation open to it. One is ontological, referring to the human mind as being social (existing as social entity). Here the notion of "genesis" indicates the principal fact that there was a history of the emergence of the mind in a social context. But the process of that emergence is not elaborated. The ontological focus on sociogenesis merely does not forget that what is, was once becoming to be.

The second interpretational alley of sociogenesis focuses on the process of emergence of psychological phenomena through social means. Here the focus on development is crucial. It is precisely this interpretation that offers a new road to empirical work for psychologists. At the same time, it is exactly the developmental orientation that has been vanishing from psychology's sphere of attention over the last century. Developmental ideas in the work of Janet, Baldwin, Piaget, Vygotsky, Mead, Krueger, Sander, and others have been translated back into nondevelopmental theoretical notions. Thus, Piaget's developmental equilibration theory has been overlooked in favor of declaring him to be a "stage theorist," and Sander's focus on constructivity of the *Aktualgenese* process became translated into the notion of sequential order of unfolding of responses in microgenesis. The temporal organization of Werner's and Kaplan's "orthogenetic principle" became a-temporal in its transition to the idea of "genetic dramatism." One could (almost) formulate a general sociological law of social sciences' handling of development (as an open-ended, unpredictable, process). Whenever specific ideas reflecting such development emerge, they are soon transformed into concepts that describe outcomes of development, and do not reflect the process of development.

Intellectual Interdependency and Its Social Guidance

Aside from charting out the corpus of historically created approaches to sociogenesis, we wanted to look at the social processes involved in the construction of ideas. First of all, intellectual interdependency, as was outlined in Chapter 1, pertained to the relationship between ideas that traverse the minds of different scientists. Scientists may be skeptical of one another's ideas, or oppose them, or follow them, but in all cases we can see an active construction of novel ideas in the interdependent relation of the persons involved.

However, there is more to that: The social background in which these interpersonal dramas in science are created, is embedded in the secondary background of the highlighting of some complex of social representations (and keeping others without attention). This provides for the socially guided nature of science's participation in the wider societal world, which guides the sciences, especially social sciences, by differential valuation of different ways of thinking.

Social guidance of sciences takes different forms. First, it pertains to which research questions are valued (and which others disvalued).

In the historical period of European colonialism – continued after the demise of colonial empires – the cross-cultural comparisons of "us" (Germans, French, British, Americans) and "the others" (the "savages" or – stated along the guidelines of "political correctness" – "developing societies") was made into a formidable issue to be delegated to cultural/social anthropologists and cross-cultural psychologists. In the times of the cold war post-World War II, the issue of "The Soviet Man" was an appropriate topic to think about. After the reunification of Germany, psychologists rushed to study East-West differences within Germany (which were assumed to emerge over forty years) instead of asking questions about North-South differences (which have had about four hundred years to emerge). While concentrating on the East-West German (i.e., intra-ethnic) comparisons, German psychologists are not specifically oriented toward cross-ethnic comparisons within Germany (e.g., comparing German Germans and Turkish Germans, nowadays a formidable part of the population of Germany).

Second, the societal guidance of the social sciences orients the researchers as to how to carry out their research projects. The social guidance of social sciences in the United States has been ideologically prescriptive of quantitative approaches in the social sciences,[1] even when it is obvious that the particular phenomena of interest may not allow quantification. The reliance on the variety of statistical methods as *the* scientific method survives in spite of clear demonstrations of the limitations of these methods, and statisticians' criticisms of the inappropriate uses of these methods. The prescription for their use is social, not substantive, and constitutes not guidance but stern guarding of the kind of empirical evidence the social scientists can create.

---

[1] The first author has come across the implicit belief among social scientists in the United States that qualitative methods are perceived to be linked with a threat to the secular nature of science. Without doubt, the history of the social sciences in the United States gives many examples of how the tension between science and religion has tormented American scientists (evidence for this surfaced in Chapters 4, 5, and 6). This anchoring of the new social representation of qualitative methods in the context of historically old opposition in the U.S. society may explain the overwhelming and rigid adherence to the god of chance (or better, the deity of statistical analysis packages) in contemporary social sciences in the United States. By rejecting one religious background, its secular equivalent easily comes into being. It becomes powerful socially, as the "right methods" become imbued with supernatural powers (e.g., the easy move from strictly technical talk of "significance" to its overgeneralized form).

After World War II, the United States captured the control over the social science institutions (by way of granting and publishing power), and the social prescriptions that have emerged on the basis of particularities of U.S. history have become exported into other countries.

Development of any science on a world-wide basis is a heterogeneous affair. Some sciences move ahead in some countries very vigorously, only to become relatively stagnant in a subsequent period. The same ideas may be taken up by scientists in another country during a different decade, and developed in new directions. The latter may still be intellectually interdependent with the former, even if our tendencies to view progress in science as monotonically progressing would hide the actual ups and downs of the progress of basic ideas. Science is an intellectual enterprise that knows no country (or language) boundaries. However, the social canalization of their ways of thinking and acting is rooted in the social processes of particular societies at given historical times. This explains the jumpy, uneven, nature of developing ideas in the given area, and the world-wide "opening" of some progressive directions in some countries (while their predecessors close, or are eliminated, in other places).

Wars and other economic upheavals have had their role in this uneven history of the social sciences. The social sciences in general have been closely connected with the ideological changes that have gone hand in hand in societies preparing for, waging, and trying to overcome the war experiences. The notion of the social nature of the person has been particularly dependent upon the social atmospheres. It has been emphasized in these historical periods when social agendas of institutions called for formation (or re-formation) of human psychological types. Times of building "new society" or re-educating immigrants would bring the sociogenetic notion to the center of attention. In contrast, historical periods emphasizing selection of persons would render that idea unpopular, and would lead to acceptance of the folk model of "genetic determinism."

Third, the social guidance of intellectual interdependency suggests to scientists when to stop thinking and asking further questions. In other terms, the approximate nature of sufficient solutions to posed research questions is somewhere in the social discourse between the given science and its social background. This feature of socially guided intellectual interdependency may explain why the sociogenetic notion has not been developed very far theoretically over the last century, and why it has not led to invention of new methodology, which it clearly needs. At a certain moment in scientific explanation, scientists negotiate, between themselves, where to stop opening black boxes of the explanation of the phenomena.

We claim that these decisions are socially guided by extra-scientific orientations. This may explain why large-samples based minimal (but statistically significant) differences in psychological "measures" of something count as final results of an investigation (rather than starting points for further, in-depth inquiry). How can a science produce a myriad of results which merely indicate that something is marginally different from something else, and remain intellectually satisfied? It is possible only if scientists' curious minds are socially pacified to be satisfied with such findings. This is perhaps most evident in the case of social blocking of the innovation of methodology. It is clear that the sociogenetic orientation requires a totally new formal inferential system. The one used in nondevelopmental and nonsocial psychology – the heritage of Galton and Pearson – simply misfits with the holistic (see Chapters 7 and 8), hierarchically organized (see Chapter 3) and meaningful (Chapters 4 and 6) phenomena. Despite the recurrent claims by sociogenetic thinkers since the times of Janet, Baldwin, Mead, and Vygotsky, no systematic construction effort in the realm of research methodology can be found. Instead, there are disputes about the *replacement* of the quantitative method by an equally empiricistic qualitative method (e.g., the turn to ethnographic observations and analysis of discourse in education and cultural studies). If successful, such replacement would not solve the problem different sociogenetic thinkers have outlined: how to empirically investigate social construction processes within the progressing course of development (see Chapter 4, Baldwin's canons and postulates). A qualitative, ethnographic description of behavior in an everyday setting may have the immediate appeal of being "close to reality" (in comparison to a "standardized measure"), yet it remains equally unconnected with the theoretical propositions of sociogenetic kind. The difference of the new turn at the facade level is remarkable: Instead of numbers, researcher would look at videotapes, or listen to audiotapes. But these new kinds of newly socially legitimized data suffer from the same hurdle of interpretation that their previous (numerical) cousins: They cannot be interpreted without a clear, systematic, and explicit connection between the theoretical and empirical domains of the given science.

The Final Note: Guidance for the Sociogenesis of Sociogenesis

What was said above is clearly stated without much concern for the realm of social valuation of our efforts in this book. Yet the whole effort of writing this long and complex book was worth the while if it leads us, and our readers, further in the direction of selectively opening up more of the consensually closed black boxes of sociogenetic research. To return to the words of Ernst Cassirer – and paraphrasing them – the "wounds" that the social nature of the persons-who-are scientists inflicts upon them cannot be healed but through recognition of the specific nature of the social guidance of our sociogenetic theories. Recognizing that, we can try to transcend that guidance, perhaps finally arriving at a science in which the social nature of the human psyche is a solid a phenomenon for investigation as chemical substances or structures of the cell are for other sciences.

Bibliography

Abel'skaya, R., & Neopikhonova, O. (1932). Problema razvitiya v nemetskoy psikhologii i ee vliyanie na sovetskuyu pedologiyu i psikhologiyu. *Pedologiya*, 4, 27–36.

Addams, J. (1902). *Democracy and social ethics*. New York: The Macmillan Company.

   (1905). Problems of municipal administration. *American Journal of Sociology* 10(4), 425–444.

   (1912). Recreation as a public function in urban communities. *American Journal of Sociology*, 17, 615–619.

Ahonen, S. (1997). A transformation of history: the official representations of history in East Germany and Estonia, 1986–1991. *Culture & Psychology*, 3(1), 41–62.

Alam, C. M., & Merskey, H. (1992). The development of the hysterical personality. *History of Psychiatry*, 3, 135–165.

Allen, C. (1949). Janet and the structure of consciousness. In C. Allen, *Modern Discoveries in Medical Psychology* (pp. 32–60). London: MacMillan and Co.

Allport, G. W. (1943). The productive paradoxes of William James. *Psychological Review*, 50, 95–123.

   (1951). Dewey's individual and social psychology. In P. A. Schlipp, ed., *The philosophy of John Dewey* (pp. 265–290). New York: Tudor.

Altmann, S. P. (1903). Simmel's philosophy of money. *American Journal of Sociology*, 9, 46–68

American, S. (1898a). The movement for small playgrounds. *American Journal of Sociology*, 4, 159–170.

   (1898b). The movement for vacation schools. *American Journal of Sociology*, 4, 309–325.

Anan'ev, B. G. (1931). O nekotorykh voprosakh marksistsko-leninskoy rekonstruktsii psikhologii. *Psikhologiya*, 3–4, 325–344.

Andersson, O. (1962). *Studies in the Pre-history of Psychoanalysis*. Stockholm: Svenska Bokförlaget.

Angell, J. R. (1961). James Rowland Angell. In C. Murchison, ed., *A history of psychology in autobiography*. Vol. 3 (pp. 1–38). New York: Russell & Russell.

Aronovich, G. D., & Khotin, B. I. (1929). K voprosu o podrazhanii u obez'jan (macacus rhesus). In L. L. Vasil'ev, V. N. Mjasishchev, V. N. Osipova, A. L. Shnirman, & N. M. Shchelovanov, eds., *Novoe v refleksologii i fiziologii nervnoj sistemy* (pp. 378–397). Moscow-Leningrad: Gosudarstvennoe Izdatel'stvo.

Asendorpf, J. B., & Valsiner, J. (1992). Three dimensions of developmental perspectives. In J. B. Asendorpf, & J. Valsiner, eds., *Framing stability and change* (pp. ix–xxii). Newbury Park, CA: Sage.

Ash, M. G. (1985). Gestalt psychology: Origins in Germany and reception in the United States. In C. Buxton, ed., *Points of view in the modern history of psychology* (pp. 295–344). Orlando, FL.: Academic Press.

(1995). *Gestalt psychology in German Culture 1890–1967*. Cambridge, MA: Cambridge University Press.

Atkinson, C. (1983). *Making sense of Piaget: The philosophical roots*. London: Routledge & Kegan Paul.

Averill, J. R. (1986). The acquisition of emotions during childhood. In R. Harré, ed., *The Social Construction of Emotions* (pp. 98–118). Oxford: Blackwell.

Azam, E. (1876a). Amnésie périodique, ou dédoublement de la vie. *Annales Médico-Psychologiques*, ser. 5(16) 5–35.

(1876b). Amnésie périodique, ou doublement de la vie. *Revue Scientifique*, ser. 2, 5, 481–489.

(1876c). Le dédoublement de la personnalité. Suite de l'histoire de Félida X. *Revue Scientifique*, ser. 2(6) 265–269.

(1877). Le dédoublement de la personnalité et l'amnésie periodique. Suite de l'histoire de Félida X. Relation d'un fait nouveau du même ordre. *Revue Scientifique*, ser. 2, 7, 577–581.

(1878). La double conscience. *Revue Scientifique*, ser. 2(8) 194–196.

(1879). La double personnalité. Double conscience. Responsibilité. *Revue Scientifique*, ser. 2(8), 844–846.

Babinski, J. (1910). *De l'hypnotisme en thérapeutique et en médicine légale*. Paris: Semaine Médicale.

Bacon, F. (1620/1960). *The New Organon and Related Writings*. New York: Macmillan.

Bakhtin, M. M. (1934/1975). Slovo v romane [Discourse in the novel]. In M. Bakhtin, *Voprosy literatury i estetiki* (pp. 73–232). Moscow: Khudozhestvennaya Literatura. [in English translation Bakhtin, 1981]

Bailey, P. (1928). The psychology of human conduct. A review. *American Journal of Psychiatry*, 8, 209–234.

Baldwin, J. D. (1988). Mead and Skinner: agency and determinism. *Behaviorism*, 16, 2, 109–127.

(1989). The use and abuse of Mead: A case study. *Symbolic Interaction*, 12, 1, 53–57.

Baldwin, J. M. (1891). Suggestion in infancy. *Science*, 17 (No. 421). 113–117.

(1892a). Suggestion and will. *Proceedings of International Congress of Experimental Psychology*. Second Session (pp. 49–54). London: Williams & Norgate.

(1892b). Origin of volition in childhood. *Science*, 20 (No. 511), 286–287.

(1892c). Among the psychologists of Paris. *The Nation*, 55, No. 1413, 68.

(1892d). With Bernheim at Nancy. *The Nation*, 55, No. 1415, 101–103.

(1894). The origin of emotional expression. *Psychological Review*, 1, 610–623.

(1894a). Psychology past and present. *Psychological Review*, 1, 363–391.

(1894b). Imitation: A chapter in the natural history of consciousness. *Mind*, 3 (new series), 26–55.

(1894c). Personality-suggestion. *Psychological Review*, 1, 274–279.

(1895). *Mental development in the child and the race*. New York: Macmillan.

(1896a). Heredity and instinct I. *Science*, 3 (No. 64), 438–441.

(1896b). Heredity and instinct II. *Science*, 3 (No. 67), 558–561.

(1897a). Organic selection. *Science*, 5 (No. 121), 634–636.

(1897b). Determinate evolution. *Psychological Review*, 4, 393–401.

(1897c). *Social and ethical interpretations in mental development*. New York: MacMillan.

(1898). On selective thinking. *Psychological Review*, 5(1) 1–24.

(1902a). *Fragments in philosophy and science*. New York: Charles Scribner's Sons.

(1902b). *Development and evolution*. London: MacMillan.

(1904). The limits of pragmatism. *Psychological Review*, 11, 30–60.

(1905). Sketch of the history of psychology. *Psychological Review*. 12, 144–165.

(1906a). *Thought and things: A study of the development and meaning of thought, or genetic logic*. Vol. 1. *Functional logic, or genetic theory of knowledge*. London: Swan Sonnenschein & Co.

(1906b). Introduction to experimental logic. *Psychological Review*, 13, 388–395.

(1907a). Logical community and the differenc of discernibles. *Psychological Review*, 14, 395–402.

(1907b). On truth. *Psychological Review*, 14, 264–287.

(1908a). *Thought and things: A study of the development and meaning of thought, or genetic logic*. Vol. 2. *Experimental logic, or genetic theory of thought*. London: Swan Sonnenschein & Co.

(1908b). Knowledge and imagination. *Psychological Review*, 15, 181–196.

(1910). Report on terminology. In E. Claparède, ed., *VIme Congrès International de Psychologie* (pp. 480–481). Geneva: Kündig.

(1911a). *Thought and things: A study of the development and meaning of thought, or genetic logic*. Vol 3. *Interest and art being real logic*. London: Swan Sonnenschein & Co.

(1911b). *The individual and society*. Boston: Richard G. Badger.

(1915). *Genetic theory of reality*. New York: G. P. Putnam's Sons.

(1926). *Between two wars 1861–1921*. Vol. 1–2. Boston, MA: The Stratford Company.

(1930). James Mark Baldwin. In C. Murchison, ed., *A history of psychology in autobiography*. Vol. 1 (pp. 1–30). New York: Russell & Russell.

Baltes, P. B. (1997). Ernst E. Boesch at 80: Reflections from a student on the culture of psychology. *Culture & Psychology*, 3(3) 247–256.

Barraud, H.-J. (1971). *Freud et Janet. Etude comparée*. Toulouse: Privat.

Barrucand, D. (1967). *Histoire de l'hypnose en France*. Paris: P.U.F.

Barry, R. M. (1968). A man and a city: George Herbert Mead in Chicago. In M. Novak, ed., *American philosophy and the future: Essays for a new generation* (pp. 173–192). New York: Charles Scribner's Sons.

Bartlett, F. C. (1932/1977). *Remembering. A study in experimental and social psychology.* Cambridge: Cambridge University Press.

Bastian, A. (1868). Zur vergleichende Psychologie. *Zeitschrift für Völkerpsychologie und Sprachwissenschaft,* 5, 153–180.

Bazerman, C. (1987). Codifying the social scientific style: The APA Publication Manual as a behaviorist rhetoric. In J. S. Nelson, A. Megill & D. N. McCloskey, eds., *The rhetorics of the human sciences* (pp. 125–144). Madison, WI: University of Wisconsin Press.

Beauchesne, H. (1986). *Histoire de la psychopathologie.* Paris: P.U.F.

Beaunis, H. (1886). Un fait de suggestion mentale. *Revue Philosophique,* 11, 204.

Bechterev, V. M. (1932). *General principles of human reflexology.* New York: International Publishers.

Behrens, P. J. (1997). G. E. Müller: the third pillar of experimental psychology. In W. Bringmann, H. E. Lück, R. Miller, & C. E. Early, eds., *A pictorial history of psychology* (pp. 171–176). Chicago: Quintessence Publishing Co.

Beisel, N. (1993). Morals versus art: censorship, the politics of interpretation, and the Victorian nude. *American Sociological Review,* 58, 145–162.

Benigni, L., & Valsiner, J. (1995). "Amoral familism" and child development: Edward Banfield and the understanding of child socialization in Southern Italy. In J. Valsiner, ed., *Child development within culturally structured environments.* Vol. 3. *Comparative-cultural and constructivist perspectives* (pp. 83–104). Norwood, NJ: Ablex Publishing Corporation.

Bensaude-Vincent, B., & Stengers, I. (1996). *A history of chemistry.* Cambridge, MA: Harvard University Press.

Bergeron, M. (1960). La psychologie des conduites. *Bulletin de Psychologie,* 14, 24–28.

Bergson, H. (1886). De la simulation inconsciente dans l'état d'hypnotisme. *Revue Philosophique,* 22, 525–531.

(1939). *Matière et mémoire.* Paris: P.U.F.

(1944a). *Essai sur les données immediates de la conscience.* Paris: P.U.F.

(1944b). *Creative evolution.* New York: The Modern Library. (original edition 1907).

Bernheim, H. (1877). *Leçons de clinique médicale.* Paris: Berger-Levrault.

(1892). Sur l'amaurose et l'état hypnotique. Lettre à Janet. *Revue Générale des Sciences Pures et Appliquées,* 15 October, 691.

(1903/1995). *Hypnotisme, suggestion, psychothérapie.* Paris: Fayard.

(1911–12). Définition et valeur thérapeutique de l'hypnotisme. *Journal für Psychologie und Neurologie,* 18, 468–477.

(1913). *L'hystérie.* Paris: Octave Doin et Fils.

(1917). *Automatisme et suggestion.* Paris: Alcan.

Binet, A. (1886a). Les diverses écoles hypnotiques (discussion with Delboeuf). *Revue Philosophique,* 22, 532–538.

(1886b). Review of Bernheim, De la suggestion et de ses applications à la thérapeutique. *Revue Philosophique,* 22, 557–563.

(1889a). Recherches sur les altérations de la conscience chez les hystériques. *Revue Philosophique*, 27, 135–170.

(1889b). Sur les mouvements volontaires dans l'anesthésie hystérique. *Revue Philosophique*, 28, 470–500.

(1890). Review of P. Janet, L'automatisme psychologique. *Revue Philosophique*, 29, 186–200.

(1892). *Les alterations de la personnalité*. Paris: Alcan.

(1896). *Alterations of personality*. New York: D. Appleton and Co.

Binet, A., & Féré, C. (1887). *Le magnétisme animal*. Paris: Alcan.

Blondel, Ch. (1924). La personnalité. In G. Dumas, ed., *Traité de Psychologie. Tome II* (pp. 522–574). Paris: Alcan.

Boesch, E. E. (1991). *Symbolic action theory and cultural psychology*. New York: Springer.

(1993). The sound of the violin. *Schweizerische Zeitschrift für Psychologie*, 52, 2, 70–81.

(1997a). The story of a cultural psychologist: autobiographical observations. *Culture & Psychology*, 3(3) 257–275.

(1997b). Reasons for a symbolic concept of action. *Culture & Psychology*, 3(3) 423–431.

(1997c). *Von der Sehnsucht*. Saarbrücken: Author (privately published).

Bonjean, A. (1890). *L'hypnotisme, ses rapports avec le droit et la theurapeutique*. Paris: Baillière.

Boodin, J. (1904). Time and reality. *Psychological Review Monograph Supplements*, 6, 3 (whole no. 26), 1–119.

(1908). Truth and meaning. *Psychological Review*, 15, 172–180.

The existence of social minds. *American Journal of Sociology*, 19(1) 1–47.

(1913). Cognition and social interpretation. *American Journal of Sociology*, 20, 181–219.

(1918). Social systems. *American Journal of Sociology*, 23(6) 705–734.

(1921). The law of social participation. *American Journal of Sociology*, 27, 22–53.

Boring, E. G. (1950). *A history of experimental psychology*. New York, NY: Appleton-Century-Crofts. (2nd ed.)

Borovsky, V. M. (1926). O probleme myshlenija v psikhologii povedenija. In K. N. Kornilov, ed., *Problemy sovremennoj psikhologii* (pp. 145–151). Leningrad: Gosudarstvennoe Izdatel'stvo.

(1927a). Golovnoj mozg i povedenie. *Vestnik Kommunisticheskoj Akademii*, 23, 227–249.

(1927b). Metafisika v sravnitel'noj psikhologii. *Pod Znaniem Marksizma*, 7–8, 159–191.

Bowden, H. (1904). What is pragmatism? *Journal of Philosophy, Psychology and Scientific Methods*, 1(16) 421–427.

Brainard, P. P. (1930). The mentality of a child compared with that of apes. *Journal of Genetic Psychology*, 37, 268–292.

Branco, A. U. (1996). Constraints on the universality of psychological constructs. *Culture & Psychology*, 2, 477–483.

Branco, A. U., & Valsiner, J. (1997). Changing methodologies: A co-

constructivist study of goal orientations in social interactions. *Psychology and Developing Societies*, 9(1) 35–64.

Bringmann, W. G., Bringmann, N. J., & Ungerer, G. A. (1980). The establishment of Wundt's Laboratory: An archival and documentary study. In W. G. Bringmann, & R. D. Tweney, eds., *Wundt studies. A centennial collection* (pp. 123–157). Toronto: C. J. Hogrefe.

Bringuier, J. C. (1977). *Conversations libres avec Jean Piaget*. Paris: Laffont.

Broughton, J. M. (1981). The genetic psychology of James Mark Baldwin. *American Psychologist*, 36(4) 396–407.

Brunberg, J. J. (1988). *Fasting girls: The emergence of anorexia nervosa as a modern disease*. Cambridge, MA: Harvard University Press.

Bruner, J. S. (1990). *Acts of meaning*. Cambridge, MA: Harvard University Press.

Budagov, R. A. (1988). *Portrety jazykovedov 19–20 vv.* Moscow: Nauka.

Bühler, K. (1934/1965). *Sprachtheorie*. Jena-Stuttgart: Gustav Fischer.

(1967). Christian von Ehrenfels und Albert Einstein. In F. Weinhandl, ed., *Gestalthaftes sehen: Ergebnisse und aufgaben der Morphologie* (pp. 86–91). Darmstadt: Wissenschaftliche Buchgesellschaft.

(1990). *Theory of language: The representational function of language*. Amsterdam: John Benjamins.

Burkhardt, F. H., ed., (1984). *The works of William James. Briefer Course*. Cambridge, MA: Harvard University Press.

Burkhardt, R. W. (1984). The zoological philosophy of J. B. Lamarck. In J. B. Lamarck, *Zoological philosophy* (pp. xv–xxxix). Chicago: University of Chicago Press.

Burnham, J. C. (1956). *Lester Frank Ward in American thought*. Washington, DC: Public Affairs Press (Annals of American Sociology).

Buytendijk, F. J. J. (1928). *Psychologie des animaux*. Paris: Alcan.

Cahan, E. D. (1984). The genetic psychologies of James Mark Baldwin and Jean Piaget. *Developmental Psychology*, 20(1) 128–135.

(1992). John Dewey and human development. *Developmental Psychology*, 28(2) 205–214.

Cairns, R. B. (1980). Developmental theory before Piaget: the remarkable contributions of James Mark Baldwin. *Contemporary Psychology*, 25(6) 438–440.

(1983). The emergence of developmental psychology. In W. Kessen, ed., *Handbook of child psychology*. Vol. 1. *History, theory and methods* (pp. 41–102). New York: Wiley. (4th ed.)

(1986). Phenomena lost. In J. Valsiner, ed., *The individual subject and scientific psychology* (pp. 97–111). New York: Plenum.

(1992). The making of a developmental science: the contributions and intellectual heritage of James Mark Baldwin. *Developmental Psychology*, 28(1) 17–24.

Cairns, R. B., Elder, G. E., & Costello, E. J., eds., (1996). *Developmental science*. New York: Cambridge University Press.

Calkins, M. W., Dunlap, K., Gardiner, H. N., Ruckmick, C. A., & Warren, H. C. (1922). Definitions and limitations of psychological terms, II. *Psychological Bulletin*, 19, 230–233.

Campbell, D. T. (1988). A general 'selection theory', as implemented in biological evolution and in social-belief- transmission-with-modification in science. *Biology and Philosophy*, 3, 171–177.

Campbell, J. (1995). Community without fusion: Dewey, Mead, Tufts. In R. Hollinger & D. Depew, eds., *Pragmatism: from progressivism to postmodernism* (pp. 56–71). New York: Praeger.

Campili, G. (1886). *Il grande ipnotismo e la suggestione ipnotica nei rapporti col dirritto penale e civile*. Roma: Fratelli Boca.

Carroy, J. (1991). *Hypnose, suggestion et psychologie. L'invention de sujets*. Paris: P.U.F.

(1993). *Les personnalitées doubles et multiples. Entre science et fiction*. Paris: P.U.F.

Cassirer, E. (1929). Pathologie de la conscience symbolique. *Journal de Psychologie*, 26, 289–336.

(1942). The influence of language upon the development of scientific thought. *Journal of Philosophy*, 39(12) 309–327.

Catan, L. (1986). The dynamic display of process: Historical development and contemporary uses of the microgenetic method. *Human Development, 29*, 252–263.

Chan, A. (1985). *Children of Mao*. Seattle, WA: University of Washington Press.

Charcot, J. M. (1893). Préface. In P. Janet (1893). *Etat mental des hystériques. Les stigmates mentaux* (p. iii). Paris: Rueff.

Charpentier, R. (1927). Review of P. Janet, De l'angoisse à l'extase. *Annales Medico-Psychologiques*, 85, 376–381.

(1935). Review of P. Janet, Les débuts de l'intelligence. *Annales Medico-Psychologiques*, 93, 490–491.

(1936). Review of P. Janet, La psychologie expérimentale et comparée. *Annales Medico-Psychologiques*, 94, 481–482.

Chertok, L. (1960). A propos de la découverte de la méthode cathartique. *Bulletin de Psychologie*, 14, 33–37.

Cirillo, L., & Kaplan, B. (1983). Figurative action from the perspective of genetic-dramatism. In S. Wapner & B. Kaplan, eds., *Toward a holistic developmental psychology* (pp. 235–252). Hillsdale, NJ: Erlbaum.

Cirillo, L., & Wapner, S., eds., (1986). *Value presuppositions in theories of human development*. Hillsdale, NJ: Erlbaum.

Claparède, E. (Ed.) (1910). *VIme Congrès International de Psychologie*. Genève: Kündig.

(1910). L'unification et la fixation de la terminologie psychologique. In E. Claparède, ed., *VIme Congrès International de Psychologie* (pp. 467–479). Geneva: Kündig.

Clark, R. W. (1980). *Freud: The man and the cause*. New York: Random House (p. 134).

Cole, M. (1990). Cultural psychology: A once and future discipline? In J. Berman, ed., *Nebraska Symposium on Motivation*. Vol. 37 (pp. 279–336). Lincoln, NE: University of Nebraska Press.

(1992). Context, modularity, and the cultural constitution of development. In L. T. Winegar & J. Valsiner, eds., *Children's development within social context*. Vol. 2. *Research and methodology* (pp. 5–31). Hillsdale, NJ: Erlbaum.

(1995). Culture and cognitive development: From cross-cultural research to creating systems of cultural mediation. *Culture & Psychology*, 1(1) 25–54.

(1996) *Cultural psychology: A once and future discipline* Cambridge, MA: Harvard University Press.

Collins, J. (1968). Josiah Royce: Analyst of religion as community. In M. Novak (Ed.), *American philosophy and the future* (pp. 192–218). New York: Charles Scribner's Sons.

Cook, G. A. (1977). G. H. Mead's social behaviorism. *Journal of the History of the Behavioral Sciences*, 13, 307–316.

(1993). *George Herbert Mead: The making of a social pragmatist*. Urbana: University of Illinois Press.

Cooley, C. H. (1902). *Human nature and the social order*. New York: Charles Scribner's Sons.

(1907). Social consciousness. *American Journal of Sociology*, 12(5) 675–687.

(1908). A study of early use of self-words by a child. *Psychological Review*, 15(6) 339–357.

(1913). The sphere of pecuniary valuation. *American Journal of Sociology*, 19, 188–203.

(1925). *Social organization: A study of the larger mind*. New York: Charles Scribner's Sons.

(1926). The roots of social knowledge. *American Journal of Sociology*. 33(1) 59–79.

(1929). The life-study method as applied to rural social research. *Publications of the American Sociological Society*, 23, 248–254.

(1930). *Sociological theory and social research*. New York: Henry Holt.

Coriat, I. H. (1945). Some personal reminiscences of psychoanalysis in Boston: An autobiographical note. *The Psychoanalytic Review*, 32, 1–8.

Cornelius, H. (1897). *Psychologie als Erfahrungswissenschaft*. Leipzig: B. G. Teubner.

Courtier, J. (1910). Emploi d'un système de symboles et de signes en psychologie. In E. Claparède, ed., *Vl-me Congrès International de Psychologie* (pp. 500–527). Geneva: Kündig.

Crabtree, A. (1993). *From Mesmer to Freud: Magnetic Sleep and the Roots of Psychological Healing*. New Haven: Yale University Press.

Crocq, L., & De Verbizier, J. (1988). Le traumatisme psychologique dans l'oeuvre de Pierre Janet. *Bulletin de psychologie*, 41, 483–485.

Cronk, C. F. (1976). James and the problem of intersubjectivity: An interpretative critique. In W. R. Corti (Ed.), *The philosophy of William James* (pp. 221–244). Hamburg: Felix Meiner Verlag.

Crosland, M. (1995). Changes in chemical concepts and language in the Seventeenth Century. In U. Klein & W. Lefèvre eds., *Workshop on fundamental concepts of early modern chemistry in the context of the operational and experimental practice*. Preprint 25 (pp. 31–46). Berlin: Max-Planck-Institut für Wissenschaftsgeshichte.

Danziger, K. (1990). *Constructing the subject*. Cambridge: Cambridge University Press.

The practice of psychological discourse. In C. F. Graumann & K. J. Gergen, eds. *Historical dimensions of psychological discourse* (pp. 83–100). New York: Cambridge University Press.

Darwin, C. (1872/1965). *The expression of the emotions in man and animals.* Chicago-London: The University of Chicago Press.

Daudet, A. (1899). *Notes sur la vie.* Paris: Fasquelle.

Davis, M. M. (1906). *Gabriel Tarde: An essay in sociological theory.* New York: Doctoral Dissertation.

Deegan, M.-J. (1996). "Dear love, dear love": Feminist pragmatism and the Chicago female world of love and ritual. *Gender & Society,* 10(5) 590–607.

Deegan, M. J., & Burger, J. S. (1978). George Herbert Mead and social reform: his work and writings. *Journal of the History of the Behavioral Sciences,* 14, 362–373.

Delacroix, H. (1924). Maine de Biran et l'école médico-psychologique. *Bulletin de la Société Française de Philosophie,* 24, 51–63.

(1927). L'aphasie selon Head. *Journal de Psychologie,* 24, 285–329.

Delay, J. (1960). Pierre Janet et la tension psychologique. *Psychologie Française,* 5, 93–110.

Delboeuf, J. (1886). De l'influence de l'éducation et de l'imitation dans le somnambulisme provoqué. *Revue Philosophique,* 22, 146–171.

(1887). *De l'origine des effets curatives de l'hypnotisme: étude de psychologie expérimentale.* Paris: Alcan.

(1892). *L'hypnotisme devant les chambres législatives belges.* Paris: Alcan.

DelFattore, J. (1992). *What Johnny shouldn't read: Textbook censorship in America.* New Haven, CT: Yale University Press.

Delmas, F. A. (1923). Psychopathies organiques et psychoses constitutionelles. *Journal de Psychologie,* 20, 169–175.

Del Rio, P. (1990). La Zona de Desarollo Proximo y la Zona Sincrética de Representación: El espacio instrumental de la acción social. *Infancia y Aprendizaje,* 51–52, 191–244.

Del Rio, P., & Alvarez, A. (1995a). Tossing, praying, and reasoning: The changing architectures of mind and agency. In J. V. Wertsch, P. del Río & A. Alvarez, eds., *Sociocultural studies of mind* (pp. 215–247). Cambridge: Cambridge University Press.

De Rosa, A. S. (1994). From theory to metatheory in social representations: the lines of argument of a theoretical-methodological debate. *Social Science Information,* 33(2) 273–304.

Descartes, R. (1649–1985). The passions of the soul. In J. Cottingham. R. Stoothoff, & D. Murdoch, eds., *The philosophical writings of Descartes.* vol. 1 (pp. 328–404). Cambridge: Cambridge University Press.

Despine, P. (1870). *De la contagion morale.* Marseille: Camoin.

Dessoir, M. (1910). Das Unterbewusstsein. In E. Claparède, ed., *VIme Congrès International de Psychologie* (pp. 37–56). Genève: Kündig.

DeTocqueville, A. (1969). *Democracy in America.* Garden City: Doubleday.

Devereux, G. (1967). *From anxiety to method in the behavioral sciences.* The Hague: Mouton.

Dewey, J. (1887). Knowledge as idealisation. *Mind,* 12, 382–396.

(1891). *Psychology*. New York: American Book Company
(1894). The theory of emotion. I. Emotional attitudes. *Psychological Review*, 1(6) 553–569.
(1895). The theory of emotion. II. The significance of emotions. *Psychological Review*, 2(1) 13–32.
(1896). The reflex arc concept in psychology. *Psychological Review*, 3(3) 357–370.
(1907). The control of ideas by facts. *Journal of Philosophy, Psychology and Scientific Methods*, 4(10) 253–259.
(1908). What does pragmatism mean by practical? *Journal of Philosophy, Psychology and Scientific Methods*, 5(4) 85–99.
(1932). Prefatory remarks. In G. H. Mead, *The philosophy of the present* (pp. xxxvi–xl). Chicago: Open Court.
(1980). *The middle works, 1899–1924*, (Vol. 9). Carbondale, IL: Southern Illinois University Press.
Dilthey, W. (1895/1924). Beiträge zum studium der Individualität. In W. Dilthey, *Die geistige Welt* (pp. 241–316). Leipzig: Teubner.
Dobzhansky, T. (1955). The crisis in Soviet biology. In E. J. Simmons, ed., *Continuity and change in Russian and Soviet thought* (pp. (pp. 329–346). Cambridge, MA: Harvard University Press.
Dodds, A. E., Lawrence, J. A., & Valsiner, J. (1997). The personal and the social: Mead's theory of the generalized other. *Theory & Psychology*, 7(4) 483–503.
Dolby, R. G. A. (1977). The transmission of two new scientific disciplines from Europe to North America in the late 19th century. *Annals of Science*, 34, 287–310.
Draghiscesco, D. (1904). *Du rôle de l'individu dans le déterminisme social*. Paris: Félix Alcan.
Draguns, J. G. (1983). Why microgenesis? An inquiry on the motivational sources of going beyond the information given. *Archives of Psychology*, 135, 5–16.
(1984). Microgenesis by any other name. In W. D. Froehlich, G. Smith, J. G. Draguns, & U. Hentschel, eds., *Psychological processes in cognition and personality* (pp. 3–17). Washington, DC: Hemisphere Publishing Co.
Ducret, J. J. (1984). *Jean Piaget. Savant et philosophe*. Volume I. Genève: Droz.
Duff, K. (1902). A new factor in the elementary school curriculum. *American Journal of Sociology*, 8(2), 145–157.
Dumas, G. (1911). Contagion mentale. *Revue Philosophique*, 71, 225–244; 384–407.
(1924a). L'interpsychologie. In G. Dumas, ed., *Traité de Psychologie. Tome II* (pp. 739–764). Paris: Alcan.
(1924b). La pathologie mentale. In G. Dumas, (ed.), *Traité de Psychologie. Tome 2* (pp. 811–1006). Paris: Alcan.
(1924c). La psychologie pathologique. In G. Dumas, ed., *Traité de Psychologie. Tome 2* (pp. 1007–1070). Paris: Alcan.
(1924d). Conclusion. In G. Dumas, ed., *Traité de Psychologie. Tome 2* (pp. 1121–1158). Paris: Alcan.

(1930). Introduction à la psychologie. In G. Dumas, ed., *Nouveau Traité de Psychologie. Tome 1. Notions préliminaires Introduction. Méthodologie* (pp. 335–366). Paris: Alcan.

Ebbinghaus, H. (1885/1971). *Über das Gedächtnis.* Darmstadt: Wissenschaftliche Buchgesellschaft.

Eckensberger, L. (1990). From cross-cultural psychology to cultural psychology. *The Quarterly Newsletter of the Laboratory of Comparative Human Cognition,* 12(1) 37–52.

(1991). Moralische Urteile als handlungsleitende normative Regelsysteme im Spiegel der Kulturvergleichenden Forschung. In A. Thomas (Ed.), *Einführung in der kulturvergleichende Psychologie.* Göttingen: Hogrefe.

(1992). Agency, action, and culture: Three basic concepts for psychology in general and for cross-cultural psychology in specific. *Arbeiten der Frachrichtung Psychologie,* Universität des Saarlandes, No. 165. Saarbrücken.

(1997). The legacy of Boesch's intellectual oeuvre. *Culture & Psychology,* 3(3) 277–298.

Edwards, D. (1997). *Discourse and cognition.* London: Sage

Elias, N. (1991). *The society of individuals.* Oxford: Blackwell.

Ellenberger, H. (1970). *The discovery of the unconsciousness.* New York: Basic Books.

(1965). Charcot and the Salpêtrière school. *American Journal of Psychotherapy,* 19, 253–267.

(1966). The pathogenic secret and its therapeutics. *Journal of the History of the Behavioral Sciences,* 2, 29–42.

(1978). Pierre Janet and his American friends. In G. E. Gifford, ed., *Psychoanalysis, psychotherapy and the New England medical scene. 1894–1944* (pp. 63–72). New York: Science History Publications.

(1993). Pierre Janet, philosopher. In M. Micale, ed., (1993). *Essays of Henri F. Ellenberger in the History of Psychiatry* (pp. 155–175). Princeton, NJ: Princeton University Press.

Ellsworth, P. C. (1994). William James and emotion: is a century of fame worth a century of misunderstanding? *Psychological Review,* 101(2) 222–229.

Ellwood, C. A. (1899a). Prolegomena to social psychology I. *American Journal of Sociology,* 4(5) 656–665.

(1899b). Prolegomena to social psychology II. *American Journal of Sociology,* 4(5) 807–822.

(1899c). Prolegomena to social psychology IV. The concept of social mind. *American Journal of Sociology,* 5, 220–227.

(1901a). The theory of imitation in social psychology. *American Journal of Sociology,* 6, 731–736.

(1901b). *Some prolegomena to social psychology.* Doctoral dissertation at Department of Sociology, University of Chicago. Chicago: University of Chicago Press.

(1907). Sociology: Its problems and its relations. *American Journal of Sociology,* 13(3) 300–348.

(1910). The psychological view of society. *American Journal of Sociology,* 15, 596–618.

(1911). Marx's "economic determinism" in the light of modern psychology. *American Journal of Sociology*, 17, 35–46.

(1913). The social function of religion. *American Journal of Sociology*, 19(2) 289–307.

(1914). The eugenics movement from the standpoint of sociology. In *Eugenics: Twelve university lectures* (pp. 213–238). New York: Dodd, Mead & Co.

(1916). Objectivism in sociology. *American Journal of Sociology*, 22(3) 289–305.

(1918). Theories of cultural evolution. *American Journal of Sociology*, 23, 779–800.

(1924). The relations of sociology and social psychology. *Journal of Abnormal & Social Psychology*, 19, 3–12.

Elmgren, J. (1967). *Pierre Janets psykologi*. Stockholm: Universitetskanslersämbetet.

Engels, F. (1925/1978). *Dialektik der Natur*. Berlin: Dietz Verlag.

Engler, R. (1968). *Ferdinand de Saussure. Cours de linguistique générale: Édition critique*. Wiesbaden: Otto Harrassowitz.

Ericsson, K. A., & Simon, H. A. (1993). *Protocol analysis: Verbal reports as data*. Cambridge, MA: The MIT Press.

Ey, H. (1960). Force et faiblesses des concepts génétiques de la psychopathologie de Pierre Janet. *Bulletin de Psychologie*, 14, 50–55.

(1968). Pierre Janet: The man and the work. In B. B. Wolman, ed., *Historical roots of contemporary psychology* (pp. 177–195). New York: Harper and Row.

Fabian, R. (1993). Die Grazer Schule der Gestaltpsychologie. In H. E. Lück & R. Miller, eds., *Illustrierte Geschichte der Psychologie* (pp. 71–75). München: Quintessenz.

Faris, E. (1937). The social psychology of George Mead. *American Journal of Sociology*, 43(3) 391–403.

Farr, R. M. (1981). The social origins of the human mind: A historical note. In J. P. Forgas, ed., *Social cognition* (pp. 247–258). London: Academic Press.

(1983). Wilhelm Wundt (1832–1920) and the origins of psychology as an experimental and social science. *British Journal of Social Psychology*, 22, 289–301.

(1987). Social representations: A French tradition of research. *Journal for the Theory of Social Behaviour*, 17(4) 343–369.

(1988). The international origins of a science: Social psychology. Paper presented at the 24th International Congress of Psychology, Sydney, Australia.

(1989). The social and collective nature of representations. In J. P. Forgas & J. M. Innes, eds., *Recent advances in social psychology: An international perspective* (pp. 157–166). Amsterdam: North-Holland.

(1998). From collective to social representations: Aller et retour. *Culture & Psychology* (4) 275–296.

Faure, H. (1988). La réédition des oeuvres de Pierre Janet. *Bulletin de psychologie*, 41, 477–481.

Feigenberg, I. M. (1996). *L. S. Vygotskij: Nachalo Puti*. Jerusalem: Jerusalem Publishing Centre.

Feline, A. (1988). L'apport des concepts de Pierre Janet à la psychopharmacologie. *Bulletin de psychologie*, 41, 485–486.

Feofanov, M. P. (1932). Teoriya kul'turnogo razvitiya v pedologii kak elektricheskaya kontseptsiya, imeyushchaya v osnovnom idealisticheskie korni. *Pedologiya*, 1–2, 21–34.

Feyerabend, P. (1984). Mach's theory of research and its relation to Einstein's. *Studies in History and Philosophy of Science*, 15(1) 1–22.

Findlay, J. N. (1972). Foreword. In A. Meinong, *On emotional presentation* (pp. xi–xxvii). Evanston, IL: Northwestern University Press.

Fine, G. A. (1993). The sad demise, mysterious disappearance, and glorious triumph of symbolic interactionism. *Annual Review of Sociology*, 19, 61–87.

Fischer, H. (1928). Erlebnis und Metaphysik: zur Psychologie des metaphysischen Schaffens. *Neue Psychologische Studien*, 3, 223–437.

Fite, W. (1911). *Individualism: Four lectures on the significance of consciousness for social relations*. New York: Longmans, Green & Co.

Flick, U. (1995a). Social representations. In J. A. Smith, R. Harré, & L. Van Langenhove, eds., *Rethinking psychology* (pp. 70–96). London: Sage.

eds., (1995b). *Psychologie des sozialen*. Reinbek: Rohwolt.

Flügel, O. (1880a). Das Ich im Leben der Völker *Zeitschrift für Völkerpsychologie und Sprachwissenschaft*, 11, 43–80 and 141–160.

(1880b). Ueber die Entwicklung der sittlichen Ideen. *Zeitschrift für Völkerpsychologie und Sprachwissenschaft*, 12, 27–63; 310–334; 451–470.

Fogarty, R. S. (ed.) (1994). *Special love/special sex: An Oneida community diary*. Syracuse, NY: Syracuse University Press.

Forel, O. L. (1927). De la suggestion. *Annales Medico-Psychologiques*, 85, 443–462.

Foucault, M. (1983). *This is not a pipe*. Berkeley, CA: University of California Press.

Fouillée, A. (1889). Le sentiment de l'effort et la conscience de l'action. *Revue Philosophique*, 28, 561–582.

Frawley, R. C. (1992). Siegler and Crowley's (1991) conception of development. *American Psychologist*, 47, 1239–1240.

Freeman-Moir, D. J. (1982). The origin of intelligence. In J. M. Broughton & D. J. Freeman-Moir, eds., *The cognitive-developmental psychology of James Mark Baldwin* (pp. 127–168). Norwood, NJ: Ablex.

Galton, F. (1904). Eugenics: Its definition, scope, and aims. *American Journal of Sociology*, 10(1) 1–25.

(1905). Studies in eugenics. *American Journal of Sociology*, 11, 11–25.

Garnier, P. (1887). *L'automatisme somnambulique devant les tribunaux*. Paris: Baillière.

Gauld, A. (1992). *A history of hypnotism*. Cambridge: Cambridge University Press.

Gergen, K. J. (1985). The social constructionist movement in modern psychology. *American Psychologist* 40(3) 266–275.

(1994). *Realities and relationships: Soundings in social construction*. Cambridge, MA: Harvard University Press.

Germain, J. (1960). Pierre Janet. *Bulletin de Psychologie*, 14, 2–4.

Gigerenzer, G. (1993). The superego, the ego, and the id in statistical reasoning. In G. Keren & C. Lewis, eds., *A handbook for data analysis in the behavioral sciences: Methodological issues* (pp. 311–339). Hillsdale, NJ: Erlbaum.

Gigerenzer, G., Swijtink, Z., Porter, T., Daston, L., Beatty, J., & Krüger, L. (1989). *The empire of chance.* Cambridge: Cambridge University Press.

Gilbert, G. N., & Mulkay, M. (1984). *Opening Pandora's box: A sociological analysis of scientists' discourse.* Cambridge: Cambridge University Press.

Gilles de la Tourette, G. (1889). *L'hypnotisme at les états analogues au point de vue médico-légal.* Paris: Plon, Nourrit et Cie.

Gillette, J. M. (1914). Critical points in Ward's pure sociology. *American Journal of Sociology,* 20, 31–67.

Gley, E. (1886). A propos d'une observation de sommeil provoqué à distance. *Revue Philosophique,* 11, 425–428.

Glock, H. -J. (1986). Vygotsky and Mead on the self, meaning and internalisation. *Studies in Soviet Thought,* 31, 131–148.

Goethe, J. W. (1832/1975). *Faust.* Munchen: Beck.

Goetzmann, W. II. (1973). Introduction: The American hegelians. In W. H. Goetzmann, ed., *The American hegelians* (pp. 3–18). New York: A. Knopf.

Gould, S. J. (1977). *Ontogeny and phylogeny.* Cambridge, MA: The Belknap Press of Harvard University Press.

Graumann, C. F. (1959). Aktualgenese. *Zeitschrift für experimentelle und angewandte Psychologie,* 6, 410–448.

(1996). Psyche and her descendants. In In C. F. Graumann & K. J. Gergen, eds., *Historical dimensions of psychological discourse* (pp. 17–35). New York: Cambridge University Press.

Green, C. D. (1996). Where did the word "cognitive" come from, anyway? *Canadian Psychology,* 37(1) 31–39.

Guillaume, P. (1925/1968). *L'imitation chez l'enfant.* Paris: PUF.

Guillaume, P., & Meyerson, I. (1930a). Recherches sur l'usage de l'instrument chez les singes I. Le probleme du détour. *Journal de Psychologie,* 27, 177–236.

(1930b). Recherches sur l'usage de l'instrument chez les singes II. L'intermédiaire lié à l'objet. *Journal de Psychologie,* 28, 481–555.

Gutmann, B. (1923). Amulette und Talismane bei den Dschagganegern am Kilimandscharo. *Arbeiten zur Entwicklungspsychologie,* 6, 1–29.

(1926). Das Recht der Dschagga. *Arbeiten zur Entwicklungspsychologie,* 7, 1–734.

(1932). Die Stammeslehren der Dschagga. I. Die Vorlehren. Die Lageriehren. *Arbeiten zur Entwicklungspsychologie,* 12, 1–671.

(1935). Die Stammeslehren der Dschagga. II. Die Lehren vor der Beschneidung. *Arbeiten zur Entwicklungspsychologie,* 16, 1–642.

Gutzmann, H. (1922). Psychologie der Sprache. In G. Kafka, (ed.), *Handbuch der vergleichenden Psychologie II. Die Funktionen des normalen Seelenlebens* (pp. 3–90). München: Ernst Reinhardt.

Hacking, I. (1995). *Rewriting the soul. multiple personality and the sciences of memory.* Princeton, NJ: Princeton University Press.

Hakfoort, C. (1992). Science deified: Wilhelm Ostwald's energeticist worldview and the history of scientism. *Annals of Science*, 49, 525–544.

Haller, M. H. (1984). *Eugenics: Hereditary attitudes in American thought*. New Brunswick, NJ: Rutgers University Press.

Hamilton, J. H. (1900). A neglected principle in civic reform. *American Journal of Sociology*, 5, 746–760.

Hammer. S. (1993). Felix Krueger. In H. E. Lück & R. Miller, eds., *Illustrierte Geschichte der Psychologie* (pp. 103–105). Müchen: Quintessenz.

Harms, E. (1959). Pierre Janet. *American Journal of Psychiatry*, 115, 1036–1037.

Harré, R. (1984). *Personal being*. Cambridge, MA: Harvard University Press.

Harrington, A. (1987). *Medicine, mind, and the double brain*. Princeton, NJ: Princeton University Press.

Harris, T. L. (1891). *The new republic: A discourse of the prospects, dangers, duties and safeties of the times*. Santa Rosa, CA: Fountaingrove Press.

Harsanyi, J. C., & Selten, R. (1988). *A general theory of equilibrium selection in games*. Cambridge, MA: MIT Press.

Hart, D., Kohlberg, L., & Wertsch, J. V. (1987). The developmental social-self theories of James Mark Baldwin, George Herbert Mead, and Lev Semenovich Vygotsky. In L. Kohlberg, ed., *Child psychology and childhood education* (pp. 223–258). New York: Longman.

Hartmann, E. (1935). *Philosophy of the unconscious*. London: Kegan Paul.

Haule, J. R. (1983). Archetype and integration: Exploring the Janetian roots of analytical psychology. *Journal of Analytical Psychology*, 28, 253–267.

    (1984). From somnambulism to the archetypes: The French roots of Jung's split with Freud. *Psychoanalytic Review*, 71, 635–659.

Head, H. (1920). *Aphasia and kindred disorders of speech*. Cambridge: Cambridge University Press.

    (1921). Disorders of symbolic thinking and expression. *British Journal of Psychology*, 11(2) 179–193.

Heider, F. (1958). *The psychology of interpersonal relations*. New York: Wiley.

    (1970). Gestalt theory: Early history and reminiscenses. *Journal of the History of the Behavioral Sciences*, 6, 131–139.

Henderson, C. R. (1909). Are modern industry and city life unfavorable to the family? *American Journal of Sociology*, 14, 668–680.

Henle, M. (1977). The influence of Gestalt psychology in America. *Annals of the New York Academy of Sciences*, 291, 3–12.

Herbst, D. P. (1987). *What happens when we make a distinction: An elementary introduction to co-genetic logic*. Work Research Institute, Document No. 6, Oslo.

Héricourt, J. (1886). Un cas de somnambulisme à distance. *Revue Philosophique*, 11, 200–203.

Herman, E. (1995). *The romance of American psychology: Political culture in the age of experts*. Berkeley, CA: University of California Press.

Hermans, H. J. M. (1994). Buber on mysticism, May on creativity, and the dialogical nature of the self. *Studies in Spirituality*, 4, 279–305.

    (1995). The limitations of logic in defining the self. *Theory & Psychology*, 5(3) 375–382.

(1996). Opposites in a dialogical self: Constructs as characters. *Journal of Constructivist Psychology*, 9, 1–26.

Hermans, H. J. M., & Kempen, H. J. G. (1993). *The dialogical self: meaning as movement*. San Diego, CA: Academic Press.

Herrmann, T. (1976). Ganzheitspsychologie und Gestalttheorie. In H. Balmer, ed., *Die Psychologie des 20. Jahrhunderts. Vol 1. Die Europäische Tradition* (pp. 573–658). Zürich: Kindler-Verlag.

Hesnard, A. (1960). Un parallèle Janet-Freud. *Bulletin de Psychologie*, 14, 69–73.

Hilgard, E. R. (1977). *Divided consciousness: Multiple controls in human thought and personality*. New York: Wiley.

Hine, R. V. (1991). *Josiah Royce: From Grass Valley to Harvard*. Norman, OK: University of Oklahoma Press.

Hinshelwood, R. D. (1991). Psychodynamic psychiatry before World War I. In G. E. Berrios & H. Freeman, eds., *one hundred and fifty years of British Psychiatry 1841–1991* (pp. 197–205). London: Gaskell.

Hofstede, G. (1991). *Cultures and organizations*. NY: McGraw-Hill.

Hollinger, D. A. (1995). The problem of pragmatism in American history: a look back and a look ahead. In R. Hollinger & D. Depew, eds., *Pragmatism: from progressivism to postmodernism* (pp. 19–37). New York: Praeger.

Holmes, F. L. (1995). Concepts, operations, and the problem of "modernity" in early modern chemistry. In U. Klein & W. Lefèvre, eds., *Workshop on fundamental concepts of early modern chemistry in the context of the operational and experimental practice*. Preprint 25 (pp. 47–72). Berlin: Max-Planck-Institut für Wissenschaftsgeschichte.

Hooker, D. (1915). Social hygiene: another great social movement. *Social Hygiene*, 2, 5–10.

Horton, R. (1993). *Patterns of thought in Africa and the West*. Cambridge: Cambridge University Press.

Horton, W. M. (1924). The origin and psychological function of religion according to Pierre Janet. *American Journal of Psychology*, 35, 16–52.

Hugins, W. (Ed.). (1972). *The reform impulse, 1825–1850*. New York: Harper & Row.

Ipsen, G. (1926) Zur Theorie des Erkennens: Untersuchungen über Gestalt und Sinn sinnloser Wörter. *Neue Psychologische Studien*, 1, 3, 283–471.

(1932). Der neue Sprachbegriff. *Zeitschrift für Deutschkunde*, 46, 1–18.

Irons, D. (1895a). Prof. James' theory of emotion. *Mind*, 3, n.s. 77–97.

(1895b). Recent developments in theory of emotion. *Psychological Review*, 2, 279–284.

(1895c). The physical basis of emotion: A reply. *Mind*, 4, n.s., 92–99.

Irons, J. (1895d). Descartes and modern theories of emotion. *Philosophical Review*, 4, 291–302.

Izard, C. E. (1990). The substrates and functions of emotion feelings: William James and current emotion theory. *Personality and Social Psychology Bulletin*, 16(4) 626–635.

Jahoda, G. (1988). Critical notes and reflections on 'social representations.' *European Journal of Social Psychology*, 18, 195–209.

(1993). *Crossroads between culture and mind.* Cambridge, MA: Harvard University Press.

(1997). Wilhelm Wundt's "Völkerpsychologie". In W. Bringmann, H. E. Lück, R. Miller, & C. E. Early, eds., *A pictorial history of psychology* (pp. 148–152). Chicago: Quintessence Publishing Co.

James, W. (1884). What is an emotion. *Mind*, 9, 188–205.

(1884/1984). What is an emotion? In C. Calhoun & R. C. Solomon, eds., *What is an Emotion? Classic readings in philosophical psychology* (pp. 127–141). New York: Oxford University Press.

(1890). *Principles of psychology.* New York: Henry Holt.

(1890/1983). *The principles of psychology.* Cambridge, MA: Harvard University Press.

(1894). The physical basis of emotion. *Psychological Review.* 1, 516–529.

(1895). The knowing of things together. *Psychological Review*, 2(2) 105–117.

(1896). The will to believe. *New World*, 5, 327–347.

(1902/1985). *The varieties of religious experience.* Harmondsworth: Penguin Classics.

(1904a). The Chicago school. *Psychological Bulletin*, 1(1) 1–5.

(1904b). Does 'consciousness' exist? *Journal of Philosophy, Psychology and Scientific Methods*, 1(18) 477–491.

(1904c). A world of pure experience. I. *Journal of Philosophy, Psychology and Scientific Methods*, 1(20) 533–543.

(1904d). A world of pure experience. II. *Journal of Philosophy, Psychology and Scientific Methods*, 1(21) 561–570.

(1905). How two minds can know one thing. *Journal of Philosophy, Psychology and Scientific Methods*, 2, 176–181.

(1907a). *Pragmatism: A new name for some old ways of thinking.* London: Longmans, Green & Co.

(1907b). Pragmatism's conception of truth. *Journal of Philosophy, Psychology, and Scientific Methods*, 4(6) 141–155.

(1979). *The will to believe, and other essays in popular philosophy.* Cambridge, MA: Harvard University Press.

Janet, J. (1888). L'hystérie et l'hypnotisme, d'après la théorie de la double personnalité. *Revue Scientifique*, 25, 616–623.

(1889). Un cas d'hystérie grave. *La France Médicale*, April 6.

Janet, P. (1876). La notion de la personnalité. *Revue Scientifique*, ser. 2(5) 574–575.

(1884a). De la suggestion dans l'état d'hypnotisme. *La Revue Politique et Littéraire*, 21, 100–104.

(1884b). De la suggestion dans l'état d'hypnotisme. *La Revue Politique et Littéraire*, 21, 129–132.

(1884c). De la suggestion dans l'état d'hypnotisme. *La Revue Politique et Littéraire*, 21, 178–185.

(1884d). De la suggestion dans l'état d'hypnotisme. *La Revue Politique et Littéraire*, 21, 198–203.

(1897). *Principes de métaphysique et de psychologie.* Paris: Delagrave.

(1886a). Note sur quelques phénomènes de somnambulisme. *Revue Philosophique*, 22, 190–198.

(1886b). Deuxième note sur le sommeil provoqué a distance at la suggestion mentale pendant l'état somnambulique. *Revue Philosophique*, 22, 212–223.

(1886c). Les actes inconscients et le dédoublement de la personalité pendant le somnambulisme provoqué. *Revue Philosophique*, 22, 577–592.

(1886d). Les phases intermédiaires de l'hypnotisme. *Revue Scientifique*, 19, 577–587.

(1886e). Deuxième note sur le sommeil provoqué a distance at la suggestion mentale pendant l'état somnambulique. *Bulletins de la Société de Psychologie Physiologique*, 2, 70–80.

(1887). L'anesthésie systématisée et la dissociation des phénomènes psychologiques. *Revue Philosophique*, 23, 449–472.

(1888). Les actes inconscients et la mémoire pendant le somnambulisme. *Revue Philosophique*, 25, 238–279.

(1889a). *L'automatisme psychologique. Thèse*. Paris: Alcan.

(1889b). *Baco Verulamius. Alchemicis philosophis quid debuerit*. Angers: Imprimerie Burdin.

(1890). Une altération de la faculté de localiser les sensations. *Revue Philosophique*, 29, 659–664.

(1891). Etude sur un cas d'aboulie et d'idées fixes. *Revue Philosophique*, 31, 258–287, 382–407.

(1892a). Etude sur quelques cas d'amnésie antérograde dans la maladie de la désagrégation psychologique. In *International Congres of Experimental Psychology* (pp. 26–30). London: Williams & Norgate.

(1892b). Le spiritisme contemporain. *Revue Philosophique*, 33, 414–442.

(1892c). Le congrès international de psychologie expérimentale. *Revue Générale des Sciences Pures et Appliquées*, 3, 15 September, 609–616.

(1892d). Réponse à une lettre de Bernheim. *Revue Générale des Sciences Pures et Appliquées*, 15 October, 691.

(1892e). L'anesthesie hystérique. *Archives de Neurologie*, 23, 323–352.

(1892f). La suggestion chez les hystériques. *Archives de Neurologie*, 24, 448–470.

(1893a). *Etat mental des hystériques. Les stigmates mentaux*. Paris: Rueff.

(1893b). L'amnesie continue. *Revue Générale des Sciences Pures et Appliquées*, 4, 30 March, 167–179.

(1893c). Quelques définitions récentes de l'hystérie. *Archives de Neurologie*, 25, 417–438; 26, 1–29.

(1893d). Review of H. Tuke, A Dictionary of Psychological Medicine. *Brain*, 16, 286–302.

(1894a). Histoire d'une idée fixe. *Revue Philosophique*, 37, 121–168.

(1894b). *Etat mental des hystériques. Les accidents mentaux*. Paris: Rueff.

(1894c). *Der Geisteszustand der Hysterischen. Die psychische Stigmata*. Leipzig: Deuticke.

(1894d). Un cas de possession et d'exorcisme moderne. *Bulletin des travaux de l'Université de Lyon*, 8, 41–57.

(1895a). J.-M. Charcot. Son oeuvre psychologique. *Revue Philosophique*, 39, 569–604.

(1895b). Rapport sur Durand, Le merveilleux scientifique. *Annales Medico-Psychologiques, Vllle série*, 1, 447–455.

(1895c). Note sur quelques spasmes des muscles du tronc chez les hystériques. *La France Médicale*, 42, 769–776.

(1895d). Aboulie. In Ch. Richet, *Dictionnaire de physiologie*. Tome 1 (pp. 9–13). Paris: Alcan.

(1895e). Amnésie. In Ch. Richet, *Dictionnaire de physiologie*. Tome 1 (pp. 431–436). Paris: Alcan.

(1895f). Anesthésie. In Ch. Richet, *Dictionnaire de physiologie*. Tome 1 (pp. 431–436). Paris: Alcan.

(1895g). Attention. In Ch. Richet, *Dictionnaire de physiologie*. Tome 1 (pp. 431–436). Paris: Alcan.

(1896a). Résumé historique des études sur le sentiment de la personnalité. *Revue Scientifique*, 33, 97–103.

(1896b). *Manuel de philosophie du baccalauréat de l'enseignement secondaire classique*. Paris: Nony.

(1897a). L'influence somnambulique et le besoin de direction. *Revue Philosophique*, 43, 113–143.

(1897b). Sur la divination par les miroirs et les hallucinations subconscientes. *Bulletin des travaux de l'Université de Lyon*, 2, 261–274.

(1897c). L'insomnie par idée fixe subconsciente. *La Presse Médicale, 5*, 41–44.

(1898). *Névroses et idées fixes*. Vol. 1. Paris: Alcan.

(1903a). *Les obsessions et la psychasthénie*. Vol. 1. Paris: Alcan.

(1903b). *Nevrozy i fiksirovannye idei*. St. Petersburg: O. N. Popov.

(1907a/1965). *The mayor symptoms of hysteria*. New York-London: Hafner Publishing Company. (2nd ed.)

(1907b). The subconscious. *The Journal of Abnormal Psychology*, 2, 58–67.

(1909a). Délire systématique à la suite des pratiques du spiritisme. *Revue Neurologique*, 17, 432–435.

(1909b). Délire systématique à la suite des pratiques du spiritisme. *L'Encéphale*, 4, 363–368.

(1910a). *Les névroses*. Paris: Flammarion.

(1910b). Une Félida artificielle. *Revue Philosophique*, 59, 329–357; 483–529.

(1910c). Le subconscient. *Scientia*, 7, 64–79.

(1910d). Les problèmes du subconscient. In E. Claparède, ed., *Vlme Congrès International de Psychologie* (pp. 57–70). Genève: Kündig.

(1910e). The subconscious. In Münsterberg, H., Ribot, Th., Janet, P., Jastrow, J., Hart, B., & Prince, M., *Subconscious phenomena* (pp. 53–70). Boston: Richard G. Badger.

(1910–11). Les problèmes de la suggestion. *Journal für Psychologie und Neurologie*, 17, 323–343.

(1911). *Nevrozy*. Moscow: Kosmos.

(1913a). La psycho-analyse. In *XVIIth International Congress of Medicine* (pp. 13–64).

(1913b). *Psikhicheskij avtomatizm*. Moscow.

(1914a). La psycho-analyse, rapport au XVlle Congrès international de Médecine de Londres. *Journal de Psychologie*, 11, 1–36; 97–130.

(1914b). Janet über die Psychoanalyse. *Zentralblatt für Psychoanalyse und Psychotherapie*, 4, 309–316.

(1915a). La tension psychologique et ses oscillations. *Journal de Psychologie*, 12, 165–193.

(1915b). Valeur de la psycho-analyse de Freud. *Revue de Psychothérapie et de Psychologie Appliquée*, 29, 82–83.

(1915c). Psychoanalysis. *Journal of Abnormal Psychology*, 9, 1–35; 153–187.

(1917). L'oeuvre psychologique de Th. Ribot. *Journal de Psychologie*, 14, 268–282.

(1919). *Les médications psychologiques*. Paris: Alcan.

(1920a). Les oscillations de l'activité mentale. *Journal de Psychologie*, 17, 31–44.

(1920b). La tension psychologique, ses degrés, ses oscillations. La force et la tension psychologique. *British Journal of Medical Psychology*, 1, 1–15.

(1921a). Les oscillations de l'activité mentale. *Journal de Psychologie*, 18, 140–145.

(1921b). La tension psychologique, ses degrés et ses oscillations. La hiérarchie des tendances, *British Journal of Medical Psychology*, 1, 144–164.

(1921c). La tension psychologique, ses degrés et ses oscillations. Les oscillations du niveau mental. *British Journal of Medical Psychology*, 1, 209–224.

(1923a/1980). *La médecine psychologique*. Paris: Flammarion.

(1923b). La tension psychologique et ses oscillations. In G. Dumas, *Traité de psychologie*. Tome 1 (pp. 919–952). Paris: Alcan.

(1925). *Psychological Healing*. New York: The MacMillan Company.

(1926a). *Psicología de los Sentimientos*. Mexico: Libraria Franco-Americana.

(1926b). *De l'angoisse à l'extase*. Vol. 1. Paris: Alcan.

(1926c). *Psychologie experimentale. Les stades de l'évolution psychologique*. Paris: Chahine.

(1928a). *L'évolution de la mémoire et de la notion du temps*. Paris: Chahine.

(1928b). *De l'angoisse à l'extase*. Vol. II. Paris: Alcan.

(1928c). Fear of action as an essential element in the sentiment of melancholia. In M. L. Reymert, ed., *Feelings and emotions. The Wittenberg Symposium* (pp. 297–317). Worcester, MA: Clark University Press.

(1929). *L'évolution psychologique de la personnalité*. Paris: Chahine.

(1930a). Psychologie et graphologie. *L'Hygiène Mentale*, 25, 191–194.

(1930b). L'analyse psychologique. In C. Murchison, *Psychologies of 1930* (pp. 369–373). Worcester, MA: Clark University Press.

(1930c/1961). Pierre Janet. In C. Murchison, ed., *A history of psychology in autobiography*. Vol. 1 (pp. 123–133). New York: Russell & Russell.

(1932). *L'amour et la haine*. Paris: Maloine.

(1935). *Les débuts de l'intelligence*. Paris: Flammarion.

(1936). *L'intelligence avant le langage*. Paris: Flammarion.

(1937a). Les troubles de la personnalité sociale. *Annales Médico-Psychologiques*, 95, 149–200; 421–468.

(1937b). Le langage inconsistent. *Theoria*, 3, 57–71.

(1937c). Psychological strength and weakness in mental diseases. In *Harvard tercentenary publications. Factors determining behavior* (pp. 64–106). Cambridge, MA: Harvard University Press.

(1937d). Psychological strength and weakness in mental diseases. In *Factors determining human behavior* (pp. 64–106), Cambridge, MA: Harvard University Press.

(1938). La psychologie de la conduite. In H. Wallon, ed., *Encyclopédie Française*. Tome 8. La vie mentale (pp. 11–16). Paris: Larousse.

(1946). Auto-biographie psychologique. *Les Études Philosophiques*, 2, 81–87.

Joas, H. (1985). *G. H. Mead: A contemporary re-examination of his thought*. Cambridge, MA: MIT Press.

Jodelet, D. (1991). *Madness and social representations: Living with the mad in one French community*. Berkeley, CA: University of California Press.

Jones, E. (1911). The pathology of morbid anxiety. *The Journal of Abnormal Psychology*, 5, 81–106.

(1914–15). Professor Janet on psychoanalysis: A rejoinder. *The Journal of Abnormal Psychology*, 9, 400–410.

(1959). *Free associations. Memories of a psycho-analyst*. London: The Hogarth Press.

(1974). *Sigmund Freud: Life and work. Vol. II. Years of maturity*. London: The Hogarth Press.

(1980). *Sigmund Freud: Life and work. Vol. I. The young Freud*. London: The Hogarth Press.

Joravsky, D. (1989). *Russian psychology: A critical history*. Oxford: Blackwell

(1992). Comparative psychology in Russia. *International Journal of Comparative Psychology*, 6, 56–60.

Josephs, I. E. (1998a). Constructing one's self in the city of the silent: dialogue, symbols, and the role of "as-if" in self development. *Human Development*, 41(3) 180–195.

(1998b). Do you know Ragnar Rommetveit? On dialogue and silence, poetry and pedantry, and cleverness and wisdom in psychology. *Culture & Psychology*, 4, 189–212.

Josephs, I. E., & Valsiner, J. (1998). How does autodialogue work? *Social Psychology Quarterly*, 61(1) 68–83.

Kabanov, N. (1913). *Vspomogatel'nyj mezhdunarodnyj yazyk Esperanto*. Moscow: Izdanie Posrednika.

Kafka, G. (1922). Tierpsychologie. In G. Kafka, *Handbuch der vergleichenden Psychologie* (pp. 11–144). München: Verlag von Ernst Reinhardt.

Kaiser, D. (1994). Bringing human actors back on stage: The personal context of the Einstein-Bohr debate. *British Journal for the History of Science*, 27(93) Part 2, 129–152.

Kakar, S. (1996). Religious conflict in the modern world. *Social Science Information*, 35(3) 447–458.

Kaplan, B. (1955). Some psychological methods for the investigation of expressive language. In H. Werner, ed., *On expressive language* (pp. 19–27). Worcester, MA: Clark University Press.

(1966). The "latent content" of Heinz Werner's comparative-developmental approach. In S. Wapner & B. Kaplan, eds., *Heinz Werner 1890–1964: papers in memoriam* (pp. 33–39). Worcester, MA: Clark University Press.

(1983). Genetic-dramatism: Old wine in new bottles. In S. Wapner & B. Kaplan, eds., *Toward a holistic developmental psychology* (pp. 53–74). Hilldale, NJ: Erlbaum.

(1986). Value presuppositions in theories of human development. In L. Cirillo & S. Wapner, eds., *Value presuppositions in theories of human development* (pp. 89–103). Hillsdale, NJ: Erlbaum.

(1992). Strife on systems: Tensions between organismic and developmental points of view. *Theory & Psychology*, 2(4) 431–443.

(1994). Is the concept of development applicable to art? In M. B. Franklin & B. Kaplan, eds., *Development and the arts: Critical perspectives* (pp. 3–10). Hillsdale, NJ: Erlbaum.

Keizer, B. (1994). *Het refrein is Hein*. Nijmegen: SUN.

Keller, E. F. (1996). The dilemma of scientific subjectivity in postvital culture. In P. Galison & D. J. Stump, eds., *The disunity of science: Boundaries, contexts, and power* (pp. 417–427). Stanford: Stanford University Press.

Kellog, W. N., & Kellog, L. A. (1933). *The ape and the child*. New York: McGraw-Hill.

Khotin, B. I. (1992). Biological psychology as a science. *International Journal of Comparative Psychology*, 6, 10–36.

Kim, U. (1994). Individualism and collectivism: conceptual clarification and elaboration. In U Kim, H. C. Triandis, Ç. Kagitçibasi, S-C Choi & G. Yoon, eds., *Individualism and collectivism: Theory, method, and applications* (pp. 19–40). Thousand Oaks, CA: Sage.

King, E. G. (1990). Reconciling democracy and the crowd in turn-of-century American social-psychological thought. *Journal of the History of the Behavioral Science*, 26(4) 334–344.

Kitchener, R. F. (1986). *Piaget's theory of knowledge. Genetic epistemology & scientific reason*. New Haven: Yale University Press.

Klein, U. (1995). Experimental practice and layers of knowledge in early modern chemistry. In U. Klein & W. Lefèvre, eds., *Workshop on fundamental concepts of early modern chemistry in the context of the operational and experimental practice*. Preprint 25 (pp. 73–110). Berlin: Max-Planck-Institut für Wissenschaftsgeschichte.

Klemm, O. (1938). Gedanken über seelische Anpassung. *Archiv für die gesamte Psychologie*, 100, 387–400.

(1961). Otto Klemm. In C. Murchison, ed., *A history of psychology in autobiography*. Vol. 3 (pp. 153–180). New York: Russell & Russell.

Knorr Cetina, K. (1992). The couch, the cathedral, and the laboratory: On the relationship between experiment and laboratory in science. In A. Pickering, ed., *Science as practice and culture* (pp. 113–138). Chicago: University of Chicago Press.

(1996). The care of the self and blind variation: The disunity of two leading sciences. In P. Galison & D. J. Stump, eds., *The disunity of science: Boundaries, contexts, and power* (pp. 287–310). Stanford: Stanford University Press.

Knox, J. E., & Stevens, C. (1993). Vygotsky and Soviet Russian defectology. In

R. W. Rieber & A. S. Carton, eds., *The collected works of L. S. Vygotsky. Vol. 2. The fundamentals of defectology* (pp. 1–25). New York-London: Plenum Press.

Koch, S. (1992). Psychology's Bridgman vs. Bridgman's Bridgman. *Theory & Psychology*, 2(3) 261–290.

Koffka, K. (1922). Perception: An introduction to the Gestalt-theorie. *Psychological Bulletin*, 19, 531–585.

———— (1924). Introspection and the method of psychology. *British Journal of Psychology*, 15, 149–161. (Russian translation 1926).

———— (1925a). *Die Grundlagen der psychischen Entwicklung*. Osterwieck am Harz: A. W. Zickfeldt (Russian translation 1934).

———— (1925b). Psychologie. In M. Dessoir, ed., *Lehrbuch der Philosophie. Band II. Die Philosophie in ihren Einzelgebieten* (pp. 495–603). Berlin: Ullstein.

———— (1926). Samonablyudenie i metod psikhologii. In K. Kornilov, ed., *Problemy sovremennoy psikhologii* (pp. 179–192). Leningrad: GIZ.

———— (1932). Preodolenie mekhanisticheskikh i vitalisticheskikh techenij v sovremennoj psikhologii. *Psikhologija*, 5(1–2) 59–69.

———— (1934). *Osnovy psikhicheskogo razvitija*. Moscow-Leningrad: Gosudarstvennoe Social'no-Ekonomicheskoe Izdatel'stvo.

Kohlberg, L. (1969). Stage and sequence: The cognitive-developmental approach to moralization. In D. Goslin, ed., *Handbook of socialization theory and research*. Chicago: Rand McNally.

———— (1982). Moral development. In J. M. Broughton & D. J. Freeman-Moir, eds., *The cognitive-developmental psychology of James Mark Baldwin* (pp. 277–325). Norwood, NJ: Ablex.

Köhler, W. (1915). Optische Untersuchungen am Schimpansen und am Haushuhn. *Abhandlungen der Königlich Preussischen Akademie der Wissenschaften*, 3, 3–70.

———— (1917a). Die Farbe der Sehdinge beim Schimpansen und beim Haushuhn. *Zeitschrift für Psychologie*, 77, 248–255.

———— (1917b). *Intelligenzprüfungen an Anthropoiden*. Berlin: Königliche Akademie der Wissenschaften.

———— (1918). Nachweis einfacher Strukturfunktionen beim Schimpansen und beim Haushuhn. *Abhandlungen der Königlich Preussischen Akademie der Wissenschaften*, 2, 3–101.

———— (1920). *Die physischen Gestalten in Ruhe und im stationären Zustand: Eine naturphilosophische Untersuchung*. Erlangen: Verlag der Philosophischen Akademie.

———— (1921a). Die Methoden der psychologischen Forschung an Affen. In E. Abderhalden, ed., *Handbuch der biologischen Arbeitsmethoden* (Abt. 6, Teil D) (pp. 69–120). Berlin: Urban & Schwarzenberg.

———— (1921b). *Intelligenzprüfungen an Menschenaffen*. Berlin: Julius Springer (Russian translation 1930).

———— (1922). Zur Psychologie des Schimpansen. *Psychologische Forschung*, 1, 2–46.

———— (1924). *Gestalt psychology*. New York: Liveright Publishing Corporation.

———— (1928). Bemerkungen zur Gestalttheorie. Im Anschluss an Rignanos Kritik. *Psychologische Forschung*, 11, 188–234.

(1929). La perception humaine. *Journal de psychologie*, 27, 5–30.

(1930). *Issledovanie intellekta chelovekopodobnykh obez'jan*. Moscow: Izdatel'stvo Kommunisticheskoj Akademii.

(1933). *Psychologische Probleme*. Berlin: Verlag von Julius Springer.

Kojevnikov, A. (1996). *Games of Soviet democracy: Ideological discussions in sciences around 1948 reconsidered*. Preprint 37. Berlin: Max-Planck-Institut für Wissenschaftsgeschichte.

Kozulin, A. (1990). *Vygotsky's psychology: A biography of ideas*. New York: Harvester Wheatsheaf.

Kragh, U., & Smith, G. eds., (1970). *Percept-genetic analysis*. Lund: Gleerups.

Krementsov, N. L. (1992). V. A. Wagner and the origin of Russian ethology. *International Journal of Comparative Psychology*, 6, 61–70.

Kretschmer, E. (1929). *Körperbau und Charakter*. Berlin: Julius Springer.

Krueger, F. (1903). *Zur Psychologie der wissenschaflichen Arbeitsgliederung*. Lecture for Habilitation, Leipzig, April, 28.

(1906). Die Theorie der Konsonanz. *Psychologische Studien*, 1, 305–387.

(1913a). New aims and tendencies in psychology. *Philosophical Review*, 22(3) 251–264.

(1913b). Magical factors in the first development of human labor. *American Journal of Psychology*, 24, 256–261.

(1915). Über Entwicklungspsychologie. *Arbeitzen zur Entwicklungspsychologie*, 1, 1 (pp. 1–232). Leipzig: Wilhelm Engelmann.

(1922). Wilhelm Wundt als deutscher Denker. In A. Hoffmann, ed., *Wilhelm Wundt. Eine Würdigung* (pp. 1–44). Erfurt: Kenferschen Buchhandlung.

(1926). Über psychische Ganzheit. *Neue Psychologische Studien*, 1, 1–121.

(1928a). Das Wesen der Gefühle. *Archiv für die gesamte Psychologie*, 65, 91–128.

(1928b). The essence of feeling. In M. L. Reymert, ed., *Feelings and emotions: The Wittenberg symposium* (pp. 58–86). Worcester, MA: Clark University Press.

(1928c). Wissenschaften und der Zusammenhang des Wirklichen. *Neue Psychologische Studien*, Bd. 3, ix–xxvii.

(1935). Psychologie des Gemeinschaftslebens. In O. Klemm, ed., *Psychologie des Gemeinschaftsleben. Berichte über den XIV Kongress der Deutsche Gesellschaft für Psychologie in Tübingen, 1934* (pp. 5–62). Jena: Gustav Fischer.

Kuhn, T. (1970). *The structure of scientific revolutions*. Chicago: University of Chicago Press.

Kuklick, B. (1995). American philosophy and its lost public. In R. Hollinger & D. Depew, eds., *Pragmatism: From progressivism to postmodernism* (pp. 142–152). New York: Praeger.

Kuklick, H. (1980). Boundary maintenance in American sociology: limitations to academic "professionalization." *Journal of the History of the Behavioural Sciences*, 16, 201–219.

Kurazov, I. F. (1931). *Vvedenie v istoricheskuju psikhologiju*. Moscow-Leningrad: Gosudarstvennoe Sotsial'no-Ekonomicheskoe Izdatel'stvo.

Laboratory of Comparative Human Cognition (1983). Culture and cognitive development. In W. Kessen, ed., *Handbook of child psychology*. Vol. 1. *History, theory & methods* (pp. 295–356). New York: Wiley.

La Mettrie, J. O. de (1748/1981). *L'homme machine*. Paris: Denoël/Gonthier.

Ladame, P. L. (1888). *L'hypnotisme et la médecine légale*. Lyon: Storck.

Ladygina-Kohts, N. N. (1923). *Issledovanie poznavatel'nykh sposobnostej shimpanze*. Moscow-Petrograd: Gosudarstvennoe Izdatel'stvo.

(1928a). Recherches sur l'intelligence du chimpanzé. *Journal de Psychologie*, 25, 255–275.

(1928b). *Prisposobitel'nye motornye navyki makaka v usloviyakh eksperimenta. K voprosu o "trudovykh protsessakh" nizshikh obez'yan*. Moscow: Izdanie Gosudarstvennogo Darvinovskogo Muzeya.

(1930). Les aptitudes motrices adaptives du singe inférieur. *Journal de Psychologie*, 27, 412–447.

(1935). *Ditya shimpanze i ditya cheloveka v ikh instinktakh, emotsiyakh, igrakh, privychkakh i vyrazhitel'nykh dvizheniyakh*. Moscow: Trudy Muzeya.

(1937). La conduite du petit du chimpanzé et de l'enfant de l'homme. *Journal de Psychologie*, 34, 494–531.

(1959). *Konstruktivnaya i orudiynaya deyatel'nost' vysshikh obezyan (shimpanze)*. Moscow: Izdatel'stvo Akademii Nauk SSSR.

(1982). Infant ape and human child. *Storia e Critica della Psicologia*, 3, 122–189.

Ladygina-Kohts, N. N., & Dembovskii, Y. N. (1969). The psychology of primates. In M. Cole & I. Maltzman, eds., *A handbook of contemporary Soviet psychology* (pp. 41–70). New York: Basic Books.

Lafforgue, J. (1887). *Contribution à l'étude médico-légale de l'hypnotisme*. Paris: Ph.D. Bordeaux.

Lalande, A. (1930). La psychologie, ses divers objets et ses méthodes. In G. Dumas, ed., *Nouveau Traité de Psychologie. Tome 1. Notions préliminaires. Introduction. Méthodologie* (pp. 367–419). Paris: Alcan.

Lang, A. (1992). Kultur als "externe Seele"–eine semiotish-ökologische Perspektive. In C. Allesch, E. Billmann-Mahecha & A. Lang, eds., *Psychologische Aspekte des kulturellen Wandels*. Wien: Verlag des V.w.G.Ö.

(1993). Non-Cartesian artefacts in dwelling activities: Steps towards a semiotic ecology. *Schweizerische Zeitschrift für Psychologie*, 52(2) 138–147.

Lang, A. (1997). Thinking rich as well as simple: Boesch's cultural psychology in semiotic perspective. *Culture & Psychology*, 3(3) 383–394.

Lang, P. J. (1994). The varieties of emotional experience: A meditation on James-Lange theory. *Psychological Review*, 101, 2, 211–221.

Latour, B. (1987). *Science in action*. Cambridge, MA: Harvard University Press.

(1993). *We have never been modern*. Cambridge, MA: Harvard University Press.

Latour, B. & Woolgar, S. (1979). *Laboratory life: The social construction of scientific facts*. Beverly Hills, CA: Sage.

Lazarus, M., & Steinthal, H. (1860). Einleitende Gedanken über Völkerpsychologie. *Zeitschrift für Völkerpsychologie und Sprachwissenschaft*, 1, 1–73.

Le Bon, G. (1894). *Psychologie des foules*. Paris: Alcan.

(1895). *Lois psychologiques de l'évolution des peuples*. Paris: Alcan (2nd ed.)

(1911). *Les opinions et les croyances: génèse-évolution*. Paris: Flammarion.

Lee, B. (1982). Cognitive development and the self. In J. M. Broughton & D. J. Freeman-Moir, eds., *The cognitive-developmental psychology of James Mark Baldwin* (pp. 169–210). Norwood, NJ: Ablex.

Legrand du Saulle, H. (1864). *La folie devant les tribunaux*. Paris: Savy.

(1877). *Etude médico-légale sur les épileptiques*. Paris: Delahaye.

(1883). *Les hystériques, leur état physique et mental, actes insolites, délictueux et criminels*. Paris: Baillière.

Lester F. W. (1913). *American Journal of Sociology*, 19, 61–78.

Leuba, J. H. (1913). Sociology and psychology. *American Journal of Sociology*, 19, 323–342.

Leudar, I. (1991). Sociogenesis, coordination, and mutualism. *Journal for the Theory of Social Behaviour*, 21(2) 197–220.

Levitin, K. (1982). *One is not born a personality*. Moscow: Progress Publishers.

(1990). *Lichnost'ju ne rozhdajutsja*. Moscow: Nauka.

Lévy-Bruhl, L. (1910). *Les fonctions mentales dans les sociétés inférieures*. Paris: Alcan.

(1922). *La mentalité primitive*. Paris: Retz.

Lewin, K. (1927). Gesetz und Experiment in der Psychologie. *Symposion*, 1, 375–421.

Libbrecht, K., & Quackelbeen, J. (1995). On the early history of male hysteria and psychic trauma: Charcot's influence on Freudian thought. *Journal of the History of the Behavioral Sciences*, 31, 370–384.

Liébeault, A. A. (1866). *Du sommeil et des états analogues considéré surtout au point de vue de l'action du moral sur le physique*. Paris: Masson.

(1889). *Le sommeil provoqué et les états analogues*. Paris: Doin.

(1891). *Thérapeutique suggestive. Son mécanisme, propriétés diverses du sommeil provoqué et des états analogues*. Paris: Doin.

Liégeois, J. (1884). *De la suggestion hypnotique dans ses rapports avec le droit civil et le droit criminel*. Paris: Picard.

(1889). *De la suggestion et du somnambulisme dans leur rapports avec la jurisprudence et la médecine légale*. Paris: Doin.

(1892). Hypnotisme et criminalité. *Revue Philosophique*, 33, 233–272.

Linell, P. (1992). The embeddedness of decontextualization in the contexts of social practices. In A. H. Wold (Ed.), *The dialogical alternative: Towards a theory of language and mind* (pp. 253–271). Oslo: Scandinavian University Press.

Linell, P. (1996). Troubles with mutualities: Towards a dialogical theory of misunderstanding and miscommunication. In I. Markova, C. G. Graumann & K. Foppa (eds.), *Mutualities in dialogue* (pp. 176–213). Cambridge: Cambridge University Press.

Lipps, T. (1926). *Psychological studies*. Baltimore, MD: Williams & Wilkins.

Lorenz, K. (1965). Preface. In Ch. Darwin, *The expression of the emotions in man and animals* (pp. ix–xiii). Chicago-London: The University of Chicago Press.

Löwy, I. (1992). The strength of loose concepts-boundary concepts, federative experimental strategies and disciplinary growth: the case of immunology. *History of Science*, 30(90) Part 4, 376–396.

(1996). *Between bench and bedside*. Cambridge, Ma: Harvard University Press.

Lück, H. E. (1993). Kurt Lewin: A German-Jewish psychologist. *Journal of Psychology and Judaism*, 17, 153–168.

Luczynski, J. (1997). The multivoicedness of historical representations in a changing sociocultural context: Young Polish adults' representations of World War II. *Culture & Psychology*, 3(1), 21–40.

Luria, A. R. (1926). Nauchnaya khronika. Moskovskji gosudarstvennyj institut eksperimental'noj psikhologii v 1924 godu. In K. N. Kornilov, ed. *Problemy sovremennoj psikhologii* (pp. 244–252). Leningrad: Gosudarstvennoe Izdatel'stvo.

Lyman Wells, F. (1912). Critique of impure reason. *The Journal of Abnormal Psychology*, 6, 89–93.

MacDonald, R. (1912). The social basis of individuality. *American Journal of Sociology*, 18(1) 1–20.

MacLean, A. M. (1903). The sweat-shop in summer. *American Journal of Sociology*, 9, 289–309.

Macmillan, M. B. (1979). Delboeuf and Janet as influences in Freud's treatment of Emmy von N. *Journal of the History of the Behavioral Sciences*, 15, 299–309.

Mahoney, M. J. (1989). Participatory epistemology and psychology of science. In B. Gholson, W. R. Shadish, & A. C. Houts, eds. *Psychology of science: Contributions to metascience* (pp. 138–164). Cambridge: Cambridge University Press.

Maiers, W. (1988). Has psychology exaggerated its "natural science character"? In W. J. Baker, L. P. Mos, H. V. Rappard & H. J. Stam, eds. *Recent trends in theoretical psychology* (pp. 133–143). New York: Springer.

Malakhovskaya, D. B. (1992a). Boris Iosifovich Khotin (1895–1950). *International Journal of Comparative Psychology*, 6, 3–4.

(1992b). From the history of comparative psychology in the USSR. *International Journal of Comparative Psychology*, 6, 50–55.

Malvano, L. (1997). The myth of youth in images: Italian fascism. In G. Levi and J-C. Schmitt, eds., *A history of young people in the West*. Vol. 2. (pp. 232–256). Cambridge, MA: Harvard University Press.

Mantell, U. (1936). Aktualgenetische Untersuchungen an Situationsdarstellung. *Neue Psychologische Studien*, 13(2) 4–95.

Marková, I. (1990). A three-step process as a unit of analysis in dialogue. In I. Marková & K. Foppa, eds. *The dynamics of dialogue* (pp. 129–146). Hemel Hempstead: Harvester.

(1994). Mutual construction of asymmetries. In P. van Geert & L. Mos, eds. *Annals of theoretical psychology*. Vol. 10. New York: Plenum.

Markus, H., & Kitayama, S. (1991). Culture and the self: Implications for cognition, emotion, and motivation. *Psychological Review*, 98(2) 224–253.

Markus, H., & Nurius, P. (1986). Possible selves. *American Psychologist*, 41, 9, 954–969.

Markus, H., & Wurf, E. (1987). The dynamic self-concept: A social psychological perspective. *Annual Review of Psychology*, 38, 299–337.

Mason, P. (1996). On producing the (American) exotic. *Anthropos*, *91*, 139–151.

Maudsley, H. (1876). *Le crime et la folie*. Paris: Baillière.

Mayo, E. (1952). *The psychology of Pierre Janet*. London: Routledge & Kegan Paul.

McCagg, W. O., & Seigelbaum, L., eds. (1989). *The disabled in the Soviet Union: past and present: theory and practice*. Pittsburgh, PA: University of Pittsburgh Press.

McDermott, J. J. (1995). Introduction to the new edition. In J. Royce, *The philosophy of loyalty* (pp. vii–xxi). Nashville, TN: Vanderbilt University Press.

McDougall, W. (1937). Tendencies, as indispensable postulates of all psychology. In H. Piéron & I. Meyerson, eds., *Onzième Congrès International de Psychologie* (pp. 157–170). Agen: Imprimerie Moderne.

McPhail, C., & Rexroat, C. (1979). Mead vs. Blumer: The divergent methodological perspectives of social behaviorism and symbolic interactionism. *American Sociological Review*, 44, 449–467.

Mead, G. H. (1894a). Herr Lasswitz on energy and epistemology. *Psychological Review*, 1, 172–175.

(1894b). Review of K. Lasswitz, Die moderne Energetik in ihrer Bedeutung fürdie Erkenntniskritik. *Psychological Review*, *1*, 210–213.

(1895a). Review of: An introduction to comparative psychology, of C. L. Morgan. *Psychological Review*, 2, 399–402.

(1895b). A theory of emotions from the physiological standpoint. *Psychological Review*, 2, 162–164.

(1899). The working hypothesis in social reform. *American Journal of Sociology*, 5, 367–371.

(1899). Review of: The psychology of socialism by Gustave LeBon. *American Journal of Sociology*, 5(3) 404–412.

(1903). The definition of the psychical. *Decennial Publications of the University of Chicago*, First Series, Vol. 3. *Investigations representing the departments* (pp. 3–38). Chicago: University of Chicago Press.

(1904a). The relations of psychology and philology. *Psychological Bulletin*, 1, 11, 375–391.

(1904b). Image or sensation. *Journal of Philosophy, Psychology and Scientific Methods*, 1, 604–607.

(1905). Review of D. Draghiscesco, 'De role de l'individu dans le determinisme social' and D. Draghiscesco, 'Le probleme du determinisme, determinisme biologique and determinisme social', *Psychological Bulletin*, 5, 399–405.

(1906). The imagination in Wundt's treatment of myth and religion. *Psychological Bulletin*, 3, 393–399.

(1907). Social evolution. Review of L'Évolution créatrice of H. Bergson. *Psychological Bulletin*, 4, 379–384.

(1908a). The philosophical basis of ethics. *International Journal of Ethics*, 18, 311–323.

(1908b). McDougall's social psychology. *Psychological Bulletin*, 5, 385–391.

(1909). Social psychology as counterpart to physiological psychology. *Psychological Bulletin*, 6(12) 401–408.

(1910a). The psychology of social consciousness implied in instruction. *Science*, 31, No. 801, 688–693.

(1910b). Social consciousness and the consciousness of meaning. *Psychological Bulletin*, 7(12) 397–405.

(1911). Review of: Individualism: Four lectures on the significance of consciousness for social relations by Warner Fite. *Psychological Bulletin*, 8, 323–328.

(1912). The mechanism of social consciousness. *Journal of Philosophy*, 9, 401–406.

(1913). The social self. *Journal of Philosophy*, 10, 374–380.

(1917). Scientific method and individual thinker. In *Creative intelligence: Essays in the pragmatic attitude* (pp. 176–227). New York: Henry Holt & Co.

(1918). The psychology of punitive justice. *American Journal of Sociology*, 23(5) 577–602.

(1923). Scientific method and the moral sciences. *International Journal of Ethics*, 33(3) 229–247.

(1925). The genesis of the self and social control. *International Journal of Ethics*, 35, 251–277.

(1930a). The philosophies of Royce, James, and Dewey in their American setting. *International Journal of Ethics*, 40, 211–231.

(1930b). Cooley's contribution to American social thought. *American Journal of Sociology*, 35(5) 693–706.

(1932). *The philosophy of the present*. Chicago: Open Court.

(1934). *Mind, self and society from the standpoint of a social behaviorist*. Chicago: University of Chicago Press.

(1936). *Movements of thought in the nineteenth century*. Chicago: University of Chicago Press.

(1938). *The philosophy of the act*. Chicago: University of Chicago Press.

Mecacci, L. (1979). *Brain and history*. New York: Brunner/Mazel.

(1992). Another lost world of Russian psychology. *International Journal of Comparative Psychology*, 6, 71–74.

Meinong, A. (1902/1983). *On assumptions*. Berkeley, CA: University of California Press.

(1917/1972). *On emotional presentation*. Evanston, IL.: Northwestern University Press.

Meira, L. (1995). The microevolution of mathematical representations in children's activity. *Cognition and Instruction*, 13(2) 269–313.

Melk-Koch, M. (1989). *Auf der Suche nach der menschlichen Gesellschaft: Richard Thurnwald*. Berlin: Staatliche Museen Preussicher Kulturbesitz.

Menon, U., & Shweder, R. A. (1994). Kali's tongue: Cultural psychology and the power of 'shame' in Orissa. In S. Kitayama & H. Markus, eds., *Emotion and culture* (pp 237–280). Washington, DC: American Psychological Association.

Merton, R. K. (1936). Puritanism, pietism, and science. *Sociological Review*, 28(1) 1–30.

Metzger, W. (1965). The historical background for national trends in psychology: German psychology. *Journal of the History of the Behavioral Sciences*, 1, 109–115.

Meyerson, I. (1947). Pierre Janet et la théorie des tendances. *Journal de Psychologie*, 40, 5–19.

Micale, M. (1993a). On the 'disappearance' of hysteria: A study in the clinical (ed.) deconstruction of a diagnosis. *Isis*, 84, 496–526.

(1993b). *Essays of Henri F. Ellenberger in the history of psychiatry*. Princeton, NJ: Princeton University Press.

(1995). *Approaching hysteria: Disease and its interpretations*. Princeton, NJ: Princeton University Press.

Michaud, E. (1997). Soldiers of an idea: Young people under the Third Reich. In G. Levi and J-C. Schmitt, eds., *A history of young people in the West*. Vol. 2 (pp. 257–280). Cambridge, MA: Harvard University Press.

Milet, J. (1973). Gabriel Tarde (1843–1904). In A. M. Rocheblave-Spenlé, & J. Milet, eds., *G. Tarde: Ecrits de psychologie sociale* (pp. 9–24). Toulouse: Privat.

Milliken, O. J. (1898). The movement for vacation schools. *American Journal of Sociology*, 4, 289–308.

Milne Bramwell, J. (1903/1956). *Hypnotism: Its history, practice and theory*. New York: The Institute for Research in Hypnosis and The Julian Press.

Minkowski, E. (1960). A propos des dernières publications de Pierre Janet. *Bulletin de Psychologie*, 14, 121–127.

Misiti, R. (1982). Introduction: Ladygina-Kohts and Soviet comparative psychology. *Storia e Critica della Psicologia*, 3, 109–121.

Mitter, P. (1992). *Much maligned monsters: A history of European reactions to Indian art*. Chicago: University of Chicago Press.

Monroe, P. (1895). English and American Christian Socialism: An estimate. *American Journal of Sociology*, 1, 50–68.

Moody, E., Markova, I., & Plichtova, J. (1995). Lay representations of democracy: a study in two cultures. *Culture & Psychology*, 1(4) 423–453.

Morawski, J. (1996). Principles of selves: The rhetoric of introductory textbooks in American psychology. In C. F. Graumann & K. J. Gergen, eds., *Historical dimensions of psychological discourse* (pp. 145–162). New York: Cambridge University Press.

Moreau de Tours, J. (1859). *La psychologie morbide*. Paris: Masson.

Morgan, C. L. (1894). *An introduction to comparative psychology*. London: Walter Scott.

(1896). On modification and variation. *Science*, 4 (99), 733–740.

Morris, C. W. (1934). Preface to *Mind, self and society* (pp. v–vii). Chicago: University of Chicago Press.

Moscovici, S. (1961). *La psychanalyse: son image et son public*. Paris: PUF.

(1968). *Essai sur l'histoire humaine de la nature*. Paris:

(1972). *La societe contra nature*. Paris: Union Generale

(1974). *Hommes domestiques et hommes sauvages*. Paris: Union Generale.

(1976). *Society against nature: The emergence of human societies*. Atlantic Highlands, NJ: Humanities Press.

(1981a). On social representations. In J. P. Forgas, ed., *Social cognition* (pp. 181–209). London: Academic Press.

(1981b). *L'âge des foules: Un traité historique de psychologie des masses.* Paris: Fayard.

(1982). The coming era of representations. In J.-P. Codol & J.-P. Leyens, eds., *Cognitive analysis of social behavior* (pp. 115–150). The Hague: Martinus Nijhoff.

(1985). *The age of the crowd: A historical treatise on mass psychology.* Cambridge: Cambridge University Press.

(1987). The conspiracy mentality. In C. F. Graumann & S. Moscovici, eds., *Changing conceptions of conspiracy* (pp. 151–169). New York: Springer.

(1988a). Crisis of communication and crisis of explanation. In W. Schönpflug, ed., *Bericht über der 36. Kongress der Deutschen Gesellschaft für Psychologie in Berlin.* Vol. 2 (pp. 94–109). Göttingen: Hogrefe.

(1988b). Notes towards a description of social representations. *European Journal of Social Psychology,* 18, 211–250.

(1990). Social psychology and developmental psychology: Extending the conversation. In G. Duveen & B. Lloyd, eds., *Social representations and the development of knowledge* (pp. 164–185). Cambridge: Cambridge University Press.

(1991). Experiment and experience: An intermediate step from Sherif to Asch. *Journal for the Theory of Social Behaviour,* 21(3) 253–268.

(1993). Toward a social psychology of science. *Journal for the Theory of Social Behaviour,* 23(4) 343–374.

(1994). Social representations and pragmatic communication. *Social Science Information,* 33(2) 163–177.

(1995). Geschichte und Aktualität sozialer Repräsentationen. In U. Flick, ed., *Psychologie des sozialen.* (pp. 266–314). Reinbek: Rohwolt.

Moscovici, S. & Marková, I, (1998). Presenting social representations: a conversation. *Culture & Psychology* 4, 3, 371–410.

Mucchielli, L. (1994a). Sociologie et psychologie en France, l'appel à un territoire commun: vers une psychologie collective (1890–1940). *Revue de Synthèse,* 445–483.

(1994b). Durkheim ou la révolution des sciences humaines. *La Recherche,* 268, 896–902.

Much, N. C., & Harré, R. (1994). How psychologies "secrete" moralities. *New Ideas in Psychology,* 12(3) 291–321.

Mueller, R. H., (1976). A chapter in the history of the relationship between psychology and sociology in America: James Mark Baldwin. *Journal of the History of the Behavioral Sciences,* 12, 240–253.

Mulkay, M. (1993). Rhetorics of hope and fear in the great embryo debate. *Social Studies of Science,* 23, 721–742.

Müller, K. (1996). *Allgemeine systemtheorie.* Opladen: Westdeutscher Verlag.

Münsterberg, H., (ed.), (1910). *Subconscious phenomena.* Boston: Richard G. Badger.

Murphy, A. E. (1932). Preface to *The philosophy of the present* (pp. vii–viii). Chicago: Open Court.

Myers, G. E. (1986). *William James: His life and thought.* New Haven, CT: Yale University Press.

Newman, D., Griffin, P., & Cole, M. (1989). *The construction zone: Working for cognitive change in school.* Cambridge: Cambridge University Press.

Nye, R. A. (1975). *The origins of crowd psychology: Gustave Le Bon and the crisis of mass democracy in the Third Republic.* London: Sage.

Obeyesekere, G. (1981). *Medusa's hair.* Chicago: University of Chicago Press.

(1984). *The cult of the goddess Pattini.* Chicago: University of Chicago Press.

(1990). *The work of culture.* Chicago: University of Chicago Press.

Ochorowicz, J. (1909). Hypnotisme et mesmérisme. In Ch. Richet, ed., *Dictionnaire de physiologie.* Tome 8 (pp. 709–778). Paris: Alcan.

Oliveira, Z. M. R., & Valsiner, J. (1997). Play and imagination: The psychological construction of novelty. In A. Fogel, M. Lyra, & J. Valsiner, eds., *Dynamics and indeterminism in developmental and social processes* (pp. 119–133). Hillsdale, NJ: Erlbaum.

Osborn, H. F. (1896). Ontogenetic and phylogenetic variation. *Science*, 4 (100), 786–789.

O'Shea, M. V. (1906). Notes on education for social efficiency. *American Journal of Sociology*, 11, 646–654.

Ovsiankina, M. (1928). Die Wiederaufnahme unterbrochener Handlungen. *Psychologische Forschung*, 11, 302–379.

Parker, W. B. (Ed.) (1909). *Psychotherapy: A course of reading in sound psychology, sound medicine, and sound religion.* New York: Centre Publishing Co.

Parodi, D. (1925). La philosophie française de 1918 à 1925. *Revue Philosophique*, 99, 359–383.

Parsons, M. (1982). Aesthetic development. In J. M. Broughton & D. J. Freeman-Moir, eds., *The cognitive-development psychology of James Mark Baldwin* (pp. 389–433). Norwood, NJ: Ablex.

Pavlov, I. P. (1928/1963). *Lectures on conditioned reflexes.* New York: International Publishers.

(1933). Les sentiments d'emprise et la phase ultraparadoxale. Lettre ouverte au professeur Pierre Janet. *Journal de Psychologie*, 30, 849–854.

Payer, L. (1990). *Medicine and culture.* London: Victor Gollancz Ltd.

Perinbanayagam, R. S. (1975). The significance of others in the thought of Alfred Schutz, G. H. Mead, and C. H. Cooley. *Sociological Quarterly*, 16, 500–521.

Perry, C., & Laurence, J.-R (1984). Mental processing outside of awareness: The contributions of Freud and Janet. In K. S. Bowers & D. Meichenbaum, eds., *The Unconscious Reconsidered* (pp. 9–48). New York: Wiley.

Petras, J. W. (1973). George Herbert Mead's theory of self: A study in the origin and convergence of ideas. *Canadian Review of Sociology and Anthropology*, 10, 148–159.

Phillips, W. (1947). The problem defined: Portrait of the artist as an American. *Horizon*, No. 93–94, 12–19.

Piaget, J. (1982). Reflections on Baldwin. In J. M. Broughton & D. J. Freeman-Moir, eds., *The cognitive-developmental psychology of James Mark Baldwin* (pp. 80–86). Norwood, NJ: Ablex.

Pickering, A. (1995). *The mangle of practice: Time, agency, and science.* Chicago: University of Chicago Press.

(1992). *Science as practice and culture.* Chicago: University of Chicago Press.

Piéron, H. (1937). Allocution. In H. Piéron & I. Meyerson, (eds.), *Onzième Congrès International de Psychologie* (pp. 507–514). Agen: Imprimerie Moderne.

(1960). Conscience et conduite chez Pierre Janet. *Bulletin de Psychologie*, 14, 149–153.

Pitnam, R. K. (1987). Pierre Janet on obsessive compulsive disorders. *Archives of General Psychiatry*, 44, 226–232.

Plas, R. (1994). La psychologie pathologique d'Alfred Binet. In P. Fraisse & J. Segui, eds., *Les origines de la psychologie scientifique* (pp. 229–245). Paris: P.U.F.

Pope, H. G., Hudson, J. I., & Mialet, J.-P. (1985). Bulimia in the late nineteenth century: The observations of Pierre Janet. *Psychological Medicine*, 15, 739–743.

Potebnya, A. A. (1926/1989). Mysl i jazyk. In A. A. Potebnya, *Slovo i mif* (pp. 17–200). Moscow: Pravda.

Pressley, M. (1992). How not to study strategy discovery. *American Psychologist*, 47, 1240–1241.

Prévost, C. M. (1973a). *La psycho-philosophie de Pierre Janet.* Paris: Payot.

(1973b). *Janet, Freud, et la psychologie clinique.* Paris: Payot.

Prigogine, I. (1973). Irreversibility as a symmetry-breaking process. *Nature*, 246, 67–71.

Prince, M. (1910). The subconscious. In E. Claparède, ed., *Vlme Congrès International de Psychologie* (pp. 71–97). Genève: Kündig.

Raphelson, A. C. (1973). The pre-Chicago association of the early functionalists. *Journal of the Behavioral Sciences*, 9, 115–122.

Ratner, C. (1991). *Vygotsky's sociohistorical psychology and its contemporary applications.* New York: Plenum.

(1996). Activity as a key concept for cultural psychology. *Culture & Psychology*, 2(4) 407–434.

Raymond, F., & Janet, P. (1898). *Névroses et idées fixes.* Vol. II. Paris: Alcan.

(1903). *Les obsessions et la psychasthénie*, Vol. II. Paris: Alcan.

(1904). Dépersonnalisation et possession chez un psychasthénique. *Journal de Psychologie*, 1, 28–37.

Reed, J. (1919/1977). *Ten days that shook the world.* London: Penguin.

Renn, J. (1996). History of science as historical epistemology. Preprint 36: *Historical epistemology and the advancement of science* (pp. 1–12). Berlin: Max-Planck-Institut für Wissenschaftsgeshichte.

Report of the Committee of Ten (1912). *American Journal of Sociology*, 17, 620–636.

Reuchlin, M. (1965). The historical background for national trends in psychology: France. *Journal of the History of the Behavioral Sciences*, 1, 115–123.

(1986).*Histoire de la psychologie.* Paris: P.U.F. (13th ed.).

Revesz, G. (1924). Experiments on animal space perception. *British Journal of Psychology*, 14, 387–414.

(1925). Experimental study in abstraction in monkeys. *Journal of Comparative Psychology*, 5, 293–343.

Reymert, M. L. (1928). *Feelings and emotions*. The Wittenberg Symposium. Worcester, MA: Clark University Press.

Ribot, Th. (1888). La psychologie contemporaine. *Revue Scientifique*, 25, 449–455.

(1894). *L'hérédité psychologique*. Paris: Alcan. (5th ed.)

(1907). Le subconscient. *Revue Philosophique*, 53, 197–205.

(1930). *La psychologie des sentiments*. Paris: Alcan. (13th ed.)

Richards, R. J. (1987). James Mark Baldwin: Evolutionary biopsychology and the politics of scientific ideas. In R. J. Richards, *Darwin and the evolutionary theories of mind and behavior* (pp. 451–503). Chicago: University of Chicago Press.

Richet, Ch. (1886). Un fait de somnambulisme à distance. *Revue Philosophique*, 11, 199–200.

(1923). Réponse à M. P. Janet. A propos de métapsychique. *Revue Philosophique*, 96, 462–471.

Robinson, J. A. (1988). "What we've got here is a failure to communicate": The cultural context of meaning. In J. Valsiner, ed., *Child development within culturally structured environments*. Vol. 2. *Social co-construction and environmental guidance of development* (pp. 137–198). Norwood, NJ: Ablex.

Rocheblave-Spenlé, A. M., (1973). Gabriel Tarde et la psychologie sociale. In A. M. Rocheblave-Spenlé, & J. Milet, eds., *G. Tarde. Ecrits de psychologie sociale* (pp. 25–42). Toulouse: Privat.

Roëll, D. R. (1996). *De wereld van instinct*. Rotterdam: Erasmus Publishing.

Rogoff, B. (1982). Integrating context and cognitive development. In M. Lamb & A. Brown, eds., *Advances in developmental psychology*. Vol. 2 (pp. 125–170). Hillsdale, NJ: Erlbaum.

(1986). Adult assistance of children's learning. In T. E. Raphael, ed., *The contexts of school-based literacy* (pp. 27–40). New York: Random House.

(1990). *Apprenticeship in thinking: Cognitive development in social context* New York: Oxford University Press.

(1992). Three ways of relating person and culture. *Human Development*, 35(5) 316–320.

(1993). Children's guided participation and participatory appropriation in sociocultural activity. In R. H. Wozniak & K. W. Fischer, eds., *Development in context* (pp. 121–153). Hillsdale, NJ: Erlbaum.

(1995). Observing sociocultural activity on three planes: Participatory appropriation, guided participation, and apprenticeship. In J. V. Wertsch, P. del Río & A. Alvarez, eds., *Sociocultural studies of mind* (pp. 139–164). Cambridge: Cambridge University Press.

(1996). Developmental transitions in children's participation in sociocultural activities. In A. J. Sameroff & M. M. Haith, eds., *The five to seven year shift: The age of reason and responsibility* (pp. 273–294. Chicago: University of Chicago Press.

(1997). Evaluating development in the process of participation: Theory, methods, and practice building on each other. In E. Amsel & K. A. Renninger, eds., *Change and development: Issues of theory, method, and application* (pp. 265–285). Mahwah, NJ: Erlbaum.

Rogoff, B., Baker-Sennett, J., Lacasa, P., & Goldsmith, D. (1995). Development through participation in sociocultural activity. In J. J. Goodnow, P. J. Miller, & F. Kessel, eds. *Cultural practices as contexts for development* (pp. 45–65). San Francisco, CA: Jossey-Bass (No. 67 in New Directions for Child Development).

Rogoff, B., Chavajay, P., & Matusov, E. (1993). Questioning assumptions about culture and individuals. *Behavioral and Brain Sciences*, 16, 533–534.

Rogoff, B., & Lave, J., eds. (1984). *Everyday cognition*. Cambridge, MA: Harvard University Press.

Rommetveit, R. (1972). Linguistic and nonlinguistic components of communication: Notes on the intersection of psycholinguistic and social psychological theory. In S. Moscovici, ed., *The psychosociology of language* (pp. 357–368). Chicago: Markham Publishing Co.

(1979). On common codes and dynamic residuals in human communication. In R. Rommetveit & R. Blaker, eds., of *Studies of language, thought and verbal communication* (pp. 163–175). London: Academic Press.

(1992). Outlines of a dialogically based social-cognitive approach to human cognition and communication. In A. H. Wold, ed., *The dialogical alternative: Towards a theory of language and mind* (pp. 19–44). Oslo: Scandinavian University Press.

(1998). On human beings, computers, and representational-computational versus hermeneutic-dialogical approaches to human cognition and communication. *Culture & Psychology*, 4, 189–213.

Rosa, A. (1994). History of psychology as a ground for reflexivity. In A. Rosa & J. Valsiner, eds., *Historical and theoretical discourse*. Vol. 1 of *Explorations in socio-cultural studies* (pp. 149–167). Madrids: Fundación Infancia y Aprendizaje.

Rosa, A., Huertas, J. A., & Blanco, F. (1996). *Metodología para la historia de la psicología*. Madrid: Alianza.

Rosen, R. (1982). *The lost sisterhood*. Baltimore, MD.: Johns Hopkins University Press.

Ross, E. A. (1908). The nature and scope of social psychology. *American Journal of Sociology*, 13, 5, 577–583.

Ross, J. B. (1907). The temper of the American. *American Journal of Sociology* (13) 380–391.

Roux, J. Ch. (1909). Hystérie. In Ch. Richet, ed., *Dictionnaire de physiologie*. Tome 8 (pp. 874–907). Paris: Alcan.

Royce, J. (1892a). *The spirit of modern philosophy*. Boston: Houghton & Mifflin.

(1892b). The outlook in ethics. *International Journal of Ethics*, 2, 106–111.

(1893/1966). The two-fold nature of knowledge: imitative and reflective. *Journal of the History of Philosophy*, 4, 326–337.

(1894a). The external world and the social consciousness. *Philosophical Review*, 3(5) 513–545.

(1894b). The case of John Bunyan. *Psychological Review*, 1, 22–33, 134–151, 230–240.

(1895a). Some observations on the anomalies of self-consciousness. *Psychological Review*, 2(5) 433–457, 574–584.

(1895b). Preliminary report on imitation. *Psychological Review*, 2,(3) 217–235.

(1895c). Self-consciousness, social consciousness and nature. *Philosophical Review*, 4, 465–485, 577–602.

(1898a). The psychology of invention. *Psychological Review*, 5(2) 113–144.

(1898b). *Studies of good and evil*. New York: Appleton.

(1901). *The world and the individual*. New York: Macmillan.

(1912). *The sources of religious insight*. New York: Charles Scribner's Sons.

(1995). *The philosophy of loyalty*. Nashville, TN: Vanderbilt University Press. [original in 1908]

Rüssel, A. (1944). Das Wesen der Bewegungskoordination. *Archiv für die gesamte Psychologie*, 112, 1–22.

Ryan, M. P. (1981). *Cradle of the middle class: The family in Oneida County, New York, 1790–1865*. Cambridge: Cambridge University Press.

Rychlak, J. F. (1995). A teleological critique of modern cognitivism. *Theory & Psychhology*, 5, 4, 511–531.

Ryle, G. (1949). *The Concept of Mind*. London: Hutchinson.

Saada-Robert, M. (1992a). Understanding the microgenesis of number. In J. Bideaud, C. Meljac, & J.-P. Fischer, eds., *Pathways to number* (pp. 265–282). Hillsdale, NJ: Erlbaum.

(1992b). Sequentiality and simultaneity in the microgenesis of number. Paper read at the Jean Piaget Society, Montreal, May.

(1994). Microgenesis and situated cognitive representations. In N. Mercer & C. Coll, eds. *Explorations in socio-cultural studies*. Vol. 3. *Teaching, learning, and interaction* (pp. 55–64). Madrid: Fundación Infancia y Aprendizaje.

Samukhin, N. V., Birenbaum, G. V., & Vygotsky, L. S. (1934). K voprosu o dementsii pri bolezni Pika. *Sovetskaya Nevropatologiya, Psikhiatriya, Psikhogigiena*, 6, 97–136.

Sander, F. (1922). Wundts Prinzip der schöpferische Synthese. In A. Hoffmann, ed., *Wilhelm Wundt. Eine Würdigung* (pp. 55–58) Erfurt: Kenferschen Buchhandlung.

(1926). Über räumliche Rhytmik. *Neue Psychologische Studien*, 1, 125–158.

(1927). Ueber Gestaltqualitäten. *Proceedings of the 8th International Congress of Psychology, 1926*. (pp. 183–189). Groningen: P. Noordhoff.

(1928/1962b). Experimentelle Ergebnisse der Gestaltpsychologie. In F. Sander, & H. Volkelt, eds., *Ganzheitspsychologie* (pp. 73–112). München: C. H. Beck.

(1930). Structure, totality of experience, and Gestalt. In C. Murchison, ed., *Psychologies of 1930* (pp. 188–204). Worcester, MA: Clark University Press.

(1932a). Funktionale Struktur, Erlebnisganzheit und Gestalt. *Archiv für die gesamte Psychologie*, 85, 237–260.

(1932b). Gestaltpsychologie und Kunsttheorie. *Neue Psychologische Studien*, 4, 321–346.

(1934). Seelische Struktur und Sprache. *Neue Psychologische Studien*, 12, 59–67.

(1962a). Gestaltwerden und Gestaltzerfall. In F. Sander, & H. Volkelt, eds., *Ganzheitspsychologie* (pp. 113–117). München: C. H. Beck.

Sander, F., & Volkelt, H. (1962). *Ganzheitspsychologie: Grundlagen, Ergebnisse, Anwendungen*. München: C. H. Beck.

Sapp. J. (1994). *Evolution by association: A history of symbiosis*. New York: Oxford University Press.

Saussure, R. de (1910). Unuformigo de la scienca terminaro. In E. Claparède, ed., *VIme Congrès International de Psychologie* (pp. 482–499). Geneva: Kündig.

Schmidt. E. M. (1939). Über den Aufbau rhythmischer Gestalten. *Neue Psychologische Studien*, 14(2) 5–98.

Schubert, H.-J. (1998). Introduction. In H.-J. Schubert, ed., *Charles Horton Cooley on self and social organization* (pp. 1–31). Chicago: University of Chicago Press.

Schwalbe, M. (1988). Mead among the cognitivists: roles as performance imagery. *Journal for the Theory of Social Behaviour*, 17(2) 113–133.

Schwartz, L. (1951). *Die Neurosen und die dynamische Psychologie von Pierre Janet*. Basel: Schwabe (French translation 1955).

Scott, C. H. (1976). *Lester Frank Ward*. Boston: G. K. Hall.

Severtsov, A. N. (1921). *Etjudy po teorii evoljutsii*. Berlin: Gosudarstvennoe Izdatel'stvo RSFSR.

(1922). *Evolijutsija i psikhika*. Moscow: Izdanie M. & S. Sabashnikov.

(1927). Ueber die Beziehungen zwischen der Ontogenese und der Phylogenese der Tiere. *Jena. Zeitschrift für Naturwissenschaften*, 56,(o.s. 63), 51–180.

(1929). Direction of evolution. *Acta Zoologica*, 10, 59–141.

(1931). *Morphologische Gesetzmässigkeiten der Evolution*. Jena: Fischer.

(1949). *Sobranie Sochinenij. Tom 1. Raboty po metamerii golovy pozvonochnykh*. Moscow-Leningrad: Izdatel'stvo Akademii Nauk USSR.

Shalin, D. N. (1988). G. H. Mead, socialism, and the progressive agenda. *American Journal of Sociology*, 93(4) 913–951.

Shapin, S. (1995). Here and everywhere: Sociology of scientific knowledge. *Annual Review of Sociology*, 21, 289–321.

Shif, Zh. I. (1935). *Razvitie nauchnykh ponyatiy u shkol'nika*. Moscow-Leningrad: Gosudarstvennoe Uchebno-Pedagogicheskoe Izdatel'stvo.

Shiva, V. (1988). Reductionist science as epistemological violence. In A. Nandy, ed. *Science, hegemony and violence: A requiem to modernity* (pp. 232–256). Delhi: Oxford University Press.

Shoenberg, P. J. (1975). The symptom as stigma or communication in hysteria. *International Journal of Psychoanalytic Psychotherapy*, 4, 507–517.

Shook, J. R. (1995). Wilhelm Wundt's contribution to John Dewey's functional psychology. *Journal of the History of the Behavioral Sciences*, 31, 347–369.

Shotter, J. (1993). *Conversational realities: Constructing life through language*. London: Sage.

Showalter, E. (1997). *Hystories: Hysterical epidemics and modern culture*. London: Picador.

Shweder, R. (1984). Anthropology's romantic rebellion against the enlightenment, or there is more to thinking than reason and evidence. In R. Shweder & R. A. LeVine, eds. *Culture theory* (pp. 27–66). Cambridge: Cambridge University Press.

(1990). Cultural psychology – what is it? In J. W. Stigler, R. A. Shweder and G. Herdt, eds. *Cultural psychology* (pp. 1–43). Cambridge: Cambridge University Press.

(1992). Ghost busters in anthropology. In R. D'Andrade & C. Strauss, eds. *Human motives and cultural models* (pp. 45–57). Cambridge: Cambridge University Press.

(1995). The confessions of a methodological individualist. *Culture & Psychology*, 1(1) 115–122.

(1996a). True ethnography: The lore, the law, and the lure. In R. Jessor, A. Colby & R. A. Shweder, eds. *Ethnography and human development* (pp. 15–52). Chicago: University of Chicago Press.

(1996b). Quanta and qualia: What is the "object" of ethnographic method?. In R. Jessor, A. Colby & R. A. Shweder, eds. *Ethnography and human development* (pp. 175–182). Chicago: University of Chicago Press.

Shweder, R., Mahapatra, M., & Miller, J. G. (1987). Culture and moral development. In J. Kagan & S. Lamb, eds. *The emergence of morality in young children* (pp. 1–83). Chicago: University of Chicago Press.

Shweder, R., & Much, N. (1987). Determinations of meaning: Discourse and moral socialization. In W. M. Kurtines and J. L. Gewirtz, eds., *Moral development through social interaction* (pp. 197–244). New York: Wiley.

Shweder, R. & Sullivan, M. (1993). Cultural psychology: Who needs it? *Annual Review of Psychology*, 44, 497–523.

Sidgwick, H. (1886). The historical method. *Mind*, 11 (o.s.), 203–219.

Siegler, R. S. (1996). *Emerging minds*. New York: Oxford University Press.

Siegler, R. S., & Crowley, K. (1991). The microgenetic method: A direct means for studying cognitive development. *American Psychologist* 46, 616–620.

(1992). Microgenetic methods revisited. *American Psychologist*, 47, 1241–1243.

Simmel, G. (1884). Dantes Psychologie. *Zeitschrift für Völkerpsychologie und Sprachwissenschaft*, 20, 6–46.

(1890). Zur Psychologie der Frauen. *Zeitschrift für Völkerpsychologie und Sprachwissenschaft*, 5, 153.

(1896). Superiority and subordination as subject matter of sociology. *American Journal of Sociology*, 2(2) 167–189, and 1897, 2, 392–415.

(1898). The persistence of social groups. *American Journal of Sociology*, 3, 662–698, 829–836 and 4, 35–50.

(1900). A chapter in the philosophy of value. *American Journal of Sociology*, 5, 5, 577–603.

(1902). The number of members as determining the sociological form of the group. *American Journal of Sociology*, 8, 1–46, 158–196.

(1904). The sociology of conflict. *American Journal of Sociology*, 9, 490–525; 672–689; 798–811.

(1905). A contribution to the sociology of religion. *American Journal of Sociology*, 11, 339–376.

(1906). The sociology of secrecy and of secret societies. *American Journal of Sociology*, 11(4) 441–498.

(1909). The problem of sociology. *American Journal of Sociology*, 15(3) 289–320.

(1910). How is society possible? *American Journal of Sociology*, 16, 372–391.

Simpson, G. G. (1953). The Baldwin effect. *Evolution*, 7, 110–117.

Sinha, D., & Tripathi, R. C. (1994). Individualism in a collectivist culture: A case of coexistance of opposites. In U. Kim, H. C. Triandis, Ç. Kagitçibasi, S-C Choi & G. Yoon, eds. *Individualism and collectivism: Theory, method, and applications* (pp. 123–136). Thousand Oaks, CA: Sage.

Sjöwall, B. (1967). *Psychology of tension*. Stockholm: Svenska Bokförlaget.

Smedslund, J. (1995). Psychologic: Common sense and the pseudoempirical. In J. A. Smith. R. Harré, & L. van Langenhove, eds. *Rethinking psychology* (pp. 196–206). London: Sage.

(1997). *The structure of the common sense*. Mahwah, NJ: Erlbaum.

Smolka, A. L. B., Góes, M. C., & Pino, A. (1995). The constitution of the subject: A persistent question. In J. Wertsch & B. Rogoff, eds. *Sociocultural studies of the mind*. Cambridge: Cambridge University Press

Snow, W. F. (1915). Progress, 1900–1915. *Social Hygiene*, 2, 37–47.

Sokolov, V. E., & Baskin, L. M. (1992). Development of ethology in the USSR. *Internatinal Journal of Comparative Psychology*, 6, 75–78.

Sollier, P. (1910). Lettre au directeur. *Revue Philosophique*, 59, 550–551.

Spinoza, B. de (1677/1955). *On the improvement of the understanding: The ethics. Correspondence*. Mineola: Dover Publications.

Sprung, H. (1997). Carl Stumpf. In W. Bringmann, H. E. Lück, R. Miller, & C. E. Early, eds. *A pictorial history of psychology* (pp. 247–250). Chicago: Quintessence Publishing Co.

Stern, W. (1906). *Person und Sache: System der philosophischen Weltanschauung*. Leipzing: J. A. Barth.

(1919). *Person und Sache*. Vol. 2. *Die menschliche Persönlichkeit*. (2nd ed.). Leipzig: J. A. Barth.

(1924). Person und Sache. Vol. 3. Wertphilosophie. Leipzig: J. A. Barth.

Stevens, J. A. (1982). Children of the Revolution: Soviet Russia's homeless children (Bezprizorniki) in the 1920s. *Russian History/Histoire Russe*, 9 (2–3), 242–264.

Stocking, G. W. (1962). Lamarckianism in American social science: 1890–1915. *Journal of the History of Ideas*, 23, 239–256.

Strachey, J. (1973). *The standard edition of the complete psychological works of Sigmund Freud. Vol. II. Studies on hysteria by Josef Breuer and Sigmund Freud*. London: The Hogarth Press.

Strickland, L. H., ed., (1994). V. M. Bekhterev's *Collective reflexology*. Commack, NY: Nova Science Publishers [Russian original in 1921].

Stumpf, C. & von Hornbostel, E. (1911). Über die Bedeutung ethnologischer Untersuchungen für die Psychologie und Ästhetik der Tonkunst. *Beiträge zur Akustik und Musikwissenschaft*, 6. 102–115.

Subercaseaux, B. (1927). *Apuntes de psicologia comparada*. Santiago de Chile: Bardi.

Sulloway, F. J. (1992). *Freud, Biologist of the Mind*. Cambridge, MA: Harvard University Press.

Sully, J. (1896). Book review of Baldwin's Mental development in the child and the race. *Mind*, 5, 97–103.

Talankin, A. A. (1931a). O povorote na psikhologicheskom fronte. *Sovetskaya Psikhonevrologiya*, 2–3, 8–23.

(1931b). O "marksistskoy psikhologii" prof. Kornilova. *Psikhologiya*, 4(1) 24–43.

Tarde, G. (1884). Qu'est-ce qu'une société? *Revue Philosophique*, 18, 489–510.

(1890). *Les lois de l'imitation*. Paris: Alcan.

(1894). *Lois psychologiques de l'évolution des peuples*. Paris: Felix Alcan.

(1895). *Psychologie des foules*. Paris: Felix Alcan.

(1902). *Les lois sociales*. Paris: Alcan.

Tardieu, A (1880). *Etude médico-légale sur la folie*. Paris: Baillière.

Terman, L. M. (1921). *The intelligence of school children*. London: George G. Harrap & Co. Ltd.

Terman, L. M., Dickson, V. E., Sutherland, A. H., Franzen, R. H., Tupper, C. R., & Fernald, G. (1923). *Intelligence tests and school reorganization*. Yonkers-on-Hudson, NY: World Book Company.

Thompson, G. E. (1993). Causality in economics: Rhetorical ethic or positivist empiric? *Quality & Quantity*, 27, 47–71.

Thorndike, E. L. (1911). *Animal intelligence*. New York: Macmillan.

Tinker, M. A. (1980). Wundt's doctorate students and their theses 1875–1920. In W. G. Bringmann & R. D. Tweney, eds. *Wundt studies. A centennial collection* (pp. 269–279). Toronto: C. J. Hogrefe.

Tinterow, M. M. (1970). *Foundations of hypnosis: From Mesmer to Freud*. Springfield, IL: C. C. Thomas.

Tobolowska, J. (1911). Review of P. Janet, L'état mental des hystériques. *Journal de Psychologie*, 8, 469–472.

Triandis, H. (1994). Theoretical and methodological approaches to the study of collectivism and individualism. In U Kim, H. C. Triandis, Ç. Kagitçibasi, S-C Choi & G. Yoon, eds. *Individualism and collectivism: Theory, method, and applications* (pp. 41–51). Thousand Oaks, CA: Sage.

Triandis, H. (1995). *Individualism and collectivism*. San Francisco: Westview.

Tufts, J. H. (1904). The individual and his relation to society. *Psychological Review Monograph Supplements*, 6, 2, (whole No. 25), 1–58.

Turbiaux, M. (1960). Le centenaire de Pierre Janet à la Société Française de Psychologie. *Bulletin de Psychologie*, 14, 190–193.

Tweney, R. D., Doherty, M. E., & Mynatt, C. R. (1981). *On scientific thinking*. New York: Columbia University Press.

Vagner, V. A. (1896). *Voprosy zoopsikhologii*. St. Petersburg: Izdanie L. F. Panteleeva.

(1898). Metafizika i nauka. *Obrazovanie*, 9, 16–34.

(1901). Biologicheskij metod v zoopsikhologii. *Trudy imperatorskogo Sankt-Peterburgskogo Obshchestva Estvestoispytatelej*, 33, 1–96.

(1904). Iz istorija darvinizma v sotsiologii. *Russkaja mysl'*, 8, 1–29.

(1910). *Biologicheskie osnovanija sravnitel'noj psikhologii*. Vol. 1. St. Petersburg-Moscow: Izdanie M. O. Wol'f.

(1913). *Biologicheskie osnovanija sravnitel'noj psikhologii*. Vol. 2. St. Petersburg-Moscow; Izdanie M. O. Wol'f.

(1923). *Biopsikhologija i smezhnye nauki*. Petersburg.

(1925). *Vozniknovenie i razvitie psikhicheskikh sposobnostej*, Vol. 3. *Ot refleksov do instinktov*. Leningrad: Nachatki Znanij.

(1928). *Vozniknovenie i razvitie psikhicheskikh sposobnostej*, Vol. 5. Leningrad: Nachatki Znanij.

(1929). *Psikhologicheskie tipy i kollektivnaja psikhologija*. Leningrad: Nachatki znanij.

(1992a). From the other shore: My autobiography. *International Journal of Comparative Psychology*, 6, 37–55.

(1992b). Comparative psychology as a course of study in the university and in other higher educational institutions. *International Journal of Comparative Psychology*, 6, 5–9.

Valenstein, E. S. (1986). *Great and desperate cures*. New York, NY: Basic Books.

Valsiner, J. (1985). Common sense and psychological theories: The historical nature of logical necessity. *Scandinavian Journal of Psychology*, 26, 97–109.

(1987). *Culture and the development of children's action*. Chichester: Wiley.

(1988). *Developmental psychology in the Soviet Union*. Brighton: Harvester Press.

(1988). Ontogeny of co-construction of culture within socially organized environmental settings. In J. Valsiner, ed. *Child development within culturally structured environments*. Vol. 2. *Social co-construction and environmental guidance of development* (pp. 283–297). Norwood, NJ: Ablex.

(1989).*Human development and culture*. Lexington, MA: D. C. Heath & Co.

(1992). Interest: A metatheoretical perspective. In K. A. Renninger, S. Hidi, & A. Krapp, eds. *The role of interest in learning and development* (pp. 27–41). Hillsdale, NJ: Erlbaum.

(1993a). Making of the future: Temporality and the constructive nature of human development. In G. Turkewitz & D. Devenney, eds. *Timing as initial condition of development* (pp. 13–40). Hillsdale, NJ: Erlbaum.

(1993b). Bi-directional cultural transmission and constructive sociogenesis. In R. Maier & W. de Graaf, eds. *Mechanisms of sociogenesis* (pp. 47–70) New York: Springer. [actually 1994].

(1994a). Reflexivity in context: Narratives, hero-myths, and the making of histories in psychology. In A. Rosa & J. Valsiner, eds. *Explorations in sociocultural studies*. Vol. 1. *Historical and theoretical discourse* (pp. 169–186). Madrid: Fundacion Infancia y Aprendizaje.

(1994b). Uses of common sense and ordinary language in psychology, and beyond: a co-constructionist perspective and its implications. In J. Siegfried, ed., *The status of common sense in psychology*. (pp. 46–57). Norwood, NJ: Ablex.

(1994c). Culture and human development: a co-constructionist perspective. In P. van Geert, L. P. Mos, & W. J. Baker, eds. *Annals of Theoretical Psychology*. Vol. 10 (pp. 247–298). New York: Plenum

(1994d). Irreversibility of time and the construction of historical developmental psychology. *Mind, Culture, and Activity*, 1, 1–2, 25–42.

(1996). Co-constructionism and development: a socio-historic tradition. *Anuario de Psicologia* (Barcelona), No. 69. Pp. 63–82.

Valsiner, J., & Van der Veer, R. (1988). On the social nature of human cognition: An analysis of the shared intellectual roots of George Herbert Mead and Lev Vygotsky. *Journal for the Theory of Social Behaviour*, 18, 117–135.

(1993). The encoding of distance: The concept of the zone of proximal development and its interpretations. In R. R. Cocking & K. A. Renninger, eds. *The development and meaning of psychological distance* (pp. 35–62). Hillsdale, NJ: Erlbaum.

Van der Hart, O., Brown, P., & Van der Kolk, B. A. (1989). Pierre Janet's psychological treatment of post-traumatic stress. *Journal of Traumatic Stress*, 2, 379–395.

Van der Hart, O., & Friedman, B. (1989). A reader's guide to Pierre Janet on dissociation: A neglected intellectual heritage. *Dissociation*, 2, 3–16.

Van der Hart, O., & Horst, R. (1989). The dissociation theory of Pierre Janet. *Journal of Traumatic Stress*, 2, 397–412.

Van der Kolk, B. A., & Van der Hart, O. (1989). Pierre Janet and the breakdown of adaptation in psychological trauma. *The American Journal of Psychiatry*, 146, 1530–1540.

Van der Veer, R (1984). *Cultuur en cognitie*. Groningen: Wolters-Noordhoff.

(1994). Pierre Janet's relevance for a socio-cultural approach. In A. Rosa & J. Valsiner, eds. *Historical and theoretical discourse in social-cultural studies* (pp. 205–209). Madrid: Fundación Infancia y Aprendizaje.

(1996a). The concept of culture in Vygotsky's thinking. *Culture & Psychology*, 2, 247–263.

(1996b). Henri Wallon's theory of early child development: The role of emotions. *Developmental Review*, 16, 364–390.

(1996c). Vygotsky and Piaget: A collective monologue. *Human Development*, 39, 237–242.

(1996d). On some historical roots and present-day doubts: A reply to Nicolopoulou and Weintraub. *Culture & Psychology*, 2, 457–463.

(1997). Some major themes in Vygotsky's theoretical work. An introduction. In R. W. Rieber & J. Wollock, eds., *The collected works of L. S. Vygotsky*. Vol. 3. *Problems of the theory and history of psychology* (pp. 1–7). New York-London: Plenum Press. (translated and with an introduction by R. van der Veer).

Van der Veer, R., & Valsiner, J. (1988) Lev Vygotsky and Pierre Janet: On the origin of the concept of sociogenesis. *Developmental Review*, 8, 52–65.

(1991a). Sociogenetic perspectives in the work of Pierre Janet. *Storia della Psicologia*, 3, 6–23.

(1991b). *Understanding Vygotsky: A quest for synthesis*. Oxford: Basil Blackwell.

eds. (1994). *The Vygotsky Reader*. Oxford: Blackwell.

Van der Veer, R., & Van IJzendoorn, M. H. (1985). Vygotsky's theory of the higher psychological processes: Some criticisms. *Human Development*, 28, 1–9.

Van Geert, P. (1988). The concept of transition in developmental theories. In W. Baker, L. P. Mos, H. V. Rappard & H. J. Stam, eds. *Recent trends in theoretical psychology* (pp. 225–235). New York: Springer.

Van Ginneken, J. (1992). *Crowds, psychology, and politics, 1871–1899*. Cambridge: Cambridge University Press.

Van Hoorn, W., & Verhave, T. (1980). Wundt's changing conceptions of a general and theoretical psychology. In W. G. Bringmann & R. D. Tweney, eds., *Wundt studies. A centennial collection* (pp. 71–113). Toronto: C. J. Hogrefe.

Vari-Szilagyi, I. (1991). G. H. Mead and L. S. Vygotsky on action. *Studies in Soviet Thought*, 42, 93–121.

Varshava, B. E., & Vygotsky, L. S. (1931). *Psikhologicheskij slovar'*. Moscow: Gosudarstvennoe Uchebno-Pedagogicheskoe Izdatel'stvo.

Vidal, F. (1994). *Piaget before Piaget*. Cambridge, MA: Harvard University Press.

Vincent, G. E. (1910). The rivalry of social groups. *American Journal of Sociology*, 16, 469–484.

Volkelt, H. (1914). Über die Vorstellungen der Tiere. *Arbeiten zur Entwicklungspsychologie*, 2, 1–126.

(1922). Die Völkerpsychologie in Wundts Entwicklungsgang. In A. Hoffmann, ed., *Wilhelm Wundt. Eine Würdigung* (pp. 74–105). Erfurt: Kenferschen Buchhandlung.

(1934). Vom Wesen der Ganzqualitäten In O. Klemm, ed., *Bericht über den XIII Kongress der Deutsche Gesellschaft für Psychologie in Leipzig, 1933* (pp. 180–181). Jena: Gustav Fischer.

(1935). Kind und Familie. In O. Klemm, ed., *Psychologie des Gemeinschaftsleben. Berichte über den XIV Kongress der Deutsche Gesellschaft für Psychologie in Tübingen, 1934* (pp. 264–273). Jena: Gustav Fischer.

(1944). Abwehr eines Angriffes auf die genetische Ganzheitspsychologie. *Archiv für die gesamte Psychologie*, 112, 207–215.

(1954). Grundbegriffe der Ganzheitspsychologie. In A. Wellek, ed., *Wege zur Ganzheitspsychologie*. (pp. 1–46). München: C. H. Beck. (2nd ed.)

(1959/1962). Simultangestalten, Verlaufungsgestalten und "Einfühlung." In F. Sander, & H. Volkelt, eds. *Ganzheitspsychologie* (pp. 147–158). München: C. H. Beck.

(1963). *Grundfragen der Psychologie*. München: C. H. Beck.

Von Baer, K. E. (1828). *Über Entwicklungsgeschichte der Thiere: Beobachtung und reflexion*. Königsberg: Bornträger.

Von Dürckheim-Montmartin, K. (1954). Gemeinschaft. In A. Wellek ed., *Wege zur Ganzheitspsychologie* (pp. 195–216). München: C. H. Beck. (2nd ed.)

Vonèche, J. J. (1982). Evolution, development, and the growth of knowledge. In J. M. Broughton & D. J. Freeman-Moir, eds., *The cognitive-developmental psychology of James Mark Baldwin* (pp. 51–79). Norwood, NJ: Ablex.

Von Ehrenfels, C. (1890/1967). Über "Gestaltqualitäten. In F. Weinhandl, ed. *Gestalthaftes sehen: Ergebnisse und aufgaben der Morphologie* (pp. 11–43). Darmstadt: Wissenschaftliche Buchgesellschaft [originally in *Vierterjahreschrift für wissenschaftliche Philosophie*, 1890, 14, 242–292]

Von Hornbostel, E. (1913). Über ein akustisches Kriterium für Kulturzusammenhänge. *Beiträge zur Akustik und Musikwissenschaft*, 7, 1–21.

Von Lilienthal, K. (1887). *Der Hypnotismus und das Strafrecht*. Berlin: Verlag von Guttentag.

Von Weizsäcker, V. (1927/1957). Über medizinische Anthropologie. In V. von Weizsäcker, & D. Wyss, eds. *Zwischen Medizin und Philosophie* (pp. 97–116). Göttingen: Vandehoeck & Ruprecht.

Voutsinas, D. (1960). Hypnose, suggestion, hystérie. *Bulletin de Psychologie*, 14, 161–189.

Vucinich, A. (1988). *Darwin in Russian thought*. Berkeley: University of California Press.

Vygodskaja, G. L., & Lifanova, T. M. (1996). *Lev Semenovich Vygotskij. Zhizn'. Dejatel'nost'. Shtrikhi k portretu*. Moscow: Leont'ev Publishers.

Vygotsky, L. S. (1916a). M. Yu. Lermontov (k 75-letiyu so dnya smerti). *Novyj Put'*, 28, 7–11.

(1916b). Literaturnye zametki. "Peterburg". Roman Andreya Belogo. *Novyj Put'*, 47, 27–32.

(1916c). *Tragediya o Hamlete, printse Datskom, U. Shekspira*. Moscow: Master's Thesis.

(1917). Avodim Khoin. *Novyj Put'*, 11–12, 8–10.

(1923a). Evrejskij teatr. Sil'va. "A mensh zol men zajn". *Nash Ponedel'nik*, 30, 3.

(1923b). Evrejskij teatr. Koldun'ya. "Dos ferblonzele sheifele". *Nash Ponedel'nik*, 33, 3.

(1923c). Evrejskij teatr. Bar Kokhba. "Der eshiva bokher". *Nash Ponedel'nik*, 34, 3.

(1923d). 10 dnej, kotorye potryasli mir. *Polesskaya Pravda*, 1081, December 23.

(1925a). *Psikhologiya iskusstva*. Moscow: Doctoral Dissertation.

(1925b). Principles of social education for deaf and dumb children in Russia. In *International Conference on the Education of the Deaf* (pp. 227–237). London: William H. Taylor and Sons.

(1925/1986). *Psikhologiya iskusstva*. Moscow: Iskusstvo.

(1925/1997). Consciousness as a problem for the psychology of behavior. In R. W. Rieber & J. Wollock, eds., *The collected works of L. S. Vygotsky*. Vol. 3. *Problems of the theory and history of psychology* (pp. 63–79). New York-London: Plenum Press.

(1926a/1997). The methods of reflexological and psychological investigation. In R. W. Rieber & J. Wollock, eds., *The collected works of L. S. Vygotsky*. Vol. 3. *Problems of the theory and history of psychology* (pp. 35–49). New York-London: Plenum Press.

(1926b/1997). The historical meaning of the crisis in psychology: A methodological investigation. In R. W. Rieber & J. Wollock, eds., *The Collected Works of L. S. Vygotsky. Vol. 3., Problems of the Theory and History of Psychology* (pp. 233–343). New York-London: Plenum Press.

(1926c). *Pedagogicheskaya psikhologiya*. Moscow: Rabotnik Proshveschenia.

(1929a). Geneticheskie korni myshlenija i rechi. *Estvestvoznanie i Marksizm*, 1, 106–134.

(1929b). K voprosu ob intellekte antropoidov v svjazi s rabotami W. Köhler'a. *Estvestvoznanie i Marksizm*, 2, 131–153.

(1929c). Povedenie zhivotnykh i cheloveka. In L. S. Vygotsky (1960), *Razvitie Vysshikh Psikhicheskikh Funktsij* (pp. 397–456). Moscow: A.P.N.

(1930a). Predislovie. In W. Köhler, *Issledovanie intellekta chelovekopodobnykh obez'jan* (pp. i–xxix). Moscow: Izdatel'stvo Kommunisticheskoj Akademii.

(1930b). Strukturnaya psikhologiya. In L. S. Vygotsky, S. Gellershtein, V. Fingert, & M. Shirvindt, eds., *Osnovnye techeniya sovremennoy psikhologii* (pp. 84–125). Moscow: Gosudarstvennoe Izdatel'stvo.

(1931/1983). Istoriya razvitiya vysshikh psikhicheskikh funktsii. In A. M. Matyushkin, ed., *Sobranie sochinennii. Tom tretii. Problemy razvitiya psikhiki*. Moscow: Pedagogika.

(1931/1997). The history of the development of higher mental functions. In R. W. Rieber, ed., *The collected works of L. S. Vygotsky.* Vol. 4. *The history of the development of higher mental functions* (pp. 1–251). New York-London: Plenum Press.

(1932/1984). Lectures on psychology. In R. W. Rieber & A. S. Carton (Eds.), *The collected works of L. S. Vygotsky.* Vol. 1. *Problems of General Psychology* (pp. 289–358). New York-London: Plenum Press.

(1933/1984). Uchenie ob emotsijakh. In L. S. Vygotsky, *Sobranie Sochinenij. Tom 6. Nauchnoe Nasledstvo* (pp. 91–318). Moscow: Pedagogika.

(1934a). *Myshlenie i rech. Psikhologicheskie issledovanija*. Moscow-Leningrad: Gosudarstvennoe Social'no-Ekonomicheskoe Izdatel'stvo.

(1934b/1990). *Pensiero e linguaggio*. Rome: Editori Laterza.

(1934c/1987). Thinking and speech. In R. W. Rieber & A. S. Carton, eds., *The collected works of L. S. Vygotsky.* Vol. 1. *Problems of General Psychology* (pp. 39–285). New York-London: Plenum Press.

(1934d/1960). Problema razvitija i raspada vysshikh psikhicheskikh funkcij. In L. S. Vygotsky, *Razvitie vysshikh psikhicheskikh funkcij* (pp. 364–383). Moscow: Izdatel'stvo APN RSFSR.

(1934e/1997). Preface to Koffka. In R. W. Rieber & J. Wollock, eds., *The collected works of L. S. Vygotsky.* Vol. 3. *Problems of the theory and history of psychology* (pp. 195–232). New York-London: Plenum Press.

(1934f). Thought in schizophrenia. *Archives of Neurology and Psychiatry*, 31, 1063–1077.

(1935). *Umstvennoe razvitie detey v protsesse obucheniya*. Moscow-Leningrad: Gosudarstvennoe Uchebno-Pedagogicheskoe Izdatel'stvo.

Vygotsky, L. S., & Luria, A. R. (1930). *Etjudy po istorii povedenija. Obez'jana. Primitiv. Rebenok*. Moscow-Leningrad: Gosudarstvennoe Izdatel'stvo.

Wagner, W. (1994). Fields of research and socio-genesis of social representations: a discussion of criteria and diagnostics. *Social Science Information*, 33(2) 199–228.

(1996). Queries about social representation and construction. *Journal for the Theory of Social Behaviour*, 26(2) 95–120.

Wagner, W., Valencia, J., & Elejabarrieta, F. (1996). Relevance, discourse, and the 'hot' stable core of social representations – a structural analysis of word associations. *British Journal of Social Psychology*, 35, 331–351.

Walker, S. (1983). *Animal thought*. London: Routledge & Kegan Paul.

Wallace, D. (1967). Reflections on the education of George Herbert Mead. *American Journal of Sociology*, 72(4) 396–412.

Wallon, H. (1928). Review of P. Janet, De l'angoisse à l'extase. *Revue Philosophique*, 105, 309–312.

(1942/1970). *De l'acte à la pensée*. Paris: Flammarion.

(1960). Pierre Janet, psychologue réaliste. *Bulletin de Psychologie*, 14, 154–156.

Wapner, S., & Kaplan, B. (1964). Heinz Werner: 1890–1964. *American Journal of Psychology*, 77, 513–517.

Ward, L. F. (1883). *Dynamic sociology, or applied social science*. New York: D. Appleton and Co.

(1897). Collective telesis. *American Journal of Sociology*, 2, 801–822.

(1903). *Pure sociology: A treatise on the origin and spontaneous development of society*. New York: MacMillan.

(1913). Eugenics, euthenics, and eudemics. *American Journal of Sociology*, 18(6) 737–734.

Watson, J. B. (1913). Psychology as the behaviorist views it. *Psychological Review*, 20, 158–177.

Watson, R. I. (1965). The historical background for national trends in psychology: United States. *Journal of the History of the Behavioral Sciences*, 1, 130–138.

Wellek, A. (1935). Zur Typologie der Musikalität der deutschen Stämme. In O. Klemm, ed., *Psychologie des Gemeinschaftsleben. Berichte über den XIV Kongress der Deutsche Gesellschaft für Psychologie in Tübingen, 1934* (pp. 130–136). Jena: Gustav Fischer.

(1938). Typus und struktur. *Archiv für die gesamte Psychologie*, 100, 465–477.

(1954). Die genetische Ganzheitspsychologie der Leipziger Schule und Ihre Verzweigungen. *Neue Psychologische Studien*, 15, 1–67.

(1967). Ganzheit, Gestalt und Nichtgestalt. In F. Weinhandl, ed., *Gestalthaftes sehen: Ergebnisse und Aufgaben der Morphologie* (pp. 384–397). Darmstadt: Wissenschaftliche Buchgesellschaft.

Werner, C. W., & Altman, I. (1998). A dialectical/transactional framework for social relations: Children in secondry territories. In D. Görlitz, H.-J. Harloff, G. Mey & J. Valsiner (Eds), *Children, cities, and psychological theories: Developing relationships* (pp. 123–154). Berlin: W. de Gruyter.

Werner, H. (1919a). Über optische Rhytmik. *Archiv für die gesamte Psychologie*, 38, 115–163.

(1919b). Rhythmus, eine mehrwertige Gestaltverkettung. *Zeitschrift für Psychologie*, 82, 198–218.

(1919c). *Die Ursprünge der Metapher. Arbeiten zur Entwicklungspsychologie* (pp. 1–238). Leipzig: J. A. Barth.

(1925). *Einführung in die Entwicklungspsychologie*. Leipzig: Barth.

(1926). Über Mikromelodik und Mikroharmonik. *Zeitschrift für Psychologie*, 98, 74–89.

(1927). Ueber Pysiognomische Wahrnehmungsweisen und Ihre experimentelle Prüfung. In *Proceedings and papers of the 8th International Congress of Psychology, 1926, Groningen* (pp. 443–446). Groningen: P. Noordhoff.

(1929). Uber die Sprachphysiognomik als einer neuen Methode der vergleichenden Sprachbetrachtung. *Zeitschrift für Psychologie*, 109, 337–363.

(1930). Die Rolle der Sprachempfindung im Prozess der Gestaltung ausdrückmässig erlebter Wörter. *Zeitschrift für Psychologie* 117, 230–254.

(1931). Das Prinzip der Gestaltschichtung und seine Bedeutung im kunstwerklichen Aufbau. *Zeitschrift für angewandte Psychologie*, Beiheft 59, 241–256.

(1937). Process and achievement. *Harvard Educational Review*, 7, 353–368.

(1938). William Stern's personalistics and psychology of personality. *Character & Personality*, 7, 109–125.

(1940). Musical "micro-scales" and "micromelodies." *Journal of Psychology*, 10, 149–156.

(1946). The concept of rigidity: A critical evaluation. *Psychological Review*, 53, 1, 43–52.

(1948). *Comparative psychology of mental development*. New York: International University Press.

(1954). Change of meaning: A study of semantic processes through the experimental method. *Journal of General Psychology*, 50, 181–208.

(1956). Microgenesis and aphasia. *Journal of Abnormal & Social Psychology*, 52, 347–353.

(1957). The concept of development from a comparative and organismic point of view. In D. B. Harris, ed., *The concept of development* (pp. 125–147). Minneapolis, MN: University of Minnesota Press.

Werner, H., & Kaplan, B. (1956). The development approach to cognition: Its relevance to the psychological interpretation of anthropological and ethnolinguistic data. *American Anthropologist*, 58, 866–880.

(1984). *Symbol formation*. Hillsdale, N.J.: Erlbaum. (1st ed.: 1963).

Werner, H., & Kaplan, E. (1950). Development of word meaning through verbal context. *Journal of Psychology*, 29, 251–257.

(1952). The acquisition of word meanings. *Monographs of SRCD, No. 51*.

(1954). The word context test. *British Journal of Psychology*, 45, 134–136.

Werner, H., & Wapner, S. (1949). Sensory-tonic field theory of perception. *Journal of Personality*, 18(1) 88–107.

(1956). Sensory-tonic field theory of perception: basic concepts and experiments. *Rivista di Psicologia*, 50(4) 315–337.

Wertheimer, M. (1912a). Über das Denken der Naturvölker I: Zahlen und Zahlgebilde. *Zeitschrift für Psychologie*, 60, 321–378.

(1912b). Experimentelle Studien über das Sehen von Bewegung. *Zeitschrift für Psychologie*, 61, 161–265.

Wertsch, J. V. (1979). From social interaction to higher psychological processes: A clarification and application of Vygotsky's theory. *Human Development*, 22, 1–22.

(1981). The concept of activity in Soviet psychology: An introduction. In J. V. Wertsch, ed., *The concept of activity in Soviet psychology* (pp. 3–36). Armonk, NY: Sharpe.

(1983). The role of semiosis in L. S. Vygotsky's theory of human cognition. In B. Bain, ed., *The sociogenesis of language and human conduct* (pp. 17–31). New York: Plenum.

(1984). The zone of proximal development: Some conceptual issues. In B. Rogoff & J. V. Wertsch, eds., *Children's learning in the "zone of proximal development"* (pp. 7–17). No. 23. *New Directions for Child Development*. San Francisco: Jossey-Bass.

(1985). Adult-child interaction as a source of self-regulation in children. In S. R. Yussen, ed., *The growth of reflection in children* (pp. 69–97). Orlando, FL: Academic Press.

(1990). The voice of rationality in a sociocultural approach to mind. In L. C. Moll, ed. *Vygotsky and education* (pp. 111–126). Cambridge: Cambridge University Press.

(1991). *Voices in the mind.* Cambridge, MA: Harvard University Press.

(1997). Narrative tools of history and identity. *Culture & Psychology*, 3(1) 5–20.

Wertsch, J. V., Minick, N., & Arns, F. J. (1984). The creation of context in joint problem-solving. In B. Rogoff & J. Lave, eds., *Everyday cognition: Its development in social context* (pp. 151–171). Cambridge, MA: Harvard University Press.

White, S. (1979). Developmental psychology and Vico's concept of universal history. In G. Tagliacozzo, M. Mooney, D. P. Verene, eds., *Vico and contemporary thought* (pp. 1–13). Atlantic Highlands, NJ: Humanities Press.

Wiley, N. (1979). Notes on self genesis: From Me to We to I. *Studies in Symbolic Interaction*, 2, 87–105.

Wilson, D. J. (1995). Fertile ground: Pragmatism, science, and logical positivism. In R. Hollinger & D. Depew, eds., *Pragmatism: From progressivism to postmodernism* (pp. 122–141). New York: Praeger.

Winegar, L. T., & Valsiner, J. (1992). Re-contextualizing context: Analysis of metadata and some further elaborations. In L. T. Winegar & J. Valsiner, eds., *Children's development within social context*. Vol. 2. *Research and methodology* (pp. 249–266). Hillsdale, NJ: Erlbaum.

Winter, J. A., & Goldfield, E. C. (1991). Caregiver-child interaction in the development of self: The contributions of Vygotsky, Bruner, and Kaye to Mead's theory. *Symbolic Interaction*, 14(4) 433–447.

Wirth, W. (1961). Wilhelm Wirth. In C. Murchison, ed., *A history of psychology in autobiography*. Vol. 3 (pp. 283–327). New York: Russell & Russell.

Witkin, H. A. (1965). Heinz Werner: 1890–1964. *Child Development*, 30(2) 307–328.

Woolgar, S. (1988). *Knowledge and reflexivity.* London: Sage.

Woolston, H. B. (1912). The urban habit of mind. *American Journal of Sociology*, 17, 602–614.

Worcester, W. L. (1893). Observations on some points in James' psychology. II. Emotions. *The Monist*, 3,(2) 285–298.

Wozniak, R. (1982). Metaphysics and science, reason, and reality: The intellectual origins of genetic epistemology. In J. M. Broughton & D. J. Freeman-

Moir, eds., *The cognitive-developmental psychology of James Mark Baldwin* (pp. 13–45). Norwood, NJ: Ablex.

Wundt, W. (1900–1920). *Völkerpsychologie: Eine Untersuchung der Entwicklungsgesetze*. Vol. 1–10. Leipzig: Wilhelm Engelmann [2nd ed. 1910–20 by Alfred Kröner Verlag].

(1921). *Logik der Geisteswissenschaften*. 4th ed. Stuttgart: Ferdinand Enke.

(1973). *The language of gestures*. The Hague: Mouton.

Yerkes, R. M. (1916). The mental life of monkeys and apes: A study of ideational behavior. *Behavioral Monographs*, 3, ser. no. 12. New York: Holt.

(1925). *Almost Human*. London: Jonathan Cape.

Yerkes, R. M., & Learned, B. W. (1925). *Chimpanzee intelligence and its vocal expressions*. Baltimore, MD: Williams & Wilkins.

Yerkes, R. M., & Petrunkevitch, A. (1925). Studies of chimpanzee vision by Ladygina-Kohts. *Journal of Comparative Psychology*, 5, 99–108.

Zeigarnik, B. (1927). Das Behalten erledigter un unerledigter Handlungen. *Psychologische Forschung*, 9, 1–85.

Zueblin, C. (1898). Municipal playgrounds in Chicago. *American Journal of Sociology*, 4(2) 145–158.

Index